The PRENTICE HALL *Reader*

FOURTH EDITION

GEORGE MILLER

University of Delaware

PRENTICE HALL, Englewood Cliffs, New Jersey 07632

Library of Congress Cataloging-in-Publication Data

The Prentice Hall reader / [compiled by] George Miller.—4th ed.
    p.   cm.
   ISBN 0-13-079302-7
   1.–College readers. 2.–English language—Rhetoric. I.–Miller,
  George. II.–Prentice Hall, inc.
PE1417.P74   1994
808'.0427—dc20   94-32237
                                       CIP
                                       AC

Acquisitions editor: Alison Reeves and Phil Miller
Development editor: Mark Gallaher
Interior and cover design: Thomas Nery
Design director: Paula Martin
Manufacturing buyer: Mary Anne Gloriande
Cover Photo: Thomas McKnight *"Newport"*
Silkscreen, 22 3/4" x 45". © 1994 Thomas McKnight.

©1995, 1992, 1989, 1986 by Prentice Hall, Inc.
A Simon & Schuster Company
Englewood Cliffs, New Jersey 07632

Printed in the United States of America
10 9 8 7 6 5 4 3 2 1

ISBN 0-13-079302-7 (student text)

ISBN 0-13-183088-0 (annotated instructor's edition)

Prentice-Hall International (UK) Limited, *London*
Prentice-Hall of Australia Pty. Limited, *Sydney*
Prentice-Hall Canada Inc., *Toronto*
Prentice-Hall Hispanoamericana, S.A., *Mexico*
Prentice-Hall of India Private Limited, *New Delhi*
Prentice-Hall of Japan, Inc., *Tokyo*
Simon & Schuster Asia Pte. Ltd., *Singapore*
Editora Prentice-Hall do Brasil, Ltda., *Rio de Janeiro*

For Lisa, her book

CONTENTS

ONE

GATHERING AND USING EXAMPLES   39

NARRATION 83

DESCRIPTION 129

FOUR

DIVISION AND CLASSIFICATION   174

FIVE

COMPARISON AND CONTRAST 228

SIX

PROCESS   275

SEVEN

CAUSE AND EFFECT   328

EIGHT

NINE

ARGUMENTATION AND PERSUASION 420

TEN

REVISING   487

APPENDIX

THEMATIC
CONTENTS

AUTOBIOGRAPHY AND BIOGRAPHY

CHILDREN AND FAMILY

Contemporary Phenomena and Issues

Stereotypes, Prejudice, and the Struggle for Equality

WOMEN'S ROLES, WOMEN'S RIGHTS

GROWING OLDER

HUMOR AND SATIRE

MEN AND WOMEN

RACE, CLASS, AND CULTURE

NATURE AND THE ENVIRONMENT

PSYCHOLOGY AND BEHAVIOR

Reading, Writing, and Language

School and College

Self-Discovery

PREFACE

The Prentice Hall Reader is predicated on two premises: that reading plays a vital role in learning how to write and that writing and reading can best be organized around the traditional division of discourse into a number of structural patterns. Such a division is not the only way that the forms of writing can be classified, but it does have several advantages.

First, practice in these structural patterns encourages students to organize knowledge and to see the ways in which information can be conveyed. How else does the mind know except by classifying, comparing, defining, or seeking cause and effect relationships? Second, the most common use of these patterns occurs in writing done in academic courses. There students are asked to narrate a chain of events, to describe an artistic style, to classify plant forms, to compare two political systems, to tell how a laboratory experiment was performed, to analyze why famine occurs in Africa, to define a philosophical concept, or to argue for or against building a space station. Learning how to structure papers using these patterns is an exercise that has immediate application in students' other academic work. Finally, because the readings use these patterns as structural devices, they offer an excellent way in which to integrate reading into a writing course. Students can see the patterns at work and learn how to use them to become more effective writers and better, more efficient readers.

WHAT IS NEW IN THE FOURTH EDITION

The fourth edition of *The Prentice Hall Reader* features 60 selections, 24 of which are new, and another 11 papers written by student writers. As in the previous editions, the readings are chosen on the basis of several criteria: how well they demonstrate a particular pattern of organization, appeal to a freshman audience, and promote interesting and appropriate discussion and writing activities.

New to this edition is Chapter 10: Revising. This chapter begins with advice for students on how to analyze their own writing; how to use peer readers and a writing center or tutor; how to conference with their instructor, and how to proofread their work. The chapter presents advice from three professional writers and revisers—Peter Elbow, William Zinsser, and Donald Murray—and four examples of revisions done by professional writers. The discussion questions for each selection help focus attention on how and why the writers revised their work.

Also new to the fourth edition is an extensive appendix on finding, using, and documenting sources. Here students can find information on how to locate reference books; how to use a card or on-line library catalog; how to locate the right subject headings; how to find magazines, journals, newspapers and government documents; how to interview; how to evaluate sources; and how to integrate quoted material into their own prose. In addition, the appendix offers sample citations based on both the MLA and APA systems and reproduces with accompanying commentary a sample student research paper.

In this edition, each reading is now prefaced by two prereading questions. One asks students to *connect* the subject of the reading to their own experiences; the second asks students to *anticipate* their reading experience by trying to answer a specific question about the selection.

Each reading is now followed by a fourth writing suggestion—a journal writing exercise. The other three writing suggestions for each reading provide suggestions for writing a paragraph, an essay, and a research paper. Many of the writing suggestions are new to this edition.

A new *Instructor's Quiz Booklet*, containing a content and a vocabulary quiz for each of the selections, is available from your Prentice Hall representative.

OTHER DISTINCTIVE FEATURES OF THIS TEXT

PROSE IN REVISION

As every writing instructor knows, getting students to revise is never easy. Having finished a paper, most students do not want to see it again, let alone revise it. Furthermore, for many students revising means making word substitutions and correcting grammatical and mechanical errors—changes that instructors regard as proofreading, not revising. To help make the need for revision more vivid and to show how writers revise, the *Prentice Hall Reader* includes three features:

1. Chapter 10: Revising. A complete chapter with a lengthy introduction offers specific advice on how to revise. The chapter includes advice from three writers and then four examples of how professional writers revised their work.
2. The introduction to each chapter of readings include a first draft of a student essay, a comment on the draft's strengths and weaknesses, and a final, revised draft. These essays, realistic examples of student writing, model the student revision process.
3. The third writing suggestion after each selection is accompanied by prewriting and rewriting activities. In all, the text provides 180 specific rewriting activities to help students organize ideas and to revise what they have written.

SELECTIONS

The fourth edition of *The Prentice Hall Reader* offers instructors flexibility in choosing readings. No chapter has fewer than five selections and most have six or more. The readings are scaled in terms of length and sophistication. The selections in each chapter begin with a student essay and the selections from professional writers are arranged so that they increase in length and in difficulty and sophistication.

WRITING SUGGESTIONS

Each reading is followed by four writing suggestions: the first is a journal writing suggestion; the second calls for a paragraph-length response; the third, an essay; and the fourth, an essay involving research. Each of the suggestions is related to the content of the reading and each calls for a response in the particular pattern or mode being studied. The material in the Annotated Instructor's Edition includes a fifth writing suggestion for each reading, bringing the total number of writing suggestions in the fourth edition to 300.

INTRODUCTIONS

The introduction to each chapter offers clear and succinct advice to the student on how to write that particular type of paragraph or essay. The introductions anticipate questions, provide answers, and end with a checklist, titled "Some Things to Remember," to remind students of the major concerns they should have when writing.

HOW TO READ AN ESSAY

The first introductory section offers advice on how to read an essay, following prereading, reading and rereading models. A sample analysis of an essay by Lewis Thomas shows how to use this reading model to prepare an essay for class.

HOW TO WRITE AN ESSAY

The following section, "How to Write an Essay," offers an overview of every stage of the writing process, starting with advice on how to define a subject, purpose, and audience and an explanation of a variety of prewriting techniques. The section also shows students how to write a thesis statement, how to decide where to place that statement in an essay, and how to approach the problems of revising an essay. Finally it contains a student essay as well as two drafts of the student's two opening paragraphs.

ANNOTATED INSTRUCTOR'S EDITION

An annotated edition of *The Prentice Hall Reader* is available to instructors. Each of the selections in the text is annotated with

- A suggested link to other writing and organizational strategies found in the reading
- A Teaching Strategy that suggests ways in which to teach the reading and to keep attention focused on how the selection works as a piece of writing
- Appropriate background information that explains allusions or historical contexts
- Specific class and collaborative learning activities that can be used with the reading
- Links to Writing that suggest how to use the reader to teach specific grammatical, mechanical, and rhetorical issues in writing. These "links" provide a bridge between a handbook and *The Prentice Hall Reader.*
- Possible responses to all of the discussion questions included within the text

- Tips on "related readings" that suggest how to pair essays in the reader
- An additional writing suggestion

INSTRUCTOR'S QUIZ BOOKLET

A separate *Instructor's Quiz Booklet* for *The Prentice Hall Reader* is available from your Prentice Hall representative. The booklet contains two quizzes for each selection in the reader—one on content and the other on vocabulary. Each quiz has five multiple-choice questions. The quizzes are intended to be administered and graded quickly. They provide the instructor with a brief and efficient means of testing the student's ability to extract significant ideas from the readings and of demonstrating his or her understanding of certain vocabulary words as they are used in the essays. Keys to both content and vocabulary quizzes are included at the back of the *Quiz Booklet*.

TEACHING WRITING WITH "THE PRENTICE HALL READER"

A separate manual on planning the writing and the reading in a composition course is available from your Prentice Hall representative. Primarily addressed to the new graduate teaching assistant or the adjunct instructor, the manual includes sections on teaching the writing process, including how to use prewriting activities, to conference, to design and implement collaborative learning activities, and to grade. In addition, it provides advice on how to plan a class discussion of a reading and how to avoid pointless discussions. An appendix contains an index to all of the activities and questions in *The Prentice Hall Reader* that involve grammatical, mechanical, sentence- or paragraph-level subjects, three additional sample syllabi, and a variety of sample course materials including self-assessment sheets, peer editing worksheets, and directions for small group activities.

ACKNOWLEDGMENTS

Although writing is a solitary activity, no one can write without the assistance of others. This text owes much to many people: To the staff at Prentice Hall who have continued to play a large role in helping to develop this reader, especially Phil Miller, President, Humanities and Social Science; Alison Reeves, Executive Editor, English, who has been supportive and patient; David Schecter, editorial assistant; Mark Gallaher, the Development Editor on this edition, who was a constant source of ideas and advice; and Gina Sluss, Executive Marketing Manager.

To my reviewers, who wrote extensive critiques of the manuscript and made many helpful suggestions: Carolyn R. Allison, Essex Community College; Will Hochman, University of Southern Colorado; Mary Joseph, Lander College; Shelby Pierce, Owens Technical College.

To Laurie LoSasso-Casey and Andrea Newlyn, my editorial assistants on this edition, whose energies and thoroughness made my work easier. To the writing program staff at the University of Delaware and the students in my own writing classes, who tested materials, offered suggestions, and contributed essays to the introductions. To my wife Vicki, who encourages and understands. And finally to my children, Lisa, Jon, Craig, Valerie, Eric, Evan, Adam, and Alicia and Eric Gray, who have learned over the years to live with a father who writes.

George Miller
University of Delaware

THE NEW YORK TIMES SUPPLEMENTS PROGRAM

THE NEW YORK TIMES and PRENTICE HALL are sponsoring Themes of the Times; a program designed to enhance student access to current information of relevance in the classroom.

Through this program, the core subject matter provided in the text is supplemented by a collection of time-sensitive articles from one of the world's most distinguished newspapers, THE NEW YORK TIMES. These articles demonstrate the vital, ongoing connection between what is learned in the classroom and what is happening in the world around us.

To enjoy the wealth of information of THE NEW YORK TIMES daily, a reduced subscription rate is available in deliverable areas. For information, call toll-free: 1-800-631-1222.

PRENTICE HALL and THE NEW YORK TIMES are proud to co-sponsor Themes of the Times. We hope it will make the reading of both textbooks and newspapers a more dynamic, involving process.

How to Read
an Essay

When your grade in most writing courses is determined by the papers that you write, rather than by examinations based on the essays that you read in the course, you might wonder why any instructor would assign "readings" in a writing course. How do these two seemingly very different activities fit together?

How Does Reading Help You Write?

You read in a writing course for three purposes: First, the essays are a source of information: you learn by reading and what you learn can then, in turn, be used in your writing. Any paper that involves research, for example, requires selective, critical reading on your part as you search for and evaluate sources. Second, readings offer a perspective on a particular subject, one with which you might agree or disagree. In this sense readings can serve as catalysts or stimuli to provoke writing. Many of the writing suggestions in this text grow out of the readings, asking you to explore some aspect of the subject more fully, to reply to a writer's position, or to expand on or refine that position. Finally, readings offer models to a writer; they show you how another writer dealt with a particular subject or a particular writing problem, and they demonstrate writing strategies. Other writing suggestions in this text ask you to employ the same strategy used in a reading with a different subject in an essay of your own.

The first two purposes—readings as a source of information or as a stimulus to writing—are fairly obvious, but the third purpose might seem confusing. Exactly how are you, as a student writer, to use an essay written by a professional writer as an example or model? Are you to suppose to sound like E. B. White or Joan Didion or Maya Angelou? Are you to imitate their styles or the structures that they use in their essays?

To model, in the sense that the word is being used here, does not mean to produce an imitation. You are not expected to use the same organizational structure or to imitate someone else's style, tone, or approach. Rather, what you can learn from these writers is how to handle information; how to adapt writing to a particular audience; how to structure the body of an essay; how to begin, make transitions, and end; how to construct effective paragraphs and achieve sentence variety. In short, the readings represent an album of performances, examples that you can use to study writing techniques.

Models or examples are important to you as a writer because you learn to write effectively in the same way that you learn to do any other activity. You study the rules or advice on how it is done; you practice, especially under the watchful eye of an instructor or a coach; and you study how others have mastered similar problems and techniques. A young musician learns how to read music and play an instrument, practices daily, studies with a teacher, and listens to and watches how other musicians play. A baseball player learns the proper offensive and defensive techniques, practices daily, is supervised by a coach, and listens to the advice and watches the performance of other players. As a writer in a writing class, you do the same thing: follow the advice offered by your instructor and textbooks, practice by writing and revising, listen to the advice and suggestions of your fellow students, and study the work of other writers.

HOW DOES WRITING HELP YOU READ?

Reading and writing actually benefit each other: being a good reader will help you become a more effective writer and being a good writer will help you become a more effective reader. As a writer, you learn how to pattern an essay, how to use examples to support a thesis, how to structure an argument, how to make an effective transition from one point to another. You learn how to write beginnings, middles, and ends, and most especially you learn how essays can be organized. For example, through reading you learn that comparison and contrast essays can be organized in either the subject-by-subject or the point-by-point pattern, that narratives are structured chronologically, and that cause and effect analyses are linear and sequential. When you read other essays, you look for structure and pattern, realizing that such devices are not only creative tools you use in writing, but also analytical ones that can be used in reading. By revealing to you an underlying organizational pattern, such devices help you understand what the essay says. In order to become an efficient reader, however, you need to exercise the same care and attention that you do when you write. You do that by becoming an active rather than a passive reader.

ACTIVE RATHER THAN PASSIVE READING

Every reader first reads a piece of writing for plot or subject matter. On that level, the reader wants to know what happens, what is the subject, whether it is new or interesting. Generally that first reading is done quickly, even, in a sense, superficially. The reader is a spectator waiting passively to be entertained or informed. Then, if it is important for the reader to use that piece of writing in some way, to understand it in detail and in depth, the next stage of active reading begins. On this level, the reader asks questions, seeks answers, looks for organizational structures, and concentrates on themes and images or on the thesis and the quality of evidence presented. Careful reading requires this active participation of the reader. Writing and reading are, after all, social acts and as such they involve an implied contract between a writer and an audience. A writer's job is to communicate clearly and effectively; a reader's job is to read attentively and critically.

Because as a reader you need to become an active participant in this process of communication, you should always read any piece of writing you are using in a course or on your job more than just once. Rereading an essay or a textbook involves the same types of critical activities that you use when rereading a poem, a novel, or a play, and demands your attention and your active involvement as a reader. You must examine how the author embodies meaning or purpose in prose. You must seek answers to a variety of questions: How does the author structure the essay? How does the author select, organize, and present information? To whom is the author writing? How does that audience influence the essay?

You can increase your effectiveness as an active and critical reader by following the same three-stage model that you use as a writer: divide your time into prereading, reading, and rereading activities.

PREREADING

Before you begin reading an essay in this text, look first at the biographical headnote that describes the author and her or his work and that identifies where and when the essay was originally published, including any special conditions or circumstances that surrounded or influenced its publication. The headnote ends with two "Before Reading" questions that encourage you to connect aspects of the reading to your experiences, and to anticipate the writer's thought. A careful reading of this material can help prepare you to read the essay.

Look next at the text of the essay itself. What does the title tell you about the subject or the tone? A serious, dignified title such as "The Value of Children: A Taxonomical Essay" (p. 219) sets up a very different set of expectations than a playful title such as "You Have Definitely Won!" (p. 73). Page through the essay—are there any obvious subdivisions in the text (extra spaces, sequence markers, subheadings) that signal an organizational pattern? Does the paragraphing suggest a particular structure? You might also read the first sentence in every paragraph to get a general sense of what the essay is about and where the author is going.

Finally, look at the series of questions that follow each selection. Those questions always ask about subject and purpose, structure and audience, and vocabulary and style. Read through them so that you know what to look for when you read the essay. Before you begin to read, make sure that you have a pen or pencil, some paper on which to take notes, and a dictionary in which to check the meanings of unfamiliar words.

READING

When you begin to read a selection in this book, you already have an important piece of information about its structure. Each selection was chosen to demonstrate a particular type of writing (narration, description, exposition, and argumentation) and a particular pattern of organization (chronological, spatial, division and classification, comparison and contrast, process, cause and effect, definition, induction or deduction). As you read, think about how the author organized the essay. On a separate sheet of paper, construct a brief outline. That will help you focus your attention on how the whole essay is put together.

Remember that an essay will typically express a particular idea or assertion **(thesis)** about a **subject** to an **audience** for a particular reason **(purpose)**. Probably one reading of an essay will be enough for you to answer questions about **subject**, but you may have to reread the essay several times in order to identify the author's **thesis** and **purpose**. Keep these three elements separate and clear in your own mind. It will help to answer each of the following questions as you read and reread:

1. **Subject:** What is this essay about?
2. **Thesis:** What particular point is the author trying to make about this subject?
3. **Audience:** To whom is the author writing? Where did the essay first appear? How does its intended audience help shape the essay and influence its language and style?
4. **Purpose:** Why is the author writing this? Is the intention to entertain? To inform? To persuade?

Effective writing contains specific, relevant details and examples. Look carefully at the writer's choice of examples. Remember that the author made a conscious decision to include each of these details. Ideally, each is appropriate to the subject and each contributes to the thesis and purpose.

REREADING

Rereading, like rewriting, is not always a discrete stage in a linear process. Just as you might pause after writing several sentences and then go back and make some immediate changes, so as a reader, you might stop at the end of a paragraph and then go back and reread what you have just read. Depending upon the difficulty of the essay, it might take several rereadings for you to be able to answer the questions posed above about the writer's thesis and purpose. Even if you feel certain about your understanding of the essay, a final rereading is important.

In that rereading, focus on the essay as an example of a writer's craft. Look carefully at the paragraphing. How effective is the introduction to the essay? The conclusion? Have you ever used a similar strategy to begin or end an essay? How do both reflect the writer's purpose? Audience? Pay attention to the writer's sentence structures. How do these sentences differ from the ones that you typically write? Does the author employ a variety of sentence types and lengths? Is there anything unusual about the author's word choices? Do you use a similar range of vocabulary when you write? Remember that the writer of essays is just as conscious of craft as the poet, the novelist, or the playwright.

A SAMPLE READING

Before you begin reading in the fourth edition of *The Prentice Hall Reader*, you can see how to use these techniques of prereading, reading, and rereading in the following essay, which has been annotated over the course of several readings. Following the essay are the reader's prereading, reading, and rereading notes.

ON CLONING A HUMAN BEING

Lewis Thomas

Lewis Thomas (1913–1993) was born in Flushing, New York, and received his M.D. from Harvard University. He served on the medical faculty at Johns Hopkins, Tulane, Cornell, and Yale, before assuming the position of chancellor of the Memorial Sloan-Kettering Cancer Center in New York. Thomas published widely in his research specialty, pathology, the study of diseases and their causes.

In 1971, he began contributing a 1200-word monthly column, focusing on current topics related to medicine and biological science, to the New England Journal of Medicine. *Titled "Notes of a Biology Watcher," the column proved highly popular with professionals who subscribed to the journal as well as nonspecialists. Several collections of these essays have been published, including* The Lives of a Cell: Notes of a Biology Watcher *(1974),* The Medusa and the Snail *(1979),* Late Night Thoughts on Listening to Mahler's Ninth Symphony *(1983), and* Fragile Species *(1992).*

In "On Cloning a Human Being," originally published in the New England Journal of Medicine, *Thomas sets out to analyze the effect that an experiment to clone a human being would have on the rest of the world.*

BEFORE READING

Connecting: What do you know about cloning, both in fact and from science fiction? Do you find cloning a positive technological development or a frightening one?

Anticipating: What seems to be Thomas's attitude toward cloning? As a scientist, does he express the opinion you expect?

It is now theoretically possible to recreate an iden- 1
tical creature from any animal or plant, from the
DNA contained in the nucleus of any somatic cell.
A single plant root-tip cell can be teased and seduced into conceiving a perfect copy of the whole
plant; a frog's intestinal epithelial cell possesses the
complete instructions needed for a new, same frog.

Definition of cloning

If the technology were further advanced, you could do this with a human being, and there are now startled predictions all over the place that this will in fact be done, someday, in order to provide a version of immortality for carefully selected, especially valuable people.

2   The cloning of humans is on most of the lists of things to worry about from Science, along with behavior control, genetic engineering, transplanted heads, computer poetry, and the unrestrained growth of plastic flowers.

Joking here.

3   Cloning is the most dismaying of prospects, mandating as it does the elimination of sex with only a metaphoric elimination of death as compensation. It is almost no comfort to know that one's cloned, identical surrogate lives on, especially when the living will very likely involve edging one's real, now aging self off to the side, sooner or later. It is hard to imagine anything like filial affection or respect for a single, unmated nucleus; harder still to think of one's new, self-generated self as anything but an absolute, desolate orphan. Not to mention the complex interpersonal relationship involved in raising one's self from infancy, teaching the language, enforcing discipline, instilling good manners, and the like. How would you feel if you became an incorrigible juvenile delinquent by proxy at the age of fifty-five?

Two versions of the same person living at once – the original and the clone. Wild idea.

proxy: person acting for another person

4   The public questions are obvious. Who is to be selected, and on what qualifications? How to handle the risks of misused technology, such as self-determined cloning by the rich and powerful but socially objectionable, or the cloning by governments of dumb, docile masses for the world's work? What will be the effect on all the uncloned rest of us of human sameness? After all, we've accustomed ourselves through hundreds of millennia to the continual exhilaration of uniqueness; each of us is totally different, in a fundamental sense, from all the other four billion. Selfness is an essential fact of life. The thought of human nonselfness, precise sameness, is terrifying, when you think about it.

4-paragraph introduction sets up negatives about cloning

5   Well, don't think about it, because it isn't a probable possibility, not even as a long shot for the dis-

Thesis: Cloning human beings is not really possible.

How to Read an Essay

tant future, in my opinion. I agree that you might clone some people who would look amazingly like their parental cell donors, but the odds are that they'd be almost as different as you or me, and certainly more different than any of today's identical twins.

The time required for the experiment is only one of the problems, but a formidable one. Suppose you wanted to clone a prominent, spectacularly successful diplomat, to look after the Middle East problems of the distant future. You'd have to catch him and persuade him, probably not very hard to do, and extirpate a cell. But then you'd have to wait for him to grow up through embryonic life and then for at least forty years more, and you'd have to be sure all observers remained patient and unmeddlesome through his unpromising, ambiguous childhood and adolescence.

Reason 1: Time involved

↳ *"valuable person"*

Moreover, you'd have to be sure of recreating his environment, perhaps down to the last detail. "Environment" is a word which really means people, so you'd have to do a lot more cloning than just the diplomat himself.

Reason 2: Environment would have to be created

This is a very important part of the cloning problem, largely overlooked in our excitement about the cloned individual himself. You don't have to agree all the way with B. F. Skinner to acknowledge that the environment does make a difference, and when you examine what we really mean by the word "environment" it comes down to other human beings. We use euphemisms and jargon for this, like "social forces," "cultural influences," even Skinner's "verbal community," but what is meant is the dense crowd of nearby people who talk to, listen to, smile or frown at, give to, withhold from, nudge, push, caress, or flail out at the individual. No matter what the genome says, these people have a lot to do with shaping a character. Indeed, if all you had was the genome, and no people around, you'd grow a sort of vertebrate plant, nothing more.

To be the same, the clone would have to have the same environment

genome: genetic organism

So, to start with, you will undoubtedly need to clone the parents. No question about this. This means the diplomat is out, even in theory, since you couldn't have gotten cells from both his parents at the time when he was himself just recognizable as an early social treasure. You'd have to limit the list of clones to people already certified as sufficiently valuable for the effort, with both parents still alive. The parents would need cloning and, for consistency, their parents as well. I suppose you'd also need the usual informed-consent forms, filled out and signed, not easy to get if I know parents, even harder for grandparents.

10 But this is only the beginning. It is the whole family that really influences the way a person turns out, not just the parents, according to current psychiatric thinking. Clone the family.

11 Then what? The way each member of the family develops has already been determined by the environment set around him, and this environment is more people, people outside the family, schoolmates, acquaintances, lovers, enemies, car-pool partners, even, in special circumstances, peculiar strangers across the aisle on the subway. Find them, and clone them.

12 But there is no end to the protocol. Each of the outer contacts has his own surrounding family, and his and their outer contacts. Clone them all.

13 To do the thing properly, with any hope of ending up with a genuine duplicate of a single person, you really have no choice. You must clone the world, no less.

14 We are not ready for an experiment of this size, nor, I should think, are we willing. For one thing, it would mean replacing today's world by an entirely identical world to follow immediately, and this means no new, natural, spontaneous, random, chancy children. No children at all, except for the manufactured doubles of those now on the scene. Plus all those identical adults, including all of today's politicians, all seen double. It is too much to contemplate.

15 Moreover, when the whole experiment is finally finished, fifty years or so from now, how could you get a responsible scientific reading on the outcome? Somewhere in there would be the original clonee, probably lost and overworked, now well into middle age, but everyone around him would be precise du-

Handwritten margin notes:
Causal chain: clone parents, grandparents, family, people outside the family who came in contact with the individual, the whole world.

Isn't this an exaggeration?

He's really joking here

plicates of today's everyone. It would be today's same world, filled to overflowing with duplicates of today's people and their same, duplicated problems, probably all resentful at having had to go through our whole thing all over, sore enough at the clone to make endless trouble for him, if they found him.

[margin note: With the world cloned, everything would be the same, leading to dissatisfaction]

And obviously, if the whole thing were done precisely right, they would still be casting about for ways to solve the problem of universal dissatisfaction, and sooner or later they'd surely begin to look around at each other, wondering who should be cloned for his special value to society, to get us out of all this. And so it would go, in regular cycles, perhaps forever. 16

I once lived through a period when I wondered what Hell could be like, and I stretched my imagination to try to think of a perpetual sort of damnation. I have to confess, I never thought of anything like this. 17

I have an alternative suggestion, if you're looking for a way out. Set cloning aside, and don't try it. Instead, go in the other direction. Look for ways to get mutations more quickly, new variety, different songs. Fiddle around, if you must fiddle, but never with ways to keep things the same, no matter who, not even yourself. Heaven, somewhere ahead, has got to be a change. 18

[margin note: The author's real purpose comes out here; ties to paragraph 4.]

Prereading Notes

The headnote indicates that the author, Lewis Thomas, was a physician and medical researcher and that most of his essays--including this one--were written for *The New England Journal of Medicine*. These facts and the title "On Cloning a Human Being" initially suggest that this will be a pretty serious, probably dry essay and that it may be full of a lot of technical information. However, scanning the essay by looking at the first sentence in each paragraph shows the tone to be fairly informal: Paragraph 5, for example, begins "Well, don't think about it. . . ." It is also clear from a quick scan of the essay that it is really on *not* cloning a human being. Thomas is focusing on the problems

involved in cloning human beings and seems to say
that it will never happen.

Reading Notes

Outline:
par. 1   Introduction to cloning and predictions
that "especially valuable people" will be cloned
par. 2-4   Worries about cloning
par. 5   Thomas says cloning "isn't a probable
possibility"
par. 6   Reason 1: Too much time involved in any
experiment with human cloning
par. 7-15   Reason 2: Since individuals are shaped
by their environments, to clone a person would
require cloning his or her parents, grandparents,
the whole family, "the world, no less." People are
not ready to replace today's world with "an entirely
identical world to follow immediately," so everyone
would hate the original clonee for causing all the
trouble.
par. 16   The cloning cycle would have to start
again to duplicate someone who could "solve the
problem of universal dissatisfaction" with the
original cloning experiment.
par. 17   To Thomas, this would be worse than Hell.
par. 18   Instead of cloning, it would be better to
experiment with "ways to get mutations more quickly,
new variety, different songs."

     After an initial reading, it is clear that
Thomas's subject is cloning and predictions that
"valuable people" will be cloned experimentally in
the future. He states his thesis explicitly in
paragraph 5: Cloning "isn't a probable possibility,
not even as a long shot for the distant
future. . . ." Even though the essay was written for
The New England Journal of Medicine, it would seem
that Thomas intended to reach a general educated
audience; for example, he includes very little
specialized terminology and doesn't assume any
particular medical or scientific expertise. His
purpose seems to be basically to inform, to explain
to his audience why cloning of human beings isn't
likely to happen in the future.

But in explaining why human beings aren't likely to be cloned, Thomas gives reasons that seem exaggerated. Could it really be necessary to clone the whole world, as he says? Why would he want to suggest that the effects of cloning a single human being would be so drastic?

Rereading Notes

Rereading the essay reveals that Thomas is deliberately pushing the idea of cloning a human being to the point of absurdity. His tone is humorous from the beginning: In paragraph 2, for example, he lists as some of our worries about Science "transplanted heads, computer poetry, and the unrestrained growth of plastic flowers." When he describes the effects of an experiment in cloning an important diplomat and what would really be required to clone a human being (pars. 10-13), he builds each paragraph up to its logical--and increasingly absurd--conclusion: "Clone the family." "Find them, and clone them." "Clone them all." "You must clone the world, no less." In paragraph 14 he pushes the absurdity one step further, imagining a world where there are no longer unique children who grow up to be unique adults but only identical doubles of those who already exist--"including all of today's politicians. . . . It is too much to contemplate." The next two paragraphs continue in this vein, ending with the most absurd idea of all: that another cloning would have to take place of the person who could get everyone out of this mess. "And so it would go," Thomas says, "in regular cycles, perhaps forever."

Thomas is saying that it is absurd to imagine that an exact replica of another human being could ever be cloned; given the fact that the clone would necessarily grow up under different influences, the two might look alike but "they'd be almost as different as you and me, and certainly more different than any of today's identical twins" (paragraph 5). Moreover, an even more substantial point emerges on rereading: There can be no benefit from cloning human beings to begin with. "Precise

sameness," Thomas says, "is terrifying" (paragraph
4), an idea that he returns to in his conclusion,
where he suggests that it is better for humans to
experiment with "mutations," "variety," and "change"
than with clones.

Thomas's purpose, therefore, seems to be more
than simply informing readers about the
impossibility of creating a human clone; at the
core, he is arguing for a view of human nature that
recognizes the value of "variety" over some standard
of "perfection" and his method is to do so in an
entertainingly humorous way.

Each of the essays in the fourth edition of *The Prentice Hall
Reader* will repay you for the time and effort you put into reading it
carefully and critically. Each essay shows an artful craftsperson at
work, solving the problems inherent in communicating experiences,
feelings, ideas, and opinions to an audience. Each writer is someone
from whom you, as a reader and as a thinker, can learn. So when your
instructor assigns a selection from the text, remember that as a reader
you must assume an active role. Don't assume that reading an essay
once—to see what it is "about"—will mean that you are prepared to
write about it or that you have learned all that you can learn from the
essay. Ask questions, seek answers to those questions, analyze, and
reread.

SOME THINGS TO REMEMBER WHEN READING

1. Read the headnote to the selection. How does this information help you to understand the writer and the context in
   which the selection was written?
2. Look at the questions that precede and follow each reading.
   They will help focus your attention on the important aspects
   of the selection. After you read, write out answers to each
   question.
3. Read through the selection first to see what happens and to
   satisfy your curiosity.
4. Reread the selection several times, taking notes or underlining as you go.
5. Write or locate in the essay a thesis statement. Remember

that the thesis is the particular point that the writer is trying to make about the subject.

6. Define a purpose for the essay. Why is the writer writing? Does the author make that purpose explicit?

7. Imagine the audience for such an essay. Who is the likely reader? What does that reader already know about the subject? Is the reader likely to have any preconceptions or prejudices about the subject?

8. Isolate a structure in the selection. How is it put together? Into how many parts can it be divided? How do those parts work together? Outline the essay.

9. Be sure that you understand every sentence. How does the writer vary the sentence structures?

10. Look up every word that you cannot define with some degree of certainty. Remember that you might misinterpret what the author is saying if you simply skip over the unfamiliar words.

11. Reread the essay one final time, reassembling its parts into the artful whole that it was intended to be.

How to Write
an Essay

Watching a performance, whether it is athletic or artistic, our attention is focused on the achievement displayed in that moment. In
concentrating on the performance, however, we might forget about
the extensive practice that lies behind that achievement. Writing is no
different. Typically, writers rely on perspiration, not inspiration. An
effective final product depends upon careful preliminary work.

A WRITER'S SUBJECT

The first step in writing is to determine a subject, what a piece of
writing is about. The majority of writing tasks that you face either in
school or on the job require you to write in response to a specific assignment. Your instructor, for example, might ask you to use the specific writing suggestions that follow each reading in this book. Before
you begin work on any writing assignment, take time to study what is
being asked. What limits have already been placed on the assignment? What are the key words (for example, "compare," "analyze,"
"define") used in the assignment?

Once you have a subject, the next step is to restrict, focus, or
narrow that subject into a workable topic. Although the words "subject" and "topic" are sometimes used interchangeably, think of "subject" as the broader, more general word. You move from a subject to
a "topic" by limiting or restricting what you will include or cover.
The shift from subject to topic is a gradual one that is not marked by
a clearly definable line. Just remember that a topic is a more restricted
version of a larger subject.

A WRITER'S PURPOSE

A writer writes to fulfill three fundamental purposes: *to entertain, to inform,* and *to persuade.* Obviously, those purposes are not necessarily separate: an interesting, maybe even humorous, essay that documents the health hazards caused by smoking can, at the same time, attempt to persuade the reader to give up smoking. In this case the main purpose is still persuasion; entertainment and information play subordinate roles in catching the reader's interest and in documenting with appropriate evidence the argument being advanced.

These three purposes are generally associated with the traditional division of writing into four forms—narration, description, exposition (including classification, comparison and contrast, process, cause and effect, and definition), and argumentation. *Narrative* or *descriptive essays* typically tell a story or describe a person, object, or place in order to entertain a reader and re-create the experience. *Expository essays* primarily provide information for a reader. *Argumentative* or *persuasive essays,* on the other hand, seek to move a reader, to gain support, to advocate a particular type of action.

A WRITER'S AUDIENCE

Audience is a key factor in every writing situation. Writing is, after all, a form of communication and as such implies an audience. In many writing situations, your audience is a controlling factor that affects both the content of your paper and the style in which it is written. An effective writer learns to adjust to an audience and to write for that audience; for a writer, like a performer, needs and wants an audience.

Writers adjust their style and tone on a spectrum ranging from informal to formal. Articles that appear in popular, wide-circulation magazines often are written in the first person, use contractions, favor popular and colloquial words, and contain relatively short sentences and paragraphs. Articles in more scholarly journals exhibit a formal style that involves an objective and serious tone, a more learned vocabulary, and longer and more complicated sentence and paragraph constructions. In the informal style the writer injects his or her personality into the prose; in the formal style the writer remains detached and impersonal. A writer adopts whatever style seems appropriate for a particular audience or context. An effective writer does not have just one style or voice, but many.

SOME THINGS TO REMEMBER

Before you begin even to prewrite, you need to think about your subject, purpose, and audience. Remind yourself of their importance in your writing process by jotting down responses to the following:

1. My general subject is _____.

2. My more specific topic is _____.

3. My purpose is to _____.

4. My intended audience is _____.

A WRITER'S INFORMATION

What makes writing entertaining, informative, or persuasive is information—specific, relevant detail. If you try to write without gathering information, you end up skimming the surface of your subject, even if you "know" something about it.

How you go about gathering information on your topic depends upon your subject and your purpose for writing. Some topics, such as those involving a personal experience, require a memory search; other assignments, such as describing a particular place, require careful observation. Essays that convey information or argue particular positions often demand information that must be gathered through research. Some possible strategies for gathering information and ideas about your topic are listed below. Before you start this step in your prewriting, remember three things.

First, **remember that different tactics work for different topics and for different writers.** You might find that freewriting is great for some assignments, but not for others. As a writer, explore your options. Don't rule out any strategy until you have tried it. Second, **remember that prewriting activities sometimes produce information and sometimes just produce questions that you will then need to answer.** In other words, prewriting often involves learning what you don't know, what you need to find out. Learning to ask the right questions is just as important as knowing the right answers. Third, **remember that these prewriting activities are an excellent way in which to find a focus, to narrow a subject, or to suggest a working plan for your essay.** As you begin to explore a subject or topic, the possibilities spread out before you. Try not to be

How to Write an Essay

wedded to a particular topic or thesis until you have explored a subject through prewriting activities.

LISTING DETAILS FROM PERSONAL EXPERIENCE OR OBSERVATION

Even your most unforgettable experience has probably been forgotten in part. If you are going to re-create it for a reader, you will have to do some active searching among your memories. By focusing your attention you can slowly recall more details. Ask yourself a series of questions about the chronology of the experience. For example, start with a particular detail and then try to stimulate your memory: What happened just before? Just after? Who was there? Where did the experience take place? Why did it happen? When did it happen? How did it happen?

Sense impressions, like factual details, decay from memory. In the height of the summer, it is not easy to recall a crisp fall day. Furthermore, sensory details are not always noticed, let alone recorded. How many times have you passed by a particular location without really seeing it?

Descriptions, like every other form of writing, demand specific information, and the easiest way to gather that detail is to observe. Before you try to describe a person, place, or object, take some time to list specific details on a piece of paper. At first record everything you notice. Do not worry about having too much, for you can always edit later. At this stage it is better to have too much than to have too little.

The next step is to decide what to include in your description and what to exclude. As a general principle, an effective written description does not try to record everything. The selection of detail should be governed by your purpose in the description. Ask yourself what you are trying to show or reveal. For what reason? What is particularly important about this person, place, or object? A description is not the verbal equivalent of a photograph or a tape recording.

FREEWRITING

Putting words down on a page or a computer screen can be very intimidating. Your editing instincts immediately want to take over—are the words spelled correctly? Are the sentences complete? Do they contain any mechanical or grammatical errors? Not only must you express your ideas in words, but suddenly those words must be the correct words.

When you translate thoughts into written words and then edit those words at the same time, writing can seem impossible. Instead of allowing ideas to take shape in words or allowing the writing to stimulate your thinking, you become fearful of committing anything to paper.

Writing, however, can stimulate thought. Every writer has experienced times when an idea became clear because it was written down. If those editing instincts can be turned off, you can use writing as a way of generating ideas about a paper.

Freewriting is an effective way to deal with this dilemma. Write without stopping for a fixed period of time—a period as short as ten minutes or as long as an hour. Do not stop; do not edit; do not worry about mistakes. You are looking for a focus point—an idea or a subject for a paper. You are trying to externalize your thinking into writing. What emerges is a free association of ideas. Some are relevant; some are worthless. After you have ideas on paper, you can then decide what is worth saving, developing, or simply throwing away.

JOURNALS

A daily journal can be an effective seedbed of ideas for writing projects. Such a journal should not be a daily log of your activities (got up, went to class, had lunch), but instead a place where you record ideas, observations, memories, feelings. Set aside a specific notebook or a pad of paper in which to keep your journal. Try to write for at least ten minutes every day. Over a period of time—such as a semester—you will be surprised how many ideas for papers or projects you will accumulate. When you are working on a paper, you might want to confine part of your daily journal entries to that particular subject.

BRAINSTORMING AND MAPPING

A brainstorm is an oral freewriting in which a group of people jointly try to solve a problem by spontaneously contributing ideas. Whatever comes to mind, no matter how obvious or unusual, gets said. Hopefully out of the jumble of ideas that surface, some possible solutions to the problem will be found.

Although brainstorming is by definition a group activity, it can also be done by the individual writer. In the center of a blank sheet of paper, write down a key word or phrase referring to your subject. Then in the space around your subject, quickly jot down any ideas that come to mind. Do not write in sentences—just key words and phrases. Because you are not filling consecutive lines with words and because you have space in which the ideas can be arranged, this form of brainstorming often suggests structural relationships. You can increase the usefulness of such an idea generator by adding graphic devices such as circles, arrows, or connecting lines to indicate the possible relationships among ideas. These devices can be added to your brainstorming sheet later, and they become a map to the points you might want to cover in your essay.

FORMAL QUESTIONING

One particularly effective way to gather information on any topic is to ask yourself questions about it. This allows you to explore the subject from a variety of different angles. After all, the secret to finding answers always lies in knowing the right questions to ask. A good place to start is with the list of questions below. Remember, though, that not every question is appropriate for every topic.

Illustration
1. What examples of _____ can be found?
2. In what ways are these things examples of _____?
3. What details about _____ seem the most important?

Comparison and Contrast
1. To what is _____ similar? List the points of similarity.
2. From what is _____ different? List the points of difference.
3. Which points of similarity or difference seem most important?
4. What does the comparison or contrast tell the reader about _____?

Division and Classification
1. Into how many parts can _____ be divided?
2. How many parts is _____ composed of?
3. What other category of things is _____ most like?
4. How does _____ work?
5. What are _____'s component parts?

Process
1. How many steps or stages are involved in _____?
2. In what order do those steps or stages occur?

Cause and Effect
1. What precedes _____?
2. Is that a cause of _____?
3. What follows _____?

4. Is that an effect of _____?

5. How many causes of _____ can you find?

6. How many effects of _____ can you find?

7. Why does _____ happen?

Definition

1. How is _____ defined in a dictionary?

2. Does everyone agree about the meaning of _____?

3. Does _____ have any connotations? What are they?

4. Has the meaning of _____ changed over time?

5. What words are synonymous with _____?

Argument and Persuasion

1. How do your readers feel about _____?

2. How do you feel about _____?

3. What are the arguments in favor of _____? List those arguments in order of strength.

4. What are the arguments against _____? List those arguments in order of strength.

INTERVIEWING

Typically you gather information for college papers by locating printed sources—books, articles, reports. Depending upon your topic, however, printed sources are not always available. In that case, people often represent a great source of information for a writer. Obviously you should choose someone who has special credentials or knowledge about the subject.

Interviewing requires some special skills and tact. When you first contact someone to request an interview, always explain who you are, what you want to know, and how you will use the information. Remember that specific questions will produce more useful information than general ones. Take notes that you can expand later, or use a tape recorder. Keep attention focused on the information that you need, and do not be afraid to ask questions to keep your informant on the subject. If you plan to use direct quotations, make sure that the wording is accurate. If possible, check the quotations with your source one final time.

A WRITER'S THESIS

For informative and argumentative essays, the information-gathering stage of the writing process is the time in which to sharpen your topic

How to Write an Essay

and to define first a tentative or working thesis for your paper and then a final thesis. Even narrative and descriptive essays may be strengthened by the development of a thesis at this stage.

Thesis is derived from a Greek word that means "placing" or "position" or "proposition." When you formulate a thesis, you are defining your position on the subject. A thesis lets your reader know exactly where you stand. Because it represents your "final" position, a thesis is typically something that you develop and refine as you move through the prewriting stage, testing out ideas and gathering information. Don't try to start with a final thesis; begin with a tentative thesis (also called a *hypothesis*, from the Greek for "supposition"). Allow your final position to emerge based on what you have discovered in the prewriting stage.

Before you write a thesis statement, you need to consider the factors that will control or influence the form your thesis will take. For example, a thesis is a reflection of your purpose in writing. If your purpose is to persuade your audience to do or to believe something, your thesis will urge the reader to accept that position. If your purpose is to convey information to your reader, your thesis will forecast your main points and indicate how your paper will be organized.

Your thesis will also be shaped by the scope and length of your paper. Your topic and your thesis must be manageable within the space you have available; otherwise, you end up skimming the surface. A short paper requires a more precise focus than a longer one. As a result, when you move from subject to topic to thesis, make sure that each step is more specific and has an increasingly sharper focus. To check that focusing process, ask yourself the following questions:

What is my general subject?

What is my specific topic within that general subject area?

What is my position on that specific topic?

WRITING A THESIS STATEMENT

When you have answered the questions about your purpose, when you have sharpened your general subject into a topic, when you have defined your position toward that topic, you are ready to write a thesis statement. The process is simple. You write a thesis statement by linking together your topic and your position on that topic.

Subject: Violence on television

Topic: The impact that viewing televised violence has on young children

Thesis: Televised violence makes young children numb to violence in the real world, distorts their perceptions of how people behave, and teaches them how to be violent.

An effective thesis, like any position statement, has a number of characteristics.

1. A thesis should clearly signal the purpose of the paper.

2. A thesis should state or take a definite position. It tells the reader what will be covered in the paper.

3. A thesis should express that definite position in precise, familiar terms. Avoid vague, abstract, or complicated technical terms.

4. A thesis should offer a position that can be explored or expanded within the scope of the paper. Remember that in moving from a general subject to a thesis, you have narrowed and sharpened your focus.

PLACING A THESIS IN YOUR PAPER

Once you have written a thesis for your paper or essay, you must make two final decisions. First, you have to decide whether to include that explicit statement in your paper or just allow your paper's structure and content to imply that thesis. Second, if you decide to include a thesis statement, you must then determine where to place it in your paper. For example, should it appear in the first paragraph or at some point later in the paper?

If you look carefully at examples of professional writing, you will discover that neither question has a single answer. Writers make these decisions based upon the type of paper they are writing. As a student, however, you can follow several guidelines. Most pieces of writing done in college—either papers or essay examinations—should have explicit thesis statements. Typically, those statements should be placed early in the paper (although the thesis for a narrative or descriptive essay may typically come at the end). The thesis will not always be in the first paragraph since your introduction might be designed to attract a reader's attention. Nevertheless, placing a thesis statement early in your paper will guarantee that the reader knows exactly what to expect.

Every argumentative or persuasive paper should have an explicitly stated thesis. Where you place that thesis depends upon whether the paper is structured deductively or inductively. Since a deductive argument begins with a general truth and then moves to a specific application of that truth, such an arrangement requires that the thesis be stated early. On the other hand, since an inductive argument moves in the opposite direction, starting with specific evidence and then moving to a conclusion, such an arrangement requires that the thesis be withheld until near the end of the paper.

Similarly, whenever your strategy in a paper is to build to a conclusion, a realization, or a discovery, you can withhold an explicit statement of your thesis until late in the paper. An early statement would spoil the suspense.

REVISING AN ESSAY

The idea of revising a paper may not sound appealing in the least. By the time you have finished the paper, the last thing you want to do is to revise it. Nevertheless, revising is a crucial step in the writing process, one you cannot afford to skip.

The word *revision* literally means "to see again." You do not revise a paper just by proofreading it for mechanical and grammatical errors, which is an expected final step in the writing process. Instead, a revision takes place after a draft of a whole paper or part of it has been completed, after a period of time has elapsed and you have had a chance to get some advice or criticism on what you wrote, after you can see what you wrote, not what you *think* you wrote. Revision should also involve an active, careful scrutiny on your part of every aspect of your paper—your subject, thesis, purpose, audience, paragraph structures, sentence constructions, and word choice.

BEGINNING A REVISION

Revision should start not with the smallest unit—the choice of a particular word—but with the largest—the choice of subject, thesis, purpose, audience, and organization. A revision in its broadest sense involves a complete rethinking of a paper from idea through execution. Once you have finished a paper, think first about these five groups of questions—if possible, write out answers to each:

1. What is my *subject*? Is it too large? Too small? Is it interesting? Is it fresh or informative?
2. What is my *thesis*? Do I have a precise position on my subject? Have I stated that thesis in a single sentence? Do I see the difference between having a subject and having a thesis?
3. What is my *purpose*? Why did I write *this* paper? Have I expressed my purpose in my thesis statement? Is everything in the paper related to that purpose?

4. Whom do I imagine as my *audience*? Who will read this? What do they already know about the subject? Have I written the paper with that audience in mind?
5. How is my paper *structured*? Have I followed the advice on structure given in the chapter introductions to this text? Is the organization of my paper clear and inevitable? Can it be outlined easily? Have I provided enough examples and details?

USING THE ADVICE OF OTHERS

Another great help in revising is to find an editor/critic. If your writing instructor has the time to look at your draft or if your college or university has a writing center or a writing tutor program, you can get the advice of an experienced, trained reader. If your paper or part of it is discussed in class, listen to your classmates' comments as a way of gauging how successful your writing has been. If your writing class uses peer editing, you can study the responses of your editors for possible areas for revision.

Peer evaluation works best when readers start with a series of specific directions—questions to answer or things for which to look. If you are interested in trying peer evaluation, you and a classmate could start with an editing checksheet adapted from the "Some Things to Remember" section at the end of each introductory chapter in this book. Whenever you are responding to someone else's writing, remember that your comments are always more valuable if they are specific and suggest ways in which changes could be made.

It is often difficult to accept criticism, but if you want to improve your writing skills, you need someone to say, "why not do this?" After all, you expect that an athletic coach or a music or dance teacher will offer criticism. Your writing instructor plays the same role, and the advice and criticism he or she offers is meant to make your writing more effective; it is not intended as a personal criticism of you or your abilities.

JUDGING LENGTH

After you have finished a draft of a paper, look carefully at how your response measures up to your instructor's guidelines about the length of the paper. Such guidelines are important for they give you some idea of the amount of space that you will need to develop and illustrate your thesis sufficiently. If your papers are consistently short, you probably have not included enough examples or illustrating details. Writing the suggested number of words does not, of course, guarantee a good essay, but writing only half of the suggested number because you fail to develop and illustrate your thesis can result in a lower grade.

Similarly, if your papers consistently exceed your instructor's guidelines, you have probably not sufficiently narrowed your subjects or you may have included too many details and examples. Of the material available to support, develop, and illustrate a thesis, some is more significant and relevant than the rest. Never try to include everything—select the best, the most appropriate, the most convincing.

CHECKING PARAGRAPHS

The qualities of a good paragraph—things like unity, coherence, organization, completeness—have been stressed in every writing course you have taken. When you revise your paper, look carefully at each paragraph to see if it exhibits those qualities. How often have you paragraphed? If you have only one or two paragraphs in a several-page essay, you have not clearly indicated the structure of your essay to your reader or your essay does not have a clear, logical organization. On the other hand, if you have many short paragraphs, you are overparagraphing, probably shifting ideas too quickly and failing to develop each one adequately. A good paragraph is meaty; a good essay is not a string of undeveloped ideas or bare generalizations.

IS AN ERROR-FREE PAPER AN "A" PAPER?

Although good, effective writing is mechanically and grammatically correct, you cannot reverse the equation. It is perfectly possible to write a paper that has no "errors" but that is still a poor paper. An effective paper fulfills the requirements of the assignment, has something interesting or meaningful to say, includes specific evidence and examples rather than vague generalizations. Effective writing is a combination of many factors: appropriate content, a focused purpose, a clear organization, and effective expression.

Although perfect grammar and mechanics do not make a perfect paper, such things are important. Minor errors are like static in your writing. Too many of them distract your reader and focus the reader's attention not on your message, but on your faulty expression. Minor errors can undermine your reader's confidence in you as a

qualified authority. If you make careless errors in spelling or punctuation, for example, your reader might assume that you made similar
errors in reporting information. So while a revision is not just a
proofreading, proofreading should be a part of the revision process.

A STUDENT WRITER'S REVISION PROCESS

The writing and rewriting process as outlined in this section can be
seen in the evolution of Tina Burton's "The Watermelon Wooer."
Tina's essay was written in response to a totally open assignment: she
was just to write an essay using examples, due in three weeks. The
openness of the assignment proved initially frustrating to Tina.
When she first began work on an essay, she started with a completely
different topic. That weekend, however, she went home to visit her
parents. Her grandfather had died just a few months before and the
family was sorting through some photographs and reminiscing about
him. Suddenly, Tina had the idea she wanted: she would write about
her grandfather and her ambivalent feelings toward him. Once she
had defined this specific topic, she also determined her purpose (to
inform about her grandfather and her mixed feelings, as well as to entertain through a vivid description of this unusual old man), and her
audience (her instructor and classmates).

Tina's first written work on the assignment came when she
made a list of about thirty things that she remembered about him.
"The list had to be cut," Tina said, "so I marked off those things
which were too bawdy or too unbelievable." "I wanted to portray him
as sympathetic," she added, "but I was really afraid that the whole
piece would come off as too sentimental or drippy."

At the next class meeting, the instructor set aside some time for
prewriting activities. The teacher recommended that the students try
either a freewriting or a brainstorming exercise. Tina did the brainstorming that appears on the following page.

EARLIER DRAFT

From here, Tina wrote a complete draft in one sitting. She had the
most difficulty with the beginning of the essay. "I kept trying to describe him, but I found that I was including too much," she commented. The breakthrough came through the advice of two other
students in the class. The first page of the first draft of Tina's essay
follows. The handwritten comments were provided by Kathrine
Varnes.

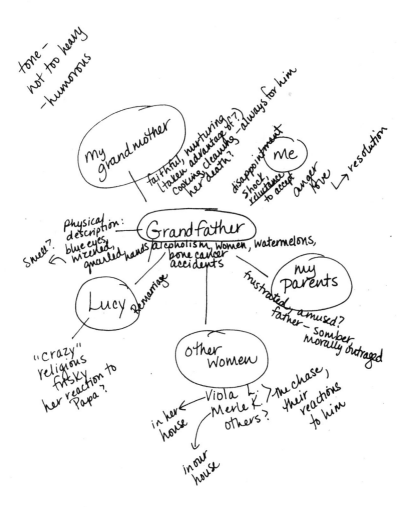

tone –
not too heavy
– humorous

my grandmother

faithful, nurturing?
(taken advantage of?)
cooking, cleaning, –always for him
her death?

me

disappointment
shock,
reluctance
to accept
anger
love
→ resolution

physical
description:
blue eyes,
wrinkled,
gnarled hands
Smell?

Grandfather

alcoholism, Women, watermelons,
bone cancer
accidents

my
Parents

frustrated,
amused?
father – somber
morally outraged

Lucy

Remarriage

"crazy"
religious
frisky
her reaction to
Papa?

other
Women

Viola L.
Merle K.
others?

the chase,
their reactions
to him

in her
house

in our
house

The Watermelon Wooer

When someone you love dearly behaves in
a manner that offends you, do you stop
loving that person? Do you lose all respect
for that person because you cannot forget

~~repulsive [?]~~

the act (that you judged as repulsive) (On the

Eventually,?

contrary), you might (eventually) fondly recall

*I have a
personal
dislike for
this 3-word
transition

the once offensive behavior. (Perhaps,) in

time, you might even understand why you

so?

found the behavior loathesome. Maybe, you

will reach a point in time when you will be

Some way
to
condense?

unable to think of your loved one without

thinking of the once questionable behavior.

Such is the case with my grandfather.

Before I tell the story of how my
grandfather behaved in ways that I could
neither understand nor tolerate, I must

introduce?

first (give some background information on)
him. A wizened little man with dancing blue
eyes and hands gnarled from years of
carpentry work, "Papa" was a notorious
womanizer and an alcoholic. Born and raised

in Halifax County, Virginia, he spent most
of his life building houses, distilling and
selling corn liquor, and chasing women.
After he and my grandmother had been married
for thirty years or so, he decided to
<u>curtail some of his wild behavior and treat</u>   *both of these*
                                                      things? or
<u>her with more respect</u>. Actually, he remained   *respect by*
                                                      curtailing?
faithful to her only after he discovered
that she was ill and probably wouldn't be
around to feed and nurture him for much
longer. ~~So, as you can see,~~ my grandfather
                                  _
(*didn't*
 does not) have a spotless, or even a remotely
   reputation
commendable record of personal achievements. *) use alternative*
                                              diction to
                                              soften tone?

REVISED DRAFT

"Kathrine wanted me to condense and to find a way in which to jump
right into the essay," Tina noted. "She also said, 'you're trying to tell
too much. Let the story tell itself. Try to think of one thing that
might capture something essential or important about him.'" In a
second peer editing, Tina sought the advice of Stephen Palley, another classmate. Stephen offered these comments on this first page of
the second draft.

                                          characterize an essential
        The Watermelon Wooer   *part of his eccentricity*
my ~~grandfather~~ never really (settled down)
        Let me tell you a story about my   *Intro?*
                               ←
grandfather~~--and, I guess, me too. I don't~~

~~pretend to know whether my story will shock,~~

~~offend, amuse, or bore.~~ I only know that I

feel the need to tell the ~~story.~~ it

For a time he

~~Before I tell the story of how my~~

~~grandfather~~ behaved in ways that I could

but eventually

neither understand nor tolerate, I must

(I see him now)   Let me introduce

first introduce him. A wizened little man

with ~~dancing blue eyes~~ and hands ~~gnarled~~

~~from years of carpentry work,~~ "Papa" was a

notorious womanizer and an alcoholic. Born

and raised in Halifax County, Virginia, he

spent most of his life building houses,

distilling and selling corn liquor, and

chasing women. After he and my grandmother

had been married for thirty years or so, he

decided to show her some respect by

curtailing his wild behavior. Actually, he

remained faithful to her only after he

discovered that she was ill and probably

wouldn't be around to feed and nurture him

for much longer. Papa didn't have a spotless

reputation.

smell?
It's funny
but when
I think of my
grandfather
I think 1st
of the way
he smelled

Hilter
ponies,
fertilizer

"Stephen offered me quite a few helpful suggestions," Tina recalled, "but he also suggested something that I just didn't quite feel comfortable with." As you can see in the revised draft, Tina had queried Stephen about possibly including her memories of odor. In a conversation Stephen urged Tina to substitute memories of smells for memories of sight. In the end, though, Tina observed, "I just couldn't do what Stephen suggested."

FINAL DRAFT

Before the three weeks were over, Tina actually wrote five separate drafts of her essay. "Everything here is true," she said, "but I worried so much about what I included, because I didn't want to embarrass anyone in my family." "Throughout the process," she added, "I was also worried about my tone. I wanted it to be funny; I wanted my readers to like my grandfather and his watermelon adventures."

Reproduced below is Tina's final draft of her essay. Note that she concludes with a thesis that summarizes her main point.

The Watermelon Wooer

Tina M. Burton

I see him now, sprawled on our couch, clutching a frayed afghan, one brown toenail escaping his sock. His darting eyes are betraying his withered body.

Born and raised in backwoods Virginia, my grandfather spent most of his life building houses, distilling and selling corn liquor, and chasing women. After he and my grandmother had been married for thirty years or so, he decided to show her some respect by curtailing his wild behavior. Actually, he remained faithful to her only after he discovered that she was ill and probably wouldn't be around to feed and nurture him much longer. Papa didn't have a spotless reputation.

Because he'd been on the wagon for several years and hadn't had any affairs for the last ten years, my family thought that Papa would continue to behave in a "respectable" manner even after my grandmother died. I guess we were hoping for some sort of miracle. After my grandmother died in 1983, Papa became a rogue again: he insisted on reveling in wild abandon. When my father found out that Papa was drinking heavily again and crashing his car into mailboxes, houses, and other large obstacles, he asked Papa to move into our house. The fact that three of Papa's female neighbors had complained to the police about Papa's exposing himself probably had something to do with my father's decision.

The year that Papa lived with us rivaled the agony of Hell.

I was always Papa's favorite grandchild, his "gal," and I worshipped him from the time that I was old enough to spend summers with him on his farm. Until I saw him every day, witnessed for myself his sometimes lewd behavior and his odd personality quirks, I never really believed the stories about him that I had heard from my mother and father. Every morning, he baited my mother with comments like "the gravy's too thick," "my room's too cold," "your kids are too loud," and "the phone rings too often." Against my mother's wishes, he smoked in the house. In mixed company, he gleefully explained how to have sex in an inner tube in the ocean without getting caught and gave detailed physical descriptions of the women he'd had sex with. It surprised me how much my opinion of Papa changed in one year.

During this one year, Papa did many things that I thought were embarrassing and inexcusable. I came face-to-face with the "dark" side of his personality. One week after moving into my parents' home, Papa began to sneak the orange juice from the refrigerator and doctor it with Smirnoff's vodka. I knew he'd been pickling his brain with alcohol for years and that this was part of the disease, but he'd said that he'd gone dry. Besides, he was violating my father's most important rule: no alcohol in the house. I didn't know that his drinking was only the first of a long line of incredible acts.

The behaviors that ultimately endeared Papa to me, that made me forgive him his shortcomings, are also those which I recall with a great deal of sadness. These are the memories of him that I

treasure, the stories that I will tell to my
grandchildren when they are old enough to deal with
graphic material. A year ago, I never would have
believed that I could fondly remember, much less
write about, these episodes.

For about a year, Papa engaged in what I refer
to as the "watermelon affairs." Perhaps because he
had lived on a vegetable farm for the majority of
his life Papa had a special affinity for a wide
variety of fruits and vegetables. Especially dear to
him were watermelons. So, he assumed that other
elderly people, particularly women, shared his
proclivity for produce. One week after he moved into
my parent's house, he embarked upon his mission--to
woo with watermelons as many women as he could.

A shrewd man, possessed of a generous supply of
common sense and watermelons, Papa decided to seduce
a woman who lived very close to him. This woman
happened to be my maternal grandmother who also
lived in our house. Unaware of his lascivious
intentions and bent on helping him assuage his grief
over the loss of his wife, Grandmother Merle
prepared special meals for Papa and spent long hours
conversing with him about farming, grandchildren,
and life in the "Old South." Merle assumed that the
watermelons Papa brought to her were nothing more
than a token of his appreciation for her kindness.
When Papa grabbed a part of Merle that she preferred
to remain untouched, these conversations came to an
abrupt halt. Of course, we were mortified by his
inappropriate behavior, but I suspect that my
parents secretly were amused. While Papa's
indiscretion with Merle was upsetting, at least no
one other than members of my immediate family knew
about the incident. His next romantic adventure
earned him immediate notoriety in the neighborhood.
One afternoon, huge watermelon in hand, he trotted
over to visit Viola Lampson, a decrepit and cranky
elderly woman with whom my family had been friendly
for twenty years. Twenty minutes after Papa entered
her house, the police came. Poor Viola was in a
state of disrepair because my grandfather had been
chasing her around her kitchen table demanding
kisses. Fortunately, the policeman who arrived at

the scene of the crime was quite understanding and polite; he advised my father to keep a careful watch on Papa at all times. My somber father was very embarrassed. Finally, we were all beginning to see the relationship between watermelons and women. He'd disappear with a watermelon and return with the police.

I was mortified by Papa's lecherous desire for other women. After all, wasn't he supposed to be grieving over the death of my grandmother, his wife of fifty years? I resigned myself to the fact that I never would love him or respect him in the manner that I once had. For a while, I avoided his company and refused to answer his frequent questions about why I was avoiding him. I didn't think about why he was behaving the way he was; I simply cast judgement on his behavior and shut myself off from him. Not until Papa remarried did I even try to understand his needs or his behavior.

Approximately one year after his wife died, Papa remarried. Finally, he found a woman who not only loved watermelon but also loved him and his frisky behavior. Lucy, often referred to as "crazy Lucy" by her neighbors who had heard her speak of miracle healings and visions of Christ, wed Papa and took him into her already jam-packed home. Amazingly, she convinced him to stop drinking and to refrain from molesting other women. She could not, however, convince Papa to "get the religion" as she called it. My family was nonplussed both by Papa's decision to remarry at age 77 and to stop drinking after all these years. We all were annoyed by the fact that Lucy convinced him to do in several months what we had been trying to get him to do for many years.

Not until I learned that Papa was dying of bone cancer did I try to understand why he needed to remarry and why I found that fact unbearable. Until this time, I harbored the feeling that Papa somehow was degrading the memory of my grandmother by remarrying. His attempted seductions of women disturbed me, but his decision to marry Lucy saddened me. Only after I spent many afternoons with Papa and Lucy did I realize that they truly loved each other. More importantly, I realized that Papa,

devastated by his wife's death, was afraid to be
alone in his old age. Perhaps sensing his illness,
even though he knew nothing of its development at
this time, he wanted to recapture some of his
stamina, some of his youth. He really wasn't
searching for someone to replace my grandmother: he
simply wanted to have a companion to comfort him, to
distract him from his grief.

Fortunately, I accepted Papa's actions and
resolved my conflict with him before he died. Once
again, I was his "gal" in spirit, and I even came to
love and respect Lucy. Now, I find that I cannot
conjure images of Papa without thinking of
watermelons and his romantic escapades. The acts
that once troubled me eventually allowed me to
glimpse the frail side of my grandfather, to see him
as a human being possessed of fears and flaws rather
than a cardboard ideal.

SOME THINGS TO REMEMBER WHEN REVISING

1. Put your paper aside for a period of time before you attempt
   to revise it.

2. Seek the advice of your instructor or a writing center tutor,
   or the help of classmates.

3. Reconsider your choice of topic. Were you able to treat it
   adequately in the space you had available?

4. State your thesis in a sentence as a way of checking your
   content. Is everything in the paper relevant to that thesis?

5. Check to make sure that you have given enough examples to
   clarify your topic, to support your argument, or to make
   your thesis clear. Relevant specifics convince and interest a
   reader.

6. Look through the advice given in each of the introductions
   to this text. Have you organized your paper carefully? Is its
   structure clear?

7. Define your audience. To whom are you writing? What assumptions have you made about your audience? What
   changes are necessary to make your paper clear and interesting to that audience?

8. Check the guidelines your instructor provided. Have you
   done what was asked? Is your paper too short or too long?

9. Examine each sentence to make sure that it is complete and grammatically correct. Try for a variety of sentence structures and lengths.

10. Look carefully at each paragraph. Does it obey the rules for effective paragraph construction? Do your paragraphs clearly indicate the structure of your essay?

11. Check your word choice. Have you avoided slang, jargon, and clichés? Have you used specific words? Have you used appropriate words for your intended audience?

12. Proofread one final time.

GATHERING AND USING EXAMPLES

Effective writing in any form depends upon details and examples. Relevant details and examples make writing interesting, informative, and persuasive. If you try to write without having gathered these essential specifics, you are forced to skim the surface of your subject, relying on generalizations, incomplete and sometimes inaccurate details, and unsubstantiated opinions.

Without specifics, even a paper with a strong, clearly stated thesis becomes superficial. How convinced would you be by the following argument?

> In their quest for big-time football programs, American universities have lost sight of their educational responsibilities. Eager for the revenues and alumni support that come with winning teams, universities exploit their football players. They do not care if the players get an education. They care only that they remain academically eligible to play for four seasons. At many schools only a small percentage of these athletes graduate. Throughout their college careers, they are encouraged to take easy courses and to put athletics first. It does not matter how they perform in the classroom as long as they distinguish themselves every Saturday afternoon. This exploitation should not be allowed to continue. Universities have a responsibility to educate their students, not to use them to gain publicity and to raise money.

Even if you agree with the writer's thesis, the paragraph does not go beyond the obvious. The writer generalizes, and probably distorts as a result. What the reader gets is an opinion unsupported by any evidence. For example, you might reasonably ask questions about the statement, "At many schools only a small percentage of these athletes graduate." How many schools? How small a percentage? How does this percentage compare with that of non-athletes? After all, not everyone who starts college ends up graduating. To persuade your reader—and even to interest your reader—you need specific information, details and examples that illustrate the points you are trying to make.

WHERE CAN YOU FIND DETAILS AND EXAMPLES?

Basically, you gather details and examples either from your own experiences and observations or from research. Your sources vary depending upon what you are writing about. For example, *Life* magazine once asked writer Malcolm Cowley for an essay on what it was like to turn 80. Cowley was already 80 years old, so he had a wealth of firsthand experiences from which to draw. Since nearly all of Cowley's readers were younger than 80, he decided to show his readers what it was like to be old by providing a simple list that begins like this:

> The body and its surroundings have their messages for him, or only one message: "You are old." Here are some of the occasions on which he receives the message:
>
> —when it becomes an achievement to do thoughtfully, step by step, what he once did instinctively
>
> —when his bones ache
>
> —when there are more and more little bottles in the medicine cabinet, with instructions for taking four times a day
>
> —when he fumbles and drops his toothbrush (butterfingers)
>
> —when his face has bumps and wrinkles, so that he cuts himself while shaving (blood on the towel)
>
> —when year by year his feet seem farther from his hands
>
> —when he can't stand on one leg and has trouble pulling on his pants
>
> —when he hesitates on the landing before walking down a flight of stairs
>
> —when he spends more time looking for things misplaced than he spends using them after he (or more often his wife) has found them

—when he falls asleep in the afternoon

—when it becomes harder to bear in mind two things at once

—when a pretty girl passes him in the street and he doesn't turn his head

Much of what you might be writing about, however, lies outside of your own experiences and observations. David Guterson, for example, set out to write a magazine article for *Harper's* about the Mall of America in Minneapolis. He chose to begin his essay with a series of facts:

> Last April, on a visit to the new Mall of America near Minneapolis, I carried with me the public-relations press kit provided for the benefit of reporters. It included an assortment of "fun facts" about the mall: 140,000 hot dogs sold each week, 10,000 permanent jobs, 44 escalators and 17 elevators, 12,750 parking places, 13,300 short tons of steel, $1 million in cash disbursed weekly from 8 automatic-teller machines. Opened in the summer of 1992, the mall was built on the 78-acre site of the former Metropolitan Stadium, a five-minute drive from the Minneapolis–St. Paul International Airport. With 4.2 million square feet of floor space—including twenty-two times the retail footage of the average American shopping center—the Mall of America was "the largest fully enclosed combination retail and family entertainment center in the United States."

The accumulation of facts—taken from the press kit—becomes a way of catching the reader's attention. In a nation impressed by size, what better way to "capture" the country's largest mall than by heaping up facts and statistics.

As the examples in this chapter show, writers sometimes draw only upon their personal experiences, as Anna Quindlen does in "The Name Is Mine." Other times, though, writers mix examples drawn from their personal experiences with information gathered from outside sources. Deborah Tannen in "Wears Jump Suit, Sensible Shoes, Uses Husband's Last Name" starts with her observations of a small group of women and men at an academic conference and then interprets those observations using linguistic research. Tim Johnson in "You Have Definitely Won!" combines his own reactions to the magazine stamp sheet promotions with a series of quotations from relevant experts who comment on the honesty and the history of such advertising schemes. Regardless of where you find them, remember that specific, relevant details and examples are very important in anything you write. They add life and interest to your writing, and they support or illustrate the points you are trying to make.

How Do I Gather Details and Examples from My Experiences?

Even when you are narrating an experience that happened to you, or describing something that you saw, you will have to spend some time remembering the event, sorting out the details of the experience, and deciding which examples best support the point that you are trying to make. The best place to start in your memory and observation search is with the advice offered in "How to Write an Essay" (pp. 16–38).

Many of the essays in this and later chapters begin with the writer's memories, experiences, and observations. Anna Quindlen, for example, draws only on a series of experiences in her married life to write "The Name Is Mine." Similarly, Bob Greene's "Cut" begins with his own experience. Even when writers add information taken from sources outside of their own experiences—as do Deborah Tannen in "Wears Jump Suit, Sensible Shoes, Uses Husband's Last Name," Maxine Hong Kingston in "The Wild Man of the Green Swamp," and Tim Johnson in "You Have Definitely Won!"—observation and personal experience may still play a significant role.

How Do I Gather Information from Outside Sources?

When you think about researching a subject, you might think only of going to a library to look up your topic in a card catalog, a periodical index, or a database. But you can find information in many other ways. Presumably, Maxine Hong Kingston found the story of the "Wild Man" in a newspaper. She does not, however, just recount the story as a newspaper reporter might: she connects the story with her own experiences and observations. Deborah Tannen in "Wears Jump Suit, Sensible Shoes, Uses Husband's Last Name" begins with a series of observations she makes while watching the participants at a conference. She combines those observations with other pieces of information that she acquired from the research that she and other scholars have done in the field of linguistics. Tim Johnson in "You Have Definitely Won!," a feature article from a Sunday magazine supplement in a large city newspaper, finds his details and examples in the places you might expect a feature writer to use—primarily from personal observation and from interviews with knowledgeable sources. The experiences of other people can also be excellent sources of information. Bob Greene, for example, recounts the experiences of four men who were also "cut" from athletic teams when they were young.

When you use information gathered from outside sources—whether those sources are written texts or interviews—it is important that you document those sources. While it is true that articles in newspapers and magazines do not provide the type of documentation that you find in a paper written for a college course, nevertheless you are a student and not a reporter. Be sure to ask your instructor how you are to document quotations and paraphrases—is it all right just to mention the sources in the text or do you need to provide formal parenthetical documentation? Additional advice and sample papers can be found in the appendix, "Finding, Using, and Documenting Sources," p. 549. Be sure to read that material before you hand in a paper that uses outside sources.

HOW MANY EXAMPLES ARE ENOUGH?

It would make every writer's job much easier if there were a single, simple answer to the question of how many examples to use. Instead, the answer is "enough," "enough to interest the reader," "enough to convince the reader." Sometimes one fully developed example might be enough. The advertisements for organizations such as Save the Children often tell the story of a specific child in need of food and shelter. The single example, accompanied with a photograph, is enough to persuade many people to sponsor a child. Maxine Hong Kingston in "The Wild Man of the Green Swamp" focuses on one example—using that example as a way to make her point about how society as a whole views an "outsider."

Other times you might need to use many details and examples. Deborah Tannen begins by watching three women at a conference. She uses her observations as a basis from which to generalize about how society "marks" women, but not men. In "Cut," Bob Greene writes about how being "cut" from the junior high school basketball team changed his life. To support his thesis and extend it beyond his own personal experience, Greene includes the stories of four other men who had similar experiences. But why give five examples of the same experience? Why not three or seven? There is nothing magical about the number five—Greene might have used five because he had that much column space in the magazine—but the five give authority to Greene's assertion, or at least they create the illusion of authority. To prove the validity of Greene's thesis would require a proper statistical sample. Only then could it be said with some certainty that the experience of being "cut" makes men superachievers later in life. In most writing situations, however, such thoroughness is not needed. If the details and examples are well chosen and relevant, the reader is likely to accept your assertions.

SAMPLE STUDENT ESSAY

Frank Smite, recently divorced and recently returned to college, chose to work on an essay about the difficulties that older, single or newly-single people have in meeting people to date. "Young college kids have it easy," Frank complained, "you are constantly surrounded by eligible people your own age. Try meeting someone when you're thirty-five, slightly balding, just divorced, and working all day." His first draft of the opening of his essay appears below:

```
              My Search for Love
    My wife and I separated and then quickly
divorced a year ago. I figured that I would be able
to forget some of the pain by returning to dating.
At first, I was excited about the prospect of
meeting new people. It made me feel young again.
Besides, this time I'd be able to avoid the problems
that led to my divorce. While I'm not exactly a male
movie star--I'm thirty-five, a little overweight,
kind of thin on the top, and have one daughter who I
desperately miss seeing every day--I figured that
romance was just around the corner.
    It wasn't until I started to look for people to
ask out that I realized how far away that corner
was. Frankly, in my immediate world, there seemed to
be no one who was roughly my age and unmarried.
That's when I began to look at the various ways that
people in my situation can meet people. I attended
several meetings of the local Parents Without
Partners group, but that didn't seem promising; I
joined a computerized dating service; and, believe
it or not, I started reading the "personals" in the
newspaper.
```

When Frank came to revise his essay, he had his instructor's comments and the reactions of several classmates. Everyone agreed that he had an excellent subject and some good detail, but several readers were a little troubled by Frank's overuse of "I." One reader asked Frank if he could make his essay focus a little less on his own immediate experience and a little more on what anyone in his position might do. His instructor suggested that with the right type of revision, Frank might be able to publish his essay in the local newspaper—after all, she noted, many people are in the same situation. His instructor also suggested that Frank might eliminate the reference to his daughter and how much he misses her. Although those feelings are important, that is not where Frank wanted to center the essay. Frank liked the idea of sharing his experiences with a wider audience. His revised introduction—complete with a new title—follows:

Looking for Love

Ask any single or divorced adult about the problems of meeting "prospective partners" and you are likely to get a litany of complaints and horrifying experiences. No longer can people rely on introductions from well-meaning friends. After all, most of those friends are also looking for love. Matchmaking has become big business--even, in fact, a franchised business.

Today the search for love takes many forms, from bar hopping, to organizations such as Parents Without Partners, to computerized and videotaped "search services," to singles groups organized around a shared concern (for example, those who are concerned about the environment or who love books). A little more desperate (and risky and certainly tacky) is the newspaper classified. Titled "Getting Personal" in my local newspaper, advertisements typically read like this one running today: "Single white female, pretty, petite blond, 40's ISO [in search of] WM [white male] for a perfect relationship (it does exist!)."

SOME THINGS TO REMEMBER

1. Use details and examples—effective writing depends upon them.
2. For some subjects, you can find the illustrations you need from your own experiences and observations. You will proba-

bly need, however, to work at remembering and gathering those specifics.

3. For some subjects you will need some type of research—interviewing people, looking material up in your school's library, connecting your observations with knowledge that you have acquired in other courses or situations.

4. Choose examples that are relevant and accurate. Quality is more important than quantity. Make sure your examples support your argument or illustrate the points you are trying to make. If you use an outside authority—either an interview or a printed source—make sure that the source is knowledgeable and reliable. Remember also to document those sources.

5. The number of details and examples you need necessarily varies. Sometimes one will do; sometimes you will need many. If you want your readers to do or to believe something, you will need to supply some evidence to gain their support or confidence.

The Name Is Mine
Anna Quindlen

*Born in 1953, Anna Quindlen attended Barnard College in New York City.
She has enjoyed a successful career at the* New York Times, *where she has
written three different weekly columns, including her current syndicated column, "Public & Private," for which she won the 1992 Pulitzer Prize for
commentary. Two collections of her columns have been published, in addition
to a children's book,* The Tree That Came to Stay *(1992) and a novel,*
Object Lessons *(1991). Currently, she is working on a second novel.*

    *This essay first appeared in "Life in the 30's," a weekly column that
Quindlen wrote for the* Times *from 1986 to 1988. Based on her own experiences as a mother, a wife, and a journalist, the column attracted millions
of readers and was syndicated in some sixty other newspapers. She ended the
column because of its personal nature: "It wasn't just that I was in the spotlight; it was like I was in the spotlight naked. . . . 'Life in the 30's' was
where I became public property."*

    *Here Quindlen remembers why she did not take her husband's name
when they married. "This is a story about a name," she writes. "The name
is mine. I was given it at birth, and I have never changed it, although I
married."*

BEFORE READING

Connecting: Can you remember times when your "identity" was defined not by yourself but by your association with someone else, when
you were the child *of*, the sibling *of*, the spouse *of*, the parent *of*, the
employee *of*? How did these occasions make you feel?

Anticipating: Every decision we make has consequences—some of
which we are immediately aware of and some of which only emerge
later. What are the consequences of Quindlen's decision not to take
her husband's name?

I am on the telephone to the emergency room of the local hospital.   1
My elder son is getting stitches in his palm, and I have called to make
myself feel better, because I am at home, waiting, and my husband is
there, holding him. I am 34 years old, and I am crying like a child,

making a slippery mess of my face. "Mrs. Krovatin?" says the nurse, and for the first time in my life I answer "Yes."

2   This is a story about a name. The name is mine. I was given it at birth, and I have never changed it, although I married. I could come up with lots of reasons why. It was a political decision, a simple statement that I was somebody and not an adjunct of anybody, especially a husband. As a friend of mine told her horrified mother, "He didn't adopt me, he married me."

3   It was a professional and a personal decision, too. I grew up with an ugly dog of a name, one I came to love because I thought it was weird and unlovable. Amid the Debbies and Kathys of my childhood, I had a first name only my grandmothers had and a last name that began with a strange letter. "Sorry, the letters, I, O, Q, U, V, X, Y and Z are not available," the catalogues said about monogrammed key rings and cocktail napkins. Seeing my name in black on white at the top of a good story, suddenly it wasn't an ugly dog anymore.

4   But neither of these are honest reasons, because they assume rational consideration, and it so happens that when it came to changing my name, there was no consideration, rational or otherwise. It was mine. It belonged to me. I don't even share a checking account with my husband. Damned if I was going to be hidden beneath the umbrella of his identity.

5   It seemed like a simple decision. But nowadays I think the only simple decisions are whether to have grilled cheese or tuna fish for lunch. Last week, my older child wanted an explanation of why he, his dad and his brother have one name, and I have another.

6   My answer was long, philosophical and rambling—that is to say, unsatisfactory. What's in a name? I could have said disingenuously. But I was talking to a person who had just spent three torturous, exhilarating years learning names for things, and I wanted to communicate to him that mine meant something quite special to me, had seemed as form-fitting as my skin, and as painful to remove. Personal identity and independence, however, were not what he was looking for; he just wanted to make sure I was one of them. And I am—and then again, I am not. When I made this decision, I was part of a couple. Now, there are two me's, the me who is the individual and the me who is part of a family of four, a family of four in which, in a small way, I am left out.

7   A wise friend who finds herself in the same fix says she never wants to change her name, only to have a slightly different identity as a family member, an identity for pediatricians' offices and parent-teacher conferences. She also says that the entire situation reminds her of the women's movement as a whole. We did these things as individuals, made these decisions about ourselves and what we wanted

Gathering and Using Examples

to be and do. And they were good decisions, the right decisions. But we based them on individual choice, not on group dynamics. We thought in terms of our sense of ourselves, not our relationships with others.

Some people found alternative solutions: hyphenated names, 8 merged names, matriarchal names for the girls and patriarchal ones for the boys, one name at work and another at home. I did not like those choices; I thought they were middle grounds, and I didn't live much in the middle ground at the time. I was once slightly disdainful of women who went all the way and changed their names. But I now know too many smart, independent, terrific women who have the same last names as their husbands to be disdainful anymore. (Besides, if I made this decision as part of a feminist world view, it seems dishonest to turn around and trash other women for deciding as they did.)

I made my choice. I haven't changed my mind. I've just changed 9 my life. Sometimes I feel like one of those worms I used to hear about in biology, the ones that, chopped in half, walked off in different directions. My name works fine for one half, not quite as well for the other. I would never give it up. Except for that one morning when I talked to the nurse at the hospital, I always answer the question "Mrs. Krovatin?" with "No, this is Mr. Krovatin's wife." It's just that I understand the down side now.

When I decided not to disappear beneath my husband's um- 10 brella, it did not occur to me that I would be the only one left outside. It did not occur to me that I would ever care—not enough to change, just enough to think about the things we do on our own and what they mean when we aren't on our own anymore.

QUESTIONS ON SUBJECT AND PURPOSE

1. Why did Quindlen not change her last name when she married?
2. How does she feel about her decision now?
3. Since Quindlen does not plan to change her name, what purpose might she have in writing the essay?

QUESTIONS ON STRATEGY AND AUDIENCE

1. The essay could begin at the second paragraph. Why might Quindlen have chosen to begin the essay with the telephone call experience?

2. In paragraph 9, Quindlen returns to the incident at the hospital. How does this device help hold the essay together?
3. The essay appeared in a column headed "Life in the 30's." How might that affect the nature of the audience who might read the essay?

QUESTIONS ON VOCABULARY AND STYLE

1. At the beginning of paragraphs 2 and 9, Quindlen uses three very short simple sentences in a row. Why?
2. Twice in the essay (paragraphs 4 and 10), Quindlen refers to coming under her husband's "umbrella." What is the effect of such an image?
3. Be able to define the following words: *disingenuously* (paragraph 6) and *disdainful* (8).

WRITING SUGGESTIONS

1. **For your Journal**. Do you have any desire to change your name? If so, why? If not, why not? In your journal explore what changing or not changing your name might mean. Would "you" be any different?
2. **For a Paragraph**. In a paragraph explore the meaning that you find in your name. You can choose your first or last name, or even a nickname. How does that name define you?
3. **For an Essay**. In paragraph 6, Quindlen remarks, "there are two me's, the me who is the individual and the me who is part of a family of four. . . ." Everyone experiences such moments of awareness. Think about those times when you have been "two," and in an essay explore the dilemma posed by being an individual and, at the same time, a part of a larger whole.

Prewriting:
a. Make a list of relationships that might have produced similar experiences (you and your family, you and your friends, you and a social group).
b. Select one of those relationships and freewrite about it, trying to focus on a significant and specific decision you made.
c. Remember that the experience will have to be narrated in a time sequence, either starting with the decision and then tracing the consequences, or starting with the consequences and then flashing back to the decision.

Gathering and Using Examples

Rewriting:

  a. Try, if you have not already done so, to imitate Quindlen's strategy of "hooking" the reader into the essay.

  b. Experiment with a different time sequence (as described in c above) for your essay. Does the other sequence work any more effectively?

  c. Try to find someone to read your essay—a friend, room-mate, classmate, or tutor in a writing center. Ask your reader for some constructive criticism and then listen to what you hear.

4. For Research. How widespread and recent is the phenomenon of women not taking their husbands' names? Research the problem through periodical sources in your college's library and through interviews. Then, using that research, write an essay for one of the following audiences:

  a. An article intended for a male audience

  b. An article intended for an unmarried female audience who might be considering such a decision

  c. A traditional research paper for a college course

CUT

Bob Greene

Bob Greene was born in Columbus, Ohio, in 1947 and received a B.J. from Northwestern University in 1969. He has been a columnist for the Chicago Sun-Times, *the* Chicago Tribune, *and* Esquire, *as well as a contributing correspondent for "ABC News Nightline." His books include* Running: A Nixon-McGovern Campaign Journal *(1973),* American Beat *(1983), and* Hang Time: Days, Dreams and Destinations with Michael Jordan *(1992). Recently, he wrote his first novel,* All Summer Long *(1993), about three men who meet at a twenty-fifth high school reunion.*

Greene is, in many ways, a reporter of everyday events. He rarely tries to be profound, but concentrates instead on "human interest" stories, the experiences that we all share. In this essay from Esquire, *a magazine aimed at a male audience, Greene relates the stories of five successful men who shared the experience of being "cut from the team." Does being "cut," Greene wonders, make you a superachiever later in life?*

BEFORE READING

Connecting: Was there ever a time when you realized that you were not going to be allowed to participate in something that you wanted very much? Did someone tell you, "you're not good enough," or did you realize it yourself?

Anticipating: Writers recount personal experiences for some reason, and that reason is never just "here is what happened to me"; instead, writers focus on the significance of the experience. What significance does Greene see in these narratives?

1   I remember vividly the last time I cried. I was twelve years old, in the seventh grade, and I had tried out for the junior high school basketball team. I walked into the gymnasium; there was a piece of paper tacked to the bulletin board.

2   It was a cut list. The seventh-grade coach had put it up on the board. The boys whose names were on the list were still on the team; they were welcome to keep coming to practices. The boys whose

     How to Read an Essay

names were not on the list had been cut; their presence was no longer desired. My name was not on the list.

I had not known the cut was coming that day. I stood and stared   3
at the list. The coach had not composed it with a great deal of subtlety; the names of the very best athletes were at the top of the sheet of paper, and the other members of the squad were listed in what appeared to be a descending order of talent. I kept looking at the bottom of the list, hoping against hope that my name would miraculously appear there if I looked hard enough.

I held myself together as I walked out of the gym and out of the   4
school, but when I got home I began to sob. I couldn't stop. For the first time in my life, I had been told officially that I wasn't good enough. Athletics meant everything to boys that age; if you were on the team, even a substitute, it put you in the desirable group. If you weren't on the team, you might as well not be alive.

I had tried desperately in practice, but the coach never seemed   5
to notice. It didn't matter how hard I was willing to work; he didn't want me there. I knew that when I went to school the next morning I would have to face the boys who had not been cut—the boys whose names were on the list, who were still on the team, who had been judged worthy while I had been judged unworthy.

All these years later, I remember it as if I were still standing   6
right there in the gym. And a curious thing has happened: in traveling around the country, I have found that an inordinately large proportion of successful men share that same memory—the memory of being cut from a sports team as a boy.

I don't know how the mind works in matters like this; I don't   7
know what went on in my head following that day when I was cut. But I know that my ambition has been enormous ever since then; I know that for all of my life since that day, I have done more work than I had to be doing, taken more assignments than I had to be taking, put in more hours than I had to be spending. I don't know if all of that came from a determination never to allow myself to be cut again— never to allow someone to tell me that I'm not good enough again— but I know it's there. And apparently it's there in a lot of other men, too.

Bob Graham, thirty-six, is a partner with the Jenner & Block law   8
firm in Chicago. "When I was sixteen, baseball was my whole life," he said. "I had gone to a relatively small high school, and I had been on the team. But then my family moved, and I was going to a much bigger high school. All during the winter months I told everyone that

I was a ballplayer. When spring came, of course I went out for the team.

9   "The cut list went up. I did not make the team. Reading that cut list is one of the clearest things I have in my memory. I wanted not to believe it, but there it was.

10   "I went home and told my father about it. He suggested that maybe I should talk to the coach. So I did. I pleaded to be put back on the team. He said there was nothing he could do; he said he didn't have enough room.

11   "I know for a fact that it altered my perception of myself. My view of myself was knocked down; my self-esteem was lowered. I felt so embarrassed; my whole life up to that point had revolved around sports, and particularly around playing baseball. That was the group I wanted to be in—the guys on the baseball team. And I was told that I wasn't good enough to be one of them.

12   "I know now that it changed me. I found out, even though I couldn't articulate it at the time, that there would be times in my life when certain people would be in a position to say 'You're not good enough' to me. I did not want that to happen ever again.

13   "It seems obvious to me now that being cut was what started me in determining that my success would always be based on my own abilities, and not on someone else's perceptions. Since then I've always been something of an overachiever; when I came to the law firm I was very aggressive in trying to run my own cases right away, to be the lead lawyer in the cases with which I was involved. I made partner at thirty-one; I never wanted to be left behind.

14   "Looking back, maybe it shouldn't have been that important. It was only baseball. You pass that by. Here I am. That coach is probably still there, still a high school baseball coach, still cutting boys off the baseball team every year. I wonder how many hundreds of boys he's cut in his life?"

15   Maurice McGrath is senior vice-president of Genstar Mortgage Corporation, a mortgage banking firm in Glendale, California. "I'm forty-seven years old, and I was fourteen when it happened to me, and I still feel something when I think about it," he said.

16   "I was in the eighth grade. I went to St. Philip's School in Pasadena. I went out for the baseball team, and one day at practice the coach came over to me. He was an Occidental College student who had been hired as the eighth-grade coach.

17   "He said, 'You're no good.' Those were his words. I asked him why he was saying that. He said, 'You can't hit the ball. I don't want you here.' I didn't know what to do, so I went over and sat off to the

side, watching the others practice. The coach said I should leave the practice field. He said that I wasn't on the team, and that I didn't belong there anymore.

"I was outwardly stoic about it. I didn't want anyone to see how 18 I felt. I didn't want to show that it hurt. But oh, did it hurt. All my friends played baseball after school every day. My best friend was the pitcher on the team. After I got whittled down by the coach, I would hear the other boys talking in class about what they were going to do at practice after school. I knew that I'd just have to go home.

"I guess you make your mind up never to allow yourself to be 19 hurt like that again. In some way I must have been saying to myself, 'I'll play the game better.' Not the sports game, but anything I tried. I must have been saying, 'If I have to, I'll sit on the bench, but I'll be part of the team.'

"I try to make my own kids believe that, too. I try to tell them 20 that they should show that they're a little bit better than the rest. I tell them to think of themselves as better. Who cares what anyone else thinks? You know, I can almost hear that coach saying the words. 'You're no good.'"

Author Malcolm MacPherson (*The Blood of His Servants*), forty, lives 21 in New York. "It happened to me in the ninth grade, at the Yalesville School in Yalesville, Connecticut," he said. "Both of my parents had just been killed in a car crash, and as you can imagine, it was a very difficult time in my life. I went out for the baseball team, and I did pretty well in practice.

"But in the first game I clutched. I was playing second base; the 22 batter hit a pop-up, and I moved back to catch it. I can see it now. I felt dizzy as I looked up at the ball. It was like I was moving in slow motion, but the ball was going at regular speed. I couldn't get out of the way of my own feet. The ball dropped to the ground. I didn't catch it.

"The next day at practice, the coach read off the lineup. I was- 23 n't on it. I was off the squad.

"I remember what I did: I walked. It was a cold spring after- 24 noon, and the ground was wet, and I just walked. I was living with an aunt and uncle, and I didn't want to go home. I just wanted to walk forever.

"It drove my opinion of myself right into a tunnel. Right into a 25 cave. And when I came out of the cave, something inside of me wanted to make sure in one manner or another that I would never again be told I wasn't good enough.

26   "I will confess that my ambition, to this day, is out of control. It's like a fire. I think the fire would have pretty much stayed in control if I hadn't been cut from that team. But that got it going. You don't slice ambition two ways; it's either there or it isn't. Those of us who went through something like that always know that we have to catch the ball. We'd rather die than have the ball fall at our feet.

27   "Once that fire is started in us, it never gets extinguished, until we die or have heart attacks or something. Sometimes I wonder about the home-run hitters; the guys who never even had to worry about being cut. They may have gotten the applause and the attention back then, but I wonder if they ever got the fire. I doubt it. I think maybe you have to get kicked in the teeth to get the fire started.

28   "You can tell the effect of something like that by examining the trail you've left in your life, and tracing it backward. It's almost like being a junkie with a need for success. You get attention and applause and you like it, but you never quite trust it. Because you know that back then you were good enough if only they would have given you a chance. You don't trust what you achieve, because you're afraid that someone will take it away from you. You know that it can happen; it already did.

29   "So you try to show people how good you are. Maybe you don't go out and become Dan Rather; maybe you just end up owning the Pontiac dealership in your town. But it's your dealership, and you're the top man, and every day you're showing people that you're good enough."

30   Dan Rather, fifty-two, is anchor of the CBS *Evening News*. "When I was thirteen, I had rheumatic fever," he said. "I became extremely skinny and extremely weak, but I still went out for the seventh-grade baseball team at Alexander Hamilton Junior High School in Houston.

31   "The school was small enough that there was no cut as such; you were supposed to figure out that you weren't good enough, and quit. Game after game I sat at the end of the bench, hoping that maybe this was the time I would get in. The coach never even looked at me; I might as well have been invisible.

32   "I told my mother about it. Her advice was not to quit. So I went to practice very day, and I tried to do well so that the coach would be impressed. He never even knew I was there. At home in my room I would fantasize that there was a big game, and the three guys in front of me would all get hurt, and the coach would turn to me and put me in, and I would make the winning hit. But then there'd be another game, and the late innings would come, and if we were way

ahead I'd keep hoping that this was the game when the coach would put me in. He never did.

"When you're that age, you're looking for someone to tell you you're okay. Your sense of self-esteem is just being formed. And what that experience that baseball season did was make me think that perhaps I wasn't okay.

"In the last game of the season something terrible happened. It was the last of the ninth inning, there were two outs, and there were two strikes on the batter. And the coach turned to me and told me to go out to right field.

"It was a totally humiliating thing for him to do. For him to put me in for one pitch, the last pitch of the season, in front of all the other boys on the team . . . I stood out there for that one pitch, and I just wanted to sink into the ground and disappear. Looking back on it, it was an extremely unkind thing for him to have done. That was nearly forty years ago, and I don't know why the memory should be so vivid now; I've never known if the coach was purposely making fun of me—and if he was, why a grown man would do that to a thirteen-year-old boy.

"I'm not a psychologist. I don't know if a man can point to one event in his life and say that that's the thing that made him the way he is. But when you're that age, and you're searching for your own identity, and all you want is to be told that you're all right . . . I wish I understood it better, but I know the feeling is still there."

QUESTIONS ON SUBJECT AND PURPOSE

1. Greene's "cuts" all refer to not making an athletic team. What other kinds of "cuts" can you experience?
2. It is always risky to speculate on an author's purpose, but why would Greene write about this? Why reveal to everyone something that hurt so much?
3. How might Greene have gone about gathering examples of other men's similar experiences? Why would they be willing to contribute? Would everyone who has been cut be so candid?
4. What can be said in the coaches' defense? Should everyone who tries out be automatically guaranteed a place on the team?

QUESTIONS ON STRATEGY AND AUDIENCE

1. Greene structures his essay in an unusual way. How can the

essay be divided? Why give a series of examples of other men who were "cut"?

2. How many examples are enough? What if Greene had used two examples? Eight examples? How would either extreme have influenced your reaction as a reader?

3. Greene does not provide a final concluding paragraph. Why?

4. Are you skeptical after you have finished the essay? Does everyone react to being cut in the same way? What would it take to convince you that these reactions are typical?

QUESTIONS ON VOCABULARY AND STYLE

1. How would you characterize the tone of Greene's essay? How is it achieved? Through language? Sentence structure? Paragraphing?

2. Why does Greene allow each man to tell his own story? Why not just summarize their experiences? Each story is enclosed in quotation marks. Do you think that these were the exact words of each man? Why?

3. What do *inordinately* (paragraph 6) and *stoic* (18) mean?

WRITING SUGGESTIONS

1. **For your Journal.** Greene attributes enormous significance to a single experience; he feels it literally changed his entire life. Try to remember some occasions when a disappointment seemed to change your life by changing your expectations for yourself. In your journal, list some possible instances, and then explore one.

2. **For a Paragraph.** As children, we imagine ourselves doing or being anything that we want. As we grow older, however, we discover that our choices become increasingly more limited; in fact, each choice we make seems to cut off whole paths of alternative choices. We cannot be or do everything that we once thought we could. Choose a time in your life when you realized that a particular expectation or dream would never come true. In a paragraph, narrate that experience. Remember to make the significance of your realization clear to your reader.

3. **For an Essay.** Describe an experience similar to the one that Greene narrates. It might have happened in an academic

course during your school years, in a school or community activity, in athletics, or on the job: we can be "cut," "released," or "fired" from almost anything. Remember to make your narrative vivid through the use of detail and to make the significance of your narrative clear to the reader.

Prewriting:
a. Make a list of some possible events about which to write.
b. Select one of those events and brainstorm. Jot down whatever you remember about the event and your reactions to it. Do not worry about writing complete sentences.
c. Use the details generated from your brainstorming in your essay. Do not try to include every detail, but select those that seem the most revealing. Always ask yourself, how important is this detail?

Rewriting:
a. Remember that in writing about yourself it is especially important to keep your readers interested. They need to feel how significant this experience was. Do not just *tell* them; *show* them. One way to do this is to dramatize the experience. Did you?
b. Look carefully at your introduction. Do you begin in a vivid way? Does it make your reader want to keep reading? Test it by asking friends or relatives to read just the opening paragraphs.
c. How effective is your conclusion? Do you just stop? Do you just repeat in slightly altered words what you said in your introduction? Try to find another possible ending.

4. **For Research**. Check the validity of Greene's argument. What can you find in your library about the psychological effects of such vivid rejections? A reference librarian can help you start your search for information. Use that research in an essay about the positive or negative effects of such an experience. Remember to document your sources. You might write your paper in one of the following forms (each of which has a slightly different audience):

a. A conventional research paper for a college course.
b. An article for a popular magazine (for example, *Esquire, Working Woman, Parents'*).
c. A feature article for your school's newspaper.

WEARS JUMP SUIT,
SENSIBLE SHOES,
USES HUSBAND'S LAST NAME

Deborah Tannen

Deborah Tannen was born in 1945 in Brooklyn, New York, and received a Ph.D. from the University of California, Berkeley. Among her many publications dealing with interpersonal communication are two studies intended for the general reader: That's Not What I Meant!: How Conversational Style Makes or Breaks Your Relations with Others *(1986) and* You Just Don't Understand: Women and Men in Conversation *(1990). In 1992, she conducted a seminar on gender differences in communication for U.S. senators shortly after Justice Clarence Thomas's Supreme Court nomination hearings.*

Tannen has remarked about her writing: "I see one of my missions— the presentation of linguistic research to a general audience—as a means of understanding human communication and improving it." In this essay, published in the Sunday magazine section of The New York Times, *Tannen combines personal observation and research to explain to her audience how language and culture "mark" women in ways they do not men.*

BEFORE READING

Connecting: Look carefully at how you are dressed right now. What do your hairstyle, clothes, and shoes say about you? To what extent do you project this image intentionally?

Anticipating: The distinction between "marked" and "unmarked" is crucial to Tannen's observations and argument. What exactly do the terms mean?

1   Some years ago I was at a small working conference of four women and eight men. Instead of concentrating on the discussion I found myself looking at the three other women at the table, thinking how each had a different style and how each style was coherent.

2   One woman had dark brown hair in a classic style, a cross between Cleopatra and Plain Jane. The severity of her straight hair was

softened by wavy bangs and ends that turned under. Because she was beautiful, the effect was more Cleopatra than plain.

The second woman was older, full of dignity and composure. Her hair was cut in a fashionable style that left her with only one eye, thanks to a side part that let a curtain of hair fall across half her face. As she looked down to read her prepared paper, the hair robbed her of bifocal vision and created a barrier between her and the listeners. 3

The third woman's hair was wild, a frosted blond avalanche falling over and beyond her shoulders. When she spoke she frequently tossed her head, calling attention to her hair and away from her lecture. 4

Then there was makeup. The first woman wore facial cover that made her skin smooth and pale, a black line under each eye and mascara that darkened already dark lashes. The second wore only a light gloss on her lips and a hint of shadow on her eyes. The third had blue bands under her eyes, dark blue shadow, mascara, bright red lipstick and rouge; her fingernails flashed red. 5

I considered the clothes each woman had worn during the three days of the conference. In the first case, man-tailored suits in primary colors with solid-color blouses. In the second, casual but stylish black T-shirts, a floppy collarless jacket and baggy slacks or a skirt in neutral colors. The third wore a sexy jump suit; tight sleeveless jersey and tight yellow slacks; a dress with gaping armholes and an indulged tendency to fall off one shoulder. 6

Shoes? No. 1 wore string sandals with medium heels; No. 2, sensible, comfortable walking shoes; No. 3, pumps with spike heels. You can fill in the jewelry, scarves, shawls, sweaters—or lack of them. 7

As I amused myself finding coherence in these styles, I suddenly wondered why I was scrutinizing only the women. I scanned the eight men at the table. And then I knew why I wasn't studying them. The men's styles were unmarked. 8

The term "marked" is a staple of linguistic theory. It refers to the way language alters the base meaning of a word by adding a linguistic particle that has no meaning on its own. The unmarked form of a word carries the meaning that goes without saying—what you think of when you're not thinking anything special. 9

The unmarked tense of verbs in English is the present—for example, *visit*. To indicate past, you mark the verb by adding *ed* to yield *visited*. For future, you add a word: *will visit*. Nouns are presumed to be singular until marked for plural, typically by adding *s* or *es*, so *visit* becomes *visits* and *dish* becomes *dishes*. 10

11   The unmarked forms of most English words also convey "male." Being male is the unmarked case. Endings like *ess* and *ette* mark words as "female." Unfortunately, they also tend to mark them for frivolousness. Would you feel safe entrusting your life to a doctorette? Alfre Woodard, who was an Oscar nominee for best supporting actress, says she identifies herself as an actor because "actresses worry about eyelashes and cellulite, and women who are actors worry about the characters we are playing." Gender markers pick up extra meanings that reflect common associations with the female gender: not quite serious, often sexual.

12   Each of the women at the conference had to make decisions about hair, clothing, makeup and accessories, and each decision carried meaning. Every style available to us was marked. The men in our group had made decisions, too, but the range from which they chose was incomparably narrower. Men can choose styles that are marked, but they don't have to, and in this group none did. Unlike the women, they had the option of being unmarked.

13   Take the men's hair styles. There was no marine crew cut or oily longish hair falling into eyes, no asymmetrical, two-tiered construction to swirl over a bald top. One man was unabashedly bald; the others had hair of standard length, parted on one side, in natural shades of brown or gray or graying. Their hair obstructed no views, left little to toss or push back or run fingers through and, consequently, needed and attracted no attention. A few men had beards. In a business setting, beards might be marked. In this academic gathering, they weren't.

14   There could have been a cowboy shirt with string tie or a three-piece suit or a necklaced hippie in jeans. But there wasn't. All eight men wore brown or blue slacks and nondescript shirts of light colors. No man wore sandals or boots; their shoes were dark, closed, comfortable and flat. In short, unmarked.

15   Although no man wore makeup, you couldn't say the men didn't wear makeup in the sense that you could say a woman didn't wear makeup. For men, no makeup is unmarked.

16   I asked myself what style we women could have adopted that would have been unmarked, like the men's. The answer was none. There is no unmarked woman.

17   There is no woman's hair style that can be called standard, that says nothing about her. The range of women's hair styles is staggering, but a woman whose hair has no particular style is perceived as not caring about how she looks, which can disqualify her for many positions, and will subtly diminish her as a person in the eyes of some.

18   Women must choose between attractive shoes and comfortable shoes. When our group made an unexpected trek, the woman who

wore flat, laced shoes arrived first. Last to arrive was the woman in spike heels, shoes in hand and a handful of men around her.

If a woman's clothing is tight or revealing (in other words, sexy), it sends a message—an intended one of wanting to be attractive, but also a possibly unintended one of availability. If her clothes are not sexy, that too sends a message, lent meaning by the knowledge that they could have been. There are thousands of cosmetic products from which women can choose and myriad ways of applying them. Yet no makeup at all is anything but unmarked. Some men see it as a hostile refusal to please them.

19

Women can't even fill out a form without telling stories about themselves. Most forms give four titles to choose from. "Mr." carries no meaning other than that the respondent is male. But a woman who checks "Mrs." or "Miss" communicates not only whether she has been married but also whether she has conservative tastes in forms of address—and probably other conservative values as well. Checking "Ms." declines to let on about marriage (checking "Mr." declines nothing since nothing was asked), but it also marks her as either liberated or rebellious, depending on the observer's attitudes and assumptions.

20

I sometimes try to duck these variously marked choices by giving my title as "Dr."—and in so doing risk marking myself as either uppity (hence sarcastic responses like "Excuse *me!*") or an overachiever (hence reactions of congratulatory surprise like "Good for you!")

21

All married women's surnames are marked. If a woman takes her husband's name, she announces to the world that she is married and has traditional values. To some it will indicate that she is less herself, more identified by her husband's identity. If she does not take her husband's name, this too is marked, seen as worthy of comment: she has *done* something; she has "kept her own name." A man is never said to have "kept his own name" because it never occurs to anyone that he might have given it up. For him using his own name is unmarked.

22

A married woman who wants to have her cake and eat it too may use her surname plus his, with or without a hyphen. But this too announces her marital status and often results in a tongue-tying string. In a list (Harvey O'Donovan, Jonathan Feldman, Stephanie Woodbury McGillicutty), the woman's multiple name stands out. It is marked.

23

I have never been inclined toward biological explanations of gender differences in language, but I was intrigued to see Ralph Fasold bring biological phenomena to bear on the question of linguistic marking

24

in his book "The Sociolinguistics of Language." Fasold stresses that language and culture are particularly unfair in treating women as the marked case because biologically it is the male that is marked. While two X chromosomes make a female, two Y chromosomes make nothing. Like the linguistic markers *s*, *es* or *ess*, the Y chromosome doesn't "mean" anything unless it is attached to a root form—an X chromosome.

25   Developing this idea elsewhere, Fasold points out that girls are born with fully female bodies, while boys are born with modified female bodies. He invites men who doubt this to lift up their shirts and contemplate why they have nipples.

26   In his book, Fasold notes "a wide range of facts which demonstrates that female is the unmarked sex." For example, he observes that there are a few species that produce only females, like the whiptail lizard. Thanks to parthenogenesis, they have no trouble having as many daughters as they like. There are no species, however, that produce only males. This is no surprise, since any such species would become extinct in its first generation.

27   Fasold is also intrigued by species that produce individuals not involved in reproduction, like honeybees and leaf-cutter ants. Reproduction is handled by the queen and a relatively few males; the workers are sterile females. "Since they do not reproduce," Fasold says, "there is no reason for them to be one sex or the other, so they default, so to speak, to female.

28   Fasold ends his discussion of these matters by pointing out that if language reflected biology, grammar books would direct us to use "she" to include males and females and "he" only for specifically male referents. But they don't. They tell us that "he" means "he or she," and that "she" is used only if the referent is specifically female. This use of "he" as the sex-indefinite pronoun is an innovation introduced into English by grammarians in the 18th and 19th centuries, according to Peter Mühlhäusler and Rom Harré in "Pronouns and People." From at least about 1500, the correct sex-indefinite pronoun was "they," as it still is in casual spoken English. In other words, the female was declared by grammarians to be the marked case.

29   Writing this article may mark me not as a writer, not as a linguist, not as an analyst of human behavior, but as a feminist—which will have positive or negative, but in any case powerful, connotations for readers. Yet I doubt that anyone reading Ralph Fasold's book would put that label on him.

30   I discovered the markedness inherent in the very topic of gender after writing a book on differences in conversational style based on geographical region, ethnicity, class, age and gender. When I was interviewed, the vast majority of journalists wanted to talk about the

differences between women and men. While I thought I was simply describing what I observed—something I had learned to do as a researcher—merely mentioning women and men marked me as a feminist for some.

When I wrote a book devoted to gender differences in ways of 31 speaking, I sent the manuscript to five male colleagues, asking them to alert me to any interpretation, phrasing or wording that might seem unfairly negative toward men. Even so, when the book came out, I encountered responses like that of the television talk show host who, after interviewing me, turned to the audience and asked if they thought I was male-bashing.

Leaping upon a poor fellow who affably nodded in agreement, 32 she made him stand and asked, "Did what she said accurately describe you?" "Oh, yes," he answered. "That's me exactly." "And what she said about women—does that sound like your wife?" "Oh yes," he responded. "That's her exactly." "Then why do you think she's male-bashing?" He answered, with disarming honesty, "Because she's a woman and she's saying things about men."

To say anything about women and men without marking one- 33 self as either feminist or anti-feminist, male-basher or apologist for men seems as impossible for a woman as trying to get dressed in the morning without inviting interpretations of her character.

Sitting at the conference table musing on these matters, I felt 34 sad to think that we women didn't have the freedom to be unmarked that the men sitting next to us had. Some days you just want to get dressed and go about your business. But if you're a woman, you can't, because there is no unmarked woman.

QUESTIONS ON SUBJECT AND PURPOSE

1. What exactly does Tannen mean when she says, "there is no unmarked woman" (paragraph 34)?
2. Some of Tannen's examples deal with personal appearance and some deal with language. Why does she blend the two subjects?
3. Why does Tannen introduce the theories of Ralph Fasold in paragraphs 24–28?

QUESTIONS ON STRATEGY AND AUDIENCE

1. What types of "evidence" or examples does Tannen use in her essay?
2. How does that evidence reflect her audience? What assumptions might she make about her audience?

3. Why might Tannen have given the essay this particular title? Why not something like "Marking and Unmarking: The Significance of Dress, Language, Biology, and Culture"?

QUESTIONS ON VOCABULARY AND STYLE

1. Why might Tannen have chosen to write in the first person ("I")? What effect does that choice have on her essay? On the reader?

2. During the first section of her essay (paragraphs 2–7) how and why does Tannen uses parallelism?

3. Be prepared to define the following words: *scrutinizing* (paragraph 8), *unabashedly* (13), *trek* (18), *myriad* (19), *parthenogenesis* (26), *affably* (32).

WRITING SUGGESTIONS

1. For your Journal. Tannen makes her observations of women and men while attending an academic conference. Make some observations of your own. Study the dress of each of your instructors over a period of several days. In your journal, keep a record of what you see. Another possibility would be to do the same with people in your workplace. Speculate on what the dress of each reveals.

2. For a Paragraph. Using one or more of your instructors as your subject, write a paragraph describing clothing, makeup, and so forth, and analyzing possible significance of these choices of dress.

3. For an Essay. In paragraph 11, Tannen gives several examples of how English marks the feminine form of a noun with endings such as *ess* and *ette*. In an essay explore more fully how English gender markings "reflect common association with the female gender: not quite serious, often sexual" (paragraph 11). Your essay should include a number of examples and should explore the significance of this phenomenon of "diminishing" the female.

Prewriting:

a. Make a list of nouns that are used to describe jobs or professions. Are there differences in the masculine and feminine forms of the noun? Are different words used to signal a male worker and a female worker?

b. Ask your friends and classmates to add to your list. Check through a dictionary; watch as you read newspapers and magazines. Try to gather additional examples over several days.

c. Formulate a thesis (perhaps the same one that Tannen uses) on the basis of the examples that you have found. Then use that thesis to select the most relevant examples from your list.

Rewriting:

a. Remember that the quality of your examples and your analysis are more important than the quantity of your evidence. Look carefully at each example and discard any that seem weak.

b. Ask your friends and classmates to read your essay. Can they think of additional examples that might work? Do they feel that you have clearly demonstrated the "truth" of your thesis?

c. Try for an interesting title and an effective opening. Remember that you want to "hook" your reader: you want to keep the reader's attention.

4. For Research. Is Tannen's observation that "there is no unmarked woman" true for every culture? Select another culture and research the extent to which women in that culture are "marked" as well. Remember that you might come to the same conclusion as Tannen does, but you will need a number of relevant examples to support that conclusion. A good place to start your research would be with the Library of Congress Subject Headings—ask your reference librarian for help. Be sure to document your sources.

THE WILD MAN
OF THE GREEN SWAMP

Maxine Hong Kingston

Maxine Hong Kingston was born in 1940 in Stockton, California. She received a B.A. from the University of California before moving to Hawaii, where she taught high school English and mathematics for twelve years. Her writing blends myth, legend, history, and autobiography, mixing fiction and nonfiction, while exploring the ways in which her Chinese heritage and American lifestyle intermingle. The Woman Warrior: Memoirs of a Girlhood Among Ghosts *(1976) earned a National Book Critics Circle Award, and* China Men *(1980) won an American Book Award. Her latest book is the novel* Tripmaster Monkey: His Fake Book *(1988).*

"The Wild Man of the Green Swamp" is an excerpt from China Men, *a book of fact and fiction, myth and history, that tells the story of several generations of the men in Kingston's family.*

BEFORE READING

Connecting: Can you remember a time that in encountering a culture different from your own, you misinterpreted someone else's behavior? Or a time that someone unfamiliar with your culture misinterpreted your behavior?

Anticipating: How does Kingston invite us to "see" the Wild Man? Do we see him differently as the narrative unfolds?

1   For eight months in 1975, residents on the edge of Green Swamp, Florida, had been reporting to the police that they had seen a Wild Man. When they stepped toward him, he made strange noises as in a foreign language and ran back into the saw grass. At first, authorities said the Wild Man was a mass hallucination. Man-eating animals lived in the swamp, and a human being could hardly find a place to rest without sinking. Perhaps it was some kind of a bear the children had seen.

2   In October, a game officer saw a man crouched over a small fire, but as he approached, the figure ran away. It couldn't have been a bear

because the Wild Man dragged a burlap bag after him. Also, the fire was obviously man-made.

The fish-and-game wardens and the sheriff's deputies entered 3 the swamp with dogs but did not search for long; no one could live in the swamp. The mosquitoes alone would drive him out.

The Wild Man made forays out of the swamp. Farmers en- 4 countered him taking fruit and corn from the turkeys. He broke into a house trailer, but the occupant came back, and the Wild Man escaped out a window. The occupant said that a bad smell came off the Wild Man. Usually, the only evidence of him were his abandoned campsites. At one he left the remains of a four-foot-long alligator, of which he had eaten the feet and tail.

In May a posse made an air and land search; the plane signaled 5 down to the hunters on the ground, who circled the Wild Man. A fish-and-game warden "brought him down with a tackle," according to the news. The Wild Man fought, but they took him to jail. He looked Chinese, so they found a Chinese in town to come translate.

The Wild Man talked a lot to the translator. He told him his 6 name. He said he was thirty-nine years old, the father of seven children, who were in Taiwan. To support them, he had shipped out on a Liberian freighter. He had gotten very homesick and asked everyone if he could leave the ship and go home. But the officers would not let him off. They sent messages to China to find out about him. When the ship landed, they took him to the airport and tried to put him on an airplane to some foreign place. Then, he said, the white demons took him to Tampa Hospital, which is for insane people, but he escaped, just walked out and went into the swamp.

The interpreter asked how he lived in the swamp. He said he 7 ate snakes, turtles, armadillos, and alligators. The captors could tell how he lived when they opened up his bag, which was not burlap but a pair of pants with the legs knotted. Inside, he had carried a pot, a piece of sharpened tin, and a small club, which he had made by sticking a railroad spike into a section of aluminum tubing.

The sheriff found the Liberian freighter that the Wild Man had 8 been on. The ship's officers said that they had not tried to stop him from going home. His shipmates had decided that there was something wrong with his mind. They had bought him a plane ticket and arranged his passport to send him back to China. They had driven him to the airport, but there he began screaming and weeping and would not get on the plane. So they had found him a doctor, who sent him to Tampa Hospital.

Now the doctors at the jail gave him medicine for the mosquito 9 bites, which covered his entire body, and medicine for his stomachache. He was getting better, but after he'd been in jail for three days, the U.S. Border Patrol told him they were sending him back. He became hysterical. That night, he fastened his belt to the bars, wrapped it around his neck, and hung himself.

10   In the newspaper picture he did not look very wild, being led by the posse out of the swamp. He did not look dirty, either. He wore a checkered shirt unbuttoned at the neck, where his white undershirt showed; his shirt was tucked into his pants; his hair was short. He was surrounded by men in cowboy hats. His fingers stretching open, his wrists pulling apart to the extent of the handcuffs, he lifted his head, his eyes screwed shut, and cried out.

11   There was a Wild Man in our slough too, only he was a black man. He wore a shirt and no pants, and some mornings when we walked to school, we saw him asleep under the bridge. The police came and took him away. The newspaper said he was crazy; it said the police had been on the lookout for him for a long time, but we had seen him every day.

QUESTIONS ON SUBJECT AND PURPOSE

1. Why does Kingston refer to the man as "Wild Man"? What expectations does that phrase arouse in a reader?
2. When does Kingston stop using the phrase "Wild Man"? Why might she have changed the way she refers to the man?
3. Kingston never explicitly interprets the incident for her audience. What significance could a reader see in the story?

QUESTIONS ON STRATEGY AND AUDIENCE

1. Where might you expect to read an article with a title like "The Wild Man of the Green Swamp"? Why might Kingston have chosen to title the piece in this way?
2. Why does Kingston add paragraph 11? How does this additional information influence our reading of the "Wild Man"?
3. How does Kingston manipulate the narrative so as to control what we as readers learn?

QUESTIONS ON VOCABULARY AND STYLE

1. What is the effect of the details that Kingston gives us in paragraph 7? Why tell us this?

2. How would you characterized the "style" of Kingston's piece? What do her word choices and sentence structures, for example, suggest about the audience to whom she is writing?

3. Be prepared to define the following words: *hallucination* (paragraph 1), *forays* (4), *slough* (11).

WRITING SUGGESTIONS

1. For your Journal. Unfortunately, people often react negatively to "difference"—sometimes with suspicion or hostility, sometimes with fear or at least discomfort. In your journal, explore a memory or two when you encountered such negative reactions—either your own, or those of others. Did these reactions ever change?

2. For a Paragraph. Using the material from one of the experiences you recorded in your journal, write a paragraph in which you describe the experience. Remember that you are not just recording something that happened: you are doing so for a reason. You might try allowing your reason or thesis to be implied rather than explicitly stated.

3. For an Essay. If our instinctive reaction to difference is to fear it rather than to welcome it, how can we change our reactions? In an essay, explore the problem and possible solutions. Use examples from your own experience, or from the experiences of others, to illustrate your essay. Do not just narrate events; be sure to advance or argue for a strategy for change.

Prewriting:

a. Make a list of relevant illustrations from your own experience.

b. Ask friends or classmates to contribute examples from their experiences. Make sure that each possible example is relevant.

c. For each possible example, jot down what it reveals. Remember that you are not just documenting the reaction. You are looking as well for ways in which that initial reaction was changed.

Rewriting:

a. Have you argued for a strategy for change? Put that strategy into a single sentence—a thesis sentence.

b. Ask friends or classmates to read your essay. How do they react to your examples? Do your illustrations support the points that you are trying to make? Use your readers' reactions to rethink your choice of examples.

c. Remember that several important, developed examples are more effective than many somewhat irrelevant or sketchy examples. Did you adequately develop your examples?

4. **For Research**. It is easy to view the people who "panhandle" on the street, or who "dive" into dumpsters (like Lars Eighner in Chapter 6), or who sleep in doorways and abandoned buildings as "wild" people. They are certainly "outside" of our own experiences. What do we know about those who are homeless in America? Who are they? In a research paper, explore the problem of defining these people. Use your information to "argue" for how this knowledge ought to shape a response to the problem of helping others.

YOU HAVE DEFINITELY WON!

Tim Johnson

Tim Johnson was born in Hammond, Indiana, and earned a B.A. in economics and political science from Yale University. He has been a newspaper reporter and copy editor for several newspapers, and a writer for the international aid organization Oxfam America. Since 1989, he has been a copy editor for the Philadelphia Inquirer.

"You Have Definitely Won!" appeared in the Sunday magazine supplement of the Philadelphia Inquirer. *Johnson commented about the essay: "It took me a while. I tend to be someone who researches things too much. I never think I know enough. I debated back and forth whether to make it first person. There's a prejudice in newspaper work against first-person writing. Finally, I just broke down. After I wrote a few paragraphs, I decided it had to be in the first person."*

BEFORE READING

Connecting: How much "junk" mail do you and your family receive each week? Did you ever think someone might write a "story" about something as common and universal as publishers' sweepstakes?

Anticipating: Knowing as most of us do that the "odds of being picked from tens of millions are uniformly dismal," why is it that people fill out these entry forms? Or, similarly, why do people buy lottery tickets?

I'm not sure why, but whenever one of those big, breathless envelopes arrives in the mail bearing offers of multi-million-dollar prizes and cheap magazine subscriptions and thumbnail portraits of Ed McMahon, I find myself wondering how Henry Kissinger handles solicitations like this. ("Congratulations on becoming a finalist Henry A. Kiffinger. . . .") Is it possible that he sits at his desk, with several calls on hold, pasting stamps onto his claim sheet? Does he wonder, with some annoyance, if the misspelling of his name will disqualify him for the multimillions? Is one of the calls to Ed McMahon?

Unlikely, of course, but no more so than my chances of winning the multimillions. Kissinger probably has an attache who opens his mail and takes care of all his magazine orders and sweepstakes entries, while I have to decide for myself whether my presumptive claim to the multimillions is worth a cheap subscription to, say, House Beautiful.

3   It's a decision many of us have to make repeatedly, not just for Ed McMahon's American Family Publishers, but for other magazine stamp-sheet companies that run sweepstakes—the renowned Publishers Clearing House with its intimate executive memo ("Personally I'm very happy you can be our next big winner Henry A. Kiffinger . . ."), the much smaller but comparably exclusive Magazine Marketplace ("Each week we select customers who meet special qualifications . . . and this week we chose you Henry A. Kiffinger") and the even smaller but better punctuated Magazine Express ("Isn't it time your luck changed for the better, Henry A. Kiffinger?"), not to mention the venerable Reader's Digest, which stands apart as an actual publisher ("Henry A. Kiffinger will be an instant millionaire").

4   Mail it in or pitch it? This is a decision often made in some torment, as you ask yourself: If I go through with this moderately degrading stamp-pasting routine and mail the certificate in, does that imply that I'm falling for this intellectually insulting sales pitch and that therefore I'm not, well, very bright?

5   Annoying as this last question is, there's some relief in knowing that no one else is in a position to answer it or even pose it publicly except the postal service, the stamp-sheet company and your attache (if you have one), all of whose discretion you should be able to count on. The stamp-sheet companies are so discreet, in fact, that they won't even say how many multimillions of these offers they send out, much less who mails them back. So you can go ahead and enter, secure in the knowledge that your broodings (*Am I a sucker? Does this subscription to House Beautiful really enhance my infinitesimal chances?*) will stay private. Unless of course you win the big one, in which case multimillions of people will find out you entered and thus, ipso facto, made a fool of yourself.

6   I pitch it.

7   Now comes a postcard from a company I have never heard of professing to be "final notice" that I have *definitely won* one of three prizes. Chances are this means a day trip to the Pinelands. I know this because my wife and I responded to one of these cards once. The prize we were obviously in line for was a portable TV, and we just happened to be in the market for a cheap one. So we drove down to the Pinelands, endured a grueling three-hour hard sell for timesharing in a trailer park, and collected a cheap, battery-powered TV without batteries that we later sold for a price that almost covered the

cost of the trip. In other words, considering that we actually received one of the prizes we had *definitely won*, we made out rather well.

But I don't want to press my luck any further, so this postcard 8 goes straight in the trash, as do other *you-have-definitely-won-one-of-these* promotions. Bogus prize notifications are, as a state official in Harrisburg puts it, "probably one of the fastest growing scams in the United States."

"We are getting thousands of complaints," said Rick Hicks, di- 9 rector of the Bureau of Consumer Protection of the Pennsylvania Attorney General's Office. "Every week, some new contest appears. Generally, they offer some fabulous prize through calling a 900 number. Or paying a fee for a catalogue of goods that are overpriced anyway. Or an initiation fee." The sleazier operations induce you to pay something for the award you have *definitely won*—much more than you ever get back.

The New Jersey Division of Consumer Affairs brings forth the 10 cautionary tale of an elderly woman from Flemington who lost $230,000 over three years to sweepstakes and other promotions, and who in one instance was told over the phone that she'd won a million dollars, but that she first had to buy some things and send a check for $14,600, which she did, only to receive a couple of watches and an air filter.

And then there's the 90-year-old man in New Jersey who lost a 11 more modest total of $20,000. For educational purposes, the Division of Consumer Affairs maintains a traveling archive of the promotional mail he received in one month—210 solicitations in January 1993, seeking fees from $1 to $350.

The storied victims of contest fraud are just about always el- 12 derly. Can it be that the wisdom and sagacity of advanced age come only at the price of hood-winkability? It's hard to imagine that being true in Kissinger's case. Still, he turned 70 last year, and it's not inconceivable that he's slightly more vulnerable now than he was at the height of his powers, back in the '70s. He must have people who are adept at weeding out the fraudulent mail and phone solicitations. I'd be very, very surprised if Kissinger's attache were a member of the gullible elderly set. Come to think of it, I'd also be very, very surprised if I won the Publishers Clearing House sweepstakes.

In the spectrum of mail-order sweepstakes, ranging from the 13 cynically sinister ripoffs to the innocent diversions with real payoffs, the magazine stamp-sheet promotions seem to fall more toward the legitimate end. So say some of the watchdogs, anyway. Hicks, in what might be construed as something just short of a resounding endorsement in these litigious times, said Publishers Clearing House and its ilk "tend to be unactionable from an unfair-trade-practices perspective. Those guys aren't the real problem."

14   John Barker, vice president of the National Consumers League, said: "There's no reason someone shouldn't send stuff into Publishers Clearing House. It's harmless." This from an organization that receives about 200 telephone complaints a day about sweepstakes, mostly from definite winners.

15   "Publishers Clearing House is a high-integrity operation," said Stephen Wigginton, circulation director of a magazine that should know something about consumer fraud—Consumer Reports, which is included in the Publishers Clearing House stamp sheet. "They award the prizes they say they do."

16   I pick the big envelope out of the trash. I brush off the orange pulp. After a few minutes on the radiator, the official certificate is as dry as ever, and it flattens out quite nicely beneath a copy of *War and Peace*.

17   With the envelope's contents arrayed on the kitchen table, I'm not sure where to begin. There's the official certificate, displaying the personal $10 million-prize-winning numbers and a picture of an eagle, all on some sort of hard-currency-inspired design. There's a rather long personal letter from Ed McMahon in several typefaces, and some photos of previous winners that look a bit like wanted posters, not terribly flattering, and a couple of brochures for lesser prizes, and a Stage 3 Upgrade Card, whatever that is, and a return envelope that does not have Ed McMahon's picture on it, plus of course the stamp sheet—a perforated swatch of colorful stickers imprinted with the nameplates of about 120 magazines.

18   Now most Americans, hearing a description of this inventory and asked to identify it, would probably say Publishers Clearing House. Only the cognoscenti are likely to recognize it as American Family Publishers', and that's ironic because by all accounts both companies operate on roughly the same scale of megamailings and offer many of the same magazines for the same prices, and they both promise a $10 million prize that you're about as likely to win as you are to receive a long, personal letter from Ed McMahon sharing his thoughts on Tolstoy's theory of history.

19   So, back to the task at hand, which is (and here is where a college education comes in handy) to read as little of this stuff on the kitchen table as possible, but still field a valid sweepstakes entry. The only problem is that this approach plays right into American Family's hands, because the more cursorily I scan these materials, the more likely I am to come away with the impression that if I want to collect the multimillions, I'd better order a magazine.

This goes to the the heart of the matter. No sign of Kissinger 20
here—presumably he arrived at this point long ago and moved on—
but the $10 million question remains: Do you have to subscribe to
win?

The law says no. A random-giveaway contest that you have to 21
pay to enter is not a sweepstakes, it's a lottery, which is illegal to operate unless you're a church or a state.

The stamp-sheet companies, not surprisingly, also say no. "No 22
purchase necessary to enter and win," reads an American Family dis-
claimer. "We *really mean it* when we say there's NO PURCHASE
NECESSARY to enter our Sweeps and win," reads a brochure from
Publishers Clearing House. "You *never* have to buy anything or pay
anything to claim your prize."

This brochure has a reassuring air of probity and restraint (only 23
three typefaces). It's titled "Everything you ever wanted to know
about Publishers Clearing House Sweepstakes (and more!)," but it
turns out to be not much help if you want to know about how, in the
fall of 1992, more than 2,000 unopened entries wound up on a street
in Queens, where they were found by sanitation workers.

Publishers Clearing House said the dumping was a mistake and 24
blamed an outside mail-processing firm. Nevertheless, the find
prompted several nonsubscribing contestants to file a lawsuit, which
Publishers Clearing House settled out of court by promising that
everyone who had received a mailing would be eligible for the next
$10 million prize. (The company no longer uses outside mail proces-
sors and opens every envelope itself, according to spokesman David
Sayer, who also points out that 11 of the last 17 Publishers Clearing
House millionaires were nonsubscribers.)

American Family now faces a similar lawsuit, filed by the same 25
New Jersey lawyer, Jeffrey Herrmann, and based in part on another
sighting of unopened entries—this time, being hauled out of a warehouse in Tampa, Fla. American Family has maintained, in a court
document, that it doesn't have to open the mail from nonsubscribers
because their sweepstakes entry numbers are scanned through a window in the return envelope.

Well, I'm prepared to give both companies the benefit of the 26
doubt on the dumping, and even on the brochures and disclaimers.
What bothers me is that they *still* try to goad or intimidate me into
ordering, through devices like "Yes" and "No" stickers on the return
envelope, or "express" stickers implying that subscribers' sweepstakes
entries will get special treatment.

And so it has come to this: a closer look at the Stage 3 Upgrade 27
Card.

"WARNING: IF YOU DO NOT UPGRADE YOUR 28

STATUS BY ORDERING, YOU COULD FORFEIT ANY RIGHTS TO FUTURE MAILINGS."

29   I pitch it again, all of it.

30   It's true that the stamp-sheet magazine prices are pretty good. The regular subscription price is usually discounted, as much as 50 percent in some cases. Sweepstakes contestants who want to subscribe just send the money to the stamp-sheet company, which then collects a commission that is typically 75 percent, 85 percent or more, according to people in the industry.

31   I pull the big envelope out of the trash again, along with the other American Family paraphernalia. I shake off the coffee grounds.

32   The radiator dries off the stamp sheet, but the stains are harder to overlook now, and the Tolstoy isn't quite as effective this time.

33   So, what sort of magazine wants to be listed in a sweepstakes promotion? At first glance, the diversity of these stamps defies generalization. You have your special-interest magazines—American Handgunner, Astrology, Barbie, Car and Driver, I Love Cats, Horticulture, Magic Crochet and Vegetarian Times, to name a few. You have magazines for old folks (Successful Retirement), kids (Sesame Street), people who want to live a long time (Longevity), politically correct programmers (PC Computing), employed women with children (Working Mother), people who live in houses (Home), current Christians (Christianity Today) and on and on, as well as the usual checkout-counter varieties like the big three news magazines, TV Guide, US, Ebony, Better Homes and Gardens, Reader's Digest.

34   One thing they do seem to have in common is that they're not particularly high-brow. You won't find stamps for the New York Review of Books or the New England Journal of Medicine or even the new New Yorker. No, Reader's Digest is more like it.

35   I can't be too hard on Reader's Digest. After all, it was Reader's Digest that invented the mass-market mail-order sweepstakes as we now know it, or misconstrue it.

36   No single Digest employee can take full credit for it, any more than any one physicist deserves credit for, say, the Manhattan Project. But Tony Arau, now president of a direct-mail consulting firm in Valley Forge, was one of the principals. Back in 1959, when Arau was copy and creative chief of the Digest's book and record division, Digest founder DeWitt Wallace asked him to design a promotional contest.

37   In those days, random-give-away promotions typically took the form of people sending in boxtops, one of which would eventually be pulled out of a drum by somebody wearing a blindfold. By contrast, Arau recalled recently, what Wallace had in mind was an editorial-

style contest of the sort that was also common then, such as "Why I Like the Digest" in 25 words or less.

Arau thought about it for a few months, without coming up with anything, before he hit on his revolutionary idea: a sweepstakes using a computer to pick a random, winning number at the outset of the contest. 38

"The whole idea behind it," Arau said, "was that *you may already have won.* That was the whole gimmick." 39

And that's what made it possible for stamp-sheet companies and many others to send you oversize envelopes announcing in big, exciting type that you've hit the jackpot, subject of course to the condition, spelled out in little boring type, that you hold a pre-selected number. 40

Well, you don't have to be a nuclear physicist to appreciate the Manhattan Project. But I suspect you do have to be a direct-mail expert to fully comprehend why YOU MAY ALREADY HAVE WON is immeasurably profitable and enticing, while the boxtop era's "You may win later" is bankrupt and discredited. 41

Since probability clearly has nothing to do with this disparity—your odds of being picked from tens of millions are uniformly dismal, no matter when the picking is done—I suspect the difference must have something to do with fate. 42

Perhaps when people are told they *may already have won,* they feel a subliminal connection to destiny—a destiny mediated by blind faith and ritual (stamp-pasting), a destiny pre-determined by mysterious, unseen forces (direct-mail experts) that confer rewards (jackpot) and punishments (continuing life as you're living it) for unknown reasons. 43

Nah. 44

It all really defies understanding, like war and peace. That's why I haven't given up on winning the multimillions or, just as improbably, getting a longish letter from Ed McMahon explaining what he thinks Tolstoy would make of all this. 45

Sure, I fantasize about what I'd do with the prize money, just as the sweepstakes promoters invariably encourage me to (yep, I'd buy me a magazine), but when I get tired of that, I imagine what the letter might say. 46

In his jovial, avuncular way, Ed would tell me about how Tolstoy believed history to be a huge, ungainly process aggregated from the world's multiplicity of tiny, individual forces. And that no one can know what will result from the interplay of all those forces, least of all the great men who profess to be in control, but are really just along for the ride. And that no one can be sure what brought about, 47 say, the end of the Cold War or the ascendancy of Kissinger or the rise of *The Tonight Show* or the demise of Ed's old show, *Who Do You Trust*, but that, at the same time, no one can be certain that these disparate developments didn't result at least in part from the synchronized hopes and actions of multimillions of people who paste stamps and mail them in and dream of winning the big one. And that therefore, I'd better get my entry in before it's too late.

QUESTIONS ON SUBJECT AND PURPOSE

1. Henry Kissinger was Secretary of State under President Richard Nixon, and continues to be a highly respected (and highly paid) advisor in international affairs. Why might Johnson make reference to him in the essay, and why is his name occasionally misspelled?

2. Beginning with paragraph 7, Johnson digresses from his comments about the magazine stamp-sheet promotions to write about "bogus prize notifications." Why does he include this section?

3. Did reading the essay change your view of such publisher promotions? Are you now more or less likely to return the card? Buy a subscription? Do you think Johnson wanted to persuade you one way or another?

QUESTIONS ON STRATEGY AND AUDIENCE

1. How does Johnson's account of his own experience with the sweepstakes entry function in the essay?

2. What are Johnson's primary sources of information in the essay?

3. What expectations could Johnson have about his audience?

QUESTIONS ON VOCABULARY AND STYLE

1. What is the effect of Johnson's use of the first person ("I")?

2. At a number of points in the essay, Johnson sets off single sentences or words as separate paragraphs. Where does he do that and why? What do these instances have in common?

3. Be prepared to define the following words and phrases: *attache* (paragraph 2), *presumptive* (2), *venerable* (3), *discretion* (5), *ipso facto* (5), *sagacity* (12), *gullible* (12), *litigious* (13), *ilk* (13),

cognoscenti (18), *cursorily* (19), *probity* (23), *goad* (26), *misconstrue* (35), *subliminal* (43), *avuncular* (47).

WRITING SUGGESTIONS

1. **For your Journal.** What is it that makes people, yourself included perhaps, take chances on such "long shots"? In your journal, speculate on some reasons. You might want to focus on yourself, or you might want to talk with friends and relatives to see if they can offer any reasons.

2. **For a Paragraph.** In a paragraph, using the examples that you gathered in your journal writing, describe the appeal that such chance-taking has. If you are using yourself as an example, write in the first person. If you are using other people as examples, be sure to integrate some quotations.

3. **For an Essay.** How do companies, organizations, and charities compete for your money through direct mail advertising? Using the mail that you, your friends, and your family receive for at least one week, write an essay in which you describe and classify the nature of the various sales appeals that advertisers use. If you do not receive enough mail, consider adding in advertisements from magazines and newspapers for products and services that are also sold through direct mail advertising.

Prewriting:

a. Spend at least a week gathering examples of direct mail advertising—for magazines, for credit cards, for products, for charities, whatever. Be sure to get a substantial body of evidence from which to work.

b. Read through all of the advertisements and sort them out, by the nature of the appeals, into a series of categories. Are there distinctly different strategies that are used by particular advertisers?

c. Look at the advice offered in Chapter 4 about classification. This can help you organize the body of your essay.

Rewriting:

a. Have you quoted from the advertisements? If not, do so to make your examples more vivid. Johnson, for example, selectively and effectively quotes parts of the messages from the magazine stamp-sheet promotions.

b. Remember that you are looking to define the major strategies—not all of the minor details. Be sure that your examples are developed and vivid; but do not try to be all-inclusive in your analysis.

c. Try to find both an appropriate title (notice that Johnson quotes a sentence from the advertisement) and a strong, effective opening paragraph. Ask your friends and classmates to evaluate both your title and your opening paragraph(s).

4. **For Research**. Using Johnson's essay as a model, imagine that you are an investigative reporter on assignment for a Sunday newspaper. You are to write a feature article for a general readership about a current phenomenon. It can be national in scope or limited to your local community, or even your campus. Your research could involve some library work, but it could also involve interviewing relevant experts. Even though you are writing this as a feature article, be sure to document your sources for your instructor on a separate sheet of paper.

NARRATION

When a friend asks, "What did you do last night?" you reply with a narrative: "After the chemistry midterm was over at 8:30, we went to Shakey's for pizza. Then we stopped at the bowling alley for a couple of games, and about 11 we split up and I went back to the dorm for some serious sleeping." A narrative is a story, and all stories, whether they are personal narratives, or novels, or histories, have the same essential ingredients: a series of events arranged in a chosen order and told by a narrator for some particular purpose. Your reply, for example, exhibits all four elements: a series of events (the four things you did last evening) arranged in an order (chronological) and told by a narrator ("I," a first-person narrator) for some particular purpose (to answer your friend's question).

Any type of writing can and does use narration; it is not something found only in personal experience essays or fiction. Narration can also be used to provide evidence in an argument. Bob Greene in "Cut" (Chapter 1) groups five personal narrative examples to support his assertion that being cut from an athletic team can make you a superachiever in life. Narration can also be found mixed with description in William Least Heat-Moon's "Nameless, Tennessee" (Chapter 3) or underlying a persuasive essay in Richard Rodriguez's "None of This Is Fair" (Chapter 9). In fact, there are examples of narration in the readings found in every chapter of this text.

WHAT DO YOU INCLUDE IN A NARRATIVE?

No one, probably not even your mother, wants to hear everything you did today. Readers, like listeners, want you to exercise selection, for some things are more important or interesting than others. Historians have to select out of a mass of data what they will include and emphasize. They cannot tell the whole story, for if they did, the reader would get entangled in trivia, and the significant shape and meaning of the narrative would be lost. Even in personal experiences you condense and select. Generally you need to pare away, to cut out the unnecessary and the uninteresting. What you include depends, of course, on what happened and, more importantly, upon the purpose or meaning that you are trying to convey.

HOW DO YOU STRUCTURE A NARRATIVE?

Time structures all narratives, although events do not always need to be arranged in chronological order. A narrative can begin at one point in time and then "flash back" to an earlier action or event. Langston Hughes's "Salvation" begins with a narrator looking back at an experience that occurred when he was thirteen, although the story itself is told in the order in which it happened. The most typical inversion is to begin at the end of the narrative and then to move backward in time to explain how that end was reached. More complex narratives, such as Judith Ortiz Cofer's "Silent Dancing," may shift several times back and forth between incidents in the past, or between the past and the present. Two cautions are obvious: first, do not switch time too frequently, especially in short papers; second, make sure that the switches are clearly marked for your reader.

Remember as well that you control where your narrative begins and ends. For example, the experience that E. B. White narrates in "Once More to the Lake" began when he and his son arrived at the lake and ended with their departure. The essay, however, begins with a flashback to his first summer at the lake thirty-seven years earlier. It ends as he watches his son pull on a cold, soggy bathing suit. The essay builds to that single moment of insight, and so this scene serves as the appropriate end of the narrative. It would have been anticlimactic for White to have added another paragraph detailing their final departure from the lake. Do not feel the need to "finish" the story if, in fact, you have achieved your purpose. Try to build to a climactic moment and end there.

Writers frequently change or modify an actual personal experience in order to tell the story more effectively, heighten the tension, or make their purpose clearer. In her essay "On Keeping a Notebook" (Chapter 6), Joan Didion remarks:

> I tell what some would call lies. "That's simply not true," the members of my family frequently tell me when they come up against my memory of a shared event. "The party was *not* for you, the spider was *not* a black widow, *it wasn't that way at all.*" Very likely they are right, for not only have I always had trouble distinguishing between what happened and what merely might have happened, but I remain unconvinced that the distinction, for my purposes, matters.

Whenever you recall an experience, even if it just happened last week, you do not necessarily remember it exactly as it happened. The value of a personal narrative does not rest in accuracy to the original experience. It does not matter, for example, whether the scene with sister Monroe in the Christian Methodist Episcopal Church occurred exactly as Maya Angelou describes it years later. What does matter is that it could have happened and that it is faithful to the purpose Angelou intends.

HOW ARE NARRATIVES TOLD?

Two things are especially important in relating your narrative. First, you need to choose a point of view from which to tell the story. Personal experience narratives, such as those by Hughes, Angelou, and White, are generally told in the first person: the narrator is an actor in the story. Historical narratives and narratives used as illustrations in a larger piece of writing are generally told in the third person. The historian, for example, is outside the narrative and provides an objective view of the actions described. Judith Ortiz Cofer mixes first-person and third-person narration as she shifts from relating her own childhood experiences to recalling a home movie of a family party. Point of view can vary in one other way. The narrator can reveal only his or her own thoughts (and so use what is known as the limited point of view), or the narrator can reveal what anyone else in the narrative thinks or feels (and so use the omniscient, or all-knowing, point of view).

Second, you need to decide whether you are going to "show" or "tell" or mix the two. You "show" in a narrative by dramatizing a scene and creating dialogue. Hughes re-creates his experience for the reader by showing what happened and by recording some of the conversation that took place the night he was "saved from sin." The other option is "telling," that is, summarizing what happened. E. B. White tells the reader what he experienced and how he felt. He never dramatizes a particular scene and he never uses dialogue. Showing makes a narrative more vivid, for it allows the reader to experience the scene directly. Telling, on the other hand, allows you to include a greater number of events and details. Either way, selectivity is necessary. Hughes does not dramatize all of the events that happened; White does not summarize day-to-day activities. Each writer selects those moments which best give shape and significance to the experience.

WHAT DO YOU WRITE ABOUT IF NOTHING EVER HAPPENED TO YOU?

It is easy to assume that the only things worth writing about are once-in-a-lifetime experiences—a heroic or death-defying act, a personal tragedy, an Olympic medal-winning performance. But a good personal experience narrative does not need to be based on an extraordinary experience. In fact, ordinary experiences, because they are about things familiar to every reader, are the best sources for personal narratives. There is nothing extraordinary, for example, about the events related in Langston Hughes's "Salvation," even though Hughes's experience was a turning point in his life. Annie Dillard relates the sort of childhood experience that any one of us might have had; there is certainly nothing earth-shaking in her encounter with the angry man at whom she and her friend have thrown snowballs, though she tells the story with great zest. E. B. White's return to the lake where he summered as a child, and even his feelings as he watches his son, are ordinary experiences shared and understood by every parent revisiting the past.

The secret to writing a good personal experience narrative lies in two areas. First, you must tell your story artfully. Following the advice outlined in this introduction is a good way to ensure that your narrative will be constructed as effectively as possible. Just telling what happened is not enough, though, for you must do a second, equally important thing: you must reveal a purpose in your tale. Purposes can be many. You might offer insight into human behavior or motivation; you might mark a significant moment in your life; you might reveal an awareness of what it is to be young and to have dreams; you might reflect on the precariousness of life and inevitability of change and decay. What is important is that your narrative have a point, a reason for being, and that you make the reason clear to your reader.

SAMPLE STUDENT ESSAY

Hope Zucker decided to write about a powerful childhood memory—a pair of red shoes that became her "ruby slippers" and the key to the Land of Oz.

EARLIER DRAFT

My New Shoes

When you are four years old anything longer than five minutes feels like eternity, so when the clerk told me and my mom that it would take three to four weeks for my new shoes to arrive, I was almost in tears. Since seeing *The Wizard of Oz*, I had thought of little else other than owning a pair of ruby slippers. My dreams were full of spinning houses, little munchkins, flying monkeys, and talking lions. All I wanted was to be Dorothy, and the shoe store had made a promise to find me a pair of red mary-janes which would hopefully take me to Munchkin Land and Oz.

For the next three weeks I made all the preparations I could think of in order to become Dorothy. It did not matter how convincing Judy Garland was because I knew in my heart that I was the true Dorothy. I sang "Somewhere Over the Rainbow" day and night, and I played dress up with an old light blue checked dress of my mother's. I even went as far as to carry my dog in a basket, but that did not work out too well. I had my mom braid my long brown hair, and after I insisted, she tied a light blue ribbon around each braid. I skipped wherever I went, and I even went as far as coloring part of our driveway with chalk to create my very own yellow brick road.

The only thing missing to my new persona was my ruby slippers. After my mother explained to me that three weeks really was not that far off in the future. I decided to help the store in their search for my red mary-janes. For a month I called the store everyday when I got home from preschool. Mr. Rogers and Big Bird could wait because there was nothing in the whole wide world that was more important than my red patent leather shoes. By the end of the month, the nice little old ladies at the store knew me by name and thought that I was the cutest child. Lucky for them, they did not have to put up with me.

Finally, after what seemed like years, the lady on the other side of the phone said that yes, my shiny red shoes had arrived. Now I had only to plead with my mother to get her to make a special trip into the city. After a few days of delay and a great deal of futile temper tantrums, my mom took me to the store. I could hardly contain my excitement. During the ride, I practiced the one and only line that only the real Dorothy could say, "There's no place like home." And of course, I clicked my beat up boondockers three times each time I recited my part. It was all practice for the real thing.

As we pulled into the parking lot, all the little old ladies inside the store waved to me as if they had been expecting me for days. I finally got to see my shoes, and they were as perfect as I knew they'd be. I was practically jumping out of my seat when she began to remove the stiff tissue paper surrounding my shoes, so rather than wait for her to fit my little feet into my slippers, I grabbed them from her and did it myself. They were the prettiest pair of shoes any girl could have!

For the next few weeks I was Dorothy and I'd stop everyone I'd see in order to prove it by tapping my heels together and saying, "There's no place like home." But soon my feet grew too big for my ruby slippers, and as I graduated into the next larger size, I no longer wanted to be Dorothy. As I grew up, so did my dreams. Cinderella, now she was someone to be! Yet, once again that phase, like the phases I am going through now, passed fairly quickly.

Hope made enough copies of her essay so that the whole class could read and then discuss it. After reading her essay to the class, Hope asked her classmates for their reactions. Several students suggested that she tighten her narrative, eliminating those details that were not essential to the story. Most of their suggestions were centered in paragraphs 4 and 5. "Why mention Mr. Rogers and Big Bird?" someone asked. "I didn't want you to have to wait several days to pick them up, and I didn't want to be reminded of your temper," commented another. When Hope came to revise her draft, she used this advice. She also eliminated a number of clichés and made a significant change in the ending of the paper. Notice how much more effective the final version is as the result of these minor revisions.

REVISED DRAFT

The Ruby Slippers

To a four-year old, anything longer than five minutes feels like eternity, so when the clerk told me and my mom that it would take three to four weeks for my new shoes to arrive, I was almost in tears. Since seeing *The Wizard of Oz*, I had thought of little else other than owning a pair of ruby slippers. My dreams were full of spinning houses, little munchkins, flying monkeys, and talking lions. All I wanted was to be Dorothy, and the shoe store had made a promise to find me a pair of red mary-janes which would hopefully take me to Munchkin Land and Oz.

For the next three weeks I made all the preparations I could think of in order to become Dorothy. It did not matter how convincing Judy Garland was because I knew in my heart that I was the true Dorothy. I sang "Somewhere Over the Rainbow" day and night, and I played dress up with an old light blue checked dress of my mother's. I even went as far as to carry my dog in a basket. My mom braided my long brown hair, and after I insisted, she tied a light blue ribbon around each braid. I skipped everywhere I went and colored part of our driveway with chalk to create my very own yellow brick road.

The only thing missing was my ruby slippers. After my mother explained that three weeks really was not that far off, I decided to help the store in their search for my red mary-janes. For a month I called the store everyday when I got home from preschool. By the end of the month, the ladies at the store knew me by name.

Finally, the woman on the other end of the phone said that yes, my shiny red shoes had arrived. I could hardly contain my excitement. During the ride, I practiced the one line that only the real Dorothy could say, "There's no place like home." And of course, I clicked my beat up loafers three times each time I recited that line. It was all practice for the real thing.

As we pulled into the parking lot, all the ladies inside the store waved to me as if they had been expecting me. I finally got to see my shoes, and they were as perfect as I had imagined. I was practically jumping out of my seat when she began to remove the stiff tissue paper surrounding my shoes, so rather than wait for her to fit my little feet into my slippers, I grabbed them from her and did it myself. They were the prettiest pair of shoes any girl could have!

For the next few weeks I was Dorothy and I'd stop everyone I'd see in order to prove it by tapping my heels together and saying, "There's no place like home." But soon my feet grew too big for my ruby slippers, and as I graduated into the next larger size, I no longer wanted to be Dorothy. As I grew up, so did my dreams.

SOME THINGS TO REMEMBER

1. Decide first why you are telling the reader *this* story. You must have a purpose clearly in mind.
2. Choose an illustration, event, or experience that can be covered adequately within the space limitations you face. Do not try to narrate the history of your life in an essay!
3. Decide on which point of view you will use. Do you want to be a part of the narrative or an objective observer? Which is more appropriate for your purpose?

4. Keeping your purpose in mind, select those details or events which seem the most important or the most revealing.

5. Arrange those details in an order—either a strict chronological one or one that employs a flashback. Remember to keep your verb tenses consistent and to signal any switches in time.

6. Remember the differences between showing and telling. Which method will be better for your narrative?

SALVATION

Langston Hughes

*Born in Joplin, Missouri, Langston Hughes (1902–1967) was an impor-
tant figure in the Harlem Renaissance. He is best known for his jazz- and
blues-inspired poetry, though he was also a talented prose writer and playwright. Among his writings are* Simple Speaks His Mind *(1950), the first
of four volumes of some of his best-loved stories; and* Ask Your Mama: 12
Moods for Jazz *(1961), one of his later, angry collections of poetry, fueled
by emotions surrounding the civil rights movements.*

The Big Sea: An Autobiography *(1940), published when Hughes
was thirty-eight years old, is a memoir of his early years, consisting of a series of short narratives focusing on events and people. After the death of his
grandmother, Hughes was raised by Auntie Reed, one of his grandmother's
friends. Uncle Reed, Auntie's husband, was, as Hughes notes in* The Big
Sea, *"a sinner and never went to church as long as he lived . . . but both of
them were very good and kind. . . . And no doubt from them I learned to
like both Christians and sinners equally well."*

BEFORE READING

Connecting: Was there a time in your teenage years when you were
disappointed by someone or something?

Anticipating: No narrative recounts every minute of an experience.
Writers must leave out far more than they include. What events con-
nected with this experience does Hughes leave out of his narrative?
Why?

1   I was saved from sin when I was going on thirteen. But not really
saved. It happened like this. There was a big revival at my Auntie
Reed's church. Every night for weeks there had been much preaching, singing, praying, and shouting, and some very hardened sinners
had been brought to Christ, and the membership of the church had
grown by leaps and bounds. Then just before the revival ended, they
held a special meeting for children, "to bring the young lambs to the
fold." My aunt spoke of it for days ahead. That night I was escorted

to the front row and placed on the mourners' bench with all the other young sinners, who had not yet been brought to Jesus.

My aunt told me that when you were saved you saw a light, and something happened to you inside! And Jesus came into your life! And God was with you from then on! She said you could see and hear and feel Jesus in your soul. I believed her. I had heard a great many old people say the same thing and it seemed to me they ought to know. So I sat there calmly in the hot, crowded church, waiting for Jesus to come to me. 2

The preacher preached a wonderful rhythmical sermon, all moans and shouts and lonely cries and dire pictures of hell, and then he sang a song about the ninety and nine safe in the fold, but one little lamb was left out in the cold. Then he said: "Won't you come? Won't you come to Jesus? Young lambs, won't you come?" And he held out his arms to all us young sinners there on the mourners' bench. And the little girls cried. And some of them jumped up and went to Jesus right away. But most of us just sat there. 3

A great many old people came and knelt around us and prayed, old women with jet-black faces and braided hair, old men with work-gnarled hands. And the church sang a song about the lower lights are burning, some poor sinners to be saved. And the whole building rocked with prayer and song. 4

Still I kept waiting to *see* Jesus. 5

Finally all the young people had gone to the altar and were saved, but one boy and me. He was a rounder's son named Westley. Westley and I were surrounded by sisters and deacons praying. It was very hot in the church, and getting late now. Finally Westley said to me in a whisper: "God damn! I'm tired o' sitting here. Let's get up and be saved." So he got up and was saved. 6

Then I was left all alone on the mourner's bench. My aunt came and knelt at my knees and cried, while prayers and song swirled all around me in the little church. The whole congregation prayed for me alone, in a mighty wail of moans and voices. And I kept waiting serenely for Jesus, waiting, waiting—but he didn't come. I wanted to see him, but nothing happened to me. Nothing! I wanted something to happen to me, but nothing happened. 7

I hear the songs and the minister saying: "Why don't you come? My dear child, why don't you come to Jesus? Jesus is waiting for you. He wants you. Why don't you come? Sister Reed, what is this child's name?" 8

"Langston," my aunt sobbed. 9

"Langston, why don't you come? Why don't you come and be saved? Oh, Lamb of God! Why don't you come?" 10

11   Now it was really getting late. I began to be ashamed of myself, holding everything up so long. I began to wonder what God thought about Westley, who certainly hadn't seen Jesus either, but who was now sitting proudly on the platform, swinging his knickerbockered legs and grinning down at me, surrounded by deacons and old women on their knees praying. God had not struck Westley dead for taking his name in vain or for lying in the temple. So I decided that maybe to save further trouble, I'd better lie, too, and say that Jesus had come, and get up and be saved.

12   So I got up.

13   Suddenly the whole room broke into a sea of shouting, as they saw me rise. Waves of rejoicing swept the place. Women leaped in the air. My aunt threw her arms around me. The minister took me by the hand and led me to the platform.

14   When things quieted down, in a hushed silence, punctuated by a few ecstatic "Amens," all the new young lambs were blessed in the name of God. Then joyous singing filled the room.

15   That night, for the last time in my life but one—for I was a big boy twelve years old—I cried. I cried, in bed alone, and couldn't stop. I buried my head under the quilts, but my aunt heard me. She woke up and told my uncle I was crying because the Holy Ghost had come into my life, and because I had seen Jesus. But I was really crying because I couldn't bear to tell her that I had lied, that I had deceived everybody in the church, that I hadn't seen Jesus, and that now I didn't believe there was a Jesus any more, since he didn't come to help me.

QUESTIONS ON SUBJECT AND PURPOSE

1. Who narrates the story? From what point in time is it told?

2. What does the narrator expect to happen when he is to be saved? What does happen?

3. Why does the narrator cry at the end of the story?

4. What was Hughes's attitude toward his experience when it first happened? At the time he originally wrote this selection? How does the opening sentence reflect that change in attitude?

QUESTIONS ON STRATEGY AND AUDIENCE

1. Why did Hughes not tell the story in the present tense? How would doing so change the story?

2. How much dialogue is used in the narration? Why does Hughes not use more?
3. Why does Hughes blend telling with showing in the story?
4. How much time is represented by the events in the story? Where does Hughes compress the time in his narrative? Why does he do so?

QUESTIONS ON VOCABULARY AND STYLE

1. What is the effect of the short paragraphs (5, 9, and 12)? How does Hughes use paragraphing to help shape his story?
2. How much description does Hughes include in his narrative? What types of details does he single out?
3. What is the effect of the exclamation marks used in paragraph 2?
4. Try to identify or explain the following phrases: *the ninety and nine safe in the fold* (paragraph 3), *the lower lights are burning* (4), *a rounder's son* (6), *knickerbockered legs* (11).

WRITING SUGGESTIONS

1. **For your Journal.** What can you remember from your early teenage years? In your journal first make a list of significant moments—both the high and low points—and then re-create one moment in prose.
2. **For a Paragraph.** We have all been disappointed by someone or something in our life. Single out a particular moment from your past. After spending some time remembering what happened and how you felt, narrate that experience for a general reader in a paragraph. Remember that your paragraph must reveal what the experience meant to you. Try using some dialogue.
3. Have you ever experienced anything that changed your life? It does not need to be a dramatic change—perhaps just a conviction that you will *never* do that again or that you will *always* be sure to do that again. In an essay, narrate for a reader that experience. Remember that your narrative should illustrate or prove the experience's significance to you.

Prewriting:
a. Divide your prewriting sessions for this paper into a series of activities done on different days. On day one,

concentrate just on making a list of possible vivid experiences—a near miss, a careless moment, a time you were caught, a stupid choice.

b. On day two, spend half an hour freewriting about two of the events from your list. Try to do one writing in the morning and one in the afternoon. Do not worry about writing complete, correct sentences. Do not stop during the writing.

c. On day three, spend an hour thinking about one of the two events. Jot down as much detail as you can remember.

d. On day four, write a draft of the essay, using the details gathered from the activities above.

Rewriting:

a. A successful narrative has a shape and a purpose. You do not need to include everything that happened, just those events relevant to the experience and its effect on you. Look again at the narratives included in this chapter. Notice what they include and exclude. Does your narrative show the same economy?

b. Did you use any dialogue? Sparing use will probably make your narrative more vivid—that is, it will show rather than tell.

c. Is the order of events clear to the reader? Is the story told in a strict chronological order? Did you use flashbacks? Think about other possible arrangements for your narrative.

4. For Research. Does Hughes seem to be serious about his experience—did he "lose" his faith as a result of what happened? Locate other examples of Hughes's writing (check your college's library catalogue for books by Hughes). Then, in an essay, analyze the significance (or insignificance) of this event in Hughes's writing. Be sure to formulate an explicit thesis about the importance of the event in Hughes's work.

SISTER MONROE

Maya Angelou

Maya Angelou was born Marguerita Johnson in St. Louis, Missouri, in 1928. A talented performing artist as well as a poet and autobiographer, Angelou has used much of her writing to explore American black female identity. Among her many accomplishments, she was coordinator for the Southern Christian Leadership Conference, and she was invited by President Clinton to compose and perform a poem for the 1993 Presidential inaugural, "On the Pulse of Morning." Her most significant writings have been her five volumes of autobiography (1970–1987); her most recent book is Wouldn't Take Nothing for my Journey Now *(1993).*

The following selection is from the first of Angelou's memoirs, I Know Why the Caged Bird Sings *(1970), a work that describes her early years in Stamps, Arkansas. One critic called that work a "revealing portrait of the customs and harsh circumstances of black life in the segregated South." Here in a brilliantly comic moment, Angelou recalls how Sister Monroe "got the spirit" one Sunday morning at church.*

BEFORE READING

Connecting: As a spectator, when do you find a physical mishap, such as a fight or fall, comic? What is necessary for us to laugh at "slapstick comedy" and not be concerned about the welfare of the people involved?

Anticipating: How does Angelou create humor in this narrative? What makes it funny?

In the Christian Methodist Episcopal Church the children's section   1
was on the right, cater-cornered from the pew that held those ominous women called the Mothers of the Church. In the young people's section the benches were placed close together, and when a child's legs no longer comfortably fitted in the narrow space, it was an indication to the elders that that person could now move into the intermediate area (center church). Bailey and I were allowed to sit with the other children only when there were informal meetings, church socials or the like. But on the Sundays when Reverend Thomas

preached, it was ordained that we occupy the first row, called the mourners' bench. I thought we were placed in front because Momma was proud of us, but Bailey assured me that she just wanted to keep her grandchildren under her thumb and eye.

2   Reverend Thomas took his text from Deuteronomy. And I was stretched between loathing his voice and wanting to listen to the sermon. Deuteronomy was my favorite book in the Bible. The laws were so absolute, so clearly set down, that I knew if a person truly wanted to avoid hell and brimstone, and being roasted forever in the devil's fire, all she had to do was memorize Deuteronomy and follow its teaching, word for word. I also liked the way the word rolled off the tongue.

3   Bailey and I sat alone on the front bench, the wooden slats pressing hard on our behinds and the backs of our thighs. I would have wriggled just a bit, but each time I looked over at Momma, she seemed to threaten, "Move and I'll tear you up," so, obedient to the unvoiced command, I sat still. The church ladies were warming up behind me with a few hallelujahs and praise the Lords and Amens, and the preacher hadn't really moved into the meat of the sermon.

4   It was going to be a hot service.

5   On my way into church, I saw Sister Monroe, her open-faced gold crown glinting when she opened her mouth to return a neighborly greeting. She lived in the country and couldn't get to church every Sunday, so she made up for her absences by shouting so hard when she did make it that she shook the whole church. As soon as she took her seat, all the ushers would move to her side of the church because it took three women and sometimes a man or two to hold her.

6   Once she hadn't been to church for a few months (she had taken off to have a child), she got the spirit and started shouting, throwing her arms around and jerking her body, so that the ushers went over to hold her down, but she tore herself away from them and ran up to the pulpit. She stood in front of the altar, shaking like a freshly caught trout. She screamed at Reverend Taylor. "Preach it. I say, preach it." Naturally he kept on preaching as if she wasn't standing there telling him what to do. Then she screamed an extremely fierce "I said, preach it" and stepped up on the altar. The Reverend kept on throwing out phrases like home-run balls and Sister Monroe made a quick break and grasped for him. For just a second, everything and everyone in the church except Reverend Taylor and Sister Monroe hung loose like stockings on a washline. Then she caught the minister by the sleeve of his jacket and his coattail, then she rocked him from side to side.

7   I have to say this for our minister, he never stopped giving us the lesson. The usher board made its way to the pulpit, going up both aisles with a little more haste than is customarily seen in church. Truth to tell, they fairly ran to the minister's aid. Then two of the deacons,

in their shiny Sunday suits, joined the ladies in white on the pulpit, and each time they pried Sister Monroe loose from the preacher he took another deep breath and kept on preaching, and Sister Monroe grabbed him in another place, and more firmly. Reverend Taylor was helping his rescuers as much as possible by jumping around when he got a chance. His voice at one point got so low it sounded like a roll of thunder, then Sister Monroe's "Preach it" cut through the roar, and we all wondered (I did, in any case) if it would ever end. Would they go on forever, or get tired out at last like a game of blindman's bluff that lasted too long, with nobody caring who was "it"?

I'll never know what might have happened, because magically the pandemonium spread. The spirit infused Deacon Jackson and Sister Willson, the chairman of the usher board, at the same time. Deacon Jackson, a tall, thin, quiet man, who was also a part-time Sunday school teacher, gave a scream like a falling tree, leaned back on thin air and punched Reverend Taylor on the arm. It must have hurt as much as it caught the Reverend unawares. There was a moment's break in the rolling sounds and Reverend Taylor jerked around surprised, and hauled off and punched Deacon Jackson. In the same second Sister Willson caught his tie, looped it over her fist a few times, and pressed down on him. There wasn't time to laugh or cry before all three of them were down on the floor behind the altar. Their legs spiked out like kindling wood. 8

Sister Monroe, who had been the cause of all the excitement, walked off the dais, cool and spent, and raised her flinty voice in the hymn, "I came to Jesus, as I was, worried, wounded, and sad, I found in Him a resting place and He has made me glad." 9

The minister took advantage of already being on the floor and asked in a choky little voice if the church would kneel with him to offer a prayer of thanksgiving. He said we had been visited with a mighty spirit, and let the whole church say Amen. 10

On the next Sunday, he took his text from the eighteenth chapter of the Gospel according to St. Luke, and talked quietly but seriously about the Pharisees, who prayed in the streets so that the public would be impressed with their religious devotion. I doubt that anyone got the message—certainly not those to whom it was directed. The deacon board, however, did appropriate funds for him to buy a new suit. The other was a total loss. 11

QUESTIONS ON SUBJECT AND PURPOSE

1. Who is the narrator? How old does she seem to be? How do you know?

2. Why does Sister Monroe behave as she does?

3. How does the section on the narrator and Bailey act as a preface to the story of Sister Monroe? Is it relevant, for example, that the narrator's favorite book of the Bible is Deuteronomy?

QUESTIONS ON STRATEGY AND AUDIENCE

1. Part of the art of narration is knowing what events to select. Look carefully at Angelou's story of Sister Monroe (paragraphs 5 to 9). What events does she choose to include in her narrative?

2. How is Sister Monroe described? Make a list of all of the physical particulars we are given about her. How, other than direct description, is Sister Monroe revealed to the reader?

3. What shift occurs between paragraphs 5 and 6? Did you notice it the first time you read the selection?

QUESTIONS ON VOCABULARY AND STYLE

1. Other than a few words uttered by Sister Monroe, Angelou uses no other dialogue in the selection. How, then, is the story told? What advantage does this method have?

2. Writing humor is never easy. Having a funny situation is essential, but, in addition, the story must be told in the right way. (Remember how people can ruin a good joke?) How does Angelou's language and style contribute to the humor in the selection?

3. How effective are the following images:
   a. "She stood in front of the altar, shaking like a freshly caught trout" (paragraph 6).
   b. "The Reverend kept on throwing out phrases like home-run balls" (6).
   c. "Everyone in the church . . . hung loose like stockings on a washline" (6).
   d. "Their legs spiked out like kindling wood" (8).

WRITING SUGGESTIONS

1. **For your Journal.** Observe people for a day. In your journal, make a list of the funny or comic moments that you notice.

Select one of those moments and first describe the situation you witnessed, then analyze why it seemed funny to you.

2. **For a Paragraph.** Everyone has experienced a funny, embarrassing moment—maybe it happened to you or maybe you just witnessed it. In a paragraph, narrate that incident for your reader. Remember to keep the narrative focused.

3. **For an Essay.** Select a "first" from your experience—your first day in junior high school, your first date, your first time driving a car, your first day on a job or at college. Re-create that first for your reader. Remember to shape your narrative and select only important, contributing details. Focus your narrative around a significant aspect of that first experience, whether it was funny or serious.

Prewriting:

a. Several days before your essay is due, set aside an hour to comb your memories for some significant "firsts." Make a list of possibilities, jotting down whatever details you remember. Let the list rest for a day before looking at it again.

b. Scan your list and select the most promising item. For another hour jot down randomly whatever you remember. Focus on re-creating the event in your memory. One detail often triggers others. Do not try to write yet; just gather details.

c. Remember that your narrative needs to hinge on a significant feature—it can be an insight (such as in Hughes's "Salvation" or White's "Once More to the Lake") or a serious or comic pattern (as in "Sister Monroe"). Write down an explicit statement of what it is you want to reveal in your narrative. Use that statement to decide what details to include and what to exclude.

Rewriting:

a. After completing your draft, go back and look at the purpose statement you wrote in prewriting. Carefully test each detail you included to see if it relates to that intended purpose. Omit any irrelevant or inappropriate details.

b. Look at your conclusion. How did you end? Did you lead up to a climactic moment, or did you end with a flat conclusion ("And so you can see why this experience was important to me")? Compare how the writers in this chapter end their narratives.

4. **For Research.** What is an autobiography? Is it always a factual account of events in the writer's life? Is it ever "made up" or fictional? Is it ever propagandistic? What purposes do autobiographies have? Select an autobiography written by someone who interests you—check your college's library catalogue for possibilities. Then analyze that work as an autobiography. Do not summarize. Instead, formulate a thesis about what you see as the writer's sense of purpose in the book. Support your argument with evidence from the text and be sure to document your quotations.

ON BEING CHASED
Annie Dillard

*Born in Pittsburgh in 1945, Annie Dillard received an M.A. in English
from Hollins College in Virginia. A poet, essayist, and novelist, she served as
a contributing editor of* Harper's *for a number of years. Her many nonfiction works include the Pulitzer Prize-winning* Pilgrim at Tinker Creek
(1974), and she recently published her first novel, The Living *(1992).*

In An American Childhood *(1987), the book in which the following essay originally appeared as a chapter, Dillard recalls her childhood. One
reviewer observed that the book is "less about a coming-to-age than about a
coming-to-consciousness, a consciousness so heightened by what appears to be
an overactive autonomic nervous system that one sometimes fears her nerves
will burst through her skin." In "On Being Chased," Dillard describes how
at the age of seven she discovered an adult who knew "what I thought only
children who trained at football knew: that you have to fling yourself at what
you're doing, you have to point yourself, forget yourself, aim, dive."*

BEFORE READING

Connecting: Dillard narrates an episode that occurred when she was
seven years old. Can you remember an intensely felt event that occurred in your life at about that same age? Can you recall it in the
same detail?

Anticipating: Every child has been lectured to by an adult for committing an inappropriate act. Few, however, have probably found the
experience worth remembering. What is it about this experience that
fascinates Dillard?

Some boys taught me to play football. This was fine sport. You   1
thought up a new strategy for every play and whispered it to the others. You went out for a pass, fooling everyone. Best, you got to throw
yourself mightily at someone's running legs. Either you brought him
down or you hit the ground flat out on your chin, with your arms
empty before you. It was all or nothing. If you hesitated in fear, you
would miss and get hurt: you would take a hard fall while the kid got
away, or you would get kicked in the face while the kid got away. But

if you flung yourself wholeheartedly at the back of his knees—if you gathered and joined body and soul and pointed them diving fearlessly—then you likely wouldn't get hurt, and you'd stop the ball. Your fate, and your team's score, depended on your concentration and courage. Nothing girls did could compare with it.

2   Boys welcomed me at baseball, too, for I had, through enthusiastic practice, what was weirdly known as a boy's arm. In winter, in the snow, there was neither baseball nor football, so the boys and I threw snowballs at passing cars. I got in trouble throwing snowballs, and have seldom been happier since.

3   On one weekday morning after Christmas, six inches of new snow had just fallen. We were standing up to our boot tops in snow on a front yard on trafficked Reynolds Street, waiting for cars. The cars traveled Reynolds Street slowly and evenly; they were targets all but wrapped in red ribbons, cream puffs. We couldn't miss.

4   I was seven; the boys were eight, nine, and ten. The oldest two Fahey boys were there—Mikey and Peter—polite blond boys who lived near me on Lloyd Street, and who already had four brothers and sisters. My parents approved Mikey and Peter Fahey. Chickie McBride was there, a tough kid, and Billy Paul and Mackie Kean too, from across Reynolds, where the boys grew up dark and furious, grew up skinny, knowing, and skilled. We had all drifted from our houses that morning looking for action, and had found it here on Reynolds Street.

5   It was cloudy but cold. The cars' tires laid behind them on the snowy street a complex trail of beige chunks like crenellated castle walls. I had stepped on some earlier; they squeaked. We could have wished for more traffic. When a car came, we all popped it one. In the intervals between cars we reverted to the natural solitude of children.

6   I started making an iceball—a perfect iceball, from perfectly white snow, perfectly spherical, and squeezed perfectly translucent so no snow remained all the way through. (The Fahey boys and I considered it unfair actually to throw an iceball at somebody, but it had been known to happen.)

7   I had just embarked on the iceball project when we heard tire chains come clanking from afar. A black Buick was moving toward us down the street. We all spread out, banged together some regular snowballs, took aim, and, when the Buick drew nigh, fired.

8   A soft snowball hit the driver's windshield right before the driver's face. It made a smashed star with a hump in the middle.

9   Often, of course, we hit our target, but this time, the only time in all of life, the car pulled over and stopped. Its wide black door opened; a man got out of it, running. He didn't even close the car door.

He ran after us, and we ran away from him, up the snowy 10
Reynolds sidewalk. At the corner, I looked back; incredibly, he was
still after us. He was in city clothes: a suit and tie, street shoes. Any
normal adult would have quit, having sprung us into flight and made
his point. This man was gaining on us. He was a thin man, all action.
All of a sudden, we were running for our lives.

Wordless, we split up. We were on our turf; we could lose our- 11
selves in the neighborhood backyards, everyone for himself. I paused
and considered. Everyone had vanished except Mikey Fahey, who was
just rounding the corner of a yellow brick house. Poor Mikey, I
trailed him. The driver of the Buick sensibly picked the two of us to
follow. The man apparently had all day.

He chased Mikey and me around the yellow house and up a 12
backyard path we knew by heart: under a low tree, up a bank, through
a hedge, down some snowy steps, and across the grocery store's delivery driveway. We smashed through a gap in another hedge, entered
a scruffy backyard and ran around its back porch and tight between
houses to Edgerton Avenue; we ran across Edgerton to an alley and
up our own sliding woodpile to the Halls' front yard; he kept coming. We ran up Lloyd Street and wound through mazy backyards toward the steep hilltop at Willard and Lang.

He chased us silently, block after block. He chased us silently 13
over picket fences, through thorny hedges, between houses, around
garbage cans, and across streets. Every time I glanced back, choking
for breath, I expected he would have quit. He must have been as
breathless as we were. His jacket strained over his body. It was an immense discovery, pounding into my hot head with every sliding, joyous step, that this ordinary adult evidently knew what I thought only
children who trained at football knew: that you have to fling yourself
at what you're doing, you have to point yourself, forget yourself, aim,
dive.

Mikey and I had nowhere to go, in our own neighborhood or 14
out of it, but away from this man who was chasing us. He impelled us
forward; we compelled him to follow our route. The air was cold;
every breath tore my throat. We kept running, block after block; we
kept improvising, backyard after backyard, running a frantic course
and choosing it simultaneously, failing always to find small places or
hard places to slow him down, and discovering always, exhilarated,
dismayed, that only bare speed could save us—for he would never
give up, this man—and we were losing speed.

He chased us through the backyard labyrinths of ten blocks be- 15
fore he caught us by our jackets. He caught us and we all stopped.

We three stood staggering, half blinded, coughing, in an obscure 16
hilltop backyard: a man in his twenties, a boy, a girl. He had released

our jackets, our pursuer, our captor, our hero: he knew we weren't going anywhere. We all played by the rules. Mikey and I unzipped our jackets. I pulled off my sopping mittens. Our tracks multiplied in the backyard's new snow. We had been breaking new snow all morning. We didn't look at each other. I was cherishing my excitement. The man's lower pants legs were wet; his cuffs were full of snow, and there was a prow of snow beneath them on his shoes and socks. Some trees bordered the little flat backyard, some messy winter trees. There was no one around: a clearing in a grove, and we the only players.

17   It was a long time before he could speak. I had some difficulty at first recalling why we were there. My lips felt swollen; I couldn't see out of the sides of my eyes; I kept coughing.

18   "You stupid kids," he began perfunctorily.

19   We listened perfunctorily indeed, if we listened at all, for the chewing out was redundant, a mere formality, and beside the point. The point was that he had chased us passionately without giving up, and so he had caught us. Now he came down to earth. I wanted the glory to last forever.

20   But how could the glory have lasted forever? We could have run through every backyard in North America until we got to Panama. But when he trapped us at the lip of the Panama Canal, what precisely could he have done to prolong the drama of the chase and cap its glory? I brooded about this for the next few years. He could only have fried Mikey Fahey and me in boiling oil, say, or dismembered us piecemeal, or staked us to anthills. None of which I really wanted, and none of which any adult was likely to do, even in the spirit of fun. He could only chew us out there in the Panamanian jungle, after months or years of exalting pursuit. He could only begin, "You stupid kids," and continue in his ordinary Pittsburgh accent with his normal righteous anger and the usual common sense.

21   If in that snowy backyard the driver of the black Buick had cut off our heads, Mikey's and mine, I would have died happy, for nothing has required so much of me since as being chased all over Pittsburgh in the middle of winter—running terrified, exhausted—by this sainted, skinny, furious red-headed man who wished to have a word with us. I don't know how he found his way back to his car.

QUESTIONS ON SUBJECT AND PURPOSE

1. In what sense is the chase for Dillard a "glory" she wanted to "last forever" (paragraph 19)?

2. What is unexpected about the driver's behavior?

3. How does Dillard feel about her pursuer?

QUESTIONS ON STRATEGY AND AUDIENCE

1. How do the first two paragraphs of the essay serve as an introduction to the episode with the snowballs and the chase?
2. When and how does Dillard describe the man?
3. What expectations could Dillard have of her readers?

QUESTIONS ON VOCABULARY AND STYLE

1. What is particularly appropriate about the one-sentence description of the man's legs (paragraph 16): "The man's lower pants legs were wet; his cuffs were full of snow, and there was a prow of snow beneath them on his shoes and socks"?
2. Be prepared to discuss the effect created by each of the following sentences:
   a. "The cars' tires laid behind them on the snowy street a complex trail of beige chunks like crenellated castle walls" (paragraph 5).
   b. "He could only begin, 'You stupid kids,' and continue in his ordinary Pittsburgh accent with his normal righteous anger and the usual common sense" (paragraph 20).
3. Be able to define the following words: *crenellated* (paragraph 5), *reverted* (5), *nigh* (7), *prow* (16), *perfunctorily* (18).

WRITING SUGGESTIONS

1. **For your Journal**. In your journal, make a list of some of your memorable childhood experiences dealing with adults. What do you remember about each of these scenes? Looking back, can you attribute a value or lesson to each experience? Try to do so for at least some.
2. **For a Paragraph**. Many childhood experiences acquire meaning or significance only as we grow older. Select a time in your youth when you were confronted by the adult world. In a paragraph, narrate the experience and reveal as well what it has taught you about life or about dealing with or being an adult.
3. **For an Essay**. Select a remembered experience from your past, although not necessarily one from your childhood. The experience should reveal something significant about you or about life in general. It should have a thesis, a point you wish to make. In an essay, re-create that experience for your readers. Make sure that the narrative has that central focus or thesis.

Prewriting:

a. Over a period of a day or two, keep a list of possible experiences about which you might write.

b. For each of the most promising possibilities, finish the following sentence: "The significance of this experience was. . . ."

c. Select two of those experiences and freewrite for 15 minutes about each.

Rewriting:

a. Remember that a narrative must have a beginning, middle, and end. Check your narrative to make sure that you come to the climactic moment in the story and then immediately conclude. Compare your ending to those used in the readings in this chapter.

b. Try changing the time sequence of your narrative. If you told the story in chronological order, try using a flashback to begin the story. If you began with a flashback, try a strict chronological order. Which seems to work better?

c. Remember to keep descriptive details to an effective minimum. Too much description slows down the story. Go through your narrative and underline all of the instances in which you described something. Are there too many?

4. For Research. To what extent do all autobiographical memoirs tell a similar story? In your college's library, find several books similar to Dillard's *An American Childhood*—that is, books that record an author's childhood years (for example, works by Maya Angelou or Richard Rodriguez). Read them, and then in a research paper using these texts as examples, discuss the similarities that all share. To what extent are childhood memories universal rather than unique? Alternatively, you might concentrate on examining Dillard's memoir in detail. Test the assertion of one critic about the text that is quoted in the biographical note at the start of this essay. To what extent is *An American Childhood* a book about "Coming-to-consciousness"?

SILENT DANCING
Judith Ortiz Cofer

Judith Ortiz Cofer was born in Hormigueros, Puerto Rico, in 1952. Her family settled in Paterson, New Jersey, in 1954, but because her father was in the U.S. Navy, mother and children periodically returned to Puerto Rico while his fleet was on maneuvers. She earned her M.A. in English from Florida Atlantic University in 1977. Today, she lives on a farm in rural Louisville, Georgia, and teaches English at the University of Georgia. She has published three books of poetry—one of which, Peregrina, *won a major poetry award in 1985—and a collection of essays. Her first novel,* The Line of the Sun *(1989), was nominated for the Pulitzer Prize in 1990. Her most recent book is* The Latin Deli: Prose and Poetry *(1993).*

In "Silent Dancing," the title essay from her collection Silent Dancing: A Partial Remembrance of a Puerto Rican Childhood *(1990), Cofer remembers her youth in Paterson, New Jersey. In a 1992 interview in* Kenyon Review, *she noted: "It deals with culture and language as well as climate. As a child going back and forth to Puerto Rico, I became very observant; I guess children who are lonely because they are dislocated and relocated geographically and emotionally become observers of life."*

BEFORE READING

Connecting: Can you remember an occasion when you (or someone else in your family) felt uncomfortable because of who or what you were? That feeling could have been connected to something cultural, social, economic, or even physical.

Anticipating: In the essay, Cofer has a dual focus: the first half of the essay deals with her experiences as a child in Paterson; the second half is about a New Year's Eve party that was captured in a home movie. What is the connection between the two parts of the essay? Why might she link these memories together?

We have a home movie of this party. Several times my mother and I have watched it together, and I have asked questions about the silent revelers coming in and out of focus. It is grainy and of short duration, but it's a great vis- 1 *ual aid to my memory of life at that time. And it is in color—the only complete scene in color I can recall from those years.*

2   We lived in Puerto Rico until my brother was born in 1954. Soon after, because of economic pressures on our growing family, my father joined the United States Navy. He was assigned to duty on a ship in Brooklyn Yard—a place of cement and steel that was to be his home base in the States until his retirement more than twenty years later. He left the Island first, alone, going to New York City and tracking down his uncle who lived with his family across the Hudson River in Paterson, New Jersey. There my father found a tiny apartment in a huge tenement that had once housed Jewish families but was just being taken over and transformed by Puerto Ricans, overflowing from New York City. In 1955 he sent for us. My mother was only twenty years old, I was not quite three, and my brother was a toddler when we arrived at El Building, as the place had been christened by its newest residents.

3   My memories of life in Paterson during those first few years are all in shades of gray. Maybe I was too young to absorb vivid colors and details, or to discriminate between the slate blue of the winter sky and the darker hues of the snow-bearing clouds, but that single color washes over the whole period. The building we lived in was gray, as were the streets, filled with slush the first few months of my life there. The coat my father had bought for me was similar in color and too big; it sat heavily on my thin frame.

4   I do remember the way the heater pipes banged and rattled, startling all of us out of sleep until we got so used to the sound that we automatically shut it out or raised our voices above the racket. The hiss from the valve punctuated my sleep (which has always been fitful) like a nonhuman presence in the room—a dragon sleeping at the entrance of my childhood. But the pipes were also a connection to all the other lives being lived around us. Having come from a house designed for a single family back in Puerto Rico—my mother's extended-family home—it was curious to know that strangers lived under our floor and above our heads, and that the heater pipe went through everyone's apartment. (My first spanking in Paterson came as a result of playing tunes on the pipes in my room to see if there would be an answer.) My mother was as new to this concept of beehive life as I was, but she had been given strict orders by my father to keep the doors locked, the noise down, ourselves to ourselves.

5   It seems that Father had learned some painful lessons about prejudice while searching for an apartment in Paterson. Not until years later did I hear how much resistance he had encountered with

landlords who were panicking at the influx of Latinos into a neighborhood that had been Jewish for a couple of generations. It made no difference that it was the American phenomenon of ethnic turnover which was changing the urban core of Paterson, and that the human flood could not be held back with an accusing finger.

"You Cuban?" one man had asked my father, pointing at his 6 name tag on the navy uniform—even though my father had the fair skin and light brown hair of his northern Spanish background, and the name Ortiz is as common in Puerto Rico as Johnson is in the United States.

"No," my father had answered, looking past the finger into his 7 adversary's angry eyes. "I'm Puerto Rican."

"Same shit." And the door closed. 8

My father could have passed as European, but we couldn't. My 9 brother and I both have our mother's black hair and olive skin, and so we lived in El Building and visited our great-uncle and his fair children on the next block. It was their private joke that they were the German branch of the family. Not many years later that area too would be mainly Puerto Rican. It was as if the heart of the city map were being gradually colored brown—*café con leche* brown. Our color.

The movie opens with a sweep of the living room. It is "typical" immigrant 10 *Puerto Rican decor for the time: the sofa and chairs are square and hard-looking, upholstered in bright colors (blue and yellow in this instance) and covered with the transparent plastic that furniture salesmen then were so adept at convincing women to buy. The linoleum on the floor is light blue; where it had been subjected to spike heels, as it was in most places, there were dime-size indentations all over it that cannot be seen in this movie. The room is full of people dressed up: dark suits for the men, red dresses for the women. When I have asked my mother why most of the women are in red that night, she has shrugged and said, "I don't remember. Just a coincidence." She doesn't have my obsession for assigning symbolism to everything.*

The three women in red sitting on the couch are my mother, my 11 *eighteen-year-old cousin, and her brother's girlfriend. The* novia *is just up from the Island, which is apparent in her body language. She sits up formally, her dress pulled over her knees. She is a pretty girl, but her posture makes her look insecure, lost in her full-skirted dress, which she has carefully tucked around her to make room for my gorgeous cousin, her future sister-in-law. My cousin has grown up in Paterson and is in her last year of high school. She doesn't have a trace of what Puerto Ricans call* la mancha *(literally, the stain: the mark of the new immigrant—something about the posture, the voice, or the humble demeanor that makes it obvious to everyone the person has just arrived on the mainland). My cousin is wearing a tight, sequined, cocktail dress. Her brown hair has been lightened with peroxide around the bangs, and she is holding a cigarette expertly between her fingers, bringing it up to her mouth in a sensuous arc of her arm as she talks animatedly. My mother, who has come up to sit between the two women, both only a few years younger than herself, is somewhere between the poles they represent in our culture.*

12   It became my father's obsession to get out of the barrio, and thus we were never permitted to form bonds with the place or with the people who lived there. Yet El Building was a comfort to my mother, who never got over yearning for *la isla*. She felt surrounded by her language: the walls were thin, and voices speaking and arguing in Spanish could be heard all day. *Salsas* blasted out of radios, turned on early in the morning and left on for company. Women seemed to cook rice and beans perpetually—the strong aroma of boiling red kidney beans permeated the hallways.

13   Though Father preferred that we do our grocery shopping at the supermarket when he came home on weekend leaves, my mother insisted that she could cook only with products whose labels she could read. Consequently, during the week I accompanied her and my little brother to La Bodega—a hole-in-the-wall grocery store across the street from El Building. There we squeezed down three narrow aisles jammed with various products. Goya and Libby's— those were the trademarks that were trusted by her *mamá*, so my mother bought many cans of Goya beans, soups, and condiments, as well as little cans of Libby's fruit juices for us. And she also bought Colgate toothpaste and Palmolive soap. (The final *e* is pronounced in both these products in Spanish, so for many years I believed that they were manufactured on the Island. I remember my surprise at first hearing a commercial on television in which "Colgate" rhymed with "ate.") We always lingered at La Bodega, for it was there that Mother breathed best, taking in the familiar aromas of the foods she knew from Mamá's kitchen. It was also there that she got to speak to the other women of El Building without violating outright Father's dictates against fraternizing with our neighbors.

14   Yet Father did his best to make our "assimilation" painless. I can still see him carrying a real Christmas tree up several flights of stairs to our apartment, leaving a trail of aromatic pine. He carried it formally, as if it were a flag in a parade. We were the only ones in El Building that I knew of who got presents on both Christmas and *día de Reyes*, the day when the Three Kings brought gifts to Christ and to Hispanic children.

15   Our supreme luxury in El Building was having our own televi-

sion set. It must have been a result of Father's guilt feelings over the isolation he had imposed on us, but we were among the first in the barrio to have one. My brother quickly became an avid watcher of Captain Kangaroo and Jungle Jim, while I loved all the series showing families. By the time I started first grade, I could have drawn a map of Middle America as exemplified by the lives of characters in *Father Knows Best, The Donna Reed Show, Leave It to Beaver, My Three Sons,* and (my favorite) *Bachelor Father,* where John Forsythe treated his adopted teenage daughter like a princess because he was rich and had a Chinese houseboy to do everything for him. In truth, compared to our neighbors in El Building, *we* were rich. My father's navy check provided us with financial security and a standard of living that the factory workers envied. The only thing his money could not buy us was a place to live away from the barrio—his greatest wish, Mother's greatest fear.

In the home movie the men are shown next, sitting around a card table set 16 *up in one corner of the living room, playing dominoes. The clack of the ivory pieces was a familiar sound. I heard it in many houses on the Island and in many apartments in Paterson. In* Leave It to Beaver, *the Cleavers played bridge in every other episode; in my childhood, the men started every social occasion with a hotly debated round of dominoes. The women would sit around and watch, but they never participated in the games.*

Here and there you can see a small child. Children were always 17 *brought to parties and, whenever they got sleepy, were put to bed in the host's bedroom. Babysitting was a concept unrecognized by the Puerto Rican women I knew: a responsible mother did not leave her children with any stranger. And in a culture where children are not considered intrusive, there was no need to leave the children at home. We went where our mother went.*

Of my preschool years I have only impressions: the sharp bite of the 18 wind in December as we walked with our parents toward the brightly lit stores downtown; how I felt like a stuffed doll in my heavy coat, boots, and mittens; how good it was to walk into the five-and-dime and sit at the counter drinking hot chocolate. On Saturdays our whole family would walk downtown to shop at the big department stores on Broadway. Mother bought all our clothes at Penney's and Sears, and she liked to buy her dresses at the women's specialty shops like Lerner's and Diana's. At some point we'd go into Woolworth's and sit at the soda fountain to eat.

We never ran into other Latinos at these stores or when eating 19 out, and it became clear to me only years later that the women from El Building shopped mainly in other places—stores owned by other

Puerto Ricans or by Jewish merchants who had philosophically accepted our presence in the city and decided to make us their good customers, if not real neighbors and friends. These establishments were located not downtown but in the blocks around our street, and they were referred to generically as La Tienda, El Bazar, La Bodega, La Botánica. Everyone knew what was meant. These were the stores where your face did not turn a clerk to stone, where your money was as green as anyone else's.

20   One New Year's Eve we were dressed up like child models in the Sears catalogue: my brother in a miniature man's suit and bow tie, and I in black patent-leather shoes and a frilly dress with several layers of crinoline underneath. My mother wore a bright red dress that night, I remember, and spike heels; her long black hair hung to her waist. Father, who usually wore his navy uniform during his short visits home, had put on a dark civilian suit for the occasion: we had been invited to his uncle's house for a big celebration. Everyone was excited because my mother's brother Hernan—a bachelor who could indulge himself with luxuries—had bought a home movie camera, which he would be trying out that night.

21   Even the home movie cannot fill in the sensory details such a gathering left imprinted in a child's brain. The thick sweetness of women's perfumes mixing with the ever-present smells of food cooking in the kitchen: meat and plantain *pasteles*, as well as the ubiquitous rice dish made special with pigeon peas—*gandules*—and seasoned with precious *sofrito* sent up from the Island by somebody's mother or smuggled in by a recent traveler. *Sofrito* was one of the items that women hoarded, since it was hardly ever in stock at La Bodega. It was the flavor of Puerto Rico.

22   The men drank Palo Viejo rum, and some of the younger ones got weepy. The first time I saw a grown man cry was at a New Year's Eve party: he had been reminded of his mother by the smells in the kitchen. But what I remember most were the boiled *pasteles*, plantain or yucca rectangles stuffed with corned beef or other meats, olives, and many other savory ingredients, all wrapped in banana leaves. Everybody had to fish one out with a fork. There was always a "trick" *pastel*—one without stuffing—and whoever got that one was the "New Year's Fool."

23   There was also the music. Long-playing albums were treated like precious china in these homes. Mexican recordings were popular, but the songs that brought tears to my mother's eyes were sung by the melancholy Daniel Santos, whose life as a drug addict was the stuff of legend. Felipe Rodríguez was a particular favorite of couples, since he

sang about faithless women and brokenhearted men. There is a snatch of one lyric that has stuck in my mind like a needle on a worn groove: *De piedra ha de ser mi cama, de piedra la cabezera . . . la mujer que a mi me quiera . . . ha de quererme de veras. Ay, Ay, Ay, corazón, porque no amas . . .* I must have heard it a thousand times since the idea of a bed made of stone, and its connection to love, first troubled me with its disturbing images.

The five-minute home movie ends with people dancing in a circle—the creative filmmaker must have set it up, so that all of them could file past him. It is both comical and sad to watch silent dancing. Since there is no justification for the absurd movements that music provides for some of us, people appear frantic, their faces embarrassingly intense. It's as if you were watching sex. Yet for years, I've had dreams in the form of this home movie. In a recurring scene, familiar faces push themselves forward into my mind's eye, plastering their features into distorted close-ups. And I'm asking them: "Who is *she?*" Who is the old woman I don't recognize? Is she an aunt? Somebody's wife? Tell me who she is."

  24

"See the beauty mark on her cheek as big as a hill on the lunar landscape of her face—well, that runs in the family. The women on your father's side of the family wrinkle early; it's the price they pay for that fair skin. The young girl with the green stain on her wedding dress is *la novia*—just up from the Island. See, she lowers her eyes when she approaches the camera, as she's supposed to. Decent girls never look at you directly in the face. *Humilde*, humble, a girl should express humility in all her actions. She will make a good wife for your cousin. He should consider himself lucky to have met her only weeks after she arrived here. If he marries her quickly, she will make him a good Puerto Rican-style wife; but if he waits too long, she will be corrupted by the city, just like your cousin there."

  25

"She means me. I do what I want. This is not some primitive island I live on. Do they expect me to wear a black mantilla on my head and go to mass every day? Not me. I'm an American woman, and I will do as I please. I can type faster than anyone in my senior class at Central High, and I'm going to be a secretary to a lawyer when I graduate. I can pass for an American girl anywhere—I've tried it. At least for Italian, anyway—I never speak Spanish in public. I hate these parties, but I wanted the dress. I look better than any of these *humildes* here. *My* life is going to be different. I have an American boyfriend. He is older and has a car. My parents don't know it, but I sneak out of the house late at night sometimes to be with him. If I marry him, even my name will be American. I hate rice and beans—that's what makes these women fat."

  26

27   "Your *prima* is pregnant by that man she's been sneaking around with. Would I lie to you? I'm your *tiá política*, your great-uncle's common-law wife—the one he abandoned on the Island to go marry your cousin's mother. *I* was not invited to this party, of course, but I came anyway. I came to tell you that story about your cousin that you've always wanted to hear. Do you remember the comment your mother made to a neighbor that has always haunted you? The only thing you heard was your cousin's name, and then you saw your mother pick up your doll from the couch and say: 'It was as big as this doll when they flushed it down the toilet.' This image has bothered you for years, hasn't it? You had nightmares about babies being flushed down the toilet, and you wondered why anyone would do such a horrible thing. You didn't dare ask your mother about it. She would only tell you that you had not heard her right, and yell at you for listening to adult conversations. But later, when you were old enough to know about abortions, you suspected.

28   "I am here to tell you that you were right. Your cousin was growing an *americanito* in her belly when this movie was made. Soon after, she put something long and pointy into her pretty self, thinking maybe she could get rid of the problem before breakfast and still make it to her first class at the high school. Well, *niña*, her screams could be heard downtown. Your aunt, her *mamá*, who had been a midwife on the Island, managed to pull the little thing out. Yes, they probably flushed it down the toilet. What else could they do with it—give it a Christian burial in a little white casket with blue bows and ribbons? Nobody wanted that baby—least of all the father, a teacher at her school with a house in West Paterson that he was filling with real children, and a wife who was a natural blonde.

29   "Girl, the scandal sent your uncle back to the bottle. And guess where your cousin ended up? Irony of ironies. She was sent to a village in Puerto Rico to live with a relative on her mother's side: a place so far away from civilization that you have to ride a mule to reach it. A real change in scenery. She found a man there—women like that cannot live without male company—but believe me, the men in Puerto Rico know how to put a saddle on a woman like her. *La gringa*, they call her. Ha, ha, ha. *La gringa* is what she always wanted to be . . ."

30   The old woman's mouth becomes a cavernous black hole I fall into. And as I fall, I can feel the reverberations of her laughter. I hear the echoes of her last mocking words: *la gringa, la gringa!* And the conga line keeps moving silently past me. There is no music in my dream for the dancers.

31   When Odysseus visits Hades to see the spirit of his mother, he makes an offering of sacrificial blood, but since all the souls crave an audience with the living, he has to listen to many of them before he

can ask questions. I, too, have to hear the dead and the forgotten speak in my dream. Those who are still part of my life remain silent, going around and around in their dance. The others keep pressing their faces forward to say things about the past.

My father's uncle is last in line. He is dying of alcoholism, 32 shrunken and shriveled like a monkey, his face a mass of wrinkles and broken arteries. As he comes closer I realize that in his features I can see my whole family. If you were to stretch that rubbery flesh, you could find my father's face, and deep within *that* face—my own. I don't want to look into those eyes ringed in purple. In a few years he will retreat into silence, and take a long, long time to die. *Move back, Tío, I tell him. I don't want to hear what you have to say. Give the dancers room to move. Soon it will be midnight. Who is the New Year's Fool this time?*

QUESTIONS ON SUBJECT AND PURPOSE

1. To what does the title "Silent Dancing" refer?
2. When was the home movie taken? What is the relationship between the movie and the story that Cofer narrates about her childhood?
3. Cofer never explicitly states what her thesis or point is. What, though, does the essay seem to be about?

QUESTIONS ON STRATEGY AND AUDIENCE

1. How do the sections of the narrative that are printed in italic type differ from the rest of the essay? Why might Cofer place them in italics?
2. Toward the end of the essay (paragraphs 25–29), Cofer appears to quote other speakers. Who speaks each of these paragraphs? How do you know?
3. What does Cofer's handling of the Spanish words and phrases suggest about her sense of her audience?

QUESTIONS ON VOCABULARY AND STYLE

1. Why might Cofer choose to dramatize the encounter between her father and the landlord (paragraphs 5–8)?
2. In paragraph 29, Cofer repeats the Spanish phrase *la gringa*. What does that phrase mean? Can you guess from its context?

3. Be prepared to define the following words: *revelers* (paragraph 1), *demeanor* (11), *animatedly* (11), *permeated* (12), *fraternizing* (13), *intrusive* (17), *crinoline* (20), *ubiquitous* (21)

WRITING SUGGESTIONS

1. **For your Journal.** In your journal, jot down a list of family events that you remember from childhood. Is there one in particular that you would like to have on videotape? Explore why that one event would be important to you.

2. **For a Paragraph.** A substantial part of Cofer's essay is the description of a family New Year's Eve party. Most families have certain holiday rituals that characterize the family and its culture. Select such an occasion and narrate in a paragraph what typically happens. Remember as well to suggest what it is about this ritual or occasion that is so characteristic of your family and its culture.

3. **For an Essay.** It is natural, especially for young people, to want to assimilate themselves into the dominant group—to wear the same clothes, to speak in the same way, to share the group's values. Choose a time when you modified your behavior or values because of your desire to be "like" others. Narrate the event, but at the same time explore why you did what you did and how it made you feel. Were you compromising something? Were you glad to be rid of your "difference"?

Prewriting:

a. Make a list of as many times as you remember that you sought to conform. Add to the list over a period of several days. Try to capture a mental picture of each particular moment.

b. Try freewriting for five to ten minutes about each decision. Which ones seem the most detailed and most significant?

c. Remember that you are narrating a decision. Your narrative must have a beginning, middle, and end. Be sure to structure your account of the decision so that it has the shape necessary for a story.

Rewriting:

a. Look again at the draft of your narrative. Have you explored why you made the decision to conform and how it made you feel? The purpose of the narrative is more than just to tell the story.

b. Underline those sections of your narrative that deal with your attitude toward this decision. Have you revealed your feelings without directly telling the reader how you felt?

c. Remember to catch your reader's attention in the first paragraph. Look closely at your introduction. Ask a friend to read just that paragraph. Does your friend want to keep reading?

4. **For Research.** To what extent does Cofer explore a similar theme in her other work? Locate other examples of Cofer's writing (see the headnote and check the catalogue and databases available in your library). Then, in an essay, analyze Cofer's writing to isolate her central concerns. Be sure to formulate a thesis about the themes that occur in her writing—do not just summarize her work. Another possibility would be to compare Cofer's work with that of another writer who concentrates on his or her alienating experiences in American culture—excellent choices would be Richard Rodriguez, Amy Tan, or N. Scott Momaday.

ONCE MORE TO THE LAKE

E. B. White

Elwyn Brooks White (1899–1985) was born in Mount Vernon, New York, and received a B.A. from Cornell in 1921. In 1925 White began writing for The New Yorker *and was one of the mainstays of that magazine, his precise, ironic, nostalgic prose style closely associated with its own. His books include the children's classic* Charlotte's Web *(1952) and the widely used prose guide,* Elements of Style *(1959), White's revision of a text by his freshman English professor, William Strunk.*

As a child White summered with his parents and five brothers and sisters on a lake in Maine. He later commented: "It was sheer enchantment. We Whites were city people—everything about Belgrade [the area] was a new experience. . . . The delicious smells and sounds . . . are still with me after these many years of separation." In "Once More to the Lake" White revisits the lake in Maine where he summered as a child. Taking his son with him, White discovers that their identities merge: "I began to sustain the illusion that he was I, and therefore, by simple transposition, that I was my father."

BEFORE READING

Connecting: What place in your past holds a special significance for you? A park? A relative's house or apartment? Somewhere you lived? Somewhere you visited regularly?

Anticipating: In narrating his return to the lake with his son, White concentrates on certain memories and experiences. He does not tell us everything that happened. As you read, notice what White includes. What do the individual moments have in common?

1   One summer along about 1904, my father rented a camp on a lake in Maine and took us all there for the month of August. We all got ringworm from some kittens and had to rub Pond's Extract on our arms and legs night and morning, and my father rolled over in a canoe with all his clothes on; but outside of that the vacation was a success and from then on none of us ever thought there was any place in the world like that lake in Maine. We returned summer after summer—

always on August 1st for one month. I have since become a salt-water man, but sometimes in summer there are days when the restlessness of the tides and the fearful cold of the sea water and the incessant wind that blows across the afternoon and into the evening make me wish for the placidity of a lake in the woods. A few weeks ago this feeling got so strong I bought myself a couple of bass hooks and a spinner and returned to the lake where we used to go, for a week's fishing and to revisit old haunts.

I took along my son, who had never had any fresh water up his   2
nose and who had seen lily pads only from train windows. On the journey over to the lake I began to wonder what it would be like. I wondered how time would have marred this unique, this holy spot—the coves and streams, the hills that the sun set behind, the camps and the paths behind the camps. I was sure that the tarred road would have found it out and I wondered in what other ways it would be desolated. It is strange how much you can remember about places like that once you allow your mind to return into the grooves that lead back. You remember one thing, and that suddenly reminds you of another thing. I guess I remembered clearest of all the early mornings, when the lake was cool and motionless, remembered how the bedroom smelled of the lumber it was made of and of the wet woods whose scent entered through the screen. The partitions in the camp were thin and did not extend clear to the top of the rooms, and as I was always the first up I would dress softly so as not to wake the others, and sneak out into the sweet outdoors and start out in the canoe, keeping close along the shore in the long shadows of the pines. I remembered being very careful never to rub my paddle against the gunwale for fear of disturbing the stillness of the cathedral.

The lake had never been what you would call a wild lake. There   3
were cottages sprinkled around the shores, and it was in farming country although the shores of the lake were quite heavily wooded. Some of the cottages were owned by nearby farmers, and you would live at the shore and eat your meals at the farmhouse. That's what our family did. But although it wasn't wild, it was a fairly large and undisturbed lake and there were places in it which, to a child at least, seemed infinitely remote and primeval.

I was right about the tar: it led to within half a mile of the shore.   4
But when I got back there, with my boy, and we settled into a camp near a farmhouse and into the kind of summertime I had known, I could tell that it was going to be pretty much the same as it had been before—I knew it, lying in bed the first morning, smelling the bedroom, and hearing the boy sneak quietly out and go off along the shore in a boat. I began to sustain the illusion that he was I, and therefore, by simple transposition, that I was my father. This sensation

persisted, kept cropping up all the time we were there. It was not an entirely new feeling, but in this setting it grew much stronger. I seemed to be living a dual existence. I would be in the middle of some simple act, I would be picking up a bait box or laying down a table fork, or I would be saying something, and suddenly it would be not I but my father who was saying the words or making the gesture. It gave me a creepy sensation.

5   We went fishing the first morning. I felt the same damp moss covering the worms in the bait can, and saw the dragonfly alight on the tip of my rod as it hovered a few inches from the surface of the water. It was the arrival of this fly that convinced me beyond any doubt that everything was as it always had been, that the years were a mirage and there had been no years. The small waves were the same, chucking the rowboat under the chin as we fished at anchor, and the boat was the same boat, the same color green and the ribs broken in the same places, and under the floor-boards the same fresh-water leavings and debris—the dead helgramite, the wisps of moss, the rusty discarded fishhook, the dried blood from yesterday's catch. We stared silently at the tips of our rods, at the dragonflies that came and went. I lowered the tip of mine into the water, tentatively, pensively dislodging the fly, which darted two feet away, poised, darted two feet back, and came to rest again a little farther up the rod. There had been no years between the ducking of this dragonfly and the other one— the one that was part of memory. I looked at the boy, who was silently watching his fly, and it was my hands that held his rod, my eyes watching. I felt dizzy and didn't know which rod I was at the end of.

6   We caught two bass, hauling them in briskly as though they were mackerel, pulling them over the side of the boat in a businesslike manner without any landing net, and stunning them with a blow on the back of the head. When we got back for a swim before lunch, the lake was exactly where we had left it, the same number of inches from the dock, and there was only the merest suggestion of a breeze. This seemed an utterly enchanted sea, this lake you could leave to its own devices for a few hours and come back to, and find that it had not stirred, this constant and trustworthy body of water. In the shallows, the dark, water-soaked sticks and twigs, smooth and old, were undulating in clusters on the bottom against the clean ribbed sand, and the track of the mussel was plain. A school of minnows swam by, each minnow with its small individual shadow, doubling the attendance, so clear and sharp in the sunlight. Some of the other campers were in swimming, along the shore, one of them with a cake of soap, and the water felt thin and clear and unsubstantial. Over the years there had been this person with the cake of soap, this cultist, and here he was. There had been no years.

Up to the farmhouse to dinner through the teeming, dusty 7
field, the road under our sneakers was only a two-track road. The
middle track was missing, the one with the marks of the hooves and
splotches of dried, flaky manure. There had always been three tracks
to choose from in choosing which track to walk in; now the choice
was narrowed down to two. For a moment I missed terribly the middle alternative. But the way led past the tennis court, and something
about the way it lay there in the sun reassured me; the tape had loos-
ened along the backline, the alleys were green with plantains and
other weeds, and the net (installed in June and removed in September) sagged in the dry noon, and the whole place steamed with mid-
day heat and hunger and emptiness. There was a choice of pie for
dessert, and one was blueberry and one was apple, and the waitresses
were the same country girls, there having been no passage of time,
only the illusion of it as in a dropped curtain—the waitresses were
still fifteen; their hair had been washed, that was the only difference—they had been to the movies and seen the pretty girls with the
clean hair.

Summertime, oh summertime, pattern of life indelible, the 8
fadeproof lake, the woods unshatterable, the pasture with the sweet-
fern and the juniper forever and ever, summer without end; this was
the background, and the life along the shore was the design, the cottages with their innocent and tranquil design, their tiny docks with
the flagpole and the American flag floating against the white clouds in
the blue sky, the little paths over the roots of the trees leading from
camp to camp and the paths leading back to the outhouses and the
can of lime for sprinkling, and at the souvenir counters at the store
the miniature birchbark canoes and the post cards that showed things
looking a little better than they looked. This was the American family at play, escaping the city heat, wondering whether the newcomers
in the camp at the head of the cove were "common" or "nice," wondering whether it was true that the people who drove up for Sunday
dinner at the farmhouse were turned away because there wasn't
enough chicken.

It seemed to me, as I kept remembering all this, that those times 9
and those summers had been infinitely precious and worth saving.
There had been jollity and peace and goodness. The arriving (at the
beginning of August) had been so big a business in itself, at the rail-
way station the farm wagon drawn up, the first smell of the pine-
laden air, the first glimpse of the smiling farmer, and the great
importance of the trunks and your father's enormous authority in
such matters, and the feel of the wagon under you for the long ten-
mile haul, and at the top of the last long hill catching the first view of
the lake after eleven months of not seeing this cherished body of

water. The shouts and cries of the other campers when they saw you, and the trunks to be unpacked, to give up their rich burden. (Arriving was less exciting nowadays, when you sneaked up in your car and parked it under a tree near the camp and took out the bags and in five minutes it was all over, no fuss, no loud wonderful fuss about trunks.)

10   Peace and goodness and jollity. The only thing that was wrong now, really, was the sound of the place, an unfamiliar nervous sound of the outboard motors. This was the note that jarred, the one thing that would sometimes break the illusion and set the years moving. In those other summertimes all motors were inboard; and when they were at a little distance, the noise they made was a sedative, an ingredient of summer sleep. They were one-cylinder and two-cylinder engines, and some were make-and-break and some were jump-spark, but they all made a sleepy sound across the lake. The one-lungers throbbed and fluttered, and the twin-cylinder ones purred and purred, and that was a quiet sound too. But now the campers all had outboards. In the daytime, in the hot mornings, these motors made a petulant, irritable sound; at night, in the still evening when the afterglow lit the water, they whined about one's ears like mosquitoes. My boy loved our rented outboard, and his great desire was to achieve singlehanded mastery over it, and authority, and he soon learned the trick of choking it a little (but not too much), and the adjustment of the needle valve. Watching him I would remember the things you could do with the old one-cylinder engine with the heavy flywheel, how you could have it eating out of your hand if you got really close to it spiritually. Motor boats in those days didn't have clutches, and you would make a landing by shutting off the motor at the proper time and coasting in with a dead rudder. But there was a way of reversing them, if you learned the trick, by cutting the switch and putting it on again exactly on the final dying revolution of the flywheel, so that it would kick back against compression and begin reversing. Approaching a dock in a strong following breeze, it was difficult to slow up sufficiently by the ordinary coasting method, and if a boy felt he had complete mastery over his motor, he was tempted to keep it running beyond its time and then reverse it a few feet from the dock. It took a cool nerve, because if you threw the switch a twentieth of a second too soon you would catch the flywheel when it still has speed enough to go up past center, and the boat would leap ahead, charging bull-fashion at the dock.

11   We had a good week at the camp. The bass were biting well and the sun shone endlessly, day after day. We would be tired at night and lie down in the accumulated heat of the little bedrooms after the long hot day and the breeze would stir almost imperceptibly outside and the smell of the swamp drift in through the rusty screens. Sleep would

Narration

come easily and in the morning the red squirrel would be on the roof, tapping out his gay routine. I kept remembering everything, lying in bed in the mornings—the small steamboat that had a long rounded stern like the lip of a Ubangi, and how quietly she ran on the moonlight sails, when the older boys played their mandolins and the girls sang and we ate doughnuts dipped in sugar, and how sweet the music was on the water in the shining night, and what it had felt like to think about girls then. After breakfast we would go up to the store and the things were in the same place—the minnows in a bottle, the plugs and spinners disarranged and pawed over by the youngsters from the boys' camp, the fig newtons and the Beeman's gum. Outside, the road was tarred and cars stood in front of the store. Inside, all was just as it had always been, except that there was more Coca Cola and not so much Moxie and root beer and birch beer and sarsaparilla. We would walk out with a bottle of pop apiece and sometimes the pop would backfire up our noses and hurt. We explored the streams, quietly, where the turtles slid off the sunny logs and dug their way into the soft bottom; and we lay on the town wharf and fed worms to the tame bass. Everywhere we went I had trouble making out which was I, the one walking at my side, the one walking in my pants.

One afternoon while we were there at that lake a thunderstorm   12
came up. It was like the revival of an old melodrama that I had seen long ago with childish awe. The second-act climax of the drama of the electrical disturbance over a lake in America had not changed in any important respect. This was the big scene, still the big scene. The whole thing was so familiar, the first feeling of oppression and heat and a general air around camp of not wanting to go very far away. In midafternoon (it was all the same) a curious darkening of the sky, and a lull in everything that had made life tick; and then the way the boats suddenly swung the other way at their moorings with the coming of a breeze out of the new quarter, and the premonitory rumble. Then the kettle drum, then the snare, then the bass drum and cymbals, then crackling light against the dark, and the gods grinning and licking their chops in the hills. Afterward the calm, the rain steadily rustling in the calm lake, the return of light and hope and spirits, and the campers running out in joy and relief to go swimming in the rain, their bright cries perpetuating the deathless joke about how they were getting simply drenched, and the children screaming with delight at the new sensation of bathing in the rain, and the joke about getting drenched linking the generations in a strong indestructible chain. And the comedian who waded in carrying an umbrella.

When the others went swimming my son said he was going in   13
too. He pulled his dripping trunks from the line where they had hung

all through the shower, and wrung them out. Languidly, and with no thought of going in, I watched him, his hard little body, skinny and bare, saw him wince slightly as he pulled up around his vitals the small, soggy, icy garment. As he buckled the swollen belt suddenly my groin felt the chill of death.

QUESTIONS ON SUBJECT AND PURPOSE

1. Why does White go "once more" to the lake?
2. In what ways does White's son remind him of himself as a child? Make a list of the similarities he notices.
3. What is the meaning of the final sentence? Why does he feel "the chill of death"?
4. White's essay has achieved the status of a classic. Unquestionably White is an excellent writer, but surely the popularity of the essay depends upon something more. What else might account for that popularity?

QUESTIONS ON STRATEGY AND AUDIENCE

1. How does White structure his narrative? What events does he choose to highlight?
2. No narrative can record everything, and this is certainly not an hour-by-hour account of what happened. What does White ignore? Why, for example, does he end his narrative before the end of the actual experience (that is, leaving the lake)?
3. Why is his son never described?
4. What assumptions does White make about his audience?

QUESTIONS ON VOCABULARY AND STYLE

1. At several points White has trouble distinguishing between who is the son and who is the father. Select one of those scenes and examine how White describes the moment. How does the prose capture that confusion?
2. Can you find examples of figurative language—similes and metaphors, for example—in White's essay? Make a list.
3. Be able to define the following words: *placidity* (paragraph 1), *gunwale* (2), *primeval* (3), *teeming* (7), *premonitory* (12), *languidly* (13).

WRITING SUGGESTIONS

1. **For your Journal**. In the second paragraph, White observes: "It is strange how much you can remember about places like that once you allow your mind to return into the grooves that lead back. You remember one thing, and that suddenly reminds you of another thing." In your journal, try what he suggests. Pick a particular event you remember from childhood. Record the details that you remember.

2. **For a Paragraph**. Select one of the events that you listed in Suggestion 1 and, in a paragraph, narrate your experience. Do not feel that your experience has to be bizarre or death-defying; readers are attracted as well by the universal—the well-told, shaped, common experience. Remember this as you move from a private journal entry to this "public" paragraph (that is, one that has an audience larger than yourself).

3. **For an Essay**. Look for a moment or an experience in your memories that brought an insight. Suddenly you saw or you understood or you knew. Narrate the experience but build to the moment of your understanding.

   Prewriting:

   a. Make a list of your most powerful memories. Just list the events first. Later go back and make notes on each one.

   b. Select a promising event. Set aside an hour to think about what happened. Try to remember what happened just before and just after. Who else was there? What were you wearing?

   c. Complete the following sentence: "The insight that I am trying to reveal is _____." Use that statement to check over your prewriting notes.

   d. Study White's essay or Hughes's as possible structural models.

   Rewriting:

   a. Once your draft is finished, set it aside for at least a day. When you look at it again, check every detail against the purpose statement you wrote as a prewriting activity.

   b. Check to make sure you have used vivid verbs and concrete nouns. Do not overuse adjectives or adverbs.

   c. Just as the ending of a narrative should come to a climactic end, so its introduction ought to plunge the reader into the experience. Check to make sure you begin and end quickly and definitely.

4. For Research. What is your earliest memory? What factors control that aspect of our memories? Is it possible to remember events that took place before you could talk? What kinds of early memories are most easily recalled? In a research paper, provide some answers to these questions. Since memory plays such a significant role in everyone's life, you can assume that any audience will be interested in opinions that scientists now hold of this subject. You might prepare your paper in one of the following formats:

a. A traditional research paper for a college course, or

b. A feature article for a popular magazine.

Be sure to document your sources.

DESCRIPTION

You have bought a car—your first—and understandably you can hardly wait to tell your friends. "What does it look like?" they ask and you modestly reply, "A silver-gray '86 Ford Escort with red racing stripes and gray leather seats." What you have done is provide a description; you have given your listeners enough information to allow them to form a mental picture of your new (and used) car. Like narration, description is an everyday activity. You describe to a friend what cooked snails really taste like, how your favorite perfume smells, how your body feels when you have a fever, how a local rock band sounded last night. Description re-creates sense impressions, ideas, and feelings by translating them into words.

That translation is not always easy. For one thing, when you have a first-hand experience, all of your senses are working at the same time: you see, taste, smell, feel, hear; you experience feelings and have thoughts about the experience. When you convey that experience to a reader or a listener, you can only record one sense impression at a time. Furthermore, sometimes it is difficult to find an adequate translation for a particular sense impression—how do you describe the smell of musk perfume or the taste of freshly squeezed orange juice? On the other hand, the translation into words offers two distinct advantages: first, ideally it isolates the most important aspects of the experience, ruling out anything else that might distract your reader's attention; second, it makes those experiences more permanent. Sensory impressions decay in seconds, but written descriptions survive indefinitely.

Consider, for example, Darcy Frey's description of Russell Thomas, a star basketball player at a Brooklyn, New York, high school, as he practices on a playground in August:

> At this hour Russell usually has the court to himself; most of the other players won't come out until after dark, when the thick humid air begins to stir with night breezes and the court lights come on. But this evening is turning out to be a fine one—cool and foggy. The low, slanting sun sheds a feeble pink light over the silvery Atlantic a block away, and milky sheets of fog roll off the ocean and drift in tatters along the project walkways. The air smells of sewage and saltwater. At the far end of the court, where someone has torn a hole in the chicken wire fence, other players climb through and begin warming up.

Traditionally, descriptions are divided into two categories: objective and subjective. In objective description you record details without making any personal evaluation or reaction. For example, Roger Angell, offers this purely objective description of a baseball, recording weight, dimensions, colors, and material:

> It weighs just five ounces and measures between 2.86 and 2.94 inches in diameter. It is made of a composition-cork nucleus encased in two thin layers of rubber, one black and one red, surrounded by 121 yards of tightly wrapped blue-gray wool yarn, 45 yards of white wool yarn, 53 more yards of blue-gray wool yarn, 150 yards of fine cotton yarn, 53 more yards of blue-gray wool yarn, 150 yards of fine cotton yarn, a coat of rubber cement, and a cowhide (formerly horsehide) exterior, which is held together with 216 slightly raised red cotton stitches.

Few descriptions outside of science writing, however, are completely objective. Instead of trying to include every detail, writers choose details carefully. That process of selection is determined by the writer's purpose and by the impression that the writer wants to create. For example, when Tracy Kidder in "Linda Manor" describes the view of the nursing home, he offers his readers a perspective of what he sees: ". . . its grounds were often empty. Their quietude lent a secretive quality to the sprawling, low-roofed building . . . surrounded by wintry woods and dormant grass as white as a nurse's starched uniform." Not everyone looking at that view would have "seen" what Kidder saw.

In subjective description, you are free to interpret the details for your reader; your reactions and descriptions can be emotional and value loaded. When Gretel Ehrlich in "A River's Route" describes the river as a "white chute tumbling over soft folds of conglomerate rock—brown bellies," the reader immediately knows that this is not the type of description that would be found in a geology textbook.

Descriptions serve a variety of purposes, but in every case it is important to make that purpose clear to your reader. Sometimes description is done solely to record the facts, as in Angell's description of the baseball, or to evoke an atmosphere, as in Darcy Frey's description of an August evening at a basketball court in Brooklyn. More often, description is used as support for other purposes. Gretel Ehrlich, in describing her journey to the source of the river, is not trying to describe accurately a landscape. Instead, she uses description to emphasize the oneness that links people and nature.

How Do You Describe an Object or a Place?

The first task in writing a description is to decide what you want to describe. As in every other writing task, making a good choice means that the act of writing will be easier and probably more successful. Before you begin, keep two things in mind: first, there is rarely any point in describing a common object or place—something every reader has seen—unless you do it in a fresh and perceptive way. Roger Angell describes a baseball, but he does so by dissecting it, giving a series of facts about its composition. Probably most of Frey's readers had at least seen pictures of a project playground, but after reading his description, what they are left with is a sense of vividness—this passage evokes or re-creates in our minds a mental picture of that evening.

Second, remember that your description needs to create a focused impression. To do that, you need to select details which contribute to your purpose. That will give you a way of deciding which details out of the many available are relevant. Details in a description must be carefully chosen and arranged; otherwise, your reader will be overwhelmed or bored by the accumulation of detail.

How Do You Describe a Person?

Before you begin to describe a person, remember an experience that everyone has had. You have read a novel and then seen a film or a made-for-television version, and the two experiences did not mesh. The characters, you are convinced, just did not *look* like the actors and actresses: "She was thinner and blond" or "He was all wrong—not big enough, not rugged enough." Any time you read a narrative that contains a character—either real or fictional—you form a mental picture of the person, and that picture is generally not based upon any physical description that the author has provided. In fact, in many narratives, authors provide only minimal description of the people involved. For example, if you look closely at Elizabeth Wong's description of her grandmother, you will find only one physical detail: her height. Of the Thurmond Watts family in William Least Heat-Moon's "Nameless, Tennessee," the details are just as few: Thurmond himself is "tall" and "thin"; but his wife Miss Ginny, his sister-in-law Marilyn, and his daughter Hilda are not physically described at all. In both narratives, however, you get a vivid sense of the people being described.

Fictional characters or real people are created or revealed primarily through ways other than direct physical description. What a person does or says, for example, also reveals personality. The reader "sees" Popo in Wong's essay through what she does; the ways in which she behaves; the things, people, and values important to her. Those details, finally, are the things most important about her. The Wattses, in Heat-Moon's narrative, are revealed by how they react, what they say, how their speech sounds, what they consider to be important. These are the key factors in re-creating Heat-Moon's experience for the reader.

In fact, descriptions of people should not try to be verbal portraits recording physical attributes in photographic detail. Words finally are never as efficient in doing that as photographs. If the objective in describing a person is not photographic accuracy, what then is it? Go back to the advice offered earlier in this introduction: decide first what impression you want to create in your reader. Why are you describing this person? What is it about this person that is worth describing? In all likelihood the answer will be something other than physical attributes. Once you know what that something is, you can then choose those details which best reveal or display the person.

How Do You Organize a Description?

You have found a subject; you have studied it—either first-hand or in memory; you have decided upon a reason for describing this particular subject; you have selected details which contribute to that reason or purpose. Now you need to organize your paragraph or essay. Descriptions, like narratives, have principles of order, although the principles vary depending upon what sense impressions are involved. When the primary descriptive emphasis is on seeing, the most obvious organization is spatial—moving from front to back, side to side, outside to inside, top to bottom, general to specific. The description moves as a camera would. Roger Angell's description of a baseball moves outward from the cork nucleus, through the layers of rubber, wool yarn, and rubber cement, to the cowhide exterior.

Other sense experiences might be arranged in order of importance, from the most obvious to the least—the loudest noise at the concert, the most pervasive odor in the restaurant—or even in chronological order. Kidder's description of Lou Freed, for example, follows Lou as he exits his room, walks down the hallway to turn on the night-lights, and returns to his room.

DOES DESCRIPTION MEAN LOTS OF ADJECTIVES AND ADVERBS?

Remember that one-sentence description of your car: "A silver-gray '86 Ford Escort with red racing stripes and gray leather seats." Your audience would have no trouble creating a vivid mental picture from that little bit of information, because it has seen an Escort before. The noun provides the primary image. The three adjectives describe color. The point is that you can create an image without providing a mountain of adjectives and adverbs—just as you imagine what a character looks like without being told. When Elizabeth Wong writes of her grandmother, she does not describe what she looked like. Instead, she catches her actions at a special moment: "When my Popo opened a Christmas gift, she would shake it, smell it, listen to it. She would size it up. She would open it nimbly, with all enthusiasm and delight, and even though the mittens were ugly or the blouse too small or the card obviously homemade, she would coo over it as if it were the baby Jesus." One of the greatest dangers in writing a description lies in trying to describe too much, trying to qualify every noun with at least one adjective and every verb with an adverb. Precise, vivid nouns and verbs will do most of the work for you.

SAMPLE STUDENT ESSAY

Nadine Resnick chose to describe her favorite childhood toy—a stuffed doll she had named Natalie.

Pretty in Pink

Standing in the middle of the aisle, staring up at the world as most children in nursery school do, something pink caught my eye. Just like Rapunzel in her high tower, there was a girl inside a cardboard and plastic prison atop a high shelf smiled down at me. I pointed to the doll and brought her home with me that same day. Somehow I knew that she was special.

She was named Natalie. I do not know why, but the name just seemed perfect, like the rest of her. Natalie was less than twelve inches tall and wore a pink outfit. Her hands and grimacing face were made of plastic while the rest of her body was stuffed with love. She had brown eyes and brown hair, just like me, which peeked through her burgundy and pink-flowered bonnet. Perhaps the most unusual feature about her was that my mom had tattooed my name on her large bottom so that if Natalie ever strayed from me at nursery school or at the supermarket, she would be able to find me.

There was some kind of magic about Natalie's face. I think it was her grin from ear to ear. Even if I had played with her until she was so dirty that most of her facial features were hidden, Natalie's never-ending smile usually shown through. When I neglected her for days to play with some new toy and then later returned, her friendly smirk was still there. When I was left home alone for a few hours, her smile assured me that I need not be afraid. Natalie's bright smile also cheered me up when I was sick or had a bad day. And she always had enough hugs for me.

As I was growing up, Natalie and her beaming face could usually be found somewhere in my room--on my bed, in her carriage, hiding under a pile of junk, and later piled in my closet with the rest of my other dolls and stuffed animals. When I got older, I foolishly decided that I no longer needed such childish toys. So I put Natalie and the rest of my stuffed animals in a large black plastic bag in a

dark corner of the basement. I now realize that the
basement really is not an honorable place for
someone who has meant so much to me. But, I will bet
that she is still smiling anyway.

Nadine had a chance to read her essay to a small group of classmates during a collaborative editing session. Everyone liked the essay
and most of their suggested changes were fairly minor. For example,
several people objected to her choice of the words "grimaced" and
"smirk," feeling that such words were not appropriate choices for a
lovable doll. Another student, however, suggested a revision in the
final paragraph. "It seems like you put her farther and farther away
from you as you got older. Why don't you emphasize that distancing
by having it occur in stages?" he commented. When Nadine rewrote
her essay, she made a number of minor changes in the first three paragraphs and then followed her classmate's idea in the fourth paragraph.

REVISED DRAFT

Natalie

Standing in the store's aisle, staring up at the
world as most pre-school children do, something pink
caught my eye. Just like Rapunzel in her high tower,
a girl trapped inside a cardboard and plastic prison
atop a high shelf smiled down at me. I pointed to
the doll and brought her home with me that same day.
Somehow I knew that she was special.

She was named Natalie. I do not know why, but
the name just seemed perfect, like the rest of her.
Natalie was less than twelve inches tall and wore a
pink outfit. Her hands and smiling face were made of
plastic while the rest of her body was plumply
stuffed. Just like me, she had brown eyes and brown
hair which peeked through her burgundy and pink-
flowered bonnet. Perhaps her most unusual feature
was my name tattooed on her bottom so that if
Natalie ever strayed from me at nursery school or at
the supermarket, she would be able to find me.

Natalie's face had a certain glow, some kind of
magic. I think it was her grin from ear to ear.
After I had played with her, no matter how dirty her

face was, Natalie's never-ending smile still beamed through. When I neglected her for days to play with some new toy and then later returned, her friendly grin was still there. Years later, when I was old enough to be left home alone for a few hours, her smile assured me that I need not be afraid. Natalie's bright smile also cheered me up when I was sick or had a bad day. And she always had enough hugs for me.

As I was growing up, Natalie and her beaming face could usually be found somewhere in my room. However, she seemed to move further away from me as I got older. Natalie no longer slept with me; she slept in her own carriage. Then she rested on a high shelf across my room. Later she made her way into my closet with the rest of the dolls and stuffed animals that I had outgrown. Eventually, I decided that I no longer needed such childish toys, so I put Natalie and my other stuffed animals in a large black plastic bag in a dark cellar corner. Even though I abandoned her, I am sure that Natalie is still smiling at me today.

SOME THINGS TO REMEMBER

1. Choose your subject carefully, making sure that you have a specific reason or purpose in mind for whatever you describe.
2. Study or observe your subject—try to see it or experience it in a fresh way. Gather details; make a list; use all your senses.
3. Use your purpose as a way of deciding which details ought to be included and which excluded.
4. Choose a pattern of organization to focus your reader's attention.
5. Use precise, vivid nouns and verbs, as well as adjectives and adverbs, to create your descriptions.

Description

A PRESENT FOR POPO

Elizabeth Wong

Elizabeth Wong was born in Los Angeles, California, in 1958, the daughter of Chinese immigrants. Before receiving an M.F.A. from New York University in 1991, she worked as a newspaper journalist and television reporter in several California cities. Since then, she has written three plays— Letters to a Student Revolutionary *(1991),* Kimchee and Chitlins *(1992), and* China Doll *(1992)—and a monthly Op-Ed column for the* Los Angeles Times; *she also writes for television.*

In an interview about her writing published in Unbroken Thread: An Anthology of Plays by Asian American Women *(1993), Wong commented on her original feelings about being raised in Chinatown: "I didn't want to have anything to do with all these people who talked with accents, who didn't read the things that I read or see the movies I saw. . . . I didn't have anything in common with these people." She continued, "It wasn't until I became a playwright that I began to like myself the way I am." This essay first appeared as a* Los Angeles Times *Op-Ed column in December, 1992.*

BEFORE READING

Connecting: What memories or associations come immediately to mind when you think about one of your parents or grandparents?

Anticipating: Wong is writing about her memories of her maternal grandmother. Out of the many memories that she has, why might she select the ones that she does? How does each included detail affect our sense of Popo?

When my Popo opened a Christmas gift, she would shake it, smell it, listen to it. She would size it up. She would open it nimbly, with all enthusiasm and delight, and even though the mittens were ugly or the blouse too small or the card obviously homemade, she would coo over it as if it were the baby Jesus.

Despite that, buying a gift for my grandmother was always problematic. Being in her late 80s, Popo didn't seem to need any more sweaters or handbags. No books certainly, as she only knew six words of English. Cosmetics might be a good idea, for she was just a wee bit vain.

3　　But ultimately, nothing worked. "No place to put anything anyway," she used to tell me in Chinese. For in the last few years of her life, Popo had a bed in a room in a house in San Gabriel owned by one of her sons. All her belongings, her money, her very life was now co-opted and controlled by her sons and their wives. Popo's daughters had little power in this matter. This was a traditional Chinese family.

4　　For you see, Popo had begun to forget things. Ask her about something that happened 20 years ago, and she could recount the details in the heartbeat of a New York minute. But it was those niggling little everyday matters that became so troubling. She would forget to take her heart medicine. She would forget where she put her handbag. She would forget she talked to you just moments before. She would count the few dollars in her billfold, over and over again. She would ask me for the millionth time, "So when are you going to get married?" For her own good, the family decided she should give up her beloved one-room Chinatown flat. Popo herself recognized she might be a danger to herself, "I think your grandmother is going crazy," she would say.

5　　That little flat was a bothersome place, but Popo loved it. Her window had a view of several import-export shops below, not to mention the grotesque plastic hanging lanterns and that nasty loudspeaker serenading tourists with 18 hours of top-40 popular hits.

6　　My brother Will and I used to stand under her balcony on Mei Ling Way, shouting up, "Grandmother on the Third Floor! Grandmother on the Third Floor!" Simultaneously, the wrinkled faces of a half-dozen grannies would peek cautiously out their windows. Popo would come to the balcony and proudly claim us: "These are my grandchildren coming to take me to *dim sum*." Her neighbors would cluck and sigh, "You have such good grandchildren. Not like mine."

7　　In that cramped room of Popo's, I could see past Christmas presents. A full-wall collage of family photos that my mother and I made together and presented one year with lots of fanfare. Popo had attached additional snapshots by way of paper clips and Scotch tape. And there, on the window sill, a little terrarium to which Popo had tied a small red ribbon. "For good luck," as she gleefully pointed out the sprouting buds. "See, it's having babies."

8　　Also, there were the utility shelves on the wall, groaning from a wide assortment of junk, stuff and whatnot. Popo was fond of salvaging discarded things. After my brother had installed the shelving, she did a little jig, then took a whisk broom and lightly swept away any naughty spirits that might be lurking on the walls. "Shoo, shoo,

shoo, away with you, Mischievous Ones!" That apartment was her independence, and her pioneer spirit was everywhere in it.

Popo was my mother's mother, but she was also a second 9
mother to me. Her death was a great blow. The last time I saw her was Christmas, 1990, when she looked hale and hearty. I thought she would live forever. Last October, at 91, she had her final heart attack. The next time I saw her, it was at her funeral.

An open casket, and there she was, with a shiny new penny 10
poised between her lips, a silenced warrior woman. Her sons and daughters placed colorful pieces of cloth in her casket. They burned incense and paper money. A small marching band led a New Orleans-like procession through the streets of Chinatown. Popo's picture, larger than life, in a flatbed truck to survey the world of her adopted country.

This little 4-foot, 9-inch woman had been the glue of our fam- 11
ily. She wasn't perfect, she wasn't always even nice, but she learned from her mistakes, and, ultimately, she forgave herself for being human. It is a lesson of forgiveness that seems to have eluded her own sons and daughters.

And now she is gone. And with her—the tenuous, cohesive ties of 12
blood and duty that bound us to family. My mother predicted that once the distribution of what was left of Popo's estate took place, no further words would be exchanged between Popo's children. She was right.

But this year, six of the 27 grandchildren and two of the 18 13
great-grandchildren came together for a holiday feast of honey-baked ham and mashed potatoes. Not a gigantic family reunion. But I think, for now, it's the one yuletide present my grandmother might have truly enjoyed.

Merry Christmas, Popo! 14

QUESTIONS ON SUBJECT AND PURPOSE

1. What is the "occasion" for Wong to write about her grandmother? What prompted the essay?

2. Why might Wong have chosen to write about the death of her grandmother? What might have been her motives?

3. Why would be a reader be interested in a tribute to someone else's grandmother?

QUESTIONS ON STRATEGY AND AUDIENCE

1. How does the idea of a "present" unify the essay?

2. How much of Popo's life is included in the essay? On what time period, for example, does Wong focus?
3. Does there seem to be more than one "audience" (that is, someone other than the general reader of the newspaper) for Wong's essay?

QUESTIONS ON VOCABULARY AND STYLE

1. At a number of points in the essay, Wong "quotes" Popo. Why? What is the effect of these bits of conversation?
2. What is the effect of the final line of the essay?
3. Be prepared to define the following words: *niggling* (paragraph 4), *collage* (7), *tenuous* (12).

WRITING SUGGESTIONS

1. **For your Journal.** Select a vivid memory that involves a parent or grandparent. In your journal, describe for yourself what you remember. Do not worry about trying to be too focused. Concentrate on recovering memories.
2. **For a Paragraph.** In a paragraph, try to "capture" a relative. Remember that your description needs a central focus or purpose: Why are you writing about this person? What is important for the reader to know about this person? Select details to reveal your relative's personality.
3. **For an Essay.** In writing about Popo, Wong achieves two purposes: she memorializes her grandmother and she comments on her family. In an essay, try for a similar effect. Who, for example, is important to holding your family together? Who has "taught" the family a "lesson"? Who has caused the family a "problem"?

Prewriting:
a. Make a list of everyone in your family. If necessary, include even cousins.
b. Next to each name, jot down your associations with that person. Try freewriting or clustering ideas for those people who look most promising as subjects.
c. Finish the following sentence: "The significance of this person is _____."

Rewriting:

a. Ask a friend or classmate to read your essay. Once your reader has finished, ask your reader to finish the test sentence you wrote for item c under *Prewriting*. Did your reader see the significance that you intended?

b. Did you reveal that significance—it could also be called a thesis—at the beginning of the essay or at the end? Try placing it in the other position. What impact does that move have on the essay?

c. Have you created a vivid sense of the person? Ask your reader, "Can you see or imagine this person?" Remember that you do not have to "photograph"—that is, record a series of physical details—to achieve that effect.

4. For Research. Select someone famous who has died within the last year. Using the periodical indexes and databases in your college library, locate at least six articles in periodicals and reference works written about the person before his or her death. Then use that research to write a tribute. Do not just report facts; be sure to have a central focus or thesis about the person's significance. Remember to document your information and quotations.

LINDA MANOR

Tracy Kidder

Tracy Kidder was born in New York City in 1945. Before receiving an M.F.A. from the University of Iowa in 1974, he served in Vietnam as an army intelligence officer. He has built a very successful career as a nonfiction author, writing numerous newspaper and magazine articles and four nonfiction books, including The Soul of a New Machine *(1982), for which he won a Pulitzer Prize and the American Book Award.*

Commenting on his writing, Kidder said: "The thing that I concern myself with is narrative characters. The ingredients of a good narrative are characters, bringing people to life on the page. . . . The engine of narrative is human motivation. With nonfiction, of course, you're stuck with what is, what was. I don't like to invent quotes. I try to make it as accurate as I can. But within those boundaries, what really interests me is some kind of marriage of all these things."

Kidder immerses himself in the subjects about which he writes, as in his latest book, Old Friends *(1993), about a nursing home called Linda Manor. Prior to writing* Old Friends, *Kidder, for a year, spent a large part of each day watching and talking with the people who lived and worked there.*

BEFORE READING

Connecting: What must it be like to be old, infirm, and ill? Is someone in your family in this position? Is someone in a nursing home like Linda Manor? How would you feel about living there?

Anticipating: If you were trying to describe a place or a building, how would you organize that description? Does Kidder organize his description the same way you would?

1   Inside Linda Manor, upstairs on Forest View, the lights in the corridors brighten. The living room windows begin to reflect the lights on the plastic Christmas tree, and the view through those windows is fading, the woods growing thicker, the birches glowing in the dusk. At the west end of Forest View's longer corridor, a white-haired woman in a plain housedress and sneakers leans against the heating register, a cane in her hands, and she gazes out at clouds. She is very

forgetful and yet very nostalgic and, of all the people who live here, the most devoted to windows. "They come and go," she says of the clouds. "I guess that's to be expected. First they're dark and then they're light. First they're there and then they're gone." She makes a small laugh. She goes on gazing through the glass. "I don't know what all this business is about, living this way. I tried to figure it out, but I can't." The clouds hovering above the silhouette of the far ridge are sharply etched, clouds of the north wind, dark gray in the last light of a sky that is still too bright for stars.

The light seeps away. The windows at the ends of Forest View's 2 corridors throw back watery images of carpeted corridors that could belong to a clean motel. It is night. Lou Freed comes out of his room, down on the north hall just past the elevators. Lou is small and plump in the middle, with fleecy white hair and thick, dark-framed glasses. Behind the lens, the lid of his left eye droops. His close-cropped mustache is a dash of white across his face. His forehead and cheeks are deeply furrowed. Lou wears a look of concentration as he comes out into the hall. He holds a cane in his right hand. Its black shaft is striped like a barber pole with yellowish tape. Lou applied the tape several years ago when his eyes began to fail and he couldn't cross a street very quickly anymore. He used to hold the cane aloft as he crossed, hoping it would catch the attention of drivers. He no longer has to worry about crossing streets, but he's left the tape in place since coming here, on the theory that it will help him to spot his cane if he should misplace it. He never does misplace it.

As he walks, Lou leans on his cane, but not heavily. Now and 3 then he extends it forward, searching for possible obstructions. Lou walks with his legs spread well apart, his left arm swinging free and a little away from his torso while his right arm works the cane. He crosses the corridor perpendicularly and then turns south, following the carpet's border, traveling in a slow, sturdy gait, like an old sailor crossing a rolling deck, passing along a wall equipped with an oak handrail and adorned with cream-colored wallpaper and rose-colored moldings, passing several numbered bedroom doors of blond oak veneer and framed prints of flowers and puppies and English hunting scenes.

The nurses' station, enclosed with a Formica counter, is brightly 4 lit as always. Lou stops at the corner of the station. He shifts his cane to his left hand and slides his right hand up the wall until it touches the edge of a four-gang light switch. His fingers are nimble. They move with a confident inquisitiveness, but they fumble slightly over the plate of the light switch. This isn't the switch that Lou wants. He finds the one he wants by finding this one first. His hand pauses here tonight, however. The plastic plate surrounding these four switches feels warm. In Lou's experience, this sometimes signifies a circuit overload. Nothing serious, but he'll have to remember to tell Bruce, the director of maintenance, tomorrow.

5   Lou's hand moves on across the wall, fingers fumbling again until they strike a two-gang switch. Then with a flick of the forefinger, joyous in its certainty, Lou throws both switches up, and in all the bedrooms of Forest View the night lights come on.

6   Night lights are important. They might save other residents from falling on the way to their bathrooms in the middle of the night. They might save Lou from such a fate. April, one of the aides, has forgotten to turn them on. Or else she's been too busy. When that happens, Lou does the job. He doesn't mind. It is a job.

7   "Hi, Lou." A nurse, a young woman in slacks—the nurses here don't wear uniforms—stands nearby, behind the medication cart, studying her records.

8   "Hi," Lou says. "Who's that?"

9   "Eileen," she says, adding, "Lou, did you get your iron today?"

10   Lou lifts his right arm and makes as if to flex his biceps. His arms are thin. The flesh sags from them. But some muscle rises. "Pretty soon I'll be sweating rust." Lou has a soft, gravelly voice.

11   The nurse chuckles. Lou smiles. Then he shifts his cane to his right hand, his face grows serious again, and he starts slowly back down the carpeted hallway toward his room. As Lou nears the doorway, he hears the sound of screeching tires. He enters to the sound of gunfire.

12   Within, the lights are out and the curtains drawn. Lou's roommate, Joe Torchio, lies on his back on the bed nearer the door, a baldheaded, round-faced, round-bellied man. In the changeable glow of his TV, Joe looks beached and bristly. Lou feels his way past Joe to the other side of the room, and in a while he begins to get ready for bed. The charge nurse knocks. Joe flicks his remote control at the TV, leaving it lit but mute, and the nurse enters, carrying pills.

13   Back in his eighties, Lou knew all the names and functions of his medicines. Now he takes too many to remember, though he still makes inquiries about new ones now and then. Joe has said he doesn't know what pills the nurses give him and he doesn't care. "If they want to kill me, go ahead," Joe likes to say, and Lou replies, "Joe, don't talk that way." But Lou says he isn't worried either, because the pills he takes all have arrows on them, to tell them where to go once they get inside. The nurse laughs: Lou and Joe may take a lot of pills, but they are among the most physically healthy of Linda Manor's residents.

14   Joe turns his head on his pillow and looks at Lou, who has climbed into his bed and under the covers. "We're the best!" Joe exclaims.

"God help the others if we're the best," Lou says. 15

"Anyway, I can't read." 16

"I could read if I could see." 17

"I have half a brain, and you can't see," Joe says. 18

"And so betwixt us both, we licked the platter clean," Lou says. 19
He smiles, the covers pulled up to his chin, and he sighs. "Ahh, dear.
It's a great life, if you don't weaken."

Joe aims his remote control at the TV. The sounds of a car 20
chase resume, and Lou drifts off to sleep.

• • •

It seemed so new a place for people so old. Linda Manor had 21
opened for business only a little more than a year ago. It stood in
what had been a hay field, in a suburban-bucolic setting, on Route 9
a few miles west of downtown Northampton, Massachusetts. The de-
veloper named Linda Manor after one of his daughters. The building
had balconies and balcony railings along its flat roofs and wide frieze
boards under its eaves. Out front there was a portico, supported on
four Doric columns, and two tall flagpoles, also a little fountain, like
a child's wading pool. And everything, except for the brick walls, was
painted white. The building looked not quite finished, like the parts
of a giant wedding cake laid side to side.

The obligation of finding a nursing home for a sick, aged per- 22
son usually falls to a daughter. On any given day in the region, a middle-aged woman would be looking around for an acceptable
establishment. There were a few. But there were also places where the
stench of urine got in one's clothes like tobacco smoke, where four,
sometimes five, elderly people lay jammed in tiny rooms, where residents sat tied to wheelchairs and strapped to beds, where residents
weren't allowed to bring with them any furniture of their own or to
have private phones or to use the public pay phone without nurses listening in. One woman, on a recent tour of a nearby place, had been
shown a room with a dead resident in it. Some nursing homes looked
fancy and well kept but were all veneer. When Linda Manor's portico
hove into view, it looked like one of those.

• • •

What most people take for granted is unusual in nursing 23
homes. Linda Manor had some unusually pleasant qualities. The staff
wasn't the largest per resident in the area, but large by the prevailing
standards and far larger than the state required. Every room in the
building got natural light. There was a small greenhouse. Residents
were allowed to bring their own furnishings and to have their own
telephones. Most rooms contained two beds. A few were singles. And
none of the residents was tied up. This policy of "no restraints" was

rare in the world of nursing homes. The local newspaper carried a long story about it when Linda Manor first opened. The publicity helped to make the policy work. A good reputation meant lots of applications for beds. The management could afford to turn away the very violent and most floridly demented.

24   Some residents were brought from great distances, from places like Florida and California, to be near their families. Most came from western Massachusetts, and collectively they made up a fairly accurate cross section of the area's old people. A few were wealthy. About 30 percent paid the high private rate. Medicaid and Medicare paid the room and board for most. Some owned nothing when they arrived. One man did not even own a change of clothes; several of the staff rummaged through their husbands' closets and outfitted him.

25   Periodically, wheelchair vans or ambulances or private cars parked in front of the portico and new residents were escorted in, a few on their own feet, others in wheelchairs, some on gurneys. New residents arrived from hospitals mainly, and occasionally from other nursing homes. Some arrived directly from their own or their children's homes, and for them the transition tended to be hardest. Some newcomers left their relatives' cars only after coaxing. And, on the other hand, a few residents would say that they felt sad but relieved when they arrived. The eighty-five-year-old woman, for instance, who had lived alone in a two-story house, crawling up and down the stairs, bathing herself with talcum powder for fear of the tub, subsisting mostly on tea and toast.

26   A few people died within days of arriving—one on her very first day—and it was hard to resist a Victorian explanation, that they died of broken hearts. More often, though, the physical health of new residents stabilized or even improved, in some cases because they had received marginal care and feeding before. Some residents merely stopped here, to rest and receive a few months of therapy, on the way home from the hospital. One well-traveled, well-read woman declared, soon after arriving, that she never played bingo in her life and did not intend to start now. She stayed at Linda Manor for a year, read most of Proust, and then returned home. But hers was an exceptional case.

27   By this time, December 1990, Linda Manor was running at capacity—121 beds, all full. Most of the residents were over 70 years old. The oldest had reached her 103rd year in remarkably good health. About two thirds were women, a figure in line with national actuarial figures. It went without saying that everyone had an illness. Most had several.

• • •

28   Linda Manor's grounds were often empty. Their stillness lent a secretive quality to the sprawling, low-roofed building—set back from busy Route 9, surrounded by wintry woods and dormant grass, adorned with Greco-Roman columns, balconies and parapets, all as white as a nurse's starched uniform. As one stared at it, the place grew odder in the mind. The building looked so provisional. So new and yet containing so much of the past. Many residents remembered World War I as if it had ended yesterday. Some remembered first-hand accounts of the Civil War. They were like immigrants arriving in a new land with long lives behind them, obliged to inhabit a place that was bound to seem less real than the places they recalled. For most of those long-lived, ailing people, Linda Manor represented all the permanence that life still had to offer. It was their home for the duration, their last place on earth.

QUESTIONS ON SUBJECT AND PURPOSE

1. Kidder's purpose is to describe a place, the Linda Manor nursing home. Why, then, does he devote so much space to the description of Lou Freed?

2. Toward the end, Kidder observes about Linda Manor: "As one stared at it, the place grew odder in the mind" (paragraph 28). What might he mean by that observation?

3. Does Kidder ever seem to be judgmental? Can you tell how he feels about what he sees?

QUESTIONS ON STRATEGY AND AUDIENCE

1. Kidder could have set his description of Linda Manor in any season or at any time of the day. How might the atmosphere be different if the narrative were set in spring or summer? In the morning?

2. How does Kidder structure his description? How can it be divided?

3. What expectations might Kidder have about his audience?

QUESTIONS ON VOCABULARY AND STYLE

1. The nursing home is named Linda Manor. What does the word "manor" mean? In what sense is this place a "manor"?

2. In the final paragraph, Kidder writes of the residents: "They were like immigrants arriving in a new land with long lives behind them. . . ." That sentence offers an example of what figure of speech? Why might Kidder use that figure of speech?

3. Be prepared to define the following words: *bucolic* (paragraph 21), *floridly* (23), *demented* (23), *provisional* (28).

WRITING SUGGESTIONS

1. For your Journal. How would you describe your parents' attitudes toward their parents? How would you describe your attitudes toward your grandparents? In your journal, explore both subjects. (If you are an older student, you might rather explore your and your children's attitudes toward your own parents.)

2. For a Paragraph. Most people "personalize" their space. Every dorm room, bedroom, or apartment might be exactly the same size as the others in the complex or house, but each looks different because a unique person occupies it. In a paragraph, describe such a place, taking care to focus on how the physical space reveals something about its occupant.

3. For an Essay. Writing about a close friend or a relative is never easy: you know too much and so cannot be completely objective. Still, writing about such a person is a way to order your experience, record your memories, and memorialize your friend or relative. Write an essay about someone who has touched your life. Do not just describe the person; also make the reader understand what is important to you about this person. Why should the reader be "introduced" to him or her?

Prewriting:

a. Spend some time thinking about possible subjects. Once you have listed three or four possibilities, try freewriting about each for ten or fifteen minutes. Write whatever comes to mind about the person and your feelings.

b. Finish the following sentence: "My reader should be introduced to the person because _____." Do not just fill in the sentence with a vague phrase like "she is interesting."

c. Do not try to describe the person photographically. Select details that reveal personality and the qualities that you wish to emphasize.

Rewriting:

a. Ask a friend or classmate to read your essay. Once your reader has finished, ask her or him to finish the test sentence you wrote for item b under *Prewriting*. Does your reader see the purpose you intended?

b. Look carefully at the structure of your essay. Is it strictly chronological? Would it be better to start with a flashback, or to order your material in some other way? Jot down an outline for an alternate structure, even if you are basically satisfied with your own.

c. Realistically, how good is your title? Does it catch your reader's attention? Or is it something flat like "My Aunt Carol."

4. For Research. America is a society that worships youth and shuns old age. Old people are often not figures to be respected or honored, but burdens to be cared for by hired professionals. In many other societies, however, the elderly are treated very differently. Research a society that honors its old. Do not just report on how the elderly are seen or treated in this society. Formulate a thesis that explains why this society behaves in this way.

NAMELESS, TENNESSEE

William Least Heat-Moon

William Least Heat-Moon was born William Trogdon in Missouri in 1939 and earned a Ph.D. in English from the University of Missouri in 1973. Trogdon's father created his pen name in memory of their Sioux forefather. His books include the best-selling Blue Highways: A Journey into America *(1982) and the recent* PrairyErth *(1991), the result of four years of research into the history, geology, geography, and sociology of Chase County, Kansas.*

Blue Highways is the account of Heat-Moon's 14,000-mile journey *through American backroads in a converted van called "Ghost Dancing." Its title refers to the blue ink used by map-publisher Rand McNally to indicate smaller, or secondary, roads. In this chapter from that work, Heat-Moon describes his experiences at a general store in Nameless, Tennessee, where he meets Thurmond and Virginia Watts, living in a world seemingly untouched by time.*

BEFORE READING

Connecting: If you could get in an automobile and drive off—and time, money, and responsibilities posed no obstacles—where would you go?

Anticipating: "Nameless, Tennessee" does more than just faithfully record everything Heat-Moon saw while visiting the Wattses. The narrative has a central focus that controls the selection of detail. What is that focus?

1   Nameless, Tennessee, was a town of maybe ninety people if you pushed it, a dozen houses along the road, a couple of barns, same number of churches, a general merchandise store selling Fire Chief gasoline, and a community center with a lighted volleyball court. Behind the center was an open-roof, rusting metal privy with PAINT ME on the door, in the hollow of a nearby oak lay a full pint of Jack Daniel's Black Label. From the houses, the odor of coal smoke.

2   Next to a red tobacco barn stood the general merchandise with a poster of Senator Albert Gore, Jr., smiling from the window. I

knocked. The door opened partway. A tall, thin man said, "Closed up. For good," and started to shut the door.

"Don't want to buy anything. Just a question for Mr. Thurmond Watts." 3

The man peered through the slight opening. He looked me over. "What question would that be?" 4

"If this is Nameless, Tennessee, could he tell me how it got that name?" 5

The man turned back into the store and called out, "Miss Ginny! Somebody here wants to know how Nameless come to be Nameless." 6

Miss Ginny edged to the door and looked me and my truck over. Clearly, she didn't approve. She said, "You know as well as I do, Thurmond. Don't keep him on the stoop in the damp to tell him." Miss Ginny, I found out, was Mrs. Virginia Watts, Thurmond's wife. 7

I stepped in and they both began telling the story, adding a detail here, the other correcting a fact there, both smiling at the foolishness of it all. It seems the hilltop settlement went for years without a name. Then one day the Post Office Department told the people if they wanted mail up on the mountain they would have to give the place a name you could properly address a letter to. The community met; there were only a handful, but they commenced debating. Some wanted patriotic names, some names from nature, one man recommended in all seriousness his own name. They couldn't agree, and they ran out of names to argue about. Finally, a fellow tired of the talk; he didn't like the mail he received anyway. "Forget the durn Post Office," he said. "This here's a nameless place if I ever seen one, so leave it be." And that's just what they did. 8

Watts pointed out the window. "We used to have signs on the road, but the Halloween boys keep tearin' them down." 9

"You think Nameless is a funny name," Miss Ginny said. "I see it plain in your eyes. Well, you take yourself up north a piece to Difficult or Defeated or Shake Rag. Now them are silly names." 10

The old store, lighted only by three fifty-watt bulbs, smelled of coal oil and baking bread. In the middle of the rectangular room, where the oak floor sagged a little, stood an iron stove. To the right was a wooden table with an unfinished game of checkers and a stool made from an apple-tree stump. On shelves around the walls sat earthen jugs with corncob stoppers, a few canned goods, and some of the two thousand old clocks and clockworks Thurmond Watts owned. Only one was ticking, the others he just looked at. I asked how long he'd been in the store. 11

"Thirty-five years, but we closed the first day of the year. We're hopin' to sell it to a churchly couple. Upright people. No athians." 12

13   "Did you build this store?"

14   "I built this one, but it's the third general store on the ground. I fear it'll be the last. I take no pleasure in that. Once you could come in here for a gallon of paint, a pickle, a pair of shoes, and a can of corn."

15   "Or horehound candy," Miss Ginny said. "Or corsets and salves. We had cough syrups and all that for the body. In season, we'd buy and sell blackberries and walnuts and chestnuts, before the blight got them. And outside, Thurmond milled corn and sharpened plows. Even shoed a horse sometimes."

16   "We could fix up a horse or a man or a baby," Watts said.

17   "Thurmond, tell him we had a doctor on the ridge in them days."

18   "We had a doctor on the ridge in them days. As good as any doctor alivin'. He'd cut a crooked toenail or deliver a woman. Dead these last years."

19   "I got some bad ham meat one day," Miss Ginny said, "and took to vomitin'. All day, all night. Hangin' on the drop edge of yonder. I said to Thurmond, 'Thurmond, unless you want shut of me, call the doctor.'"

20   "I studied on it," Watts said.

21   "You never did. You got him right now. He come over and put three drops of iodeen in half a glass of well water. I drank it down and the vomitin' stopped with the last swallow. Would you think iodeen could do that?"

22   "He put Miss Ginny on one teaspoon of spirits of ammonia in well water for her nerves. Ain't nothin' works better for her to this day."

23   "Calms me like the hand of the Lord."

24   Hilda, the Wattses' daughter, came out of the backroom. "I remember him," she said. "I was just a baby. Y'all were talkin' to him, and he lifted me up on the counter and gave me a stick of Juicy Fruit and a piece of cheese."

25   "Knew the old medicines," Watts said. "Only drugstore he needed was a good kitchen cabinet. None of them anteebeeotics that hit you worsen your ailment. Forgotten lore now, the old medicines, because they ain't profit in iodeen."

26   Miss Ginny started back to the side room where she and her sister Marilyn were taking apart a duck-down mattress to make bolsters. She stopped at the window for another look at Ghost Dancing. "How do you sleep in that thing? Ain't you all cramped and cold?"

27   "How does the clam sleep in his shell?" Watts said in my defense.

"Thurmond, get the boy a piece of buttermilk pie afore he goes on." 28

"Hilda, get some buttermilk pie." He looked at me. "You like good music?" I said I did. He cranked up an old Edison phonograph, the kind with the big morning-glory blossom for a speaker, and put on a wax cylinder. "This will be 'My Mother's Prayer,'" he said. 29

While I ate buttermilk pie, Watts served as disc jockey of Nameless, Tennessee. "Here's 'Mountain Rose.'" It was one of those moments that you know at the time will stay with you to the grave: the sweet pie, the gaunt man playing the old music, the coals in the stove glowing orange, the scent of kerosene and hot bread. "Here's 'Evening Rhapsody.'" The music was so heavily romantic we both laughed. I thought: It is for this I have come. 30

Feathered over and giggling, Miss Ginny stepped from the side room. She knew she was a sight. "Thurmond, give him some lunch. Still looks hungry." 31

Hilda pulled food off the woodstove in the backroom: home-butchered and canned whole-hog sausage, home-canned June apples, turnip greens, cole slaw, potatoes, stuffing, hot cornbread. All delicious. 32

Watts and Hilda sat and talked while I ate. "Wish you would join me." 33

"We've ate," Watts said. "Cain't beat a woodstove for flavorful cookin'." 34

He told me he was raised in a one-hundred-fifty-year-old cabin still standing in one of the hollows. "How many's left," he said, "that grew up in a log cabin? I ain't the last surely, but I must be climbin' on the list." 35

Hilda cleared the table. "You Watts ladies know how to cook." 36

"She's in nursin' school at Tennessee Tech. I went over for one of them football games last year there at Coevul." To say *Cookeville*, you let the word collapse in upon itself so that it comes out "Coevul." 37

"Do you like football?" I asked. 38

"Don't know. I was so high up in that stadium, I never opened my eyes." 39

Watts went to the back and returned with a fat spiral notebook that he set on the table. His expression had changed. "Miss Ginny's *Deathbook*." 40

The thing startled me. Was it something I was supposed to sign? He opened it but said nothing. There were scads of names written in a tidy hand over pages incised to crinkliness by a ballpoint. Chronologically, the names had piled up: Wives, grandparents, a still-born infant, relatives, friends close and distant. Names, names. After 41 each, the date of the unknown finally known and transcribed. The last entry bore yesterday's date.

42 "She's wrote out twenty years' worth. Ever day she listens to the hospital report on the radio and puts the names in. Folks come by to check a date. Or they just turn through the books. Read them like a scrapbook."

43 Hilda said, "Like Saint Peter at the gates inscribin' the names."

44 Watts took my arm. "Come along." He led me to the fruit cellar under the store. As we went down, he said, "Always take a newborn baby upstairs afore you take him downstairs, otherwise you'll incline him downwards."

45 The cellar was dry and full of cobwebs and jar after jar of home-canned food, the bottles organized as a shopkeeper would: sausage, pumpkin, sweet pickles, tomatoes, corn relish, blackberries, peppers, squash, jellies. He held a hand out toward the dusty bottles. "Our to-morrows."

46 Upstairs again, he said, "Hope to sell the store to the right folk. I see now, though, it'll be somebody offen the ridge. I've studied on it, and maybe it's the end of our place." He stirred the coals. "This store could give a comfortable livin', but not likely get you rich. But just gettin' by is dice rollin' to people nowadays. I never did see my day guaranteed."

47 When it was time to go, Watts said, "If you find anyone along your ways wants a good store—on the road to Cordell Hull Lake—tell them about us."

48 I said I would. Miss Ginny and Hilda and Marilyn came out to say goodbye. It was cold and drizzling again. "Weather to give a man the weary dismals," Watts grumbled. "Where you headed from here?"

49 "I don't know."

50 "Cain't get lost then."

51 Miss Ginny looked again at my rig. It had worried her from the first as it had my mother. "I hope you don't get yourself kilt in that durn thing gallivantin' around the country."

52 "Come back when the hills dry off," Watts said. "We'll go lookin' for some of them round rocks all sparkly inside."

53 I thought a moment. "Geodes?"

54 "Them's the ones. The country's properly full of them."

QUESTIONS ON SUBJECT AND PURPOSE

1. At one point in the narrative (paragraph 30), Heat-Moon remarks, "I thought: It is for this I have come." What does he seem to be suggesting? What is the "this" that he finds in Nameless?

2. Why do "Miss Ginny's *Deathbook*" (paragraph 40) and the "fruit cellar" (44) seem appropriate details?
3. What might have attracted Heat-Moon to this place and these people? What does he want you to sense? Is there anything in his description and narrative that suggests how he feels about Nameless?

QUESTIONS ON STRATEGY AND AUDIENCE

1. After you have read the selection, describe each member of the Watts family. Describe the exterior and interior of their store. Then carefully go through the selection and see how many specific descriptive details Heat-Moon uses. List them.
2. What devices other than direct description does Heat-Moon use to create the sense of place and personality? Make a list and be prepared to tell how those devices work.
3. How is the narrative arranged? Is the order just spatial and chronological?
4. This selection is taken from *Blue Highways: A Journey into America*, a bestseller for nearly a year. Why would a travel narrative—full of stories such as this—be so appealing to an American audience?

QUESTIONS ON VOCABULARY AND STYLE

1. Heat-Moon attempts to reproduce the pronunciation of some words—for example, *athians* (paragraph 12), *iodeen* (21), and *anteebeeotics* (25). Make a list of all such phonetic spellings. Why does Heat-Moon do this? Do you think he captures all of the Wattses' accent or just some part of it? Is the device effective?
2. Examine how Heat-Moon uses dialogue in his description. How are the Wattses revealed by what they say? How much of what was actually said during the visit is recorded? Can you find specific points in the story where Heat-Moon obviously omits dialogue?
3. Try to define or explain the following words and phrases: *horehound candy* (paragraph 15), *bolsters* (26), *buttermilk pie* (28), *incised to crinkliness by a ballpoint* (41), *weary dismals* (48), *gallivantin' around* (51).

WRITING SUGGESTIONS

1. **For your Journal**. Have you ever encountered or experienced a person, a place, or an event that seemed cut off from the modern world? In your journal try to recall a few such experiences.

2. **For a Paragraph**. Virtually every campus has a building or a location that has acquired a strange or vivid name (for example, the cafeteria in the Student Center known as "The Scrounge"). In a paragraph, describe such a place to a friend who has never seen it. Remember to keep a central focus—you want to create an atmosphere more than you want to try to write a verbal photograph.

3. **For an Essay**. Look for an unusual business in your town or city (a barber shop, a food co-op, a delicatessen or diner, a second-hand clothing store, a specialized boutique). In an essay, describe the place. Your essay will need to have a focus—a central impression or thesis—that will govern your selection of details. It will probably work best if you also include some descriptions of people and dialogue.

Prewriting:

a. Take a walk and make a list of possible places.

b. Visit one or more of them and take notes on what you see. Imagine yourself as a newspaper reporter. If people are present, try to write down exactly what they say.

c. Decide on a particular quality or feeling or idea that you want to convey about this place. Write a statement of purpose.

d. Do not "overpeople" your description. Do not try to describe every character completely. Reveal personality through significant detail and dialogue.

Rewriting:

a. Check to make sure that you have made effective use of verbs and nouns. Do not rely on adjectives and adverbs to do the work of description.

b. Using your statement of purpose, check every detail that you included in your essay. Does it belong? Does it relate to that stated purpose?

4. **For Research**. Heat-Moon is fascinated by unusual names, and often drives considerable distances to visit towns with names such as Dime Box, Hungry Horse, Liberty Bond, Ninety-Six, and Tuba City. Choose an unusual place name

(town, river, subdivision, topographical feature) from your home state and research the origin of the name. A reference librarian can show you how to locate source materials. If possible, you could contact your local historical society or public library for help or interview some knowledgeable local residents. Using your research, write an essay about how that name was chosen. Remember to document your sources.

A RIVER'S ROUTE

Gretel Ehrlich

Gretel Ehrlich was born in Santa Barbara, California, and educated at Bennington College, the New School of Social Research, and the UCLA Film School. In 1976, Ehrlich visited Wyoming on a Public Broadcasting assignment to film sheep ranchers in the Bighorn Mountains. She moved there a few years later, exchanging a big city lifestyle for a sheeprancher's existence. A poet, film editor, novelist, and essayist, Ehrlich has contributed to Harper's *since 1985. She is best known for* The Solace of Open Spaces *(1985), a collection of essays about impressions of and incidents in her new Wyoming life, as well as her recovery from personal tragedy.*

"A River's Route" was published as the introduction to the Sierra Club's wilderness wall calendar in 1989. It reached other audiences when it was also published in Harper's *(December 1988) and in* Montana Spaces: Essays and Photographs in Celebration of Montana *(1988). In her search for a river's origin, Ehrlich discovers far more than a literal spring, for she finds that "to trace the history of a river, or a raindrop . . . is also to trace the history of the soul, the history of the mind descending and arising in the body."*

BEFORE READING

Connecting: Regardless of the nature of the landscape that surrounds us, we react to it in some way—even if only by ignoring it. Have you ever seen your surroundings in some way other than literally—for example, skyscrapers as symbolic of modern life; polluted waters as symbolic of a careless, industrial society? How might you interpret the landscape that surrounds you?

Anticipating: Ehrlich records the observations she makes on a hike up a mountain. Despite the abundance of details, Ehrlich does more than just "photograph" what she sees. What significance does she find in her journey?

1   It's morning in the Absaroka Mountains. The word *absaroka* means "raven" in the Crow language, though I've seen no ravens in three days. Last night I slept with my head butted against an Englemann

spruce, and on waking the limbs looked like hundreds of arms swinging in a circle. The trunk is bigger than an elephant's leg, bigger than my torso. I stick my nose against the bark. Tiny opals of sap stick to my cheeks and the bark breaks up, textured: red and gray, coarse and smooth, wet and flaked.

A tree is an aerial garden, a botanical migration from the sea, from those earliest plants, the seaweeds; it is a purchase on crumbled rock, on ground. The human, standing, is only a different upsweep and articulation of cells. How tree-like we are, how human the tree. 2

But I've come here to seek out the source of a river, and as we make the daylong ascent from a verdant valley, I think about walking and wilderness. We use the word "wilderness," but perhaps we mean wildness. Isn't that why I've come here? In wilderness, I seek the wildness in myself—and in so doing, come on the wildness everywhere around me because, being part of nature, I'm cut from the same cloth. 3

Following the coastline of a lake, I watch how wind picks up water in dark blasts and drops it again. Ducks glide in Vs away from me, out onto the fractured, darkening mirror. I stop. A hatch of mayflies powders the air and the archaic, straight-winged dragonflies hang, blunt-nosed, above me. A friend talks about aquatic bugs: water beetles, spinners, assassin bugs, and one that hatches, mates, and dies in a total life-span of two hours. At the end of the meadow, the lake drains into a fast-moving creek. I quicken my pace and trudge upward. Walking is also an ambulation of mind. The human armor of bones rattles, fat rolls, and inside this durable, fleshy prison of mine, I make a beeline toward otherness, lightness, or, maybe like a moth, toward flame. 4

Somewhere along the trail I laugh out loud. How shell-like the body seems suddenly—not fleshy at all, but inhuman and hard. And farther up, I step out of my body though I'm still held fast by something, but what? I don't know. 5

How foolish the preparations for wilderness trips seem now. We pore over our maps, chart our expeditions. We "gear up" at trailheads with pitons and crampons, horsepacks and backpacks, fly rods and cameras, forgetting the meaning of simply going, of lifting thought-covers, of disburdenment. I look up from these thoughts. A blue heron rises from a gravel bar and glides behind a gray screen of dead trees, appears in an opening where an avalanche downed pines, and lands again on water. 6

I stop to eat lunch. Ralph Waldo Emerson wrote, "The Gautama said that the first men ate the earth and found it sweet." I eat baloney and cheese and think about eating the earth. It's another way of framing our wonder in which the width of the mouth stands for the 7

generous palate of consciousness. I cleanse my palate with miner's let-
tuce and stream water and try to imagine what kinds of sweetness the
earth provides: the taste of glacial flour, or the mineral taste of basalt,
the fresh and foul bouquets of rivers, the desiccated, stinging flavor of
a snow-storm—like eating red ants, my friend says.

8   As I begin to walk again it occurs to me that this notion of "eating the earth" is not about gluttony, hedonism, or sin, but, rather, unconditional love. Everywhere I look I see the possibility of love. To
find wildness, I must first offer myself up, accept all that comes before
me: a bullfrog breathing hard on a rock; moose tracks under elk scats;
a cloud that looks like a clothespin; a seep of water from a high cirque,
black on brown rock, draining down from the brain of the world.

9   At tree line, birdsong stops. I'm lifted into another movement of
music, one with no particular notes, only windsounds becoming wa-
tersounds, becoming windsounds. Above, a cornice crowns a ridge and
melts into a teal and turquoise lake, like a bladder leaking its wine.

10   On top of Marston Pass I'm in a ruck of steep valleys and gray,
treeless peaks. The alpine carpet, studded with red paint-brush and
alpine buttercups, gives way to rock. Now all the way across a vertiginous valley, I see where water oozes from moss and mud, how, at its
source, it quickly becomes something else.

11   Emerson also said: "Every natural fact is an emanation, and that
from which it emanates is an emanation also, and from every emanation is a new emanation." The ooze, the source of a great river, is now
a white chute tumbling over soft folds of conglomerate rock—brown
bellies. Now wind tears at it, throwing sheets of water to another part
of the mountainside; soft earth gives way under my feet, clouds spill
upward and spit rain. Isn't everything redolent with loss, with momentary radiance, a coming to different ground? Stone basins catch the waterfall, spill it again, like thoughts strung together, laddered down.

12   I see where meltwater is split by a rock—half going west to the
Pacific, the other going east to the Atlantic, for this is the Continental Divide. Down the other side the air I gulp feels softer. Ice spans
and tunnels the creek, then, when night comes but before the full
moon, falling stars have the same look as that white chute of water,
falling against the rock of night.

13   To rise above tree line is to go above thought and after, the de-
scent back into birdsong, bog orchids, willows, and firs, is to sink into
the preliterate parts of ourselves. It is to forget discontent, undisci-
plined needs. Here the world is only space, raw loneliness, green valleys hung vertically. Losing myself to it—if I can—I do not fall. . . or,
if I do, I'm only another cataract of water.

Wildness has no conditions, no sure routes, no peaks or goals, 14
no source that is not instantly becoming something more than itself,
then letting go of that, always becoming. It cannot be stripped of its
complexity by CAT scan or telescope. Rather, it is a many-pointed
truth, almost a bluntness, a sudden essence like the wild strawberries
strung along the ground on scarlet runners under my feet. Wildness
is source and fruition at once, as if every river circled round, the
mouth eating the tail—and the tail, the source.

Now I am camped among trees again. Four yearling moose, 15
their chestnut coats shiny from a summer's diet of willow shoots,
tramp past my bedroll and drink from a spring that issues sulfurous
water. The ooze, the white chute, the narrow stream—now almost a
river—joins this small spring and slows into skinny oxbows and deep
pools before breaking again on rock, a stepladder of sequined riffles.

To trace the history of a river, or a raindrop, as John Muir 16
would have done, is also to trace the history of the soul, the history of
the mind descending and arising in the body. In both, we constantly
seek and stumble on divinity, which, like the cornice feeding the lake
and the spring becoming a waterfall, feeds, spills, falls, and feeds itself
over and over again.

QUESTIONS ON SUBJECT AND PURPOSE

1. Literally, what event does Ehrlich describe in the essay?
2. How does this description differ from what you might expect
   in a description of a journey?
3. What purpose might Ehrlich have in writing the essay?

QUESTIONS ON STRATEGY AND AUDIENCE

1. How does the metaphor of a "journey" or a search for origins
   structure the essay?
2. What is the difference between "wilderness" and "wildness"?
   Check the two words in a dictionary.
3. This essay appeared in a Sierra Club wilderness wall calendar.
   How might the place of publication influence the essay?

QUESTIONS ON VOCABULARY AND STYLE

1. As Ehrlich makes her way up and then back down the mountain, how does her description of the river (and the bodies of
   water along the way) change?

2. In what possible way does anyone "eat the earth" (paragraphs 7 and 8)?

3. Be prepared to define the following words: *purchase* (paragraph 2), *articulation* (2), *verdant* (3), *ambulation* (4), *disburdenment* (6), *palate* (7), *desiccated* (7), *hedonism* (8), *cirque* (8), *cornice* (9), *teal* (9), *ruck* (10), *vertiginous* (10), *emanation* (11), *redolent* (11), *yearling* (15), *oxbow* (15), *riffle* (15).

WRITING SUGGESTIONS

1. For your Journal. Sometimes being in an environment or landscape different from the one you that are used to triggers a fresh perspective. Go somewhere that you do not see or visit everyday—walk another way home or visit a nearby park. Look carefully at what you see. In your journal, record your impression of this "new" landscape.

2. For a Paragraph. Look around your room, refrigerator, apartment, home, or yard, and find some living or organic object. Spend some time "seeing" and studying this object. Look for something significant about it—maybe what the object seems to represent or symbolize, maybe just a fresh way of seeing the ordinary. In a paragraph, describe your object.

3. For an Essay. Nature can be seen and interpreted in many ways. Select a landscape or a natural event and in an essay describe it to your reader in such a way as to reveal a significance other than just scientific or photographic reality.

Prewriting:

a. Make a list of possible subjects—a thunderstorm, a park, a hurricane, a clear night, a fog, a bed of flowers. Try to select something that you can directly experience.

b. Next to each subject, write down what you see as "revealed" in each—for example, indifference, benevolence, or hostility toward man.

c. Select two of the most promising subjects and make a list of possible descriptive details to use. Remember that each detail needs to be connected with the significance that you are trying to convey.

Rewriting:

a. Check to make sure that you have used vivid nouns and verbs to carry most of the descriptive burden. Do not use too many adjectives and adverbs.

b. Go through your essay and underline every descriptive detail. Are there too many? Are you trying to make the reader see too much? Are all of the details related to the significance that you are trying to reveal?

c. Have you been too heavy-handed in emphasizing the significance that you see? Remember you are trying to reveal significance, you are not lecturing your reader on the significance.

4. For Research. How have other writers "seen" nature? Select an author who has written about nature, and formulate a thesis about how that writer sees nature in her or his work. You can use the Library of Congress Subject Headings in your school's library to locate possible authors (start with the heading "Nature"). Your instructor can also suggest some possibilities (for example, poets such as William Wordsworth or Gerard Manley Hopkins; essayists such as Annie Dillard or Henry David Thoreau). Your library will have collections of nature-related literature as well.

THE INHERITANCE OF TOOLS
Scott Russell Sanders

Born in Memphis, Tennessee, in 1945, Scott Russell Sanders received a Ph.D. from Cambridge University. Currently a professor of English at Indiana University, Sanders is a novelist, an essayist, and a science fiction writer. He has contributed fiction and essays to numerous journals and magazines, and has published fourteen books, including his most recent, Staying Put: Making a Home in a Restless World *(1993).*

Sanders writes often about his childhood and his efforts to "ground" himself. In another of his collections of essays, Secrets of the Universe *(1991), Sanders describes growing up with an alcoholic father, noting that he "wants to drag into the light what eats at me—the fear, the guilt, the shame—so that my own children may be spared." In this personal essay, occasioned by his father's death, Sanders explores the "inheritance" that adheres to four tools passed through four generations of his family.*

BEFORE READING

Connecting: Can you think of something that you learned how to do from a family member or friend?

Anticipating: In what ways is "The Inheritance of Tools" an appropriate title for the essay? What is the essay about?

1   At just about the hour when my father died, soon after dawn one February morning when ice coated the windows like cataracts, I banged my thumb with a hammer. Naturally I swore at the hammer, the reckless thing, and in the moment of swearing I thought of what my father would say: "If you'd try hitting the nail it would go in a whole lot faster. Don't you know your thumb's not as hard as that hammer?" We both were doing carpentry that day, but far apart. He was building cupboards at my brother's place in Oklahoma; I was at home in Indiana putting up a wall in the basement to make a bedroom for my daughter. By the time my mother called with news of his death—the long distance wires whittling her voice until it seemed too thin to bear the weight of what she had to say—my thumb was swollen. A week or so later a white scar in the shape of a crescent

moon began to show above the cuticle, and month by month it rose across the pink sky of my thumbnail. It took the better part of a year for the scar to disappear, and every time I noticed it I thought of my father.

The hammer had belonged to him, and to his father before him. The three of us have used it to build houses and barns and chicken coops, to upholster chairs and crack walnuts, to make doll furniture and book shelves and jewelry boxes. The head is scratched and pockmarked, like an old plowshare that has been working rocky fields, and it gives off the sort of dull sheen you see on fast creek water in the shade. It is a finishing hammer, about the weight of a bread loaf, too light, really, for framing walls, too heavy for cabinetwork, with a curved claw for pulling nails, a rounded head for pounding, a fluted neck for looks, and a hickory handle for strength.

The present handle is my third one, bought from a lumberyard in Tennessee down the road from where my brother and I were helping my father build his retirement house. I broke the previous one by trying to pull sixteen-penny nails out of floor joists—a foolish thing to do with a finishing hammer, as my father pointed out. "You ever hear of a crowbar?" he said. No telling how many handles he and my grandfather had gone through before me. My grandfather used to cut down hickory trees on his farm, saw them into slabs, cure the planks in his hayloft, and carve handles with a drawknife. The grain in hickory is crooked and knotty, and therefore rough, hard to split, like the grain in the two men who owned this hammer before me.

After proposing marriage to a neighbor girl, my grandfather used this hammer to build a house for his bride on a stretch of river bottom in northern Mississippi. The lumber for the place, like the hickory for the handle, was cut on his own land. By the day of the wedding he had not quite finished the house, and so right after the ceremony he took his wife home and put her to work. My grandmother had worn her Sunday dress for the wedding, with a fringe of lace tacked on around the hem in honor of the occasion. She removed this lace and folded it away before going out to help my grandfather nail siding on the house. "There she was in her good dress," he told me some fifty-odd years after that wedding day, "holding up them long pieces of clapboard while I hammered, and together we got the place covered up before dark." As the family grew to four, six, eight, and eventually thirteen, my grandfather used this hammer to enlarge his house room by room, like a chambered nautilus expanding his shell.

By and by the hammer was passed along to my father. One day he was up on the roof of our pony barn nailing shingles with it, when I stepped out the kitchen door to call him for supper. Before I could yell, something about the sight of him straddling the spine of that roof and swinging the hammer caught my eye and made me hold my tongue. I was five or six years old, and the world's commonplaces were still news to me. He would pull a nail from the pouch at his waist, bring the hammer down, and a moment later the *thunk* of the blow would reach my ears. And that is what had stopped me in my tracks and stilled my tongue, that momentary gap between seeing and hearing the blow. Instead of yelling from the kitchen door, I ran to the barn and climbed two rungs up the ladder—as far as I was allowed to go—and spoke quietly to my father. On our walk to the house he explained that sound takes time to make its way through air. Suddenly the world seemed larger, the air more dense, if sound could be held back like any ordinary traveler.

6   By the time I started using this hammer, at about the age when I discovered the speed of sound, it already contained houses and mysteries for me. The smooth handle was one my grandfather had made. In those days I needed both hands to swing it. My father would start a nail in a scrap of wood, and I would pound away until I bent it over.

7   "Looks like you got ahold of some of those rubber nails," he would tell me. "Here, let me see if I can find you some stiff ones." And he would rummage in a drawer until he came up with a fistful of more cooperative nails. "Look at the head," he would tell me. "Don't look at your hands, don't look at the hammer. Just look at the head of that nail and pretty soon you'll learn to hit it square."

8   Pretty soon I did learn. While he worked in the garage cutting dovetail joints for a drawer or skinning a deer or tuning an engine, I would hammer nails. I made innocent blocks of wood look like porcupines. He did not talk much in the midst of his tools, but he kept up a nearly ceaseless humming, slipping in and out of a dozen tunes in an afternoon, often running back over the same stretch of melody again and again, as if searching for a way out. When the humming did cease, I knew he was faced with a task requiring great delicacy or concentration, and I took care not to distract him.

9   He kept scraps of wood in a cardboard box—the ends of two-by-fours, slabs of shelving and plywood, odd pieces of molding—and everything in it was fair game. I nailed scraps together to fashion what I called boats or houses, but the results usually bore only faint resemblance to the visions I carried in my head. I would hold up these constructions to show my father, and he would turn them over in his hands admiringly, speculating about what they might be. My cobbled-together guitars might have been alien spaceships, my barns might have been models of Aztec temples, each wooden contraption might have been anything but what I had set out to make.

10   Now and again I would feel the need to have a chunk of wood shaped or shortened before I riddled it with nails, and I would clamp

it in a vise and scrape at it with a handsaw. My father would let me lacerate the board until my arm gave out, and then he would wrap his hand around mine and help me finish the cut, showing me how to use my thumb to guide the blade, how to pull back on the saw to keep it from binding, how to let my shoulder do the work.

"Don't force it," he would say, "just drag it easy and give the teeth a chance to bite." 11

As the saw teeth bit down, the wood released its smell, each kind with its own fragrance, oak or walnut or cherry or pine—usually pine because it was the softest, easiest for a child to work. No matter how weathered and gray the board, no matter how warped and cracked, inside there was this smell waiting, as of something freshly baked. I gathered every smidgen of sawdust and stored it away in coffee cans, which I kept in a drawer of the workbench. When I did not feel like hammering nails I would dump my sawdust on the concrete floor of the garage and landscape it into highways and farms and towns, running miniature cars and trucks along miniature roads. Looming as huge as a colossus, my father worked over and around me, now and again bending down to inspect my work, careful not to trample my creations. It was a landscape that smelled dizzyingly of wood. Even after a bath my skin would carry the smell, and so would my father's hair, when he lifted me for a bedtime hug. 12

I tell these things not only from memory but also from recent observation, because my own son now turns blocks of wood into nailed porcupines, dumps cans full of sawdust at my feet and sculpts highways on the floor. He learns how to swing a hammer from the elbow instead of the wrist, how to lay his thumb beside the blade to guide a saw, how to tap a chisel with a wooden mallet, how to mark a hole with an awl before starting a drill bit. My daughter did the same before him, and even now, on the brink of teenage aloofness, she will occasionally drag out my box of wood scraps and carpenter something. So I have seen my apprenticeship to wood and tools reenacted in each of my children, as my father saw his own apprenticeship renewed in me. 13

The saw I use belonged to him, as did my level and both of my squares, and all four tools had belonged to his father. The blade of the saw is the bluish color of gun barrels, and the maple handle, dark from the sweat of hands, is inscribed with curving leaf designs. The level is a shaft of walnut two feet long, edged with brass and pierced by three round windows in which air bubbles float in oil-filled tubes of glass. The middle window serves for testing if a surface is horizontal, the others for testing if a surface is plumb or vertical. My grand- 14 father used to carry this level on the gun-rack behind the seat in his pickup, and when I rode with him I would turn around to watch the bubbles dance. The larger of the two squares is called a framing square, a flat steel elbow, so beat up and tarnished you can barely make out the rows of numbers that show how to figure the cuts on rafters. The smaller one is called a try square, for marking right angles, with a blued steel blade for the shank and a brass-faced block of cherry for the head.

15　　　I was taught early on that a saw is not to be used apart from a square: "If you're going to cut a piece of wood," my father insisted, "you owe it to the tree to cut it straight."

16　　　Long before studying geometry, I learned there is a mystical virtue in right angles. There is an unspoken morality in seeking the level and the plumb. A house will stand, a table will bear weight, the sides of a box will hold together only if the joints are square and the members upright. When the bubble is lined up between two marks etched in the glass tube of a level, you have aligned yourself with the forces that hold the universe together. When you miter the corners of a picture frame, each angle must be exactly forty-five degrees, as they are in the perfect triangles of Pythagoras, not a degree more or less. Otherwise the frame will hang crookedly, as if ashamed of itself and of its maker. No matter if the joints you are cutting do not show. Even if you are butting two pieces of wood together inside a cabinet, where not one except a wrecking crew will ever see them, you must take pains to insure that the ends are square and the studs are plumb.

17　　　I took pains over the wall I was building on the day my father died. Not long after that wall was finished—paneled with tongue-and-groove boards of yellow pine, the nail holes filled with putty and the wood all stained and sealed—I came close to wrecking it one afternoon when my daughter ran howling up the stairs to announce that her gerbils had escaped from their cage and were hiding in my brand new wall. She could hear them scratching and squeaking behind her bed. Impossible! I said. How on earth could they get inside my drum-tight wall? Through the heating vent, she answered. I went downstairs, pressed my ear to the honey-colored wood, and heard the *scritch scritch* of tiny feet.

18　　　"What can we do?" my daughter wailed. "They'll starve to death, they'll die of thirst, they'll suffocate."

19　　　"Hold on," I shouted, "I'll think of something."

20　　　While I thought and she fretted, the radio on her bedside table delivered us the headlines. Several thousand people had died in a city in India from a poisonous cloud that had leaked overnight from a chemical plant. A nuclear-powered submarine had been launched. Rioting continued in South Africa. An airplane had been hijacked in

Description

the Mediterranean. Authorities calculated that several thousand homeless people slept on the streets within sight of the Washington Monument. I felt my usual helplessness in face of all these calamities. But here was my daughter weeping because her gerbils were holed up in a wall. This calamity I could handle.

"Don't worry," I told her. "We'll set food and water by the heating vent and lure them out. And if that doesn't do the trick, I'll tear the wall apart until we find them." 21

She stopped crying and gazed as me. "You'd really tear it apart? Just for my gerbils? The *wall?*" Astonishment slowed her down only for a second, however, before she ran to the workbench and began tugging at drawers, saying, "Let's see, what'll we need? Crowbar. Hammer. Chisels. I hope we don't have to use them—but just in case." 22

We didn't need the wrecking tools. I never had to assault my handsome wall, because the gerbils eventually came out to nibble at a dish of popcorn. But for several hours I studied the tongue-and-groove skin I had nailed up on the day of my father's death, considering where to begin prying. There were no gaps in that wall, no crooked joints. 23

I had botched a great many pieces of wood before I mastered the right angle with a saw, botched even more before I learned to miter a joint. The knowledge of these things resides in my hands and eyes and the webwork of muscles, not in the tools. There are machines for sale—powered miter boxes and radial-arm saws, for instance—that will enable any casual soul to cut proper angles in boards. The skill is invested in the gadget instead of the person who uses it, and this is what distinguishes a machine from a tool. If I had to earn my keep by making furniture or building houses, I suppose I would buy powered saws and pneumatic nailers; the need for speed would drive me to it. But since I carpenter only for my own pleasure or to help neighbors or to remake the house around the ears of my family, I stick with hand tools. Most of the ones I own were given to me by my father, who also taught me how to wield them. The tools in my work-bench are a double inheritance, for each hammer and level and saw is wrapped in a cloud of knowing. 24

All of these tools are a pleasure to look at and to hold. Merchants would never paste NEW NEW NEW! signs on them in stores. Their designs are old because they work, because they serve their purpose well. Like folksongs and aphorisms and the grainy bits of language, these tools have been pared down to essentials. I look at my claw hammer, the distillation of a hundred generations of carpenters, and consider that it holds up well beside those other classics— Greek vases, Gregorian chants, *Don Quixote*, barbed fish hooks, 25 candles, spoons. Knowledge of hammering stretches back to the earliest humans who squatted beside fires chipping flints. Anthropologists have a lovely name for those unworked rocks that served as the earliest hammers. *Dawn stones*, they are called. Their only qualification for the work, aside from hardness, is that they fit the hand. Our ancestors used them for grinding corn, tapping awls, smashing bones. From dawn stones to this claw hammer is a great leap in time, but no great distance in design or imagination.

26   On that iced-over February morning when I smashed my thumb with the hammer, I was down in the basement framing the wall that my daughter's gerbils would later hide in. I was thinking of my father, as I always did whenever I built anything, thinking how he would have gone about the work, hearing in memory what he would have said about the wisdom of hitting the nail instead of my thumb. I had the studs and plates nailed together all square and trim, and was lifting the wall into place when the phone rang upstairs. My wife answered, and in a moment she came to the basement door and called down softly to me. The stillness in her voice made me drop the framed wall and hurry upstairs. She told me my father was dead. Then I heard the details over the phone from my mother. Building a set of cupboards for my brother in Oklahoma, he had knocked off work early the previous afternoon because of cramps in his stomach. Early this morning, on his way into the kitchen of my brother's trailer, maybe going for a glass of water, so early that no one else was awake, he slumped down on the linoleum and his heart quit.

27   For several hours I paced around inside my house, upstairs and down, in and out of every room, looking for the right door to open and knowing there was no such door. My wife and children followed me and wrapped me in arms and backed away again, circling and staring as if I were on fire. Where was the door, the door, the door? I kept wondering. My smashed thumb turned purple and throbbed, making me furious. I wanted to cut it off and rush outside and scrape away the snow and hack a hole in the frozen earth and bury the shameful thing.

28   I went down into the basement, opened a drawer in my workbench, and stared at the ranks of chisels and knives. Oiled and sharp, as my father would have kept them, they gleamed at me like teeth. I took up a clasp knife, pried out the longest blade and tested the edge on the hair of my forearm. A tuft came away cleanly, and I saw my father testing the sharpness of tools on his own skin, the blades of axes and knives and gouges and hoes, saw the red hair shaved off in patches from his arms and the backs of his hands. "That will cut bear," he would say. He never cut a bear with his blades, now my

blades, but he cut deer, dirt, wood. I closed the knife and put it away. Then I took up the hammer and went back to work on my daughter's wall, snugging the bottom plate against a chalkline on the floor, shimming the top plate against the joists overhead, plumbing the studs with my level, making sure before I drove the first nail that every line was square and true.

QUESTIONS ON SUBJECT AND PURPOSE

1. What is the subject of Sanders's essay? Is it tools? His father's death?
2. Is Sanders's father or grandfather (or his children) ever described in the story? How are they revealed to the reader?
3. What "door" (paragraph 27) is Sanders searching for?
4. What exactly has Sanders inherited from his father?

QUESTIONS ON STRATEGY AND AUDIENCE

1. How does Sanders use time to structure his essay? Is the story told in chronological order?
2. What is the function of each of the following episodes or events in the essay?
   a. The sore thumb
   b. "A mystical virtue in right angles" (paragraph 16)
   c. The wall he was building
3. What expectations does Sanders seem to have about his audience?

QUESTIONS ON VOCABULARY AND STYLE

1. How much dialogue does Sanders use in the story? What does the dialogue contribute?
2. Throughout the essay, Sanders makes use of many effective similes and metaphors. Make a list of six such devices. What does each contribute to the essay? How fresh and arresting are these images?
3. Be able to define each of the following words or phrases: *plowshare* (paragraph 2), *sixteen-penny nails* (3), *chambered nautilus* (4), *rummage* (7), *lacerate* (10), *smidgen* (12), *plumb* (14), *miter* (24), *aphorisms* (25), *shimming* (28).

WRITING SUGGESTIONS

1. **For your Journal.** The word "inheritance" probably suggests to you money or property that is bequeathed to a descendent. But you can "inherit" many things that are far less tangible. In your journal, explore what you might have inherited from someone in your family—maybe it is a talent, an interest, an ability, an obsession.

2. **For a Paragraph.** Study the childhood scenes or episodes that Sanders includes in his essay—for example, calling his father to supper (paragraph 5), hammering nails (6–9), landscaping with sawdust (12). Notice how Sanders re-creates sensory experiences. Then in a paragraph re-create a similar experience from your childhood. Remember to evoke sensory impressions for your reader—a sight, a sound, a smell, a touch.

3. **For an Essay.** Think about a skill, talent, or even a habit that you have learned from or share with a family member. In addition to the ability or trait, what else have you "inherited"? How does it affect your life? In an essay describe the inheritance and its effect on you.

   Prewriting:

   a. Divide a piece of paper into two columns. In the left-hand column, make a list of possible subjects. Work on the list over a period of several days. In the space to the right of this list jot down the significance that you see in such an inheritance.

   b. Select one of the items from your list and freewrite for 15 minutes. Concentrate on the significance of this ability or trait in your life. How has it shaped or altered your life, your perceptions? Reread what you have just written. Then freewrite for another 15 minutes.

   c. Like Sanders, you will be dealing with two "times" in the essay—your childhood and your present. Notice how Sanders manipulates time in his essay. He does not narrate the story in a strict chronological sequence. Experiment with time as an organizational strategy in your essay. Outline two or more structures for the essay.

   Rewriting:

   a. Check your essay to see if you have used vivid verbs and concrete nouns. Watch that you do not overwork adjectives and adverbs.

Description

b. Did you include dialogue in your essay? If not, try adding some. Remember, though, that dialogue slows the pace of a story. Do not overuse it.

c. Look carefully at your conclusion. You want to end forcefully; you want to emphasize the significance of your inheritance. Reread your essay several times and then try freewriting a new conclusion. Try for a completely new ending. If you are using a peer reader, ask that reader to judge both conclusions.

4. For Research. The passing on of traditional crafts or skills is an important part of cultural tradition. Choose a society that interests you, and find a particular craft that is preserved from one generation to another. It might also be something that has been preserved in your family's religious or ethnic heritage. In a research paper, document the nature of the craft and the methods by which the culture ensures its transmission. What is important about this craft? What does it represent to that society? Why bother to preserve it?

DIVISION AND CLASSIFICATION

Division and classification are closely related methods of analysis, but you can remember the difference by asking yourself whether you are analyzing a single thing or analyzing two or more things. Division occurs when a single subject is subdivided into its parts. To list the ingredients in a can of soup or a box of cereal is to perform a division. The key is that you begin with a single thing.

In the following excerpt from a "chemistry primer" for people interested in cooking, Harold McGee uses division twice—first to subdivide the atom into its smaller constituent particles and second to subdivide the "space" within the atom into two areas (nucleus and shell):

> An atom is the smallest particle into which an element can be sub-divided without losing its characteristic properties. The atom too is divisible into smaller particles, *electrons*, *protons*, and *neutrons*, but these are the building blocks of all atoms, no matter of what element. The different properties of the elements are due to the varying combinations of subatomic particles contained in their atoms. The Periodic Table arranges the elements in order of the number of protons contained in one atom of each element. That number is called the atomic number.
>
> The atom is divided into two regions: the nucleus, or center in which the protons and neutrons are located, and a surrounding "orbit," or more accurately a "cloud" or "shell," in which the electrons move continuously. Both protons and neutrons weigh about 2000 times as much as electrons, so practically all of an atom's mass is concentrated in the nucleus.

Similarly, Paul Bodanis in an essay later in this chapter uses division to structure his discussion of "What's in Your Toothpaste?"; Bodanis analyzes the composition of toothpaste, offering some surprising insights into the "ingredients" we brush with every morning. Gail Sheehy in "Predictable Crises in Adulthood" also uses division when she marks off six stages that typically occur in the lives of every adult between the ages of eighteen and fifty. Sheehy does not classify the lives of many adults; rather, she divides adulthood into a series of stages or periods.

Division, then, is used to show the components of a larger subject; it helps the reader understand a complex whole by considering it in smaller units.

Classification, instead of starting with a single subject and then subdividing it into smaller units, begins with two or more items which are then grouped or classified into categories. Newspapers, for example, contain "classified" sections in which advertisements for the same type of goods or services are grouped or classified together. A classification must have at least two categories. Depending upon how many items you start with and how different they are, you can end up having quite a few categories. You probably remember, in at least rough form, the taxonomic classification you learned in high school biology. It begins by setting up as many as five kingdoms (animals, plants, monera, fungi, and protista) and then moves downward to increasingly narrower categories (phylum or division, class, order, family genus, species).

Most classifications outside of the sciences are not as precisely and hierarchically defined. For example, E. B. White uses classification to discuss the three different groups of people who make up New York City:

> There are roughly three New Yorks. There is, first, the New York of the man or woman who was born here, who takes the city for granted and accepts its size and its turbulence as natural and inevitable. Second, there is the New York of the commuter—the city that is devoured by locusts each day and spat out each night. Third, there is the New York of the person who was born somewhere else and came to New York in quest of something. Of these three trembling cities the greatest is the last—the city of final destination, the city that is a goal.

In this chapter, Bernard R. Berelson's classification of the reasons people want children is precisely and logically ordered—something we would expect in an essay that is titled "The Value of Children: A Taxonomical Essay" and that uses headings to display its organizational pattern clearly. In contrast, Mary Mebane in "Shades of Black" uses classification in subtle ways—not once, but four times in the essay.

How Do You Choose a Subject?

In choosing your subject for either division or classification, be sure to avoid the obvious approach to the obvious subject. Every teacher has read at some point a classification essay placing teachers into three groups based solely on the grade level at which they teach: elementary school teachers teach in elementary school, middle school teachers teach in middle school, and high school teachers teach in high school. Although the classification is complete and accurate, such a subject and approach are likely to lead you into writing that is boring and simply not worth either your time or your reader's. No subject is inherently bad, but if you choose to write about something common, you need to find an interesting angle from which to approach it. Before you begin to write, answer two questions: first, what is your purpose? and second, will your reader learn something or be entertained by what you plan to write?

How Do You Divide or Classify a Subject?

Since both division and classification involve separation into parts—either dividing a whole into pieces or sorting many things into related groups or categories—you have to find ways in which to divide or group. Those ways can be objective and formal, such as the classification schemes used by biologists, or subjective and informal like Susan Allen Toth's scheme in "Cinematypes." Either way, several things are particularly important.

First, you subdivide or categorize for a reason or a purpose, and your division or classification should be made with that end in mind. Bernard R. Berelson in the "The Value of Children: A Taxonomical Essay" places people's reasons for wanting children into six categories: biological, cultural, political, economic, familial, and personal. His purpose is to explain the various factors that motivate people to *want* children, and these six categories represent the spectrum of reasons why adults *want* children. Berelson does not include, for example, a category labeled "accidental," for such a heading would lie outside of and be irrelevant to his stated purpose.

Second, your division or classification must be complete—you cannot omit pieces or leave items unclassified. How complete your classification needs to be depends upon your purpose. Given the limited purpose that Toth has, it is sufficient to offer just three types of dates. They do not represent all possible dates, but in the comic context of Toth's essay, the three are enough to establish her point. Berelson, on the other hand, sets out to be exhaustive, to isolate all of the reasons people at any time or in any place have wanted children. As a result, he has to include some categories that are essentially irrelevant for most Americans. For example, probably few if any Americans ever want children because of political reasons, that is, because their government encourages them to do so. But in some societies at certain periods of time political reasons have been important. Therefore, Berelson must include that category as well.

Third, the categories or subdivisions you establish need to be parallel in form. In mathematical terms, the categories should share a lowest common denominator. A simple and fairly effective test for parallelism is to see whether your categories are all phrased in similar grammatical terms. Berelson, for example, defines his categories (the reasons for wanting children) in exactly parallel form:

> the biological
> the cultural
> the political
> the economic
> the familial
> the personal
>> personal power
>> personal competence
>> personal status
>> personal extension
>> personal experience
>> personal pleasure

For this reason you should not establish a catch-all category which you label something like "other." When Berelson is finished with his classification scheme, no reasons for wanting children are left unaccounted for; everything fits into one of the six subdivisions.

Finally, your categories or subdivisions should be mutually exclusive; that is, items should belong in only one category. Toth's "cinematypes" cannot be mistaken for one another.

How Do You Structure a Division or Classification Essay?

The body of a division or classification essay will have as many parts as you have subdivisions or categories. Each subdivision or category will probably be treated in a single paragraph or in a group of related paragraphs. Toth, for example, uses a very symmetrical form in her essay: she organizes "Cinematypes" around the three different men with whom she has gone to the movies, treating each date in three paragraphs. Not every essay will be so evenly and perfectly divided. The central portion of Sheehy's "Predictable Crises of Adulthood" covers the six stages of adulthood in sections of varying length.

Once you have decided how many subdivisions or categories you will have and how long each one will be, you still have to decide in what order to arrange those parts or categories. Sometimes you must devise your own order. Toth, for example, could have arranged her "cinematypes" in any order. Nothing in the material itself determines the sequence. However, not all divisions or classifications have the same flexibility in their arrangement. Some invite, or imply, or even demand a particular order. Because she is tracing the chronological development of adults, Sheehy has a built-in order that she has to follow. Her essay would not have made sense if she organized her division in any other way. Similarly, if you were classifying films using the ratings established by the motion picture industry, you would essentially have to follow the G, PG, PG13, R, NC-17, and X sequence. Although you could begin at either end, it would not make sense to begin with any of the four middle categories.

Having an order underlying your division or classification can be a great help for both you and your reader. It allows you to know where to place each section, dictating the order you will follow. It gives your reader a clear sense of direction. Berelson, for example, in "The Value of Children: A Taxonomical Essay," arranges his reasons why people have children in an order that "starts with chemistry and proceeds to spirit." That is, he deals first with the biological reasons for wanting children and moves finally to the most spiritual of reasons—love.

Sample Student Essay

April Lavallee found a subject to divide in another course she was taking. Notice how the division is similar to, but not identical with, a process analysis. April's purpose is not to tell the reader how memory works—such a subject would probably be too complicated for a short paper. Instead, April uses the accepted three-part division of memory to show why we remember some things but not others.

EARLIER DRAFT

Improving Your Memory

While attempting to memorize chapter upon chapter of unlearned material the night before a test, what college student would not want to learn more about the workings of our memory system with the hope, perhaps, of shortening the duration of time required to learn a unit of material? The first step in the process of increasing memory is to learn more about the workings and structures of our memory systems. Although controversial, the information-processing model of memory described here is a widely accepted model of our memory system and its components. This model breaks our memory down into three principal storage structures, each corresponding to a stage of processing of a stimulus. Information about a particular stimulus is entered, or registered, in the first of these structures, known as the Sensory Register, by means of one or more of the five senses. It is held here very briefly--for approximately 250 msec to 2 seconds--in raw sensory form, and eventually decays and vanishes completely. Once recognized, information can pass to the next storage structure-- the Short-Term Memory (STM). Information is stored here not as raw sensory data, but as familiar recognizable patterns. By the use of rehearsal, information may be retained here for much longer than in the Sensory Register, but without the use of this, the information decays just as in the Sensory Register. Another limitation, in addition to time, on STM is the amount of material which can be stored at one time in STM, even with the help of rehearsal. The generally accepted number of items which can be held in STM is approximately seven, varying by two depending upon the individual. According to this model, increased repetition leads the information to

storage in long-term memory, the third of the
storage structures. This structure is relatively
permanent and contains all of our knowledge about
the world. Any limit on the amount of material this
structure is capable of holding has not been
established and is seemingly nonexistent, seeing
that the amount that we can learn appears to be
unlimited. Learning of material such as this can aid
the diligent student in perfecting memory strategies
designed to enhance his memory capabilities.

   The strength of April's essay is that it has specific information
to convey, information April had available because she was also taking
a psychology course that semester. When her classmates had a chance
to read her opening sentences on a mimeographed handout, several
were anxious to read on—"anything to help with studying," remarked
one student. But as soon as April heard that response, she realized a
problem. Her opening sentences and her title seem to promise advice
on how to improve memory. In fact, the essay analyzes the three divisions that constitute memory. As a result of the students' responses,
April decided to rewrite her introduction and conclusion to reflect
her real subject. In the process of revising, April decided as well to
emphasize the three-part division of memory even more by introducing paragraph divisions into her paper.

REVISED DRAFT

The Structure of Memory

   George Washington was our first President; the
North defeated the South in the Civil War; the
Japanese bombed Pearl Harbor during World War II;
and the whale is the largest living mammal. These
statements have nothing in common except that
practically every American knows them. Although they
are unimportant to our everyday lives, we can
remember facts such as these, but we cannot remember
where our keys are when we are late for work. We can
recite the Pledge of Allegiance, but we cannot
remember the seven digits the telephone operator
just gave us. Why is this?

The information-processing model used to describe how our memories work helps explain phenomena such as these. This model defines three principal storage structures, each of which corresponds to a stage in the processing of a stimulus. Information is first entered or registered by means of one or more of the five senses in the Sensory Register. It is held here briefly--for approximately 250 msec to 2 seconds--in raw sensory form, and eventually decays and vanishes completely.

Once the information is recognized it can pass to the next storage structure--the Short-Term Memory (STM). Information is stored here as familiar, recognizable patterns. By the use of rehearsal (forced recall and repetition), information can be retained here for much longer than in the Sensory Register. Without rehearsal, though, the information decays just as it does in the Sensory Register. Another limitation, in addition to time, on STM is the amount of material that can be stored here at one time, even with the help of rehearsal. The generally accepted number of items that can be held in STM is seven, plus or minus two depending on the individual.

With increased repetition, information is transferred from STM to Long-Term Memory (LTM), the third of the storage structures. This structure is relatively permanent and contains all of our knowledge about the world. Apparently LTM is unlimited in the amount of information it can hold. The secret to remembering is to get the information into LTM, so next time pay attention and rehearse that telephone number or the location of your keys and sunglasses. Then you won't forget.

SOME THINGS TO REMEMBER

1. In choosing a subject for division or classification ask yourself: first, what is my purpose? and second, will my reader learn something or be entertained by my paper?
2. Remember that your subdivision or classification should reflect your purpose—that is, the number of categories or parts is related to what you are trying to do.

3. Make sure that your division or classification is complete. Do not omit any pieces or items. Everything should be accounted for.

4. Take care that the parts or categories are phrased in parallel form.

5. Avoid a category labeled something such as "other" or "miscellaneous."

6. Remember to make your categories or subdivisions mutually exclusive.

7. Once you have established your subdivisions, check to see whether there is an order implied or demanded by your subject.

8. As you move from one subdivision to another, provide markers for the reader so that the parts are clearly labeled.

WHAT'S IN YOUR TOOTHPASTE
Paul Bodanis

Raised in Chicago, Paul Bodanis earned a degree in mathematics from the University of Chicago and did postgraduate work in theoretical biology and population genetics. He traveled to London and then to Paris, where he began his journalism career as a copyboy at the International Herald Tribune. *Bodanis has a special talent for explaining complex concepts in simple, yet entertaining, language. He has written three books:* The Body Book: A Fantastic Voyage to the World Within *(1984);* The Secret House *(1986); and* The Secret Garden: Dawn to Dusk in the Astonishing Hidden World of the Garden *(1992).*

This essay is excerpted from his second book The Secret House *(1986). One reviewer noted: "The book explores the gee-whiz science that sits unnoticed under every homeowner's nose." If you are appalled to discover what is in your toothpaste, you ought to read Bodanis's account of some mass-produced ice cream that contains "leftover cattle parts that no one else wants."*

BEFORE READING

Connecting: Most of us are well aware of the toxic nature of some common products, but there are many others that we assume are safe—maybe even good for us. Think about those things that you use, eat, or drink every day. Which ones have you never worried about?

Anticipating: Is Bodanis being fair and objective in his essay? How can you judge?

Into the bathroom goes our male resident, and after the most pressing need is satisfied it's time to brush the teeth. The tube of toothpaste is squeezed, its pinched metal seams are splayed, pressure waves are generated inside, and the paste begins to flow. But what's in this toothpaste, so carefully being extruded out?

Water mostly, 30 to 45 percent in most brands: ordinary, everyday simple tap water. It's there because people like to have a big gob of toothpaste to spread on the brush, and water is the cheapest stuff there is when it comes to making big gobs. Dripping a bit from the tap onto your brush would cost virtually nothing; whipped in with the rest of the toothpaste the manufacturers can sell it at a neat and accountant-pleasing $2 per pound equivalent. Toothpaste manufacture is a very lucrative occupation.

3   Second to water in quantity is chalk: exactly the same material that schoolteachers use to write on blackboards. It is collected from the crushed remains of long-dead ocean creatures. In the Cretaceous seas chalk particles served as part of the wickedly sharp outer skeleton that these creatures had to wrap around themselves to keep from getting chomped by all the slightly larger other ocean creatures they met. Their massed graves are our present chalk deposits.

4   The individual chalk particles—the size of the smallest mud particles in your garden—have kept their toughness over the aeons, and now on the toothbrush they'll need it. The enamel outer coating of the tooth they'll have to face is the hardest substance in the body— tougher than skull, or bone, or nail. Only the chalk particles in toothpaste can successfully grind into the teeth during brushing, ripping off the surface layers like an abrading wheel grinding down a boulder in a quarry.

5   The craters, slashes, and channels that the chalk tears into the teeth will also remove a certain amount of build-up yellow in the carnage, and it is for that polishing function that it's there. A certain amount of unduly enlarged extra-abrasive chalk fragments tear such cavernous pits into the teeth that future decay bacteria will be able to bunker down there and thrive; the quality control people find it almost impossible to screen out these errant super-chalk pieces, and government regulations allow them to stay in.

6   In case even the gouging doesn't get all the yellow off, another substance is worked into the toothpaste cream. This is titanium dioxide. It comes in tiny spheres, and it's the stuff bobbing around in white wall paint to make it come out white. Splashed around onto your teeth during the brushing it coats much of the yellow that remains. Being water soluble it leaks off in the next few hours and is swallowed, but at least for the quick glance up in the mirror after finishing it will make the user think his teeth are truly white. Some manufacturers add optical whitening dyes—the stuff more commonly found in washing machine bleach—to make extra sure that that glance in the mirror shows reassuring white.

7   These ingredients alone would not make a very attractive concoction. They would stick in the tube like a sloppy white plastic lump, hard to squeeze out as well as revolting to the touch. Few consumers would savor rubbing in a mixture of water, ground-up blackboard chalk, and the whitener from latex paint first thing in the morning.

To get around that finicky distaste the manufacturers have mixed in a host of other goodies.

To keep the glop from drying out, a mixture including glycerine glycol—related to the most common car antifreeze ingredient—is whipped in with the chalk and water, and to give *that* concoction a bit of substance (all we really have so far is wet colored chalk) a large helping is added of gummy molecules from the seaweed *Chondrus Crispus*. This seaweed ooze spreads in among the chalk, paint, and antifreeze, then stretches itself in all directions to hold the whole mass together. A bit of paraffin oil (the fuel that flickers in camping lamps) is pumped in with it to help the moss ooze keep the whole substance smooth.

With the glycol, ooze, and paraffin we're almost there. Only two major chemicals are left to make the refreshing, cleansing substance we know as toothpaste. The ingredients so far are fine for cleaning, but they wouldn't make much of the satisfying foam we have come to expect in the morning brushing.

To remedy that every toothpaste on the market has a big dollop of detergent added too. You've seen the suds detergent will make in a washing machine. The same substance added here will duplicate that inside the mouth. It's not particularly necessary, but it sells.

The only problem is that by itself this ingredient tastes, well, too like detergent. It's horribly bitter and harsh. The chalk put in toothpaste is pretty foul-tasting too for that matter. It's to get around that gustatory discomfort that the manufacturers put in the ingredient they tout perhaps the most of all. This is the flavoring, and it has to be strong. Double rectified peppermint oil is used—a flavorer so powerful that chemists know better than to sniff it in the raw state in the laboratory. Menthol crystals and saccharin or other sugar simulators are added to complete the camouflage operation.

Is that it? Chalk, water, paint, seaweed, antifreeze, paraffin oil, detergent, and peppermint? Not quite. A mix like that would be irresistible to the hundreds of thousands of individual bacteria lying on the surface of even an immaculately cleaned bathroom sink. They would get in, float in the water bubbles, ingest the ooze and paraffin, maybe even spray out enzymes to break down the chalk. The result would be an uninviting mess. The way manufacturers avoid that final obstacle is by putting something in to kill the bacteria. Something good and strong is needed, something that will zap any accidentally intrudant bacteria into oblivion. And that something is formaldehyde—the disinfectant used in anatomy labs.

So it's chalk, water, paint, seaweed, antifreeze, paraffin oil, detergent, peppermint, formaldehyde, and fluoride (which can go some way towards preserving children's teeth)—that's the usual mixture raised to the mouth on the toothbrush for a fresh morning's clean. If it sounds too unfortunate, take heart. Studies show that thorough brushing with just plain water will often do as good a job.

QUESTIONS ON SUBJECT AND PURPOSE

1. Bodanis explains to the reader what toothpaste is composed of. Is his description objective? Could it appear, for example, in an encyclopedia?
2. After reading the essay, you might feel that Bodanis avoids certain crucial issues about the composition of toothpaste. Does he raise for you any questions that he does not answer?
3. What might Bodanis's purpose be? Is he arguing for something? Is he attacking something?

QUESTIONS ON STRATEGY AND AUDIENCE

1. How does Bodanis seem to arrange or order his division?
2. Bodanis gives the most space (three paragraphs) to chalk. Why? What is his focus in the section?
3. What could Bodanis expect about his audience?

QUESTIONS ON VOCABULARY AND STYLE

1. How would you characterize the tone of the essay?
2. Bodanis links most of the ingredients to their use in another product. Find these links and be prepared to comment on the effect that these linkages have on the reader.
3. Be prepared to define the following words: *splayed* (paragraph 1), *extruded* (1), *lucrative* (2), *aeons* (4), *abrading* (4), *carnage* (5), *errant* (5), *finicky* (7), *dollop* (10), *gustatory* (11), *tout* (11), *intrudant* (12).

WRITING SUGGESTIONS

1. **For your Journal**. Over a period of several days keep a list of every product that you use or consume—everything from a lip balm, to a cosmetic, to an after-shave cologne, to a mouth-

wash, to a piece of chewing gum. When you really start to think about it, which ones would you like to know more about?

2. **For a Paragraph.** Select a common food or beverage and sub-divide it into its constituent parts. Use the contents label on the package as a place to start. You could use either the list of ingredients or the nutrition information. Present your division in a paragraph. Do not just describe what you find; rather, develop an attitude or thesis toward those findings. Bodanis, for example, certainly expresses (and implies) how he feels about what he finds in toothpaste.

3. **For an Essay.** Americans exhibit widely differing attitudes to-ward the food they eat, in large part because they have the greatest choice of any people in the world. In an essay, classify the American eater. You can approach your subject from a se-rious or a comic point of view. Do not just describe types; your essay should either state or imply your feelings or judg-ments about your findings. Try to establish somewhere be-tween four and six categories.

Prewriting:

a. Establish, through observation, a series of types. Visit a su-permarket, a health food co-op, a fast food restaurant, a sandwich shop, a vegetarian restaurant. Consult the Yellow Pages for a listing of food suppliers and restaurants. Jot down your observations on the diversity of food and eaters around you.

b. Interview several people who have strong feelings about food or whose food habits are strikingly different from your own.

c. Plan out a strategy for organizing your categories—look, for example, at the organizational plans used by Sheehy and Berelson.

Rewriting:

a. Check to see if your categories are stated in parallel form. On a separate sheet of paper, jot down the key word or phrase for each one. Are they in parallel grammatical form?

b. Are there adequate links or transitions from one category to another in your essay? Compare your links to those used by Sheehy and Berelson.

c. Find a peer reader and ask for an honest reaction to your paper and its organization.

4. **For Research**. Americans have become increasingly concerned about the additives that are put into food. Research the nature of food additives. How many are there? In general, what do they do? Develop a classification scheme to explain the largest groups or subdivisions. Be sure to adopt a stand or thesis about the use of such additives, and be sure to document your sources.

CINEMATYPES

Susan Allen Toth

*Born in Ames, Iowa, in 1940, Susan Allen Toth graduated from Smith College and Berkeley and received a Ph.D. from the University of Minnesota in 1969. She taught English at San Francisco State College and now teaches at Macalester College in Minnesota. Toth has contributed articles and stories to a wide range of magazines and newspapers. She has written two memoirs—*Blooming: A Small Town Girlhood *(1981) and* Ivy Days: Making My Way Out East *(1984).*

In "Cinematypes," originally published in Harper's, *Toth classifies the men who take her to movies: Aaron likes art films; Pete, films with redeeming social value; and Sam, movies that are entertaining. But her own passion, Toth confesses, is for old Technicolor musicals and films in which "the men and women always like each other."*

BEFORE READING

Connecting: Think about the people who are or have been significant in your life. What characteristics do they share? Are you drawn to the same type of person? To radically different types of people?

Anticipating: The core of Toth's essay describes her experiences going to the movies with three different men. Why should the reader care? Does Toth have a reason for relating these experiences—a larger purpose or thesis?

Aaron takes me only to art films. That's what I call them, anyway: 1
strange movies with vague poetic images I don't always understand.
Long dreamy movies about a distant Technicolor past, even longer
black-and-white movies about the general meaninglessness of life.
We do not go unless at least one reputable critic has found the cine-
matography superb. We went to the *The Devil's Eye*, and Aaron
turned to me in the middle and said, "My God, this is *funny*." I do not
think he was pleased.

When Aaron and I go to the movies, we drive our cars sepa- 2
rately and meet by the box office. Inside the theater he sits tentatively
in his seat, ready to move if he can't see well, poised to leave if the

film is disappointing. He leans away from me, careful not to touch the bare flesh of his arm against the bare flesh of mine. Sometimes he leans so far I am afraid he may be touching the woman on his other side. If the movie is very good, he leans forward, too, peering between the heads of the couple in front of us. The light from the screen bounces off his glasses; he gleams with intensity, sitting there on the edge of his seat, watching the screen. Once I tapped him on the arm so I could whisper a comment in his ear. He jumped.

3   After *Belle de Jour* Aaron said he wanted to ask me if he could stay overnight. "But I can't," he shook his head mournfully before I had a chance to answer, "because I know I never sleep well in strange beds." Then he apologized for asking. "It's just that after a film like that," he said, "I feel the need to assert myself."

4   Pete takes me only to movies that he thinks have redeeming social value. He doesn't call them "films." They tend to be about poverty, war, injustice, political corruption, struggling unions in the 1930s, and the military-industrial complex. Pete doesn't like propaganda movies, though, and he doesn't like to be too depressed, either. We stayed away from *The Sorrow and the Pity*; it would be, he said, just too much. Besides, he assured me, things are never that hopeless. So most of the movies we see are made in Hollywood. Because they are always topical, these movies offer what Pete calls "food for thought." When we saw *Coming Home*, Pete's jaw set so firmly with the first half-hour that I knew we would end up at Poppin' Fresh Pies afterward.

5   When Pete and I go to the movies, we take turns driving so no one owes anyone else anything. We leave the car far from the theater so we don't have to pay for parking space. If it's raining or snowing, Pete offers to let me off at the door, but I can tell he'll feel better if I go with him while he finds a spot, so we share the walk too. Inside the theater Pete will hold my hand when I get scared if I ask him. He puts my hand firmly on his knee and covers it completely with his own hand. His knee never twitches. After a while, when the scary part is past, he loosens his hand slightly and I know that is a signal to take mine away. He sits companionably close, letting his jacket just touch my sweater, but he does not infringe. He thinks I ought to know he is there if I need him.

6   One night, after *The China Syndrome*, I asked Pete if he wouldn't like to stay for a second drink, even though it was past midnight. He thought a while about that, considering my offer from all possible angles, but finally he said no. Relationships today, he said, have a tendency to move too quickly.

Sam likes movies that are entertaining. By that he means 7
movies that Will Jones in the *Minneapolis Tribune* loved and either
Time or *Newsweek* rather liked; also movies that do not have sappy
love stories, are not musicals, do not have subtitles, and will not force
him to think. He does not go to movies to think. He liked *California
Suite* and *The Seduction of Joe Tynan*, though the plots, he said, could
have been zippier. He saw it all coming too far in advance, and that
took the fun out. He doesn't like to know what is going to happen. "I
just want my brain to be tickled," he says. It is very hard for me to
pick out movies for Sam.

When Sam takes me to the movies, he pays for everything. He 8
thinks that's what a man ought to do. But I buy my own popcorn, because he doesn't approve of it; the grease might smear his flannel
slacks. Inside the theater, Sam makes himself comfortable. He takes
off his jacket, puts one arm around me, and all during the movie he
plays with my hand, stroking my palm, beating a small tattoo on my
wrist. Although he watches the movie intently, his body operates on
instinct. Once I inclined my head and kissed him lightly just behind
his ear. He beat a faster tattoo on my wrist, quick and musical, but he
didn't look away from the screen.

When Sam takes me home from the movies, he stands outside 9
my door and kisses me long and hard. He would like to come in, he
says regretfully, but his steady girlfriend in Duluth wouldn't like it.
When the *Tribune* gives a movie four stars, he has to save it to see
with her. Otherwise her feelings might be hurt.

I go to some movies by myself. On rainy Sunday afternoons I 10
often sneak into a revival house or a college auditorium for old Technicolor musicals, *Kiss Me Kate*, *Seven Brides for Seven Brothers*,
Calamity Jane, even once, *The Sound of Music*. Wearing saggy jeans so
I can prop my feet on the seat in front, I sit toward the rear where no
one can see me. I eat large handfuls of popcorn with double butter.
Once the movie starts, I feel completely at home. Howard Keel and
I are old friends; I grin back at him on the screen. I know the sound
tracks by heart. Sometimes when I get really carried away I hum
along with Kathryn Grayson, remembering how I once thought I
would fill out a formal like that. I am rather glad now I never did.
Skirts whirl, feet tap, acrobatic young men perform impossible feats,
and then the camera dissolves into a dream sequence I know I can
comfortably follow. It is not, thank God, Bergman.

If I can't find an old musical, I settle for Hepburn and Tracy, 11
vintage Grant or Gable, on adventurous days Claudette Colbert or
James Stewart. Before I buy my ticket I make sure it will all end hap-

pily. If necessary, I ask the girl at the box office. I have never seen *Stella Dallas* or *Intermezzo*. Over the years I have developed other peccadilloes: I will, for example, see anything that is redeemed by Thelma Ritter. At the end of *Daddy Long Legs* I wait happily for the scene when Fred Clark, no longer angry, at last pours Thelma a convivial drink. They smile at each other, I smile at them, I feel they are smiling at me. In the movies I go to by myself, the men and women always like each other.

QUESTIONS ON SUBJECT AND PURPOSE

1. Characterize each of Toth's cinematypes. How is each type revealed?
2. What types of movies does Toth go to alone? What common characteristics do they have?
3. Why does Toth end with the remark: "In the movies I go to by myself, the men and women always like each other"?

QUESTIONS ON STRATEGY AND AUDIENCE

1. Why does Toth begin as she does? Why not give an introductory paragraph? What would be the effect of such a paragraph?
2. Why does Toth end each of the three narrative "types" with a comment on the male-female relationship?
3. Does Toth's essay capture your interest? It is, after all, one person's experiences with three types of film-watchers. Why should we as readers be interested in the essay?

QUESTIONS ON VOCABULARY AND STYLE

1. How does Toth use parallel structures in her essay? How many different types of parallelism can you find? How does each function?
2. How would you characterize the tone of Toth's essay? How is it achieved? Be able to point to at least three different devices or techniques.
3. Be able to define the following words: *tattoo* (paragraph 8), *peccadilloes* (11), *convivial* (11).

WRITING SUGGESTIONS

1. **For your Journal.** In your journal, make a list of the people

who have been significant in your life. You can either confine yourself to one category (for example, "significant others," "role models/mentors," or "friends") or you can mix categories. After each name try to capture in a sentence or two what was most significant or important about that person.

2. **For a Paragraph.** Using the journal entries above as a prewriting exercise, see if you can establish a classification scheme for those people to whom you are attracted. In a paragraph, classify the characteristics of those people. Try to find a coherent thesis to explain what you discover. Does this scheme reveal, for example, anything about your needs or values?

3. **For an Essay.** Make a list of two dozen or more recent films (from the last six months). Check your list against newspaper and magazine listings to make sure that it is fairly representative of what has been released, and not just movies you have seen. Then, using the list, devise a scheme of classification for these films. In addition to being descriptive, try to explain as well what such a classification reveals about our society and our tastes. Other possible subjects might include video or computer games, best-selling books, television shows, musical groups.

Prewriting:

a. Check a metropolitan newspaper. If necessary, do so in your campus library. Most Friday, Saturday, or Sunday editions include brief reviews of the new films. That will help you construct your scheme.

b. Talk to relatives and friends about recent films as well. That will give you an additional body of information.

c. Write the relevant pieces of information about each film on index cards. Sort the cards into as many categories as seem appropriate. Remember, however, that you do not want twelve categories, each of which contains a single example. Try to create a scheme that contains three to six categories.

Rewriting:

a. Look again at how you organized your classification scheme. Why begin with that category? Why end with that one? Complete the following: "The ordering principle in my essay is _____."

b. Since your reader will not have seen every one of these films, you will have to summarize each in a sentence or two. On the other hand, your essay should not consist just of summaries of the films. Make a copy of your paper and highlight in colored pen all of the sentences that summarize plot. Then look at what remains. Have you defined and analyzed the categories as well?

c. Find a peer reader and ask for some honest criticism. Did the reader find the essay interesting? Is the scheme too obvious? Are there enough examples to explain your categories?

4. **For Research**. What is "hot" and why? Select a range of popular items—for example, clothing styles, films, activities or sports, music, books, life-styles—that seem particularly important or popular right now. Collectively, what do these things say about our society and our values? In a research paper, classify what those items seem to have in common. Taken as a whole, how do they help define American society in the 1990s? Be sure to document your sources wherever appropriate.

PREDICTABLE CRISES OF ADULTHOOD

Gail Sheehy

Born in 1937 in Mamaroneck, New York, Gail Sheehy graduated from the University of Vermont with a double major in English and home economics. Her work includes numerous magazine articles, for which she won Best Magazine Writer from the Washington Journalism Review *in 1991. She has written ten books, including the best-selling,* Passages: The Predictable Crises of Adult Life *(1976). A sequel,* The Silent Passage: Menopause *(1992), has also brought her wide acclaim. Sheehy's books frequently have had the exploration of character development as their central theme. "I'm interested in human behavior and human growth," she has said. "I'm very hopeful about long-term maturing of civilized people[s], so I'm always fascinated by tracking how it happens in individuals."*

The following selection is taken from an introductory chapter of Passages, *a book which describes six different stages in adult life. The research for the book was drawn from 115 in-depth interviews Sheehy did with educated, middle-class people between the ages of 18 and 55. The appeal and influence of the book has lasted long after its initial publication. In a 1991 survey done by the Library of Congress and the Book-of-the-Month Club,* Passages *was ranked ninth among those books which have most influenced people.*

BEFORE READING

Connecting: How do you feel about knowing that there are "predictable" crises ahead in your life? Have you encountered any of the stages that Sheehy describes?

Anticipating: Although Sheehy's essay covers the period from ages 18 to 50, the majority of the essay is devoted to the period from the late 20s to the late 30s. Why?

We are not unlike a particularly hardy crustacean. The lobster grows by developing and shedding a series of hard, protective shells. Each time it expands from within, the confining shell must be sloughed off. 1

It is left exposed and vulnerable until, in time, a new covering grows to replace the old.

2   With each passage from one stage of human growth to the next we, too, must shed a protective structure. We are left exposed and vulnerable—but also yeasty and embryonic again, capable of stretching in ways we hadn't known before. These sheddings may take several years or more. Coming out of each passage, though, we enter a longer and more stable period in which we can expect relative tranquillity and a sense of equilibrium regained. . . .

3   As we shall see, each person engages the steps of development in his or her own characteristic *step-style*. Some people never complete the whole sequence. And none of us "solves" with one step—by jumping out of the parental home into a job or marriage, for example—the problems in separating from the caregivers of childhood. Nor do we "achieve" autonomy once and for all by converting our dreams into concrete goals, even when we attain those goals. The central issues or tasks of one period are never fully completed, tied up, and cast aside. But when they lose their primacy and the current life structure has served its purpose, we are ready to move on to the next period.

4   Can one catch up? What might look to others like listlessness, contrariness, a maddening refusal to face up to an obvious task may be a person's own unique detour that will bring him out later on the other side. Developmental gains won can later be lost—and rewon. It's plausible, though it can't be proven, that the mastery of one set of tasks fortifies us for the next period and the next set of challenges. But it's important not to think too mechanistically. Machines work by units. The bureaucracy (supposedly) works step by step. Human beings, thank God, have an individual inner dynamic that can never be precisely coded.

5   Although I have indicated the ages when Americans are likely to go through each stage, and the differences between men and women where they are striking, do not take the ages too seriously. The stages are the thing, and most particularly the sequence.

6   Here is the briefest outline of the developmental ladder.

PULLING UP ROOTS

7 Before 18, the motto is loud and clear: "I have to get away from my parents." But the words are seldom connected to action. Generally still safely part of our families, even if away at school, we feel our autonomy to be subject to erosion from moment to moment.

8   After 18, we begin Pulling Up Roots in earnest. College, military service, and short-term travels are all customary vehicles our so-

ciety provides for the first round trips between family and a base of one's own. In the attempt to separate our view of the world from our family's view, despite vigorous protestations to the contrary—"I know exactly what I want!"—we cast about for any beliefs we can call our own. And in the process of testing those beliefs we are often drawn to fads, preferably those most mysterious and inaccessible to our parents.

Whatever tentative memberships we try out in the world, the   9
fear haunts us that we are really kids who cannot take care of ourselves. We cover that fear with acts of defiance and mimicked confidence. For allies to replace our parents, we turn to our contemporaries. They become conspirators. So long as their perspective meshes with our own, they are able to substitute for the sanctuary of the family. But that doesn't last very long. And the instant they diverge from the shaky ideals of "our group," they are seen as betrayers. Rebounds to the family are common between the ages of 18 and 22.

The tasks of this passage are to locate ourselves in a peer group   10
role, a sex role, an anticipated occupation, an ideology or world view. As a result, we gather the impetus to leave home physically and the identity to *begin* leaving home emotionally.

Even as one part of us seeks to be an individual, another part   11
longs to restore the safety and comfort of merging with another. Thus one of the most popular myths of this passage is: We can piggyback our development by attaching to a Stronger One. But people who marry during this time often prolong financial and emotional ties to the family and relatives that impede them from becoming self-sufficient.

A stormy passage through the Pulling Up Roots years will   12
probably facilitate the normal progression of the adult life cycle. If one doesn't have an identity crisis at this point, it will erupt during a later transition, when the penalties may be harder to bear.

THE TRYING TWENTIES

The Trying Twenties confront us with the question of how to take   13
hold in the adult world. Our focus shifts from the interior turmoils of late adolescence—"Who am I?" "What is truth?"—and we become almost totally preoccupied with working out the externals. "How do I put my aspirations into effect?" "What is the best way to start?" "Where do I go?" "Who can help me?" "How did *you* do it?"

In this period, which is longer and more stable compared with   14
the passage that leads to it, the tasks are as enormous as they are exhilarating: To shape a Dream, that vision of ourselves which will gen-

---

erate energy, aliveness, and hope. To prepare for a lifework. To find a mentor if possible. And to form the capacity for intimacy, without losing in the process whatever consistency of self we have thus far mustered. The first test structure must be erected around the life we choose to try.

15   Doing what we "should" is the most pervasive theme of the twenties. The "shoulds" are largely defined by family models, the press of the culture, or the prejudices of our peers. If the prevailing cultural instructions are that one should get married and settle down behind one's own door, a nuclear family is born. If instead the peers insist that one should do one's own thing, the 25-year-old is likely to harness himself onto a Harley-Davidson and burn up Route 66 in the commitment to have no commitments.

16   One of the terrifying aspects of the twenties is the inner conviction that the choices we make are irrevocable. It is largely a false fear. Change is quite possible, and some alteration of our original choices is probably inevitable.

17   Two impulses, as always, are at work. One is to build a firm, safe structure for the future by making strong commitments, to "be set." Yet people who slip into a ready-made form without much self-examination are likely to find themselves *locked in*.

18   The other urge is to explore and experiment, keeping any structure tentative and therefore easily reversible. Taken to the extreme, these are people who skip from one trial job and one limited personal encounter to another, spending their twenties in the *transient* state.

19   Although the choices of our twenties are not irrevocable, they do set in motion a Life Pattern. Some of us follow the locked-in pattern, others the transient pattern, the wunderkind pattern, the caregiver pattern, and there are a number of others. Such patterns strongly influence the particular questions raised for each person during each passage. . . .

20   Buoyed by powerful illusions and belief in the power of the will, we commonly insist in our twenties that what we have chosen to do is the one true course in life. Our backs go up at the merest hint that we are like our parents, that two decades of parental training might be reflected in our current actions and attitudes.

21   "Not me," is the motto, "I'm different."

CATCH-30

22 Impatient with devoting ourselves to the "shoulds," a new vitality springs from within as we approach 30. Men and women alike speak of feeling too narrow and restricted. They blame all sorts of things, but what the restrictions boil down to are the outgrowth of career

Division and Classification

and personal choices of the twenties. They may have been choices perfectly suited to that stage. But now the fit feels different. Some inner aspect that was left out is striving to be taken into account. Important new choices must be made, and commitments altered or deepened. The work involves great change, turmoil, and often crisis—a simultaneous feeling of rock bottom and the urge to bust out.

One common response is the tearing up of the life we spent 23 most of our twenties putting together. It may mean striking out on a secondary road toward a new vision or converting a dream of "running for president" into a more realistic goal. The single person feels a push to find a partner. The woman who was previously content at home with children chafes to venture into the world. The childless couple reconsiders children. And almost everyone who is married, especially those married for seven years, feels a discontent.

If the discontent doesn't lead to a divorce, it will, or should, call 24 for a serious review of the marriage and of each partner's aspirations in their Catch-30 condition. The gist of that condition was expressed by a 29-year-old associate with a Wall Street law firm:

"I'm considering leaving the firm. I've been there four years 25 now; I'm getting good feedback, but I have no clients of my own. I feel weak. If I wait much longer, it will be too late, too close to that fateful time of decision on whether or not to become a partner. I'm success-oriented. But the concept of being 55 years old and stuck in a monotonous job drives me wild. It drives me crazy now, just a little bit. I'd say that 85 percent of the time I thoroughly enjoy my work. But when I get a screwball case, I come away from court saying, 'What am I doing here?' It's a *visceral* reaction that I'm wasting my time. I'm trying to find some way to make a social contribution or a slot in city government. I keep saying, 'There's something more.'"

Besides the push to broaden himself professionally, there is a 26 wish to expand his personal life. He wants two or three more children. "The concept of a home has become very meaningful to me, a place to get away from troubles and relax. I love my son in a way I could not have anticipated. I never could live alone."

Consumed with the work of making his own critical life-steer- 27 ing decisions, he demonstrates the essential shift at this age: an absolute requirement to be more self-concerned. The self has new value now that his competency has been proved.

His wife is struggling with her own age-30 priorities. She wants 28 to go to law school, but he wants more children. If she is going to stay home, she wants him to make more time for the family instead of taking on even wider professional commitments. His view of the bind, of what he would most like from his wife, is this:

29

"I'd like not to be bothered. It sounds cruel, but I'd like not to have to worry about what she's going to do next week. Which is why I've told her several times that I think she should do something. Go back to school and get a degree in social work or geography or whatever. Hopefully that would fulfill her, and then I wouldn't have to worry about her line of problems. I want her to be decisive about herself."

30 The trouble with his advice to his wife is that it comes out of concern with *his* convenience, rather than with *her* development. She quickly picks up on this lack of goodwill: He is trying to dispose of her. At the same time, he refuses her the same latitude to be "selfish" in making an independent decision to broaden her own horizons. Both perceive a lack of mutuality. And that is what Catch-30 is all about for the couple.

ROOTING AND EXTENDING

31 Life becomes less provisional, more rational and orderly in the early thirties. We begin to settle down in the full sense. Most of us begin putting down roots and sending out new shoots. People buy houses and become very earnest about climbing career ladders. Men in particular concern themselves with "making it." Satisfaction with marriage generally goes downhill in the thirties (for those who have remained together) compared with the highly valued, vision-supporting marriage of the twenties. This coincides with the couple's reduced social life outside the family and the in-turned focus on raising their children.

THE DEADLINE DECADE

32 In the middle of the thirties we come upon a crossroads. We have reached the halfway mark. Yet even as we are reaching our prime, we begin to see there is a place where it finishes. Time starts to squeeze.

33 The loss of youth, the faltering of physical powers we have always taken for granted, the fading purpose of stereotyped roles by which we have thus far identified ourselves, the spiritual dilemma of having no absolute answers—any or all of these shocks can give this passage the character of crisis. Such thoughts usher in a decade between 35 and 45 that can be called the Deadline Decade. It is a time of both danger and opportunity. All of us have the chance to rework the narrow identity by which we defined ourselves in the first half of life. And those of us who make the most of the opportunity will have a full-out authenticity crisis.

34 To come through this authenticity crisis, we must reexamine our purposes and reevaluate how to spend our resources from now

on. "Why am I doing all this? What do I really believe in?" No matter what we have been doing, there will be parts of ourselves that have been suppressed and now need to find expression. "Bad" feelings will demand acknowledgment along with the good.

It is frightening to step off onto the treacherous footbridge 35 leading to the second half of life. We can't take everything with us on this journey through uncertainty. Along the way, we discover that we are alone. We no longer have to ask permission because we are the providers of our own safety. We must learn to give ourselves permission. We stumble upon feminine or masculine aspects of our natures that up to this time have usually been masked. There is grieving to be done because an old self is dying. By taking in our suppressed and even our unwanted parts, we prepare at the gut level for the reintegration of an identity that is ours and ours alone—not some artificial form put together to please the culture or our mates. It is a dark passage at the beginning. But by disassembling ourselves, we can glimpse the light and gather our parts into a renewal.

Women sense this inner crossroads earlier than men do. The 36 time pinch often prompts a woman to stop and take an all-points survey at age 35. Whatever options she has already played out, she feels a "my last chance" urgency to review those options she has set aside and those that aging and biology will close off in the *now foreseeable* future. For all her qualms and confusion about where to start looking for a new future, she usually enjoys an exhilaration of release. Assertiveness begins rising. There are so many firsts ahead.

Men, too, feel the time push in the mid-thirties. Most men re- 37 spond by pressing down harder on the career accelerator. It's "my last chance" to pull away from the pack. It is no longer enough to be the loyal junior executive, the promising young novelist, the lawyer who does a little *pro bono* work on the side. He wants now to become part of top management, to be recognized as an established writer, or an active politician with his own legislative program. With some chagrin, he discovers that he has been too anxious to please and too vulnerable to criticism. He wants to put together his own ship.

During this period of intense concentration on external ad- 38 vancement, it is common for men to be unaware of the more difficult, gut issues that are propelling them forward. The survey that was neglected at 35 becomes a crucible at 40. Whatever rung of achievement he has reached, the man of 40 usually feels stale, restless, burdened, and unappreciated. He worries about his health. He wonders, "Is this all there is?" He may make a series of departures from well established lifelong base lines, including marriage. More and more men are seeking second careers in midlife. Some become self-destructive. And many men in their forties experience a major shift of emphasis away from pouring all their energies into their own advancement. A more tender, feeling side comes into play. They become interested in developing an ethical self.

RENEWAL OR RESIGNATION

39 Somewhere in the mid-forties, equilibrium is regained. A new stability is achieved, which may be more or less satisfying.

40 If one has refused to budge through the midlife transition, the sense of staleness will calcify into resignation. One by one, the safety and supports will be withdrawn from the person who is standing still. Parents will become children; children will become strangers; a mate will grow away or go away; the career will become just a job—and each of these events will be felt as an abandonment. The crisis will probably emerge again around 50. And although its wallop will be greater, the jolt may be just what is needed to prod the resigned middle-ager toward seeking revitalization.

41 On the other hand . . .

42 If we have confronted ourselves in the middle passage and found a renewal of purpose around which we are eager to build a more authentic life structure, these may well be the best years. Personal happiness takes a sharp turn upward for partners who can now accept the fact: "I cannot expect *anyone* to fully understand me." Parents can be forgiven for the burdens of our childhood. Children can be let go without leaving us in collapsed silence. At 50, there is a new warmth and mellowing. Friends become more important than ever, but so does privacy. Since it is so often proclaimed by people past midlife, the motto of this stage might be "No more bullshit."

QUESTIONS ON SUBJECT AND PURPOSE

1. In what senses are these crises "predictable"? What does that word suggest?
2. How sharply drawn—and how ironclad—are Sheehy's divisions? Why?
3. What purpose might Sheehy have in writing?

QUESTIONS ON STRATEGY AND AUDIENCE

1. What is the effect of subdividing the text by using headings?
2. Why might Sheehy choose to use "we" instead of "one" or "he" or "she"?

Division and Classification

3. How precisely can you define Sheehy's audience? What features of the selection suggest that definition?

QUESTIONS ON VOCABULARY AND STYLE

1. Why might Sheehy begin with the analogy to the lobster? What is appropriate about that analogy?
2. Why might Sheehy "quote" the response of a 29-year-old in paragraphs 25, 26, and 29?
3. Be prepared to define the following words: *sloughed* (1), *autonomy* (3), *impetus* (10), *wunderkind* (19), *chafes* (23), *visceral* (25), *"pro bono"* (37), *chagrin* (37), *calcify* (40).

WRITING SUGGESTIONS

1. **For your Journal.** Think about your friends who are roughly the same age as you. Can you see in their lives and your own any similarities so far? In your journal, make a list of your contemporaries, and jot down what has happened to them, what decisions they are faced with, what questions or problems seem most important to them.
2. **For a Paragraph.** Natural processes, such as the stages of development in the life cycle, provide good examples of how division differs from classification. To analyze such processes, you must subdivide a whole into its parts rather than separate many things into categories. Select any natural process—perhaps from a course you are taking this semester or term—and describe in a substantial paragraph its major stages or subdivisions.
3. **For an Essay.** Sheehy begins her division with people older than 18. Drawing from your own life experiences, and those of your siblings, children, and friends, construct a division that covers the teenage years—from 13 to 19. What subdivisions seem common to Americans between those ages? Other possibilities might be to focus on very young children (if you have children of your own), or to focus on people age 50 and older.

Prewriting:
a. If you are analyzing the teenage years, take six sheets of blank paper, and on the top of each, write a different age. Then on the page below, list everything that you can think of that happened to you (and to your siblings or children, if

relevant) during that year. Work on your sheets over a several-day period.

b. Brainstorm with a friend or family member about the significant moments or events that occurred during those years. Take notes. Do you see any general patterns beginning to emerge?

c. Reread the Sheehy article. Notice how she establishes her subdivisions, how she characterizes each. As you plan your subdivisions, ask yourself if you have provided similar significant generalizations about each stage.

Rewriting:

a. Look back over your notes from your brainstorming session. Did anyone say something that might be quoted? Notice how Sheehy uses quotations in her text. Try the same device in yours.

b. As a rule of thumb, try for no more than three subdivisions. Remember that Sheehy covered 30 to 35 years in six stages.

c. Look at your introduction. Have you tried to catch your reader's interest? Or have you written a standard thesis introduction ("Teenagers pass through three distinct stages on their way to adulthood")? How would *Time* or *Newsweek* begin a story on this topic?

4. For Research. Sheehy ends her division with those aged 50. Obviously, however, adults continue to develop and change until death. Drawing upon published research and interviews with those over 50, write a research paper in which you identify the stages through which older Americans pass. Be sure to document your sources wherever appropriate.

SHADES OF BLACK
Mary Mebane

Mary Elizabeth Mebane (1933–1992), novelist, teacher, and civil rights activist, was born in Durham, North Carolina. She received her Ph.D. at the University of North Carolina. Her writings deal mainly with the African American experience in the South and the new consciousness that was born during the years of the civil rights movement. Her most widely acclaimed books are her autobiographies: Mary *(1981) and* Mary, Wayfarer *(1983).*

In her autobiographies, Mebane recounts her struggles to escape poverty and prejudice. The prejudice she encountered was not just from whites. In Mary, *the book from which this selection is taken, Mebane details her treatment by both her family and by other African Americans. In this excerpt, she describes the particular prejudice encountered by "black black" women.*

BEFORE READING

Connecting: Probably no one is able to escape being prejudiced in one way or another, even if we do not show it overtly. Is there someone—either a particular person or a member of a particular group—toward whom you either feel or exhibit prejudice?

Anticipating: Mebane mixes personal experience with observations on human behavior. How does that strategy contribute to the effectiveness of her writing? What if, for example, she had just discussed the prejudice in general terms?

During my first week of classes as a freshman, I was stopped one day 1
in the hall by the chairman's wife, who was indistinguishable in color
from a white woman. She wanted to see me, she said.

This woman had no official position on the faculty, except that 2
she was an instructor in English; nevertheless, her summons had to
be obeyed. In the segregated world there were (and remain) gross
abuses of authority because those at the pinnacle, and even their
spouses, felt that the people "under" them had no recourse except to
submit—and they were right except that sometimes a black who got
sick and tired of it would go to the whites and complain. This course
of action was severely condemned by the blacks, but an interesting

thing happened—such action always got positive results. Power was thought of in negative terms: I can deny someone something, I can strike at someone who can't strike back, I can ride someone down; that proves I am powerful. The concept of power as a force for good, for affirmative response to people or situations, was not in evidence.

3   When I went to her office, she greeted me with a big smile. "You know," she said, "you made the highest mark on the verbal part of the examination." She was referring to the examination that the entire freshman class took upon entering the college. I looked at her but I didn't feel warmth, for in spite of her smile her eyes and tone of voice were saying, "How could this black-skinned girl score higher on the verbal than some of the students who've had more advantages than she? It must be some sort of fluke. Let me talk to her." I felt it, but I managed to smile my thanks and back off. For here at North Carolina College at Durham, as it had been since the beginning, social class and color were the primary criteria used in determining status on the campus.

4   First came the children of doctors, lawyers, and college teachers. Next came the children of public-school teachers, businessmen, and anybody else who had access to more money than the poor black working class. After that came the bulk of the student population, the children of the working class, most of whom were the first in their families to go beyond high school. The attitude toward them was: You're here because we need the numbers, but in all other things defer to your betters.

5   The faculty assumed that light-skinned students were more intelligent, and they were always a bit nonplussed when a dark-skinned student did well, especially if she was a girl. They had reason to be appalled when they discovered that I planned to do not only well but better than my light-skinned peers.

6   I don't know whether African men recently transported to the New World considered themselves handsome or, more important, whether they considered African women beautiful in comparison with Native American Indian women or immigrant European women. It is a question that I have never heard raised or seen research on. If African men considered African women beautiful, just when their shift in interest away from black black women occurred might prove to be an interesting topic for researchers. But one thing I know for sure: by the twentieth century, really black skin on a woman was considered ugly in this country. This was particularly true among those who were exposed to college.

7   Hazel, who was light brown, used to say to me, "You are *dark*, but not *too* dark." The saved commiserating with the damned. I had

the feeling that if nature had painted one more brushstroke on me, I'd have had to kill myself.

Black skin was to be disguised at all costs. Since a black face is 8 rather hard to disguise, many women took refuge in ludicrous makeup. Mrs. Burry, one of my teachers in elementary school, used white face powder. But she neglected to powder her neck and arms, and even the black on her face gleamed through the white, giving her an eerie appearance. But she did the best she could.

I observed all through elementary and high school that for var- 9 ious entertainments the girls were placed on the stage in order of color. And very black ones didn't get into the front row. If they were past caramel-brown, to the back row they would go. And nobody questioned the justice of these decisions—neither the students nor the teachers.

One of the teachers at Wildwood School, who was from the 10 Deep South and was just as black as she could be, had been a strict enforcer of these standards. That was another irony—that someone who had been judged outside the realm of beauty herself because of her skin tones should have adopted them so wholeheartedly and applied them herself without question.

One girl stymied that teacher, though. Ruby, a black cherry of 11 a girl, not only got off the back row but off the front row as well, to stand alone at stage center. She could outsing, outdance, and outdeclaim everyone else, and talent proved triumphant over pigmentation. But the May Queen and her Court (and in high school, Miss Wildwood) were always chosen from among the lighter ones.

When I was a freshman in high school, it became clear that a 12 light-skinned sophomore girl named Rose was going to get the "best girl scholar" prize for the next three years, and there was nothing I could do about it, even though I knew I was the better. Rose was caramel-colored and had shoulder-length hair. She was highly favored by the science and math teacher, who figured the averages. I wasn't. There was only one prize. Therefore, Rose would get it until she graduated. I was one year behind her, and I would not get it until after she graduated.

To be held in such low esteem was painful. It was difficult not to 13 feel that I had been cheated out of the medal, which I felt that, in a fair competition, I perhaps would have won. Being unable to protest or do anything about it was a traumatic experience for me. From then on I instinctively tended to avoid the college-exposed dark-skinned male, knowing that when he looked at me he saw himself and, most of the time, his mother and sister as well, and since he had rejected his blackness, he had rejected theirs and mine.

Oddly enough, the lighter-skinned black male did not seem to 14 feel so much prejudice toward the black black woman. It was no accident, I felt, that Mr. Harrison, the eighth-grade teacher, who was reddish-yellow himself, once protested to the science and math teacher about the fact that he always assigned sweeping duties to Doris and Ruby Lee, two black black girls. Mr. Harrison said to them one day, right in the other teacher's presence, "You must be some bad girls. Every day I come down here ya'll are sweeping." The science and math teacher got the point and didn't ask them to sweep any-more.

15   Uneducated black males, too, sometimes related very well to the black black woman. They had been less firmly indoctrinated by the white society around them and were more securely rooted in their own culture.

16   Because of the stigma attached to having dark skin, a black black woman had to do many things to find a place for herself. One possibility was to attach herself to a light-skinned woman, hoping that some of the magic would rub off on her. A second was to make herself sexually available, hoping to attract a mate. Third, she could resign herself to a more chaste life-style—either (for the professional woman) teaching and work in established churches or (for the uneducated woman) domestic work and zealous service in the Holy and Sanctified churches.

17   Even as a young girl, Lucy had chosen the first route. Lucy was short, skinny, short-haired, and black black, and thus unacceptable. So she made her choice. She selected Patricia, the lightest-skinned girl in the school, as her friend, and followed her around. Patricia and her friends barely tolerated Lucy, but Lucy smiled and doggedly hung on, hoping that some who noticed Patricia might notice her, too. Though I felt shame for her behavior, even then I understood.

18   As is often the case of the victim agreeing with and adopting the attitudes of oppressor, so I have seen it with black black women. I have seen them adopt the oppressor's attitude that they are nothing but "sex machines," and their supposedly superior sexual perform-ance becomes their sole reason for being and for esteeming them-selves. Such women learn early that in order to make themselves attractive to men they have somehow to shift the emphasis from physical beauty to some other area—usually sexual performance. Their constant talk is of their desirability and their ability to gratify a man sexually.

19   I knew two such women well—both of them black black. To hear their endless talk of sexual conquests was very sad. I have never seen the category that these women fall into described anywhere. It is not that of promiscuity or nymphomania. It is the category of total self-rejection: "Since I am black, I am ugly, I am nobody. I will per-

form on the level that they have assigned to me." Such women are the pitiful results of what not only white America but also, and more important, black America has done to them.

Some, not taking the sexuality route but still accepting black society's view of their worthlessness, swing all the way across to intense religiosity. Some are staunch, fervent workers in the more traditional Southern churches—Baptist and Methodist—and others are leaders and ministers in the lower status, more evangelical Holiness sects.

Another avenue open to the black black woman is excellence in a career. Since in the South the field most accessible to such women is education, a great many of them prepared to become teachers. But here, too, the black black woman had problems. Grades weren't given to her lightly in school, nor were promotions on the job. Consequently, she had to prepare especially well. She had to pass examinations with flying colors or be left behind; she knew that she would receive no special consideration. She had to be overqualified for a job because otherwise she didn't stand a chance of getting it—and she was competing only with other blacks. She had to have something to back her up: not charm, not personality—but training.

The black black woman's training would pay off in the 1970s. With the arrival of integration the black black woman would find, paradoxically enough, that her skin color in an integrated situation was not the handicap it had been in an all-black situation. But it wasn't until the middle and late 1960s, when the post-1945 generation of black males arrived on college campuses, that I noticed any change in the situation at all. *He* wore an afro and *she* wore an afro, and sometimes the only way you could tell them apart was when his afro was taller than hers. Black had become beautiful, and the really black girl was often selected as queen of various campus activities. It was then that the dread I felt at dealing with the college-educated black male began to ease. Even now, though, when I have occasion to engage in any type of transaction with a college-educated black man, I gauge his age. If I guess he was born after 1945, I feel confident that the transaction will turn out all right. If he probably was born before 1945, my stomach tightens, I find myself taking shallow breaths, and I try to state my business and escape as soon as possible.

QUESTIONS ON SUBJECT AND PURPOSE

1. What kinds of prejudice and discrimination did Mebane encounter? What were the reasons for that discrimination?

2. How does Mebane mix personal experience with commentary on human behavior? Does the mixture seem to work? What does it add to the selection?

3. What is Mebane's purpose in writing?

QUESTIONS ON STRATEGY AND AUDIENCE

1. How is classification used in the selection? How many classifications are made?
2. How is the selection structured? Make a sketchy outline of the organization. What does it reveal?
3. How does Mebane use examples in her classification scheme? Are there examples for all of the categories? Why or why not?

QUESTIONS ON VOCABULARY AND STYLE

1. How does Mebane describe the shades of black? What types of adjectives, for example, does she use?
2. What is the difference between "established churches" and "Holy and Sanctified churches" (paragraph 16)? Why does Mebane use the capital letters?
3. Be able to define the following words: *fluke* (paragraph 3), *nonplussed* (5), *commiserate* (7), *stymied* (11), *traumatic* (13), *indoctrinated* (15), *chaste* (16), *staunch* (20).

WRITING SUGGESTIONS

1. **For your Journal.** Spend a day being very conscious of your own behavior and the behavior of others around you. In your journal, keep a list of every instance in which you saw prejudiced behavior. Such behavior might be based on physical appearance, socioeconomic background, sexual orientation, age, gender, race, or anything else.
2. **For a Paragraph.** In a paragraph, explore one of the types of prejudice that you recorded in your journal. Classify the reactions that you observed in others or in yourself.
3. **For an Essay.** Have you or a friend ever been classified by someone and discriminated against as a result? In an essay, use your experience to show how and why that classification was made. If you have not had this experience, turn the question around. Have you ever classified someone and discriminated against that person as a result?

Prewriting:

a. If you have encountered discrimination, you will probably have a wide range of experiences from which to draw. If you have not, you will need to examine closely your own behavior. Either way, make a list of possible experiences.

b. Remember that prejudices are based on stereotypes that distort, reduce, ridicule. Your essay should expose the inadequacies of such ways of thinking; it should not celebrate any form of discrimination.

c. Once you have gathered examples, you must decide which ones you will include. As you saw in Chapter 1, sometimes one well-developed, appropriate example is enough; other times, a number of examples are necessary. Do not try to include every experience. Decide which ones on your list seem most promising.

d. Try freewriting about each of the examples. Set each of those freewritings aside until it is time to assemble a draft of the complete essay.

Rewriting:

a. Remember that your examples should reveal the discrimination at work. Do not just tell your readers; show them. Look carefully at your draft to see if you have made the examples dramatic and vivid enough.

b. In drawing upon your experiences in this way, your essay will probably make use of narrative as well as classification strategies. Look back through Chapter 2 to review the principles of effective narration. See how closely you followed that advice.

c. Once you have a draft of your essay, spend some time rereading and studying Mebane's essay. Notice how she tells her story, how she reveals prejudice, how she makes transitions from one aspect of the topic to another.

4. For Research. Research the problems encountered in interracial, interreligious, intercultural, or same-sex relationships. What types of prejudice do couples encounter? Classify those prejudices. In addition to library research, you might want to interview some people involved in these relationships. Be sure to have a controlling thesis and to document your sources wherever appropriate.

FACES OF THE ENEMY

Sam Keen

Sam Keen was raised in Maryville, Tennessee, and graduated from Prince-ton with a Ph.D. in philosophy. He is sometimes called a "vagabond philoso-pher" because his writing frequently blends psychology, philosophy, and theology. He has written over ten books, including his recent best-seller, Fire in the Belly: On Being a Man *(1991).*

In his book Faces of the Enemy *(1985), which was made into an award-winning television program, Keen blends psychology and sociology to discuss how paranoia and the "hostile imagination" cast our enemies into stereotypical images of evil. This essay, which first appeared in* Esquire, *is a synopsis of that book. "Wars come and go," writes Keen, "the images we use to dehumanize our enemies remain strangely the same."*

BEFORE READING

Connecting: Can you remember a time when you regarded some-one as your "enemy" or someone saw you as the "enemy"? To what extent did "name calling," for example, reveal something about the process of dehumanization that went on in that relationship?

Anticipating: Keen's examples are drawn from wars. In what other contexts does the same type of distancing or dehumanization take place? Can you apply Keen's categories in other situations? Could you add other categories?

1   The world, as always, is debating the issues of war and peace. Con-servatives believe safety lies in more arms and increased firepower. Liberals place their trust in disarmament and a nuclear freeze. I sug-gest we will be saved by neither fire nor ice, that the solutions being offered by the political right and left miss the mark. Our problem lies not in our technology, but in our minds, in our ancient tendency to create our enemies in our own imagination.

2   Our best hope for avoiding war is to understand the psychology of this enmity, the ways in which our mind works to produce our habits of paranoia, projection, and the making of propaganda. How do we create our enemies and turn the world into a killing ground?

We first need to answer some inevitable objections, raised by 3
the advocates of power politics, who say: "You can't psychologize political conflict. You can't solve the problem of war by studying perception. We don't *create* enemies. There are real aggressors—Hitler,
Stalin, Qaddafi."

True: There are always political, economic, and territorial 4
causes of war. Wars come and go; the images we use to dehumanize
our enemies remain strangely the same. The unchanging projections
of the hostile imagination are continually imposed onto changing historical circumstances. Not that the enemy is innocent of these projections—as popular wisdom has it, paranoids sometimes have *real*
enemies. Nevertheless, to understand the hostile imagination we
need to temporarily ignore the question of guilt and innocence. Our
quest is for an understanding of the unchanging images we place on
the enemy.

THE ENEMY AS CREATED BY PARANOIA

Paranoia is not an occasional individual pathology, but rather it is the 5
human condition. History shows us that, with few exceptions, social
cohesion within tribes is maintained by paranoia: when we do not
have enemies, we invent them. The group identity of a people depends on division between insiders and outsiders, us and them, the
tribe and the enemy.

The first meaning of *the enemy* is simply the stranger, the alien. 6
The bond of tribal membership is maintained by projecting hostile
and divisive emotions upon the outsider. Paranoia forms the mold
from which we create enemies.

In the paranoid imagination, *alien* means the same as *evil*, while 7
the tribe itself is defined as good: a single network of malevolent intent stretches over the rest of the world. "They" are out to get "us."
All occurrences prove the basic assumption that an outside power is
conspiring against the community.

THE ENEMY AS ENEMY OF GOD

In the language of rhetoric, every war is a crusade, a "just" war, a bat- 8
tle between good and evil. Warfare is a ritual in which the sacred
blood of our heroes is sacrificed to destroy the enemies of God.

We like to think that theocracies and holy wars ended with the 9
coming of the Industrial Revolution and the emergence of secular
cultures in the West. Yet in World War I the kaiser was pictured as
the devil; in World War II both Germany and the U.S. proclaimed
Gott mit uns, "In God We Trust"; each accused the other of being
Christ-killers. Sophisticated politicians may insist that the conflict

between the U.S. and the USSR is a matter of pragmatic power politics, but theological dimensions have not disappeared. President Reagan warns us against "the aggressive impulses of an evil empire" and asks us to "pray for the salvation of all those who live in totalitarian darkness, pray they will discover the joy of knowing God."

10   By picturing the enemy as the enemy of God we convert the guilt associated with murder into pride. A warrior who kills such an enemy strikes a blow for truth and goodness. Remorse isn't necessary. The warrior engaged in righteous battle against the enemies of God may even see himself as a priest, saving his enemy from the grip of evil by killing him.

THE ENEMY AS BARBARIAN

11   The enemy not only is a demon but is also a destroyer of culture. If he is human at all, he is brutish, dumb, and cruel, lower on the scale of evolution than The People. To the Greeks he was a barbarian. To the Americans he was, most recently, a "gook" or "slant." To the South African he is a black or "colored."

12   The barbarian theme was used widely in World War II propaganda by all participants. Nazi anti-semitic tracts contrasted the sunny, healthy Aryan with the inferior, dark, and contaminated races—Jews, Gypsies, Eastern Europeans. American soldiers were pictured as Chicago-style gangsters. Blacks were portrayed as quasigorillas despoiling the artistic achievements of European civilization. One poster used in Holland warned the Dutch that their supposed "liberators" were a mélange of KKK, jazz-crazed blacks, convicts, hangmen, and mad bombers. In turn, the U.S. frequently pictured the Germans as a Nazi horde of dark monsters on a mindless rampage.

13   The image of the barbarian represents a force to be feared: power without intelligence, matter without mind, an enemy that must be conquered by culture. The warrior who defeats the barbarian is a culture hero, keeping the dark powers in abeyance.

THE ENEMY AS RAPIST

14   Associated with the enemy as barbarian is the image of the enemy as rapist, the destroyer of motherhood.

15   As rapist, the enemy is lust defiling innocence. He is according to Nazi propaganda the Jew who lurks in the shadows waiting to seduce Aryan girls. Or in the propaganda of the Ku Klux Klan he is the black man with an insatiable lust for white women. In American war posters he is the Jap carrying away the naked Occidental woman.

Division and Classification

The portrait of the enemy as rapist, destroyer of the madonna, 16
warns us of danger and awakens our pornographic imagination by reminding us of the enticement of rape. The appeal to sexual adventure
is a sine qua non in motivating men to go to war: To the warrior belong the spoils, and chief among the spoils are the enemy's women.

THE ENEMY AS BEAST, INSECT, REPTILE

The power of bestial images to degrade is rooted in the neurotic 17
structure of the hostile imagination. Karen Horney has shown that
neurosis always involves a movement between glorified and degraded
images of the self. In warfare we act out a mass neurosis whereby we
glorify ourselves as agents of God and project our feelings of degradation and impotence upon the enemy. We are suprahuman; therefore they must be subhuman. By destroying the bestial and
contaminated enemy we can gain immortality, escape evil, transcend
decay and death.

THE ENEMY AS DEATH

In the iconography of propaganda, the enemy is the bringer of death. 18
He is Death riding on a bomb, the Grim Reaper cutting down youth
in its prime. His face is stripped of flesh, his body a dangling skeleton.

War is an irrational ritual. Generation after generation we sac- 19
rifice our substance in a vain effort to kill some essential enemy. Now
he wears an American or Soviet face. A moment ago he was a Nazi, a
Jew, a Moslem, a Christian, a pagan. But the true face of the enemy,
as Saint Paul said, is Death itself. The unconscious power that motivates us to fight for Peace, kill for Life, is the magical assumption that
if we can destroy this particular enemy we can defeat Death.

Lying within each of us is the desire for immortality. And be- 20
cause this near-instinctive desire for immortality is balanced by the
precariously repressed fear that death might really eradicate all traces
of our existence, we will go to any extreme to reassure ourselves. By
submitting to the divine ordeal of war, in which we are willing to die
or kill the enemy who *is* Death, we affirm our own deathlessness.

THE RELUCTANT KILLERS

It is easy to despair when we look at the human genius for creating 21
enemies in the image of our own disowned vices. When we add our
mass paranoia and projection to our constantly progressing weapons
technology, it seems we are doomed to destroy ourselves.

But the persistent archetypal images of the enemy may point in 22
a more hopeful direction. We demean our enemies not because we

are instinctively sadistic, but because it is difficult for us to kill others whom we recognize as fully human beings. Our natural empathy, our instinct for compassion, is strong: society does what it must to attempt to overcome the moral imperative that forbids us from killing.

23   Even so, the effort is successful only for a minority. In spite of our best propaganda, few men and women will actually try to kill an enemy. In his book *Men Against Fire*, Brigadier General S.L.A. Marshall presents the results of his study of American soldiers under fire during World War II. He discovered that *in combat* the percentage of men who would fire their rifle at the enemy *even once* did not rise above 25 percent, and the more usual figure was 15 percent. He further discovered that the fear of killing was every bit as strong as the fear of dying.

24   If it is difficult to mold men into killers, we may still hope to transform our efforts from fighting an outward enemy to doing battle with our own paranoia. Our true war is our struggle against the antagonistic mind. Our true enemy is our propensity to make enemies. The highest form of moral courage requires us to look at ourselves from another perspective, to repent, and to reown our own shadows. True self-knowledge introduces self-doubt into our minds. And self-doubt is a healthy counterbalance to the dogmatic, self-righteous certainty that governs political rhetoric and behavior; it is, therefore, the beginning of compassion.

QUESTIONS ON SUBJECT AND PURPOSE

1. According to Keen, why do we give "faces" to our enemies?
2. What characteristics do all of the "faces" share?
3. Why might Keen be writing about this subject? What might he hope to accomplish?

QUESTIONS ON STRATEGY AND AUDIENCE

1. Into how many categories does Keen classify the images that we create of our enemies?
2. How are those categories ordered or arranged?
3. Obviously Keen's essay has the greatest meaning when a nation is at war. However, what other possible applications might his audience find in this essay?

QUESTIONS ON VOCABULARY AND STYLE

1. Why might Keen have used the word "face" rather than "image"?

2. Keen's essay contains quite a few words that readers might need to check in a dictionary. On the other hand, the essay is still informal in tone and quite readable. What does this mixture suggest about Keen's sense of his readers?

3. Be prepared to define the following words: *enmity* (1), *paranoia* (2), *pathology* (5), *divisive* (6), *malevolent* (7), *theocracies* (9), *totalitarian* (9), *despoiling* (12), *melange* (12), *rampage* (12), *abeyance* (13), *defiling* (15), *insatiable* (15), *sine qua non* (16), *bestial* (17), *neurosis* (17), *iconography* (18), *eradicate* (19), *archetypal* (22), *demean* (22), *propensity* (24)

WRITING SUGGESTIONS

1. For your Journal. Many of Keen's observations are equally applicable in any situation involving prejudice and bigotry. Select one type of prejudice common in our society—perhaps it has been directed at you—and in your journal explore the significance of the "faces" or the "names" that are associated with that prejudice.

2. For a Paragraph. Stereotypes are also "faces." Select a stereotype, and explore in a paragraph the associations that are instantly made with that stereotype. How are these associations reductive and dehumanizing? Be sure to formulate a thesis that explains what is going on in the process—do not just record a series of observations.

3. For an Essay. The "them–us" distinction underlies all forms of prejudice and bigotry. Select a common form of prejudice (such as one based on race, religion, nationality, gender, age, sexual orientation, or physical or mental characteristics), and classify the types of "faces" that are assigned to that group. What do such "faces" reveal about us?

Prewriting:

a. Brainstorm for a possible topic. Spend some time just making a list of possibilities. Add to your list over a three-day period.

b. Rule off a sheet of paper into six equal blocks. Down the left-hand margin list your possible topics. Then in the five blocks running from left to right, list the various categories that each topic suggests.

c. Examine your grid carefully. How many categories or subdivisions have you established for each topic? Remember that you ought to have at least three. Check to make sure that the categories are parallel in form.

Rewriting:

a. Look carefully at your introduction. Do you attempt to catch your reader's attention? Reread the body of your essay several times. Now freewrite a new introduction to your paper. Imagine that your article will appear in a magazine, so work to grab and hold your reader's interest.

b. Have you provided enough examples and details for each category? Remember that your paragraphs need to be developed. No body paragraph in this type of essay should be only two or three sentences in length.

c. Look back at how you arranged the parts in your classification scheme. Is this the best order? How did you decide which parts to place first and last? The order should be a conscious decision on your part. Make a copy of your paper, cut it apart, and rearrange the body paragraphs. Experiment—even if you decide to stay with your original plan.

4. For Research. Although Keen's examples include no contemporary religious, ethnic, or nationalistic conflicts, we do not, unfortunately, need to look very hard to find similar examples in the late 1990s. Choose one of the many conflicts that rage today (for example, in southern Africa, the mideast, central Europe), and research how each side characterizes its opposition, the "faces" each side uses to depict its enemy. Classify these images in a research paper, explaining how they fuel or contribute to the conflict. Be sure to document your sources wherever appropriate.

THE VALUE OF CHILDREN:
A TAXONOMICAL ESSAY

Bernard R. Berelson

Bernard R. Berelson (1912–1979) was born in Spokane, Washington, and received a Ph.D. from the University of Chicago. He divided his time between the academic world and the world of international development assistance. In 1962, he joined the Population Council, eventually serving as its president until his retirement in 1974. Berelson published extensively on population policy and the prospects for fertility declines in developing countries.

Berelson's concern with population policy is obvious in this essay reprinted from the Annual Report *of the Population Council. Using a clear scheme of classification, Berelson analyzes the reasons why people want children.*

BEFORE READING

Connecting: The phrase, "the value of children," might seem a little unusual. What, for example, was your "value" to your parents? If you have children, in what sense do they have "value" to you?

Anticipating: Despite the many reasons for having or wanting children, people in many societies today consciously choose to limit the number of children that they have. How might Berelson explain this phenomenon?

Why do people want children? It is a simple question to ask, perhaps an impossible one to answer. 1

Throughout most of human history, the question never seemed to need a reply. These years, however, the question has a new tone. It is being asked in a nonrhetorical way because of three revolutions in thought and behavior that characterize the latter decades of the twentieth century: the vital revolution in which lower death rates have given rise to the population problem and raise new issues about human fertility; the sexual revolution from reproduction; and the women's revolution, in which childbearing and –rearing no longer are being accepted as the only or even the primary roles of half the 2 human race. Accordingly, for about the first time, the question of why people want children now can be asked, so to speak, with a straight face.

3 "Why" questions of this kind, with simple surfaces but profound depths, are not answered or settled; they are ventilated, explicated, clarified. Anything as complex as the motives for having children can be classified in various ways, and any such taxonomy has an arbitrary character to it. This one starts with chemistry and proceeds to spirit.

THE BIOLOGICAL

4 Do people innately want children for some built-in reason of physiology? Is there anything to maternal instinct, or parental instinct? Or is biology satisfied with the sex instinct as the way to assure continuity?

5 In psychoanalytic thought there is talk of the "child-wish," the "instinctual drive of physiological cause," "the innate femaleness of the girl direct(ing) her development toward motherhood," and the wanting of children as "the essence of her self-realization," indicating normality. From the experimental literature, there is some evidence that man, like other animals, is innately attracted to the quality of "babyishness."

6 If the young and adults of several species are compared for differences in bodily and facial features, it will be seen readily that the nature of the difference is apparently the same almost throughout the phylogenetic scale. Limbs are shorter and much heavier in proportion to the torso in babies than in adults. Also, the head is proportionately much larger in relation to the body than is the case with adults. On the face itself, the forehead is more prominent and bulbous; the eyes large and perhaps located as far down as below the middle of the face, because of the large forehead. In addition, the cheeks may be round and protruding. In many species there is also a greater degree of overall fatness in contrast to normal adult bodies. . . . In man, as in other animals, social prescriptions and customs are not the sole or even primary factors that guarantee the rearing and protection of babies. This seems to indicate that the biologically rooted releaser of babyishness may have promoted infant care in primitive man before societies ever were formed, just as it appears to do in many animal species. Thus this releaser may have a high survival value for the species of man.*

*Eckhard H. Hess, "Ethology and Developmental Psychology," in Paul H. Musser, ed., *Carmichael's Manual of Child Psychology*, Vol. 1 (New York: Wiley, 1970), pp. 20–21.

In the human species the question of social and personal moti- 7
vation distinctively arises, but that does not necessarily mean that the
biology is completely obliterated. In animals the instinct to reproduce
appears to be all; in humans is it something?

THE CULTURAL

Whatever the biological answer, people do not want all the children 8
they physically can have—no society, hardly any woman. Everywhere
social traditions and social pressures enforce a certain conformity to
the approved childbearing pattern, whether large numbers of children in Africa or small numbers in Eastern Europe. People want children because that is "the thing to do"—culturally sanctioned and
institutionally supported, hence about as natural as any social behavior can be.

Such social expectations, expressed by everyone toward every- 9
one, are extremely strong in influencing behavior even on such an important element in life as childbearing and on whether the outcome
is two children or six. In most human societies, the thing to do gets
done, for social rewards and punishments are among the most powerful. Whether they produce lots of children or few and whether the
matter is fully conscious or not, the cultural norms are all the more
effective if, as often, they are rationalized as the will of God or the
hand of fate.

THE POLITICAL

The cultural shades off into political considerations: reproduction for 10
the purposes of a higher authority. In a way, the human responsibility to perpetuate the species is the grandest such expression—the
human family pitted politically against fauna and flora—and there always might be people who partly rationalize their own childbearing
as a contribution to that lofty end. Beneath that, however, there are
political units for whom collective childbearing is or has been explicitly encouraged as a demographic duty—countries concerned with
national glory or competitive political position; governments concerned with the supply of workers and soldiers; churches concerned
with propagation of the faith or their relative strength; ethnic minorities concerned with their political power; linguistic communities
competing for position; clans and tribes concerned over their relative
status within a larger setting. In ancient Rome, according to the Oxford English Dictionary, the proletariat—from the root *proles*, for
progeny—were "the lowest class of the community, regarded as contributing nothing to the state but offspring": and a proletaire was
"one who served the state not with his property but only with his offspring." The world has changed since then, but not all the way.

11   As the "new home economics" is reminding us in its current attention to the microeconomics of fertility, children are economically valuable. Not that that would come as a surprise to the poor peasant who consciously acts on the premise, but it is clear that some people want children or not for economic reasons.

12   Start with the obvious case of economic returns from children that appears to be characteristic of the rural poor. To some extent, that accounts for their generally higher fertility than that of their urban and wealthier counterparts: labor in the fields; hunting, fishing, animal care; help in the home and with the younger children; dowry and "bride-wealth"; support in later life (the individualized system of social security).

13   The economics of the case carries through on the negative side as well. It is not publicly comfortable to think of children as another consumer durable, but sometimes that is precisely the way parents do think of them, before conception: another child or a trip to Europe; a birth deferred in favor of a new car, the nth child requiring more expenditure on education or housing. But observe the special characteristics of children viewed as consumer durables: they come only in whole units; they are not rentable or returnable or exchangeable or available on trial; they cannot be evaluated quickly; they do not come in several competing brands or products; their quality cannot be pretested before delivery; they usually are not available for appraisal in large numbers in one's personal experience; they themselves participate actively in the household's decisions. And in the broad view, both societies and families tend to choose standard of living over number of children when the opportunity presents itself.

THE FAMILIAL

14   In some societies people want children for what might be called familial reasons: to extend the family line or the family name; to propitiate the ancestors; to enable the proper functioning of religious rituals involving the family (e.g., the Hindu son needed to light the father's funeral pyre, the Jewish son needed to say Kaddish for the dead father). Such reasons may seem thin in the modern, secularized society but they have been and are powerful indeed in other places.

15   In addition, one class of family reasons shares a border with the following category, namely, having children in order to maintain or improve a marriage: to hold the husband or occupy the wife; to repair or rejuvenate their marriage; to increase the number of children on the assumption that family happiness lies that way. The point is underlined by its converse: in some societies the failure to bear chil-

dren (or males) is a threat to the marriage and a ready cause for divorce.

Beyond all that is the profound significance of children to the very institution of the family itself. To many people, husband and wife alone do not seem a proper family—they need children to enrich the circle, to validate its family character, to gather the redemptive influence of offspring. Children need the family, but the family seems also to need children, as the social institution uniquely available, at least in principle, for security, comfort, assurance, and direction in a changing, often hostile, world. To most people, such a home base, in the literal sense, needs more than one person for sustenance and in generational extension. 16

THE PERSONAL

Up to here the reasons for wanting children primarily refer to instrumental benefits. Now we come to a variety of reasons for wanting children that are supposed to bring direct personal benefits. 17

Personal Power. As noted, having children sometimes gives one parent power over the other. More than that, it gives the parents power over the child(ren)—in many cases, perhaps most, about as much effective power as they ever will have the opportunity of exercising on an individual basis. They are looked up to by the child(ren), literally and figuratively, and rarely does that happen otherwise. Beyond that, having children is involved in a wider circle of power: 18

> In most simple societies the lines of kinship are the lines of political power, social prestige and economic aggrandizement. The more children a man has, the more successful marriage alliances he can arrange, increasing his own power and influence by linking himself to men of greater power or to men who will be his supporters. . . . In primitive and peasant societies, the man with few children is the man of minor influence and the childless man is virtually a social nonentity.* 19

Personal Competence. Becoming a parent demonstrates competence in an essential human role. Men and women who are closed off from other demonstrations of competence, through lack of talent or educational opportunity or social status, still have this central one. For males, parenthood is thought to show virility, potency, *machismo.* For females it demonstrates fecundity, itself so critical to an acceptable life in many societies. 20

Personal Status. Everywhere parenthood confers status. It is an 21

---

*Burton Benedict, "Population Regulation in Primitive Societies," in Anthony Ellison, *Population Control* (London: Penguin, 1970), pp. 176–77.

---

accomplishment open to all, or virtually all, and realized by the over-whelming majority of adult humankind. Indeed, achieving parent-hood surely must be one of the two most significant events in one's life—that and being born in the first place. In many societies, then and only then is one considered a real man or a real woman.

22   Childbearing is one of the few ways in which the poor can com-pete with the rich. Life cannot make the poor man prosperous in ma-terial goods and services but it easily can make him rich with children. He cannot have as much of anything else worth having, except sex, which itself typically means children in such societies. Even so, the poor still are deprived by the arithmetic; they have only two or three times as many children as the rich whereas the rich have at least forty times the income of the poor.

23   *Personal Extension.* Beyond the family line, wanting children is a way to reach for personal immortality—for most people, the only way available. It is a way to extend oneself indefinitely into the future. And short of that, there is simply the physical and psychological ex-tension of oneself in the children, here and now—a kind of narcis-sism: there they are and they are mine (or like me).

24
> *Look in thy glass and tell the face thou viewest,*
> *Now is the time that face should form another;*
> *But if thou live, remember'd not to be,*
> *Die single, and thine image dies with thee.*
>   *—Shakespeare's Sonnets, III*

25   *Personal Experience.* Among all the activities of life, parenthood is a unique experience. It is a part of life, or personal growth, that sim-ply cannot be experienced in any other way and hence is literally an indispensable element of the full life. The experience has many pro-found facets: the deep curiosity as to how the child will turn out; the renewal of self in the second chance; the reliving of one's own child-hood; the redemptive opportunity; the challenge to shape another human being; the sheer creativity and self-realization involved. For a large proportion of the world's women, there was and probably still is nothing else for the grown female to do with her time and energy, as society defines her role. And for many women, it might be the most emotional and spiritual experience they ever have and perhaps the most gratifying as well.

26   *Personal Pleasure.* Last, but one hopes not least, in the list of rea-sons for wanting children is the altruistic pleasure of having them, caring for them, watching them grow, shaping them, being with

them, enjoying them. This reason comes last on the list but it is typically the first one mentioned in the casual inquiry: "because I like children." Even this reason has its dark side, as with parents who live through their children, often to the latter's distaste and disadvantage. But that should not obscure a fundamental reason for wanting children: love.

There are, in short, many reasons for wanting children. Taken 27 together, they must be among the most compelling motivations in human behavior: culturally imposed, institutionally reinforced, psychologically welcome.

QUESTIONS ON SUBJECT AND PURPOSE

1. What is "the value of children"? How many different values does Berelson cite?

2. Berelson gives positive, negative, and neutral reasons for wanting children. Is the overall effect of the essay positive, negative, or neutral?

3. Which of Berelson's reasons seem most relevant in American society today? Which seem least relevant?

QUESTIONS ON STRATEGY AND AUDIENCE

1. How does Berelson organize his classification? Can you find an explicit statement of organization?

2. Could the classification have been organized in a different way? Would that have changed the essay in any way?

3. How effective is Berelson's introduction? His conclusion? Suggest other ways in which the essay could have begun or ended.

QUESTIONS ON VOCABULARY AND STYLE

1. Berelson asks a number of rhetorical questions (see Glossary). Why does he ask them? Does he answer them? Does he "ventilate," "explicate," and "clarify" them (paragraph 3)?

2. Describe the tone of Berelson's essay—what does he sound like? Be prepared to support your statement with some specific illustrations from the text.

3. Be able to define the following words: *taxonomy* (paragraph 3), *physiology* (4), *phylogenetic* (6), *bulbous* (6), *sanctioned* (8), *fauna*

and flora (10), *demographic* (10), *consumer durable* (13), *propitiate* (14), *sustenance* (16), *aggrandizement* (19), *nonentity* (19), *"machismo"* (20), *fecundity* (20), *narcissism* (23).

WRITING SUGGESTIONS

1. **For your Journal.** In your journal, explore the reasons why you do or do not want to have children. Would you choose to limit the number of children that you have? Why, or why not?

2. **For a Paragraph.** Using your journal writing as a starting point, in a paragraph classify the reasons for your decision. Focus on two or three reasons at most and be sure to have some logical order to your arrangement.

3. **For an Essay.** Few issues are so charged in American society today as abortion. In an essay, classify the reasons why people are either pro-choice or pro-life. Despite your personal feelings on the topic, try in your essay to be as objective as possible. Do not write an argument for or against abortion or a piece of propaganda.

Prewriting:

a. Interview twenty fellow students, asking their feelings about the subject. Try to get a broad spectrum of different ages, religions, and social and economic backgrounds, as well as a balance in terms of gender.

b. Analyze your own feelings on the subject.

c. If your instructor approves the use of outside sources, you can search for additional information from the many organizations on both sides of the issue. Your campus's health service will probably also have information.

Rewriting:

a. Look carefully at the organizational principle you have used in the body of your essay. How did you decide which reasons to put first? Which last? Try reordering the body of your paper.

b. Have you avoided emotionally charged language? Remember you are not trying to "defend" a position or to prove how wrong the other side is; you are trying to classify the reasons people feel as they do—whether or not you agree with them.

c. Ask several peers to read your essay and to provide honest reactions to what you have written. Are they in agreement? Consider their reactions in revising your paper.

4. **For Research.** Studies have shown that as countries become increasingly industrialized, their population growth approaches zero. For example, India's fertility rate has declined from six infants per female reproductive lifetime to four. In China, the rate is now 2.3 (zero growth is 2.1). In a research paper, explore how increasingly industrialized societies—such as India, China, Costa Rica, or Sri Lanka—have changed their views of the "value" of children. Be sure to document your sources wherever appropriate.

COMPARISON AND CONTRAST

Whenever you decide between two alternatives, you make a comparison and contrast. Which portable cassette player is the better value or has the more attractive set of features? Which professor's section of introductory sociology should you register for in the spring semester? In both cases you make the decision by comparing alternatives on a series of relevant points and then deciding which has the greater advantages.

In comparison and contrast, subjects are set in opposition in order to reveal their similarities and differences. Comparison involves finding similarities between two or more things, people, or ideas; contrast involves finding differences. Comparison and contrast writing tasks can involve, then, three activities: emphasizing similarities, emphasizing differences, or emphasizing both.

John Fischer uses comparison in this paragraph to emphasize the similarities between Ukrainians and Texans:

> The Ukrainians are the Texans of Russia. They believe they can fight, drink, ride, sing, and make love better than anybody else in the world, and if pressed will admit it. Their country, too, was a borderland—that's what Ukraine means—and like Texas it was originally settled by outlaws, horse thieves, land-hungry farmers, and people who hadn't made a go of it somewhere else. Some of these hard cases banded together, long ago, to raise hell and livestock. They called themselves Cossacks, and they would have felt right at home in any Western movie. Even today the Ukrainians cherish a wistful tradition of horsemanship, although most of them would feel as uncomfortable in a saddle as any Dallas banker. They still like to wear knee-high boots and big, furry hats, made of gray or Persian lamb, which are the local equivalent of the Stetson.

Fischer emphasizes only similarities. He tries to help his readers understand a foreign country by likening it to a place far more familiar to most Americans.

On the other hand, Henry Petroski, in his essay "The Gleaming Silver Bird and the Rusty Iron Horse," contrasts air travel to train travel, emphasizing their differences.

> The airplane lets us fly and forget. We are as gods, even in coach class, attended by young, smiling stewards and stewardesses who bring us food, drink, and entertainment. From the window of the airplane we marvel at the cities far beneath us, at the great land formations and waterways, and at the clouds. Political boundaries are forgotten, and the world is one. Everything is possible.
>
> Nothing is forgotten on the train, however. The right of way is strewn with the detritus of technology, and technology's disruptiveness is everywhere apparent. Outside the once-clean picture window of the train, which has probably slowed down to pass over a deteriorating roadbed under repair, one sees not heaven in the clouds but the graveyards of people and machines. One cannot help but notice how technology has changed the land and the lives of those who live beside the rails. The factory abandoned is a blight not easily removed; the neglected homes of myriad factory (and railroad?) workers are not easily restored.

Like every writing task, comparison and contrast is done to achieve a particular purpose. In practical situations you use it to help make a decision. You compare cassette players or professors in order to make an intelligent choice. In academic situations comparison and contrast allows you to compare carefully and thoroughly, on a point-by-point basis, two or more subjects.

HOW DO YOU CHOOSE A SUBJECT?

Many times, especially on examinations in other academic courses, the subject for comparison and contrast is already chosen for you. On an economics examination you are asked, "What are the main differences between the public and private sectors?" In political science you are to "compare the political platforms of the Republican and Democratic parties in the last presidential election." Other times, however, you must choose the subject for comparison and contrast.

The choice of subject is crucial. It is best to limit your paragraph or essay to subjects that have obvious similarities or differences.

William Zinsser compares his writing process to Dr. Brock's; Suzanne Britt Jordan contrasts thin and fat people; Elena Asturias contrasts the different values of Latin American and American society; Bruce Catton pairs Grant and Lee, the two Civil War generals.

Two other cautions are also important. First, make sure that you have a reason for making the comparison or contrast, that it will reveal something new or important and so give your comparison or contrast an interesting thesis. Wendell Berry, for example, first contrasts Kentucky road builders of 1797 with the Indians who had occupied the land, exploring the differences between a road and a path. He then compares those early road builders with road builders of today, showing that both groups share the same basic attitude toward the landscape. In both instances, Berry is trying to make a point about our attitudes toward the landscape in which we live, concluding that we have not progressed much since 1797. Second, limit your comparison and contrast to important points; do not try to cover everything. Berry, for example, concentrates on the way his subjects view and adapt to the landscape; similarly, Marcia Aldrich only focuses on the attitudes toward hair that the women in her family share.

Do You Always Find Both Similarities and Differences?

You can compare and contrast only if there is some basic similarity between the two subjects: John Fischer compares two *groups of people*—Ukrainians and Texans; Henry Petroski compares two *modes of transportation*—the airplane and the railroad. There is no point in comparing two totally unrelated subjects, so, while the mind could be compared to a computer since both process information, there would be no reason to compare a computer to an airplane. Remember, too, that some similarities will be obvious and hence not worth writing about. It would be pointless for William Zinsser to observe that both he and Dr. Brock write on word processors, use dictionaries, or work best in the quiet of their studies. This does not mean that similarities are not important or should not be mentioned. Bruce Catton, after spending most of his essay pointing out differences between Grant and Lee, ends with the similarities the two men share.

Once you have chosen your subject, make a list of the possible points of comparison and contrast. Be sure that those points are shared. William Zinsser, for example, organizes his comparison and contrast around six questions. To each of the six, Zinsser gives first

Dr. Brock's response and then his own. The contrast depends upon the two responses to each of the six questions. If Dr. Brock had answered one group of three and Zinsser a different group of three, the contrast would not have worked.

How Do You Use Analogy, Metaphor, and Simile?

Writing a comparison often involves constructing an analogy, an extended comparison in which something complex or unfamiliar is likened to something simple or familiar. The reason for making the analogy is to help your reader understand or visualize the more complex or unfamiliar more easily. For example, if you are trying to explain how the hard disk on your computer is organized, you might use the analogy of a file cabinet. The hard disk, you write, is the file cabinet which is partitioned off into directories (the file drawers) each of which contains subdirectories (the hanging folders) which in turn contain the individual files (the manila folders in which documents are stored).

Analogies are also used to provide a new way of seeing something. J. Anthony Lukas, for example, explains his attraction to the game of pinball by an analogy:

> Pinball is a metaphor for life, pitting man's skill, nerve, persistence, and luck against the perverse machinery of human existence. The playfield is rich with rewards: targets that bring huge scores, bright lights, chiming bells, free balls, and extra games. But is it replete with perils, too: culs-de-sac, traps, gutters, and gobble holes down which the ball may disappear forever.

Luka's analogy does not seek to explain the unfamiliar. Probably every reader has seen a pinball game. Rather, the analogy invites the reader to see the game in a fresh way. The suggested similarity might help the reader understand why arcade games—such as pinball—have a particular significance or attraction.

Two common forms of analogy used in writing are metaphor and simile. A metaphor directly identifies one thing with another. A rocky rapids on a river is, to Gretel Ehrlich, a "step-ladder of sequined riffles." To Gail Sheehy, adults moving toward maturity are lobsters who periodically shed their shells in order to grow. A simile, as its name suggests, is also a comparison based on a point or points of similarity. A simile differs from a metaphor by using the words "like" or "as" to link the two things being compared. In this sense, a simile suggests, rather than directly establishes, the comparison. On that February morning when his father died, Scott Russell Sanders saw that the ice "coated the windows like cataracts." Seventeenth-century poet Robert Herrick found a witty similarity: "Fain would I kiss my Julia's dainty leg, / Which is as white and hairless as an egg."

Be careful when you create analogies, similes, and metaphors; do not try, for example, to be too clever. On the other hand, do not avoid such devices altogether. Even though these compressed comparisons are used sparingly in most expository prose, they can be particularly effective tools when you want to construct a comparison.

HOW DO YOU STRUCTURE A COMPARISON AND CONTRAST?

Comparison and contrast is not only an intellectual process but also a structural pattern that can be used to organize paragraphs and essays. In comparing and contrasting two subjects, three organizational models are available.

1. *Subject-by-Subject*: you can treat all of subject A and then all of subject B (A123, B123)
2. *Point-by-Point*: you can organize by the points of comparison—point 1 in A then point 1 in B (A1/B1, A2/B2, A3/B3)
3. *Mixed Sequence*: you can mix the two patterns together

The three alternatives can be seen in the essays included in this chapter.

SUBJECT-BY-SUBJECT

Bruce Catton's comparison of Robert E. Lee and Ulysses S. Grant uses the subject-by-subject pattern. Paragraphs 5 and 6 of that essay are devoted to Lee; paragraphs 7, 8, and 9 to Grant; paragraph 10 to Lee; paragraph 11 to Grant. As Catton's example suggests, the subject-by-subject pattern for comparison and contrast works in paragraph units. If your comparison paper is fairly short, you could treat all of subject A in a paragraph or group of paragraphs and then all of subject B in a paragraph or group of paragraphs. If your paper is fairly long and the comparisons are fairly complicated, you might want to use either the point-by-point or mixed pattern.

William Zinsser's comparison of his writing process with that of Dr. Brock uses a point-by-point pattern of contrast. The two authors take turns responding to a series of six questions asked by students. The essay then follows a pattern that can be described as A1B1, A2B2, A3B3, A4B4, A5B5, A6B6. In replying to the fourth question, for example, about whether or not feeling "depressed or unhappy" will affect their writing, Brock and Zinsser reply:

[A4]   "Probably it will," Dr. Brock replied. "Go fishing. Take a walk."

[B4]   "Probably it won't," I said. "If your job is to write every day, you learn to do it like any other job."

The point-by-point, or alternating, pattern emphasizes the individual points of comparison or contrast rather than the subject as a whole. In college writing, this pattern most frequently devotes a sentence, a group of sentences, or a paragraph to each point, alternating between subject A and subject B. If you use the alternating pattern, you must decide how to order your points—for instance, by beginning or by ending with the strongest or most significant.

MIXED SEQUENCE

In longer pieces of writing, writers typically mix the subject-by-subject and point-by-point patterns. Such an arrangement provides variety for the reader. Suzanne Britt Jordan in her comparison of thin and fat people uses a mixed pattern, so mixed, in fact, that at times it is not easy to see the underlying structure. The essay begins with a subject-by-subject pattern. It is not until the end of her second paragraph, for example, that she even mentions fat people. At other points, such as in paragraph 5, she will start with an explicit point-by-point contrast: "Thin people believe in logic. Fat people see all sides."

SAMPLE STUDENT ESSAY

John Straumanis is a hurdler on the university's track team. For a comparison and contrast paragraph, John chose a familiar subject, and the first draft of his paragraph, which follows, began with a reference to his own experiences.

EARLIER DRAFT

The 120 and 440 Yard Hurdles

Many people have asked me why there are two hurdle races in track and field. Of course they are referring to the 120 yard and the 440 yard hurdles. Sure, both have ten barriers, but it's because they have almost nothing else in common is my usual reply. The 120 yard hurdle race, being the shorter of the two, is an all-out sprint where speed is of the essence. It is also a fairly simple race. Once the hurdling skill is perfected, most hurdlers run the race without even looking at the hurdles. There are always eight steps to the first hurdle, three steps in between each, then an all-out dash to the finish line. On the other hand, the 440 yard race is one of the most demanding and grueling races invented. It matches the speed of the quartermiler with the skill of a hurdler and the stamina to combine the two. The number of steps in this race varies especially towards the end, so the runner must constantly pay attention to and reanalyze the race. The 440 yard race is also more exciting. More strategy is involved, and every runner's strategy is a little bit different. The race can break open at any minute. These races are so different that many hurdlers do not compete in both, but decide to specialize.

After John had written his first draft, he stopped by the university's Writing Center to talk with a staff member. The first question his tutor asked was, "Why introduce yourself in the first three sentences?" John replied that he was a hurdler and that was why people asked him the question. After a discussion John and his tutor decided that he had two obvious options: either explain his credentials to the reader or drop the personal reference altogether. John felt that since the information he provided was factual and not open to dispute, it was not necessary for him to establish his authority. In the conference John and his tutor also talked about how he had structured his comparison/contrast. The draft paragraph first lists a similarity (each race has ten barriers) and then moves to a subject-by-subject pattern, treating first the 120 yard race and then the 440 yard race. The spacing of the hurdles in the 120 yard race is defined by the number of steps the racer takes, but not as much information is given about the spacing in the 440 yard race. John and his tutor agreed that the reader would probably wonder about that difference. In his revision, John changed his opening sentences, added some new information, and tightened his prose.

REVISED DRAFT

The Highs and Lows of Hurdling

Track and field competition includes two hurdle races: the 120 yard and the 440 yard. Although both races have ten barriers or hurdles, they have almost nothing else in common. The greater distance in the 440 yard race means that the hurdles must be spaced farther apart. In the 120 yard race it is 15 yards to the first hurdle and then 10 yards between each subsequent one. In the 440 yard race it is 49 1/4 yards to the first hurdle and 38 1/4 yards between each. The height of the hurdles is also different: 36 inches in the 440 yard race and 42 inches in the 120 yard race. Because of the distance, the 120 yard race is an all-out sprint where speed is crucial. It is also a fairly simple race. Once the hurdling skill is perfected, most hurdlers run the race without ever looking at the barriers. The number of steps in the 120 yard race is, therefore, constant--eight steps to the first hurdle, three in between, and then a dash to the finish line. On the other hand, the 440 yard race is one of the most demanding and grueling. It requires the speed of a quartermiler and the skill of a hurdler. The number of steps in this race varies, especially near the end, so the runner must constantly pay attention to and reanalyze the race. The 440 yard race is also more exciting since strategy is involved and every runner's strategy is slightly different. The race can break open at any second. The two races are so different, in fact, that many hurdlers choose to specialize in one rather than try to compete in both.

SOME THINGS TO REMEMBER

1. Limit your comparison and contrast to subjects that can be adequately developed in a paragraph or an essay.

2. Make sure that the subjects you are comparing and contrasting have some basic similarities. Make a list of similarities and differences before you begin to write.

3. Decide why the comparison or contrast is important. What does it reveal? Remember to make the reason clear to the reader.

4. Decide what points of comparison or contrast are the most important or the most revealing. In general, omit any points of comparison that would be obvious to anybody.

5. Decide which of the three patterns of comparison and contrast best fits your purpose: subject-by-subject, point-by-point, or mixed.

6. Remember to make clear to your reader when you are switching from one subject to another or from one point of comparison to another.

THE TRANSACTION:
TWO WRITING PROCESSES

William Zinsser

*William Zinsser was born in New York in 1922 and received a B.A. from
Princeton in 1944. For thirteen years he was an editor, critic, and editorial
writer with the* New York Herald Tribune. *He left in 1959 to become a
freelance writer and has since written regularly for leading magazines, including* The New Yorker, The Atlantic, *and* Life. *During the 1970s he
taught nonfiction writing and humor writing and was master of Branford
College at Yale University. Currently, Zinsser teaches at the New School and
serves as a consultant on the art of writing, working with colleges, newspapers, and corporations. He is the author of fifteen books, including* On Writing Well: An Informal Guide to Writing Nonfiction *(now in its 5th
edition), a textbook classic of which* The New York Times *wrote: "It belongs on any shelf of serious reference works for writers."*

*In this selection from that book, Zinsser dramatizes two completely
different attitudes toward writing. As someone who earns his living as a
writer, Zinsser sees writing as hard work. "The only way to learn to write,"
he has observed, "is to force yourself to produce a certain number of words on
a regular basis." In an interview he once remarked: "I don't think writing
is an art. I think sometimes it's raised to an art, but basically it's a craft, like
cabinet-making or carpentry."*

BEFORE READING

Connecting: If you had to describe your writing process to a group
of younger students, what would you say?

Anticipating: Why should writing seem so easy to Brock and so difficult to Zinsser? If he finds it so difficult, why does Zinsser continue
to write?

About ten years ago a school in Connecticut held "a day devoted to the 1
arts," and I was asked if I would come and talk about writing as a vo-
cation. When I arrived I found that a second speaker had been invited—Dr. Brock (as I'll call him), a surgeon who had recently begun

to write and had sold some stories to national magazines. He was going to talk about writing as an avocation. That made us a panel, and we sat down to face a crowd of student newspaper editors, English teachers and parents, all eager to learn the secrets of our glamorous work.

2   Dr. Brock was dressed in a bright red jacket, looking vaguely bohemian, as authors are supposed to look, and the first question went to him. What was it like to be a writer?

3   He said it was tremendous fun. Coming home from an arduous day at the hospital, he would go straight to his yellow pad and write his tensions away. The words just flowed. It was easy.

4   I then said that writing wasn't easy and it wasn't fun. It was hard and lonely, and the words seldom just flowed.

5   Next Dr. Brock was asked if it was important to rewrite. Absolutely not, he said. "Let it all hang out," and whatever form the sentences take will reflect the writer at his most natural.

6   I then said that rewriting is the essence of writing. I pointed out that professional writers rewrite their sentences repeatedly and then rewrite what they have rewritten. I mentioned that E. B. White and James Thurber rewrote their pieces eight or nine times.

7   "What do you do on days when it isn't going well?" Dr. Brock was asked. He said he just stopped writing and put the work aside for a day when it would go better.

8   I then said that the professional writer must establish a daily schedule and stick to it. I said that writing is a craft, not an art, and that the man who runs away from his craft because he lacks inspiration is fooling himself. He is also going broke.

9   "What if you're feeling depressed or unhappy?" a student asked. "Won't that affect your writing?"

10   Probably it will, Dr. Brock replied. Go fishing. Take a walk.

11   Probably it won't, I said. If your job is to write every day, you learn to do it like any other job.

12   A student asked if we found it useful to circulate in the literary world. Dr. Brock said that he was greatly enjoying his new life as a man of letters, and he told several stories of being taken to lunch by his publisher and his agent at chic Manhattan restaurants where writers and editors gather. I said that professional writers are solitary drudges who seldom see other writers.

13   "Do you put symbolism in your writing?" a student asked me.

14   "Not if I can help it," I replied. I have an unbroken record of missing the deeper meaning in any story, play or movie, and as for dance and mime, I have never had even a remote notion of what is being conveyed.

15   "I *love* symbols!" Dr. Brock exclaimed, and he described with gusto the joys of weaving them through his work.

So the morning went, and it was a revelation to all of us. At the end Dr. Brock told me he was enormously interested in my answers—it had never occurred to him that writing could be hard. I told him I was just as interested in *his* answers—it had never occurred to me that writing could be easy. (Maybe I should take up surgery on the side.) 16

As for the students, anyone might think we left them bewildered. But in fact we probably gave them a broader glimpse of the writing process than if only one of us had talked. For of course there isn't any "right" way to do such intensely personal work. There are all kinds of writers and all kinds of methods, and any method that helps people to say what they want to say is the right method for them. . . . 17

QUESTIONS ON SUBJECT AND PURPOSE

1. Zinsser uses contrast to make a point about how people write. What is that point?
2. How effective is the beginning? Would the effect have been lost if Zinsser had opened with a statement similar to his final sentence?
3. What process do you use when you write? Does it help in any way to know what other people do? Why? Why not?

QUESTIONS ON STRATEGY AND AUDIENCE

1. Which method of development does Zinsser use for his example? How many points of contrast does he make?
2. Would it have made any difference if he had used another pattern of development? Why?
3. How effective are the short paragraphs? Should they be longer?

QUESTIONS ON VOCABULARY AND STYLE

1. What makes Zinsser's story humorous? Try to isolate several aspects of humor.
2. Zinsser uses a number of parallel structures in his narrative. Make a list of them and be prepared to show how they contribute to the narrative's effectiveness.
3. Be able to explain or define the following: *avocation* (paragraph 1), *bohemian* (2), *arduous* (3), *drone* (12), *mime* (14), *gusto* (15).

WRITING SUGGESTIONS

1. **For your Journal**. How do you feel about writing? How do you feel about having other people read your writing? Is writing a source of great anxiety? Of pleasure? In your journal, explore those feelings.

2. **For a Paragraph**. Using the details provided by Zinsser, rewrite the narrative using a subject-by-subject pattern. Choose either writer and put together his advice in a single paragraph. Be sure to formulate a topic sentence that will control the paragraph.

3. **For an Essay**. Let's be honest—writing instructors and textbooks offer one view of the writing process, but the practice of most writers can differ sharply. Prewriting and revising get squeezed out when a paper is due and only one night is available. In an essay, compare and contrast your typical behavior as a writer with the process outlined in this text. Do not be afraid to be truthful.

Prewriting:

   a. For 15 minutes freewrite on the topic. Do not stop to edit or check spelling. Just write without stopping about how you write your papers—or how you wrote them before you took this course. Take a short break and then write for another 15 minutes.

   b. Based on what you have learned so far in the course, make a list of some steps involved in the writing process. Be sure to include some details or examples under each step.

   c. On a separate sheet of paper, divided into halves, list the stages of the ideal writing process on the left-hand side and the stages of your typical (or former) writing process on the right-hand side.

   d. Before you begin, weigh the three possible structures for your paper—point-by-point, subject-by-subject, or the mixed sequence. Consider all the alternatives.

Rewriting:

   a. Look carefully at the points of comparison or contrast that you have chosen. Are they the most important? The most revealing?

   b. Have you adequately developed each point? Have you included appropriate details and examples? Check to make sure that your body paragraphs are more than two or three sentences in length.

    c. Copy your introduction onto a separate sheet of paper. Show it to some friends and ask them to be honest—do they want to keep reading? Or is this just another boring English essay?

4. For Research. Compare the creative processes of two or more artists. You can choose painters, musicians, dancers, writers, actors—anyone involved in the creative arts. Check your library's catalogue and the various periodical indexes and databases for books and articles about the creative work of each person. Try to locate interviews or statements in which the artists talk about how they work. If you are having trouble locating information, ask a reference librarian to help you. Be sure to document your sources.

GROWING UP IN THE U.S.:
A FIRST GENERATION LOOK

Elena Asturias

Born in San Francisco in 1963, Elena Asturias was raised in Guatemala and the United States. She earned a law degree at the McGeorge Law School of the University of the Pacific and a Masters of Law at Georgetown University. A lawyer and political activist, Asturias is vice-president of the Latino Lawyers of San Francisco, an organization committed to raising society's awareness about the ways laws and public policy affect the Latin American community.

This essay originally appeared in Intercambios, *a bilingual magazine published in Los Angeles by the National Network of Hispanic Women.*

BEFORE READING

Connecting: Everyone in the United States, including Native Americans, is descended from immigrants. Whether you are first-generation or twelfth-generation, who were your immigrant ancestors?

Anticipating: To what extent has being a member of a group—ethnic, racial, religious, gender, or socioeconomic—influenced you? How does that "membership" contribute to your identity?

1   When I was three, the name I learned to print was Elena María del Pilar Asturias Texidor. It would be shortened in school to Elena Asturias and, on occasion, altered by monolingual nuns to Helen.

2   Growing up in the United States as a first generation Hispana has had its advantages and disadvantages. Assimilating an awareness of two cultures adds breadth to one's perspective. Among the most utilitarian benefits for society at large is the ability to share different traditions, cultures, and perspectives with others. The constant arrival of new immigrants nourishes this diversity, recharging society and inspiring those already here.

3   However, I do not consider myself a typical Hispana, but rather just one example of a Latin American raised in the U.S. My parents are both educators. My father, a retired university professor, is from

Quezaltenango, Guatemala, and my mother, a community college administrator, was born in Fajardo, Puerto Rico. Although both cultures share common themes, there are tremendous differences in their respective traditions and attitudes. In our family, we often joked that theirs was an "inter-racial marriage."

Summers were spent in Guatemala, and we occasionally vacationed on La Perla del Caribe, renting a home on the beach. The time spent visiting our parents' homelands bound us to their cultures and nurtured an appreciation for the roots they had sown in us. 4

My sister and I were educated in the American school system and the Latin American social system. We learned to behave properly at home, which included sitting and conversing with adults rather than entrenching ourselves in a world all our own. Our parents instilled in us the importance of caring for elderly and ill family members with constancy and patience. The traditional strength of the Latin family helped us as we developed a bicultural existence in the United States. 5

Preserving the language of their homelands was also of great importance to my parents. We spoke only Spanish at home, though both my parents speak flawless English. Help with school work was the only exception to this rule; it was generously given in English. We read *Don Quixote* as well as *Cinderella*. Our childrens' songs were those of CriCri, not the U.S. equivalent. Raised to respect our families, along with a healthy dose of fear lest we bring shame upon those we loved, we were motivated to study, learn and serve our community. 6

Our parents' firm commitment to community service is perhaps the most unique heirloom handed down to us as children. They took us on peace marches in the 60s and 70s even before we were able to walk. I vividly recall the view perched atop my father's shoulders of a massive swell of humanity marching for peace. 7

My parents also taught us about our family history: how our grandfather was jailed and had to flee Guatemala because of his involvement in land reform; how he received the Orden del Quetzal, the highest medal given to a civilian, for his work in vaccinating an entire region of Guatemala. These and other similar stories gave us a special sense of pride in our heritage and obligation to our community. 8

As teenagers, my mother enlisted our help in the political campaigns she supported. We distributed leaflets, made phone calls, canvassed to get the vote out and were accustomed to attending and helping organize fundraisers and other political events. This involvement in the U.S. political process helped us see that individuals can make a difference and that opportunities to do so are there for achievement. 9

What we learned and lived at home set us up for very real confrontations with the world outside our four walls. The early curfews, 10 the chaperons, the conservative manner we dressed—all contributed to the feeling that we were different. Our parents explained that these differences would add something extra to our characters. We were special, not different, and therefore more was expected of us. What made these "extra" requirements feasible was our parents' ability to balance our strict upbringing with the love and attention we needed.

11 Although some advantages of growing up in the U.S. are harder to measure, I gained a type of personal strength, self-reliance and independence I may not have found if I'd been raised in the more sheltered home life of the traditional Latin American household. However, there are trade-offs—the security and stability, the sense of belonging, of knowing one's roots fostered in a strong Latin home are often sacrificed to the risktaking needed to maximize one's potential in the U.S.

12 The more I visited my Latin American cousins and relatives, the more I began to notice a growing distance in our attitudes over politics, social issues and familial questions. Our educations were shaping us into citizens of our respective countries with correspondent attitudes and concerns. Although we retained similar cultural values and traditions, the older we got the less we agreed on the international scale.

13 We celebrated Christmas on December 24th as well as the Three Kings Day, preparing for the arrival of the giftbearers with cereal for the camels and wine for the weary travelers. Mornings of January 6th meant awakening early and rushing downstairs to check shoes left by the door for our unwrapped gifts and the remains of the goodies we'd left. Special occasions were celebrated with tamales, *paches* (Guatemala) and *pasteles* (Puerto Rico) and *Las Mañanitas* was recited on our birthdays. The outward manifestations of Latin American culture were not only for our enjoyment, but for the enjoyment of our non-Latin friends who were always included in these celebrations.

14 Perhaps the most poignant loss on a personal level is the inability to express myself as well in Spanish as in English. It's difficult when you're educated in one language to theorize in another or to write on topics as fluidly. My hope lies in the adage "practice makes perfect!"

15 If our upbringing taught us anything it is that as Hispanas transplanted as such in the U.S., we have a responsibility to educate society in the depth and beauty of our Latin American heritage and the immense contribution we can make to this country. By helping new arrivals and those less fortunate, we ensure the survival of our identity and the reinforcement of our values. To reiterate an appropriate verse of Jose Martí, recently quoted in Los Angeles at the Na-

tional Network of Hispanic Women's Round-table, "... *No hay caminos, los caminos se forman al hacer—no para nosotros pero para los por venir*" ("There are no established roads; roads are built by doing, not for ourselves, but for those to come").

QUESTIONS ON SUBJECT AND PURPOSE

1. What does Asturias see as the strengths of the Latin American social system compared to the general U.S. system?
2. What does Asturias see as the strengths of the U.S. school (and social) system?
3. In light of the final paragraph of her essay, what seems to be Asturias's purpose in writing?

QUESTIONS ON STRATEGY AND AUDIENCE

1. Why might Asturias begin her essay with the reference to her name and how it was shortened?
2. In addition to contrasting Latin American values to American values, what other contrast does Asturias introduce into her essay?
3. Given both its place of publication (see the headnote) and the final paragraph of the essay, what expectations would Asturias have of her audience?

QUESTIONS ON VOCABULARY AND STYLE

1. How many examples of parallel structure can you find in the essay? How do they help the reader?
2. How would you characterize Asturias's tone in the essay? How is that tone achieved?
3. Be prepared to define the following words: *monolingual* (paragraph 1), *assimilating* (2), *utilitarian* (2), *nurtured* (4), *feasible* (10), *poignant* (14).

WRITING SUGGESTIONS

1. **For your Journal.** Do you define your identity by connecting yourself with any particular culture or group—based, perhaps, on national origin or race, on religion, on gender, on age, or on socioeconomic factors. In your journal, explore any such possible connections.

2. **For a Paragraph**. Asturias stresses the value of cultural diversity—to the individual and to society—by concentrating on her own experiences. To what extent have you experienced the value of diversity? Do you welcome it? Do you fear it? In a paragraph, explore your feelings about encountering cultures different from your own. Be honest. Try to start with a specific example.

3. **For an Essay**. Cultural diversity is not limited just to people from different countries or different racial backgrounds. People of different ages, religious faiths, socioeconomic backgrounds, even value systems can have substantial conflicts and disagreements. Using your own experiences, compare and contrast the behavioral patterns and values of any two people. Go beyond just listing differences or similarities; find a thesis to link together your observations.

Prewriting:

a. Think about people—a friend, for example—whose behaviors and values are different from yours. Have you ever suddenly realized that the two of you see things in completely different ways? Have you ever suddenly understood something about your friend's behavior or values? Brainstorm about such moments.

b. Once you have developed a list of such experiences, select those examples in which the contrast was most obvious and vivid.

c. Write out a thesis statement that will serve to link together your observations. Try to make it specific.

Rewriting:

a. Look again at how you arranged the body of your essay. Is there a definite order in which you have presented the contrasts? What is it? Is any other order possible? If you used a point-by-point organization, reorganize your essay using a subject-by-subject arrangement.

b. Convert the list of things to remember at the end of this chapter's introduction into a list of questions. Use those questions as a way of re-seeing your draft.

c. Ask a classmate or a peer to read your essay. Ask your reader to comment on your choice of examples, your organizational pattern, and your thesis statement.

4. **For Research**. Write a research paper on the significant differences between two cultural groups. The two cultures can

both be foreign, one can be foreign and the other American, or both can be subcultures within American society. In addition to library research, you will probably want to interview people. Remember to develop a central thesis about the cultural differences and to use specific examples. Do not overgeneralize and be wary of making biased judgments. Be sure to acknowledge your sources wherever appropriate.

THAT LEAN AND HUNGRY LOOK

Suzanne Britt Jordan

Suzanne Britt Jordan was born in Winston-Salem, North Carolina, and attended Salem College and Washington University. She has been a columnist for the Raleigh News and Observer *and* Stars and Stripes, *European edition, and has written for other newspapers and news magazines. She is currently teaching at Meredith College in Raleigh, North Carolina. Jordan's books include a collection of essays,* Show and Tell *(1982);* Skinny People Are Dull and Crunchy Like Carrots *(1982), an expansion of her essay "That Lean and Hungry Look"; and* A Writer's Rhetoric *(1988), a college textbook.*

This essay originally appeared in the "My Turn" column of Newsweek *magazine. "Thin people need watching," she asserts, and after years of watching, she has reached a conclusion: "I don't like what I see."*

BEFORE READING

Connecting: Despite that fact that many Americans are overweight, our society associates fatness with many negative images. What are some immediate stereotypes that fat people bring to mind?

Anticipating: Should thin people be offended by the way they are ridiculed in Jordan's essay?

1 Caesar was right. Thin people need watching. I've been watching them for most of my adult life, and I don't like what I see. When these narrow fellows spring at me, I quiver to my toes. Thin people come in all personalities, most of them menacing. You've got your "together" thin person, your mechanical thin person, your condescending thin person, your tsk-tsk thin person, your efficiency-expert thin person. All of them are dangerous.

2 In the first place, thin people aren't fun. They don't know how to goof off, at least in the best, fat sense of the word. They've always got to be adoing. Give them a coffee break, and they'll jog around the block. Supply them with a quiet evening at home, and they'll fix the screen door and lick S&H green stamps. They say things like "there aren't enough hours in the day." Fat people never say that. Fat people think the day is too damn long already.

Comparison and Contrast

Thin people make me tired. They've got speedy little metabo-   3
lisms that cause them to bustle briskly. They're forever rubbing their
bony hands together and eyeing new problems to "tackle." I like to
surround myself with sluggish, inert, easy-going fat people, the kind
who believe that if you clean it up today, it'll just get dirty again
tomorrow.

Some people say the business about the jolly fat person is a   4
myth, that all of us chubbies are neurotic, sick, sad people. I disagree.
Fat people may not be chortling all day long, but they're a hell of a lot
nicer than the wizened and shriveled. Thin people turn surly, mean,
and hard at a young age because they never learn the value of a hot-
fudge sundae for easing tension. Thin people don't like gooey soft
things because they themselves are neither gooey nor soft. They are
crunchy and dull, like carrots. They go straight to the heart of the
matter while fat people let things stay all blurry and hazy and vague,
the way things actually are. Thin people want to face the truth. Fat
people know there is no truth. One of my thin friends is always staring at complex, unsolvable problems and saying, "The key thing
is. . . ." Fat people never say that. They know there isn't any such
thing as the key thing about anything.

Thin people believe in logic. Fat people see all sides. The sides   5
fat people see are rounded blobs, usually gray, always nebulous and
truly not worth worrying about. But the thin person persists. "If you
consume more calories than you burn," says one of my thin friends,
"you will gain weight. It's that simple." Fat people always grin when
they hear statements like that. They know better.

Fat people realize that life is illogical and unfair. They know   6
very well that God is not in his heaven and all is not right with the
world. If God was up there, fat people could have two doughnuts and
a big orange drink anytime they wanted it.

Thin people have a long list of logical things they are always   7
spouting off to me. They hold up one finger at a time as they reel off
these things, so I won't lose track. They speak slowly as if to a young
child. The list is long and full of holes. It contains tidbits like "get a
grip on yourself," "cigarettes kill," "cholesterol clogs," "fit as a fiddle," "ducks in a row," "organize," and "sound fiscal management."
Phrases like that.

They think these 2,000-point plans lead to happiness. Fat peo-   8
ple know happiness is elusive at best and even if they could get the
kind thin people talk about, they wouldn't want it. Wisely, fat people
see that such programs are too dull, too hard, too off the mark. They
are never better than a whole cheesecake.

Fat people know all about the mystery of life. They are the ones   9
acquainted with the night, with luck, with fate, with playing it by ear.

One thin person I know once suggested that we arrange all the parts of a jigsaw puzzle into groups according to size, shape, and color. He figured this would cut the time needed to complete the puzzle by at least 50 percent. I said I wouldn't do it. One, I like to muddle through. Two, what good would it do to finish early? Three, the jigsaw puzzle isn't the important thing. The important thing is the fun of four people (one thin person included) sitting around a card table, working a jigsaw puzzle. My thin friend had no use for my list. Instead of joining us, he went outside and mulched the boxwoods. The three remaining fat people finished the puzzle and made chocolate, double-fudged brownies to celebrate.

10   The main problem with thin people is they oppress. Their good intentions, bony torsos, tight ships, neat corners, cerebral machinations, and pat solutions loom like dark clouds over the loose, comfortable, spread-out, soft world of the fat. Long after fat people have removed their coats and shoes and put their feet up on the coffee table, thin people are still sitting on the edge of the sofa, looking neat as a pin, discussing rutabagas. Fat people are heavily into fits of laughter, slapping their thighs and whooping it up, while thin people are still politely waiting for the punch line.

11   Thin people are downers. They like math and morality and reasoned evaluation of the limitations of human beings. They have their skinny little acts together. They expound, prognose, probe, and prick.

12   Fat people are convivial. They will like you even if you're irregular and have acne. They will come up with a good reason why you never wrote the great American novel. They will cry in your beer with you. They will put your name in the pot. They will let you off the hook. Fat people will gab, giggle, guffaw, gallumph, gyrate, and gossip. They are generous, giving, and gallant. They are gluttonous and goodly and great. What you want when you're down is soft and jiggly, not muscled and stable. Fat people know this. Fat people have plenty of room. Fat people will take you in.

QUESTIONS ON SUBJECT AND PURPOSE

1. What is the subject of Jordan's essay? What expectations does she think that her audience might have about that subject?

2. What major points of contrast between thin and fat people does Jordan isolate?

3. Is there anything serious about Jordan's essay, or is she just trying to make us laugh?

QUESTIONS ON STRATEGY AND AUDIENCE

1. Does Jordan use the point-by-point or the subject-by-subject pattern for her essay?
2. Would it make any difference if Jordan's essay were written from the other point of view—that is, a thin person making fun of fat people? Why or why not?
3. The essay originally appeared in the "My Turn" column of *Newsweek* magazine. In identifying the author, presumably quoting from something that Jordan wrote about herself, *Newsweek* offered this descriptive sentence: "Stately, plump Jordan teaches English at North Carolina State University." Why?

QUESTIONS ON VOCABULARY AND STYLE

1. Characterize the tone of Jordan's essay. What types of sentence structure does she use most frequently? Does she ever write sentence fragments? What types of words does she use?
2. Why might Jordan use so much alliteration in the final paragraph?
3. Be prepared to define the following words: *condescending* (paragraph 1), *inert* (3), *chortling* (4), *wizened* (4), *surly* (4), *nebulous* (5), *machinations* (10), and *rutabagas* (10).

WRITING SUGGESTIONS

1. **For your Journal**. It is a rare person who has not at some point in his or her life been the subject of ridicule. Perhaps it had to do with a physical trait (wearing eyeglasses or being very tall), a habit, a lack of coordination, a stupid nickname—whatever. In your journal, explore such a memory. If you wanted to turn that prejudice around, as Jordan does, what would have been your opposite?
2. **For a Paragraph**. Using a tone similar to Jordan's, write a paragraph in which you take one side of a traditional pairing such as:
   a. short people/tall people
   b. early risers/late sleepers
   c. tidy people/sloppy people
   d. savers/spenders

3. **For an Essay**. Society has many stereotypes, often even conflicting ones. In a serious essay, contrast a pairing such as the ones listed below. Be sure to explore the cultural stereotype(s) that we have constructed.

   a. smokers/nonsmokers

   b. drinkers/nondrinkers

   c. suntanned people/untanned people

   d. tall people/short people

Prewriting:

   a. Jot down some possible subjects on a sheet of paper. For each one, describe the stereotype that society has created. What associations immediately come to mind?

   b. Look for public manifestations of that stereotype. For example, how is such a person portrayed on television, in commercials or advertisements? Are there clichés associated with the stereotype?

   c. Free associate with a group of friends. "When I say . . . , what do you think of?" Take notes on their reactions.

Rewriting:

   a. Look again at how you have arranged your points of contrast. Have you used a subject-by-subject approach or a point-by-point one? Justify in a sentence or two your choice of strategy.

   b. Check each body paragraph. Does each have a single focus point? Does each contain enough detail? Remember that paragraphs should contain more than a couple of sentences but should not go on for a page or more.

   c. Ask two friends or classmates to read your essay and then describe to you what they liked best and least. Listen to them. Do not let them just say that it is good—you want constructive criticism.

4. **For Research**. Select a stereotype that has changed in recent decades. For example, attitudes toward cigarette smokers have changed sharply in the past few years. Research those changing stereotypes. You might consult old issues of popular magazines in your school's library for visual examples of that stereotype. Check as well in both general and specialized periodical indexes for shifting public or scientific attitudes toward your subject. Be sure to document your sources wherever appropriate.

GRANT AND LEE:
A STUDY IN CONTRASTS
Bruce Catton

Born in Petoskey, Michigan, the son of a Congregationalist minister, Bruce Catton (1899–1978) attended Oberlin College in 1916 but left to serve in World War I. After the war, Catton became a journalist, writing for the Cleveland News, *the* Cleveland Plain Dealer, *and the* Boston American, *as well as editing* American Heritage. *Catton won the Pulitzer Prize and the National Book Award for* A Stillness at Appomattox *(1953). This, along with such works as* Mr. Lincoln's Army *(1951), and* This Hallowed Ground *(1956), rank him as one of the country's major Civil War historians, although he never took a college history course.*

As this essay demonstrates, Catton's approach to history emphasized the personalities of those who made it. Catton's classic essay was first a radio address, part of a series of broadcasts made by American historians, which he later revised for printed publication.

BEFORE READING

Connecting: What associations do you already make regarding these two Civil War generals? What do you recall about them?

Anticipating: What is it about Grant and Lee that interests Catton? What do they symbolize for him?

When Ulysses S. Grant and Robert E. Lee met in the parlor of a 1 modest house at Appomattox Court House, Virginia, on April 9, 1865, to work out the terms for the surrender of Lee's Army of Northern Virginia, a great chapter in American life came to a close, and a great new chapter began.

These men were bringing the Civil War to its virtual finish. To 2 be sure, other armies had yet to surrender, and for a few days the fugitive Confederate government would struggle desperately and vainly, trying to find some way to go on living now that its chief support was gone. But in effect it was all over when Grant and Lee signed the papers. And the little room where they wrote out the terms was the scene of one of the poignant, dramatic contrasts in American history.

3   They were two strong men, these oddly different generals, and they represented the strengths of two conflicting currents that, through them, had come into final collision.

4   Back of Robert E. Lee was the notion that the old aristocratic concept might somehow survive and be dominant in American life.

5   Lee was tidewater Virginia, and in his background were family, culture, and tradition . . . the age of chivalry transplanted to a New World which was making its own legends and its own myths. He embodied a way of life that had come down through the age of knighthood and the English country squire. America was a land that was beginning all over again, dedicated to nothing much more complicated than the rather hazy belief that all men had equal rights, and should have an equal chance in the world. In such a land Lee stood for the feeling that it was somehow of advantage to human society to have a pronounced inequality in the social structure. There should be a leisure class, backed by ownership of land; in turn, society itself should be keyed to the land as the chief source of wealth and influence. It would bring forth (according to this ideal) a class of men with a strong sense of obligation to the community; men who lived not to gain advantage for themselves, but to meet the solemn obligations which had been laid on them by the very fact that they were privileged. From them the country would get its leadership; to them it could look for the higher values—of thought, of conduct, of personal deportment—to give it strength and virtue.

6   Lee embodied the noblest elements of this aristocratic ideal. Through him, the landed nobility justified itself. For four years, the Southern states had fought a desperate war to uphold the ideals for which Lee stood. In the end, it almost seemed as if the Confederacy fought for Lee; as if he himself was the Confederacy . . . the best thing that the way of life for which the Confederacy stood could ever have to offer. He had passed into legend before Appomattox. Thousands of tired, underfed, poorly clothed Confederate soldiers, long-since past the simple enthusiasm of the early days of the struggle, somehow considered Lee the symbol of everything for which they had been willing to die. But they could not quite put this feeling into words. If the Lost Cause, sanctified by so much heroism and so many deaths, had a living justification, its justification was General Lee.

7   Grant, the son of a tanner on the Western frontier, was everything Lee was not. He had come up the hard way, and embodied nothing in particular except the eternal toughness and sinewy fiber of the men who grew up beyond the mountains. He was one of a body of men who owed reverence and obeisance to no one, who were self-

reliant to a fault, who cared hardly anything for the past but who had a sharp eye for the future.

These frontier men were the precise opposites of the tidewater aristocrats. Back of them, in the great surge that had taken people over the Alleghenies and into the opening Western country, there was a deep implicit dissatisfaction with a past that had settled into grooves. They stood for democracy, not from any reasoned conclusion about the proper ordering of human society, but simply because they had grown up in the middle of democracy and knew how it worked. Their society might have privileges, but they would be privileges each man had won for himself. Forms and patterns meant nothing. No man was born to anything, except perhaps to a chance to show how far he could rise. Life was competition.

Yet along with this feeling had come a deep sense of belonging to a national community. The Westerner who developed a farm, opened a shop or set up in business as a trader, could hope to prosper only as his own community prospered—and his community ran from the Atlantic to the Pacific and from Canada down to Mexico. If the land was settled, with towns and highways and accessible markets, he could better himself. He saw his fate in terms of the nation's own destiny. As its horizons expanded, so did his. He had, in other words, an acute dollars-and-cents stake in the continued growth and development of his country.

And that, perhaps, is where the contrast between Grant and Lee becomes most striking. The Virginia aristocrat, inevitably, saw himself in relation to his own region. He lived in a static society which could endure almost anything except change. Instinctively, his first loyalty would go to the locality in which that society existed. He would fight to the limit of endurance to defend it, because in defending it he was defending everything that gave his own life its deepest meaning.

The Westerner, on the other hand, would fight with an equal tenacity for the broader concept of society. He fought so because everything he lived by was tied to growth, expansion, and a constantly widening horizon. What he lived by would survive or fall with the nation itself. He could not possibly stand by unmoved in the face of an attempt to destroy the Union. He would combat it with everything he had, because he could only see it as an effort to cut the ground out from under his feet.

So Grant and Lee were in complete contrast, representing two diametrically opposed elements in American life. Grant was the modern man emerging; beyond him, ready to come on the stage, was the great age of steel and machinery, of crowded cities and a restless, burgeoning vitality. Lee might have ridden down from the old age of chivalry, lance in hand, silken banner fluttering over his head. Each man was the perfect champion of his cause, drawing both his strengths and his weaknesses from the people he led.

13   Yet it was not all contrast, after all. Different as they were—in background, in personality, in underlying aspiration—these two great soldiers had much in common. Under everything else, they were marvelous fighters. Furthermore, their fighting qualities were really very much alike.

14   Each man had, to begin with, the great virtue of utter tenacity and fidelity. Grant fought his way down the Mississippi Valley in spite of acute personal discouragement and profound military handicaps. Lee hung on in the trenches at Petersburg after hope itself had died. In each man there was an indomitable quality . . . the born fighter's refusal to give up as long as he can still remain on his feet and lift his two fists.

15   Daring and resourcefulness they had, too; the ability to think faster and move faster than the enemy. These were the qualities which gave Lee the dazzling campaigns of Second Manassas and Chancellorsville and won Vicksburg for Grant.

16   Lastly, and perhaps greatest of all, there was the ability, at the end, to turn quickly from war to peace once the fighting was over. Out of the way these two men behaved at Appomattox came the possibility of a peace of reconciliation. It was a possibility not wholly realized, in the years to come, but which did, in the end, help the two sections to become one nation again . . . after a war whose bitterness might have seemed to make such a reunion wholly impossible. No part of either man's life became him more than the part he played in their brief meeting in the McLean house at Appomattox. Their behavior there put all succeeding generations of Americans in their debt. Two great Americans, Grant and Lee—very different, yet under everything very much alike. Their encounter at Appomattox was one of the great moments of American history.

QUESTIONS ON SUBJECT AND PURPOSE

1. According to Catton, what were the differences between Grant and Lee? What were the similarities?

2. How were both men representative of America?

3. Why does Catton use contrast in order to make his main point? What is that point?

QUESTIONS ON STRATEGY AND AUDIENCE

1. How does Catton structure his essay? Does he use the subject-by-subject pattern or the point-by-point pattern?

2. How does the structure of the last four paragraphs differ from that of the first part of the essay?

3. Catton devotes most of the essay to contrasting Grant and Lee. How then does he manage to emphasize finally the similarities between the two? Why does he do so?

4. Catton was a very popular historian of the American Civil War. What would be the range of audiences to whom Catton's essay might appeal? What does Catton expect of his audience?

QUESTIONS ON VOCABULARY AND STYLE

1. How does Catton use paragraphing in his essay to make his argument clearer?

2. Does Catton show any bias in his comparison? Is there any point in the essay when it appears that he favors one man over the other?

3. Be able to define the following words: *poignant* (paragraph 2), *sinewy* (7), *obeisance* (7), *tenacity* (11), *diametrically* (12), *burgeoning* (12), *indomitable* (14).

WRITING SUGGESTIONS

1. **For your Journal.** If you had to select someone who represented or symbolized something in American society in the 1990s, who would you choose and why? In your journal, jot down a series of possibilities. To the side of each name, indicate what this particular person seems to you to represent about our society.

2. **For a Paragraph.** Start with your journal entry for the previous question. Who would represent an opposing figure to this person? In a paragraph, pair off the two figures. Be sure to indicate what each represents and why. Given that you are working with just a paragraph, you might want to try the subject-by-subject pattern as an organizational model.

3. **For an Essay.** In an essay, contrast two aspects or segments of American society. Your contrast might be based on geography (the East versus the West), on population (rural versus urban), on sex (women versus men), on age (young versus old), on political viewpoint (liberal versus conservative), or on another similar opposition. Be careful to avoid stereotypes. Remember as well to have a thesis that explains the significance or reason for making the contrast.

Prewriting:

a. Make a list of possible oppositions. Try for at least ten possible topics. Work on your list over a two-day period.

b. Select two of the most promising and interesting oppositions and freewrite for twenty minutes about each member of the pair. Do not worry about proofreading what you write; just try to explore your ideas.

c. Write an explicit and precise thesis statement that explains the significance that you see in the opposition.

Rewriting:

a. Look at how you organized your essay. Did you use a subject-by-subject, point-by-point, or mixed sequence? Would it be possible to use an arrangement other than the one you chose for the draft? Experiment using photocopies, scissors, and tape or the cut-and-paste function of your word processor.

b. Find two readers. Once they have finished reading your draft, ask them to answer each of the following questions. First, what is the paper's thesis? Second, which points of contrast seem the most important and which the least? Compare their answers. Do they parallel your own answers to those questions?

c. Honestly evaluate your conclusion. Did you have trouble ending? Put your paper away, and then try freewriting a new ending. Force it to be different from your original conclusion.

4. For Research. Choose two figures from history or two people of some current notoriety (for example, politicians, world leaders, entertainers, artists, musicians, athletes, scientists). Research your two subjects. (This will probably be easier to do if your subjects are either historical or are quite controversial.) Then in a paper contrast the two. Remember that there must be some basis or reason—a thesis—that makes it clear why you are contrasting these two people. Be sure to document your sources wherever appropriate.

THEY KNEW BUT LITTLE
Wendell Berry

Writer, environmentalist, and farmer, Wendell Berry was born in Henry County, Kentucky, in 1934. Thirty years later, he returned to his birthplace to raise his family and develop a close connection to the land. He earned a master's degree in English from the University of Kentucky in 1957, where he has taught English for about 20 years. In his essays, novels, short stories, and poetry, Berry is always concerned with the values of rural life and with our impact on the natural environment.

Commenting on his connection with "place" and with history, Berry has said: "If you live in the presence of your history, it's harder to be arrogant. If you are not living in the presence of what you've done, which will always include some damage, it's too easy to be arrogant or silly. That's why some kind of social stability is necessary so that people aren't, all the time, escaping from their own history and the damage they've done." The following is excerpted from an essay titled, "A Native Hill."

BEFORE READING

Connecting: Americans seem to have a fascination with roads, especially wide, smooth concrete highways, two-, four-, or six lanes wide, that stretch toward the horizon. What is particularly American about roads or highways?

Anticipating: We probably think of ourselves as more sophisticated or sensitive than those settlers who first explored and developed our country. Would Berry agree?

I am forever being crept up on and newly startled by the realization   1
that my people established themselves here by killing or driving out the original possessors, by the awareness that people were once bought and sold here by my people, by the sense of the violence they have done to their own kind and to each other and to the earth, by the evidence of their persistent failure to serve either the place or their own community in it. I am forced, against all my hopes and inclinations, to regard the history of my people here as the progress of

the doom of what I value most in the world: the life and health of the earth, the peacefulness of human communities and households.

2   And so here, in the place I love more than any other and where I have chosen among all other places to live my life, I am more painfully divided within myself than I could be in any other place.

3   I know of no better key to what is adverse in our heritage in this place than the account of "The Battle of the Fire-Brands," quoted in Collins' *History of Kentucky* "from the autobiography of Rev. Jacob Young, a Methodist minister." The "Newcastle" referred to is the present-day New Castle, the county seat of Henry County. I give the quote in full:

4   The costume of the Kentuckians was a hunting shirt, buckskin pantaloons, a leathern belt around their middle, a scabbard, and a big knife fastened to their belt; some of them wore hats and some caps. Their feet were covered with moccasins, made of dressed deer skins. They did not think themselves dressed without their powder-horn and shot-pouch, or the gun and the tomahawk. They were ready, then, for all alarms. They knew but little. They could clear ground, raise corn, and kill turkeys, deer, bears, and buffalo; and, when it became necessary, they understood the art of fighting the Indians as well as any men in the United States.

5   Shortly after we had taken up our residence, I was called upon to assist in opening a road from the place where Newcastle now stands, to the mouth of Kentucky river. That country, then, was an unbroken forest; there was nothing but an Indian trail passing the wilderness. I met the company early in the morning, with my axe, three days' provisions, and my knapsack. Here I found a captain, with about 100 men, all prepared to labor; about as jovial a company as I ever saw, all good-natured and civil. This was about the last of November, 1797. The day was cold and clear. The country through which the company passed was delightful; it was not a flat country, but, what the Kentuckians called, rolling ground—was quite well stored with lofty timber, and the undergrowth was very pretty. The beautiful canebrakes gave it a peculiar charm. What rendered it most interesting was the great abundance of wild turkeys, deer, bears, and other wild animals. The company worked hard all day, in quiet, and every man obeyed the captain's orders punctually.

6   About sundown, the captain, after a short address, told us the night was going to be very cold, and we must make very large fires. We felled the hickory trees in great abundance; made great log-heaps, mixing the dry wood with the green hickory; and, laying down a kind of sleepers under the pile, elevated the heap and caused it to burn rapidly. Every man had a water vessel in his knapsack; we searched for and found a stream of water. By this time, the fires were showing to great advantage; so we warmed our cold victuals, ate our

suppers, and spent the evening in hearing the hunter's stories relative to the bloody scenes of the Indian war. We then heard some pretty fine singing, considering the circumstances.

Thus far, well; but a change began to take place. They became very rude, and raised the war-whoop. Their shrill shrieks made me tremble. They chose two captains, divided the men into two companies, and commenced fighting with the firebrands—the log heaps having burned down. The only law for their government was, that no man should throw a brand without fire on it—so that they might know how to dodge. They fought, for two or three hours, in perfect good nature; till brands became scarce, and they began to violate the law. Some were severely wounded, blood began to flow freely, and they were in a fair way of commencing a fight in earnest. At this moment, the loud voice of the captain rang out above the din, ordering every man to retire to rest. They dropped their weapons of warfare, rekindled the fires, and laid down to sleep. We finished our road according to directions, and returned home in health and peace.

The significance of this bit of history is in its utter violence. The work of clearing the road was itself violent. And from the orderly violence of that labor, these men turned for amusement to disorderly violence. They were men whose element was violence; the only alternatives they were aware of were those within the comprehension of main strength. And let us acknowledge that these were the truly influential men in the history of Kentucky, as well as in the history of most of the rest of America. In comparison to the fatherhood of such as these, the so-called "founding fathers" who established our political ideals are but distant cousins. It is not John Adams or Thomas Jefferson whom we see night after night in the magic mirror of the television set; we see these builders of the road from New Castle to the mouth of the Kentucky River. Their reckless violence has glamorized all our trivialities and evils. Their aggressions have simplified our complexities and problems. They have cut all our Gordian knots. They have appeared in all our disguises and costumes. They have worn all our uniforms. Their war whoop has sanctified our inhumanity and ratified our blunders of policy.

To testify to the persistence of their influence, it is only necessary for me to confess that I read the Reverend Young's account of them with delight; I yield a considerable admiration to the exuberance and extravagance of their fight with the firebrands; I take a certain pride in belonging to the same history and the same place that they belong to—though I know that they represent the worst that is in us, and in me, and that their presence in our history has been ruinous, and that their survival among us promises ruin.

"They knew but little," the observant Reverend says of them, and this is the most suggestive thing he says. It is surely understandable and pardonable, under the circumstances, that these men were ignorant by the standards of formal schooling. But one immediately reflects that the American Indian, who was ignorant by the same standards, nevertheless knew how to live in the country without making violence the invariable mode of his relation to it; in fact, from the ecologist's or the conservationist's point of view, he did it *no* violence. This is because he had, in place of what we would call education, a fully integrated culture, the content of which was a highly complex sense of his dependence on the earth. The same, I believe, was generally true of the peasants of certain old agricultural societies, particularly in the Orient. They belonged by an intricate awareness to the earth they lived on and by, which meant that they respected it, which meant that they practiced strict economies in the use of it.

11   The abilities of those Kentucky road builders of 1797 were far more primitive and rudimentary than those of the Stone Age people they had driven out. They could clear the ground, grow corn, kill game, and make war. In the minds and hands of men who "know but little"—or little else—all of these abilities are certain to be destructive, even of those values and benefits their use may be intended to serve.

12   On such a night as the Reverend Young describes, an Indian would have made do with a small shelter and a small fire. But these road builders, veterans of the Indian War, "felled the hickory trees in great abundance; made great log-heaps . . . and caused [them] to burn rapidly." Far from making a small shelter that could be adequately heated by a small fire, their way was to make no shelter at all, and heat instead a sizable area of the landscape. The idea was that when faced with abundance one should consume abundantly—an idea that has survived to become the basis of our present economy. It is neither natural nor civilized, and even from a "practical" point of view it is to the last degree brutalizing and stupid.

13   I think that the comparison of these road builders with the Indians, on the one hand, and with Old World peasants on the other, is a most suggestive one. The Indians and the peasants were people who belonged deeply and intricately to their places. Their ways of life had evolved slowly in accordance with their knowledge of their land, of its needs, of their own relation of dependence and responsibility to it. The road builders, on the contrary, were *placeless* people. That is why they "knew but little." Having left Europe far behind, they had not yet in any meaningful sense arrived in America, not yet having *devoted* themselves to any part of it in a way that would produce the intricate knowledge of it necessary to live in it without destroying it. Because they belonged to no place, it was almost inevitable that they should behave violently toward the places they came to. We *still* have not, in any meaningful way, arrived in America. And in spite of our great

reservoir of facts and methods, in comparison to the deep earthly wisdom of established peoples we still know but little.

But my understanding of this curiously parabolic fragment of 14 history will not be complete until I have considered more directly that the occasion of this particular violence was the building of a road. It is obvious that one who values the idea of community cannot speak against roads without risking all sorts of absurdity. It must be noticed, nevertheless, that the predecessor to this first road was "nothing but an Indian trail passing the wilderness"—a path. The Indians, then, who had the wisdom and the grace to live in this country for perhaps ten thousand years without destroying or damaging any of it, needed for their travels no more than a footpath; but their successors, who in a century and a half plundered the area of at least half its topsoil and virtually all of its forest, felt immediately that they had to have a road. My interest is not in the question of whether or not they *needed* the road, but in the fact that the road was then, and is now, the most characteristic form of their relation to the country.

The difference between a path and a road is not only the obvi- 15 ous one. A path is little more than a habit that comes with knowledge of a place. It is a sort of ritual of familiarity. As a form, it is a form of contact with a known landscape. It is not destructive. It is the perfect adaptation, through experience and familiarity, of movement to place; it obeys the natural contours; such obstacles as it meets it goes around. A road, on the other hand, even the most primitive road, embodies a resistance against the landscape. Its reason is not simply the necessity for movement, but haste. Its wish is to *avoid* contact with the landscape; it seeks so far as possible to go over the country, rather than through it; its aspiration, as we see clearly in the example of our modern freeways, is to be a bridge; its tendency is to translate place into space in order to traverse it with the least effort. It is destructive, seeking to remove or destroy all obstacles in its way. The primitive road advanced by the destruction of the forest; modern roads advance by the destruction of topography.

That first road from the site of New Castle to the mouth of the 16 Kentucky River—lost now either by obsolescence or metamorphosis—is now being crossed and to some extent replaced by its modern descendant known as I-71, and I have no wish to disturb the question of whether or not *this* road was needed. I only want to observe that it bears no relation whatever to the country it passes through. It is a pure abstraction, built to serve the two abstractions that are the poles of our national life: commerce and expensive pleasure. It was built, not according to the lay of the land, but according to a blueprint. Such homes and farmlands and woodlands as happened to be in its way are now buried under it. A part of a hill near here that would have caused it to turn aside was simply cut down and disposed of as thoughtlessly as the pioneer road builders would have disposed of a tree. Its form is the form of speed, dissatisfaction, and anxiety. It represents the ultimate in engineering sophistication, but the crudest possible valuation of life in this world. It is as adequate a symbol of our relation to our country now as that first road was of our relation to it in 1797.

QUESTIONS ON SUBJECT AND PURPOSE

1. What both horrifies and fascinates Berry about "the battle of the firebrands"?
2. What significance does Berry see in the sentence "They knew but little" that he quotes from the history?
3. Why does Berry set up the contrasts he does? What point might he be trying to make to a modern reader?

QUESTIONS ON STRATEGY AND AUDIENCE

1. What are the major contrasts that Berry sets up in his essay? Are there any comparisons (that is, does he note any similarities)?
2. What is the difference between a "path" and a "road"?
3. What impact might the historical example (paragraphs 4–7) have on Berry's audience?

QUESTIONS ON VOCABULARY AND STYLE

1. What does Berry mean when he says of the road builders, "They have cut all our Gordian knots"? What does the expression mean? (Consult a dictionary for help.)
2. Berry directly quotes a very long passage from another text in his essay (paragraphs 4–7). Why does he do so? Why not just paraphrase or summarize the account?
3. Be prepared to define the following words: *jovial* (paragraph 5), *victuals* (6), *din* (7), *ratified* (8), *rudimentary* (11), *parabolic* (14), *aspiration* (15), *traverse* (15).

WRITING SUGGESTIONS

1. **For your Journal**. Think about the differences between doing something an "old" way and doing that same thing a

"new" and "more efficient" way. Try to focus on something that you have yourself experienced. In your journal, contrast the two ways. What is lost? What is gained?

2. **For a Paragraph.** Using your journal writing as a starting place, write a paragraph in which you explore the contrast between doing something an "old" and a "new" way. Like Berry, you should take a stand about the change, but the change could be either negative or positive. Express that stand in a topic sentence.

3. **For an Essay.** For Berry the road is the perfect symbol of how modern Americans stand in relation to their environment. A road "violates," while a path "preserves"; while a path is the "perfect adaptation, through experience and familiarity, of movement to place," a road "embodies a resistance against the landscape." What other symbols could be used to set up a similar contrast? For an essay, select two objects or places (for example, a typical suburban grass lawn and a wild meadow), two actions (cooking a meal from scratch or microwaving a "frozen entree"), or two values (moving slowly in order to see the landscape or racing through it to arrive quickly), and explore the contrast. You should take a stand (which you should express in a thesis), but your stand could be that the change is positive rather than negative.

Prewriting:

a. Brainstorm a list of possible symbols or subjects. Keep your list over a period of several days. Ask friends to suggest contrasts to you.

b. Select the most promising contrast and, on a sheet of paper divided down the middle, list on either side the points of contrast. What can you say about each?

c. Draft a thesis statement, making sure that it is precise. It should take a side; it should also forecast what is to come in your essay.

Rewriting:

a. Look over your paper carefully. Have you focused on the significant contrasts—those that suggest the symbolic importance of this change or difference? Make sure that you connect your observations to a larger point about change in American society.

b. Look at your title. It is really effective, or is it plain and uninspired? On another sheet of paper or on your computer screen, write ten different titles, pushing yourself if necessary, so you have several possibilities from which to choose.

c. Look at your organizational pattern. Do you begin or end with the most significant contrast? What would be the effect of changing the order?

4. **For Research.** Berry, a small farmer himself, feels very strongly about the disappearance of small family farms in the United States. (In 1972 he published *The Unsettling of America: Culture and Agriculture*, a book that has been characterized as launching the "modern movement for sustainable agriculture".) Berry believes that the United States would be better off if a greater percentage of American citizens farmed the land. In a research paper, explore the contrasts between the small family farm and agribusiness. What are we losing? What have we gained? Is it realistic to think that this country could support more small family farms? Is it desirable? Be sure to take a stand—do not just report—and remember to document your sources wherever appropriate.

HAIR
Marcia Aldrich

Marcia Aldrich received her Ph.D. from the University of Washington in 1987. She is currently on the faculty at Michigan State University, where she specializes in twentieth-century poetry. Her current work includes a scholarly study of the American poet Louise Bogan.

The following essay, published in Northwest Review, *is from a collection titled "Girl Rearing," a manuscript consisting of twenty-six essays, one for each letter of the alphabet. When asked about the demands of such an organizational pattern, Aldrich commented that she saw herself "as a poet in training" and that working within certain sets of forms, such as the twenty-six letters of the alphabet, was actually a stimulus to her writing. Each of the essays, like "Hair," is what Aldrich calls "creative nonfiction" in that they all involve both direct autobiography and a form of heightened poetic license.*

BEFORE READING

Connecting: What influences the way you choose your hairstyle? Have you fastened on one style, or are you, like Aldrich, "in the business of transforming" yourself?

Anticipating: What do hair and hairstyles come to represent in Aldrich's essay? What might changing one's hairstyle signify?

I've been around and seen the Taj Mahal and the Grand Canyon and   1
Marilyn Monroe's footprints outside Grauman's Chinese Theater,
but I've never seen my mother wash her own hair. After my mother
married, she never washed her own hair again. As a girl and an unmarried woman—yes—but, in my lifetime, she never washed her hair
with her own two hands. Upon matrimony, she began weekly treks to
the beauty salon where Julie washed and styled her hair. Her appointment on Fridays at two o'clock was never canceled or resched-
uled; it was the bedrock of her week, around which she pivoted and
planned. These two hours were indispensable to my mother's routine,
to her sense of herself and what, as a woman, she should concern herself with—not to mention their being her primary source of information about all sorts of things she wouldn't otherwise come to know.

With Julie my mother discussed momentous decisions concerning hair color and the advancement of age and what could be done about it, hair length and its effect upon maturity, when to perm and when not to perm, the need to proceed with caution when a woman desperately wanted a major change in her life like dumping her husband or sending back her newborn baby and the only change she could effect was a change in her hair. That was what Julie called a "dangerous time" in a woman's life. When my mother spoke to Julie, she spoke in conspiratorial, almost confessional, tones I had never heard before. Her voice was usually tense, on guard, the laughter forced, but with Julie it dropped much lower, the timbre darker than the upper-register shrills sounded at home. And most remarkably, she listened to everything Julie said.

2   As a child I was puzzled by the way my mother's sense of self-worth and mood seemed dependent upon how she thought her hair looked, how the search for the perfect hair style never ended. Just as Mother seemed to like her latest color and cut, she began to agitate for a new look. The cut seemed to have become a melancholy testimony, in my mother's eyes, to time's inexorable passage. Her hair never stood in and of itself; it was always moored to a complex set of needs and desires her hair couldn't in itself satisfy. She wanted her hair to illuminate the relationship between herself and the idea of motion while appearing still, for example. My mother wanted her hair to be fashioned into an event with a complicated narrative past. However, the more my mother attempted to impose a hair style pulled from an idealized image of herself, the more the hair style seemed to be at odds with my mother. The more the hair style became substantial, the more the woman underneath was obscured. She'd riffle through women's magazines and stare for long dreamy hours at a particular woman's coiffure. Then she'd ask my father in an artificially casual voice: "How do you think I'd look with really short hair?" or "Would blonde become me?" My father never committed himself to an opinion. He had learned from long experience that no response he made could turn out well; anything he said would be used against him, if not in the immediate circumstances, down the line, for my mother never forgot anything anyone ever said about her hair. My father's refusal to engage the "hair question" irritated her.

3   So too, I was puzzled to see that unmarried women washed their own hair, and married women, in my mother's circle at least, by some unwritten dictum never touched their own hair. I began studying before and after photographs of my mother's friends. These photographs were all the same. In the pre-married mode, their hair was soft and unformed. After the wedding, the women's hair styles bore the stamp of property, looked constructed from grooming talents not

their own, hair styles I'd call produced, requiring constant upkeep and technique to sustain the considerable loft and rigidity—in short, the antithesis of anything I might naively call natural. This was hair no one touched, crushed, or ran fingers through. One poked and prodded various hair masses back into formation. This hair presented obstacles to embrace, the scent of the hair spray alone warded off man, child, and pests. I never saw my father stroke my mother's head. Children whimpered when my mother came home fresh from the salon with a potent do. Just when a woman's life was supposed to be opening out into daily affection, *the* sanctioned affection of husband and children, the women of my mother's circle encased themselves in a helmet of hair not unlike Medusa's.

In so-called middle age, my mother's hair never moved, never   4 blew, never fell in her face: her hair became a museum piece. When she went to bed, she wore a blue net, and when she took short showers, short because, after all, she wasn't washing her hair and she was seldom dirty, she wore a blue plastic cap for the sake of preservation. From one appointment to the next, the only change her hair could be said to undergo was to become crestfallen. Taking extended vacations presented problems sufficiently troublesome to rule out countries where she feared no beauty parlors existed. In the beginning, my parents took overnighters, then week jaunts, and thereby avoided the whole hair dilemma. Extending their vacations to two weeks was eventually managed by my mother applying more hair spray and sleeping sitting up. But after the two-week mark had been reached, she was forced to either return home or venture into an unfamiliar salon and subject herself to scrutiny, the kind of scrutiny that leaves no woman unscathed. Then she faced Julie's disapproval, for no matter how expensive and expert the salon, my mother's hair was to be lamented. Speaking just for myself, I had difficulty distinguishing Julie's cunning from the stranger's. In these years my mother's hair looked curled, teased, and sprayed into a waved tossed monument with holes poked through for glasses. She believed the damage done to her hair was tangible proof she had been somewhere, like stickers on her suitcases.

My older sisters have worked out their hair positions differ-   5 ently. My oldest sister's solution has been to fix upon one hair style and never change it. She wants to be thought of in a singular fashion. She may vary the length from long to longer, but that is the extent of her alteration. Once, after having her first baby, the "dangerous time" for women, she recklessly cut her hair to just below the ear. She immediately regretted the decision and began growing it back as she walked home from the salon, vowing not to repeat the mistake. Her signature is dark, straight hair pulled heavily off her face in a large silver clip, found at any Woolworth's. When one clip breaks, she buys another just like it. My mother hates the timelessness of my sister's hair. She equates it with a refusal to face growing old. My mother says, "It's immature to wear your hair the same way all your life." My sister replies,

6   "It's immature to never stop thinking about your hair. If this hair style was good enough when I was twenty, it's good enough when I'm forty, if not better."

7   "But what about change?" my mother asks.

8   "Change is overrated," my sister says, flipping her long hair over her shoulder definitively. "I feel my hair."

9   My other sister was born with thin, lifeless, nondescript hair: a cross she has had to bear. Even in the baby pictures, the limp strands plastered on her forehead in question marks wear her down. Shame and self-effacement are especially plain in the pictures where she posed with our eldest sister, whose dark hair dominates the frame. She's spent her life attempting to disguise the real state of her hair. Some years she'd focus on style, pulling it back in ponytails so that from the front no one could see there wasn't much hair in the back. She tried artless, even messy styles—as if she had just tied it up any old way before taking a bath or bunched it to look deliberately snarled. There were the weird years punctuated by styles that looked as if she had taken sugar water and lemon juice and squeezed them onto her wet hair and then let them crystallize. The worst style was when she took her hair and piled it on the top of her head in a cone shape and then crimped the ponytail into a zigzag. Personally, I thought she had gone too far. No single approach solved the hair problem, and so now, in maturity, she combines the various phases of attack in hope something will work. She frosts both the gray strands and the pale brown, and then perms for added body and thickness. She's forced to keep her hair short because chemicals do tend to destroy. My mother admires my sister's determination to transform herself, and never more than in my sister's latest assault upon middle age. No one has known for many years nor does anyone remember what the untreated color or texture of either my mother's or my sister's hair might be.

10   As the youngest by twelve years, there was little to distract Mother's considerable attention from the problem of my hair. I had cowlicks, a remarkable number of them, which like little arrows shot across my scalp. They refused to be trained, to lie down quietly in the same direction as the rest of my hair. One at the front insisted on sticking straight up while two on either side of my ears jutted out seeking sun. The lack of uniformity, the fact that my hair had a mind of its own, infuriated my mother and she saw to it that Julie cut my hair as short as possible in order to curtail its wanton expression. Sit-

Comparison and Contrast

ting in the swivel chair before the mirror while Julie snipped, I felt invisible, as if I was unattached to my hair.

Just when I started to menstruate, my mother decided the battle plan needed a change, and presto, the page boy replaced the pixie. Having not outgrown the thicket of cowlicks, Mother bought a spectrum of brightly colored stretch bands to hold my hair back off my face. Then she attached thin pink plastic curlers with snap-on lids to the ends of my hair to make them flip up or under, depending on her mood. The stretch bands pressed my hair flat until the very bottom, at which point the ends formed a tunnel with ridges from the roller caps—a point of emphasis, she called it. Coupled with the aquamarine eyeglasses, newly acquired, I looked like an overgrown insect that had none of its kind to bond with.

However, I was not alone. Unless you were the last in a long line of sisters, chances were good that your hair would not go unnoticed by your mother. Each of my best friends was subjected to her mother's hair dictatorship, although with entirely different results. Perry Jensen's mother insisted that all five of her daughters peroxide their hair blonde and pull it back into high ponytails. All the girls' hair turned green in the summer from chlorine. Melissa Matson underwent a look-alike "home perm" with her mother, an experience she never did recover from. She developed a phobic reaction to anything synthetic, which made life very expensive. Not only did mother and daughter have identical tight curls and wear mother-daughter outfits, later they had look-alike nose jobs.

In my generation, many women who survived hair bondage to their mothers now experiment with hair styles as one would test a new design: to see how it works, what it will withstand, and how it can be improved. Testing requires boldness, for often the style fails dramatically, as when I had my hair cut about a half inch long at the top, and it stood straight up like a tacky shag carpet. I had to live with the results, bear daily witness to the kinks in its design for nine months until strategies of damage control could be deployed. But sometimes women I know create a look that startles in its originality and suggests a future not yet realized.

The women in my family divide into two general groups: those who fasten upon one style, become identified with a look, and are impervious to change, weathering the years steadfastly, and those who, for a variety of reasons, are in the business of transforming themselves. In my sister's case, the quest for perfect hair originates in a need to mask her own appearance; in my mother's case, she wants to achieve a beauty of person unavailable in her own life story. Some women seek transformation, not out of dissatisfaction with themselves, but because hair change is a means of moving along in their lives. These women create portraits of themselves that won't last forever, a new hair style will write over the last.

15   Since my mother dictated my hair, I never took a stand on the hair issue. In maturity, I'm incapable of assuming a coherent or consistent philosophy. I have wayward hair: it's always becoming something else. The moment it arrives at a recognizable style, it begins to undo itself, it grows, the sun colors it, it waves. When one hair pin goes in, another seems to come out. Sometimes I think I should follow my oldest sister—she claims to never give more than a passing thought to her hair and can't see what all the angst is about. She asks, "Don't women have better things to think about than their hair?"

16   I bite back: "But don't you think hair should reflect who you are?"

17   "To be honest, I've never thought about it. I don't think so. Cut your hair the same way, and lose yourself in something else. You're distracted from the real action."

18   I want to do what my sister says, but when I walk out into shop-lined streets, I automatically study women's hair and always with the same question: How did they arrive at their hair? Lately, I've been feeling more and more like my mother. I hadn't known how to resolve the dilemma until I found Rhonda. I don't know if I found Rhonda or made her up. She is not a normally trained hairdresser: she has a different set of eyes, unaffected. One day while out driving around to no place in particular, at the bottom of a hill, I found: "Rhonda's Hair Salon—Don't Look Back" written on a life-size cardboard image of Rhonda. Her shop was on the top of this steep orchard-planted hill, on a plateau with a great view that opened out and went on forever. I parked my car at the bottom and walked up. Zigzagging all the way up the hill, leaning against or sticking out from behind the apple trees, were more life-size cardboard likenesses of Rhonda. Except for the explosive sunbursts in her hair, no two signs were the same. At the bottom, she wore long red hair falling below her knees and covering her entire body like a shawl. As I climbed the hill, Rhonda's hair gradually became shorter and shorter, and each length was cut differently, until when I reached the top, her head was shaved and glistening in the sun. I found Rhonda herself out under one of the apple trees wearing running shoes. Her hair was long and red and looked as if it had never been cut. She told me she had no aspirations to be a hairdresser, "she just fell into it." "I see hair," she continued, "as an extension of the head and therefore I try to do hair with a lot of thought." Inside there were no mirrors, no swivel chairs, no machines of torture with their accompanying stink. She said, "Nothing is permanent, nothing is forever. Don't feel hampered or hemmed in by the shape of your face or the shape of your

past. Hair is vital, sustains mistakes, can be born again. You don't have to marry it. Now tip back and put your head into my hands."

QUESTIONS ON SUBJECT AND PURPOSE

1. What seems ironic to Aldrich about her mother's choice of hairstyle after she married and had children?
2. How does Aldrich group the women in her family on the basis of their attitudes toward hair?
3. Toward the end of the essay (paragraph 13), Aldrich writes of "hair bondage"? What does she mean by this phrase?

QUESTIONS ON STRATEGY AND AUDIENCE

1. Aldrich contrasts the hair of unmarried and married women in her mother's circle of friends. What is the difference?
2. In addition to contrasts between married and unmarried women, what other contrasts does Aldrich point out?
3. Are the experiences Aldrich relates with Rhonda (paragraph 18) true?

QUESTIONS ON VOCABULARY AND STYLE

1. At three points in the essay (paragraphs 5–8, 15–17, and the end of 18) Aldrich includes short exchanges of dialogue. What is the effect of these three sections?
2. Why might Aldrich choose to write in the first person? Why not, for example, "tell" more of the story using dialogue?
3. Be prepared to define the following words: *timbre* (paragraph 1), *inexorable* (2), *coiffure* (2), *dictum* (3), *unscathed* (4), *self-effacement* (9), *curtail* (10), *phobic* (12), *angst* (15).

WRITING SUGGESTIONS

1. **For your Journal**. Does anyone in your immediate family have an attitude similar to those Aldrich describes toward hair and hairstyles or toward anything comparable (clothes or shoes, for example)? In your journal, explore those attitudes.
2. **For a Paragraph**. Using your journal writing as a starting point, develop in a paragraph either a comparison or a contrast between the person you described there and yourself (or someone else you know). For example, "I share my father's

obsession about . . ."; or "My mother and my youngest sister are exact opposites when it comes to. . . ."

3. For an Essay. In what ways have your values, expectations, and behavior been shaped or influenced by your parents? Compare your generation to your parents' generation. How are you similar, and how are you different? What explains those similarities and differences? (You might alternatively choose to compare yourself to a younger generation.)

Prewriting:
a. Start a list of those things that seem most characteristic of your generation. What do you notice about people who are your age? How do they differ from people who are older or younger? Work on your list over a period of several days.
b. Start a list of those things that seem most characteristic of your parents' (or children's) generation. Interview some people in that age range. How would they characterize themselves?
c. Formulate a thesis that links your observations in the previous two prewriting activities.

Rewriting:
a. Read each paragraph with a critical eye. Is every sentence relevant? Do you have a clear, controlling focus for each paragraph? If not, do some editing.
b. Write out your thesis statement on a separate sheet of paper. Is it specific? Does it argue for the link between the two generations? Does it tell the reader what specifically to expect in the paper? If not, do some editing.
c. On a separate sheet of paper, jot down the thing that troubles you most about your paper. Allow a day to pass and then try to solve that one problem. If your college has a writing center or a peer tutoring program, take your specific problem (and your paper) there.

4. **For Research**. Society seems to expect that its youth will "rebel" and seek ways in which to express individuality and independence—through such choices as life-style, clothing, hairstyle, even body art. In a researched essay, explore how youth in either another time or another culture have reacted to their parents. Remember to do more than just report on how these young people behaved or dressed; rather, posit a thesis that offers your interpretation of this behavior as originating in some reaction to the previous generation. Contrast one generation with another, and be sure to document your sources wherever appropriate.

PROCESS

What do a recipe in a cookbook, a discussion of how the body converts food into energy and fat, a description of how igneous rocks are formed, and three sentences from your college's registration office on how to drop or add a course have in common? Each is a process analysis—either a set of directions for how to do something (make lasagna or drop a course) or a description of how something happens or is done (food is converted or rocks are formed). These two different types of process writing have two different purposes.

The function of a set of directions is to allow the reader to duplicate the process. For example, *The Amy Vanderbilt Complete Book of Etiquette* offers the following step-by-step advice to the young executive woman about how to handle paying for a business lunch or dinner.

> No one likes a man who is known never to pick up a check. In today's world, people are going to feel the same about a woman who is known never to pick up a tab. The woman executive is going to have to learn how to pay gracefully when it's her turn.
>
> In order to save embarrassment all around, who will pay for the next business lunch should be decided without question in advance. If it's a woman's turn, she should make it very clear over the telephone or face to face when the appointment is made that she will be paying. She has only to say with a smile that it really *is* her turn. She should name the time and the place, call the restaurant, and make the reservation in her name.
>
> At the end of lunch she should unobtrusively ask for the bill, add the waiter's tip to the total without an agonizing exercise in mathematics, and then use her credit card or sign her name and her company's address to the back of the check (if she has a charge ac-

count there). If she does this quietly, no one around them need be aware of her actions.

Lars Eighner in "My Daily Dives in the Dumpster" describes both how to "dive" into dumpsters and what the process eventually taught him about life and human acquisitiveness. Diane Cole offers the reader suggestions on how to respond to distasteful and bigoted remarks. Not every example of process is a set of directions about how to do something. Process can also be used to tell the reader how something happens or is made. Harold McGee, for example, explains to his readers how chewing gum, the quintessential American product, is made. McGee's paragraph is not a recipe. Instead, its function is to provide a general view of the manufacturing process.

> Today, chewing gum is made mostly of synthetic polymers, especially styrene-butadiene rubber and polyvinyl acetate, though 10 to 20% of some brands is still accounted for by chicle or jelutong, a latex from the Far East. The crude gum base is first filtered, dried, and then cooked in water until syrupy. Powdered sugar and corn syrup are mixed in, then flavorings and softeners—vegetable oil derivatives that make the gum easier to chew—and the material is cooked, kneaded to an even, smooth texture, cut, rolled thin, and cut again into strips, and packaged. The final product is about 60% sugar, 20% corn syrup, and 20% gum materials.

Elizabeth Kolbert in "Birth of a TV Show" describes the process by which the television networks acquire their new shows; Diane Ackerman tells us "Why Leaves Turn Color in the Fall." Judith Viorst in "How Books Helped Shape My Life" and Joan Didion in "On Keeping a Notebook" also describe processes not meant to be done or imitated by the reader. Didion, for example, does not offer the reader advice on how to keep a notebook, but rather describes how and why *she* keeps a notebook.

How Do You Choose a Subject to Write About?

Choosing a subject is not a problem if you have been given a specific assignment—to describe how a congressional bill becomes a law, how a chemistry experiment was performed, how to write an A paper for your English course. Often, however, you have to choose your own subject. Several considerations are crucial in making that decision.

First, choose a subject that can be adequately described or analyzed in the space you have available. When Judith Viorst in "How

Books Helped Shape My Life" catalogs the heroines with whom she identified on her "journey into young womanhood," she isolates six examples, one from each stage of her own development. She does not try to identify every influential heroine or every possible influence; she confines her analysis to these six examples.

Second, in a process analysis, as in any other writing assignment, identify the audience to whom you are writing. What does that audience already know about your subject? Are you writing to a general audience, an audience of your fellow classmates, or a specialized audience? You do not want to bore your reader with the obvious, nor do you want to lose your reader in a tangle of unfamiliar terms and concepts. Your choice of subject and certainly your approach to it should be determined by your audience. Elizabeth Kolbert's article on how television programs are developed appeared in the "Living Arts" section of *The New York Times*, read by people interested in aspects of the entertainment business. Judith Viorst's essay originally appeared in *Redbook*, a magazine that targets its audience as "women 18–34 years old," obviously a group of readers who would identify with Viorst's experience. Identifying your audience—what they might be interested in, what they already know—will help in both selecting a subject and deciding on how or what to write about it. Subjects can generally be approached from a number of different points of view. A process essay on how to apply eye makeup reaches a large but still limited audience (women who wear eye makeup), but an essay explaining the process of developing, testing, and marketing a new brand of eye makeup would have, potentially, a much broader audience.

HOW DO YOU STRUCTURE A PROCESS PAPER?

If you have ever tried to assemble something from a set of directions, you know how important it is that each step or stage in the process be clearly defined and properly placed in the sequence. Because process always involves a series of events or steps that must be done or must occur in proper order, the fundamental structure for a process paragraph or essay will be chronological.

Since proper order is essential, begin your planning by making a list of the various steps in the process. Once your list seems complete, arrange the items in the order in which they are performed or in which they occur. Check to make sure that nothing has been omitted or misplaced. If your process is a description of how to do or make something, you should check your arranged list by performing the process according to the directions you have assembled so far. This ordered list will serve as the outline for your process paper.

Converting your list or outline into a paragraph or essay is the next step. Be sure that all of the phrases on your outline have been turned into complete sentences and that any technical terms have been carefully explained for your reader. You will need some way of signaling to your reader each step or stage in the process. On your list, you simply numbered the steps, but in your paragraph or essay you generally cannot use such a device. More commonly, process papers employ various types of step or time markers to indicate order. Step markers like "first," "second," and "third" can be added to the beginnings of either sentences or paragraphs devoted to each individual stage. Time markers like "begin," "next," "in three minutes," or "while this is being done" remind the reader of the proper chronological sequence. Diane Ackerman in "Why Leaves Turn Color in the Fall" carefully uses time markers to indicate stages in the sequence ("When the days begin to shorten," "by the end of autumn," "at first," "then").

SAMPLE STUDENT ESSAY

Like many college students, Lyndsey Curtis had had considerable experience waiting on customers. Lyndsey decided to use that experience as the basis for some simple but relevant advice to any salesperson:

EARLIER DRAFT

Pleasing the Customer

After 2 1/2 years working in an ice cream store and countless times being annoyed by salespeople, I have devised a surefire three-point plan to please your customers.

(1) Always greet the customer with a smile and a friendly "May I help you?" Not only does this make him or her feel good, but it has an added bonus for you: if you are friendly to the customer, he or she will be more friendly to you and less likely to give you a hard time. Sometimes this is difficult to do if you have had a hard day, but just remember that

there is nothing more aggravating than an unfriendly salesperson. If you absolutely cannot stand to smile at one more person, ask another employee to cover for you and go to the back of the store and scream. You'll feel much better and will be able to face the shoppers pleasantly.

(2) Give the customer your undivided attention. If another employee or your boss needs to know something or to have you do something immediately, then take care of it. Customers will usually understand if you interrupt them to take care of something related to business. Just don't talk about your plans for the weekend or what happened on "General Hospital" yesterday.

(3) When the customer leaves, smile and tell him or her to have a nice day or to come back soon. Let him or her know that you appreciate his or her business, and make him or her want to continue doing business with you.

The most important thing to remember is that if it weren't for the customer, you wouldn't be getting paid. If you keep this in mind, you shouldn't have any trouble following the guidelines described above.

After Lyndsey had finished a draft of her essay, she went to see her instructor for a conference. Together they discussed what she had written. The obvious strength of her essay was that its central portion—the three-step process—was logically arranged from greeting the customer to concluding the sale. Some other areas of her paper, however, needed attention. Specifically, her instructor suggested that she look again at her opening and closing paragraphs. In the introductory sentence Lyndsey tries to establish her experience both as a salesperson and as a customer, but linking the two together is confusing. In the final paragraph she could reorder the last two sentences so that the climactic statement ("you wouldn't be getting paid") comes at the end of the paper. After this discussion of rhetorical choices (choices made for reasons of effectiveness rather than correctness), Lyndsey asked about her third paragraph. She noticed that she began with a statement—"Give the customer your undivided attention"—only to qualify it in the sentence that follows. One final trouble spot was the fourth paragraph where, in attempting to be nonsexist in her use of pronouns, she was forced into the awkward "him or her." Lyndsey and her instructor arrived at the obvious way to avoid the situation—make the reference plural ("customers"). When Lyndsey revised her paper, she tried to address each of the problems that had been discussed in the conference.

REVISED DRAFT

How to Wait on a Customer

I've been on both sides of the sales counter, so I can sympathize with both parties. I've worked in an ice cream store for 2 1/2 years, and I know that some customers are obnoxious or rude. On the other hand, however, I've been annoyed by ignorant salespeople who seemed to think that helping me was a great chore. As a result of my experiences, I have devised a surefire three-point plan to please your customers.

(1) Always greet your customers with a smile and a friendly "May I help you?" Not only does this make them feel good, but it has an added bonus for you: if you are friendly to them, they will be more friendly to you and less likely to give you a hard time. Sometimes this is difficult to do if you have had a bad day, but just remember that there is nothing more aggravating than an unfriendly salesperson. If you absolutely cannot stand to smile at one more person, ask another employee to cover for you and go to the back of the store and scream! It always worked for me.

(2) Give the customers your undivided attention. They will understand an interruption due to store business, as long as you apologize for it and assure them that you will return to help them as soon as possible. Just don't talk about your plans for the weekend or what happened on "General Hospital" yesterday!

(3) When customers leave, smile and tell them to have a nice day or to come back soon. Let them know that you appreciate their business, and make them want to continue doing business with you.

If you have any trouble following the guidelines described above, just keep this in mind: if it weren't for the customers, you wouldn't be getting paid.

SOME THINGS TO REMEMBER

1. Choose a subject that can be analyzed and described within the space you have available.

2. Remember that process takes two forms reflecting its two possible purposes: first, to tell the reader how to do something; or, second, to tell the reader how something happens. Make sure that you have a purpose clearly in mind before you start your paper.

3. Identify your audience and write to that audience. Ask yourself, "Will my audience be interested in what I am writing about?" and "How much does my audience know about this subject?"

4. Make a list of the various steps or stages in the process.

5. Order or arrange a list, checking to make sure nothing is omitted or misplaced.

6. Convert the list into paragraphs using complete sentences. Remember to define any unfamiliar terms or concepts.

7. Use step or time markers to indicate the proper sequence in the process.

8. Check your process one final time to make sure that nothing has been omitted. If you are describing how to do something, use your paper as a guide to the process. If you are describing how something happens, ask a friend to read your process analysis to see whether it is clear.

BIRTH OF A TV SHOW:
A DRAMA ALL ITS OWN
Elizabeth Kolbert

Born in 1961 in New York City, Elizabeth Kolbert earned a B.A. in English from Yale in 1983. She began working as a stringer for The New York Times, *moving on to newsclerk, to chief of the* Times' *Albany bureau, and finally to reporter. While covering the 1992 presidential campaign, Kolbert became interested in the relationship between the media and politics. She now mainly writes about media issues.*

Kolbert notes that she enjoys writing articles, but "it's really important to get as close as possible to what you're writing about: if you're writing about building a house, you need to go and see an actual house being built. You can't just get information from magazine articles." Getting close, in this case having access to important meetings, was something of a problem in writing this article. The subjects, she observed, "didn't want me to see what I wanted to see."

BEFORE READING

Connecting: Viewers commonly criticize the network TV shows that run in prime time hours. Have you ever wondered how and why certain shows ever made it to network television?

Anticipating: Do you ever sense how Kolbert feels about the process that she is describing? Does she ever voice any judgment about the process? About network television?

1   It was supposed to be "Grease" updated for the 1990's and packaged for television. Every week, a bunch of high school students would grapple with—and make wisecracks about—issues of life and love. Occasionally they would break into song.

2   The idea for this musical sitcom belonged to Marta Kauffman and David Crane, who have been writing together for 16 years. A few months ago, they pitched it to a group of high-ranking ABC executives here. The reaction was immediate.

3   "As soon as a couple of words left our mouths, their eyes glazed over," said Ms. Kauffman.

"It was like all the blood drained from the room," said Mr. 4
Crane.

THE WINNOWING PROCESS

It is now the height of "development season" in the television busi- 5
ness, a period that's not really a season, and is only rarely about development. Stretching from early fall through late spring, it is a time
when writers like Ms. Kauffman and Mr. Crane watch most of their
cherished ideas turned into scrap.

At the start of the season, executives from each of the net- 6
works—CBS, NBC, ABC and Fox—listen to hundreds of writers
pitch new sitcoms. The fortunate few dozen advance to the next step:
writing scripts for the prospective shows. After examining those
scripts, the networks narrow their choices to 8 or 10, for which pilot
episodes will be filmed. From these pilots, they will eventually make
four or five new sitcoms.

Ideas for dramatic series are winnowed similarly, except that 7
even fewer dramas are made. By the time the networks' fall schedules
are fixed, sometime in mid-May, roughly 99 out of 100 of the new series that were proposed will have been relegated to oblivion.

From the networks' perspective, the point of development sea- 8
son is to obtain, for the least amount of money, the shows that are
most likely to succeed. A network pays nothing for a pitch. It pays anywhere from $50,000 to $100,000 for a script. And it pays up to $1.2
million for a pilot. (The writers and producers don't see all of this
money; the cast, the crew and the studios they all work for get a cut.)

Over the last few years, the big broadcast networks have lost 9
viewers and dollars to cable channels. So network budgets have
shrunk and the number of pilot orders has been cut almost in half.
For the people who produce television shows, the stakes and the pressure are now much higher every time they approach a network with
an idea or a script or a pilot episode. Even a cherished spot on the fall
schedule means little by itself: The networks' new cost-consciousness
dictates that new shows are often given just a few weeks (and in the
case of CBS's "South of Sunset," only one) to find an audience or be
canceled.

For writers and producers (and Mr. Crane and Ms. Kauffman 10
are both), development season is a time of unremitting insecurity. Mr.
Crane compared the process of vying for a network time slot to entering a beauty pageant and donning a bathing suit.

"You feel like Miss New Jersey," he said over lunch the other 11
day at the commissary at Warner Brothers, the studio where the
team works.

12   In their not-infrequent encounters with rejection, Ms. Kauffman and Mr. Crane are probably fairly typical of television writers here, except they are a lot more successful at getting their shows on the air.

13   Four years ago, the pair created the popular HBO series "Dream On," which is still in production. (That show, which incorporates nudity and profanity above and beyond "N.Y.P.D. Blue," could not have been made for a broadcast network.)

LOOKING AHEAD TO FALL

14   "Dream On" was followed by "The Powers That Be," which lasted for a season on NBC. Last fall the Crane-Kauffman team, along with a third partner, Kevin Bright, produced "Family Album" on CBS, which got the ax after just six episodes.

15   The set for "Family Album" had barely been dismantled before it was time to start developing ideas for the next fall. Ms. Kauffman, Mr. Crane and Mr. Bright agreed to let a reporter observe the progress of these projects through the scheduling process in May.

16   "Once 'Family Album' was done, we said, 'O.K., what are we going to do next?'" recalled Leslie Moonves, the president of Warner Brothers Television, which has more than 25 other writers working to get pilots on the air. "We do this with all our producers. We analyze what their strengths are, what kind of shows they write. In the meantime, we are gathering acorns at the various networks, trying to get a bidding war going on, trying to get some excitement about them."

17   Because of the success of "Dream On," a comedy about a sex-obsessed man who thinks in film clips, Ms. Kauffman and Mr. Crane are, in Mr. Moonves's words, a "hot commodity." All four networks are eager to work with them, though not necessarily on the shows they want to work on.

18   After several consultations with Warners, Ms. Kauffman and Mr. Crane decided to pitch three sitcoms for the fall: the musical, a show about six people in their 20's making their way in Manhattan and a series about a Staten Island teen-ager with a fertile fantasy life. In an effort to maximize their chances, they examined each network's style—although it might not seem so, people in the industry think the four networks have distinguishable tastes and preferences—and which time slots might be available at each. They decided to pitch the high-school musical to ABC, the teen-age show to Fox and the young-adult show to NBC.

19   "We felt cutting-edge-wise, Fox and NBC probably right now were better for them," Mr. Moonves said.

ABC, perhaps still cringing from the response to its last musi- 20
cal venture, "Cop Rock," turned down the show it was pitched. Fox
ordered a script. NBC was so eager to work with the pair again that,
in an unusual move, it agreed to shoot a pilot, even though no script
was in hand.

A NETWORK CONCESSION

Explaining the network's concession to Ms. Kauffman and Mr. Crane, 21
Warren Littlefield, the president of NBC Entertainment, said, "You
have to make a substantial commitment to be in business with them."
If the network eventually decides not to make a pilot episode, it will
pay a substantial penalty. (Hundreds of thousands of dollars is typical
in such cases.)

Ms. Kauffman and Mr. Crane met at Brandeis University, 22
where they both wanted to be actors. After college, they moved to
New York and began writing musical comedies together instead.
Some of these musicals, including "A . . . My Name Is Alice," and
"Upstairs at O'Neal's," ran Off Broadway. Posters for the shows now
hang in their shared office at Warner Brothers, above their desks,
which face each other.

"We actually don't get tired of each other," Ms. Kauffman said 23
of the arrangement.

"Annoyed sometimes," Mr. Crane interjected. 24

After all these years of writing together, the two have come to 25
sound alike, and their conversation has the easy, interrupt-each-other
quality one expects from a married couple, which they are not. Ms.
Kauffman is married to a composer, Michael Skloff, who has written
the opening music for some of their television shows.

EXPLORING TEEN-AGERS

To prepare for writing the script for the NBC pilot, Ms. Kauffman 26
interviewed several of the twentysomething babysitters who care for
her two young children. For the Fox show, she and Mr. Crane rented
an armful of teen-age movies, including "Risky Business" and "Say
Anything." They started to watch the Fox series "Beverly Hills
90210," trying to discern what it had that attracted so many teenagers. ("The actors are all very good looking," was Ms. Kauffman's
conclusion.)

For the last several weeks the pair have been sitting across from 27
each other, doing what television producers must often do: trying to
write funny dialogue for two different sets of characters. From the
way they talk about the characters—Harry is the lead in the Fox
script, Rachel and Monica are important figures in the NBC script—

it is clear they have been spending a lot of time with their creations. "Monica is sick of dating," Ms. Kauffman said knowingly, as if referring to a close friend. "She feels like if she has to eat another Caesar salad, she's going to die."

28   The Fox script was due first, late last month. As the deadline approached, there was a crunch. They weren't satisfied with the opening of the script and decided to rewrite it. The script was too long and had to be cut. On an easel in their office, Ms. Kauffman and Mr. Crane wrote themselves a message in black letters: "Write Faster." After some second thoughts, they crossed out "faster" and replaced it with "better."

CHANGES REQUESTED

29 Fox told the pair recently that it liked the script and wanted to shoot a pilot, but with some changes. The main character will grow up a little—he will be a junior in high school instead of a freshman, as originally planned—and a few family members, including his father, will be dropped. (As to how they will account for the absence of the father, Mr. Crane said, "Ask us in a few weeks.")

30   Pending approval of the script they just sent to NBC, Ms. Kauffman and Mr. Crane are gearing up to shoot two pilots by the end of April. Mr. Crane described their mood as "harried, happy and anxious."

31   Casting is the next step, and much of the shows' future depends on finding the right actors. This is especially true for the Fox show, which requires a dynamic young man for the lead. Ms. Kauffman and Mr. Crane are convinced that somewhere out there, the next Michael J. Fox is waiting. Now all they need to do is find him.

QUESTIONS ON SUBJECT AND PURPOSE

1. Of the three shows that Kauffman and Crane "pitch" to the networks, which two are successful?
2. None of the three shows that the writers "pitch" is a dramatic series. Why might writers avoid dramatic series?
3. What does Kolbert's purpose seem to be in writing the article?

QUESTIONS ON STRATEGY AND AUDIENCE

1. What are the stages in the "birth" of a television show?
2. As in many newspaper articles, the text is divided by a series of subheadings. What is the function of such a device?
3. To whom is Kolbert writing? How do you know?

QUESTIONS ON VOCABULARY AND STYLE

1. What role does Kolbert assume in the article? That is, does she just "report" or does she also comment on the story?
2. What types of sources does Kolbert use in her article?
3. Be prepared to define the following words: *winnowed* (paragraph 7), *relegated* (7), *unremitting* (10), *vying* (10), *discern* (26), *harried* (30).

WRITING SUGGESTIONS

1. **For your Journal.** Kolbert describes the process by which networks acquire new shows. How do you acquire or select something? Jot down a list of things that you have recently selected or acquired—anything from choosing an elective this semester, to buying a new material possession, to selecting a friend. Did you follow a process—maybe implicitly rather than explicitly—in making your decision? Next to each item on the list make some brief notes about your decision-making process.
2. **For a Paragraph.** Using your journal activity as a prewriting, write a paragraph in which you explain to a reader how to make a decision in selecting or acquiring a particular thing.
3. **For an Essay.** Every college major, no matter how structured, allows students to choose certain "electives." Students choose those electives on the basis of many factors, including such things as the time of day the course is offered, the difficulty of the course, their interest in the subject matter, the value that the course might have in helping them get a job or improve their resume. Write an essay (or an article) for your college's newspaper describing for other students how to select an elective. What process should students follow?

   Prewriting:
   a. Interview a substantial number of students, asking each one how and why they chose a particular elective. After the course ended, did they still think that they had made the right decision?
   b. Brainstorm about your prospective audience. Who reads the student newspaper? What is the composition of the undergraduate class? Are many of the students returning adults? Do most of your classmates work while attending school?
   c. Check your college's undergraduate catalog. How many electives do you have in your major? Read through the undergraduate course offerings to see how many different courses there are from which you can choose.

Rewriting:

a. Did you choose to write as an objective, detached reporter or as the filtering consciousness ("I")? Reconsider that choice by rewriting a paragraph or two using the opposite strategy. Which seems more effective?

b. Make sure that the steps or stages in the process of selecting are clearly marked and called out.

c. Look again at your title. Remember that newspaper readers scan the pages quickly and that you must capture their attention. Your article is potentially of great value to every reader.

4. **For Research.** The process of creating television shows, as Kolbert describes it, seems disturbingly risky. No wonder so many shows fail. What, though, makes a show a success? Select a television show that went on to many successful seasons (for example, *All in the Family* or *Married with Children*) or one that created a dedicated following (for example, *Star Trek* or *Northern Exposure*) and trace in a researched paper the process by which this show managed to triumph over the odds. The reference room of your college's library will have a number of books that will help you trace the history of such shows. Some shows are also the subject of critical study as well. Be sure to document your sources wherever appropriate.

WHY LEAVES TURN COLOR
IN THE FALL

Diane Ackerman

Diane Ackerman, a poet and nature writer, was born in Waukegan, Illinois, in 1948. During her twenties, she published three books of poetry while earning an M.F.A. and a Ph.D. in English from Cornell University. Widely regarded as a gifted lyric poet, she incorporates a surprising amount of scientific fact into her work, breaking through the traditional barrier between poetry and science. Ackerman has also published four books of nonfiction which exhibit the same unquenchable curiosity and precise metaphor that characterize her poetry. Her most recent prose work is The Moon by Whale Light and Other Adventures Among Bats, Crocodilians, Penguins, and Whales *(1991).*

"Why Leaves Turn Color in the Fall" is from A Natural History of the Senses *(1990), a bestselling book that has been called, an "encyclopedia of the senses . . . an intriguing assortment of history, biology, anthropology, cultural fact, and folklore, woven together with poetic inspiration to celebrate the faculties of human perception."*

BEFORE READING

Connecting: For understandable reasons we rarely think about the wonders of the natural processes that surround us. Think about something that is happening in the natural world around you right now—the blue sky, the wind, clouds, snow, blooming flowers. Can you explain how that something is happening?

Anticipating: In what ways does Ackerman's account of the coloring of leaves seem different from what you might expect to read in a science textbook?

The stealth of autumn catches one unaware. Was that a goldfinch 1
perching in the early September woods, or just the first turning leaf?
A red-winged blackbird or a sugar maple closing up shop for the winter? Keen-eyed as leopards, we stand still and squint hard, looking for signs of movement. Early-morning frost sits heavily on the grass, and

turns barbed wire into a string of stars. On a distant hill, a small square of yellow appears to be a lighted stage. At last the truth dawns on us: Fall is staggering in, right on schedule, with its baggage of chilly nights, macabre holidays, and spectacular, heart-stoppingly beautiful leaves. Soon the leaves will start cringing on the trees, and roll up in clenched fists before they actually fall off. Dry seedpods will rattle like tiny gourds. But first there will be weeks of gushing color so bright, so pastel, so confettilike, that people will travel up and down the East Coast just to stare at it—a whole season of leaves.

2   Where do the colors come from? Sunlight rules most living things with its golden edicts. When the days begin to shorten, soon after the summer solstice on June 21, a tree reconsiders its leaves. All summer it feeds them so they can process sunlight, but in the dog days of summer the tree begins pulling nutrients back into its trunk and roots, pares down, and gradually chokes off its leaves. A corky layer of cells forms at the leaves' slender petioles, then scars over. Undernourished, the leaves stop producing the pigment chlorophyll, and photosynthesis ceases. Animals can migrate, hibernate, or store food to prepare for winter. But where can a tree go? It survives by dropping its leaves, and by the end of autumn only a few fragile threads of fluid-carrying xylem hold leaves to their stems.

3   A turning leaf stays partly green at first, then reveals splotches of yellow and red as the chlorophyll gradually breaks down. Dark green seems to stay longest in the veins, outlining and defining them. During the summer, chlorophyll dissolves in the heat and light, but it is also being steadily replaced. In the fall, on the other hand, no new pigment is produced, and so we notice the other colors that were always there, right in the leaf, although chlorophyll's shocking green hid them from view. With their camouflage gone, we see these colors for the first time all year, and marvel, but they were always there, hidden like a vivid secret beneath the hot glowing greens of summer.

4   The most spectacular range of fall foliage occurs in the northeastern United States and in eastern China, where the leaves are robustly colored, thanks in part to a rich climate. European maples don't achieve the same flaming reds as their American relatives, which thrive on cold nights and sunny days. In Europe, the warm, humid weather turns the leaves brown or mildly yellow. Anthocyanin, the pigment that gives apples their red and turns leaves red or red-violet, is produced by sugars that remain in the leaf after the supply of nutrients dwindles. Unlike the carotenoids, which color carrots, squash, and corn, and turn leaves orange and yellow, anthocyanin varies from year to year, depending on the temperature and amount of sunlight. The fiercest colors occur in years when the fall sunlight is strongest

and the nights are cool and dry (a state of grace scientists find vexing to forecast). This is also why leaves appear dizzyingly bright and clear on a sunny fall day: The anthocyanin flashes like a marquee.

Not all leaves turn the same colors. Elms, weeping willows, and 5 the ancient ginkgo all grow radiant yellow, along with hickories, aspens, bottlebrush buckeyes, cottonweeds, and tall, keening poplars. Basswood turns bronze, birches bright gold. Water-loving maples put on a symphonic display of scarlets. Sumacs turn red, too, as do flowering dogwoods, black gums, and sweet gums. Though some oaks yellow, most turn a pinkish brown. The farmlands also change color, as tepees of cornstalks and bales of shredded-wheat-textured hay stand drying in the fields. In some spots, one slope of a hill may be green and the other already in bright color, because the hillside facing south gets more sun and heat than the northern one.

An odd feature of the colors is that they don't seem to have any 6 special purpose. We are predisposed to respond to their beauty, of course. They shimmer with the colors of sunset, spring flowers, the tawny buff of a colt's pretty rump, the shuddering pink of a blush. Animals and flowers color for a reason—adaptation to their environment—but there is no adaptive reason for leaves to color so beautifully in the fall any more than there is for the sky or ocean to be blue. It's just one of the haphazard marvels the planet bestows every year. We find the sizzling colors thrilling, and in a sense they dupe us. Colored like living things, they signal death and disintegration. In time, they will become fragile and, like the body, return to dust. They are as we hope our own fate will be when we die: Not to vanish, just to sublime from one beautiful state into another. Though leaves lose their green life, they bloom with urgent colors, as the woods grow mummified day by day, and Nature becomes more carnal, mute, and radiant.

We call the season "fall," from the Old English *feallan*, to fall, 7 which leads back through time to the Indo-European *phol*, which also means to fall. So the word and the idea are both extremely ancient, and haven't really changed since the first of our kind needed a name for fall's leafy abundance. As we say the word, we're reminded of that other Fall, in the garden of Eden, when fig leaves never withered and scales fell from our eyes. Fall is the time when leaves fall from the trees, just as spring is when flowers spring up, summer is when we simmer, and winter is when we whine from the cold.

Children love to play in piles of leaves, hurling them into the 8 air like confetti, leaping into soft unruly mattresses of them. For children, leaf fall is just one of the odder figments of Nature, like hailstones or snowflakes. Walk down a lane overhung with trees in the never-never land of autumn, and you will forget about time and death, lost in the sheer delicious spill of color. Adam and Eve concealed their nakedness with leaves, remember? Leaves have always hidden our awkward secrets.

9   But how do the colored leaves fall? As a leaf ages, the growth hormone, auxin, fades, and cells at the base of the petiole divide. Two or three rows of small cells, lying at right angles to the axis of the petiole, react with water, then come apart, leaving the petioles hanging on by only a few threads of xylem. A light breeze, and the leaves are airborne. They glide and swoop, rocking in invisible cradles. They are all wing and may flutter from yard to yard on small whirlwinds or updrafts, swiveling as they go. Firmly tethered to earth, we love to see things rise up and fly—soap bubbles, balloons, birds, fall leaves. They remind us that the end of a season is capricious, as is the end of life. We especially like the way leaves rock, careen, and swoop as they fall. Everyone knows the motion. Pilots sometimes do a maneuver called a "falling leaf," in which the plane loses altitude quickly and on purpose, by slipping first to the right, then to the left. The machine weighs a ton or more, but in one pilot's mind it is a weightless thing, a falling leaf. She has seen the motion before, in the Vermont woods where she played as a child. Below her the trees radiate gold, copper, and red. Leaves are falling, although she can't see them fall, as she falls, swooping down for a closer view.

10   At last the leaves leave. But first they turn color and thrill us for weeks on end. Then they crunch and crackle underfoot. They *shush*, as children drag their small feet through leaves heaped along the curb. Dark, slimy mats of leaves cling to one's heels after a rain. A damp, stuccolike mortar of semidecayed leaves protects the tender shoots with a roof until spring, and makes a rich humus. An occasional bulge or ripple in the leafy mounds signals a shrew or a field mouse tunneling out of sight. Sometimes one finds in fossil stones the imprint of a leaf, long since disintegrated, whose outlines remind us how detailed, vibrant, and alive are the things of this earth that perish.

QUESTIONS ON SUBJECT AND PURPOSE

1. According to Ackerman, why do leaves turn color?
2. From the point of view of a naturalist, what is surprising about the fact that fall leaves offer such a vivid show of color?
3. Obviously Ackerman is not writing a textbook explanation of why leaves turn color and fall. What then does she seem to be doing?

QUESTIONS ON STRATEGY AND AUDIENCE

1. How does Ackerman use process in her essay?
2. In paragraph 7, Ackerman digresses to discuss the significance of the word "fall." How is this material related to the point she is trying to make in the essay?
3. What assumptions does Ackerman make about her audience?

QUESTIONS ON VOCABULARY AND STYLE

1. How effective is Ackerman's introductory paragraph? What is she trying to do?
2. What figure of speech is Ackerman using in each of the following examples:
   a. "Keen-eyed as leopards. . . ." (paragraph 1)
   b. "Early-morning frost sits heavily on the grass. . . ." (1)
   c. "The anthocyanin flashes like a marquee." (4)
   d. "Children love to play in piles of leaves, hurling them into the air like confetti, leaping into soft unruly mattresses of them." (8)
3. Be prepared to define the following words: *stealth* (paragraph 1), *edicts* (2), *petioles* (2), *xylem* (2), *vexing* (4), *dupe* (6), *carnal* (6), *tethered* (9), *capricious* (9), *careen* (9).

WRITING SUGGESTIONS

1. **For your Journal**. Observe the physical world around you. Select a natural phenomenon that is occurring, one that you would like to have explained. Brainstorm a list of promising topics. Do not worry about trying to explain each; just try to find phenomena that seem promising subjects.
2. **For a Paragraph**. In an interview, Ackerman once observed that she tries to be "open," to be "completely available to experience every second." In contrast, probably most of the time we are "closed," that is, we ignore the sea of sense impressions that surround us. Select an experience and try to be open. Record the experience as it happens using a process strategy. You do not need to explain "how" something happens scientifically; instead, explain "how" you perceive and experience it.
3. **For an Essay**. Using the paragraph writing strategy outlined in item 2, write an essay in which you record how and what

you perceive in a sense experience—a sound, a sight, a taste, a touch. Focus this time on what the experience reveals either about yourself or about the world. Do not just record; record for a reason, developing a thesis that controls your essay.

Prewriting:

a. Gather experiences for at least two days. Try out or pay attention to a variety of sense experiences. Remember you are not looking for the bizarre or the shocking. You want to see the extraordinary in the ordinary.

b. Select two of the most promising experiences and freewrite for fifteen minutes about each. At the end, try to sum up in each case your central observations.

c. Select an organizational order. What options do you have in arranging the middle of the essay? Experiment with at least two different patterns.

Rewriting:

a. Look again at your thesis statement. Is it precise? Are you making an assertion about this experience and what it reveals?

b. Ask a peer reader or a classmate to read over your essay. Then show your reader your thesis statement. Does the essay reflect that statement?

c. Never underestimate the power of a good title. Try to write at least six different titles for your paper. Ask some friends to comment on each.

4. For Research. Go back to your journal writing in item 1, and choose one of the topics that you included on your list. Research the phenomenon in your school's library. The reference room ought to have a variety of sources that will help you. In a research paper, explain how the phenomenon works. Try, as Ackerman does, to provoke a little mystery or wonder. Be sure to acknowledge your sources wherever appropriate.

MY DAILY DIVES
IN THE DUMPSTER

Lars Eighner

Born in 1948, Lars Eighner grew up in Houston, Texas. He attended the University of Texas at Austin but dropped out before graduation to do social work. In the mid-1980s, he lost his job as an attendant at a mental institution, which launched him on a three-year nightmare as a homeless person, with his dog, Lizbeth, as his companion. After publishing short stories in a variety of periodicals aimed at gay audiences, Eighner began to attract mainstream attention with the publication of short essays about homelessness in The Threepenny Review, The Utne Reader, *and* Harper's *in the late 1980s. He later reworked these as a book,* Travels with Lizbeth *(1993), the final manuscript of which was written on a personal computer that Eighner found in a dumpster.*

In the introduction to Travels with Lizbeth, *Eighner notes, "When I began this account I was living under a shower curtain in a stand of bamboo in a public park. I did not undertake to write about homelessness, but wrote what I knew, as an artist paints a still life, not because he is especially fond of fruit, but because the subject is readily at hand."*

BEFORE READING

Connecting: If you came across someone "diving" into a dumpster, what assumptions would you be likely to make about that person?

Anticipating: One would hope that few of Eighner's readers will ever have to "dive" into dumpsters in order to survive. What then can readers "learn" from his essay?

I began Dumpster diving about a year before I became homeless.   1

I prefer the term "scavenging" and use the word "scrounging"   2
when I mean to be obscure. I have heard people, evidently meaning to be polite, use the word "foraging," but I prefer to reserve that word for gathering nuts and berries and such, which I do also, according to the season and opportunity.

3   I like the frankness of the word "scavenging." I live from the refuse of others. I am a scavenger. I think it a sound and honorable niche, although if I could I would naturally prefer to live the comfortable consumer life, perhaps—and only perhaps—as a slightly less wasteful consumer owing to what I have learned as a scavenger.

4   Except for jeans, all my clothes come from Dumpsters. Boom boxes, candles, bedding, toilet paper, medicine, books, a typewriter, a virgin male love doll, change sometimes amounting to many dollars: All came from Dumpsters. And, yes, I eat from Dumpsters too.

5   There are a predictable series of stages that a person goes through in learning to scavenge. At first the new scavenger is filled with disgust and self-loathing. He is ashamed of being seen and may lurk around trying to duck behind things, or he may try to dive at night. (In fact, this is unnecessary, since most people instinctively look away from scavengers.)

6   Every grain of rice seems to be a maggot. Everything seems to stink. The scavenger can wipe the egg yolk off the found can, but he cannot erase the stigma of eating garbage from his mind.

7   This stage passes with experience. The scavenger finds a pair of running shoes that fit and look and smell brand-new. He finds a pocket calculator in perfect working order. He finds pristine ice cream, still frozen, more than he can eat or keep. He begins to understand: People do throw away perfectly good stuff, a lot of perfectly good stuff.

8   At this stage he may become lost and never recover. All the Dumpster divers I have known come to the point of trying to acquire everything they touch. Why not take it, they reason, it is all free. This is, of course, hopeless, and most divers come to realize that they must restrict themselves to items of relatively immediate utility.

9   The finding of objects is becoming something of an urban art. Even respectable, employed people will sometimes find something tempting sticking out of a Dumpster or standing beside one. Quite a number of people, not all of them of the bohemian type, are willing to brag that they found this or that piece in the trash.

10   But eating from Dumpsters is the thing that separates the dilettanti from the professionals. Eating safely involves three principles: using the senses and common sense to evaluate the condition of the found materials; knowing the Dumpsters of a given area and checking them regularly; and seeking always to answer the question, Why was this discarded?

11   Perhaps everyone who has a kitchen and a regular supply of groceries has, at one time or another, eaten half a sandwich before discovering mold on the bread, or has gotten a mouthful of milk before realizing the milk had turned. Nothing of the sort is likely to

happen to a Dumpster diver because he is constantly reminded that most food is discarded for a reason.

Yet perfectly good food can be found in Dumpsters. Canned 12 goods, for example, turn up fairly often in the Dumpsters I frequent. All except the most phobic people would be willing to eat from a can even if it came from a Dumpster. I have few qualms about dry foods such as crackers, cookies, cereal, chips, and pasta if they are free of visible contaminates and still dry and crisp. Raw fruits and vegetables with intact skins seem perfectly safe to me, excluding, of course, the obviously rotten. Many are discarded for minor imperfections that can be pared away. Chocolate is often discarded only because it has become discolored as the cocoa butter de-emulsified.

I began scavenging by pulling pizzas out of the Dumpster be- 13 hind a pizza delivery shop. In general, prepared food requires caution, but in this case I knew what time the shop closed and went to the Dumpster as soon as the last of the help left.

Because the workers at these places are usually inexperienced, 14 pizzas are often made with the wrong topping, baked incorrectly, or refused on delivery for being cold. The products to be discarded are boxed up because inventory is kept by counting boxes: A boxed pizza can be written off; an unboxed pizza does not exist. So I had a steady supply of fresh, sometimes warm pizza.

The area I frequent is inhabited by many affluent college stu- 15 dents. I am not here by chance; the Dumpsters are very rich. Students throw out many good things, including food, particularly at the end of the semester and before and after breaks. I find it advantageous to keep an eye on the academic calendar.

A typical discard is a half jar of peanut butter—though non-or- 16 ganic peanut butter does not require refrigeration and is unlikely to spoil in any reasonable time. Occasionally I find a cheese with a spot of mold, which, of course, I just pare off, and because it is obvious why the cheese was discarded, I treat it with less suspicion than an apparently perfect cheese found in similar circumstances. One of my favorite finds is yogurt—often discarded, still sealed, when the expiration date has passed—because it will keep for several days, even in warm weather.

I avoid ethnic foods I am unfamiliar with. If I do not know what 17 it is supposed to look or smell like when it is good, I cannot be certain I will be able to tell if it is bad.

No matter how careful I am I still get dysentery at least once a 18 month, oftener in warm weather. I do not want to paint too romantic a picture. Dumpster diving has serious drawbacks as a way of life.

Though I have a proprietary feeling about my Dumpsters, I 19 don't mind my direct competitors, other scavengers, as much as I hate the sodacan scroungers.

20   I have tried scrounging aluminum cans with an able-bodied companion, and afoot we could make no more than a few dollars a day. I can extract the necessities of life from the Dumpsters directly with far less effort than would be required to accumulate the equivalent value in aluminum. Can scroungers, then, are people who *must* have small amounts of cash—mostly drug addicts and winos.

21   I do not begrudge them the cans, but can scroungers tend to tear up the Dumpsters, littering the area and mixing the contents. There are precious few courtesies among scavengers, but it is a common practice to set aside surplus items: pairs of shoes, clothing, canned goods, and such. A true scavenger hates to see good stuff go to waste, and what he cannot use he leaves in good condition in plain sight. Can scroungers lay waste to everything in their path and will stir one of a pair of good shoes to the bottom of a Dumpster to be lost or ruined in the muck. They become so specialized that they can see only cans and earn my contempt by passing up change, canned goods, and readily hockable items.

22   Can scroungers will even go through individual garbage cans, something I have never seen a scavenger do. Going through individual garbage cans without spreading litter is almost impossible, and litter is likely to reduce the public's tolerance of scavenging. But my strongest reservation about going through individual garbage cans is that this seems to me a very personal kind of invasion, one to which I would object if I were a homeowner.

23   Though Dumpsters seem somehow less personal than garbage cans, they still contain bank statements, bills, correspondence, pill bottles, and other sensitive information. I avoid trying to draw conclusions about the people who dump in the Dumpsters I frequent. I think it would be unethical to do so, although I know many people will find the idea of scavenger ethics too funny for words.

24   Occasionally a find tells a story. I once found a small paper bag containing some unused condoms, several partial tubes of flavored sexual lubricant, a partially used compact of birth control pills, and the torn pieces of a picture of a young man. Clearly, the woman was through with him and planning to give up sex altogether.

25   Dumpster things are often sad—abandoned teddy bears, shredded wedding albums, despaired-of sales kits. I find diaries and journals. College students also discard their papers; I am horrified to discover the kind of paper that now merits an A in an undergraduate course.

26   Dumpster diving is outdoor work, often surprisingly pleasant. It is not entirely predictable; things of interest turn up every day, and

some days there are finds of great value. I am always very pleased when I can turn up exactly the thing I most wanted to find. Yet in spite of the element of chance, scavenging, more than most other pursuits, tends to yield returns in some proportion to the effort and intelligence brought to bear.

27   I think of scavenging as a modern form of self-reliance. After ten years of government service, where everything is geared to the lowest common denominator, I find work that rewards initiative and effort refreshing. Certainly I would be happy to have a sinecure again, but I am not heart-broken to be without one.

28   I find from the experience of scavenging two rather deep lessons. The first is to take what I can use and let the rest go. I have come to think that there is no value in the abstract. A thing I cannot use or make useful, perhaps by trading, has no value, however fine or rare it may be. (I mean useful in the broad sense—some art, for example, I would think valuable.)

29   The second lesson is the transience of material being. I do not suppose that ideas are immortal, but certainly they are longer-lived than material objects.

30   The things I find in Dumpsters, the love letters and rag dolls of so many lives, remind me of this lesson. Many times in my travels I have lost everything but the clothes on my back. Now I hardly pick up a thing without envisioning the time I will cast it away. This, I think, is a healthy state of mind. Almost everything I have now has already been cast out at least once, proving that what I own is valueless to someone.

31   I find that my desire to grab for the gaudy bauble has been largely sated. I think this is an attitude I share with the very wealthy— we both know there is plenty more where whatever we have came from. Between us are the rat-race millions who have confounded their selves with the objects they grasp and who nightly scavenge the cable channels looking for they know not what.

32   I am sorry for them.

QUESTIONS ON SUBJECT AND PURPOSE

1. Is the subject of Eighner's essay simply how to "dive" into a dumpster? What other points does he make?

2. A substantial part of the essay deals with scavenging for food. Why does Eighner devote so much space to this?

3. What larger or more general "lesson" or truth does Eighner see in his experiences? For example, for whom does Eighner say he feels sorry at the end of the essay?

QUESTIONS ON STRATEGY AND AUDIENCE

1. In what ways does the essay use process as a writing strategy?
2. What are the "predictable stages" that a scavenger goes through?
3. What assumptions does Eighner make about his audience?

QUESTIONS ON VOCABULARY AND STYLE

1. Why does Eighner prefer the term "scavenging" to a more ambiguous or better-sounding term?
2. In what way is Eighner's final sentence ironic? Why might he choose to make it a separate paragraph?
3. Be prepared to define the following words: *niche* (paragraph 3), *stigma* (6), *pristine* (7), *bohemian* (9), *dilettanti* (10), *phobic* (12), *qualms* (12), *de-emulsified* (12), *affluent* (15), *proprietary* (19), *sinecure* (27), *transience* (29), *gaudy* (31), *bauble* (31), *sated* (31).

WRITING SUGGESTIONS

1. **For your Journal.** Suppose that suddenly you found yourself without either a full-time job or without any financial support from your family. What would you do? Using an ordered sequence, plan out the steps that you would take in trying to deal with the situation.
2. **For a Paragraph.** In a world in which many Americans can find only low-paying jobs with no benefits (see Swardson's "Greetings from the Electronic Plantation" in Chapter 9), what advice could you offer to a young high school student today? In a paragraph organized according to a process structure, address that audience. Be sure to have a specific point or thesis to your paragraph. Try to avoid cliched answers; just saying "go to college," for example, is not particularly good advice since many college students are not able to find well-paying, full-time jobs.
3. **For an Essay.** Where are you going in your life, and how do you plan to get there? What are your objectives, goals, or aspirations? Where do you hope to be in ten years? In twenty years? What are you doing now to try to achieve those goals? What should you be doing? In an essay, honestly examine your directions and your actions.

Prewriting:

a. Brainstorm a list of objectives, goals, or aspirations. Be as specific as possible. Try to think ten years into the future.

b. Beside each item on your list, make another list of the steps that you are now taking that will help you reach that goal. If you find that you are having trouble with either list, you will need to spend some time trying to connect your goals with your current actions.

c. Establish an order for your actions—what is most important, what is least important? Here you should begin to establish the order you will use to present points as you develop the body of your essay.

Rewriting:

a. Check to see if your process sequence—"here is what I am doing to achieve my goals"—is clearly structured. Outline the middle of your essay as a way of checking that structure.

b. Have you tried to confront the question honestly? Have you relied on cliched answers? Ask a friend to read your essay and to respond to those two questions.

c. Look again at both your introduction and your conclusion. Do you catch the reader's interest in your introduction? Do you have a clear statement of your thesis? Does your conclusion simply repeat what you said in your introduction? Do you end, as Eighner does, on a thought-provoking note?

4. For Research. With corporate and business "downsizing," many Americans have suddenly found themselves out of work. As advice for those trapped in such a situation, write a guide to the resources available to newly unemployed. Use a process strategy as a way of providing step-by-step advice to your audience. Contact local and state agencies to see what help is available and how one goes about making an application. Be sure to document your sources—including interviews—wherever appropriate.

DON'T JUST STAND THERE

Diane Cole

Diane Cole was born in Baltimore, Maryland, in 1952. Educated at Radcliffe College (B.A.) and Johns Hopkins University (M.A.), she is a freelance journalist well versed in psychological issues, such as the "fear of finishing," and women's career issues, such as networking and professional ladder climbing. She is the author of Hunting the Headhunters: A Woman's Guide *(1988) and* After Great Pain: A New Life Emerges *(1992). She is currently working on her first novel.*

"Don't Just Stand There" originally appeared as part of a national campaign against bigotry in a special supplement to The New York Times *entitled "A World of Difference" (April 16, 1989), sponsored by the Anti-Defamation League of B'nai B'rith. Here, Cole suggests some courses of action to take when we are accosted by distasteful, sexual, or racial comments from our peers, bosses, or family members. "Shocked paralysis is often the first response," writes Cole, but she tells us we have more options than we think.*

BEFORE READING

Connecting: Can you remember a time when you were told a joke that maligned your national or ethnic origin, race, religion, gender, sexual orientation, or age? How did you respond?

Anticipating: According to Cole and the experts that she cites, what are improper responses to such distasteful or bigoted remarks?

1   It was my office farewell party, and colleagues at the job I was about to leave were wishing me well. My mood was one of ebullience tinged with regret, and it was in this spirit that I spoke to the office neighbor to whom I had waved hello every morning for the past two years. He smiled broadly as he launched into a long, rambling story, pausing only after he delivered the punch line. It was a very long pause because, although he laughed, I did not: This joke was unmistakably anti-Semitic.

2   I froze. Everyone in the office knew I was Jewish; what could he have possibly meant? Shaken and hurt, not knowing what else to do,

I turned in stunned silence to the next well-wisher. Later, still angry, I wondered, what else should I—could I—have done?

Prejudice can make its presence felt in any setting, but hearing 3 its nasty voice in this way can be particularly unnerving. We do not know what to do and often we feel another form of paralysis as well: We think, "Nothing I say or do will change this person's attitude, so why bother?"

But left unchecked, racial slurs and offensive ethnic jokes "can 4 poison the atmosphere," says Michael McQuillan, adviser for racial/ethnic affairs for the Brooklyn borough president's office. "Hearing these remarks conditions us to accept them; and if we accept these, we can become accepting of other acts."

Speaking up may not magically change a biased attitude, but it 5 can change a person's behavior by putting a strong message across. And the more messages there are, the more likely a person is to change that behavior, says Arnold Kahn, professor of psychology at James Madison University, Harrisonburg, Va., who makes this analogy: "You can't keep people from smoking in *their* house, but you can ask them not to smoke in *your* house."

At the same time, "Even if the other party ignores or discounts 6 what you say, people always reflect on how others perceive them. Speaking up always counts," says LeNorman Strong, director of campus life at George Washington University, Washington, D.C.

Finally, learning to respond effectively also helps people feel 7 better about themselves, asserts Cherie Brown, executive director of the National Coalition Building Institute, a Boston-based training organization. "We've found that, when people felt they could at least in this small way make a difference, that made them more eager to take on other activities on a larger scale," she says. Although there is no "cookbook approach" to confronting such remarks—every situation is different, experts stress—these are some effective strategies.

When the "joke" turns on who you are—as a member of an ethnic or 8 *religious group, a person of color, a woman, a gay or lesbian, an elderly person, or someone with a physical handicap—shocked paralysis is often the first response. Then, wounded and vulnerable, on some level you want to strike back.*

Lashing out or responding in kind is seldom the most effective 9 response, however. "That can give you momentary satisfaction, but you also feel as if you've lowered yourself to that other person's level," Mr. McQuillan explains. Such a response may further label you in the speaker's mind as thin-skinned, someone not to be taken seriously. Or it may up the ante, making the speaker, and then you, reach for new insults—or physical blows.

10   "If you don't laugh at the joke, or fight, or respond in kind to the slur," says Mr. McQuillan, "that will take the person by surprise, and that can give you more control over the situation." Therefore, in situations like the one in which I found myself—a private conversation in which I knew the person making the remark—he suggests voicing your anger calmly but pointedly: "I don't know if you realize what that sounded like to me. If that's what you meant, it really hurt me."

11   State how *you* feel, rather than making an abstract statement like, "Not everyone who hears that joke might find it funny." Counsels Mr. Strong: "Personalize the sense of 'this is how I feel when you say this.' That makes it very concrete"—and harder to dismiss.

12   Make sure you heard the words and their intent correctly by repeating or rephrasing the statement: "This is what I heard you say. Is that what you meant?" It's important to give the other person the benefit of the doubt because, in fact, he may *not* have realized that the comment was offensive and, if you had not spoken up, would have had no idea of its impact on you.

13   For instance, Professor Kahn relates that he used to include in his exams multiple-choice questions that occasionally contained "incorrect funny answers." After one exam, a student came up to him in private and said, "I don't think you intended this, but I found a number of those jokes offensive to me as a woman." She explained why. "What she said made immediate sense to me," he says. "I apologized at the next class, and I never did it again."

14   But what if the speaker dismisses your objection, saying, "Oh, you're just being sensitive. Can't you take a joke?" In that case, you might say, "I'm not so sure about that, let's talk about that a little more." The key, Mr. Strong says, is to continue the dialogue, hear the other person's concerns, and point out your own. "There are times when you're just going to have to admit defeat and end it," he adds, "but I have to feel that I did the best I could."

15   When the offending remark is made in the presence of others—at a staff meeting, for example—it can be even more distressing than an insult made privately.

16   "You have two options," says William Newlin, director of field services for the Community Relations division of the New York City Commission on Human Rights. "You can respond immediately at the meeting, or you can delay your response until afterward in private. But a response has to come."

17   Some remarks or actions may be so outrageous that they cannot go unnoted at the moment, regardless of the speaker or the setting. But in general, psychologists say, shaming a person in public may have the opposite effect of the one you want: The speaker will deny his offense all the more strongly in order to save face. Further, few

people enjoy being put on the spot, and if the remark really was not intended to be offensive, publicly embarrassing the person who made it may cause an unnecessary rift or further misunderstanding. Finally, most people just don't react as well or thoughtfully under a public spotlight as they would in private.

Keeping that in mind, an excellent alternative is to take the of- 18 fender aside afterward: "Could we talk for a minute in private?" Then use the strategies suggested above for calmly stating how you feel, giving the speaker the benefit of the doubt, and proceeding from there.

At a large meeting or public talk, you might consider passing the 19 speaker a note, says David Wertheimer, executive director of the New York City Gay and Lesbian Anti-Violence Project: You could write, "You may not realize it, but your remarks were offensive because. . . ."

"Think of your role as that of an educator," suggests James M. 20 Jones, Ph.D., executive director for public interest at the American Psychological Association. "You have to be controlled."

Regardless of the setting or situation, speaking up always raises 21 the risk of rocking the boat. If the person who made the offending remark is your boss, there may be an even bigger risk to consider: How will this affect my job? Several things can help minimize the risk, however. First, know what other resources you may have at work, suggests Caryl Stern, director of the A World of Difference—New York City campaign: Does your personnel office handle discrimination complaints? Are other grievance procedures in place?

You won't necessarily need to use any of these procedures, Ms. 22 Stern stresses. In fact, she advises, "It's usually better to try a one-on-one approach first." But simply knowing a formal system exists can make you feel secure enough to set up that meeting.

You can also raise the issue with other colleagues who heard the 23 remark: Did they feel the same way you did? The more support you have, the less alone you will feel. Your point will also carry more validity and be more difficult to shrug off. Finally, give your boss credit—and the benefit of the doubt: "I know you've worked hard for the company's affirmative action programs, so I'm sure you didn't realize what those remarks sounded like to me as well as the others at the meeting last week. . . ."

If, even after this discussion, the problem persists, go back for 24 another meeting, Ms. Stern advises. And if that, too, fails, you'll know what other options are available to you.

It's a spirited dinner party, and everyone's having a good time, until 25
one guest starts reciting a racist joke. Everyone at the table is white, including you. The others are still laughing, as you wonder what to say or do.

26   No one likes being seen as a party-pooper, but before deciding that you'd prefer not to take on this role, you might remember that the person who told the offensive joke has already ruined your good time.

27   If it's a group that you feel comfortable in—a family gathering, for instance—you will feel freer to speak up. Still, shaming the person by shouting 'You're wrong!" or "That's not funny!" probably won't get your point across as effectively as other strategies. "If you interrupt people to condemn them, it just makes it harder," says Cherie Brown. She suggests trying instead to get at the resentments that lie beneath the joke by asking open-ended questions: "Grandpa, I know you always treat everyone with such respect. Why do people in our family talk that way about black people?" The key, Ms. Brown says, "is to listen to them first, so they will be more likely to listen to you."

28   If you don't know your fellow guests well, before speaking up you could turn discreetly to your neighbors (or excuse yourself to help the host or hostess in the kitchen) to get a reading on how they felt, and whether or not you'll find support for speaking up. The less alone you feel, the more comfortable you'll be speaking up: "I know you probably didn't mean anything by that joke, Jim, but it really offended me. . . ." It's important to say that *you* were offended—not state how the group that is the butt of the joke would feel. "Otherwise," LeNorman Strong says, "you risk coming off as a goody two-shoes."

29   If you yourself are the host, you can exercise more control; you are, after all, the one who sets the rules and the tone of behavior in your home. Once, when Professor Kahn's party guests began singing offensive, racist songs, for instance, he kicked them all out, saying, "You don't sing songs like that in my house!" And, he adds, "they never did again."

30   *At school one day, a friend comes over and says, "Who do you think you are, hanging out with Joe? If you can be friends with those people, I'm through with you!"*

31   Peer pressure can weigh heavily on kids. They feel vulnerable and, because they are kids, they aren't as able to control the urge to fight. "But if you learn to handle these situations as kids, you'll be better able to handle them as an adult," William Newlin points out.

32   Begin by redefining to yourself what a friend is and examining what friendship means, advises Amy Lee, a human relations specialist at Panel of Americans, an intergroup-relations training and educational organization. If that person from a different group fits your requirement for a friend, ask, "Why shouldn't I be friends with Joe? We have a lot in common." Try to get more information about what-

Process

ever stereotypes or resentments lie beneath your friend's statement. Ms. Lee suggests: "What makes you think they're so different from us? Where did you get that information?" She explains: "People are learning these stereotypes from somewhere, and they cannot be blamed for that. So examine where these ideas came from." Then talk about how your own experience rebuts them.

Kids, like adults, should also be aware of other resources to back them up: Does the school offer special programs for fighting prejudice? How supportive will the principal, the teachers, or other students be? If the school atmosphere is volatile, experts warn, make sure that taking a stand at that moment won't put you in physical danger. If that is the case, it's better to look for other alternatives. 33

These can include programs or organizations that bring kids from different backgrounds together. "When kids work together across race lines, that is how you break down the barriers and see that the stereotypes are not true," says Laurie Meadoff, president of CityKids Foundation, a nonprofit group whose programs attempt to do just that. Such programs can also provide what Cherie Brown calls a "safe place" to express the anger and pain that slurs and other offenses cause, whether the bigotry is directed against you or others. 34

In learning to speak up, everyone will develop a different style and a slightly different message to get across, experts agree. But it would be hard to do better than these two messages suggested by teenagers at CityKids: "Everyone on the face of the earth has the same intestines," said one. Another added, "Cross over the bridge. There's a lot of love on the streets." 35

QUESTIONS ON SUBJECT AND PURPOSE

1. According to Cole, why should we object to "racial slurs and offensive ethnic jokes"?

2. The body of Cole's essay (paragraphs 8–34) offers strategies to use when confronting offensive remarks or jokes. How does Cole divide or organize this part of her subject?

3. What purposes might Cole have had in writing the essay?

QUESTIONS ON STRATEGY AND AUDIENCE

1. Why does Cole begin the essay with a personal example (paragraphs 1 and 2)?

2. Cole quotes a number of authorities in her essay. Why? What do the quotations and the authorities contribute to the article?

3. Why might Cole include the final section—the advice to children about handling such situations among friends? What does this section suggest about her intended audience?

QUESTIONS ON VOCABULARY AND STYLE

1. Throughout the essay Cole uses first- or second-person pronouns such as "I," "you," and "we." Why? How would the essay differ if she used "one" or "he or she"?

2. At several points (in paragraph 23, for instance), Cole suggests a possible response to a situation, enclosing that remark within quotation marks. Why might she create these imagined sentences for her reader?

3. Be prepared to define the following words: *ebullience* (paragraph 1), *tinged* (1), *rift* (17), *volatile* (33).

WRITING SUGGESTIONS

1. For your Journal. Would you honestly say that after reading Cole's essay you will respond as she suggests when you hear offensive remarks? Does it matter if they are directed at a group to which you belong or at another group? Start with a typical offensive remark that you have often heard and then plan a response to it. If you feel that you would still "just stand there," explain for yourself why you would choose not to react.

2. For a Paragraph. Studies from colleges and universities across the United States suggest that many students have "cheated" at some point during their college years. Typically, these students either plagiarized someone else's work in a paper or a laboratory report or copied answers on a quiz or exam. Suppose that a friend asks to borrow your research paper or laboratory report, explaining that he or she wants to submit it as his or her own work, or that a friend tries to "copy" answers from your paper. How can you handle such a situation? In a process paragraph, explain a procedure for replying to that person.

3. For an Essay. Cole's essay describes a process—what to do when you encounter prejudice. Select another occasion when we might need advice on how to handle a similarly awkward situation, and write an essay offering advice on what to do.

Prewriting:

a. Brainstorm about possible difficult situations—dealing with roommates, friends, or coworkers; observing a classmate cheating on a test or causing distractions in class; and so forth. Jot down as many uncomfortable situations as possible.

b. Ask some friends about similar experiences they might have had. How did they react? Try out your ideas on them.

c. Select what seems to be the most promising possibility and try freewriting for 20 minutes. Do not worry about your grammar; concentrate on getting some ideas from which to begin writing. If you are not pleased with the result, switch to another topic and try freewriting on it.

Rewriting:

a. Look carefully at the organizational strategy you have used. Are the steps in the process in a logical order? Could you, for example, construct a flow chart outlining those steps?

b. Try writing imaginary responses to the situation as Cole does. Remember to put these sentences within quotation marks. Does that strategy seem effective?

c. Reread your introduction. Does it re-create the situation for the reader? Does it catch a reader's interest? Compare your introductory strategy with that used by Cole.

4. For Research. Many colleges and universities have established policies for dealing with sexual harassment and discrimination. Research your own institution's position on these issues. See if, for example, a policy statement is available. You might also wish to interview members of the administration and faculty. Then, using your research, write an essay in which you explain to students how to handle a case of sexual harassment or discrimination.

HOW BOOKS HELPED
SHAPE MY LIFE
Judith Viorst

Judith Viorst was born in Newark, New Jersey, and educated at Rutgers University and the Washington Psychoanalytic Institute. She is a poet, journalist, and writer of fifteen children's books. She has worked as contributing editor and columnist for Redbook *magazine, and her poems and essays have appeared in major national publications. Her books for adults include* It's Hard to Be Hip over Thirty and Other Tragedies of Married Life, *a book of poems (1968),* When Did I Stop Being 20 and Other Injustices: Selected Poems from Single to Mid-Life *(1987), and* Murdering Mr. Monti *(1994), her first novel.*

"How Books Helped Shape My life" was first published in Redbook *magazine, a consideration that obviously influenced her choice of subject and approach. Viorst traces the influence of fictional heroines on her own personality—how they served "as ideals, as models, as possibilities."*

BEFORE READING

Connecting: At the start of the essay, Viorst talks about "searching for heroines who could serve as ideals, as models, as possibilities." Can you remember ever "searching" for a heroine or a hero? Is it something that only children do?

Anticipating: Viorst discusses six fictional heroines. How does she arrange her six examples? What is the central thread that provides the organization for her essay?

1   In books I've read since I was young I've searched for heroines who could serve as ideals, as models, as possibilities—some reflecting the secret self that dwelled inside me, others pointing to whole new ways that a woman (if only she dared!) might try to be. The person that I am today was shaped by Nancy Drew; by Jo March, Jane Eyre and Heathcliff's soul mate Cathy; and by other fictional females whose attractiveness or character or audacity for a time were the standards by which I measured myself.

2   I return to some of these books to see if I still understand the powerful hold that these heroines once had on me. I still understand.

Consider teen-aged Nancy Drew—beautiful, blond-haired, 3
blue-eyed girl detective—who had the most terrific life that I as a ten-year-old could ever imagine. Motherless (in other words, quite free of maternal controls), she lived with her handsome indulgent lawyer father in a large brick house set back from the street with a winding tree-lined driveway on the outside and a faithful, nonintrusive housekeeper Hannah cooking yummy meals on the inside. She also had a boy friend, a convertible, nice clothes and two close girl friends—not as perfect as she, but then it seemed to me that no one could possibly be as perfect as Nancy Drew, who in dozens and dozens of books (*The Hidden Staircase, The Whispering Statue, The Clue in the Diary, The Clue of the Tapping Heels*) was resourceful and brave and intelligent as she went around solving mysteries left and right, while remaining kind to the elderly and invariably polite and absolutely completely delightfully feminine.

I mean, what else *was* there? 4

I soon found out what else when I encountered the four March 5
sisters of *Little Women*, a sentimental, old-fashioned book about girls growing up in Civil War time in New England. About spoiled, vain, pretty Amy. And sickly, saintly Beth. And womanly, decent Meg. And about—most important of all—gawky, bookworm Jo. Dear Jo, who wasn't as flawless as the golden Nancy Drew but who showed me that girls like her—like *us*—could be heroines. Even if we weren't much to look at. Even if we were clumsy and socially gauche. And even if the transition into young womanhood often appeared to our dubious eye to be difficult and scary and even unwelcome.

Jo got stains on her dress and laughed when she shouldn't and 6
lost her temper and didn't display tact or patience or restraint. Jo brought a touch of irreverence to the cultural constraints of the world she lived in. And yet her instincts were good and her heart was pure and her headstrong ways led always to virtue. And furthermore Jo—as I yearned to be—was a writer!

In the book the years go by, Beth dies, Meg and Amy marry and 7
Jo—her fierce heart somewhat tamed—is alone. "An old maid, that's what I'm to be. A literary spinster, with a pen for a spouse, a family of stories for children, and twenty years hence a morsel of fame, perhaps!" . . . Jo sighed, as if the prospect was not inviting.

This worried young reader concurred—not inviting at all! 8

And so I was happy to read of Jo's nice suitor. Mr. Bhaer, not 9
handsome or rich or young or important or witty, but possessed of kindness and dignity and enough intelligence to understand that even a girl who wasn't especially pretty, who had no dazzling charms and who wanted to write might make a wonderful wife. And a wonderful mother. And live happily ever after.

10   What a relief!

11   What Jo and Nancy shared was active participation in life—they went out and *did*; they weren't simply done to—and they taught and promised me (at a time when mommies stayed home and there was no Women's Movement) that a girl could go out and do and still get a man. Jo added the notion that brusque, ungainly girls could go out and do and still get a man. And Jane of *Jane Eyre*, whose author once said, "I will show you a heroine as small and as plain as myself," added the further idea that such women were able to "feel just as men feel" and were capable of being just as passionate.

12   Orphaned Jane, a governess at stately Thornfield Hall, was a no-nonsense lady, cool and self-contained, whose lonely, painful childhood had ingrained in her an impressive firmness of character, an unwillingness to charm or curry favor and a sense of herself as the equal of any man. Said Jane to Mr. Rochester, the brooding, haughty, haunted master of Thornfield: "Do you think I am an automaton?—a machine without feelings? Do you think, because I am poor, obscure, plain, and little, I am soulless and heartless? You think wrong!—I have as much soul as you, and full as much heart!"

13   I loved it that such hot fires burned inside so plain a Jane. I loved her for her unabashed intensity. And I loved her for being so pure that when she learned of Mr. Rochester's lunatic wife, she sacrificed romance for honor and left him immediately.

14   For I think it's important to note that Nancy and Jo and Jane, despite their independence, were basically as good as girls can be: honest, generous, kind, sincere, reliable, respectable, possessed of absolute integrity. They didn't defy convention. They didn't challenge the rules. They did what was right, although it might cause them pain. And their virtue was always rewarded—look at Jane, rich and married at last to her Mr. Rochester. Oh, how I identified with Jane!

15   But then I read *Wuthering Heights*, a novel of soul-consuming love on the Yorkshire moors, and Catherine Earnshaw totally captured me. And she captured me, not in spite of her dangerous, dark and violent spirit, but *because* of it.

16   Cathy was as wild as the moors. She lied and connived and deceived. She was insolent, selfish, manipulative and cruel. And by marrying meek, weak Edgar instead of Heathcliff, her destiny, she betrayed a love she described in throbbing, forgettable prose as . . . elemental:

17   "My love for Heathcliff resembles the eternal rocks beneath—a source of little visible delight, but necessary. Nelly, I *am* Heathcliff—he's always, always in my mind—not as a pleasure, any more than I am always a pleasure to myself—but as my own being. . . ."

Now who, at the age of 16, could resist such quivering intensity? Who would settle for less than elemental? Must we untamed creatures of passion—I'd muse as I lay awake in my red flannel nightie—submit ourselves to conventional morality? Or could I actually choose not to be a good girl?

Cathy Earnshaw told me that I could. And so did lost Lady Brett, of *The Sun Also Rises*.

Brett Ashley was to me, at 18, free, modern, woman incarnate, and she dangled alluring new concepts before my eyes:

The value of style: "She wore a slipover jersey sweater and a tweed skirt, and her hair was brushed back like a boy's. She started all that."

The glamour of having a dark and tortured past: "Finally, when he got really bad, he used to tell her he'd kill her. . . . She hasn't had an absolutely happy life."

The excitement of nonconformity: "I've always done just what I wanted."

The importance of (understated) grace under pressure: "Brett was rather good. She's always rather good."

And the thrill of unrepressed sexuality: "Brett's had affairs with men before. She tells me all about everything."

Brett married lovelessly and drank too much and drifted too much and had an irresponsible fling with a bullfighter. But she also had class—and her own morality. She set her bullfighter free—"I'd have lived with him if I hadn't seen it was bad for him." And even though she was broke, she lied and "told him I had scads of it. . . . I couldn't take his money, you know."

Brett's wasn't the kind of morality that my mother was teaching me in suburban New Jersey. But maybe I wasn't meant for suburban life. Maybe—I would muse as I carefully lined my eyes with blue liner—maybe I'm meant for something more . . . emancipated.

I carried Brett's image with me when, after college, I lived for a while in Greenwich Village, in New York. But I couldn't achieve her desperate gallantry. And it struck me that Brett was too lonely and sad, and that Cathy had died too young (and that Scarlett O'Hara got Tara but lost her Rhett), and that maybe I ought to forget about unconventionality if the price was going to be so painfully high. Although I enjoyed my Village fling, I had no wish to live anguishedly ever after. I needed a heroine who, like me, wanted just a small taste of the wild before settling down into happy domesticity.

I found her in *War and Peace*. Her name was Natasha.

Natasha, the leading lady of this epic of Russian society during Napoleon's time, was "poetic . . . charming . . . overflowing with life," an enchanting girl whose sweet eagerness and passionate impulsivity

18

19

20

21

22

23

24

25

26

27

28

29

30

were tempered by historic and private tragedies. Betrothed to the handsome and excellent Prince Andrew, she fell in love with a heel named Anatole, and when she was warned that this foolish and dangerous passion would lead to her ruin, "I'll go to my ruin . . .," she said, "as soon as possible."

31   It ended badly with Anatole. Natasha tried suicide. Prince Andrew died. Natasha turned pale, thin, subdued. But unlike Brett and Cathy, her breach with convention was mended and, at long last, she married Pierre—a decent, substantial, loving man, the kind of man all our mothers want us to marry.

32   In marriage Natasha grew stouter and "the old fire very rarely kindled in her face now." She became an exemplary mother, an ideal wife. "She felt that her unity with her husband was maintained not by the poetic feelings that had attracted him to her but by something else—indefinite but firm as the bond between her own body and soul."

33   It sounded—if not elemental and doomed—awfully nice.

34   I identified with Natasha when, the following year, I married and left Greenwich Village. I too was ready for domesticity. And yet . . . her husband and children became "the subject which wholly engrossed Natasha's attention." She had lost herself—and I didn't want to lose me. What I needed next was a heroine who could reconcile all the warring wants of my nature—for fire and quiet, independence and oneness, ambition and love, and marriage and family.

35   But such reconciling heroines, in novels and real life, may not yet exist.

36   Nevertheless Natasha and Jane and Jo, Cathy, Nancy and Brett—each spoke to my heart and stirred me powerfully. On my journey to young womanhood I was fortunate to have them as my companions. They were, they will always remain, a part of me.

QUESTIONS ON SUBJECT AND PURPOSE

1. How many heroines does Viorst treat? What does she see in each? How are those qualities related to her own maturation?

2. When you were a child did any hero or heroine seem a particularly attractive model? Was he or she a character in a novel? Has television or film replaced novels as a source of models? Were any of these real-life models?

3. Why would any reader be interested in an essay explaining how something shaped your life? Did you find anything of interest here? If so, why? If not, why not?

QUESTIONS ON STRATEGY AND AUDIENCE

1. How does Viorst structure her essay? What progression is there? What controls the arrangement of the heroines?

2. Viorst switches the way she handles her examples when she reaches Lady Brett in *The Sun Also Rises*. Why the change?

3. For whom is Viorst writing? What expectations does she have of her audience? Can you find specific evidence to support your assumptions?

QUESTIONS ON VOCABULARY AND STYLE

1. Viorst frequently uses dashes in her sentences. What is the effect of their use?

2. Viorst seems to delight in breaking the rules we might expect writing to obey. Consider the following categories of examples and be able to show how and why each works in the essay:

   a. Informal, even casual words ("yummy," "a heel")

   b. Clichés ("solving mysteries left and right," "live happily ever after")

   c. Sentence fragments

   d. Extremely short paragraphs

3. Be able to define the following words: *gawky* (paragraph 5), *gauche* (5), *brusque* (11), *curry favor* (12), *unabashed* (13), *incarnate* (20).

WRITING SUGGESTIONS

1. **For your Journal**. Who served as your models when you were between the ages of 10 and 15? Your list can include real people and characters from films, television, or books. Next to each name try to jot down the reasons why you admired this person or character. If you find it difficult to isolate figures from that time in your life, try another age. If you can think of no such figures, speculate on why models were not attractive to you.

2. **For a Paragraph**. Select one of the figures you wrote about in your journal, and write a paragraph in which you explain why that particular model was important to you at that particular stage in your life. Remember that your goal is not just to narrate a story; you should explain what that figure meant to

you—how that figure reflected your life and values at that moment in time.

3. **For an Essay.** "How _____ Helped Shape My Life." Using Viorst's essay as a structural model, write a process analysis showing how a series of events, situations, or people helped you grow up. Subjects might include teachers, friends, or supervisors; jobs or hobbies; books or movies; or different places you've lived.

Prewriting:

a. A workable subject must meet two criteria. First, the items in the series must be parallel in form. (Viorst's are all characters from books.) Second, each item must have played a role in your life at a particular time. (Viorst's reflect her reading from age 10 to her mid-20s.) With those criteria in mind, brainstorm a list of possible subjects.

b. Narrow your list to the two best possibilities. Then decide how many time periods you could represent. Viorst includes six. That is probably too many for your essay, but be sure to have at least three. For both subjects, list in outline form the time periods you could include with an example representing each. Finally, narrow your focus to the most promising subject.

c. Develop each example for this subject clearly. Ask friends who are the same age what they remember about their growing up. Ask them to evaluate the examples you plan to use. That might help add important details.

Rewriting:

a. For each of the examples that you include, complete the following statement: "What this example meant to me was _____." Write your answers on a separate sheet of paper.

b. Look back at Viorst's essay. Not every reader has read these books, so Viorst is careful to explain exactly what was appealing or influential about each one. Have you made your essay accessible to readers?

c. The appeal of Viorst's essay is its universality. Because we all grow up and because we go through certain common stages in that process, we are interested in her analysis. Can you say the same thing about your essay? Have you made it universal enough? Will the reader want to keep reading?

Find a peer reader, and check your essay's appeal. If your reader is bored, ask why.

4. **For Research.** Viorst's essay is similar to Sheehy's "Predictable Crises of Adulthood" (Chapter 4) in that it traces the stages in Viorst's development from her preteen years to her mid-20s. To what extent does Viorst's description of her own maturation process coincide with the maturation process in other children? Are these, for example, "predictable" stages? What does research tell us about the maturation process from the preteen years to the early 20s? Your reference librarian will be able to point you to the appropriate indexes and databases to research the question. Be sure to document your sources wherever appropriate.

ON KEEPING A NOTEBOOK

Joan Didion

Joan Didion was born in Sacramento in 1934 and received a B.A. from the University of California at Berkeley in 1956. Also a novelist and screenwriter, Didion is probably best-known for her nonfiction reporting and her personal essays, the latest collection of which is After Henry *(1992), about current events of the eighties. In much of her writing she vividly portrays the personal chaos of modern American life through gripping examples and pointed direct quotations. One critic recently observed: "Didion . . . [is] practical, existential, and thoroughly informed about the facts of whatever event or subject she chooses to write about. She is voracious for facts. Her workspace must be crammed with notebooks."*

In the following selection, Didion reveals the role that her notebooks take in her writing process. Didion's essay is not a "how-to-do-something" process analysis, but she does use process to describe how and why she keeps a notebook. Along the way, she establishes some crucial distinctions between a notebook and a diary. "The point of my keeping a notebook," she writes, "has never been, nor is it now, to have an accurate factual record of what I have been doing or thinking."

BEFORE READING

Connecting: What would you expect that a writer would record in her notebook? Would it be the same as what she might record in a diary? To you, do the two words—notebook and diary—imply different types of records?

Anticipating: According to the essay, why does Didion keep notebooks?

1   "'That woman Estelle,'" the note reads, "'is partly the reason why George Sharp and I are separated today.' *Dirty crepe-de-Chine wrapper, hotel bar, Wilmington RR, 9:45 A.M.* August Monday morning."

2   Since the note is in my notebook, it presumably has some meaning to me. I study it for a long while. At first I have only the most general notion of what I was doing on an August Monday morning in the bar of the hotel across from the Pennsylvania Rail-

road station in Wilmington, Delaware (waiting for a train? missing one? 1960? 1961? why Wilmington?), but I do remember being there. The woman in the dirty crepe-de-Chine wrapper had come down from her room for a beer, and the bartender had heard before the reason why George Sharp and she were separated today. "Sure," he said, and went on mopping the floor. "You told me." At the other end of the bar is a girl. She is talking, pointedly, not to the man beside her but to a cat lying in the triangle of sunlight cast through the open door. She is wearing a plaid silk dress from Peck & Peck, and the hem is coming down.

Here is what it is: the girl has been on the Eastern Shore, and now she is going back to the city, leaving the man beside her, and all she can see ahead are the viscous summer sidewalks and the 3 A.M. long-distance calls that will make her lie awake and then sleep drugged through all the steaming mornings left in August (1960? 1961?). Because she must go directly from the train to lunch in New York, she wishes that she had a safety pin for the hem of the plaid silk dress, and she also wishes that she could forget about the hem and the lunch and stay in the cool bar that smells of disinfectant and malt and make friends with the woman in the crepe-de-Chine wrapper. She is afflicted by a little self-pity, and she wants to compare Estelles. That is what that was all about. 3

Why did I write it down? In order to remember, of course, but exactly what was it I wanted to remember? How much of it actually happened? Did any of it? Why do I keep a notebook at all? It is easy to deceive oneself on all those scores. The impulse to write things down is a peculiarly compulsive one, inexplicable to those who do not share it, useful only accidentally, only secondarily, in the way that any compulsion tries to justify itself. I suppose that it begins or does not begin in the cradle. Although I have felt compelled to write things down since I was five years old, I doubt that my daughter ever will, for she is a singularly blessed and accepting child, delighted with life exactly as life presents itself to her, unafraid to go to sleep and unafraid to wake up. Keepers of private notebooks are a different breed altogether, lonely and resistant rearrangers of things, anxious malcontents, children afflicted apparently at birth with some presentiment of loss. 4

My first notebook was a Big Five tablet, given to me by my mother with the sensible suggestion that I stop whining and learn to amuse myself by writing down my thoughts. She returned the tablet to me a few years ago; the first entry is an account of a woman who believed herself to be freezing to death in the Arctic night, only to find, when day broke, that she had stumbled onto the Sahara Desert, where she would die of the heat before lunch. I have no idea what turn of a five-year-old's mind could have prompted so insistently 5 "ironic" and exotic a story, but it does reveal a certain predilection for the extreme which has dogged me into adult life; perhaps if I were analytically inclined I would find it a truer story than any I might have told about Donald Johnson's birthday party or the day my cousin Brenda put Kitty Litter in the aquarium.

6　　So the point of my keeping a notebook has never been, nor is it now, to have an accurate factual record of what I have been doing or thinking. That would be a different impulse entirely, an instinct for reality which I sometimes envy but do not possess. At no point have I ever been able successfully to keep a diary; my approach to daily life ranges from the grossly negligent to the merely absent, and on those few occasions when I have tried dutifully to record a day's events, boredom has so overcome me that the results are mysterious at best. What is this business about "shopping, typing piece, dinner with E, depressed"? Shopping for what? Typing what piece? Who is E? Was this "E" depressed, or was I depressed? Who cares?

7　　In fact I have abandoned altogether that kind of pointless entry; instead I tell what some would call lies. "That's simply not true," the members of my family frequently tell me when they come up against my memory of a shared event. "The party was not for you, the spider was *not* a black widow, *it wasn't that way at all.*" Very likely they are right, for not only have I always had trouble distinguishing between what happened and what merely might have happened, but I remain unconvinced that the distinction, for my purposes, matters. The cracked crab that I recall having for lunch the day my father came home from Detroit in 1945 must certainly be embroidery, worked into the day's pattern to lend verisimilitude; I was ten years old and would not now remember the cracked crab. The day's events did not turn on cracked crab. And yet it is precisely that fictitious crab that makes me see the afternoon all over again, a home movie run all too often, the father bearing gifts, the child weeping, an exercise in family love and guilt. Or that is what it was to me. Similarly, perhaps it never did snow that August in Vermont; perhaps there never were flurries in the night wind, and maybe no one else felt the ground hardening and summer already dead even as we pretended to bask in it, but that was how it felt to me, and it might as well have snowed, could have snowed, did snow.

8　　*How it felt to me*: that is getting closer to the truth about a notebook. I sometimes delude myself about why I keep a notebook, imagine that some thrifty virtue derives from preserving everything observed. See enough and write it down, I tell myself and then some morning when the world seems drained of wonder, some day when I am only going through the motions of doing what I am supposed to do, which is write—on that bankrupt morning I will simply open my notebook and there it will be, a forgotten account with accumulated interest, paid passage back to the world out there: dialogue overheard in hotels and elevators and at the hatcheck counter in Pavillon (one middle-aged man shows his hat check to another and says, "That's my old football number"); impressions of Bettina Aptheker and Benjamin Sonnenberg and Teddy ("Mr. Acapulco") Stauffer; careful *aperçus* about tennis bums and failed fashion models and Greek shipping heiresses, one of whom taught me a significant lesson (a lesson I could have learned from F. Scott Fitzgerald, but perhaps we all must meet the very rich for ourselves) by asking, when I arrived to interview her in her orchid-filled sitting room on the second day of a paralyzing New York blizzard, whether it was snowing outside.

I imagine, in other words, that the notebook is about other people. But of course it is not. I have no real business with what one stranger said to another at the hatcheck counter in Pavillon; in fact I suspect that the line "That's my old football number" touched not my own imagination at all, but merely some memory of something once read, probably "The Eighty-Yard Run." Nor is my concern with a woman in a dirty crepe-de-Chine wrapper in a Wilmington bar. My stake is always, of course, in the unmentioned girl in the plaid silk dress. *Remember what it was to be me*: that is always the point.

It is a difficult point to admit. We are brought up in the ethic that others, any others, all others, are by definition more interesting than ourselves; taught to be diffident, just this side of self-effacing. ("You're the least important person in the room and don't forget it," Jessica Mitford's governess would hiss in her ear on the advent of any social occasion; I copied that into my notebook because it is only recently that I have been able to enter a room without hearing some such phrase in my inner ear.) Only the very young and the very old may recount their dreams at breakfast, dwell upon self, interrupt with memories of beach picnics and favorite Liberty lawn dresses and the rainbow trout in a creek near Colorado Springs. The rest of us are expected, rightly, to affect absorption in other people's favorite dresses, other people's trout.

And so we do. But our notebooks give us away, for however dutifully we record what we see around us, the common denominator of all we see is always, transparently, shamelessly, the implacable "I". We are not talking here about the kind of notebook that is patently for public consumption, a structural conceit for binding together a series of graceful *pensées*; we are talking about something private, about bits of the mind's string too short to use, an indiscriminate and erratic assemblage with meaning only for its maker.

12   And sometimes even the maker has difficulty with the meaning. There does not seem to be, for example, any point in my knowing for the rest of my life that, during 1964, 720 tons of soot fell on every square mile of New York City, yet there it is in my notebook, labeled "FACT." Nor do I really need to remember that Ambrose Bierce liked to spell Leland Stanford's name "£eland $tanford" or that "smart women almost always wear black in Cuba," a fashion hint without much potential for practical application. And does not the relevance of these notes seem marginal at best?:

13   In the basement museum of the Inyo County Courthouse in Independence, California, sign pinned to a mandarin coat: "This MANDARIN COAT was often worn by Mrs. Minnie S. Brooks when giving lectures on her TEAPOT COLLECTION."

Redhead getting out of car in front of Beverly Wilshire Hotel, chinchilla stole, Vuitton bags with tags reading:

MRS LOU FOX

HOTEL SAHARA

VEGAS

14   Well, perhaps not entirely marginal. As a matter of fact, Mrs. Minnie S. Brooks and her MANDARIN COAT pull me back into my own childhood, for although I never knew Mrs. Brooks and did not visit Inyo County until I was thirty, I grew up in just such a world, in houses cluttered with Indian relics and bits of gold ore and ambergris and the souvenirs my Aunt Mercy Farnsworth brought back from the Orient. It is a long way from that world to Mrs. Lou Fox's world where we all live now, and is it not just as well to remember that? Might not Mrs. Minnie S. Brooks help me to remember what I am? Might not Mrs. Lou Fox help me to remember what I am not?

15   But sometimes the point is harder to discern. What exactly did I have in mind when I noted down that it cost the father of someone I know $650 a month to light the place on the Hudson in which he lived before the Crash? What use was I planning to make of this line by Jimmy Hoffa: "I may have my faults, but being wrong ain't one of them"? And although I think it interesting to know where the girls who travel with the Syndicate have their hair done when they find themselves on the West Coast, will I ever make suitable use of it? Might I not be better off just passing it on to John O'Hara? What is a recipe for sauerkraut doing in my notebook? What kind of magpie keeps this notebook? *"He was born the night the Titanic went down."* That seems a nice enough line, and I even recall

who said it, but is it not really a better line in life than it could ever be in fiction?

But of course that is exactly it: not that I should ever use the line, but that I should remember the woman who said it and the afternon I heard it. We were on her terrace by the sea, and we were finishing the wine left from lunch, trying to get what sun there was, a California winter sun. The woman whose husband was born the night the *Titanic* went down wanted to rent her house, wanted to go back to her children in Paris. I remember wishing that I could afford the house, which cost $1,000 a month. "Someday you will," she said lazily. "Someday it all comes." There in the sun on her terrace it seemed easy to believe in someday but later I had a low-grade afternoon hangover and ran over a black snake on the way to the supermarket and was flooded with inexplicable fear when I heard the checkout clerk explaining to the man ahead of me why she was finally divorcing her husband. "He left me no choice," she said over and over as she punched the register. "He has a little seven-month-old baby by her, he left me no choice." I would like to believe that my dread then was for the human condition, but of course it was for me, because I wanted to own the house that cost $1,000 a month to rent and because I had a hangover.

It all comes back. Perhaps it is difficult to see the value in having one's self back in that kind of mood, but I do see it; I think we are well advised to keep on nodding terms with the people we used to be, whether we find them attractive company or not. Otherwise they turn up unannounced and surprise us, come hammering on the mind's door at 4 A.M. of a bad night and demand to know who deserted them, who betrayed them, who is going to make amends. We forget all too soon the things we thought we could never forget. We forget the loves and the betrayals alike, forget what we whispered and what we screamed, forget who we were. I have already lost touch with a couple of people I used to be; one of them, a seventeen-year-old, presents little threat, although it would be of some interest to me to know again what it feels like to sit on a river levee drinking vodka-and-orange-juice and listening to Les Paul and Mary Ford and their echoes sing "How High the Moon" on the car radio. (You see I still have the scenes, but I no longer perceive myself among those present, no longer could even improvise the dialogue.) The other one, a twenty-three-year old, bothers me more. She was always a good deal of trouble, and I suspect she will reappear when I least want to see her, skirts too long, shy to the point of aggravation, always the injured party, full of recriminations and little hurts and stories I do not want to hear again, at once saddening me and angering me with her vulnerability and ignorance, an apparition all the more insistent for being so long banished.

18   It is a good idea, then, to keep in touch and I suppose that keeping in touch is what notebooks are all about. And we are all on our own when it comes to keeping those lines open to ourselves: your notebooks will never help me, nor mine you. *"So what's new in the whiskey business?"* What could that possibly mean to you? To me it means a blonde in a Pucci bathing suit sitting with a couple of fat men by the pool at the Beverly Hills Hotel. Another man approaches, and they all regard one another in silence for a while. "So what's new in the whiskey business?" one of the fat men finally says by way of welcome, and the blonde stands up, arches one foot and dips it in the pool, looking all the while at the cabana where Baby Pignatari is talking on the telephone. That is all there is to that, except that several years later I saw the blonde coming out of Saks Fifth Avenue in New York with her California complexion and a voluminous mink coat. In the harsh wind that day she looked old and irrevocably tired to me, and even the skins in the mink coat were not worked the way they were doing them that year, not the way she would have wanted them done, and there is the point of the story. For a while after that I did not like to look in the mirror, and my eyes would skim the newspapers and pick out only the deaths, the cancer victims, the premature coronaries, the suicides, and I stopped riding the Lexington Avenue IRT because I noticed for the first time that all the strangers I had seen for years—the man with the seeing-eye dog, the spinster who read the classified pages every day, the fat girl who always got off with me at Grand Central—looked older than they once had.

19   It all comes back. Even that recipe for sauerkraut: even that brings it back. I was on Fire Island when I first made that sauerkraut, and it was raining, and we drank a lot of bourbon and ate the sauerkraut and went to bed at ten, and I listened to the rain and the Atlantic and felt safe. I made the sauerkraut again last night and it did not make me feel any safer, but that is, as they say, another story.

QUESTIONS ON SUBJECT AND PURPOSE

1. Why does Didion keep a notebook? What types of things does she record? How does a notebook differ from a diary?

2. In paragraph 7, Didion acknowledges that what she records did not always happen and that, for her purposes, it does not really matter. What does she mean by this? Why would she record "lies"?

3. If the notebook helps Didion remember "what it was to be me" (paragraph 9), why should anyone be interested in her essay? Is the essay as egocentric as the notebook? Is there any purpose to this other than self-discovery—what all this means to *me*, Joan Didion?

QUESTIONS ON STRATEGY AND AUDIENCE

1. The essay follows a pattern of discovery. Didion seems to discover why she keeps a notebook as she writes the essay. But that might also be a fiction. She might have known before she wrote the essay. Either way, what does such a pattern add to the essay? Why might Didion have chosen to explain in such a way?

2. How effective is the introduction? The conclusion?

3. What do the examples in her notebook tell Didion? What common thread links all of the examples she uses?

4. What expectations does Didion have of her audience? Are they realized? Use your own reading as a test.

QUESTIONS ON VOCABULARY AND STYLE

1. Why does Didion use typographical devices in the essay (things like the italics or the parentheses or the indented entries in paragraph 13)?

2. At a number of points in the essay Didion asks a group of questions about a particular entry and then goes on to answer them. What is the effect of this stylistic device? How is it related to the structure of the essay?

3. Be able to define the following: *crepe-de-Chine* (paragraph 1), *malcontent* (4), *presentiment* (4), *predilection* (5), *verisimilitude* (7), *aperçus* (8), *implacable* (11), *pensées* (11), *ambergris* (14), *recriminations* (17).

WRITING SUGGESTIONS

1. For your Journal. After carefully reading Didion's essay, write an entry modeled on the type that Didion records in her notebooks. Remember that she notes, "the point of my keeping a notebook has never been . . . to have an accurate factual record of what I have been doing or thinking." What then is the point of making entries? Answer that question by writing an entry that reveals about you what Didion's entries reveal about her.

2. **For a Paragraph.** Using the advice that Didion provides (often indirectly) write a paragraph in which you explain to a reader how to keep a notebook. Think of your paragraph as something that could be given to writers who are puzzled about the directions for the previous journal writing assignment. Make the process and the advice clear.

3. **For an Essay.** Both Didion and Judith Viorst describe by means of process how influences and experiences have shaped their lives. Look back on what has brought you here to this present moment. Then select several important events or influences that helped shape your life. Using those examples, write a process analysis on how you have come to be where you are now.

Prewriting:

a. The events/experiences/influences need to be linked only by the extent to which they helped shape your life. They can be different in form; that is, one can be a person, one an experience, one a book. You will probably need three or four at least. Brainstorm a possible list of subjects by starting with this question: "What has made me what I am?" Try to get more examples than you will eventually use. Work on your list for several days.

b. Use freewriting to develop each of the examples that you plan to use. Write for 15 minutes without stopping on each item. You might not use any of this material in your essay, but freewriting will give you a chance to experiment with what you want to say about each item.

c. Plan an organizational strategy by making an outline. The primary sequence will probably be chronological, but that is not necessary. Didion's examples are not arranged chronologically. Maybe a pattern of discovery is better. Compare the organizational patterns used by Viorst and Didion. Can you use either pattern as a model for your essay?

Rewriting:

a. Viorst and Didion use two different techniques to begin their essays; Viorst's introduction is a clear statement of her thesis. Didion's is a journalistic "hook" designed to provoke the reader's curiosity. Both are effective. Look at your introduction. Which strategy do you use? Freewrite an alternative beginning to your paper.

b. Part of the appeal of Didion's essay—like Viorst's—is its universality. We all feel the need to know who we are and who we were. Does your essay have that same appeal? Ask a peer to read your essay and then respond to the following questions: Are the experiences here common? Do you care about the narrator, or do you feel that the narrator is imposing his or her life story on you? Does the writer explain the significance of these events, experiences, and influences? Use your reader's response in revising your essay.

c. It is always good to rethink your organizational strategy. Make a copy of your essay, cut the body paragraphs apart, and rearrange them in an alternative order. (If you are working on a word processor, you can just move text blocks around.) Force yourself to experiment with this change. Is the new order any better? Even if it isn't, the process will make you look in a new way at the sequence you have used.

4. **For Research**. Didion remarks, "I think we are well advised to keep on nodding terms with the people we used to be" (paragraph 17). Is it ever possible to remember who we used to be? To what extent do we "rewrite" our lives as we grow older? Is any autobiography true? What goes into an autobiography? Research what writers have said about writing autobiography (the *Library of Congress Subject Headings* in your school's library will give you a good place to start). Then, in an essay, describe the process of writing autobiography. Be sure to document your sources wherever appropriate.

CAUSE AND EFFECT

It is a rainy morning and you are late for class. Driving to campus in an automobile with faulty brakes, you have an accident. Considering the circumstances, the accident might be attributable to a variety of causes:

> you were driving too fast
> the visibility was poor
> the roads were slippery
> the brakes did not work properly

The accident, in turn, could produce a series of consequences or effects:

> you miss class
> you get a ticket
> your license is suspended
> you injure yourself or someone else

As this suggests, cause and effect analyses frequently can go in either direction—an examination of the reasons why something occurred or of the effects or consequences that follow from a particular event or situation.

Susan Strasser, for example, uses a cause and effect strategy when she suggests that part of the popularity of fast food restaurants lies in the appeal of "stylized, repetitive, stereotyped events." Notice how Strasser structures the following paragraph to show how this ritualization is one "cause" for such restaurants' popularity:

> People arrive at McDonald's—and to a lesser extent at the other chains—knowing what they will eat, what they will pay, what to say to the counter person and how she or he will respond, what the restaurant will look like—in short, knowing exactly what to expect

and how to behave; children learn these expectations and behaviors early in life. For some, the ritual constitutes an attraction of these restaurants; they neither wish to cook nor to chat with a waitress as she intones and delivers the daily specials. The fast-food ritual requires no responsibility other than ordering (with as few words as possible) and paying; nobody has to set or clear the table, wash the dishes, or compliment the cook on her cuisine, the traditional responsibilities of husbands and children at the family dinner.*

Strasser turns her analysis of fast food restaurants in the other direction—toward effects—when she discusses how "fast food eating" has affected mealtime rituals at home:

Fast foods have changed eating habits far beyond the food itself; they have invaded the mealtime ritual even at home. The chief executive officer of Kraft, Inc., maintained that eating out accustomed people to "portion control" and therefore to accepting a processor's statement that a package of macaroni and cheese serves four. "Generally speaking," one writer claimed in *Advertising Age*, "the homemaker no longer sets the table with dishes of food from which the family fills their plates—the individual plates are filled and placed before the family, no second helpings." Eating out even accustoms diners at the same table to eating different food, putting home meals of different prepared foods within the realm of possibility and altering the nature of parental discipline; freed from the "shut up—you'll eat what we're eating" rule, children experience the pleasures and also the isolation of individual free choice at earlier ages.*

Causes and effects can be either *immediate* or *remote* with reference to time. The lists above regarding a hypothetical car accident suggest only immediate causes and effects, those things which could be most directly linked in time to the accident. Another pair of lists of more remote causes and effects could be compiled—for example, your brakes were faulty because you did not have the money to fix them, or, because of your accident, your insurance rates will go up.

Causes and effects can be either *primary* or *secondary* with reference to their significance or importance. If you had not been in a hurry and driving too fast, it might not have mattered that the visibility was poor, the roads were slippery, or your brakes were faulty. Similarly, if you or someone else had been injured, the other consequences would have seemed insignificant in comparison.

In some instances, causes and effects are linked in a *causal chain*: if you were driving too fast and tried to stop on slippery roads with

---

*Susan Strasser. *Never Done: A History of American Housework* (New York: Random House, 1982), pp. 296–97.

inadequate brakes, then each of those causes is interlinked in the inevitable accident. Likewise, the accident means that you will get a ticket, that ticket carries points against your license, your license could as a result be suspended, and either way your insurance rates will certainly climb.

WHY DO YOU WRITE
A CAUSE AND EFFECT ANALYSIS?

Cause and effect analyses are intended to explain why something happened or what the consequences are or will be of a particular occurrence. E. M. Forster in "My Wood" examines the consequences of owning property. Judith Gaines in "The 'Beefcake Years' " seeks causes or reasons for why so many advertisements today show male models in various states of undress. Carll Tucker in "Fear of Dearth" suggests reasons to explain the popularity of jogging. Joan Brumberg in "The Origins of Anorexia Nervosa" examines some causes of anorexia nervosa, tracing the disease back to its origins in middle-class families in the nineteenth century. Fox Butterfield in "Why They Excel" explores some reasons that Asian and Asian American students do so well in academic studies. Finally, Gloria Steinem in "Why Young Women Are More Conservative" analyzes for herself and her readers why women are likely to become active in the feminist movement, not during their college years, but later in life.

Cause and effect analyses can also be used to persuade readers to do or believe something. Butterfield's analysis of the cultural roots of Asian academic excellence is clearly meant to encourage readers to reevaluate their own approach toward their children's education. Steinem's explanation for the conservatism of most young women is not a direct plea for an awakening of feminine consciousness, but, after reading her essay, it would be more difficult for any reader simply to ignore the issue.

HOW DO YOU CHOOSE A SUBJECT?

In picking a subject to analyze, first remember the limits of your assignment. The larger the subject, the more difficult it will be to do justice to. Trying to analyze the causes of the Vietnam war or the effects of the national budget deficit in 500 words is an invitation to disaster. Second, make sure that the relationships you see between causes and effects are genuine. The fact that a particular event preceded another does not necessarily mean that the first caused the second. In logic this error is labeled *post hoc, ergo propter hoc* ("after this, therefore because of this").

How Do You Isolate and Evaluate Causes and Effects?

Before you begin to write, take time to analyze and, if necessary, research your subject thoroughly. It is important that your analysis consider all of the major factors involved in the relationship. Relatively few things are the result of a single cause, and rarely does a cause have a single effect. Gloria Steinem, for example, acknowledges that the answer to why young women are conservative is not a simple one—it involves a complex series of reasons.

Depending on your subject, your analysis could be based upon personal experience, thoughtful reflection and examination, or research. E. M. Forster's analysis of the effects of owning property is derived completely from studying his own reactions. Gloria Steinem's explanation comes from a decade's experience as a feminist speaker and organizer, coupled with her own personal experience as a maturing adult. Carll Tucker's playful examination of the phenomenon of jogging is a thoughtful reflection upon American values—one that required no special research but rather an application of general knowledge to a specific subject. On the other hand, Judith Gaines and Fox Butterfield draw upon research in their essays; both rely on interviews with appropriate sources and experts, and Butterfield further offers statistical evidence gleaned from library research or data base searches. Joan Jacobs Brumberg's essay is also built upon extensive research, especially in printed sources in history, literature, medicine, and psychology. As these selections show, sometimes causes and effects are certain and unquestionable. Other times, the relationships are only probable or even speculative.

Once you have gathered a list of possible causes or effects, the next step is to evaluate each item. Since any phenomenon can have many causes or many effects, you will need to select those explanations which seem most relevant or convincing. Rarely should you list every cause or every effect you can find. Generally, you choose those causes or effects which are immediate and primary, although the choice is always determined by your purpose. Tucker, for example, offers a variety of reasons why people jog, ranging from those which are immediate and personal ("to lower blood pressure," "to escape a filthy household") to those which are remote and philosophical ("modern irreligion," "fear of dearth"). He includes the spectrum because his subject is not why any particular individual jogs, but why a substantial portion of an entire nation jogs.

HOW DO YOU STRUCTURE A CAUSE AND EFFECT ANALYSIS?

By definition, causes precede effects, so a cause and effect analysis involves a linear or chronological order. Most commonly, you structure your analysis to reflect that sequence. If you are analyzing causes, typically you begin by identifying the subject that you are trying to explain and then move to analyze its causes. Carll Tucker begins with a phenomenon—jogging—that he feels is an effect or result of a set of values or concerns that are shared in our society. The rest of his essay seeks to explain why that phenomenon occurs, to explain its *causes*. Gloria Steinem begins with an observation that has grown out of her experience, that women, as they grow older, are more likely to become involved in the feminist movement. Her essay then offers an explanation for why that might be. Steinem begins with an effect and then moves to an analysis of its causes.

If you are analyzing effects, typically you begin by identifying the subject that produced the effects and then move to enumerate or explain what those effects were. E. M. Forster begins by describing how he came to purchase his "wood" and then describes four distinct effects that ownership had upon him.

Within these two structural patterns, you face one other choice: If you are listing multiple causes or effects, how do you decide in what order to treat them? That arrangement depends upon whether or not the reasons or consequences are linked in a chain. If they happen in a definite sequence, then you would arrange them in an order to reflect that sequence—normally a chronological order (this happened, then this, finally this). This linear arrangement is very similar to what you do in a process narrative except that your purpose is to answer the question "why" rather than "how." In another cause and effect essay which appears in Chapter 10, "Black Men and Public Space," Brent Staples follows a chronological pattern of development. He begins with his first experience as a night walker in Chicago and ends with his most recent experiences in Brooklyn. The essay includes a brief flashback as well, to his childhood days in Chester, Pennsylvania. As he is narrating his experiences, Staples explores the reasons why people react as they do when they encounter him at night on a city street. At the same time, Staples analyzes the impact or effects that their reactions have had on him.

But multiple causes and effects are not always linked. Steinem's causes do not occur in any inevitable chronological order, nor do Forster's effects. If the causes or effects that you have isolated are not linked in a chain, then you must find another way in which to order them. They could be organized from immediate to remote, for example. When there is a varying degree of significance or importance, the most obvious structural choice would be to arrange from the primary to the secondary or from the secondary to the primary. Before you make any arrangement, study your list of causes or effects to see whether any principle of order is evident—chronological, spatial, immediate to remote, primary to secondary. If you see a logical order, follow it.

SAMPLE STUDENT ESSAY

For a cause and effect analysis Cathy Ferguson chose to examine the effects that television's depiction of violence has on young children.

EARLIER DRAFT

TV Aggression and Children

Let's face it. Television producers are out to make money. Their main concern is with what sells. What does sell? Sensationalism. People like shocking stories. In the effort to sell, the limit of the outrageous on TV has been pushed far beyond what it was, say, ten years ago. Television aggression is one aspect of sensationalism that has been exploited to please a thrill-seeking audience. Television is not showing a greater number of aggressive scenes, but the scenes portray more violent and hostile acts. Psychologists, prompted by concerned parents, have been studying the effects of children viewing increased aggression, since the average program for kids contains 20 acts of violence per hour, while the overall average is only 7 acts of violence per hour. Research reveals three outstanding consequences of viewing greater TV hostility. First of all, TV aggression numbs children to real world violence. One experiment showed that even a brief exposure to a fairly violent show made kids indifferent to the same aggression in real life. Preschoolers are especially affected by TV violence because they are usually unable to distinguish between reality and fantasy. If they see a hostile act, they are liable to believe that it is reality, and accept it as "the norm."

This leads to the second effect of viewing TV aggression: a distorted perception of the world. Most TV shows do not present real world consequences of violence; thus children are getting a false picture of their world. Some kids are led to believe that acts of hostility are normal, common, expected even, and may lead a fearfully restricted life. In general, however, most children learn not how to be afraid of violence, but how to be violent, which is the third and most drastic effect of viewing television aggression. Almost all studies show that kids are more aggressive after they watch an aggressive show, like "Batman" or "Mighty Morphins," than after watching a pro-social show like "Barney and Friends," or a neutral show. So, although sensationalism, especially violent sensationalism, is making money for TV producers it is also creating a generation that is numb to real violence, has a distorted picture of the environment, and is itself more hostile. These effects are so palpable, it is now realized that the single best predictor of how aggressive an 18 year old will be is how much aggressive television he watched when he was 8 years old.

After Cathy handed in her first draft, she had a conference with her instructor. The instructor commented on her effective use of examples. Because the essay contains specific evidence, the cause and effect analysis seems much more convincing.

Her instructor offered some specific advice about revisions in word choice, sentence structure, and paragraph division. He noted that the essay repeated the phrase "television aggression" or a related variant seven times. Since condensed forms can be confusing, he recommended that she indicate that what she was writing about was aggression, violence, or hostility depicted on television shows. Since her first draft begins with five very short sentences and a single-word sentence fragment, he urged her to combine the sentences in order to reduce the choppy effect. Finally, he recommended that she use paragraph divisions to separate the three effects that she discusses. That division would make it easier for her reader to see the structure of the paper.

Cathy's revision addressed each of the problems that had been discussed in conference. In addition, she made a number of minor changes to tighten the prose and make it clearer.

REVISED DRAFT

The Influence of Televised Violence on Children

Let's face it. Television producers are in business to make money. Their main concern is what sells, and nothing sells better than sensationalism. In an effort to gain a larger share of the audience, television producers now treat subject matter that would never have been acceptable ten years ago. The depiction of violence on television is one aspect of that sensationalism, exploited to please a thrill-seeking audience. The number of aggressive scenes shown on television has not increased, but those scenes now portray more violent and hostile acts. This is especially true on shows aimed at children.

Psychologists, prompted by concerned parents, have begun studying the effects on children of viewing this increased aggression. The average program for children contains 20 acts of violence per hour compared to an overall average of 7 acts of violence per hour. Research reveals three significant consequences of viewing violence on television.

First, aggressive acts on television numb children to real world violence. One study showed that even a brief exposure to a fairly violent show made children indifferent to the same aggression in real life. Preschoolers are especially affected by television because they are usually unable to distinguish between reality and fantasy. If they see an aggressive act, they are likely to believe that it is real and so accept it as normal.

This potential confusion leads to the second effect of watching violence on television: a distorted perception of the world. Some children are led to believe that acts of hostility are normal, common, and even expected. As a result, these children may lead a restricted life, afraid of the violence which they imagine lurks everywhere.

In general, however, most children learn not to be afraid of violence but how to be violent--the third and most drastic effect of viewing aggression on television. Almost all studies show that children are more aggressive after they watch a show that includes violence than after watching a show that excludes it.

All three effects are so palpable that it is now realized the single best predictor of how aggressive an 18 year old will be is how much violence he watched on television when he was 8 years old.

SOME THINGS TO REMEMBER

1. Choose a topic that can be analyzed thoroughly within the limits of the assignment.

2. Decide upon a purpose: are you trying to explain or to persuade?

3. Determine an audience. For whom are you writing? What does your audience already know about your subject?

4. Analyze and research your subject. Remember to provide factual support wherever necessary. Not every cause and effect analysis can rely on unsupported opinion.

5. Be certain that the relationships you see between causes and effects are genuine.

6. Concentrate your efforts on immediate and primary causes or effects rather than on remote or secondary ones. Do not try to list every cause or every effect that you can.

7. Begin with the cause and then move to effects or begin with an effect and then move to its causes.

8. Look for a principle of order to organize your list of causes or effects. It might be chronological or spatial, for example, or it

might move from immediate to remote or from primary to secondary.

9. Remember that you are explaining why something happens or what will happen. You are not just describing how.

MY WOOD

E. M. Forster

Edward Morgan Forster (1879–1970) was born in London, England, and earned two undergraduate degrees and a master's degree from King's College, Cambridge University. He is best known as a novelist, but he also wrote short stories, literary criticism, biographies, histories, and essays. His novels, many of which have recently been made into popular films, include A Room with a View *(1908),* Howard's End *(1910), and* A Passage to India *(1924). He published two collections of essays,* Abinger Harvest *(1936) and* Two Cheers for Democracy *(1951).*

Commenting on Forster's essays, one critic wrote: "Through all the essays . . . Forster [is] a man with an alert eye for the telling detail, who responds to what he sees, reads, and hears with emotions ranging from delight to indignation, but always with intelligence and personal concern." Forster's eye for detail is apparent in this essay from Abinger Harvest. *Here Forster explores the consequences of owning property, noting that "Property produces men of weight, and it was a man of weight who failed to get into the Kingdom of Heaven."*

BEFORE READING

Connecting: What would you regard as the most important "thing" that you own? Why is it most important to you?

Anticipating: Forster observes that owning the wood made him feel "heavy." In what sense does it make him feel "heavy"?

1   A few years ago I wrote a book which dealt in part with the difficulties of the English in India. Feeling that they would have had no difficulties in India themselves, the Americans read the book freely. The more they read it the better it made them feel, and a cheque to the author was the result. I bought a wood with the cheque. It is not a large wood—it contains scarcely any trees, and it is intersected, blast it, by a public footpath. Still, it is the first property that I have owned, so it is right that other people should participate in my shame, and should ask themselves, in accents that will vary in horror, this very important question: What is the effect of property upon the character? Don't let's touch economics; the effect of private ownership upon

the community as a whole is another question—a more important question, perhaps, but another one. Let's keep to psychology. If you own things, what's their effect on you? What's the effect on me of my wood?

In the first place, it makes me feel heavy. Property does have this effect. Property produces men of weight, and it was a man of weight who failed to get into the Kingdom of Heaven. He was not wicked, that unfortunate millionaire in the parable, he was only stout; he stuck out in front, not to mention behind, and as he wedged himself this way and that in the crystalline entrance and bruised his well-fed flanks, he saw beneath him a comparatively slim camel passing through the eye of a needle and being woven into the robe of God. The Gospels all through couple stoutness and slowness. They point out what is perfectly obvious, yet seldom realized: that if you have a lot of things you cannot move about a lot, that furniture requires dusting, dusters require servants, servants require insurance stamps, and the whole tangle of them makes you think twice before you accept an invitation to dinner or go for a bathe in the Jordan. Sometimes the Gospels proceed further and say with Tolstoy that property is sinful; they approach the difficult ground of asceticism here, where I cannot follow them. But as to the immediate effects of property on people, they just show straightforward logic. It produces men of weight. Men of weight cannot, by definition, move like the lightning from the East unto the West, and the ascent of a fourteen-stone bishop into a pulpit is thus the exact antithesis of the coming of the Son of Man. My wood makes me feel heavy.

In the second place, it makes me feel it ought to be larger.

The other day I heard a twig snap in it. I was annoyed at first, for I thought that someone was blackberrying, and depreciating the value of the undergrowth. On coming nearer, I saw it was not a man who had trodden on the twig and snapped it, but a bird, and I felt pleased. My bird. The bird was not equally pleased. Ignoring the relation between us, it took fright as soon as it saw the shape of my face, and flew straight over the boundary hedge into a field, the property of Mrs. Henessy, where it sat down with a loud squawk. It had become Mrs. Henessy's bird. Something seemed grossly amiss here, something that would not have occurred had the wood been larger. I could not afford to buy Mrs. Henessy out, I dared not murder her, and limitations of this sort beset me on every side. Ahab did not want that vineyard—he only needed it to round off his property, preparatory to plotting a new curve—and all the land around my wood has become necessary to me in order to round off the wood. A boundary protects. But—poor little thing—the boundary ought in its turn to be protected. Noises on the edge of it. Children throw stones. A little more, and then a little more, until we reach the sea. Happy Canute! Happier Alexander! And after all, why should even the world be the limit of possession? A rocket containing a Union Jack, will, it is hoped, be shortly fired at the moon. Mars. Sirius. Beyond which . . . But these immensities ended by saddening me. I could not suppose that my wood was the destined nucleus of universal dominion—it is so very small and contains no mineral wealth beyond the blackberries. Nor was I comforted when Mrs. Henessy's bird took alarm for the second time and flew clean away from us all, under the belief that it belonged to itself.

5   In the third place, property makes its owner feel that he ought to do something to it. Yet he isn't sure what. A restlessness comes over him, a vague sense that he has a personality to express—the same sense which, without any vagueness, leads the artist to an act of creation. Sometimes I think I will cut down such trees as remain in the wood, at other times I want to fill up the gaps between them with new trees. But impulses are pretentious and empty. They are not honest movements towards money-making or beauty. They spring from a foolish desire to express myself and from an inability to enjoy what I have got. Creation, property, enjoyment form a sinister trinity in the human mind. Creation and enjoyment are both very, very good, yet they are often unattainable without a material basis, and at such moments property pushes itself in as a substitute, saying, "Accept me instead—I'm good enough for all three." It is not enough. It is, as Shakespeare said of lust, "the expense of spirit in a waste of shame": it is "Before, a joy proposed; behind, a dream." Yet we don't know how to shun it. It is forced on us by our economic system as the alternative to starvation. It is forced on us by an internal defect in the soul, by the feeling that in property may lie the germs of self-development and of exquisite or heroic deeds. Our life on earth is, and ought to be, material and carnal. But we have not learned to manage our materialism and carnality properly; they are still entangled with the desire for ownership, where (in the words of Dante) "Possession is one with loss."

6   And this brings us to our fourth and final point: the blackberries.

7   Blackberries are not plentiful in the meagre grove, but they are easily seen from the public footpath which traverses it, and all too easily gathered. Foxgloves, too—people will pull up the foxgloves, and ladies of an educational tendency even grub for toadstools to show them on the Monday in class. Other ladies, less educated, roll down the bracken in the arms of their gentlemen friends. There is paper, there are tins. Pray, does my wood belong to me or doesn't it? And, if it does, should I not own it best by allowing no one else to walk there? There is a wood near Lyme Regis, also cursed by a public footpath,

where the owner has not hesitated on this point. He has built high stone walls on each side of the path, and has spanned it by bridges, so that the public circulate like termites while he gorges on the blackberries unseen. He really does own his wood, this able chap. Dives in Hell did pretty well, but the gulf dividing him from Lazarus could be traversed by vision, and nothing traverses it here. And perhaps I shall come to this in time. I shall wall in and fence out until I really taste the sweets of property. Enormously stout, endlessly avaricious, pseudocreative, intensely selfish, I shall weave upon my forehead the quadruple crown of possession until those nasty Bolshies come and take it off again and thrust me aside into the outer darkness.

QUESTIONS ON SUBJECT AND PURPOSE

1. According to Forster, what are the consequences of owning property?

2. Is there any irony in buying property from the royalties earned from a book about England's problems in India?

3. What purpose(s) might Forster have had in writing the essay?

QUESTIONS ON STRATEGY AND AUDIENCE

1. In what way is this a cause and effect essay?

2. Look at the conclusion of the essay. Why does Forster end in this way? Why not add a more conventional conclusion?

3. What expectations does Forster seem to have about his audience? How do you know?

QUESTIONS ON VOCABULARY AND STYLE

1. Characterize the tone of Forster's essay. Is it formal? Informal? How is that tone achieved?

2. Forster makes extensive use of allusion in the essay. Some of the names are easily recognizable, others less so. Identify the allusions below (all but c are to Biblical stories). How does each fit into the context of the essay?

a. The wealthy man in the parable (paragraph 2)

b. Ahab and the vineyard (4)

c. Canute and Alexander (4)

d. Dives and Lazarus (7)

3. Be able to define the following words: *asceticism* (paragraph 2), *fourteen-stone* (measure of weight, 2), *depreciating* (4), *pretentious* (5), *carnal* (5), *foxgloves* (7), *bracken* (7), *avaricious* (7), *Bolshies* (Bolsheviks, 7).

WRITING SUGGESTIONS

1. For your Journal. Commenting on the second effect of owning property, Forster observes: ". . . it makes me feel it ought to be larger" (paragraph 3). To what extent does something you own make you want to own something more? Concentrate on your single most valuable (to you) possession. Does owning it ever make you want to own more? Explore the idea.

2. For a Paragraph. Select something you own that is important to you—a house, a car, a stereo system, a pet, something you use for recreation. In a paragraph, describe the consequences of owning it. How has it changed your life and behavior? Are there negative as well as positive consequences?

3. For an Essay. Extend your paragraph into an essay. Explore each of the consequences you described in a separate paragraph.

Prewriting:

a. Make a list of possible subjects. For each item try to list at least four possible effects of owning it. Do not commit to a specific subject until you have considered the range of possibilities.

b. Once you have selected an item, try freewriting for 15 minutes on each consequence of ownership. You are still gathering ideas for your essay; this material will not necessarily become part of your first draft.

c. The consequences will surely vary in terms of their significance and order of importance. Plan out an organizational strategy. Which effect should come first? Try writing each paragraph on a separate sheet of paper so that you can shuffle their order easily. Consider the alternatives.

Rewriting:

a. Make a brief outline of Forster's essay. It can be used as a model. Try to consider the author's strategy—that is, how did Forster solve the problems that this type of essay poses? Do not just imitate his form.

b. The biggest problem might come in the conclusion. Look at what you have written. Have you avoided an ending that starts, "In conclusion, there are four consequences that result from owning a _____."

c. Do you have an interesting title? Do not title your paper "My _____." Remember that titles figure significantly in arousing a reader's curiosity. Brainstorm for some possibilities. Imagine yourself as a copywriter in an advertising agency trying to sell a product.

4. For Research. Property ownership has frequently been used throughout history as a precondition for full participation in the affairs of government (voting, for example). A number of states in this country applied such a restriction until the practice was declared unconstitutional. Using outside sources, write a research essay that explains and analyzes either the reasons for, or the negative consequence of, such practices. Be sure to document your sources.

THE "BEEFCAKE YEARS"
Judith Gaines

Born in 1948, in Lincoln, Nebraska, Judith Gaines earned a B.A. in politics from the University of California at Santa Cruz. She completed her graduate thesis on violence in America at Oxford University, earning a masters in social studies. In her early writing career, she focused on rural issues, including Appalachian economic development and low-income rural women. In 1981 she began a freelance career, selling herself as a "person who would go where the Associated Press men wouldn't go," by finding interesting stories in out-of-the-way places. In 1984 she joined the Boston Globe, *and in 1988 became a reporter/columnist with what she describes as an "offbeat" beat.*

Gaines commented that the idea for "The 'Beefcake Years,'" which originally appeared in the Globe, *came when she was looking through magazines and noticing the images. "The images in movies and other areas of popular culture say a lot about who we are as a society," she observed. "I did a lot of prowling around in department stores to find out how the ads were being used and the reactions people had to them."*

BEFORE READING

Connecting: Can you think of a time when the use of an attractive, partially undressed male or female model in an advertisement prompted you to buy a particular product?

Anticipating: A "really great ad," one of Gaines's sources notes, offers the "unexpected." Why?

1 Eleven members of a men's soccer team, wearing nothing but their athletic shoes, grin at the camera in a new Adidas ad.

2 A bare-bummed adventurer endures an indignity of camping life—changing clothes in the cold—while the reader looks on.

3 A sexy young rebel, mean and muscular, smirks as he tapes his hand for boxing. In bold block letters, the caption of this cologne ad reads, "MEN ARE BACK."

4 And so they are, baring their bodies on the pages of nearly every major newsmagazine and many newspapers. In the most fetching ways.

Cause and Effect

After decades when scantily clad women have been used to lure 5
buyers to everything from soap to Subarus, advertisers have discovered they can treat men as commercial sex objects, too. "These are
the beefcake years," John Carroll, Boston advertising executive, observed recently.

What started a few years ago as an attempt to shock readers 6
with the sight of seminude males has become so mainstream—em-
bracing even underwear ads by Bloomingdale's—that some advertisers think the strategy has become almost banal.

EQUALITY

Some view the profusion of beefcake ads as evidence of a re- 7
freshing equality in exploitation. Men's bodies may never be displayed as casually or openly as women's are, but images of both sexes
"are becoming more liberated, reaching beyond the stereotypes,"
Jack Connors, CEO of the Hill, Holliday ad agency in Boston, said.

This advertising is allowing men to discover how it feels to 8
watch their kind paraded as headless heartthrobs and half-clothed
"himbos," Carroll said. "Who's going to protest? A support group for
badly built guys?"

Carroll called the approach "equality by subtraction," as ad- 9
makers drag men down to the level where women already suffer.

Others who study social imagery see a deeper trend at work. 10
What the public is seeing, they argue, is not just a beefcake parade
but dozens of different images of men that reflect the broadening
range of what being "masculine" means: burly, barechested fathers
with infants in their arms extolling the virtues of parenthood; sleek
hairless men with bodies like Greek gods, which some advertisers say
are meant to appeal to gay consumers, and ads in which women, in
business and romantic settings, are depicted in the power position.

At Boston's Wheelock College, Gail Dines, assistant professor 11
of sociology and women's studies, called the phenomenon "gender
distress." With macho, individualistic, workaholic manhood under attack and homosexuals becoming recognized as a lucrative sector of
the marketplace, what it means to be male "is up for grabs," she said.

"WHAT GENDER IS ALL ABOUT"

Although the ads "don't translate into real power-sharing be- 12
tween the sexes," Dines said, she hopes they spark discussion "of what
gender is all about." Because the images "are socially constructed,
they can be reconstructed," she said.

For those who think the use of men as sex objects signals a new 13
parity between men and women, the ads are deceiving, said Adam

Thorburn of Newton, Mass., a graduate student at Sarah Lawrence College who is researching sexism and the media.

14   He said that a key difference in how male and female bodies are used is that the men are uncovered without being exposed. Although ads with undressed females typically reveal their weakness, openness and vulnerability, males merely "show their muscularity, like a coat of armor made by their own flesh," Thorburn said.

15   Or, as Sut Jhally, communications professor at the University of Massachusetts at Amherst, put it, the men, unlike the women, have "bodies you don't mess with."

16   Jackson Katz, a former football fullback who heads Real Men, a Boston-based group fighting sexist images in contemporary culture, agrees. What's happening, he said, is a backlash.

17   As macho males find their style challenged again and again in '90s society, particularly by women, their self-image is taking a beating, according to Katz. "But one of the few areas where they still have the advantage is physical size and strength," he said.

18   So ads emphasizing male power, muscularity and control are increasingly popular, at the same time women are being shown looking thinner, younger and less threatening, Katz said.

DIVERSITY OF IMAGES

19   Poppycock, counters Connors, who sees the industry producing a diversity of masculine images, including more sensitive men showing gentleness and concern for others. "It's OK to be anything; that's the real breakthrough," he said.

20   And Ed Eskandarian, chairman of the ad firm Arnold, Fortuna, Lawner & Cabot, said women were being depicted "as smarter than ever." But, he insisted, "there's a segment of women who still idolize the dominant, daring macho type and will buy products associated with this."

21   Analysts note that the beefcake ads are not new. They began to appear several years ago when Jim Palmer, former Baltimore Orioles pitcher, shed everything but his undershorts for Jockey, and Calvin Klein began winking at gay consumers with ads featuring Adonises.

22   Sports Illustrated was so unnerved by the recent Adidas ad showing the nude soccer team (with each player's private parts artfully covered) that the editors refused to publish it, provoking a war of words between the company and the magazine.

23   "Why were they so threatened by the image of those men undressed together?" Jhally asked. "Their behavior was totally hypocritical when you consider their women's swimsuit issue."

24   According to Eskandarian, a few local publications are squea-

mish about some of the beefcake ads, airbrushing portions of bikini or underwear ads, for instance, that make men's private parts "too definable."

"Everything is banned in Boston," he said. But elsewhere most firms that display ads "don't mind the beefcake, unless it's stretching good taste, such as whips and chains." 25

In random interviews last week, consumers offered mixed reviews of the ads. 26

In the fragrance department of a Filene's department store in Braintree, Mass., dozens of posters, banners and tote bags displayed a recumbent male hunk beneath the copy: "Zino. The Fragrance of Desire." 27

All the pictures of nude male torsos "don't appeal to me, but if my fiancee walked in, she'd get me that," said Bruce Simmons, a South Boston accountant, referring to the cologne. 28

But in the Calvin Klein section of a nearby Jordan Marsh department store, where every pair of jeans included a portrait of a muscled man wearing nothing but unbuttoned and unzipped jeans, sales clerk Tracy Chaupetta said, "Women seem to like" the image. "They say they want the body, as well as the jeans." 29

Speaking for Mullen, the firm that created the ad showing the adventurer changing his clothes in the great outdoors, president James X. Mullen stressed that what was selling products "isn't nudity; it's a concept" that provides a clear and compelling representation of the product. And a really great ad also offers "the unexpected," he said. 30

The nudity surprises; it may even shock. It reaches through the clutter of contemporary images and information to grab the consumer by the pocketbook. And because ads are based on extensive consumer testing, they are "the best reflection of our times that we have," Mullen said. 31

But Carroll, for one, cautioned against reading too much into what may be only a superficial attempt to attract attention. Many ads, he said, "are just vamping." 32

QUESTIONS ON SUBJECT AND PURPOSE

1. What is Gaines trying to explain in the article?

2. According to Gaine's sources, how do "beefcake" images broaden the definition of masculinity?

3. Why doesn't Gaines offer just a single explanation for the popularity of "beefcake" advertisements?

QUESTIONS ON STRATEGY AND AUDIENCE

1. What strategy does Gaines use in her introduction? Why might she begin the article in this way?
2. What types of research did Gaines do as background for her article?
3. What expectations could Gaines have about her audience?

QUESTIONS ON VOCABULARY AND STYLE

1. In her title, why does Gaines enclose the phrase "beefcake years" in quotation marks? From where does the word *beefcake* come?
2. How does Gaines use quotations in the text? What is their role?
3. Be prepared to define the following words: *banal* (paragraph 6), *parity* (13), *recumbent* (27), *vamping* (32).

WRITING SUGGESTIONS

1. **For your Journal**. Think of several product brands that you purchase regularly—a particular brand of clothing or shoes, for example, or cosmetics, beverages, snack foods, even household items. Make a short list of such products, jotting down next to each what prompts you to purchase that particular brand. Have you ever been consciously aware that an advertisement—in print, on television, or on radio—influenced your decision?
2. **For a Paragraph**. Select a full-page advertisement from a magazine of your choice. Choose an advertisement that catches your attention. In a paragraph, analyze why that advertisement seems appealing to you.
3. **For an Essay**. At the end of her article, Gaines quotes an authority who calls advertisements "the best reflection of our times that we have." Collect a group of popular magazines—do not choose anything too specialized or scholarly—and select from them a group of advertisements that represent a fairly broad range of products. What do the advertisements, and the images that they present, seem to say about our "times." What in our culture seems to influence the types of images that we see in advertising?

Prewriting:

a. Gather a variety of magazines. You can check the current periodicals section of your college's library. Look for fifteen to twenty full-page advertisements that rely heavily on images rather than words or "copy."

b. Classify the images that you find—do they fall into distinct types or groupings? Concentrate on establishing several types of which you have a number of examples.

c. Think of the images as the result or "effect" of something in our culture. What seems to explain why an advertiser would choose this particular image to sell this particular product? Brainstorm for each group of images.

Rewriting:

a. Can you formulate a thesis that explains all of the image types that you have? Are there distinct trends or values in our culture that explain what is going on?

b. Check to make sure that you have sufficiently identified or described each type of image. In a magazine article, for example, you might find some photographic illustrations, but in your paper you will need to do what Gaines does— briefly describe the primary images.

c. Reread your introduction and your conclusion. Do you try to engage your reader at the outset? Did you write a thesis introduction? What type of conclusion did you write? Did you just repeat your crucial points in the essay? Ask a friend or classmate to comment on just the opening and closing of your paper.

4. For Research. Choose a period of the 20th century that interests you—for example, the "baby boom years" of the late 1940s and early 1950s, the "Kennedy years" of the early 1960s, even your own birth year. Using your library's collection of periodicals, search for advertisements for products from that time period. How are these advertisements a "reflection" of the age in which they were created? What insights do they offer into that time? Be sure to document your sources wherever appropriate.

FEAR OF DEARTH
Carll Tucker

Carll Tucker was born in New York City in 1951 and received a B.A. from Yale University in 1973. An editor and writer, Tucker began his career as a columnist for the Patent Trader *newspaper. He was theater critic and book columnist for the* Village Voice *from 1974 to 1977 and editor of the* Saturday Review *from 1978 to 1981. In 1986, Tucker began his own publishing company, Tucker Communications, which publishes the* Patent Trader *as well as several related publications.*

Tucker's subject in "Fear of Dearth," originally published in Saturday Review, *is jogging. In a cause and effect analysis, Tucker sets out to explain why Americans choose to jog.*

BEFORE READING

Connecting: Do you regularly exercise? Why? If you do not, why not?

Anticipating: What types of explanations for jogging does Tucker offer? Do his explanations surprise you? Why?

1   I hate jogging. Every dawn, as I thud around New York City's Central Park reservoir, I am reminded of how much I hate it. It's so tedious. Some claim jogging is thought conducive; others insist the scenery relieves the monotony. For me, the pace is wrong for contemplation of either ideas or vistas. While jogging, all I can think about is jogging—or nothing. One advantage of jogging around a reservoir is that there's no dry shortcut home.

2   From the listless looks of some fellow trotters, I gather I am not alone in my unenthusiasm: Bill-paying, it seems, would be about as diverting. Nonetheless, we continue to jog; more, we continue to *choose* to jog. From a practically infinite array of opportunities, we select one that we don't enjoy and can't wait to have done with. Why?

3   For any trend, there are as many reasons as there are participants. This person runs to lower his blood pressure. That person runs to escape the telephone or a cranky spouse or a filthy household. Another

Cause and Effect

person runs to avoid doing anything else, to dodge a decision about how to lead his life or a realization that his life is leading nowhere. Each of us has his carrot and stick. In my case, the stick is my slackening physical condition, which keeps me from beating opponents at tennis whom I overwhelmed two years ago. My carrot is to win.

Beyond these disparate reasons, however, lies a deeper cause. It is no accident that now, in the last third of the twentieth century, personal fitness and health have suddenly become a popular obsession. True, modern man likes to feel good, but that hardly distinguishes him from his predecessors. 4

With zany myopia, economists like to claim that the deeper cause of everything is economic. Delightfully, there seems no marketplace explanation for jogging. True, jogging is cheap, but then not jogging is cheaper. And the scant and skimpy equipment which jogging demands must make it a marketer's least favored form of recreation. 5

Some scout-masterish philosophers argue that the appeal of jogging and other body-maintenance programs is the discipline they afford. We live in a world in which individuals have fewer and fewer obligations. The work week has shrunk. Weekend worship is less compulsory. Technology gives us more free time. Satisfactorily filling free time requires imagination and effort. Freedom is a wide and risky river; it can drown the person who does not know how to swim across it. The more obligations one takes on, the more time one occupies, the less threat freedom poses. Jogging can become an instant obligation. For a portion of his day, the jogger is not his own man; he is obedient to a regimen he has accepted. 6

Theologists may take the argument one step further. It is our modern irreligion, our lack of confidence in any hereafter, that makes us anxious to stretch our mortal stay as long as possible. We run, as the saying goes, for our lives, hounded by the suspicion that these are the only lives we are likely to enjoy. 7

All of these theorists seem to me more or less right. As the growth of cults and charismatic religions and the resurgence of enthusiasm for the military draft suggest, we do crave commitment. And who can doubt, watching so many middle-aged and older persons torturing themselves in the name of fitness, that we are unreconciled to death, more so perhaps than any generation in modern memory? 8

But I have a hunch there's a further explanation of our obsession with exercise. I suspect that what motivates us even more than a fear of death is a fear of dearth. Our era is the first to anticipate the eventual depletion of all natural resources. We see wilderness shrinking; rivers losing their capacity to sustain life; the air, even the stratosphere, being loaded with potentially deadly junk. We see the irreplaceable 9 being squandered, and in the depths of our consciousness we are fearful that we are creating an uninhabitable world. We feel more or less helpless and yet, at the same time, desirous to protect what resources we can. We recycle soda bottles and restore old buildings and protect our nearest natural resource—our physical health—in the almost superstitious hope that such small gestures will help save an earth that we are blighting. Jogging becomes a sort of penance for our sins of gluttony, greed, and waste. Like a hair shirt or a bed of nails, the more one hates it, the more virtuous it makes one feel.

10   That is why *we* jog. Why *I* jog is to win at tennis.

QUESTIONS ON SUBJECT AND PURPOSE

1. If asked why they jog, few people would reply, "Fear of dearth." Tucker's essay does not, in fact, concentrate on the obvious and immediate reasons why people jog. Why not analyze those reasons?
2. Characterize America's ideal body types. Why are these characteristics valued? What do they reveal about our society's values and preoccupations?
3. Is Tucker being serious in his analysis? How can you tell?

QUESTIONS ON STRATEGY AND AUDIENCE

1. Tucker offers a series of reasons why people jog. Is there any principle of order underlying his arrangement of those reasons?
2. How effective is Tucker's final paragraph? Does it undercut his causal analysis in the previous paragraphs?
3. What expectations does Tucker seem to have about his audience (readers of the *Saturday Review*)? How do you know?

QUESTIONS ON VOCABULARY AND STYLE

1. How effective is Tucker's title? Why might he have chosen that particular title?
2. Be prepared to discuss how each of the following contributes to Tucker's essay:
   a. the opening sentence
   b. the "carrot and stick" image (paragraph 3)
   c. the paragraph dealing with economic causes (5)
   d. the first-person references

3. Be able to define the following words and phrases: *carrot and stick* (paragraph 3), *myopia* (5), *charismatic religions* (8), *dearth* (9), *hair shirt* (9)

WRITING SUGGESTIONS

1. For your Journal. Think about things that you regularly do and wear. Make two lists. For example, are you compulsive about working out? Do you always wear a baseball cap? Select one item from each list and explore the reasons why you do or wear this thing.

2. For a Paragraph. If you engage in any regular athletic activity, analyze the reasons why you do so. Why that activity? What appeals to you? Why bother? If you avoid any such activity, analyze why you do so. Write a paragraph analyzing the reasons for your activity or inactivity.

3. For an Essay. Select another popular American preoccupation and in an essay analyze the reasons for its popularity. Try to avoid the most obvious reasons and focus instead on what this thing or activity reveals about our society. You might consider one of the following possible topics.
   a. video games
   b. Barbie dolls or another toy
   c. a popular style of music
   d. a highly rated television show
   e. a current clothing fad
   f. radio call-in shows
   g. "fast" food or "health" food

Prewriting:
   a. Whatever you choose, it should reveal something popular, yet not obvious. Avoid a scientific or technological development unless it is something that could be considered a national obsession. Make a list of possible subjects that are central to American life today, that most people are aware of and many enjoy directly.
   b. If possible, interview some students from another country. What would they list?
   c. Remember that your essay will examine the causes of a particular effect. What are the causes of the popularity of this item? You should have multiple causes. Select your two most promising subjects and brainstorm a list of causes for each.

Rewriting:

a. Look again at your list of causes. Have you analyzed the reasons for the item's popularity? Have you given reasons that illuminate our society or our values?

b. Convert the list of things to remember at the end of the introduction to this chapter into a series of questions. Then answer each question honestly. Try to look at your paper as if someone else wrote it.

c. Presumably your essay, because it is about something that appeals to many people, should be of interest to your readers. With that in mind, try to write an introduction that stimulates reader interest. Assume your essay will appear in a popular magazine. Work to grab your reader's attention. Test your introduction on several peer readers. How do they respond? Do they want to keep reading?

4. **For Research.** An ideal man or woman today is thin, athletic, and suntanned. But what is regarded as perfect at one point in time will change in another. Research the ideal body type for both men and women at three points in the twentieth century—for example, 1900, 1940, and 1990. What did the ideal man or woman look like? How did those ideals reflect the values and concerns of society? Using your research, write an essay in which you first define those types and then analyze what they revealed about America at each point in time. Be sure to document your sources.

THE ORIGINS OF
ANOREXIA NERVOSA

Joan Jacobs Brumberg

Born in 1944 in Mount Vernon, New York, Joan Jacobs Brumberg earned a Ph.D. in American history at the University of Virginia. She is professor of human development and family studies at Cornell University. She has written many articles and two books, Mission for Life: The Story of Adoniram Judson *(1980) and* Fasting Girls: The Emergence of Anorexia Nervosa *(1988), which studies the disease from historical, social, and familial perspectives, attempting to explain why anorexia has become so prominent in recent decades. She is currently working on a book about female adolescence in the United States.*

The following selection is from Fasting Girls *and was published in* Harper's *magazine. Commenting on her explanation of the origins of anorexia nervosa, Brumberg said: "I took the position that anorexia nervosa was not only caused by culture—a position that was not popular with feminists. And I took the position that it was not only caused by a biochemical disorder, which was the medical position." Brumberg argues that psychological and family factors are also prime causes. Here she describes Victorian-era attitudes toward eating and confrontation, asking, "Why would a daughter affront her parents by refusing to eat?"*

BEFORE READING

Connecting: What attitudes toward food and toward mealtime do the members of your family share? Do you have "family" meals? Are there any rituals connected with mealtime?

Anticipating: Brumberg defines a certain environment in which anorexia nervosa emerged. What are the essential conditions of that environment?

Contrary to the popular assumption that anorexia nervosa is a peculiarly modern disorder, the malady first emerged in the Victorian era—long before the pervasive cultural imperative for a thin female body. The first clinical descriptions of the disorder appeared in England and France almost simultaneously in 1873. They were written by two well-known physicians: Sir William Withey Gull and Charles Lasègue. Lasègue, more than any other nineteenth-century doctor, captured the rhythm of repeated offerings and refusals that signaled the breakdown of reciprocity between parents and their anorexic daughter. By returning to its origins, we can see anorexia nervosa for what it is: a dysfunction in the bourgeois family system.

2   Family meals assumed enormous importance in the bourgeois milieu, in the United States as well as in England and France. Middle-class parents prided themselves on providing ample food for their children. The abundance of food and the care in its preparation became expressions of social status. The ambience of the meal symbolized the values of the family. A popular domestic manual advised, "Simple, healthy food, exquisitely prepared, and served upon shining dishes and brilliant silverware . . . a gentle blessing, and cheerful conversation, embrace the sweetest communions and the happiest moments of life." Among the middle class it seems that eating correctly was emerging as a new morality, one that set its members apart from the working class.

3   At the same time, food was used to express love in the nineteenth-century bourgeois household. Offering attractive and abundant meals was the particular responsibility and pleasure of middle-class wives and mothers. In America the feeding of middle-class children, from infancy on, had become a maternal concern no longer deemed appropriate to delegate to wet nurses, domestics, or governesses. Family meals were expected to be a time of instructive and engaging conversation. Participation was expected on both a verbal and gustatory level. In this context, refusing to eat was an unabashedly antisocial act. Anorexic behavior was antithetical to the ideal of bourgeois eating. One advice book, *Common Sense for Maid, Wife, and Mother,* stated: "Heated discussion and quarrels, fretfulness and sullen taciturnity while eating, are as unwholesome as they are unchristian."

4   Why would a daughter affront her parents by refusing to eat? Lasègue's 1873 description of anorexia nervosa, along with other nineteenth-century medical reports, suggests that pressure to marry may have precipitated the illness.

5   Ambitious parents surely understood that by marrying well, at an appropriate moment, a daughter, even though she did not carry the family name, could help advance a family's social status—particularly in a burgeoning middle-class society. As a result, the issue of marriage loomed large in the life of a dutiful middle-class daughter. Although marriage did not generally occur until the girl's early twenties, it was an event for which she was continually prepared, and a de-

sirable outcome for all depended on the ability of the parents and the child to work together—that is, to state clearly what each wanted or to read each other's heart and mind. In the context of marital expectations, a daughter's refusal to eat was a provocative rejection of both the family's social aspirations and their goodwill toward her. All of the parents' plans for her future (and their own) could be stymied by her peculiar and unpleasant alimentary nihilism.

Beyond the specific anxieties generated by marital pressure, the Victorian family milieu in America and in Western Europe harbored a mélange of other tensions and problems that provided the emotional preconditions for the emergence of anorexia nervosa. As love replaced authority as the cement of family relations, it began to generate its own set of emotional disorders. 6

Possessiveness, for example, became an acute problem in Victorian family life. Where love between parents and children was the prevailing ethic, there was always the risk of excess. When love became suffocating or manipulative, individuation and separation from the family could become extremely painful, if not impossible. In the context of increased intimacy, adolescent privacy was especially problematic: For parents and their sexually maturing daughters, what constituted an appropriate degree of privacy? Middle-class girls, for example, almost always had their own rooms or shared them with sisters, but they had greater difficulty establishing autonomous psychic space. The well-known penchant of adolescent girls for novel-reading was an expression of their need for imaginative freedom. Some parents, recognizing that their daughters needed channels for expressing emotions, encouraged diary-keeping. But some of the same parents who gave lovely marbled journals as gifts also monitored their content. Since emotional freedom was not an acknowledged prerogative of the Victorian adolescent girl, it seems likely that she would have expressed unhappiness in non-verbal forms of behavior. One such behavior was refusal of food. 7

When an adolescent daughter became sullen and chronically refused to eat, her parents felt threatened and confused. The daughter was perceived as willfully manipulating her appetite the way a younger child might. Because parents did not want to encourage this behavior, they often refused at first to indulge the favorite tastes or caprices of their daughter. As emaciation became visible and the girl looked ill, many violated the contemporary canon of prudent child-rearing and put aside their moral objections to pampering the appetite. Eventually they would beg their daughter to eat whatever she liked—and eat she must, "as a sovereign proof of affection" for them. From the parents' perspective, a return to eating was a confirmation of filial love. 8

9   The significance of food refusal as an emotional tactic within the family depended on food's being plentiful, pleasing, and connected to love. Where food was eaten simply to assuage hunger, where it had only minimal aesthetic and symbolic messages, or where the girl had to provide her own nourishment, refusal of food was not particularly noteworthy or defiant. In contrast, the anorexic girl was surrounded by a provident, if not indulgent, family that was bound to be distressed by her rejection of its largess.

10   Anorexia nervosa was an intense form of discourse that honored the emotional guidelines that governed the middle-class Victorian family. Refusing to eat was not as confrontational as yelling, having a tantrum, or throwing things; refusing to eat expressed emotional hostility without being flamboyant. And refusing to eat had the advantage of being ambiguous. If a girl repeatedly claimed lack of appetite she might indeed be ill and therefore entitled to special treatment and favors.

11   In her own way, the anorexic was respectful of what historian Peter Gay called "the great bourgeois compromise between the need for reserve and the capacity for emotion." The rejection of food, while an emotionally charged behavior, was also discreet, quiet, and ladylike. The unhappy adolescent who was in all other ways a dutiful daughter chose food refusal from within the symptom repertoire available to her. Precisely because she was not a lunatic, she selected a behavior that she knew would have some efficacy within her own family.

QUESTIONS ON SUBJECT AND PURPOSE

1. According to Brumberg, when did anorexia nervosa emerge as a definable disease? Why did it emerge in that particular time period?
2. On the basis of what Brumberg writes here, who is the most likely candidate for anorexia nervosa?
3. What purpose might Brumberg have in writing about anorexia nervosa?

QUESTIONS ON STRATEGY AND AUDIENCE

1. Why does Brumberg begin by referring to "the popular assumption that anorexia nervosa is a peculiarly modern disorder"?
2. To what extent does isolating the origins of anorexia nervosa help us to understand the disorder in young people today?

3. Brumberg uses quite a few words that might be unfamiliar to many readers. What do her vocabulary choices imply about her sense of audience?

QUESTIONS ON VOCABULARY AND STYLE

1. In paragraphs 2 and 3, Brumberg quotes from two popular domestic manuals of the nineteenth century. What do the quotations contribute to her essay?
2. In paragraph 5, Brumberg uses the phrase "alimentary nihilism" with reference to anorectics. What does the phrase mean?
3. Be prepared to define the following words: *malady* (paragraph 1), *imperative* (1), *reciprocity* (1), *dysfunction* (1), *bourgeois* (1), *milieu* (2), *ambience* (2), *wet nurses* (3), *gustatory* (3), *unabashedly* (3), *antithetical* (3), *taciturnity* (3), *burgeoning* (5), *stymied* (5), *alimentary* (5), *nihilism* (5), *melange* (6), *individuation* (7), *autonomous* (7), *penchant* (7), *prerogative* (7), *caprices* (8), *emaciation* (8), *assuage* (9), *largess* (9), *flamboyant* (10), *efficacy* (11).

WRITING SUGGESTIONS

1. **For your Journal.** How would you characterize your mealtimes? Do you care about the circumstances in which you eat? Do you have to eat with someone else? Can you just grab something on the run? Explore your attitudes toward mealtime. Do not just accept what you are doing without thinking about it. What do you expect of meals? Why?
2. **For a Paragraph.** Define your "ideal" body. Then in a second paragraph speculate on the reasons why that body type or shape seems "ideal."
3. **For an Essay.** Cultural historians have observed that American society is "obesophobic" (excessively or irrationally fearful of fat and being fat). Certainly weight consciousness permeates American society and the weight-loss industries are multi-million dollar businesses. Why?

   Prewriting:
   a. For a single day, keep a record of every reference that you encounter to being overweight—advertisements in the

media, references made by friends, remarks that you over-hear. These examples will provide detail in your essay.

b. Think about the "ideal" body types in our society. What does the ideal male or female body look like? Freewrite about that ideal as it relates to you and your friends.

c. Construct a list of possible causes that have contributed to this "fear of fat." Try to come up with at least six possible causes. Discuss possible reasons with some classmates or friends.

Rewriting:

a. Look again at your list of causes and your essay. Is there any order that seems most appropriate? Which cause ought to come first? Which last? Construct several possible out-lines or, if you are writing on a word processor, construct several different bodies for your essay. Which arrangement seems to work best?

b. Have you provided enough examples and details to support your analysis and to make your essay interesting to read? Look back over that one-day record. Have you used your best examples?

c. Think about how an article in *Time* or *Newsweek* might in-troduce such an essay. Does your introduction grab your reader's attention?

4. **For Research**. Anorexia nervosa is only one of a number of diseases that are common today but were previously unknown or undiagnosed. Other examples include Alzheimer's disease, osteoporosis, premenstrual syndrome, and chronic fatigue syndrome. Select a "new" disease or disorder and research its history. When was it first defined? What might account for its emergence during the past decade or two? Be sure to docu-ment your sources wherever appropriate.

WHY THEY EXCEL
Fox Butterfield

Born in 1939 in Lancaster, Pennsylvania, Fox Butterfield earned a B.A. and an M.A. at Harvard University. He made his mark on American journalism as a member of The New York Times *reporting team that edited* The Pentagon Papers *(1971). That book, which earned the team a 1972 Pulitzer Prize for meritorious public service, revealed the scope of U.S. involvement in the Vietnam War. In 1979, he was granted permission by the Chinese government to live in Peking as a reporter for* The New York Times. *His book,* China: Alive in the Bitter Sea *(1982), which won an American Book Award, is about his perceptions of Chinese life. Butterfield is currently the Boston bureau chief for the* Times.

"Why They Excel" originally appeared in Parade, *a Sunday newspaper magazine supplement.*

BEFORE READING

Connecting: What expectations do your parents have for you? How do those expectations influence you?

Anticipating: According to Butterfield, what are the main reasons that Asian and Asian American students excel? Would or do these reasons motivate you?

Kim-Chi Trinh was just 9 in Vietnam when her father used his 1
savings to buy a passage for her on a fishing boat. It was a costly and risky sacrifice for the family, placing Kim-Chi on the small boat, among strangers, in hopes she would eventually reach the United States, where she would get a good education and enjoy a better life. Before the boat reached safety in Malaysia, the supply of food and water ran out.

Still alone, Kim-Chi made it to the United States, coping with a 2
succession of three foster families. But when she graduated from San Diego's Patrick Henry High School in 1988, she had a straight-A average and scholarship offers from Stanford and Cornell universities.

"I have to do well—it's not even a question," said the diminu- 3
tive 19-year-old, now a sophomore at Cornell. "I owe it to my parents in Vietnam."

4   Kim-Chi is part of a tidal wave of bright, highly motivated Asian-Americans who are suddenly surging into our best colleges. Although Asian-Americans make up only 2.4 percent of the nation's population, they constitute 17.1 percent of the undergraduates at Harvard, 18 percent at the Massachusetts Institute of Technology and 27.3 percent at the University of California at Berkeley.

5   With Asians being the fastest-growing ethnic group in the country—two out of five immigrants are now Asian—these figures will increase. At the University of California at Irvine, a staggering 35.1 percent of the undergraduates are Asian-American, but the proportion in the freshman class is even higher: 41 percent.

6   Why are the Asian-Americans doing so well? Are they grinds, as some stereotypes suggest? Do they have higher IQs? Or are they actually teaching the rest of us a lesson about values we have long treasured but may have misplaced—like hard work, the family and education?

7   Not all Asians are doing equally well. Poorly educated Cambodian and Hmong refugee youngsters need special help. And Asian-Americans resent being labeled a "model minority," feeling that is just another form of prejudice by white Americans, an ironic reversal of the discriminatory laws that excluded most Asian immigration to America until 1965.

8   But the academic success of many Asian-Americans has prompted growing concern among educators, parents and other students. Some universities have what look like unofficial quotas, much as Ivy League colleges did against Jews in the 1920s and '30s. Berkeley Chancellor Ira Heyman apologized last spring for an admissions policy that, he said, had "a disproportionately negative impact on Asian-Americans."

9   I have wondered about the reason for the Asians' success since I was a fledgling journalist on Taiwan in 1969. That year, a team of boys from a poor, isolated mountain village on Taiwan won the annual Little League World Series at Williamsport, Pa. Their victory was totally unexpected. At the time, baseball was a largely unknown sport on Taiwan, and the boys had learned to play with bamboo sticks for bats and rocks for balls. But since then, teams from Taiwan, Japan or South Korea have won the Little League championship in 16 out of the 21 years. How could these Asian boys beat us at our own game?

10   Fortunately, the young Asians' achievements have led to a series of intriguing studies. "There is something going on here that we as Americans need to understand," said Sanford M. Dornbusch, a professor of sociology at Stanford. Dornbusch, in surveys of 7000 students in six San Francisco-area high schools, found that Asian-Americans consistently get better grades than any other group of stu-

dents, regardless of their parents' level of education or their families' social and economic status, the usual predictors of success. In fact, those in homes where English is spoken often, or whose families have lived longer in the United States, do slightly less well.

"We used to talk about the American melting pot as an advantage," Dornbusch said. "But the sad fact is that it has become a melting pot with low standards." 11

Other studies have shown similar results. Perhaps the most disturbing have come in a series of studies by a University of Michigan psychologist, Harold W. Stevenson, who has compared more than 7000 students in kindergarten, first grade, third grade and fifth grade in Chicago and Minneapolis with counterparts in Beijing; Sendai, Japan; and Taipei, Taiwan. On a battery of math tests, the Americans did worst at all grade levels. 12

Stevenson found no differences in IQ. But if the differences in performance are showing up in kindergarten, it suggests something is happening in the family, even before the children get to school. 13

It is here that the various studies converge: Asian parents are able to instill more motivation in their children. "My bottom line is, Asian kids work hard," said Professor Dornbusch. 14

In his survey of San Francisco-area high schools, for example, he reported that Asian-Americans do an average of 7.03 hours of homework a week. Non-Hispanic whites average 6.12 hours, blacks 4.23 hours and Hispanics 3.98 hours. Asians also score highest on a series of other measures of effort, such as fewer class cuts and paying more attention to the teacher. 15

Don Lee, 20, is a junior at Berkeley. His parents immigrated to Torrance, Calif., from South Korea when he was 5, so he could get a better education. Lee said his father would warn him about the danger of wasting time at high school dances or football games. "Instead," he added, "for fun on weekends, my friends and I would go to the town library to study." 16

The real question, then, is how do Asian parents imbue their offspring with this kind of motivation? Stevenson's study suggests a critical answer. When the Asian parents were asked why they think their children do well, they most often said "hard work." By contrast, American parents said "talent." 17

"From what I can see," said Stevenson, "we've lost our belief in the Horatio Alger myth that anyone can get ahead in life through pluck and hard work. Instead, Americans now believe that some kids have it and some don't, so we begin dividing up classes into fast learners and slow learners, where the Chinese and Japanese believe all children can learn from the same curriculum." 18

The Asians' belief in hard work also springs from their common 19 heritage of Confucianism, the philosophy of the 5th-century B.C. Chinese sage who taught that man can be perfected through practice. "Confucius is not just some character out of the past—he is an everyday reality to these people," said William Liu, a sociologist who directs the Pacific Asian-American Mental Health Research Center at the University of Illinois in Chicago.

20   Confucianism provides another important ingredient in the Asians' success. "In the Confucian ethic," Liu continued, "there is a centripetal family, an orientation that makes people work for the honor of the family, not just for themselves." Liu came to the United States from China in 1948. "You can never repay your parents, and there is a strong sense of guilt," he said. "It is a strong force, like the Protestant Ethic in the West."

21   Liu has found this in his own family. When his son and two daughters were young, he told them to become doctors or lawyers—jobs with the best guaranteed income, he felt. Sure enough, his daughters have gone into law, and his son is a medical student at UCLA, though he really wanted to be an investment banker. Liu asked his son why he picked medicine. The reply: "Ever since I was a little kid, I always heard you tell your friends their kids were a success if they got into med school. So I felt guilty. I didn't have a choice."

22   Underlying this bond between Asian parents and their children is yet another factor I noticed during 15 years of living in China, Japan, Taiwan and Vietnam. It is simply that Asian parents establish a closer physical tie to their infants than do most parents in the United States. When I let my baby son and daughter crawl on the floor, for example, my Chinese friends were horrified and rushed to pick them up. We think this constant attention is overindulgence and old-fashioned, but for Asians, who still live through the lives of their children, it is highly effective.

23   Yuen Huo, 22, a senior at Berkeley, recalled growing up in an apartment above the Chinese restaurant her immigrant parents owned and operated in Millbrae, Calif. "They used to tell us how they came from Taiwan to the United States for us, how they sacrificed for us, so I had a strong sense of indebtedness," Huo said. When she did not get all A's her first semester at Berkeley, she recalled, "I felt guilty and worked harder."

24   Here too is a vital clue about the Asians' success: Asian parents expect a high level of academic performance. In the Stanford study comparing white and Asian students in San Francisco high schools, 82 percent of the Asian parents said they would accept only an A or a B from their children, while just 59 percent of white parents set such a standard. By comparison, only 17 percent of Asian parents were

willing to accept a C, against 40 percent of white parents. On the average, parents of black and Hispanic students also had lower expectations for their children's grades than Asian parents.

Can we learn anything from the Asians? "I'm not naïve enough 25 to think everything in Asia can be transplanted," said Harold Stevenson, the University of Michigan psychologist. But he offered three recommendations.

"To start with," he said, "we need to set higher standards for our 26 kids. We wouldn't expect them to become professional athletes without practicing hard."

Second, American parents need to become more committed to 27 their children's education, he declared. "Being understanding when a child doesn't do well isn't enough." Stevenson found that Asian parents spend many more hours really helping their children with homework or writing to their teachers. At Berkeley, the mothers of some Korean-American students move into their sons' apartments for months before graduate school entrance tests to help by cooking and cleaning for them, giving the students more time to study.

And, third, schools could be reorganized to become more ef- 28 fective—without added costs, said Stevenson. One of his most surprising findings is that Asian students, contrary to popular myth, are not just rote learners subjected to intense pressure. Instead, nearly 90 percent of Chinese youngsters said they actually enjoy school, and 60 percent can't wait for school vacations to end. These are vastly higher figures for such attitudes than are found in the United States. One reason may be that students in China and Japan typically have a recess after each class, helping them to relax and to increase their attention spans. Moreover, where American teachers spend almost their entire day in front of classes, their Chinese and Japanese counterparts may teach as little as three hours a day, giving them more time to relax and prepare imaginative lessons.

Another study, prepared for the U.S. Department of Education, 29 compared the math and science achievements of 24,000 13-year-olds in the United States and five other countries (four provinces of Canada, plus South Korea, Ireland, Great Britain and Spain). One of the findings was that the more time students spent watching television, the poorer their performance. The American students watched the most television. They also got the worst scores in math. Only the Irish students and some of the Canadians scored lower in science.

"I don't think Asians are any smarter," said Don Lee, the Ko- 30 rean-American at Berkeley. "There are brilliant Americans in my chemistry class. But the Asian students work harder. I see a lot of wasted potential among the Americans."

QUESTIONS ON SUBJECT AND PURPOSE

1. According to Butterfield, what are the "causes" of the success of Asian American students?

2. Why do American students not excel to the same extent as Asian and Asian American students?

3. In addition to providing an explanation for the high achievement of Asian students, what other purpose does Butterfield seem to have? What might his American readers take from his essay?

QUESTIONS ON STRATEGY AND AUDIENCE

1. Why might Butterfield have begun with the example of Kim-Chi Trinh? Why not begin, for example, with a thesis paragraph?

2. Why might Butterfield choose to end the essay the way he does?

3. What assumptions does Butterfield seem to make about his readers? How do you know?

QUESTIONS ON VOCABULARY AND STYLE

1. What aspects of the essay suggest that Butterfield is writing for a popular rather than a scholarly audience?

2. What types of sources does Butterfield use in his essay?

3. Be prepared to define the following words: *imbue* (paragraph 17), *pluck* (18), *centripetal* (20), *rote learners* (28).

WRITING SUGGESTIONS

1. **For your Journal**. Are you "driven to excel"? In academics? In sports? In an artistic pursuit? In your career? Explore your motivations. Make a list of the ways you have sought to excel and the reasons why. On the other hand, if the phrase either frightens you or seems contrary to your thinking, explore the reasons you react that way.

2. **For a Paragraph**. Butterfield basically attributes the motivation of Asian and Asian American students to their desire to please their parents. In a paragraph, explore the typical motivations of students from another cultural group—your own or

one to which many of your friends belong. (If you are Asian or Asian American, or have many Asian American friends, you might rather critique Butterfield's analysis.)

3. **For an Essay.** Expand your paragraph into an essay. Using a cause and effect analysis, either explain what motivates a particular group of students or compare what motivates Asian or Asian American students to what motivates students from another cultural group. Try to define a specific audience—for example, readers of your college's newspaper.

Prewriting:

   a. Before you begin, think about your possible audience— their characteristics, their concerns. How will that audience influence both what you say and how you say it?

   b. Brainstorm a list of possible motivations. Also, brainstorm a list of reasons why people might *not* be motivated to excel. Consider both sides of the subject before choosing your approach.

   c. Spend 10 to 15 minutes freewriting about each item on both lists. Use these freewriting exercises to help define your subject and to analyze the possible significance or importance of each item.

Rewriting:

   a. Look again at how you have arranged or ordered the middle of your essay. Did you move from the most important to the least important cause or in the opposite direction? Try another order to see what happens.

   b. Check how you made the transitions from one reason to another. Have you used transitional devices? Do you provide the reader with a clear, logical pattern?

   c. Examine your introduction and conclusion. Put your essay aside, and, without looking at what you have already done, freewrite a new beginning and a new ending. Experiment with the strategies that Butterfield uses.

4. **For Research.** In paragraph 28, Butterfield describes some differences between Asian schools and American schools. Research the nature and methods of high school education in China, Japan, or another Pacific Rim country. Then explain in an essay how that educational system prepares and motivates students. Be sure to acknowledge your sources wherever appropriate.

WHY YOUNG WOMEN ARE MORE CONSERVATIVE

Gloria Steinem

Gloria Steinem was born in 1934 in Toledo, Ohio, and earned her B.A. in government from Smith College. She helped found New York magazine in 1968 and Ms. magazine in 1971. Steinem has earned recognition as one of the preeminent leaders of the women's liberation movement and has been active in civil rights organizations, political campaigns, and peace movements. Her latest books are Revolution from Within: A Book of Self-Esteem *(1992) and* Moving Beyond Words *(1994).*

In the following essay, Steinem starts with what appears to be a reasonable assumption—that college-age youth are more likely to be activists and open to change than their parents. But after a decade of traveling to college campuses, she has realized that her assumption is wrong. The active feminists are more likely to be middle-aged. She then goes on to explore the reasons that women, as they grow older, are more interested in the feminist movement.

BEFORE READING

Connecting: Can you think of a current issue or cause for which you are or would be willing to be an active supporter? It should be something for which you would "demonstrate" or contribute your time and money.

Anticipating: What does Steinem mean when she uses the word "conservative"? In what sense does she find young women "conservative"?

1 If you had asked me a decade or more ago, I certainly would have said the campus was the first place to look for the feminist or any other revolution. I also would have assumed that student-age women, like student-age men, were much more likely to be activist and open to change than their parents. After all, campus revolts have a long and well-publicized tradition, from the students of medieval France, whose "heresy" was suggesting that the university be separate from the church, through the anticolonial student riots of British India; from students who led the cultural revolution of the People's Repub-

lic of China, to campus demonstrations against the Shah of Iran. Even in this country, with far less tradition of student activism, the populist movement to end the war in Vietnam was symbolized by campus protests and mistrust of anyone over thirty.

It has taken me many years of traveling as a feminist speaker and organizer to understand that I was wrong about women; at least, about women acting on their own behalf. In activism, as in so many other things, I had been educated to assume that men's cultural pattern was the natural or the only one. If student years were the peak time of rebellion and openness to change for men, then the same must be true for women. In fact, a decade of listening to every kind of women's group—from brown-bag lunchtime lectures organized by office workers to all-night rap sessions at campus women's centers, from housewives' self-help groups to campus rallies—has convinced me that the reverse is more often true. Women may be the one group that grows more radical with age. Though some students are big exceptions to this rule, women in general don't begin to challenge the politics of our own lives until later.

Looking back, I realize that this pattern has been true for my life, too. My college years were full of uncertainties and the personal conservatism that comes from trying to win approval and fit into the proper grown-up and womanly role, whether that means finding a well-to-do man to be supported by or a male radical to support. Nonetheless, I went right on assuming that brave exploring youth and cowardly conservative old age were the norms for everybody, and that I must be just an isolated and guilty accident. Though every generalization based on female culture has many exceptions, and should never be used as a crutch or excuse, I think we might be less hard on ourselves and each other as students, feel better about our potential for change as we grow older—and educate reporters who announce feminism's demise because its red-hot center is not on campus—if we figured out that for most of us as women, the traditional college period is an unrealistic and cautious time. Consider a few of the reasons.

As students, women are probably treated with more equality than we ever will be again. For one thing, we're consumers. The school is only too glad to get the tuitions we pay, or that our families or government grants pay on our behalf. With population rates declining because of women's increased power over childbearing, that money is even more vital to a school's existence. Yet more than most consumers, we're too transient to have much power as a group. If our families are paying our tuition, we may have even less power.

As young women, whether students or not, we're still in the stage most valued by male-dominant cultures: we have our full potential as workers, wives, sex partners, and childbearers.

6   That means we haven't yet experienced the life events that are most radicalizing for women: entering the paid-labor force and discovering how women are treated there; marrying and finding out that it is not yet an equal partnership having children and discovering who is responsible for them and who is not; and aging, still a greater penalty for women than for men.

7   Furthermore, new ambitions nourished by the rebirth of feminism may make young women feel and behave a little like a classical immigrant group. We are determined to prove ourselves, to achieve academic excellence, and to prepare for interesting and successful careers. More noses are kept to more grindstones in an effort to demonstrate newfound abilities, and perhaps to allay suspicions that women still have to have more and better credentials than men. This doesn't leave much time for activism. Indeed, we may not yet know that it is necessary.

8   In addition, the very progress into previously all-male careers that may be revolutionary for women is seen as conservative and conformist by outside critics. Assuming male radicalism to be the measure of change, they interpret any concern with careers as evidence of "campus conservatism." In fact, "dropping out" may be a departure for men, but "dropping in" is a new thing for women. Progress lies in the direction we have not been.

9   Like most groups of the newly arrived or awakened, our faith in education and paper degrees also has yet to be shaken. For instance, the percentage of women enrolled in colleges and universities has been increasing at the same time that the percentage of men has been decreasing. Among students entering college in 1978, women *outnumbered* men for the first time. This hope of excelling at the existing game is probably reinforced by the greater cultural pressure on females to be "good girls" and observe somebody else's rules.

10   Though we may know intellectually that we need to have new games with new rules, we probably haven't quite absorbed such facts as the high unemployment rate among female Ph.D.s; the lower average salary among women college graduates of all races than among counterpart males who graduated from high school or less; the middle-management ceiling against which even those eagerly hired new business-school graduates seem to bump their heads after five or ten years; and the barrier-breaking women in nontraditional fields who become the first fired when recession hits. Sadly enough, we may have to personally experience some of these reality checks before we accept the idea that lawsuits, activism, and group pressure will have to accompany our individual excellence and crisp new degrees.

11   Then there is the female guilt trip, student edition. If we're not sailing along as planned, it must be our fault. If our mothers didn't

"do anything" with their educations, it must have been *their* fault. If we can't study as hard as we think we must (because women still have to be better prepared than men), and have a substantial personal and sexual life at the same time (because women are supposed to care more about relationships than men do), then we feel inadequate, as if each of us were individually at fault for a problem that is actually culture-wide.

I've yet to be on a campus where most women weren't worry-   12
ing about some aspect of combining marriage, children, and a career. I've yet to find one where many men were worrying about the same thing. Yet women will go right on suffering from the double-role problem and terminal guilt until men are encouraged, pressured, or otherwise forced, individually and collectively, to integrate them-selves into the "women's work" of raising children and homemaking. Until then, and until there are changed job patterns to allow equal parenthood, children will go right on growing up with the belief that only women can be loving and nurturing, and only men can be intel-lectual or active outside the home. Each half of the world will go on limiting the full range of its human talent.

Finally, there is the intimate political training that hits women   13
in the teens and early twenties: the countless ways we are still brain-washed into assuming that women are dependent on men for our basic identities, both in our work and our personal lives, much more than vice versa. After all, if we're going to enter a marriage system that's still legally designed for a person and a half, submit to an econ-omy in which women still average about fifty-nine cents on the dol-lar earned by men, and work mainly as support staff and assistants, or *co*-directors and *vice*-presidents at best, then we have to be convinced that we are not whole people on our own.

In order to make sure that we will see ourselves as half-people,   14
and thus be addicted to getting our identity from serving others, so-ciety tries hard to convert us as young women into "man junkies"; that is, into people who are addicted to regular shots of male-approval and presence, both professionally and personally. We need a man standing next to us, actually and figuratively, whether it's at work, on Saturday night, or throughout life. (If only men realized how little it matters *which* man is standing there, they would under-stand that this addiction depersonalizes them, too.) Given the danger to a male-dominant system if young women stop internalizing this political message of derived identity, it's no wonder that those who try to kick the addiction—and, worse yet, to help other women do the same—are likely to be regarded as odd or dangerous by everyone from parents to peers.

With all that pressure combined with little experience, it's no   15 wonder that younger women are often less able to support each other. Even young women who espouse feminist goals as individuals may refrain from identifying themselves as "feminist": It's okay to want equal pay for yourself (just one small reform) but it's not okay to want equal pay for women as a group (an economic revolution). Some retreat into individualized career obsessions as a way of avoiding this dangerous discovery of shared experience with women as a group. Others retreat into the safe middle ground of "I'm not a feminist but. . . ." Still others become politically active, but only on issues that are taken seriously by their male counterparts.

16   The same lesson about the personal conservatism of younger women is taught by the history of feminism. If I hadn't been conned into believing the masculine stereotype of youth as the "natural" time for freedom and rebellion, a time of "sowing wild oats" that actually is made possible by the assurance of power and security later on, I could have figured out the female pattern of activism by looking at women's movements of the past.

17   In this country, for instance, the nineteenth-century wave of feminism was started by older women who had been through the radicalizing experience of getting married and becoming the legal chattel of their husbands (or the equally radicalizing experience of not getting married and being treated as spinsters). Most of them had also worked in the antislavery movement and learned from the political parallels between race and sex. In other countries, that wave was also led by women who were past the point of maximum pressure toward marriageability and conservatism.

18   Looking at the first decade of this second wave, it's clear that the early feminist activist and consciousness-raising groups of the 1960s were organized by women who had experienced the civil rights movement, or homemakers who had discovered that raising kids and cooking didn't occupy all their talents. While most campuses of the late sixties were still circulating the names of illegal abortionists privately (after all, abortion could damage our marriage value), slightly older women were holding press conferences and speak-outs about the reality of abortions (including their own, even though that often meant confessing to an illegal act) and demanding reform or repeal of antichoice laws. Though rape had been a quiet epidemic on campus for generations, younger women victims were still understandably fearful of speaking up, and campuses encouraged silence in order to retain their reputation for safety with tuition-paying parents. It took many off-campus speak-outs, demonstrations against laws of evidence and police procedures, and testimonies in state legislatures before most student groups began to make demands on campus and local cops for greater rape protection. In fact, "date rape"—the com-

mon campus phenomenon of a young woman being raped by someone she knows, perhaps even by several students in a fraternity house—is just now being exposed. Marital rape, a more difficult legal issue, was taken up several years ago. As for battered women and the attendant exposé of husbands and lovers as more statistically dangerous than unknown muggers in the street, that issue still seems to be thought of as a largely noncampus concern, yet at many of the colleges and universities where I've spoken, there has been at least one case within current student memory of a young woman beaten or murdered by a jealous lover.

This cultural pattern of youthful conservatism makes the growing number of older women going back to school very important. They are life examples and pragmatic activists who radicalize women young enough to be their daughters. Now that the median female undergraduate age in this country is twenty-seven because so many older women have returned, the campus is becoming a major place for cross-generational connections. 19

None of this should denigrate the courageous efforts of young women, especially women on campus, and the many changes they've pioneered. On the contrary, they should be seen as even more remarkable for surviving the conservative pressures, recognizing societal problems they haven't yet fully experienced, and organizing successfully in the midst of a transient student population. Every women's history course, rape hot line, or campus newspaper that is finally covering *all* the news; every feminist professor whose job has been created or tenure saved by student pressure, or male administrator whose consciousness has been permanently changed; every counselor who's stopped guiding women one way and men another; every lawsuit that's been fueled by student energies against unequal athletic funds or graduate school requirements: all those accomplishments are even more impressive when seen against the back-drop of the female pattern of activism. 20

Finally, it would help to remember that a feminist revolution rarely resembles a masculine-style one—just as a young woman's most radical act toward her mother (that is, connecting as women in order to help each other get some power) doesn't look much like a young man's most radical act toward his father (that is, breaking the father-son connection in order to separate identities or take over existing power). 21

It's those father-son conflicts at a generational, national level that have often provided the conventional definition of revolution; yet they've gone on for centuries without basically changing the role of the female half of the world. They have also failed to reduce the level of violence in society, since both fathers and sons have included 22 some degree of aggressiveness and superiority to women in their definition of masculinity, thus preserving the anthropological model of dominance.

23   Furthermore, what current leaders and theoreticians define as revolution is usually little more than taking over the army and the radio stations. Women have much more in mind than that. We have to uproot the sexual caste system that is the most pervasive power structure in society, and that means transforming the patriarchal values of those who run the institutions, whether they are politically the "right" or the "left," the fathers or the sons. This cultural part of the change goes very deep, and is often seen as too intimate, and perhaps too threatening, to be considered as either serious or possible. Only conflicts among men are "serious." Only a takeover of existing institutions is "possible."

24   That's why the definition of "political," on campus as elsewhere, tends to be limited to who's running for president, who's demonstrating against corporate investments in South Africa, or which is the "moral" side of some conventional revolution, preferably one that is thousands of miles away.

25   As important as such activities are, they are also the most comfortable ones when we're young. They provide a sense of virtue without much disruption in the power structure of our daily lives. Even when the most consistent energies on campus are actually concentrated around feminist issues, they may be treated as apolitical and invisible. Asked "What's happening on campus?" a student may reply, "The antinuke movement," even though that resulted in one demonstration of two hours, while student antirape squads have been patrolling the campus every night for two years and women's studies have begun to transform the very textbooks we read.

26   No wonder reporters and sociologists looking for revolution on campus often miss the depth of feminist change and activity that is really there. Women students themselves may dismiss it as not political and not serious. Certainly, it rarely comes in the masculine sixties style of bombing buildings or burning draft cards. In fact, it goes much deeper than protesting a temporary symptom—say, the draft—and challenges the right of one group to dominate another, which is the disease itself.

27   Young women have a big task of resisting pressures and challenging definitions. Their increasing success is a miracle of foresight and courage that should make us all proud. But they should know that they, too, may grow more radical with age.

28   One day, an army of gray-haired women may quietly take over the earth.

QUESTIONS ON SUBJECT AND PURPOSE

1. What does Steinem mean by the word *conservative*? In what ways are young women conservative?
2. According to Steinem, what are the causes of this conservatism?
3. In what ways do women's cultural patterns differ from men's?

QUESTIONS. ON STRATEGY AND AUDIENCE

1. How does Steinem structure her cause and effect analysis? Is there a particular order to her list of causes?
2. How effective is Steinem's conclusion? Does it seem appropriate? Why or why not?
3. What assumptions does Steinem make about her audience? How are those assumptions revealed in the essay?

QUESTIONS ON VOCABULARY AND STYLE

1. Why does Steinem write in the first person ("I")? How would the essay be different if she had avoided all first-person references? If she had not interwoven her experiences with the social commentary?
2. How would you describe Steinem's tone in the essay? What does that tone come from? How formal or informal is her language? Her sentence structure?
3. Be able to define the following words: *demise* (paragraph 3), *transient* (4), *espouse* (15), *chattel* (17), *denigrate* (20).

WRITING SUGGESTIONS

1. **For your Journal**. Look around your campus; check your student newspaper and campus bulletin boards. Do you see any signs of student activism? Make a list of any "causes" that you can find. Why are these "causes" popular at this time? In your journal, speculate on the reasons for the activism that you find (or for the lack of activism that you detect).
2. **For a Paragraph**. Summarize Steinem's analysis. Do not quote her exactly. Focus instead on summarizing her reasons for this phenomenon.
3. **For an Essay**. The 1990s have been a relatively quiet time on most college campuses, with few protests about anything. Why should this be? What accounts for the quiet atmosphere

on campuses? In a cause and effect essay aimed at your college classmates, explore this situation. As a variation, you might write for an audience of parents of average college freshmen today.

Prewriting:

a. If you accept the premise that college students today are not active in social and political issues, you will need to isolate some possible reasons or causes for that apathy. Start by asking yourself what is particularly important to *you*; what are *you* concerned about? As you list the topics, try to record a reason for each concern. (For example, "I am concerned about getting a high-paying job because by the time I graduate, I will have borrowed $15,000 to finance my education.")

b. Extend your information-gathering by polling friends and classmates. Develop both a list of concerns and a list of possible explanations for those concerns. Ideally you should interview ten people, trying for a wide range of ages and backgrounds.

c. Look over the list that you have gathered. Some reasons for student concerns will be more common and more significant than others. Since you are trying to explain the generalized behavior of a large group of people, concentrate on reasons which seem primary and immediate. Place an asterisk next to those items on your lists that seem most important. Then plan an order for those items. You will need to cite at least three possible causes for the apathy of students.

Rewriting:

a. How have you defined your audience? On a separate sheet of paper, analyze the characteristics of that audience. Now look back at the draft of your essay. Have you written to that audience? List the specific ways in which your essay— in its introduction, its style, its examples—acknowledges that audience.

b. Find at least one peer reader. Ask the reader if your essay seems like an adequate (or insightful) explanation. Does the essay analyze the current college generation? Is it fair? Does it distort?

c. Although Steinem's essay is long and sophisticated, it can serve as a good structural model. Study it again as a writer looking to see how another writer handled a similar subject. You are not imitating form; you are observing technique.

4. **For Research**. On the average, women still do not earn as much money as men, although Steinem's "fifty-nine cents on the dollar" statistic increased to about seventy-one cents in the ten years after she wrote this essay. Research this problem. Why do women earn less? Present your evidence in a cause and effect analysis. Government documents are a particularly good source of information on this topic. Ask your reference or government documents librarian for help with searching for relevant documents. Remember to document your sources carefully and accurately.

EIGHT

DEFINITION

On the midterm examination in your introductory economics class only the essay question remains to be answered: "What is capitalism?" You are tempted to write the one-sentence definition you memorized from the glossary of your textbook and dash from the room. On the other hand, it is unlikely that your professor will react positively or even charitably to such a skimpy (and memorized) response. Instead, you realize that what is needed is an extended definition—one that explains what factors were necessary before capitalism could emerge, what elements are most characteristic of a capitalistic economy, how capitalism differs from other economic systems, how a capitalistic economy works, how capitalism is linked to technology and politics. What you need is a narrative, a division, a comparison and contrast, a process, and a cause and effect analysis all working together to give you a full definition of what is finally a very complex term.

When you are asked to define a word, you generally do two things: first, you provide a dictionarylike definition, normally a single sentence; and second, if the occasion demands, you provide a longer, extended definition, analyzing the subject, giving examples or details. If you use technical or specialized words that may be unfamiliar to your reader, you include a parenthetical definition: "Macroeconomics, the portion of economics concerned with large-scale movements such as inflation and deflation, is particularly interested in changes in the GNP, or gross national product."

Definitions can be denotative, connotative, or a mixture of the two. Dictionary definitions are denotative; that is, they offer a literal

and explicit definition of a word. A dictionary, for example, defines the word *prejudice* as "a judgment or opinion formed before the facts are known; preconceived idea." In most cases, however, this single sentence is not enough to give a reader a clear understanding of this word or concept.

Many words have more than just literal meanings; they also carry connotations, either positive or negative, and these connotations may make up part of an extended definition. For example, in 1944 when the United States was at war on two fronts, E. B. White was asked to write about "The Meaning of Democracy" for the Writers' War Board. White's one-paragraph response goes beyond a literal definition to explore the connotations and associations that surround the word *democracy*:

> Surely the Board knows what democracy is. It is the line that forms on the right. It is the don't in Don't Shove. It is the hole in the stuffed shirt through which the sawdust trickles; it is the dent in the high hat. Democracy is the recurrent suspicion that more than half of the people are right more than half of the time. It is the feeling of privacy in the voting booths, the feeling of communion in the libraries, the feeling of vitality everywhere. Democracy is the score at the beginning of the ninth. It is an idea which hasn't been disproved yet, a song the words of which have not gone bad. It's the mustard on the hot dog and the cream in the rationed coffee. Democracy is a request from a War Board, in the middle of a morning in the middle of a war, wanting to know what democracy is.

Democracy was, to White, not simply a form of government, but a whole way of life.

Most writing situations, especially those you encounter in college, require extended definitions. The selections in this chapter define a variety of subjects, and they suggest how differently extended definitions can be handled. Theodore Bernstein provides a denotative definition of the term *cliché* ("an overworked, commonplace expression") but surrounds that definition with examples. Rose Del Castillo Guilbault is not interested in the way a dictionary defines *macho* (typically, "a strong, virile man"); instead, she is interested in the connotations that the word carries in both the Hispanic and Anglo cultures. Judy Brady tries to define the term *wife* and the many associations that people have with that word. Amy Tan explores a definition of *mother tongue* and its impact on others. Gloria Naylor explains how the meaning of a word depends upon who uses it when she

confronts the label *nigger*. Finally, Margaret Atwood uses multiple examples to define that "capacious" topic, the *female body*.

How Much Do You Include in a Definition?

Every word, whether it refers to a specific physical object or to the most theoretical concept, has a dictionary definition. Whether that one-sentence definition is sufficient depends upon why you are defining the word. Complex words, words with many nuances and connotations, generally require a fuller definition than a single sentence can possibly provide. Moreover, one-sentence definitions often contain other words and phrases that also need to be defined.

For example, if you were asked, "What is a wife?" you could reply, "A woman married to a man." While that definition is accurate, it does not convey any sense of what such a relationship might involve. Judy Brady's "I Want a Wife" defines the word by showing what men (or some men) expect in a wife. Brady divides and lists a wife's many responsibilities—things expected of her by an actual or potential husband. Brady's essay, comically overstated as it is, offers a far more meaningful definition of the term *wife* than any one-sentence dictionary entry. Her intention surely was to reveal inequality in marriage, and she makes her point by listing a stereotypical set of male expectations.

Writing a definition is a fairly common activity in college work. In your literature course you are asked to define the romantic movement; in art history, the baroque period; in psychology, abnormal behavior. Since a single-sentence definition can never do justice to such complicated terms, an extended definition is necessary. In each case, the breadth and depth of your knowledge is being tested; your professor expects you to formulate a definition that accounts for the major subdivisions and characteristics of the subject. Your purpose is to convince your professor that you have read and mastered the assigned materials and can select and organize them, often adding some special insight of your own, into a logical and coherent response.

How Do You Structure a Definition?

Sentence definitions are relatively easy to write. You first place the word in a general class ("A wife is a *woman*") and then add any distin-

guishing features that set it apart from other members of the class ("married to a man"). But the types of definitions you are asked to write for college are generally more detailed than dictionary entries. How then do you get from a single sentence to a paragraph or an essay?

Extended definitions do not have a structure peculiar to themselves. That is, when you write a definition you do not have a predetermined structural pattern as you do with comparison and contrast, division and classification, process, or cause and effect. Instead, definitions are constructed by using all of the various strategies discussed in this book. Theodore M. Bernstein uses examples to define the term *cliché*. As the selections progress from this fairly short and simple definition to the more complex ones, the number of types of strategies that the writers employ, in addition to example, increases. Rose Del Castillo Guilbault uses contrast to establish what the word *macho* suggests to Hispanics and to Anglos. Judy Brady's definition of a wife uses division to organize the many types of responsibilities demanded of a wife. Amy Tan contrasts and classifies the many Englishes that she uses, and both Tan and Gloria Naylor use narration as vital parts of their definitions. Finally, Margaret Atwood gathers a wide range of examples to suggest the complexity involved in the phrase "the female body," ending with an imaginative contrast between the brain of a man and that of a woman.

Once you have chosen a subject for definition, think first about its essential characteristics, steps, or parts. What examples would best define it? Then plan your organization by seeing how those details can be presented most effectively to your reader. If your definition involves breaking a subject into its parts, use division or possibly even process. If you are defining by comparing your subject to another, use a comparison and contrast structure. If your subject is defined as the result of some causal connection, use a cause and effect structure. Definitions can also involve narration, description, and even persuasion. The longer the extended definition, the greater is the likelihood that your paper will involve a series of structures.

SAMPLE STUDENT ESSAY

Like many people, Lyndsey Curtis is a cat lover, and that determined her choice of subject. Lyndsey, probably influenced by having read Judy Brady's essay, decided to define the *essence* of a cat:

Felis Catus

Webster's New Collegiate Dictionary defines *cat* as "a carnivorous mammal (*Felis catus*) long domesticated and kept by man as a pet or for catching rats and mice." That is fine if you are interested in a scientific definition. In my opinion, however, it doesn't even begin to tap into the essence of that phenomenon known as "cat."

Cats perform many practical services. On cold winter nights, they keep your feet as warm as an electric blanket but without using electricity. They act as alarm clocks in the morning; it's time for you to get up when they want to be fed. Wouldn't you rather wake up to the gentle but insistent tap of a soft furry paw on your forehead than to a loud, obnoxious buzzing noise anyway? Cats are very entertaining. They are excellent subjects for photographs, as you can easily determine by setting foot inside any true cat lover's home; the walls are inevitably adorned with pictures of his or her favorite feline. They provide "musical enjoyment" for you and your neighbors when they "sing" to each other on warm summer nights. They can supply topics for hours of conversation between mutual cat lovers, who always enjoy recounting their favorite cat story. More important, however, is the emotional completeness a cat brings to your life.

When you've lived with cats your whole life as I have, you begin to realize that they are really just like people and that they become members of your family very quickly. Cats are very reliable; you can always depend on them to know when it is time to go out, when it is time to play, when it is time to eat, and when it is time to sleep (most of the day). They teach children about responsibility, love, and the importance of caring for another living being. In addition, they provide companionship for many lonely people. They sense when you are feeling upset or depressed and will always try to make you feel better by climbing up onto your lap with a great purr. A cat's love is unconditional as long as you care for him or her properly. They'll love you despite all your faults; they'll love you when it seems that no one else in the world will. They'll greet you at the door when you come home after a rough day at the office and will listen to your problems and complaints without interrupting. Cats are always there when you need a friend. B. Kliban, in his 1975 book *Cat*, put it very aptly when he defined a cat as "one Hell of a nice animal, frequently mistaken for a meatloaf."

On the peer editing checksheet for definition essays used in Lindsey's class, one of the questions concerned opening sentences: "Does the essay avoid the standard 'according to Webster . . .'?" When Lyndsey's essay was read in class during a peer editing session, several students asked about the wisdom of beginning in this way. The class agreed, however, that even though it is generally not a good idea to begin a definition with a quotation from a dictionary, the device works fairly well here since Lyndsey is trying to show how inadequate that denotative definition is. The strong point of the essay, everyone felt, was its division into "practical services" and "emotional completeness." The transition between the two halves comes smoothly and naturally. The other area that troubled the peer readers was Lyndsey's ending. As one student observed, "Your final quotation from Kliban's book seems inappropriate. You have been making some light-hearted but still serious points, and to end suddenly on such a cynical quotation introduces an abrupt change in tone." When Lyndsey came to revise her essay, she tried to address the problems that the peer editors had raised.

REVISED DRAFT

The Essence of Cat

The dictionary defines *cat* as "a carnivorous mammal (*Felis catus*) long domesticated and kept by man as a pet or for catching rats and mice." That is fine if you are interested in a scientific definition. In my opinion, however, it does not even begin to tap into the essence of that phenomenon known as "cat."

Cats perform many practical services. On cold winter nights, they keep your feet as warm as an electric blanket would, but they do it without using electricity. They act as alarm clocks in the morning; it is time to get up when they want to be fed. Wouldn't you rather wake up to the gentle but insistent tap of a soft paw on your forehead than to a loud, obnoxious buzzing noise? Cats are very entertaining. They are excellent subjects for photographs, as you can easily see from the pictures of felines that cover the walls of any true cat lover's home. They provide "musical enjoyment" for you and your neighbors, "singing" to each other on warm summer nights. They can supply topics for hours of conversation between cat lovers, who always enjoy recounting their favorite cat stories. More important, however, is the emotional completeness a cat brings to your life.

When you have lived with cats your whole life as I have, you begin to realize that they are really just like people and that they become members of your family very quickly. Cats are very reliable; you can always depend on them to know when it is time to eat, and when it is time to sleep (most of the day). They teach children about responsibility, love, and the importance of caring for another living being. In addition, they provide companionship for many lonely people. They sense when you are feeling upset or depressed and will always try to make you feel better by climbing onto your lap with a great purr. A cat's love is unconditional as long as you care for him or her properly. Cats will love you despite all your faults; they will love you when it seems that no one else in the world will. They will greet you at the door when you come home after a rough day at the office and will listen to your problems and complaints without interrupting.

Cats are always there when you need a friend.

Definition

SOME THINGS TO REMEMBER

1. Choose a subject that can be reasonably and fully defined within the limits of your paper. That is, make sure it is neither too limited nor too large.

2. Determine a purpose for your definition.

3. Spend time analyzing your subject to see what its essential characteristics, steps, or parts are.

4. Write a dictionary definition for your subject. Do this even if you are writing an extended definition. The features that set your subject apart from others in its general class reveal what must be included in your definition.

5. Choose examples that are clear and appropriate.

6. Decide which of the organizational patterns will best convey the information you have gathered.

7. Be careful about beginning, "According to Webster. . . ." There are usually more effective and interesting ways to announce your subject.

CLICHÉS
Theodore M. Bernstein

Theodore Bernstein (1904–1979) was born in New York City and educated at Columbia University. Immediately after graduation, he joined The New York Times *as a copy editor. Within the* Times *organization, he held a variety of positions, including assistant managing editor. He also edited an in-house bulletin that critiqued the writing and usage of the* Times *staff, a position that* Newsweek *magazine referred to as "linguistic policeman."*

Bernstein was an authority on English usage and served as a consultant to the Random House Dictionary *and the* American Heritage Dictionary. *His many books include* The Careful Writer: A Modern Guide to English Usage *(1965) and* Miss Thistlebottom's Hobgoblins: The Careful Writer's Guide to Taboos, Bugbears, and Outmoded Rules of English Usage *(1971). In this selection from* The Careful Writer, *Bernstein displays his usual wit and ingenuity in defining a* cliché.

BEFORE READING

Connecting: Before you begin to read, think about the word "cliché." How would you define it?

Anticipating: Do you recognize all of the examples that Bernstein gives as being clichés? If you do not recognize them as such, does that still mean that they are clichés if you use them?

1   When Archimedes' bath ran over and he discovered something about specific gravity, he was perhaps justified in sprinting into the street without his clothes and exulting. But that does not mean that every kid who sees his Saturday night bath overflow is justified in dashing outdoors naked shouting, "Eureka!" The distinction here is somewhat akin to that between the coiner of a bright phrase and the mere echoer of that phrase. It is the echoing that turns the phrase into a cliché—that is, an overworked, commonplace expression—and the echoer should realize that he has no claim to originality.

2   This is not to say that all clichés should be avoided like, shall we say, the plague. It is no more possible—or desirable—to do that than it is to abolish gravity. Many of today's clichés are likely to be tomor-

Definition

row's standard English, just as many of today's standard words were yesterday's metaphors: *thunderstruck, astonish, cuckold, conclave, sanguine,* and thousands of others that form a substantial part of any dictionary. Moreover, the cliché is sometimes the most direct way of expressing a thought. Think of the circumlocution that is avoided by saying that someone has a *dog-in-the-manger attitude*. To attempt to write around a cliché will often lead to pompous obscurity. And for a writer to decide to banish all clichés indiscriminately would be to hamstring—yes, *hamstring*—his efforts.

There are many varieties of clichés. Some are foreign phrases *(coup de grâce; et tu, Brute)*. Some are homely sayings or are based on proverbs ("You can't make an omelet without breaking eggs," *blissful ignorance*). Some are quotations ("To be or not to be"; "Unwept, unhonored, and unsung"). Some are allusions to myth or history (*Gordian knot, Achilles' heel*). Some are alliterative or rhyming phrases *(first and foremost, high and dry)*. Some are paradoxes *(in less than no time, conspicuous by its absence)*. Some are legalisms *(null and void, each and every)*. Some are playful euphemisms *(A fate worse than death, better half)*. Some are figurative phrases *(leave no stone unturned, hit the nail on the head)*. And some are almost meaningless small change *(in the last analysis, by the same token)*.

QUESTIONS ON SUBJECT AND PURPOSE

1. What is a cliché? Why are clichés so common?

2. If clichés are "overworked" and "commonplace" (paragraph 1), why not "banish" them (paragraph 2)? How would a writer know when to avoid clichés and when to use them?

3. For class discussion, list at least six additional clichés that are a part of your everyday speech. Can they be classified using the categories Bernstein mentions in the third paragraph?

QUESTIONS ON STRATEGY AND AUDIENCE

1. Why does Bernstein begin with the reference to Archimedes? Why not just begin with the definition?

2. What rhetorical structures does Bernstein use to order his paragraphs? How are they a part of his attempt at definition?

3. What expectations does Bernstein have of his audience? Find specific evidence to support your conclusions.

QUESTIONS ON VOCABULARY AND STYLE

1. In the second paragraph, Bernstein cites some examples of "yesterday's metaphors" that are "today's standard words." Check each word in a dictionary. How were these words metaphoric?

2. Why does Bernstein use clichés in his second paragraph? How many does he use?

3. Be able to define the following words: *specific gravity* (paragraph 1), *Eureka* (1), *akin* (1), *circumlocution* (2), *pompous* (2), *hamstring* (2), *euphemisms* (3).

WRITING SUGGESTIONS

1. **For your Journal.** Be conscious of the language that you hear and read for an entire day. How often do you hear or see a cliché in speaking or writing? Make a list of the clichés that you encounter in a single day. Why are there so many of them?

2. **For a Paragraph.** Select one of the following words (or a similar word) and define it in a paragraph. Consult a dictionary before beginning. Remember to use examples to make your definition clear and interesting.

   a. euphemism

   b. spoonerism

   c. malapropism

   d. cant

   e. jargon

3. **For an Essay.** Select a concept central to another academic subject you are studying this semester. Using your textbook and whatever other sources might be available, define that word or idea for a general audience. Remember to make your definition interesting through the use of appropriate examples.

   Prewriting:

   a. Remember that you will need to choose a subject that is complex enough to require an extended definition. On the other hand, you will probably want to avoid a technical subject that is of little interest to a general reader. With these two cautions in mind, use the textbooks from your other courses as guides, and make a list of possible subjects.

b. List several possibilities down the left-hand side of a sheet of paper. In the space to the right, analyze each subject from the point of view of your potential audience. What might a general audience know about this subject? Is that audience likely to be interested in or to have opinions about the subject? Answer these questions for each topic.

c. Visit the current periodicals section of your library and spend some time looking at magazines such as *Time* and *Newsweek*. If either magazine contained an article on the same subject as yours, how would it be handled? How are their articles written for a general audience? Study appropriate articles in either magazine. Pay attention to the strategy and style of the articles.

Rewriting:

a. Make a copy of your essay, and ask a peer reader to respond to it. Tell that reader to mark any section or any word in the essay that seems too technical or inadequately explained. Try to get a reader who is relatively unfamiliar with the subject.

b. Return to some sample issues of magazines such as *Time* or *Newsweek*. Study the introductions to articles with related topics. Have you used a similar strategy to begin your essay? If you have not, pretend that your essay will appear in a magazine, and try to write an introduction that your editor would like.

c. Also study the conclusions of some magazine articles. Do you conclude in a similar way? If you have not, try freewriting a new ending for your essay.

4. For Research. The reference room of your college's library will have a number of guides to English usage. Consult at least six different reference books on the subject *cliché*. Write a definition of the term with appropriate examples. You should also comment on whether clichés are ever appropriate in writing. Your essay will be used as a handout in the freshman English program at your college or university, so remember your audience. Be sure to document your sources wherever appropriate.

AMERICANIZATION IS
TOUGH ON "MACHO"

Rose Del Castillo Guilbault

Rose Del Castillo Guilbault was raised in the Salinas Valley in California. She has pursued a successful career in broadcast news as editorial and public affairs director at KGO-TV in San Francisco and as associate editor at Pacific News Service. A monthly column by her appears in the San Francisco Chronicle, *where she writes on issues affecting Spanish-speaking Americans.*

In this column, originally published in the Chronicle, *Guilbault explores the definition of "macho" in both the Hispanic and American cultures. What the word means, she notes, "depends upon which side of the border you come from."*

BEFORE READING

Connecting: What does the word *macho* suggest to you? What in a person's behavior justifies or suggests labeling him *macho*?

Anticipating: Where does Guilbault find her examples of Hispanic *macho* and American *macho*?

1   What is *macho*? That depends which side of the border you come from.

2   Although it's not unusual for words and expressions to lose their subtlety in translation, the negative connotations of *macho* in this country are troublesome to Hispanics.

3   Take the newspaper descriptions of alleged mass murderer Ramon Salcido. That an insensitive, insanely jealous, hard-drinking, violent Latin male is referred to as *macho* makes Hispanics cringe.

4   "*Es muy macho*," the women in my family nod approvingly, describing a man they respect. But in the United States, when women say, "He's so macho," it's with disdain.

5   The Hispanic *macho* is manly, responsible, hardworking, a man in charge, a patriarch. A man who expresses strength through silence. What the Yiddish language would call a *mensch*.

6   The American *macho* is a chauvinist, a brute, uncouth, selfish, loud, abrasive, capable of inflicting pain, and sexually promiscuous.

7   Quintessential *macho* models in this country are Sylvester Stal-

Definition

lone, Arnold Schwarzenegger, and Charles Bronson. In their movies, they exude toughness, independence, masculinity. But a closer look reveals their machismo is really violence masquerading as courage, sullenness disguised as silence and irresponsibility camouflaged as independence.

If the Hispanic ideal of *macho* were translated to American screen roles, they might be Jimmy Stewart, Sean Connery, and Laurence Olivier. 8

In Spanish, *macho* ennobles Latin males. In English it devalues them. This pattern seems consistent with the conflicts ethnic minority males experience in this country. Typically the cultural traits other societies value don't translate as desirable characteristics in America. 9

I watched my own father struggle with these cultural ambiguities. He worked on a farm for 20 years. He laid down miles of irrigation pipe, carefully plowed long, neat rows in fields, hacked away at recalcitrant weeds and drove tractors through whirlpools of dust. He stoically worked 20-hour days during harvest season, accepting the long hours as part of agricultural work. When the boss complained or upbraided him for minor mistakes, he kept quiet, even when it was obvious the boss had erred. 10

He handled the most menial tasks with pride. At home he was a good provider, helped out my mother's family in Mexico without complaint, and was indulgent with me. Arguments between my mother and him generally had to do with money, or with his stubborn reluctance to share his troubles. He tried to work them out in his own silence. He didn't want to trouble my mother—a course that backfired, because the imagined is always worse than the reality. 11

Americans regarded my father as decidedly un-*macho*. His character was interpreted as non-assertive, his loyalty non-ambition, and his quietness, ignorance. I once overheard the boss's son blame him for plowing crooked rows in a field. My father merely smiled at the lie, knowing the boy had done it, but didn't refute it, confident his good work was well known. But the boss instead ridiculed him for being "stupid" and letting a kid get away with a lie. Seeing my embarrassment, my father dismissed the incident, saying "They're the dumb ones. Imagine, me fighting with a kid." 12

I tried not to look at him with American eyes because sometimes the reflection hurt. 13

Listening to my aunts' clucks of approval, my vision focused on the qualities America overlooked. "He's such a hard worker. So serious, so responsible," my aunts would secretly compliment my mother. The unspoken comparison was that he was not like some of their husbands, who drank and womanized. My uncles represented the darker side of *macho*. 14

15   In a patriarchal society, few challenge their roles. If men drink, it's because it's the manly thing to do. If they gamble, it's because it's how men relax. And if they fool around, well, it's because a man simply can't hold back so much man! My aunts didn't exactly meekly sit back, but they put up with these transgressions because Mexican society dictated this was their lot in life.

16   In the United States, I believe it was the feminist movement of the early '70s that changed *macho's* meaning. Perhaps my generation of Latin women was in part responsible. I recall Chicanas complaining about the chauvinistic nature of Latin men and the notion they wanted their women barefoot, pregnant, and in the kitchen. The generalization that Latin men embodied chauvinistic traits led to this interesting twist of semantics. Suddenly a word that represented something positive in one culture became a negative prototype in another.

17   The problem with the use of *macho* today is that it's become an accepted stereotype of the Latin male. And like all stereotypes, it distorts truth.

18   The impact of language in our society is undeniable. And the misuse of *macho* hints at a deeper cultural misunderstanding that extends beyond mere word definitions.

QUESTIONS ON SUBJECT AND PURPOSE

1. According to Guilbault, what makes an Hispanic male *macho*?
2. In contrast, how does Guilbault characterize the American version of *macho*?
3. At the end of the essay, Guilbault writes, "the misuse of *macho* hints at a deeper cultural misunderstanding that extends beyond mere word definitions." To what deeper cultural misunderstanding is she referring?

QUESTIONS ON STRATEGY AND AUDIENCE

1. Why does Guilbault paragraph so frequently? What do the frequent paragraphs suggest about where the essay was first published?
2. In the central section of the essay, Guilbault writes at some length about her father. Why?
3. What does Guilbault's title suggest about her expectations of her audience?

QUESTIONS ON VOCABULARY AND STYLE

1. How does your dictionary define *macho*? From what language does the word come?

2. What are the differences between a word's denotative meaning and its connotations? Is Guilbault writing about denotation or connotation?

3. Be prepared to define the following words: *disdain* (paragraph 4), *uncouth* (6), *quintessential* (7), *recalcitrant* (10), *upbraided* (10), *menial* (11).

WRITING SUGGESTIONS

1. **For your Journal.** Make some notes toward a definition of masculinity. What traits or characteristics are suggested to you by that word? What male public figures in our society seem best to embody that definition?

2. **For a Paragraph.** Using your journal as a starting point, write a paragraph definition of the word *masculinity*. Remember that your view of *masculinity* might have much or little to do with *macho*.

3. **For an Essay.** Toward the end of her essay, Guilbault observes that *macho* has become a stereotype and that "like all stereotypes, it distorts truth." Explore another stereotype that is common in our culture. In an essay, write a definition of that stereotype using both denotative and connotative elements.

Prewriting:

a. Brainstorm a list of possible stereotypes about which to write. Ask friends and classmates to share associations or connotations that they have with each stereotype.

b. Check the term in a dictionary—as you did for *macho*—to find its denotative definition. How do the negative and positive connotations expand or change that definition?

c. Examine your stereotype as it is portrayed in our culture. How does it appear in magazines, on television, and in films? Look around, take notes, and jot down examples for your essay.

Rewriting:

a. Look again at your introduction. Have you avoided beginning with "According to Webster . . ."? Could you open with a particularly arresting example, for instance?

b. Remember that you will need to substantiate—probably through examples—the connotations you associate with the stereotype and that you will want your reader to agree that these are in fact common connotations. Ask a classmate or friend to read your essay. Does she or he agree with your definition of the stereotype?

c. Coming up with an effective, interesting title is not always an easy matter. Moreover, it does not always seem important when you are worried about finishing the essay. Look back at your title. Does it provoke reader interest? Is this a title you might find in a magazine? Brainstorm some new possibilities.

4. **For Research.** Different cultures define masculinity (or femininity) in different ways. Choose a culture different from your own and research how that culture defines either term. What is valued or expected of a male or a female? Remember that no single reference source is likely to provide a definition for you. You might have to infer values and expectations from descriptions of how that culture works. Be sure to document your sources wherever appropriate.

I WANT A WIFE

Judy Brady

Judy Brady was born in 1937 in San Francisco, California, and received a B.F.A. in painting from the University of Iowa. As a freelance writer, Brady has written essays on topics such as union organizing, abortion, and the role of women in society.

Brady's most frequently reprinted essay is "I Want a Wife," which originally appeared in Ms. *magazine in 1971. After examining the stereotypical male demands in marriage, Brady concludes, "Who wouldn't want a wife?"*

BEFORE READING

Connecting: In a relationship, what separates reasonable needs or desires from unreasonable or selfish ones?

Anticipating: What is the effect of the repetition of the phrase "I want a . . ." in the essay?

I belong to that classification of people known as wives. I am A Wife. 1
And, not altogether incidentally, I am a mother.

Not too long ago a male friend of mine appeared on the scene 2
fresh from a recent divorce. He had one child, who is, of course, with
his ex-wife. He is obviously looking for another wife. As I thought
about him while I was ironing one evening, it suddenly occurred to
me that I, too, would like to have a wife. Why do I want a wife?

I would like to go back to school so that I can become econom- 3
ically independent, support myself, and, if need be, support those dependent upon me. I want a wife who will work and send me to school.
And while I am going to school I want a wife to take care of my children. I want a wife to keep track of the children's doctor and dentist
appointments. And to keep track of mine, too. I want a wife to make
sure my children eat properly and are kept clean. I want a wife who
will wash the children's clothes and keep them mended. I want a wife
who is a good nurturant attendant to my children, who arranges for
their schooling, makes sure that they have an adequate social life with
their peers, takes them to the park, the zoo, etc. I want a wife who

takes care of the children when they are sick, a wife who arranges to be around when the children need special care, because, of course, I cannot miss classes at school. My wife must arrange to lose time at work, and not lose the job. It may mean a small cut in my wife's income from time to time, but I guess I can tolerate that. Needless to say, my wife will arrange and pay for the care of the children while my wife is working.

4   I want a wife who will take care of my physical needs. I want a wife who will keep my house clean. A wife who will pick up after me. I want a wife who will keep my clothes clean, ironed, mended, replaced when need be, and who will see to it that my personal things are kept in their proper place so that I can find what I need the minute I need it. I want a wife who cooks the meals, a wife who is a good cook. I want a wife who will plan the meals, do the necessary grocery shopping, prepare the meals, serve them pleasantly, and then do the cleaning up while I do my studying. I want a wife who will care for me when I am sick and sympathize with my pain and loss of time from school. I want a wife to go along when our family takes a vacation so that someone can continue to care for me and my children when I need a rest and change of scene.

5   I want a wife who will not bother me with rambling complaints about a wife's duties. But I want a wife who will listen to me when I feel the need to explain a rather difficult point I have come across in my course of studies. And I want a wife who will type my papers for me when I have written them.

6   I want a wife who will take care of the details of my social life. When my wife and I are invited out by my friends, I want a wife who will take care of the babysitting arrangements. When I meet people at school that I like and want to entertain, I want a wife who will have the house clean, will prepare a special meal, serve it to me and my friends, and not interrupt when I talk about the things that interest me and my friends. I want a wife who will have arranged that the children are fed and ready for bed before my guests arrive so that the children do not bother us. I want a wife who takes care of the needs of my guests so that they feel comfortable, who makes sure that they have an ashtray, that they are passed the hors d'oeuvres, that they are offered a second helping of the food, that their wine glasses are replenished when necessary, that their coffee is served to them as they like it. And I want a wife who knows that sometimes I need a night out by myself.

7   I want a wife who is sensitive to my sexual needs, a wife who makes love passionately and eagerly when I feel like it, a wife who makes sure that I am satisfied. And, of course, I want a wife who will not demand sexual attention when I am not in the mood for it. I want

a wife who assumes the complete responsibility for birth control, be-cause I do not want more children. I want a wife who will remain sex-ually faithful to me so that I do not have to clutter up my intellectual life with jealousies. And I want a wife who understands that *my* sexual needs may entail more than strict adherence to monogamy. I must, after all, be able to relate to people as fully as possible.

If, by chance, I find another person more suitable as a wife than the wife I already have, I want the liberty to replace my present wife with another one. Naturally I will expect a fresh, new life; my wife will take the children and be solely responsible for them so that I am left free. 8

When I am through with school and have a job, I want my wife to quit working and remain at home so that my wife can more fully and completely take care of a wife's duties. 9

My God, who *wouldn't* want a wife? 10

QUESTIONS ON SUBJECT AND PURPOSE

1. In what way is this a definition of a wife? Why does Brady avoid a more conventional definition?
2. Is Brady being fair? Is there anything that she leaves out of her definition that you would have included?
3. What purpose might Brady have been trying to achieve?

QUESTIONS ON STRATEGY AND AUDIENCE

1. How does Brady structure her essay? What is the order of the development? Could the essay have been arranged in any other way?
2. Why does Brady identify herself by her roles—wife and mother—at the beginning of the essay? Is that information relevant in any way?
3. What assumptions does Brady have about her audience (read-ers of *Ms.* magazine in the early 1970s)? How do you know?

QUESTIONS ON VOCABULARY AND STYLE

1. How does Brady use repetition in the essay? Why? Does it work? What effect does it create?
2. How effective is Brady's final rhetorical question? Where else in the essay does she use a rhetorical question?

3. Be able to define the following words: *nurturant* (paragraph 3), *hor d'oeuvres* (6), *replenished* (6), *monogamy* (7).

WRITING SUGGESTIONS

1. **For your Journal.** What do you look for in a possible spouse or "significant other"? Make a list of what you expect or want from a relationship with another person. Once you have brainstormed the list, rank each item in order of importance— which is most important and which least important? If you are in a relationship right now, try evaluating that relationship in light of your own priorities.

2. **For a Paragraph.** Using the material that you generated in your journal entry, write a paragraph definition of the kind of person you seek for a committed relationship. Be serious. Do not try to imitate Brady's style.

3. **For an Essay.** Define a word naming a central human relationship role, such as *husband, lover, friend, mother, father, child, sister, brother,* or *grandparent.* Define the term indirectly by showing what such a person does or should do.

Prewriting:

a. Select a word as a possible subject. Then write down a dictionary definition. The inadequacies of such a short definition (for example, *wife*: "a female partner in a marriage") will be obvious. What expectations do you have about the role or function of the person in this position? Make a list.

b. Try freewriting about the items on the list you have just made. Treat each expectation as the subject for a separate freewriting. You might not use any of the prose that you produce here; you are just trying to generate ideas.

c. Plan an organizational strategy. Look carefully at how Brady puts her essay together. How does she structure the middle of her essay? Can you use a similar structure?

Rewriting:

a. Characterize the tone of what you have written. For example, are you serious or satirical? Is it formal or informal? Does your tone complement your purpose? Look back through your essay, and imagine how it would sound to a reader.

b. Check each paragraph in your essay. Is there a consistent, unified subject for each? That unity might be expressed in an explicit topic sentence, or it might just be implicit.

c. Look again at your introduction and conclusion. Avoid imitating Brady's strategies—especially her conclusion. Look at the advice on introductions and conclusions in the Glossary. Be honest about what you have written. Could either be stronger, clearer, more interesting?

4. **For Research**. What does it mean to be a wife in another culture? Choose at least two other cultures and research those societies' expectations of a wife. Try to find cultures that show significant differences. Using your research, write an essay offering a comparative definition of *wife*. Assume that your audience is American. Be certain to document your sources.

MOTHER TONGUE
Amy Tan

Born in Oakland, California, in 1952 to Chinese immigrants, Amy Tan graduated from San Jose State University with a double major in English and Linguistics and an M.A. in Linguistics. Though her writing has been praised for its vivid language and characters, Tan did not write fiction until 1985, when she began the stories that would become her first and very successful novel, The Joy Luck Club *(1989), also a popular film. That book and her second novel,* The Kitchen God's Wife *(1991), portray the mother–daughter relationship within Chinese American and Chinese cultures.*

Tan has commented about her conversations with her parents, that when she was young, they "spoke half in English, half in Mandarin." When Tan started school, she notes, her mother "continued to talk to me in Chinese and I would answer back in English." Her parents wanted their children, she observed, "to have American circumstances and Chinese character." Tan explores the languages with which she grew up in "Mother Tongue," originally a speech, which later appeared in The Threepenny Review.

BEFORE READING

Connecting: How sensitive are you to the language that you use or your family uses? Are you ever conscious of that language? Are you ever embarrassed by it? Are you proud of it?

Anticipating: In what ways does the language of Tan and her mother "define" them in the eyes of others?

1   I am not a scholar of English or literature. I cannot give you much more than personal opinions on the English language and its variations in this country or others.

2   I am a writer. And by that definition, I am someone who has always loved language. I am fascinated by language in daily life. I spend a great deal of my time thinking about the power of language—the way it can evoke an emotion, a visual image, a complex idea, or a simple truth. Language is the tool of my trade. And I use them all—all the Englishes I grew up with.

Definition

Recently, I was made keenly aware of the different Englishes I do use. I was giving a talk to a large group of people, the same talk I had already given to half a dozen other groups. The nature of the talk was about my writing, my life, and my book, *The Joy Luck Club*. The talk was going along well enough, until I remembered one major difference that made the whole talk sound wrong. My mother was in the room. And it was perhaps the first time she had heard me give a lengthy speech, using the kind of English I have never used with her. I was saying things like, "The intersection of memory upon imagination" and "There is an aspect of my fiction that relates to thus-and-thus"—a speech filled with carefully wrought grammatical phrases, burdened, it suddenly seemed to me, with nominalized forms, past perfect tenses, conditional phrases, all the forms of standard English that I had learned in school and through books, the forms of English I did not use at home with my mother.

Just last week, I was walking down the street with my mother, and I again found myself conscious of the English I was using, the English I do use with her. We were talking about the price of new and used furniture and I heard myself saying this: "Not waste money that way." My husband was with us as well, and he didn't notice any switch in my English. And then I realized why. It's because over the twenty years we've been together I've often used that same kind of English with him, and sometimes he even uses it with me. It has become our language of intimacy, a different sort of English that relates to family talk, the language I grew up with.

So you'll have some idea of what this family talk I heard sounds like, I'll quote what my mother said during a recent conversation which I videotaped and then transcribed. During this conversation, my mother was talking about a political gangster in Shanghai who had the same last name as her family's, Du, and how the gangster in his early years wanted to be adopted by her family, which was rich by comparison. Later, the gangster became more powerful, far richer than my mother's family, and one day showed up at my mother's wedding to pay his respects. Here's what she said in part:

"Du Yusong having business like fruit stand. Like off the street kind. He is Du like Du Zong—but not Tsung-ming Island people. The local people call putong, the river east side, he belong to that side local people. That man want to ask Du Zong father take him in like become own family. Du Zong father wasn't look down on him, but didn't take seriously, until that man big like become a mafia. Now important person, very hard to inviting him. Chinese way, came only to show respect, don't stay for dinner. Respect for making big celebration, he shows up. Mean gives lots of respect. Chinese custom. Chinese social life that way. If too important won't have to stay too long. He come to my wedding. I didn't see, I heard it. I gone to boy's side, they have YMCA dinner. Chinese age I was nineteen."

7   You should know that my mother's expressive command of English belies how much she actually understands. She reads the *Forbes* report, listens to *Wall Street Week*, converses daily with her stockbroker, reads all of Shirley MacLaine's books with ease—all kinds of things I can't begin to understand. Yet some of my friends tell me they understand 50 percent of what my mother says. Some say they understand 80 to 90 percent. Some say they understand none of it, as if she were speaking pure Chinese. But to me, my mother's English is perfectly clear, perfectly natural. It's my mother tongue. Her language, as I hear it, is vivid, direct, full of observation and imagery. That was the language that helped shape the way I saw things, expressed things, made sense of the world.

8   Lately, I've been giving more thought to the kind of English my mother speaks. Like others, I have described it to people as "broken" or "fractured" English. But I wince when I say that. It has always bothered me that I can think of no way to describe it other than "broken," as if it were damaged and needed to be fixed, as if it lacked a certain wholeness and soundness. I've heard other terms used, "limited English," for example. But they seem just as bad, as if everything is limited, including people's perceptions of the limited English speaker.

9   I know this for a fact, because when I was growing up, my mother's "limited" English limited *my* perception of her. I was ashamed of her English. I believed that her English reflected the quality of what she had to say. That is, because she expressed them imperfectly her thoughts were imperfect. And I had plenty of empirical evidence to support me: the fact that people in department stores, at banks, and at restaurants did not take her seriously, did not give her good service, pretended not to understand her, or even acted as if they did not hear her.

10   My mother has long realized the limitations of her English as well. When I was fifteen, she used to have me call people on the phone to pretend I was she. In this guise, I was forced to ask for information or even to complain and yell at people who had been rude to her. One time it was a call to her stockbroker in New York. She had cashed out her small portfolio and it just so happened we were going to go to New York the next week, our very first trip outside California. I had to get on the phone and say in an adolescent voice that was not very convincing, "This is Mrs. Tan."

11   And my mother was standing in the back whispering loudly, "Why he don't send me check, already two weeks late. So mad he lie to me, losing me money."

And then I said in perfect English, "Yes, I'm getting rather concerned. You had agreed to send the check two weeks ago, but it hasn't arrived."

Then she began to talk more loudly. "What he want, I come to New York tell him front of his boss, you cheating me?" And I was trying to calm her down, make her be quiet, while telling the stockbroker, "I can't tolerate any more excuses. If I don't receive the check immediately, I am going to have to speak to your manager when I'm in New York next week." And sure enough, the following week there we were in front of this astonished stockbroker, and I was sitting there red-faced and quiet, and my mother, the real Mrs. Tan, was shouting at his boss in her impeccable broken English.

We used a similar routine just five days ago, for a situation that was far less humorous. My mother had gone to the hospital for an appointment, to found out about a benign brain tumor a CAT scan had revealed a month ago. She said she had spoken very good English, her best English, no mistakes. Still, she said, the hospital did not apologize when they said they had lost the CAT scan and she had come for nothing. She said they did not seem to have any sympathy when she told them she was anxious to know the exact diagnosis, since her husband and son had both died of brain tumors. She said they would not give her any more information until the next time and she would have to make another appointment for that. So she said she would not leave until the doctor called her daughter. She wouldn't budge. And when the doctor finally called her daughter, me, who spoke in perfect English—lo and behind—we had assurances the CAT scan would be found, promises that a conference call on Monday would be held, and apologies for any suffering my mother had gone through for a most regrettable mistake.

I think my mother's English almost had an effect on limiting my possibilities in life as well. Sociologists and linguists probably will tell you that a person's developing language skills are more influenced by peers. But I do think that the language spoken in the family, especially in immigrant families which are more insular, plays a large role in shaping the language of the child. And I believe that it affected my results on achievement tests, IQ tests, and the SAT. While my English skills were never judged as poor, compared to math, English could not be considered my strong suit. In grade school I did moderately well, getting perhaps B's, sometimes B-pluses, in English and scoring perhaps in the sixtieth or seventieth percentile on achievement tests. But those scores were not good enough to override the opinion that my true abilities lay in math and science, because in those areas I achieved A's and scored in the ninetieth percentile or higher.

16   This was understandable. Math is precise; there is only one correct answer. Whereas, for me at least, the answers on English tests
were always a judgment call, a matter of opinion and personal experience. Those tests were constructed around items like fill-in-the-
blank sentence completion, such as, "Even though Tom was
_____, Mary thought he was _____." And the
correct answer always seemed to be the most bland combinations of
thoughts, for example, "Even though Tom was shy, Mary thought he
was charming," with the grammatical structure "even though" limiting the correct answer to some sort of semantic opposites, so you
wouldn't get answers like, "Even though Tom was foolish, Mary
thought he was ridiculous." Well, according to my mother, there
were very few limitations as to what Tom could have been and
what Mary might have thought of him. So I never did well on tests
like that.

17   The same was true with word analogies, pairs of words in which
you were supposed to find some sort of logical, semantic relationship—for example, "*Sunset* is to *nightfall* as _____ is to
_____." And here you would be presented with a list of
four possible pairs, one of which showed the same kind of relation-
ship: *red* is to *stoplight, bus* is to *arrival, chills* is to *fever, yawn* is to *boring.* Well, I could never think that way. I knew what the tests were
asking, but I could not block out of my mind the images already created by the first pair, "*sunset* is to *nightfall*"—and I would see a burst
of colors against a darkening sky, the moon rising, the lowering of a
curtain of stars. And all the other pairs of words—red, bus, stoplight,
boring—just threw up a mass of confusing images, making it impossible for me to sort out something as logical as saying: "A sunset precedes nightfall" is the same as "a chill precedes a fever." The only way
I would have gotten that answer right would have been to imagine an
associative situation, for example, my being disobedient and staying
out past sunset, catching a chill at night, which turns into feverish
pneumonia as punishment, which indeed did happen to me.

18   I have been thinking about all this lately, about my mother's
English, about achievement tests. Because lately I've been asked, as a
writer, why there are not more Asian Americans represented in
American literature. Why are there few Asian Americans enrolled in
creative writing programs? Why do so many Chinese students go
into engineering? Well, these are broad sociological questions I
can't begin to answer. But I have noticed in surveys—in fact, just
last week—that Asian students, as a whole, always do significantly
better on math achievement tests than in English. And this makes me

think that there are other Asian-American students whose English spoken in the home might also be described as "broken" or "limited." And perhaps they also have teachers who are steering them away from writing and into math and science, which is what happened to me.

Fortunately, I happen to be rebellious in nature and enjoy the challenge of disproving assumptions made about me. I became an English major my first year in college, after being enrolled as premed. I started writing nonfiction as a freelancer the week after I was told by my former boss that writing was my worst skill and I should hone my talents toward account management. 19

But it wasn't until 1985 that I finally began to write fiction. And at first I wrote using what I thought to be wittily crafted sentences, sentences that would finally prove I had mastery over the English language. Here's an example from the first draft of a story that later made its way into *The Joy Luck Club*, but without this line: "That was my mental quandary in its nascent state." A terrible line, which I can barely pronounce. 20

Fortunately, for reasons I won't get into today, I later decided I should envision a reader for the stories I would write. And the reader I decided upon was my mother, because these were stories about mothers. So with this reader in mind—and in fact she did read my early drafts—I began to write stories using all the Englishes I grew up with: the English I spoke to my mother, which for lack of a better term might be described as "simple"; the English she used with me, which for lack of a better term might be described as "broken"; my translation of her Chinese, which could certainly be described as "watered down"; and what I imagined to be her translation of her Chinese if she could speak in perfect English, her internal language, and for that I sought to preserve the essence, but neither an English nor a Chinese structure. I wanted to capture what language ability tests can never reveal: her intent, her passion, her imagery, the rhythms of her speech and the nature of her thoughts. 21

Apart from what any critic had to say about my writing, I knew I had succeeded where it counted when my mother finished reading my book and gave me her verdict: "So easy to read." 22

QUESTIONS ON SUBJECT AND PURPOSE

1. What does the title "Mother Tongue" suggest?
2. How many subjects does Tan explore in the essay?
3. How does Tan feel about her mother's "tongue"?

QUESTIONS ON STRATEGY AND AUDIENCE

1. In paragraph 6, Tan quotes part of one of her mother's conversations. Why?
2. After paragraphs 7 and 17, Tan uses additional space to indicate divisions in her essay. Why does she divide the essay into three parts?
3. Tan notes in paragraph 21 that she thinks of her mother as her audience when she writes stories. Why?

QUESTIONS ON VOCABULARY AND STYLE

1. How would you characterize Tan's tone (see the Glossary for a definition) in the essay?
2. In paragraph 20, Tan quotes a "terrible line" she once wrote: "That was my mental quandary in its nascent state." What is so terrible about that line?
3. Be prepared to define the following words: *belies* (7), *empirical* (9), *benign* (14), *insular* (15), *semantic* (16), *hone* (19), *quandary* (20), *nascent* (20).

WRITING SUGGESTIONS

1. **For your Journal**. What makes up your "mother tongue"? To what extent is your language (such things as word choice, pronunciation, dialect, second language skills) influenced by your parents, your education, the part of the country in which you grew up, the influence of peers? Make a series of notes exploring those influences.
2. **For a Paragraph**. Using the information that you gathered for your journal entry, write a paragraph in which you define your "mother tongue." Try to define the influences that have shaped both how and what you say.
3. **For an Essay**. Tan suggests that a certain type or dialect of English is a language of power, that if you speak and write that English, people in authority will listen to you and respect you. How might that public, powerful English (sometimes referred to as "edited American English") be defined?

   Prewriting:
   a. Think of your own language habits. Do you, for example, speak in a different way when you address a teacher, a boss,

a member of the clergy? How do you change your language?

b. Browse through the writing textbook that you use in your freshman English course. What types of advice does the text offer about subjects such as usage and diction? Does it also define the term "dialect"?

c. Use your examples—drawn from your own experiences, from the experiences of others, from your textbook—as the basis from which to formulate a definition of the features of this public or "edited American English."

Rewriting:

a. Have you provided enough examples to support your generalizations? Go through a photocopy of your essay and underline generalizations in one color and examples in another. Is there a good balance between the two?

b. Check each individual paragraph. Is there a unified idea that controls each one? Highlight the topic sentence or key idea of each paragraph with a colored pen. If any paragraph seems less than unified, look for ways to improve it.

c. Once you have a complete draft, jot down on a separate sheet of paper what troubles you the most about the essay. What could be better? Allow a day to pass, then try to solve that problem. If your school has a writing center or a peer tutoring program, take your specific problem there.

4. For Research. Linguists have defined a wide range of dialects within the United States. Choose one of the dialects that interests you—a reference librarian or your instructor can help you find a list. You might choose one based on the geographical area in which you live or one defined by your heritage. Using the resources of your library, write a definition of that dialect. What are its distinctive features? Where did those features come from? Where is this dialect spoken within the United States? What are some particularly colorful examples? Be sure to document your sources wherever appropriate.

A WORD'S MEANING CAN OFTEN DEPEND ON WHO SAYS IT

Gloria Naylor

Gloria Naylor was born in 1950 in New York City. When Martin Luther King was assassinated, Naylor became determined to make the world a better place, and she worked as a missionary for Jehovah's Witnesses for seven years before deciding to pursue her writing interests. She graduated from Brooklyn College of the City University of New York in 1981 and then earned her M.A. in Afro-American Studies at Yale University in 1983. She has written four novels about black experience, especially the black female experience: The Women of Brewster Place *(1982),* Linden Hills *(1985),* Mama Day *(1988), and* Bailey's Cafe *(1992). She calls them her "novel quartet," and they explore the emotional, intellectual, spiritual, and sexual aspects of human experience, respectively.*

In an interview Naylor once commented on her experiences as a child in the 1960s: "They [her parents] were trying to protect us from pain. . . . They never talked much about the racial problems that were going on in America. . . . I would hear it at school and see it on television, but we never got that sort of talk in our home." Unfortunately, the protection can only work so long: "Eventually you are going to get hurt. So it is a matter of trying to ward off the moment when that would happen." "A Word's Meaning Can Often Depend on Who Says It," first published in the "Hers" column in The New York Times, *recounts the moment that the hurt first occurred for Naylor.*

BEFORE READING

Connecting: Have you ever been called a "name," a derogatory label that signaled someone's prejudice toward you? How did that act make you feel?

Anticipating: Why do people call others "names"? What are the implications of labeling people in such ways?

1   Language is the subject. It is the written form with which I've managed to keep the wolf away from the door and, in diaries, to keep my

sanity. In spite of this, I consider the written word inferior to the spoken, and much of the frustration experienced by novelists is the awareness that whatever we manage to capture in even the most transcendent passages falls far short of the richness of life. Dialogue achieves its power in the dynamics of a fleeting moment of sight, sound, smell, and touch.

I'm not going to enter the debate here about whether it is language that shapes reality or vice versa. That battle is doomed to be waged whenever we seek intermittent reprieve from the chicken and egg dispute. I will simply take the position that the spoken word, like the written word, amounts to a nonsensical arrangement of sounds or letters without a consensus that assigns "meaning." And building from the meanings of what we hear, we order reality. Words themselves are innocuous; it is the consensus that gives them true power.   2

I remember the first time I heard the word *nigger*. In my third-grade class, our math tests were being passed down the rows, and as I handed the papers to a little boy in back of me, I remarked that once again he had received a much lower mark than I did. He snatched his test from me and spit out that word. Had he called me a nymphomaniac or a necrophiliac, I couldn't have been more puzzled. I didn't know what a nigger was, but I knew whatever it meant, it was something he shouldn't have called me. This was verified when I raised my hand, and in a loud voice repeated what he had said and watched the teacher scold him for using a "bad" word. I was later to go home and ask the inevitable question that every black parent must face—"Mommy, what does *nigger* mean?"   3

And what exactly did it mean? Thinking back, I realize that this could not have been the first time the word was used in my presence. I was part of a large extended family that had migrated from the rural South after World War II and formed a close-knit network that gravitated around my maternal grandparents. Their ground-floor apartment in one of the buildings they owned in Harlem was a weekend mecca for my immediate family, along with countless aunts, uncles, and cousins who brought along assorted friends. It was a bustling and open house with assorted neighbors and tenants popping in and out to exchange bits of gossip, pick up an old quarrel, or referee the ongoing checkers game in which my grandmother cheated shamelessly. They were all there to let down their hair and put up their feet after a week of labor in the factories, laundries, and shipyards of New York.   4

Amid the clamor, which could reach deafening proportions—two or three conversations going on simultaneously, punctuated by the sound of a baby's crying somewhere in the back rooms or out on   5 the street—there was still a rigid set of rules about what was said and how. Older children were sent out of the living room when it was time to get into the juicy details about "you-know-who" up on the third floor who had gone and gotten herself "p-r-e-g-n-a-n-t!" But my parents, knowing that I could spell well beyond my years, always demanded that I follow the others out to play. Beyond sexual misconduct and death, everything else was considered harmless for our young ears. And so among the anecdotes of the triumphs and disappointments in the various workings of their lives, the word *nigger* was used in my presence, but it was set within contexts and inflections that caused it to register in my mind as something else.

6   In the singular, the word was always applied to a man who had distinguished himself in some situation that brought their approval for his strength, intelligence, or drive:

7   "Did Johnny *really* do that?"

8   "I'm telling you, that nigger pulled in $6,000 of overtime last year. Said he got enough for a down payment on a house."

9   When used with a possessive adjective by a woman—"my nigger"—it became a term of endearment for her husband or boyfriend. But it could be more than just a term applied to a man. In their mouths it became the pure essence of manhood—a disembodied force that channeled their past history of struggle and present survival against the odds into a victorious statement of being: "Yeah, that old foreman found out quick enough—you don't mess with a nigger."

10   In the plural, it became a description of some group within the community that had overstepped the bounds of decency as my family defined it. Parents who neglected their children, a drunken couple who fought in public, people who simply refused to look for work, those with excessively dirty mouths or unkempt households were all "trifling niggers." This particular circle could forgive hard times, unemployment, the occasional bout of depression—they had gone through all of that themselves—but the unforgivable sin was a lack of self-respect.

11   A woman could never be a "nigger" in the singular, with its connotation of confirming worth. The noun *girl* was its closest equivalent in that sense, but only when used in direct address and regardless of the gender doing the addressing. *Girl* was a token of respect for a woman. The one-syllable word was drawn out to sound like three in recognition of the extra ounce of wit, nerve, or daring that the woman had shown in the situation under discussion.

12   "G-i-r-l, stop. You mean you said that to his face?"

13   But if the word was used in a third-person reference or shortened so that it almost snapped out of the mouth, it always involved some element of communal disapproval. And age became an impor-

tant factor in these exchanges. It was only between individuals of the same generation, or from any older person to a younger (but never the other way around), that *girl* would be considered a compliment.

I don't agree with the argument that use of the word *nigger* at this social stratum of the black community was an internalization of racism. The dynamics were the exact opposite: the people in my grandmother's living room took a word that whites used to signify worthlessness or degradation and rendered it impotent. Gathering there together, they transformed *nigger* to signify the varied and complex human beings they knew themselves to be. If the word was to disappear totally from the mouths of even the most liberal of white society, no one in that room was naive enough to believe it would disappear from white minds. Meeting the word head-on, they proved it had absolutely nothing to do with the way they were determined to live their lives. 14

So there must have been dozens of times that *nigger* was spoken in front of me before I reached the third grade. But I didn't "hear" it until it was said by a small pair of lips that had already learned it could be a way to humiliate me. That was the word I went home and asked my mother about. And since she knew that I had to grow up in America, she took me in her lap and explained. 15

QUESTIONS ON SUBJECT AND PURPOSE

1. Are the definitions that Naylor offers denotative or connotative? See the Glossary for definitions of those two terms.
2. In what ways did Naylor's family use the word "nigger"? How does their use differ from the way in which the third-grader used the word?
3. What purpose or purposes does Naylor appear to have in the essay?

QUESTIONS ON STRATEGY AND AUDIENCE

1. Why does Naylor preface her essay with the two introductory paragraphs? Why not begin with paragraph 3?
2. In paragraphs 11–13, Naylor defines the term "girl." How does that definition fit into the essay? Why include it?
3. Naylor's essay originally appeared in *The New York Times*. What influence might the place of publication have had on the nature of the essay?

QUESTIONS ON VOCABULARY AND STYLE

1. What does Naylor seem to mean when she observes: "words themselves are innocuous; it is the consensus that gives them true power" (paragraph 2)?

2. What is the effect of the following clichés: "to keep the wolf away from the door" (paragraph 1), "the chicken and egg dispute" (2), "let down their hair" (5), "meeting the word head-on" (14).

3. Be prepared to define the following words: *innocuous* (paragraph 2), *necrophiliac* (3), *mecca* (4), *clamor* (5), *anecdotes* (5), *unkempt* (10), *trifling* (10), *connotation* (11), *stratum* (14).

WRITING SUGGESTIONS

1. **For your Journal.** Listen carefully to yourself and to those around you for at least a day. Jot down in your journal every name or label that you use or that you hear others use. What groups seem to be singled out the most often? Why?

2. **For a Paragraph.** Select a common word that has a range of connotations or associations. In a paragraph define that word by including examples of how the word might be used.

3. **For an Essay.** Write an extended definition of a word that carries a range of connotations. Remember to get your instructor's approval of your word.

   Prewriting:
   a. Make a list of at least six possibilities. Choose words that are used frequently and have a variety of meanings. Ask your friends for suggestions as well.

   b. Go to the reference room of your school's library and using a range of dictionaries, including dictionaries of slang, see how many different meanings and associations you can find.

   c. Look back over the details that you plan to include in your extended definition. What organizational strategy seems appropriate? Are you dividing the subject into parts? Are you defining through comparison? Sketch out a possible framework that organizes the examples and details you plan to use.

   Rewriting:
   a. Check your introduction. Copy it onto a separate sheet of

paper and reread it. Do you think a reader would want to continue reading? Does your introduction stimulate interest?

b. Check each individual paragraph. Is there a unified idea that controls each one? Make a copy of your essay, and highlight the topic sentence or key idea of each paragraph with a colored pen.

c. Evaluate the conclusion that you have written. Do you conclude or just stop? Do you just repeat in slightly altered words what you wrote in the introduction? Check the advice about introductions and conclusions offered in the Glossary. If your conclusion seems weak, try freewriting at least one alternative ending.

4. For Research. Research the history of one "hate" word. Where did it originate? Why? What connotations does the word have? Have those connotations changed over the years? The many dictionaries in the reference department of your college's library will be a good place in which to start your research. Be sure to document your sources wherever appropriate.

THE FEMALE BODY
Margaret Atwood

Margaret Atwood was born in Ottawa, Canada, in 1939. She received a B.A. from the University of Toronto in 1961 and earned an M.A. at Radcliffe College in 1962. A poet, essayist, short story writer, and novelist, Atwood has enjoyed critical and popular acclaim throughout her writing career, winning numerous awards and honorary degrees. Her work has explored broad themes of feminism, dystopia, and the opposition of art and nature, but always through the eyes of an individual. Her best known novel is The Handmaid's Tale *(1986), in which a totalitarian state assigns roles to women according to their reproductive abilities.*

A critic once observed that Atwood's poetry concerns "modern woman's anguish at finding herself isolated and exploited (although also exploiting) by the imposition of the sex role power structure." Here, in an essay written in response to an invitation from the Michigan Quarterly Review, *Atwood explores her reactions to the phrase "the female body."*

BEFORE READING

Connecting: What image is suggested to you by the phrase "the female body"?

Anticipating: Does Atwood's essay fulfill your expectations of an essay on the "female body"? Why or why not?

> . . . entirely devoted to the subject of "The Female
> Body." Knowing how well you have written on this
> topic . . . this capacious topic . . .
> letter from *Michigan Quarterly Review*

1

1   I agree, it's a hot topic. But only one? Look around, there's a wide range. Take my own, for instance.

2   I get up in the morning. My topic feels like hell. I sprinkle it with water, brush parts of it, rub it with towels, powder it, add lubricant. I dump in the fuel and away goes my topic, my topical topic, my

Definition

controversial topic, my capacious topic, my limping topic, my near-sighted topic, my topic with back problems, my badly behaved topic, my vulgar topic, my outrageous topic, my aging topic, my topic that is out of the question and anyway still can't spell, in its oversized coat and worn winter boots, scuttling along the sidewalk as if it were flesh and blood, hunting for what's out there, an avocado, an alderman, an adjective, hungry as ever.

2

The basic Female Body comes with the following accessories: garter belt, panti-girdle, crinoline, camisole, bustle, brassiere, stomacher, chemise, virgin zone, spike heels, nose ring, veil, kid gloves, fishnet stockings, fichu, bandeau, Merry Widow, weepers, chokers, barrettes, bangles, beads, lorgnette, feather boa, basic black, compact, Lycra stretch one-piece with modesty panel, designer peignoir, flannel nightie, lace teddy, bed, head.   3

3

The Female Body is made of transparent plastic and lights up when you plug it in. You press a button to illuminate the different systems. The circulatory system is red, for the heart and arteries, purple for the veins; the respiratory system is blue; the lymphatic system is yellow; the digestive system is green, with liver and kidneys in aqua. The nerves are done in orange and the brain is pink. The skeleton, as you might expect, is white.   4

The reproductive system is optional, and can be removed. It comes with or without a miniature embryo. Parental judgment can thereby be exercised. We do not wish to frighten or offend.   5

4

He said, I won't have one of those things in the house. It gives a young girl a false notion of beauty, not to mention anatomy. If a real woman was built like that she'd fall on her face.   6

She said, If we don't let her have one like all the other girls she'll feel singled out. It'll become an issue. She'll long for one and she'll long to turn into one. Repression breeds sublimation. You know that.   7

He said, It's not just the pointy plastic tits, it's the wardrobes. The wardrobes and that stupid male doll, what's his name, the one with the underwear glued on.   8

She said, Better to get it over with when she's young. He said, All right, but don't let me see it.   9

She came whizzing down the stairs, thrown like a dart. She was   10 stark naked. Her hair had been chopped off, her head was turned back to front, she was missing some toes and she'd been tattooed all over her body with purple ink in a scrollwork design. She hit the potted azalea, trembled there for a moment like a botched angel, and fell.

11   He said, I guess we're safe.

5

12   The Female Body has many uses. It's been used as a door knocker, a bottle opener, as a clock with a ticking belly, as something to hold up lampshades, as a nutcracker, just squeeze the brass legs together and out comes your nut. It bears torches, lifts victorious wreaths, grows copper wings and raises aloft a ring of neon stars; whole buildings rest on its marble heads.

13   It sells cars, beer, shaving lotion, cigarettes, hard liquor; it sells diet plans and diamonds, and desire in tiny crystal bottles. Is this the face that launched a thousand products? You bet it is, but don't get any funny big ideas, honey, that smile is a dime a dozen.

14   It does not merely sell, it is sold. Money flows into this country or that country, flies in, practically crawls in, suitful after suitful, lured by all those hairless pre-teen legs. Listen, you want to reduce the national debt, don't you? Aren't you patriotic? That's the spirit. That's my girl.

15   She's a natural resource, a renewable one luckily, because those things wear out so quickly. They don't make 'em like they used to. Shoddy goods.

6

16   One and one equals another one. Pleasure in the female is not a requirement. Pair-bonding is stronger in geese. We're not talking about love, we're talking about biology. That's how we all got here, daughter.

17   Snails do it differently. They're hermaphrodites, and work in threes.

7

18   Each Female Body contains a female brain. Handy. Makes things work. Stick pins in it and you get amazing results. Old popular songs. Short circuits. Bad dreams.

19   Anyway: each of these brains has two halves. They're joined together by a thick cord; neural pathways flow from one to the other, sparkles of electric information washing to and fro. Like light on waves. Like a conversation. How does a woman know? She listens. She listens in.

The male brain, now, that's a different matter. Only a thin con- 20
nection. Space over here, time over there, music and arithmetic in
their own sealed compartments. The right brain doesn't know what
the left brain is doing. Good for aiming through, for hitting the target when you pull the trigger. What's the target? Who's the target?
Who cares? What matters is hitting it. That's the male brain for you.
Objective.

This is why men are so sad, why they feel so cut off, why they 21
think of themselves as orphans cast adrift, footloose and stringless in
the deep void. What void? she asks. What are you talking about? The
void of the universe, he says, and she says Oh and looks out the window and tries to get a handle on it, but it's no use, there's too much
going on, too many rustlings in the leaves, too many voices, so she
says, Would you like a cheese sandwich, a piece of cake, a cup of tea?
And he grinds his teeth because she doesn't understand, and wanders
off, not just alone but Alone, lost in the dark, lost in the skull, searching for the other half, the twin who could complete him.

Then it comes to him: he's lost the Female Body! Look, it 22
shines in the gloom, far ahead, a vision of wholeness, ripeness, like a
giant melon, like an apple, like a metaphor for "breast" in a bad sex
novel; it shines like a balloon, like a foggy noon, a watery moon,
shimmering in its egg of light.

Catch it. Put it in a pumpkin, in a high tower, in a compound, 23
in a chamber, in a house, in a room. Quick, stick a leash on it, a lock,
a chain, some pain, settle it down, so it can never get away from you
again.

QUESTIONS ON SUBJECT AND PURPOSE

1. What appears to be the occasion for Atwood's essay?
2. In what ways might this be considered a definition of the "female body"?
3. Is it true, as Atwood notes in section 7, that the structure of
   the brain varies with gender?

QUESTIONS ON STRATEGY AND AUDIENCE

1. Why might Atwood have chosen to divide the essay as she
   does?
2. Why doesn't Atwood write transitions to bridge from one section of the essay to another instead of dividing it into sections?

3. The letter from the magazine refers to the topic as "capacious." What does that word mean? In what way does that word suggest the shape and nature of Atwood's response?

QUESTIONS ON VOCABULARY AND STYLE

1. How would you characterize Atwood's tone in the essay? (See the Glossary for a definition of *tone*.)
2. In what context might you expect to find section 3 of the essay? What does it "sound" like?
3. Be prepared to define the following words: *alderman* (paragraph 2) and *sublimation* (7).

WRITING SUGGESTIONS

1. **For your Journal**. Suppose you had been invited to write something (an essay, a poem, a story) about either the male or the female body. What would you say? In your journal, jot down some possible ideas for your response.
2. **For a Paragraph**. Select one of the ideas that you came up with in your journal writing, and expand that into a developed paragraph. Remember to use example—either a variety of different ones or a single, extended one—to develop your definition.
3. **For an Essay**. In section 5, Atwood makes numerous references to the ways in which the female body has been used to sell products. Judith Gaines in "The 'Beefcake Years'" (Chapter 7) makes a similar set of observations about how advertisers today use male bodies. Judging just from the images of women or of men presented in advertisements, write an essay about how the female or male body is defined in our culture.

Prewriting:
   a. Gather a range of magazines and look for advertisements in which women or men are used to sell particular products. If you are using magazines in your college's library, you might want to photocopy the advertisements.
   b. Make a list of what you observe in that group of advertisements. In what ways are images of women and men used? What do the images look like? Are they of a particular physical type? Is there any relationship between the image and the product?

c. Remember to consider as well what is *not* pictured or represented in the images. What types of images never appear?

Rewriting:

a. Have you provided enough examples—either by referring briefly to many or by developing a representative few in detail—to justify your definition? Check back through your draft to make sure.

b. Try outlining your draft. Do you see a clear, logical organization? Are there adequate transitions from section to section? Make a list of any problems you discover in the organization, and then devote some time to trying to solve just those problems. If your college has a writing center, ask for help there.

c. Look carefully at your conclusion. You want to end forcefully; you do not just want to repeat the same ideas and words used in your introduction. Reread your essay several times, and then try freewriting a new conclusion. Aim for a completely different ending than the one you originally wrote.

4. For Research. How have society's definitions of masculinity and femininity changed over time? Choose one of the two terms, and research its shifting definitions over the past two hundred years. What did society expect of a man or a women in 1800? In 1900? In the mid- to late 1990s? What is considered masculine or feminine? Remember that no single reference source will provide you with the answers you need. You may need to infer the definitions from the roles that society forced upon men and women and the images that represented those roles. Be sure to acknowledge your sources wherever appropriate.

ARGUMENT AND PERSUASION

We live in a world of persuasive messages—billboards, advertisements in newspapers and magazines, commercials on television and radio, signs on stores, bumper stickers, T-shirts with messages, and manufacturers' logos on clothing. Advertisements demonstrate a wide range of persuasive strategies. Sometimes they appeal to logic or reason—they ask you to compare the features and price of one automobile with those of any competitor and judge for yourself. More often, though, they appeal to your emotions or feelings—you will not be stylish unless you wear this particular brand of jeans; you are not a "real man" unless you drink this brand of beer or smoke this brand of cigarette. Arguments are frequently divided in this way—those that appeal to logic and reason and those that appeal to emotions and prejudices.

In the following paragraph, for example, Kevin Clarke appeals to logic when he argues that the "specter of chronic hunger" threatens many Americans by citing specific factual evidence to establish the magnitude of the problem:

> In March 1993, the United States reached a distressing milestone. A record 27.4 million people—about 10 percent of the nation's population and 9 million more than as recently as 1989—were receiving food stamps. Advocates think that as many as 20 million more Americans may be economically eligible for food stamps. In many ways the faces of the hungry are familiar: poor folks, old folks, people scraping by on public aid. Between half a million and a million of the country's senior citizens are malnourished; 30% of all senior citizens regularly skip meals. Native American reservations, where people have trouble reaching government support services, remain often startling pockets

of hunger. The hungry can be found among the nation's homeless and undocumented immigrants. But mostly, the hungry in the United States are still children. One child is four is growing up hungry, according to Bread for the World, a Washington-based international, interfaith policy agency.

In the face of such evidence, few readers would dispute the need to attack this problem. Later in this chapter you'll find Carl M. Cannon ("Honey, I Warped the Kids") and Alan During ("How Much Is 'Enough'?") using similar logical appeals to convince their audiences of the truth of their claims.

As an example of an argument appealing to readers' emotions, notice how the writer of this editorial from the magazine *The Disability Rag* persuasively argues against the substitution of the phrase "physically challenged" for "physically disabled":

> 'Physically challenged' attempts to conceal a crucial fact: that the reason we can't do lots of things is not because we're lazy or because we won't accept a 'challenge,' but because many things are simply beyond our control—like barriers. Like discrimination. People who favor 'physically challenged' are making a statement: Barriers, discrimination, are not *problems* for us, but *challenges*. We want those barriers, we almost seem to be saying—because by overcoming them we'll become better persons! Stronger. More courageous. After all, isn't that what challenges are for?
> Until you've made it your responsibility to get downtown, and discovered that there are no buses with lifts running on that route, you may not fully comprehend that it isn't a personal 'challenge' you're up against, but a system resistant to change.

Similarly, later in this chapter Senator Don Nickles and Aimee Berenson appeal to reader's emotions in their debate over banning HIV-inflected immigrants, as does Martin Luther King, Jr., in his famous "I Have a Dream" speech. Despite the differences in strategy, though, the objective in both argument and persuasion is the same: to persuade readers to believe or act in a certain way.

Whether you realize it or not, you already have had extensive experience in constructing arguments and in persuading an audience. Every time you try to persuade someone to do or to believe something, you have to argue. Consider a hypothetical example: You are concerned about your father's health. He smokes cigarettes, avoids exercise, is overweight, and works long hours in a stressful job. Even though you are worried, he is completely unconcerned and has always resisted your family's efforts to change his ways. Your task is to persuade him to change or modify his life-style, and doing so involves making its dangers clear, offering convincing reasons for change, and urging specific action.

Establishing the dangers is the first step, and you have a wide range of medical evidence from which to draw. That evidence involves statistics, testimony or advice from doctors, and case histories of men who have suffered the consequences of years of abusing or ignoring their health. From that body of material, you select those items which are most likely to touch your obstinate father. He might not be moved by cold statistics citing life-expectancy tables for smokers and nonexercisers, but he might be touched by the story of a friend his age who suffered a heart attack or stroke. The evidence you gather and use becomes a part of the convincing reasons for change that you offer in your argument. If your father persists in ignoring his health, he is likely to suffer some consequences. You might at this point include in your strategy emotional appeals. If he is not concerned about what will happen to him, what about his family? What will they do if he dies?

Having gotten your father to realize and acknowledge the dangers inherent in his life-style and to understand the reasons why he should make changes, it remains to urge specific action. In framing a plan for that action, you again need to consider your audience. If you urge your father to stop smoking immediately, join a daily exercise class at the local YMCA or health club, go on a thousand-calorie-a-day diet, and find a new job, chances are that he will think your proposal too drastic even to try. Instead, you might urge a more moderate plan, phasing in changes over a period of time or offering compromises (for example, that he work fewer hours).

How Do You Analyze Your Audience?

Argument or persuasion, unlike the other types of writing included in this text, has a special purpose—to persuade its audience. Because you want your reader to agree with your position or act as you urge, you need to analyze your audience carefully before you start to write. Try to answer each of the following questions:

- Who are my readers?
- What do they already know about this subject?
- How interested are they likely to be?
- How impartial or prejudiced are they going to be?

- What values do my readers share?
- Is my argument going to challenge any of my reader's beliefs or values?
- What types of evidence are most likely to be effective?
- Is my plan for requested action reasonable?

Your argumentative strategy should always reflect an awareness of your audience. Even in the hypothetical case of the unhealthy father, it is obvious that some types of evidence would be more effective than others and that some solutions or plans for action would be more reasonable and, therefore, more acceptable than others.

The second important consideration in any argument is to anticipate your audience's objections and be ready to answer them. Debaters study both sides of an argument so that they can effectively counter any opposition. In arguing the abortion issue, the Right-to-Life speaker has to be prepared to deal with subjects such as abnormal fetuses or pregnancy caused by rape or incest. The Pro-Choice speaker must face questions about when life begins and when the rights of the unborn might take precedence over the mother's rights.

WHAT DOES IT TAKE TO PERSUADE YOUR READER?

In some cases nothing will persuade your reader. For example, if you are arguing for legalized abortion, you will never convince a reader who believes that an embryo is a human being from the moment of conception. Abortion to that reader will always be murder. It is extremely difficult to argue any position that is counter to your audience's moral or ethical values. It is also difficult to argue a position that is counter to your audience's normal patterns of behavior. For example, you could reasonably argue that your readers ought to stop at all red lights and to obey the speed limit. However, the likelihood of persuading your audience to do these two things—even though not doing so breaks the law—is slim.

These cautions are not meant to imply that you should argue only "safe" subjects or that winning is everything. Choose a subject about which you feel strongly; present a fair, logical argument; express honest emotion; but avoid distorted evidence or inflammatory language. Even if no one is finally persuaded, at least you have offered a clear, intelligent explanation of your position.

In most arguments you have two possible types of support—

you can supply factual evidence, and you can appeal to your reader's values. Suppose, for example, you are arguing that professional boxing should be prohibited because it is dangerous. The reader may or may not accept your premise but at the very least would expect some support for your assertion. Your first task would be to gather evidence. The strongest evidence is factual—statistics dealing with the number of fighters each year who are fatally injured or mentally impaired. You might quote appropriate authorities—physicians, scientists, former fighters—on the risks connected with professional boxing. You might relate several instances or even a single example of a particular fighter who was killed or permanently injured while boxing. You might describe in detail how blows strike the body or head; you might trace the process by which a series of punches can cause brain damage. You might catalog the effects that years of physical punishment can produce in the human body. In your argument you might use some or all of this factual evidence. Your job as a writer is to gather the best—the most accurate and the most effective—evidence and present it in a clear and orderly way for your reader.

You can also appeal to your reader's values. You could argue that a sport in which a participant can be killed or permanently injured is not a "sport" at all. You could argue that the objective of a boxing match—to render one fighter unconscious or unable to continue—is different in kind from any other sport and not one that we, as human beings, should condone, let alone encourage. Appeals to values can be extremely effective.

Effective argumentation generally involves appealing to both reason and emotion. It is often easier to catch your reader's attention by using an emotional appeal. Demonstrators against vivisection, the dissecting of animals for laboratory research, display photographs of the torments suffered by these animals. Organizations that fight famine throughout the world use photographs of starving children. Advertisers use a wide range of persuasive tactics to touch our fears, our anxieties, our desires. But the types of argumentative writing that you are asked to do in college or in your job rarely allow for only emotional evidence.

One final thing is crucially important in persuading your reader. You must sound (and be) fair, reasonable, and credible in order to win the respect and possibly the approval of your reader. Readers distrust arguments that are loaded with unfair or inflammatory language, faulty logic, and biased or distorted evidence.

Since logic or reason is so crucial to effective argumentation, you will want to avoid logical fallacies or errors. When you construct your argument, make sure that you have avoided the following common mistakes:

- **Ad hominem argument** (literally to argue "to the person"): criticizing a person's position by criticizing his or her personal character. If an underworld figure asserts that boxing is the manly art of self-defense, you do not counter his *argument* by claiming that he makes money by betting on the fights.

- **Ad populum argument** (literally to argue "to the people"): appealing to the prejudices of your audience instead of offering facts or reasons. You do not defend boxing by asserting that it is part of the American way of life and that anyone who criticizes it is a Communist who seeks to undermine our society.

- **Appeal to an unqualified authority:** using testimony from someone who is unqualified to give it. In arguing against boxing, your relevant authorities would be physicians, or scientists, or former fighters—people who have had some direct experience. You do not quote a professional football player or your dermatologist.

- **Begging the question:** assuming as true what you are trying to prove. "Boxing is dangerous and because it is dangerous it ought to be outlawed." The first statement ("boxing is dangerous") is the premise you set out to prove, but the second statement uses that unproved premise as a basis for drawing a conclusion.

- **Either/or:** stating or implying that there are only two possibilities. Do not assert that the two choices are either to ban boxing or to allow this legalized murder to continue. Perhaps other changes might make the sport safer and hence less objectionable.

- **Faulty analogy:** using an inappropriate or superficially similar analogy as evidence. "Allowing a fighter to kill another man with his fists is like giving him a gun and permission to shoot to kill." The analogy might be vivid, but the two acts are far more different than they are similar.

- **Hasty generalization:** basing a conclusion on evidence that is atypical or unrepresentative. Do not assert that *every* boxer has suffered brain damage just because you can cite a few well-known cases.
- **Non sequitur** (literally "it does not follow"): arriving at a conclusion not justified by the premises or evidence. "My father has watched many fights on television; therefore, he is an authority on the physical hazards that boxers face."
- **Oversimplification:** suggesting a simple solution to a complex problem. "If professional boxers were made aware of the risks they take, they would stop boxing."

HOW DO YOU STRUCTURE AN ARGUMENT?

You construct an argument in either of two ways: you begin with your premise and then provide evidence or support, or you begin with your evidence and then move to your conclusion. Patricia Poore in "America's 'Garbage Crisis'" starts with a premise: "Garbage is not a serious environmental hazard." She then explains what she means by that statement and argues for treating garbage for what it is really is—"a manageable—though admittedly complex—civic issue." Roger Swardson in "Greetings from the Electronic Plantation" structures his essay in the opposite way. He begins with a narrative account of his average working day as a telephone service representative for a catalog company. It is not until about a third of the way into his essay that Swardson's point becomes clear: American business and the U.S. government have created a permanent class of working poor. There was a time, Swardson argues, when American workers could expect a living wage and job security; but today such full-time, benefit-paying jobs have been replaced by low-paying "temporary" jobs with little future and no benefits. Swardson confesses that he does not know what to do about the problem but he feels, like many Americans, that those "who have found a secure place in government, in the corporations, in wealth, have redefined the country under a different set of rules."

Swardson's essay moves basically in an inductive pattern. He starts by recounting the specifics of his working day and then moves to a general truth: we have reinstituted slavery through the creation of a class of working poor. Richard Rodriguez in "None of This Is Fair" follows a similar structural pattern by tracing his changing feelings about the kinds of affirmative action programs that advanced his own career, leading finally to his thesis that such programs often fail to help those who are really the disadvantaged.

If you are constructing an argument based upon a formal, logical progression, you can use either inductive or deductive reasoning. An *inductive* argument begins with specific evidence and then moves to a generalized conclusion to account for that evidence. The detective pieces together the evidence in an investigation and arrives at a conclusion: the butler did it.

A *deductive* argument moves in the opposite direction: it starts with a general truth and moves to a specific application of that truth. Alan Durning in "How Much Is 'Enough'?" begins with a thesis: "The richest billion people in the world have created a form of civilization so acquisitive and profligate that the planet is in danger." In the rest of the essay, Durning provides the evidence that leads him to that conclusion.

The simplest form of a deductive argument is the *syllogism*, a three-step argument involving a major premise, a minor premise, and a conclusion. Few essays—either those you write or those you read—can be reduced to a syllogism. Our thought patterns are rarely so logical, our reasoning rarely so precise. Although few essays state a syllogism explicitly, syllogisms do play a role in shaping an argument. For example, a number of essays in this reader begin with the same syllogism, even though it is not directly stated:

Major premise: All people should have equal opportunities.
Minor premise: Minorities are people.
Conclusion: Minorities should have equal opportunities.

Despite the fact that a syllogism is a precise structural form, you should not assume that a written argument will imitate it; that the first paragraph or group of paragraphs will contain a major premise; the next, a minor premise; and the final, a conclusion. Syllogisms can be basic to an argument without being a framework upon which it is constructed.

No matter how you structure your argument, one final consideration is important. Since the purpose of argumentation is to get a reader to agree with your position or to act in a particular way, it is always essential to end your paper decisively. Effective endings or conclusions to arguments can take a variety of forms. You might end with a call to action. For example, Martin Luther King's speech rises to an eloquent, rhythmical exhortation to his audience to continue to fight until they are "free at last." You might end by attacking your opposition's position, as Aimee Berenson does in arguing against a ban on HIV-inflected immigrants: "This prohibition is really a mask for a hatred of foreigners, a hatred of people of color, and a hatred of people who have HIV. That's what this is about." You might end with a relevant, thought-provoking question or quotation, as Alan Durning does when he concludes his long essay with a quotation from the ultimate American symbol of voluntary simplicity: "Maybe Henry David Thoreau had it right when he scribbled in his notebook beside Walden Pond, 'A man is rich in proportion to the things he can afford to let alone.'" Or you might end by suggesting a necessary set of steps or course of action, as Patricia Poore does when she tries to refocus her audience's attention on the real threats to our environment: "We have to protect the water supply. We must improve the quality of the air we breathe. We need a better plan for energy management. And we have to monitor toxic waste more effectively."

SAMPLE STUDENT ESSAY

Beth Jaffe decided to tackle a subject on the minds of many career-minded, dollar-conscious college students: why do you have to take so many courses outside of your major? Beth's argument is sure to arouse the attention of every advocate of a liberal arts education, and you might consider exploring the subject in an argument of your own.

EARLIER DRAFT

Reducing College Requirements

With the high costs of college still on the rise, it is not fair to make college students pay for courses labeled "requirements" which are not part of their major. Although many students want a well-rounded college education, many cannot afford to pay for one. By eliminating all of the requirements that do not pertain to a student's major, college costs could be cut tremendously. At the University of Delaware, for example, a student in the College of Arts and Science is required to take twelve credits of arts and humanities, twelve of culture and institutions of time, twelve of human beings and their environment, and thirteen of natural phenomena or science which include at least

one lab. Although some of their major courses may
fit into these categories, many others do not.
Frequently students do not like and are not
interested in the courses which fit into the four
categories and feel they are wasting their money by
paying for courses they do not enjoy, do not put
much work into, and usually do not get much out of.
It should be an option to the student to take these
extra courses. Why should a humanities or social
studies major have to take biology or chemistry?
Many of these students thought their struggle with
science was over after high school only to come to
college and find yet more "requirements" in the
sciences. Students are getting degrees in one area
of concentration. They should be able to take only
courses in their field of study and not have to waste
their money on courses they have no desire to take.

Beth's essay, with her permission, was duplicated and discussed
in class. Not surprisingly, it provoked a lively reaction. One student
asked Beth whether she was serious and exactly what it was that she
was proposing. Beth admitted that she did not advocate turning a college education into career training but that she had a number of
friends who were deeply in debt because of their four-year education.
"Why not just cut some requirements?" Beth asked. Several other students then suggested that since she did not really advocate an extreme
position, maybe she could find a compromise proposal. Her instructor
added that she might find a way of rewording her remarks about science classes. Few people, after all, are sympathetic to a position that
seems to say, "I don't want to do that. It's too hard. It's too boring."

When Beth revised her paper, she tried to follow the advice the
class had offered. In addition, she made the problem vivid by using
her roommate as an example and by pointing out what specifically
might be saved by the Jaffe proposal.

REVISED DRAFT

Lowering the Cost of a College Education

When my roommate graduates in June, she will be
$10,000 in debt. The debt did not come from spring
breaks in Fort Lauderdale or a new car. It came from

four years of college expenses, expenses that were not covered by the money she earned as a part-time waitress or by the small scholarship she was awarded annually. So now in June at age 21, with her first full-time job (assuming she gets one), Alison can start repaying her student loans.

Alison's case is certainly not unusual. In fact, because she attends a state-assisted university, her debt is less than it might be. We cannot expect education to get cheaper. We cannot expect government scholarship programs to get larger. We cannot ask that students go deeper and deeper into debt. We need a new way of combating this cost problem. We need the Jaffe proposal.

If colleges would eliminate some of the general education course requirements, college costs could be substantially lowered. At the University of Delaware, for example, a student at the College of Arts and Science is required to take twelve credits of arts and humanities, twelve of culture and the institutions of time, twelve of human beings and their environment, and thirteen of natural phenomena or science, including at least one laboratory course. Approximately half of these requirements are fulfilled by courses which are required for particular majors. The others are not, and these are likely to be courses that students are not interested in and so get little out of.

If some of these requirements were eliminated, a student would need approximately twenty-five fewer credits for a bachelor's degree. If a student took a heavier load or went to summer school, he or she could graduate either one or two semesters earlier. The result would cut college costs by anywhere from one-eighth to one-fourth.

The Jaffe proposal does decrease the likelihood that a college graduate will receive a well-rounded education. On the other hand, it allows students to concentrate their efforts in courses which they feel are relevant. Perhaps most important, it helps reduce the burden that escalating college costs have placed on all of us.

Some Things to Remember

1. Choose a subject that allows for the possibility of persuading your reader. Avoid emotionally charged subjects that resist logical examination.

2. Analyze your audience. Who are your readers? What do they already know about your subject? How are they likely to feel about it? How impartial or prejudiced are they going to be?

3. Make a list of the evidence or reasons you will use in your argument. Analyze each piece of evidence to see how effective it might be in achieving your end.

4. Honest emotion is fair, but avoid anything that is distorted, inaccurate, or inflammatory. Argue with solid, reasonable, fair, and relevant evidence.

5. Avoid the common logical fallacies listed in this introduction.

6. Make a list of all the possible counterarguments or objections your audience might have. Think of ways in which you can respond to those objections.

7. Decide how to structure your essay. You can begin with a position and then provide evidence. You can begin with the evidence and end with a conclusion. Which structure seems to fit your subject and evidence better?

8. End forcefully. Conclusions are what listeners and readers are most likely to remember. Repeat or restate your position. Drive home the importance of your argument.

SHOULD HIV-INFECTED IMMIGRANTS BE BARRED FROM THE UNITED STATES? A DEBATE

Senator Don Nickles/Aimee Berenson

Don Nickles, a U.S. Senator from Oklahoma, is the chief sponsor of a Senate measure supporting a ban that prohibits immigrants infected with the HIV virus from entering the United States. Aimee Berenson, legislative counsel with the AIDS Action Council, opposes any such ban.

"Should HIV-Infected Immigrants Be Barred from the United States?" first appeared in Health Magazine *and presents the opposing viewpoints of Nickles and Berenson regarding the quarantining of Haitians at Guantanamo Bay, Cuba. Seeking political asylum, Haitians trying to enter the country who were determined to be infected with the HIV virus were detained for some twenty months at the Guantanamo Naval Base. The larger implication of this policy is that no HIV-infected alien, no matter what his or her immediate health, economic status, or family ties to the United States, is currently allowed to enter the country.*

BEFORE READING

Connecting: Before you begin to read this debate, stop for a moment and jot down exactly what you know about being "HIV-infected." What does that term mean?

Anticipating: If you were a member of Congress and had to vote in support or in opposition to such a ban, how would you vote? Why?

SENATOR DON NICKLES: "YES"

1   Strictly as a health issue, if more HIV-positive immigrants come into the country, more Americans will get the virus and die. The Public Health Service wants to lift all restrictions on diseases except those that are communicable by airborne pathogens, like tuberculosis. They're making a serious mistake. We have always had prohibitions against immigrants with diseases like gonorrhea and syphilis. HIV is not only contagious, we do not have a cure for it. We already have

Argument and Persuasion

one million people who are HIV-positive and a quarter-million who have died. With an influx of infected immigrants the virus could really start moving in the heterosexual community, as it has in some other countries. If that happens, you can multiply the numbers several times over, I'm afraid.

On economic grounds, this is a very expensive disease to treat. Many HIV-positive people coming into the country would burden the health care system, either with the cost of their own treatment or by spreading the disease to other people, who will wind up in public hospitals. Of course, we shouldn't paint with a real broad brush. We want to be compassionate. But we don't want to allow in people with expensive medical conditions and have the taxpayers picking up the tab. Immigrants with cancer and heart problems may cost the taxpayers some money, but they're not risking other people's lives. 2

Lifting the ban on HIV-infected immigrants is a promise that Bill Clinton made to garner votes from gay rights groups, but it is not sound medical policy. It's one of the promises he made that needed to be broken. 3

AIMEE BERENSON: "NO"

This prohibition is cruel. Supporters have raised this specter: The floodgates are going to open, all these people with HIV are going to want to immigrate, they're going to drain our health care resources and infect everyone. It's crazy. There's no evidence that we're looking at huge numbers of infected people coming into this country. And HIV is not transmitted casually—if people are taught how to avoid getting it, they can avoid getting it. It's not like you are going to get the virus sitting next to somebody on a bus. 4

Our health care problem is not going to be made worse by admitting a few HIV-infected immigrants. The law already requires that immigrants show they're not going to become a public charge. In fact, people with HIV can lead long, productive lives in which they can be taxpayers and contribute to this society. 5

The United States has one of the highest rates of HIV infection in the world. To pretend that by closing our borders we are keeping out the virus is obscene, because in fact we're an exporter of AIDS. Sixty percent of the immigrants admitted in the last ten years are from countries with very low rates of infection. If they are found to be HIV-positive during legalization procedures, they are deported—despite the fact that they may well have been infected here. And we don't tell them how to avoid infecting others once they go home. We don't even necessarily tell them they have the virus. 6

This prohibition is really a mask for a hatred of foreigners, a hatred of people of color, and a hatred of people who have HIV. That's what this is about.

QUESTIONS ON SUBJECT AND PURPOSE

1. What exactly does it mean to be "HIV-positive"? Is that the same as having AIDS?
2. What is the difference between a disease transmitted by "airborne pathogens" (paragraph 1) and a disease such as HIV?
3. Which of the two positions seems most reasonable to you? Why? Do your reactions depend upon what was said or upon a preformed opinion?

QUESTIONS ON STRATEGY AND AUDIENCE

1. Traditionally, argumentation appeals to logic and reason, while persuasion appeals to emotion and sometimes prejudice. How would you label each selection?
2. What do you regard as each writer's strongest point?
3. What similar strategy do both writers use in their final paragraphs?

QUESTIONS ON VOCABULARY AND STYLE

1. Which of the two writers uses the more emotional language? Isolate some examples of that language.
2. What do these two sentences have in common:
   a. "Of course, we shouldn't paint with a real broad brush" (paragraph 2).
   b. "The floodgates are going to open ..." (4).
3. Be prepared to define the following words: *pathogens* (1), *garner* (3).

WRITING SUGGESTIONS

1. **For your Journal.** What exactly do you know about HIV infection and AIDS? In your journal make a list of what you know and what you do not know. If you have trouble making

the list or if your "do not know" list is the l[
contact your college's health or wellness cen[
information.

2. **For a Paragraph**. Beginning with your own e[
   ing your journal entry, write a paragraph in wh[
   persuade readers to learn more about the HIV [
   AIDS.

3. **For an Essay**. The 1990s have witnessed a numb[
   ing international crises: dictators and military regi[
   control of governments, civil wars, religious wars, g[
   widespread famine. The United States' efforts at int[
   to prevent these problems or to remedy them have o[
   with little success. Under the circumstances does the [
   States—one of the richest and most powerful nations [
   earth—have a moral obligation to provide a haven for [
   refugees seeking to escape dangerous civil unrest, famin[
   political, religious, and ethnic persecution? In an essay ta[
   position on this issue, and try to persuade your reader to [
   with you.

Prewriting:

a. Brainstorm a list of acceptable reasons, in your opinion, f[
   allowing and/or not allowing refugees into the country.
   Look over your list and determine which reasons seem
   more important to you than others. Make a short list of the
   strongest reasons.

b. Using your short list, brainstorm possible objections to
   each reason. Anticipate the reactions of those who will not
   agree with you.

c. Arrange your reasons in an order, deciding which reasons
   should come first, which next, and so forth. Make these decisions carefully. For example, do you want to begin or to
   end with what you feel is your strongest point?

Rewriting:

a. Reread your essay. You should be arguing for a general or
   even theoretical position, a governmental policy for admitting refugees. If you have used examples of specific groups
   of refugees, make sure they are there to support that larger
   position. In other words, do not just argue for a specific instance, such as admitting or not admitting political refugees
   from a particular country.

b. Go through your draft and underline any emotionally charged words and phrases. Look at each carefully. Are they likely to offend or alienate your audience?

c. Ask a friend to read your essay, preferably someone who has not also written on the same topic. Ask your reader for reactions. Did the reader agree with you? Why or why not? Consider that reaction when you revise your draft.

4. **For Research.** Under what circumstances can any country control who may or may not immigrate? Choose a country and research its immigration policies. How does it exclude people? Are there economic requirements? Health requirements? Are there quotas on immigrants? Are the quotas applied just to total numbers or to people from a particular country or area of the world? Once you have gathered detailed information, write a research paper in which you argue either in support of those laws or propose modification of those laws. Be sure to document your sources wherever appropriate.

HONEY, I WARPED THE KIDS

Carl M. Cannon

Carl Cannon received a degree in journalism from the University of Colorado in 1975. Currently a reporter for the Washington bureau of the Baltimore Sun, Cannon worked for several newspapers before settling in the Washington area. He has written on many subjects including children, the Washington political scene, and television.

Approached by an editor at Mother Jones *to write an article about violence on television, Cannon researched studies of the causal relationship between television viewing and violent behavior. His research led him to statistics that support what almost no one in Hollywood is willing to admit— that depictions of violence on television affect the behavior of both adults and children. In "Honey, I Warped the Kids," Cannon notes that Hollywood celebrities are often quite socially and politically active, except in the "one area over which they have control." "Honey, I Warped the Kids" has been reprinted in numerous alternative newspapers around the country.*

BEFORE READING

Connecting: Cannon observes that in the early days of television, producers and advertisers thought that television would be a force to "remake society along better lines." Based on your experiences with television, what do you think about that objective?

Anticipating: If we have known since 1956 that watching violence depicted on television (or in films) has a negative impact on children's behavior, why hasn't such violence been outlawed or eliminated?

Tim Robbins and Susan Sarandon implore the nation to treat   1
Haitians with AIDS more humanely. Robert Redford works for the
environment. Harry Belafonte marches against the death penalty. Actors and producers seem to be constantly speaking out for noble
causes far removed from their lives. But in the one area over which
they have control—the excessive violence in the entertainment industry—Hollywood activists remain silent.

The first congressional hearings on the effects of TV violence   2
took place in 1954. Although television was still relatively new, its ex-

traordinary marketing power was already evident. The tube was teaching Americans what to buy and how to act, not only in advertisements, but in dramatic shows, too.

3   Everybody from Hollywood producers to Madison Avenue ad men would boast about this power—and seek to use it on dual tracks: to make money and to remake society along better lines.

4   Because it seemed ludicrous to assert that there was only one area—the depiction of violence—where television did not influence behavior, the TV industry came up with this theory: Watching violence is cathartic. A violent person might be sated by watching a murder.

5   The notion intrigued social scientists, and by 1956 they were studying it in earnest. Unfortunately, watching violence turned out to be anything but cathartic.

6   In the 1956 study, one dozen 4-year-olds watched a "Woody Woodpecker" cartoon that was full of violent images. Twelve other preschoolers watched "Little Red Hen," a peaceful cartoon. Afterward, the children who watched "Woody Woodpecker" were more likely to hit other children, verbally accost their classmates, break toys, be disruptive, and engage in destructive behavior during free play.

7   For the next 30 years, researchers in all walks of the social sciences studied the question of whether television causes violence. The results have been stunningly conclusive.

8   "There is more published research on this topic than on almost any other social issue of our time," University of Kansas Professor Aletha C. Huston, chair of the American Psychological Association's Task Force on Television and Society, told Congress in 1988. "Virtually all independent scholars agree that there is evidence that television can cause aggressive behavior."

9   There have been some 3,000 studies of this issue—85 of them major research efforts—and they all say the same thing. Of the 85 major studies, the only one that failed to find a causal relationship between TV violence and actual violence was paid for by NBC. When the study was subsequently reviewed by three independent social scientists, all three concluded that it actually did demonstrate a causal relationship.

10   Some highlights from the history of TV violence research:

11   ■ In 1973, when a town in mountainous western Canada was wired for TV signals, University of British Columbia researchers observed first- and second-graders. Within two years, the incidence of hitting, biting, and shoving increased 160 percent.

12   ■ Two Chicago doctors, Leonard Eron and Rowell Heusmann, followed the viewing habits of a group of children for 22

years. They found that watching violence on television is the single best predictor of violent or aggressive behavior later in life, ahead of such commonly accepted factors as parents' behavior, poverty, and race.

"Television violence affects youngsters of all ages, of both genders, at all socioeconomic levels and all levels of intelligence," they told Congress in 1992. "The effect is not limited to children who are already disposed to being aggressive and is not restricted to this country."

13

- In 1988, researchers Daniel G. Linz and Edward Donnerstein of the University of California, Santa Barbara, and Steven Penrod of the University of Wisconsin studied the effects on young men of horror movies and "slasher" films.

14

They found that depictions of violence, not sex, are what desensitizes people. They divided male students into four groups. One group watched no movies, a second watched nonviolent X-rated movies, a third watched teenage sexual-innuendo movies, and a fourth watched the slasher films *Texas Chainsaw Massacre*, *Friday the 13th, Part 2*, *Maniac*, and *Toolbox Murders*.

15

All the young men were placed on a mock jury panel and asked a series of questions designed to measure their empathy for an alleged female rape victim. Those in the fourth group measured lowest in empathy for the specific victim in the experiment—and for rape victims in general.

16

The anecdotal evidence is often more compelling than the scientific studies. Ask any homicide cop from London to Los Angeles to Bangkok if TV violence induces real-life violence and listen carefully to the cynical, knowing laugh.

17

Ask David McCarthy, police chief in Greenfield, Massachusetts, why 19-year-old Mark Branch killed himself after stabbing an 18-year-old female college student to death. When cops searched his room they found 90 horror movies, as well as a machete and a goalie mask like those used by Jason, the grisly star of *Friday the 13th*.

18

Or ask Sergeant John O'Malley of the New York Police Department about a 9-year-old boy who sprayed a Bronx office building with gunfire. The boy explained to the astonished sergeant how he learned to load his Uzi-like firearm: "I watch a lot of TV."

19

Numerous groups have called, over the years, for curbing TV violence: the National Commission on the Causes and Prevention of Violence (1969), the U.S. Surgeon General (1972), the National Institute of Mental Health (1982), and the American Psychological Association (1992) among them.

20

21   During that time, cable television and movie rentals have made violence more readily available while at the same time pushing the envelope for network television. But even leaving aside cable and movie rentals, a study of TV programming from 1967 to 1989 showed only small ups and downs in violence, with the violent acts moving from one time slot to another but the overall violence rate remaining pretty steady—and pretty similar from network to network.

22   "The percent of prime-time programs using violence remains more than seven out of ten, as it has been for the entire 22-year period," researchers George Gerbner of the University of Pennsylvania Annenberg School of Communication and Nancy Signorielli of the University of Delaware wrote in 1990. For the past 22 years, they found, adults and children have been entertained by about 16 violent acts, including two murders, in each evening's prime-time programming.

23   They also discovered that the rate of violence in children's programs is three times the rate in prime-time shows. By the age of 18, the average American child has witnessed at least 18,000 simulated murders on television.

24   But all of the scientific studies and reports, all of the wisdom of cops and grief of parents have run up against Congress' quite proper fear of censorship. For years, Democratic Congressman Peter Rodino of New Jersey chaired the House Judiciary Committee and looked at calls for some form of censorship with a jaundiced eye. At a hearing five years ago, Rodino told witnesses that Congress must be a "protector of commerce."

25   "Well, we have children that we need to protect," replied Frank M. Palumbo, a pediatrician at Georgetown University Hospital and a consultant to the American Academy of Pediatrics. "What we have here is a toxic substance in the environment that is harmful to children."

26   Arnold Fege of the national PTA added, "Clearly, this committee would not protect teachers who taught violence to children. Yet why would we condone children being exposed to a steady diet of TV violence year after year?"

QUESTIONS ON SUBJECT AND PURPOSE

1. Write a thesis sentence that sums up Cannon's argument.
2. Is Cannon's approach to his subject essentially deductive or inductive? (See the chapter introduction or the Glossary for definitions of the two terms.)
3. What is Cannon arguing for?

QUESTIONS ON STRATEGY AND AUDIENCE

1. What strategy does Cannon use in his opening paragraph?
2. Why might Cannon have chosen to end his essay with two quotations?
3. What could Cannon assume about his audience?

QUESTIONS ON VOCABULARY AND STYLE

1. Does Cannon approach his subject in a detached, unbiased way, or does he reveal his prejudices? Locate two examples, perhaps in his choice of words, that support your answer.
2. What does Cannon's title, "Honey, I Warped the Kids," suggest?
3. Be prepared to define the following words: *ludicrous* (paragraph 4), *cathartic* (4), *sated* (4), *accost* (6), *innuendo* (15), *empathy* (16), *anecdotal* (17), *jaundiced* (24).

WRITING SUGGESTIONS

1. **For your Journal.** Think about your own reactions to depictions of violence. How do you react to violence in a video or computer game? In a film? In a cartoon? In a professional athletic game? Select one such example of violence you have recently witnessed, and jot down your reactions to that experience. How did it make you feel? Alternatively, you might write about how you've seen a child react to a depiction of violence.
2. **For a Paragraph.** Using the observations that you made in your journal entry, write a paragraph in which you argue that depictions of violence such as the one you describe (1) are perfectly acceptable for anyone, (2) should be banned or strictly limited, or (3) should be restricted for certain age groups. Be sure to explain why you feel as you do.
3. **For an Essay.** Assuming that Cannon is right, what might be done about this situation? In an essay, offer an agenda for change. Remember that although your audience might agree about the problem, they will not necessarily agree with the solutions that you propose. You will need to persuade your audience that your solution is reasonable and appropriate.

Prewriting:

a. Make a list of possible solutions. Try to develop each idea at least two or three sentences.

b. Make a list of possible objections to each of your suggested solutions. Again try to develop each objection in at least two or three sentences.

c. Using your two lists, brainstorm an outline for your essay. Will you begin with your premise, or will you provide evidence before presenting your conclusion? If you are presenting more than one solution, in what order will these solutions be presented?

Rewriting:

a. Find a classmate or a peer to read your essay. Ask that reader to evaluate your position. Does your reader agree? Why or why not? Listen carefully to your reader's reaction.

b. Does your essay present a premise supported by evidence or move from evidence to an ultimate conclusion? Briefly outline an alternative strategy. Which of the two arrangements seems more effective? Ask a reader to evaluate both organizational plans.

c. Look at your conclusion again. Arguments—either emotional or logical—need to end forcefully. Freewrite a totally different ending to your essay. Ask your reader to evaluate both.

4. For Research. In paragraph 24, Cannon suggests two reasons why so little has been done to limit the amount of violence depicted in the entertainment media: "Congress' quite proper fear of censorship" and the need to protect "commerce." Moreover, violence quite obviously "sells," and therefore there are enormous economic motivations for the appearance of violence in so many different forms—video and computer games, music lyrics, professional sports, and so forth. Research the other side of the argument, and present the reasons why violence is so often depicted in our culture. Be sure to document your sources wherever appropriate.

I HAVE A DREAM

Martin Luther King, Jr.

Martin Luther King, Jr. (1929–1968) was born in Atlanta, the son of a Baptist minister. Ordained in his father's church in 1947, King received a doctorate in theology from Boston University in 1955. That same year he achieved national prominence by leading a boycott protesting the segregation of the Montgomery, Alabama, city bus system, based on ideas of nonviolent civil resistance derived from Thoreau and Gandhi. A central figure in the civil rights movement, King was awarded the Nobel Peace Prize in 1964. He was assassinated in Memphis in 1968. His birthday, January 15, is celebrated as a national holiday.

King's "I Have a Dream" speech was delivered at the Lincoln Memorial to an audience of 250,000 people who assembled in Washington, D.C., on August 28, 1963. That march, commemorating in part the hundredth anniversary of Lincoln's Emancipation Proclamation, was intended as an act of "creative lobbying" to win the support of Congress and the president for pending civil rights legislation. King's speech is one of the most memorable and moving examples of American oratory.

BEFORE READING

Connecting: Probably every American has heard at least a small portion of King's speech. Before you begin to read, jot down what you know about the speech or the phrases that you remember from recordings and television clips.

Anticipating: King's speech is marked by the extensive use of images. As you read, make a note of the most powerful and recurrent images that he uses.

Five score years ago, a great American, in whose symbolic shadow we   1
stand, signed the Emancipation Proclamation. This momentous decree came as a great beacon light of hope to millions of Negro slaves who had been seared in the flames of withering injustice. It came as a joyous daybreak to end the long night of captivity.

But one hundred years later, we must face the tragic fact that   2
the Negro is still not free. One hundred years later, the life of the

Negro is still sadly crippled by the manacles of segregation and the chains of discrimination. One hundred years later, the Negro lives on a lonely island of poverty in the midst of a vast ocean of material prosperity. One hundred years later, the Negro is still languishing in the corners of American society and finds himself an exile in his own land. So we have come here today to dramatize an appalling condition.

3   In a sense we have come to our nation's capital to cash a check. When the architects of our republic wrote the magnificent words of the Constitution and the Declaration of Independence, they were signing a promissory note to which every American was to fall heir. This note was a promise that all men would be guaranteed the unalienable rights of life, liberty, and the pursuit of happiness.

4   It is obvious today that America has defaulted on this promissory note insofar as her citizens of color are concerned. Instead of honoring this sacred obligation, America has given the Negro people a bad check; a check which has come back marked "insufficient funds." But we refuse to believe that the bank of justice is bankrupt. We refuse to believe that there are insufficient funds in the great vaults of opportunity of this nation. So we have come to cash this check—a check that will give us upon demand the riches of freedom and the security of justice. We have also come to this hallowed spot to remind America of the fierce urgency of *now*. This is no time to engage in the luxury of cooling off or to take the tranquilizing drugs of gradualism. *Now* is the time to make real the promises of Democracy. *Now* is the time to rise from the dark and desolate valley of segregation to the sunlit path of racial justice. *Now* is the time to open the doors of opportunity to all of God's children. *Now* is the time to lift our nation from the quicksands of racial injustice to the solid rock of brotherhood.

5   It would be fatal for the nation to overlook the urgency of the moment and to underestimate the determination of the Negro. This sweltering summer of the Negro's legitimate discontent will not pass until there is an invigorating autumn of freedom and equality. 1963 is not an end, but a beginning. Those who hope that the Negro needed to blow off steam and will now be content will have a rude awakening if the nation returns to business as usual. There will be neither rest nor tranquility in America until the Negro is granted his citizenship rights. The whirlwinds of revolt will continue to shake the foundations of our nation until the bright day of justice emerges.

6   But there is something that I must say to my people who stand on the warm threshold which leads into the palace of justice. In the process of gaining our rightful place we must not be guilty of wrongful deeds. Let us not seek to satisfy our thirst for freedom by drink-

ing from the cup of bitterness and hatred. We must forever conduct our struggle on the high plane of dignity and discipline. We must not allow our creative protest to degenerate into physical violence. Again and again we must rise to the majestic heights of meeting physical force with soul force. The marvelous new militancy which has engulfed the Negro community must not lead us to a distrust of all white people, for many of our white brothers, as evidenced by their presence here today, have come to realize that their destiny is tied up with our destiny and their freedom is inextricably bound to our freedom. We cannot walk alone.

And as we walk, we must make the pledge that we shall march 7
ahead. We cannot turn back. There are those who are asking the devotees of civil rights, "When will you be satisfied?" We can never be satisfied as long as the Negro is the victim of the unspeakable horrors of police brutality. We can never be satisfied as long as our bodies, heavy with the fatigue of travel, cannot gain lodging in the motels of the highways and the hotels of the cities. We cannot be satisfied as long as the Negro's basic mobility is from a smaller ghetto to a larger one. We can never be satisfied as long as a Negro in Mississippi cannot vote and a Negro in New York believes he has nothing for which to vote. No, no, we are not satisfied, and we will not be satisfied until justice rolls down like waters and righteousness like a mighty stream.

I am not unmindful that some of you have come here out of 8
great trials and tribulations. Some of you have come fresh from narrow jail cells. Some of you have come from areas where your quest for freedom left you battered by the storms of persecution and staggered by the winds of police brutality. You have been the veterans of creative suffering. Continue to work with the faith that unearned suffering is redemptive.

Go back to Mississippi, go back to Alabama, go back to South 9
Carolina, go back to Georgia, go back to Louisiana, go back to the slums and ghettos of our northern cities, knowing that somehow this situation can and will be changed. Let us not wallow in the valley of despair.

I say to you today, my friends, that in spite of the difficulties and 10
frustrations of the moment I still have a dream. It is a dream deeply rooted in the American dream.

I have a dream that one day this nation will rise up and live out 11
the true meaning of its creed: "We hold these truths to be self-evident: that all men are created equal."

I have a dream that one day on the red hills of Georgia the sons 12
of former slaves and the sons of former slave owners will be able to sit down together at the table of brotherhood.

I have a dream that one day even the state of Mississippi, a 13 desert state sweltering with the heat of injustice and oppression, will be transformed into an oasis of freedom and justice.

14　　I have a dream that my four little children will one day live in a nation where they will not be judged by the color of their skin but by the content of their character.

15　　I have a dream today.

16　　I have a dream that one day the state of Alabama, whose governor's lips are presently dripping with the words of interposition and nullification, will be transformed into a situation where little black boys and black girls will be able to join hands with little white boys and white girls and walk together as sisters and brothers.

17　　I have a dream today.

18　　I have a dream that one day every valley shall be exalted, every hill and mountain shall be made low, the rough places will be made plain, and the crooked places will be made straight, and the glory of the Lord shall be revealed, and all flesh shall see it together.

19　　This is our hope. This is the faith with which I return to the South. With this faith we will be able to hew out of the mountain of despair a stone of hope. With this faith we will be able to transform the jangling discords of our nation into a beautiful symphony of brotherhood. With this faith we will be able to work together, to pray together, to struggle together, to go to jail together, to stand up for freedom together, knowing that we will be free one day.

20　　This will be the day when all of God's children will be able to sing with new meaning

> My country, 'tis of thee,
> Sweet land of liberty,
> 　Of thee I sing:
> Land where my fathers died,
> Land of the pilgrims' pride,
> From every mountain-side
> 　Let freedom ring.

21　　And if America is to be a great nation this must become true. So let freedom ring from the prodigious hilltops of New Hampshire. Let freedom ring from the mighty mountains of New York. Let freedom ring from the heightening Alleghenies of Pennsylvania!

22　　Let freedom ring from the snowcapped Rockies of Colorado!

23　　Let freedom ring from the curvaceous peaks of California!

24　　But not only that; let freedom ring from Stone Mountain of Georgia!

25　　Let freedom ring from Lookout Mountain of Tennessee!

26　　Let freedom ring from every hill and molehill of Mississippi. From every mountainside, let freedom ring.

When we let freedom ring, when we let it ring from every vil- lage and every hamlet, from every state and every city, we will be able to speed up that day when all of God's children, black men and white men, Jews and Gentiles, Protestants and Catholics, will be able to join hands and sing in the words of the old Negro spiritual, "Free at last! free at last! thank God almighty, we are free at last!"

QUESTIONS ON SUBJECT AND PURPOSE

1. What is King's dream?
2. King's essay was a speech—delivered orally before thousands of marchers and millions of television viewers. How are its oral origins revealed in the written version?
3. In what way is King's speech an attempt at persuasion? Whom was he trying to persuade to do what?

QUESTIONS ON STRATEGY AND AUDIENCE

1. Why does King begin with the words "Five score years ago"? Why does he say at the end of paragraph 6, "We cannot walk alone"? What do such words have to do with the context of King's speech?
2. How does King structure his speech? Is there an inevitable order or movement? How effective is his conclusion?
3. What expectations does King have of his audience? How do you know that?

QUESTIONS ON VOCABULARY AND STYLE

1. How many examples of figurative speech (images, metaphors, similes) can you find in the speech? What effect does such figurative language have?
2. The speech is full of parallel structures. See how many you can find. Why does King use so many?
3. Be able to define the following words: *seared* (paragraph 1), *manacles* (2), *languishing* (2), *promissory note* (3), *unalienable* (3), *invigorating* (5), *inextricably* (6), *tribulations* (8), *nullification* (16), *prodigious* (21).

WRITING SUGGESTIONS

1. **For your Journal**. It is impossible for most people to read or hear King's speech without being moved. What is it about the

speech that makes it so emotionally powerful? In your journal, speculate on the reasons the speech has such an impact. What does it suggest about the power of language?

2. **For a Paragraph.** In a paragraph argue for equality for a minority group of serious concern on your campus (the disabled, a sexual, racial, or religious minority, returning adults, commuters).

3. **For an Essay.** Expand the argument you explored in suggestion 2 above to essay length.

   Prewriting:

   a. To write convincingly about such a problem you will need specific information drawn from your own experience and/or the experiences of others. Interview several members of the minority group about whom you are writing. Take notes on index cards.

   b. Organize your cards by sorting them into groups according to topic. Make a list of those topics, and then convert the list into a working outline.

   c. What objections or reservations might your audience have? Try to imagine a critic's objections to your essay.

   Rewriting:

   a. Highlight all the specific evidence in your essay. Remember that details make an argument effective. Have you included enough? Each body paragraph needs details and examples.

   b. Check each paragraph for a unified idea. Is there a single focused idea controlling the paragraph? Jot down a key word or phrase for each paragraph.

   c. Find someone to read your essay. Does your reader find your argument fair? Convincing? If the reader disagrees, ask for specific reasons why.

4. **For Research.** According to the U.S. Census Bureau, 43 million Americans have some type of physical or mental disability. Like members of other minorities, the disabled regularly confront discrimination ranging from prejudice to physical barriers that deny them equal access to facilities. The federal government, with the passage of Title V of the Rehabilitation Act in 1973 and the Americans with Disabilities Act of 1990, has attempted to address these problems. Research the problem on your college's campus. What has been done to eliminate discrimination against the disabled? What remains to be done? Argue for the importance of such changes.

Alternatively, you might argue that the regulations are burdensome and should be abandoned. Be sure to document your sources wherever appropriate.

AMERICA'S "GARBAGE CRISIS": A TOXIC MYTH

Patricia Poore

Patricia Poore founded Garbage: The Practical Journal for the Environment, *published in Gloucester, Massachusetts. The former editor of* The Old-House Journal, *a newsletter for owners interested in the restoration of pre-World War II homes, Poore is currently the editor and publisher of* Garbage. *Exploring a range of issues,* Garbage *tackles anything dealing with waste—environmental waste, hazardous waste, solid waste, and wasted resources. Its first issue, which premiered in the fall of 1989, included articles on the waste created by food packaging materials, the use of natural pest controls, and the design of kitchen spaces for recycling.*

In Poore's "America's 'Garbage Crisis': A Toxic Myth," adapted from her article "Is Garbage an Environmental Problem?," and reprinted by Harper's Magazine *in 1994, Poore argues that garbage is not the most pressing environmental problem. The "garbage crisis" only diverts our attention, Poore contends, from more serious issues, such as protecting the nation's water supply, combating air pollution, and disposal of toxic wastes.*

BEFORE READING

Connecting: Do you or your family recycle? What do you recycle? Why? Have you ever questioned the value of recycling?

Anticipating: According to Poore, in what sense is the household garbage crisis a "toxic" myth?

1   Let us recall, for a moment, the *Mobro*—the infamous garbage barge that, in 1987, laden with an increasingly ripe pile of waste, wandered from port to port in search of a home. The *Mobro*, which was carrying plain old municipal solid waste—household garbage—occasioned headlines about the nation's looming "garbage crisis": we were throwing away too much, our landfills were running out of space, and soon the seas would be full of *Mobros*, all looking for a place to dump our trash. And yet here we are, seven years later, and our landfills are not overflowing; our waterways are not crowded with wandering barges. What happened to the garbage crisis?

The environmental movement continues to focus its attention on garbage and recycling, as if household garbage were the single most important issue we face and recycling the only solution. Of course, garbage does have an environmental impact; so does almost everything, from prairie-grass fires to the breath you just took. But, contrary to the rhetoric of some environmentalists, garbage is not a serious environmental hazard. True hazards are ones that threaten human lives and health. There are plenty of these, including toxic waste (which is quite distinct from household garbage), groundwater pollution, and urban smog. Compared with these real crises, the problems of municipal garbage disposal pale. There are times and places when household garbage *can* cause environmental problems—like when toxic runoff leaches into drinking water—but these are increasingly rare. Newer landfills are double-lined, piped, vented, leachate-tested, and eventually capped. These new standards have made current American waste management safer by far than ever before.

Some critics argue that we shouldn't downplay the threat of garbage because of its symbolic value to the environmentalist agenda. Environmental organizations are well aware of the emotional power of garbage: nothing can trigger a bounteous direct-mail response or inspire a powerful grass-roots campaign like the threat of a new landfill or incineration plant. But when symbols like the *Mobro* barge are used to divert attention and money from more pressing environmental and social problems, the symbol itself becomes a threat.

If there is a garbage crisis, it is that we are treating garbage as an environmental threat and not as what it is: a manageable—though admittedly complex—civic issue. Although many old urban landfills are reaching their capacity, the reality is that there is—and always will be—plenty of room in this country for safe landfill. We've chosen to look at garbage not as a management issue, however, but as a moral crisis. The result is that recycling is now seen as an irreproachable virtue, beyond the scrutiny of cost-benefit analysis. But in the real world, the money municipalities spend on recycling is money that can't be spent on schools, libraries, health clinics, and police. In the real world, the sort of gigantic recycling programs that many cities and towns have embarked upon may not be the best use of scarce government funds.

These programs were often sold to local tax-payers as money-saving ventures. In fact, the costs associated with consumer education, separate pickup (often in newly purchased trucks), hand- and machine-sorting, transfer stations, trucking, cleaning, and reprocessing are considerably higher than initial estimates, far higher than receipts from buyers of recyclables, and, in many areas, higher than disposal costs.

6   Putting aside financial concerns, let's consider other justifications for the recycling-above-all-else movement. Do we need recycling to extend the life of landfills? No. Landfill sites, in fact, are not scarce, and incineration remains a reasonable and safe option. The most ambitious collection programs still leave well over half of municipal waste to be disposed of, so recycling cannot completely replace disposal facilities, even if we needed it to.

7   Do we need recycling to save resources? No, not in the real world. The reason recycling is unprofitable is that most of the materials being recycled are either renewable (paper from tree farms) or cheap and plentiful (glass from silica). Aluminum *is* profitable to recycle—and private concerns were already recycling it before the legislated mandates.

8   Recycling is beginning to lose its halo as its costs become apparent and its effect on the volume of waste is found to be smaller than anticipated. Quotas and fines may force people to separate their trash, but they can't create industrial markets for the waste we recycle. Recycling can work, very effectively, on a region-by-region and commodity-by-commodity basis. But recycling as a government-mandated garbage-management option has largely failed.

9   Although the special attention we pay to garbage, to the exclusion of more serious environmental threats, may be irrational, it does make a certain emotional sense. We as individuals are intimate with our trash, which makes it a more tangible issue than, say, groundwater contamination. Nobody particularly likes garbage; nobody likes taking it out or paying to have it hauled away. We feel we should be able to control it. Furthermore, controlling it—whether by banning plastics or sorting materials neatly at curbside—alleviates consumer guilt. "There," we say, tossing our bundled newspapers on the curb, "I've done my part for the environment."

10   But for all the psychological benefit that approach may confer, it is distracting us from much more pressing national problems. Trash-handling issues should be debated and decided regionally, and those decisions have to be based, at least in part, on economics. That can't happen when one option—recycling—is elevated by environmentalist rhetoric into a national moral imperative. We have real environmental problems to worry about: We have to protect the water supply. We must improve the quality of the air we breathe. We need a better plan for energy management. And we have to monitor toxic waste more effectively. In that context, it is foolish and extremely wasteful to expend so much effort wringing our hands (and spending our money) on garbage.

QUESTIONS ON SUBJECT AND PURPOSE

1. What reservations does Poore have about the value of recycling household garbage?
2. According to Poore, what are the real threats to our environment?
3. What courses of action would Poore like to see individuals and communities take?

QUESTIONS ON STRATEGY AND AUDIENCE

1. Why might Poore begin her essay with the example of the *Mobro*?
2. Poore gives no statistics, cites no scientific studies, and quotes no experts. Do these omissions affect her argument? If not, why not?
3. What assumptions might Poore make about her audience? Remember that the essay was originally published in the magazine *Garbage: The Practical Journal for the Environment*.

QUESTIONS ON VOCABULARY AND STYLE

1. What does the word "toxic" mean?
2. How would you characterize Poore's tone in the essay? How does that tone affect her argument?
3. Be prepared to define the following words: *pale* (paragraph 2), *alleviates* (9).

WRITING SUGGESTIONS

1. **For your Journal.** To what extent has recycling become a part of your life? Do you consciously recycle garbage? What types? In your immediate environment—on your college campus, in your local community, at your place of employment—what incentives or pressures are in force to encourage recycling? For one day, pay careful attention to your environment and jot down your observations.
2. **For a Paragraph.** Separating out newspapers, glass and plastic containers, and aluminum cans is only one step that the average consumer can take to deal with the garbage crisis. Select another possibility and advocate that course of action in a paragraph directed at consumers.

3. **For an Essay**. Expand the topic that you explored in suggestion 2 into an essay. Your purpose should be to persuade consumers to do one or more things in order to help alleviate the garbage crisis.

Prewriting:

a. Make a list of possible steps that everyone could take. Possibilities might include reducing the use of fertilizers and pesticides on lawns, composting, drinking tap water rather than bottled juices, riding a bicycle to school, using rechargeable batteries. You might read Durning's "How Much is 'Enough'?" for some other possibilities.

b. Ask friends and classmates for other ideas. You might also want to contact local environmental groups for some suggestions.

c. From your list of possible actions, select a limited number that seem reasonable and valuable. Remember that you are trying to persuade your audience to do these things. You are more likely to be successful if your suggestions seem manageable to your readers.

Rewriting:

a. Once you have completed a draft of your essay, make an outline based on what you have written. Does the essay outline easily? Are some points of your argument developed in great detail and some in little detail? Use the outline to try to locate any major structural problems.

b. Have you tried to do too much? Depending upon the depth of your detail, you probably should recommend between one and, at most, four possible actions. If you try to recommend too much, your readers will be overwhelmed.

c. Remember that conclusions are very important in persuasive and argumentative essays. Plan a specific, forceful concluding strategy; do not just stop. Ask a friend or classmate to evaluate your conclusion.

4. **For Research**. How successful is recycling in your community (or in the community where your college is located)? Research recycling efforts and their costs. Is it more expensive to recycle than to dispose of garbage in other ways? Is there a ready market for recycled materials? Using information that you gather on your local level, write an essay in which you argue for or against current recycling efforts. In all likelihood, some of your research will involve interviewing knowledge-

able local experts—from municipal waste disposal authorities, to private contractors, to local environmental groups. Be sure to document your sources wherever appropriate.

How Much Is "Enough"?

Alan Durning

Alan Durning was educated at Oberlin College and Conservatory where he received degrees in music and philosophy. He is currently a senior researcher at Worldwatch Institute where he studies social and environmental problems, equity issues, and the efforts of local, grass roots initiatives to confront global problems.

Durning's "How Much is 'Enough'?" is taken from a 200-page monograph by the same name in the Worldwatch Environmental Alert Series published for the Worldwatch Institute by W.W. Norton. In both the monograph and the following condensation, Durning links consumerism to the depletion and waste of natural resources and raw materials. Dividing the world's population into groups according to income and life-style, Durning examines the energy expenditures generated by each group and advocates a return to a life-style based on sufficiency rather than on consumerism.

BEFORE READING

Connecting: How would you define "success"? What will make or does make you feel successful in life?

Anticipating: The major test of an argumentative or persuasive article is how it moves or influences its audience. How do you feel by the end of Durning's article? Have you been persuaded? Are you likely to "do" anything as a result? Why or why not?

1   Early in the post-World War II age of affluence, a U.S. retailing analyst named Victor Lebow proclaimed, "Our enormously productive economy . . . demands that we make consumption our way of life, that we convert the buying and use of goods into rituals, that we seek our spiritual satisfaction, our ego satisfaction, in consumption. . . . We need things consumed, burned up, worn out, replaced, and discarded at an ever increasing rate." Americans have risen to Mr. Lebow's call, and much of the world has followed.

2   Since 1950, American consumption has soared. Per capita, energy use climbed 60 percent, car travel more than doubled, plastics use multiplied 20-fold, and air travel jumped 25-fold.

We are wealthy beyond the wildest dreams of our ancestors; the average human living today is four-and-a-half times richer than his or her great-grandparents, and the factor is larger still among the world's consuming class. American children under the age of 13 have more spending money—$230 a year—than the 300 million poorest people in the world.   3

The richest billion people in the world have created a form of civilization so acquisitive and profligate that the planet is in danger. The lifestyle of this top echelon—the car drivers, beef eaters, soda drinkers, and throwaway consumers—constitutes an ecological threat unmatched in severity by anything but perhaps population growth. The wealthiest fifth of humankind pumps out more than half of the greenhouse gases that threaten the earth's climate and almost 90 percent of the chlorofluorocarbons that are destroying the earth's protective ozone layer.   4

Ironically, abundance has not even made people terribly happy. In the United States, repeated opinion polls of people's sense of well-being show that no more Americans are satisfied with their lot now than they were in 1957. Despite phenomenal growth in consumption, the list of wants has grown faster still.   5

Of course, the other extreme from over-consumption—poverty —is no solution to environmental or human problems: it is infinitely worse for people and equally bad for the environment. Dispossessed peasants slash-and-burn their way into the rain forests of Latin America, and hungry nomads turn their herds out onto fragile African rangeland, reducing it to desert. If environmental decline results when people have either too little or too much, we must ask ourselves: How much is enough? What level of consumption can the earth support? When does consumption cease to add appreciably to human satisfaction?   6

Answering these questions definitively is impossible, but for each of us in the world's consuming class, seeking answers may be a prerequisite to transforming our civilization into one the biosphere can sustain.   7

THE COMPULSION TO CONSUME

"The avarice of mankind is insatiable," declared Aristotle 23 centuries ago, setting off a debate that has raged ever since among philosophers over how much greed lurks in human hearts. But whatever share of our acquisitiveness is part of our nature, the compulsion to have more has never been so actively promoted, nor so easily acted upon, as it is today.   8

We are encouraged to consume at every turn by the advertising industry, which annually spends nearly $500 per U.S. citizen, by the   9 commercialization of everything from sporting events to public spaces, and, insidiously, by the spread of the mass market into realms once dominated by family members and local enterprises. Cooking from scratch is replaced by heating prepared foods in the microwave; the neighborhood baker and greengrocer are driven out by the 24-hour supermarket at the mall. As our day-to-day interactions with the economy lose the face-to-face character that prevails in surviving communities, buying things becomes a substitute source of self-worth.

10   Traditional measures of success, such as integrity, honesty, skill, and hard work, are gradually supplanted by a simple, universally recognizable indicator of achievement—money. One Wall Street banker put it bluntly to the *New York Times*: "net worth equals self-worth." Under this definition, there is no such thing as enough. Consumption becomes a treadmill with everyone judging their status by who's ahead of them and who's behind.

TECHNOLOGIES OF CONSUMPTION

11   In simplified terms, an economy's total burden on the ecological systems that undergird it is a function of three factors: the size of the human population, people's average consumption level, and the broad set of technologies—everything from mundane clotheslines to the most sophisticated satellite communications systems—the economy employs to provide for those consumption levels.

12   Transformations of agricultural patterns, transportation systems, urban design, energy use, and the like could radically reduce the total environmental damage caused by the consuming societies, while allowing those at the bottom of the economic ladder to rise without producing such egregious effects.

13   Japan, for example, uses one-third as much energy as the Soviet Union to produce a dollar's worth of goods and services, and Norwegians use half as much paper and cardboard apiece as their neighbors in Sweden, though they are equals in literacy and richer in dollar terms.

14   Eventually, though, technological change will need to be complemented by curbing our material wants. Robert Williams of Princeton University and a worldwide team of researchers conducted a careful study of the potential to reduce fossil fuels consumption through greater efficiency and use of renewable energy.

15   The entire world population, Williams concluded, could live with the quality of energy services enjoyed by West Europeans—

things like modest but comfortable homes, refrigeration for food, and ready access to public transit, augmented by limited auto use.

The study had an implicit conclusion, however: The entire 16 world population decidedly could *not* live in the style of Americans, with their larger homes, more numerous electrical gadgets, and auto-centered transportation systems.

The details of such studies will stir debate among specialists for 17 years to come. What matters for the rest of us is the lesson to hope and work for much from technological and political change, while looking to ourselves for the values changes that will also be needed.

CONSUMING DRIVES

The realities of current consumption patterns around the world point 18 toward quantitative answers to the question of how much is enough?

For three of the most ecologically important types of con- 19 sumption—transportation, diet, and use of raw materials—the world's 5.3 billion people are distributed unevenly over a vast range. Those at the bottom clearly fall beneath the "too little" line, and those at the top, the cars-meat-and-disposables class, clearly consume too much. But where in the larger middle class does "enough" lie?

About one billion people do most of their traveling—aside from 20 the occasional donkey or bus ride—on foot. Many in the walking class never go more than 100 miles from their birthplaces. Unable to get to work easily, attend school, or bring their complaints before government offices, they are severely hindered by the lack of trans-portation options.

The massive middle class of the world, numbering some three 21 billion people, travels by bus and bicycle. Mile for mile, bikes are cheaper than any other vehicles, costing under $100 in most of the Third World and requiring no fuel. They are also the most efficient form of transportation ever invented and, where not endangered by polluted air and traffic, provide their riders with healthy exercise.

The world's automobile class is relatively small: only 8 percent 22 of humans, about 400 million, own cars. The auto class's fleet of four-wheelers is directly responsible for an estimated 13 percent of carbon dioxide emissions from fossil fuels worldwide, along with air pollu-tion and acid rain, traffic fatalities numbering a quarter million an-nually, and the sprawl of urban areas into endless tract developments lacking community cohesion.

The auto class bears indirect responsibility for the far-reaching 23 impacts of their chosen vehicle. The automobile makes itself indispensable: cities sprawl, public transit atrophies, shopping centers multiply, employers scatter. Today, working Americans spend nine hours a week behind the wheel. To make these homes-away-from-home more comfortable, 90 percent of new American cars are air-conditioned, which adds emissions of gases that aggravate the greenhouse effect and deplete the ozone layer.

24 Around the world, the great marketing achievement of automobile vendors has been to turn the machine into a cultural icon. As French philosopher Roland Barthes writes, "cars today are almost the exact equivalent of the great Gothic cathedrals . . . the supreme creation of an era, conceived with passion by unknown artists, and consumed in image if not in usage by a whole population which appropriates them as purely magical objects."

25 Ironies abound: more "Eagles" drive America's expanding road network, for instance, than fly in the nation's polluted skies, and more "Cougars" pass the night in its proliferating garages than in its shrinking forests.

26 Some in the auto class are also members of a more select group: the global jet set. The four million Americans who account for 41 percent of domestic trips, for example, cover five times as many miles a year as average Americans. Furthermore, because each mile traveled by air uses more energy than a mile traveled by car, jet setters consume six-and-a-half times as much energy for transportation as ordinary car-class members.

EAT, DRINK, AND BE SUSTAINABLE

27 On the food consumption ladder, people of the world fall into three rungs reflecting calories eaten and the richness of diet. The world's 630 million poorest people lack the resources necessary to provide themselves with sufficient calories for a healthy diet, according to the latest World Bank estimates.

28 The 3.4 billion grain eaters of the world's middle class get enough calories and plenty of plant-based protein, giving them the healthiest basic diet of the world's people. They typically receive no more than 20 percent of their calories from fat, a level low enough to protect them from the consequences of excessive dietary fat.

29 The top of the ladder is populated by the meat eaters, those who obtain about 40 percent of their calories from fat. These 1.25 billion people eat three times as much fat per person as the remaining 4 billion, mostly because they eat so much red meat (see Table 1). The meat class pays the price of their diet in high death rates from the so-called diseases of affluence—heart disease, stroke, and certain types of cancer.

Argument and Persuasion

Table 1. Per-Capita Consumption of Red Meat, Selected Countries, 1989

Country	Red Meat* (pounds)
E. Germany	211
United States	168
Argentina	161
France	147
Soviet Union	126
Japan	59
Brazil	48
China	46
Egypt	26
El Salvador	10
India	3

*Beef, veal, pork, lamb, mutton, and goat in carcass weight equivalents.
Source: World Livestock Situation, Foreign Agriculture Service, USDA, Washington, D.C., March 1990.

In fact, the U.S. government, long beholden to livestock and dairy interests, now recommends a diet in which no more than 30 percent of calories come from fat. California heart specialist Dr. Dean Ornish, credited with creating the first non-drug therapy proven to reverse clogging of the arteries, prescribes a semi-vegetarian diet virtually indistinguishable from that eaten daily by peasants in China, Brazil, or Egypt.

Indirectly, the meat-eating quarter of humanity consumes almost half of the world's grain—grain that fattens the livestock they eat. They are also responsible for many of the environmental strains induced by the present global agricultural system, from soil erosion to over-pumping of underground water.

In the extreme case of American beef, producing a pound of steak requires five pounds of grain and the energy equivalent of a gallon of gasoline, not to mention the associated soil erosion, water consumption, pesticide and fertilizer runoff, groundwater depletion, and emissions of the greenhouse gas methane.

Beyond the effects of livestock production, the affluent diet rings up an ecological bill through its heavy dependence on shipping goods over great distances. One-fourth of grapes eaten in the United States are grown 7,000 miles away in Chile, and the typical mouthful of food travels 1,300 miles from farm field to dinner plate. America's far-flung agribusiness food system is only partly a product of agronomic forces. It is also a result of farm policies and health standards that favor large producers, massive government subsidies for Western irrigation water, and a national highway system that makes trucking economical by transferring the tax burden from truckers onto car drivers.

34   The thousands of small farms, bakeries, and dairies that once encircled and fed the nation's cities cannot supply chain supermarkets with sufficient quantities of perfectly uniform products to compete with the food industry conglomerates. Their lot is to slide ever closer to foreclosure while hauling their produce to struggling weekend "farmers' markets."

35   Processing and packaging add further resource costs to the affluent diet, though those costs remain largely hidden. Even relatively familiar prepared foods are surprisingly energy consumptive. Ounce for ounce, getting frozen orange juice to the consumer takes four times the energy (and several times the packaging) of providing fresh oranges. Likewise, potato chip production has four times the energy budget of potatoes.

36   The resource requirements of making the new generation of microwave-ready instant meals, loaded as they are with disposable pans and multi-layer packaging, are about ten times larger than preparing the same dishes at home from scratch.

37   Mirroring food consumption, overall beverage intake rises little between poor and rich. What changes is what people drink. The 1.75 billion people at the bottom of the beverage ladder have no option but to drink water that is often contaminated with human, animal, and chemical wastes.

38   Those in the next group up, in this case nearly two billion people, take more than 80 percent of their liquid refreshment in the form of clean drinking water. The remainder of this class's liquids come from commercial beverages such as tea, coffee, and, for the children, milk. At the quantities consumed, these beverages pose few environmental problems. They are packaged minimally, and transport energy needs are low because they are moved only short distances or in a dry form.

39   In the top class are the billion people in industrial countries. At a growing rate, they drink soft drinks, bottled water, and other prepared commercial beverages that are packaged in single-use containers and transported over great distances—sometimes across oceans.

40   Ironically, where tap water is purest and most accessible, its use as a beverage is declining. It now typically accounts for only a quarter of drinks in developed countries. In the extreme case of the United States, per-capita consumption of soft drinks rose to 47 gallons in 1989 (nearly seven times the global mean), according to the

trade magazine *Beverage Industry*. Americans now drink more soda pop than water from the kitchen sink.

THE STUFF OF LIFE

In consumption of raw materials, about one billion rural people sub- 41
sist on local biomass collected from the immediate environment. Most of what they consume each day—about a pound of grain, two pounds of fuelwood, and fodder for their animals—could be self-replenishing renewable resources. Unfortunately, because they are often pushed by landlessness and population growth into fragile, unproductive ecosystems, their minimal needs are not always met.

If these billion are materially destitute, they are part of a larger 42
group that lacks many of the benefits provided by modest use of nonrenewable resources—particularly durable things like radios, refrigerators, water pipes, high-quality tools, and carts with light-weight wheels and ball bearings. More than two billion people live in countries where per-capita consumption of steel, the most basic modern material, falls below 100 pounds a year (see Table 2).

Table 2.   Per-Capita Steel and Energy Consumption,
Selected Countries, 1987

Country	Steel (pounds)	Energy (gigajoules)
Bangladesh	11	2
Nigeria	18	5
India	44	8
Indonesia	46	8
China	141	22
Mexico	205	50
Brazil	218	22
Turkey	328	29
United States	917	280
West Germany	1005	165
Japan	1280	110
Soviet Union	1280	194

Sources: U.S. Bureau of the Census, Statistical Abstract of the United States: 1990, 110th Edition, Washington, D.C., 1990; World Resources Institute, 1990 (New York: Basic Books, 1990).

Though similar international data are not available for most 43
other basic raw materials, energy consumption can serve as a substi-

Durning / How Much Is "Enough"?   463

tute indicator since most processes that use lots of raw materials also use lots of energy. In those same countries, per-capita consumption of all types of energy (except subsistence fuelwood) is lower than 20 gigajoules per year (see Table 2).

44   Roughly one-and-a-half billion live in the middle class of materials users. Providing them with durable goods each year uses between 100 and 350 pounds of steel per capita and between 20 and 50 gigajoules per capita. At the top of the heap is the throwaway class, which uses raw materials like they're going out of style. A typical resident of the industrialized world uses 15 times as much paper, 10 times as much steel, and 12 times as much fuel as a resident of the developing world. The extreme case is again the United States, where the average person consumes most of his or her own weight in basic materials each day (see Table 3).

Table 3.   Estimated Daily U.S. Consumption
of Raw Materials, 1989

Material	Pounds (per capita)
Petroleum and Coal	40
Other Minerals	30
Agricultural Products	26
Forest Products	19
Total	115

Source: U.S. Government agencies.

45   In the throwaway economy, packaging is the essence of the product. It is at once billboard, shipping container, and preservative. Seven percent of consumer spending in the United States goes for packaging. Yet, it all ends up in the dump. Disposable goods proliferate in America and other industrial countries. Each year, Japan uses 30 million "disposable" single-roll cameras, and Americans toss away 18 billion diapers and enough aluminum cans to make about 6,000 DC-10 jet airplanes.

46   In throwaway economies, even "durable" goods are not particularly durable, nor are they easy to repair. Technological improvement would be expected to steadily raise the average working life of goods. Yet, over time, new items have fallen dramatically in price relative to repair costs, according to data compiled by the Organization for Economic Cooperation and Development. The average life span of most household appliances has stayed level. The reason is that

manufacturers have put their research dollars into lowering production costs, even if it makes repair more difficult.

Tinkerer-filmmaker Tim Hunkin spent two years poking around waste sites in England studying discarded household appliances. His findings, reported in the British magazine *New Scientist*, reveal the prevailing trend toward planned obsolescence and disposability. 47

"The machines that date back to the 1950s are very solid, made mostly of metal with everything bolted or welded together," observes Hunkin. "As the years passed, machines have become more flimsy. More parts are now made of plastic, and they are glued together rather than welded or bolted. . . . Many parts are now impossible to repair. . . . New machines are so cheap that it frequently does not pay to have a faulty appliance repaired professionally." 48

Where disposability and planned obsolescence fail to accelerate the trip from purchase to junk heap, fashion sometimes succeeds. Most clothing goes out of style long before it is worn out, but lately, the realm of fashion has colonized sports footwear, too. Kevin Ventrudo, chief financial officer of California-based L.A. Gear, which saw sales multiply fifty times in four years, told the *Washington Post*, "If you talk about shoe performance, you only need one or two pairs. If you're talking fashion, you're talking endless pairs of shoes." 49

In transportation, diet, and use of raw materials, as consumption rises on the economic scale so does waste—both of resources and of health. Bicycles and public transit are cheaper, more efficient, and healthier transport options than cars. A diet founded on the basics of grains and water is gentle to the earth and the body. And a lifestyle that makes full use of raw materials for durable goods without succumbing to the throwaway mentality is ecologically sound while still affording many of the comforts of modernity. 50

ETHICS FOR SUSTAINABILITY

When Moses came down from Mount Sinai, he could count the rules of ethical behavior on his fingers. In the complex global economy of the late 20th century, in which the simple act of turning on an air conditioner affects planetary systems, the list of rules for ecologically sustainable living could run into the hundreds. 51

The basic value of a sustainable society, the ecological equivalent of the Golden Rule, is simple: Each generation should meet its needs without jeopardizing the prospects of future generations. What is lacking is the practical knowledge—at each level of society—of what living by that principle means. 52

In a fragile biosphere, the ultimate fate of humanity may depend on whether we can cultivate a deeper sense of self-restraint, 53 founded on a widespread ethic of limiting consumption and finding non-material enrichment.

54   Those who seek to rise to this environmental challenge may find encouragement in the body of human wisdom passed down from antiquity. To seek out sufficiency is to follow the path of voluntary simplicity preached by all the sages from Buddha to Mohammed. Typical of these pronouncements is this passage from the Bible: "What shall it profit a man if he shall gain the whole world and lose his own soul?"

55   Living by this credo is not easy. As historian David Shi of Davidson College in North Carolina chronicles, the call for a simpler life is perennial through the history of the North American continent: the Puritans of Massachusetts Bay, the Quakers of Philadelphia, the Amish, the Shakers, the experimental utopian communities of the 1830s, the hippies of the 1960s, and the back-to-the-land movement of the 1970s.

56   None of these movements ever gained more than a slim minority of adherents. Elsewhere in the world, entire nations have dedicated themselves to rebuilding human character—sometimes through brutal techniques—in a less self-centered mold, and nowhere have they succeeded with more than a token few of their citizens.

57   It would be hopelessly naive to believe that entire populations will suddenly experience a moral awakening, renouncing greed, envy, and avarice. The best that can be hoped for is a gradual widening of the circle of those practicing voluntary simplicity. The goal of creating a sustainable culture, that is, a culture of permanence, is best thought of as a challenge that will last several generations.

58   Voluntary simplicity, or personal restraint, will do little good, however, if it is not wedded to bold political steps that confront the forces advocating consumption. Beyond the oft-repeated agenda of environmental and social reforms necessary to achieve sustainability, such as overhauling energy systems, stabilizing population, and ending poverty, action is needed to restrain the excesses of advertising, to curb the shopping culture, and to revitalize household and community economies as human-scale alternatives to the high-consumption lifestyle.

59   For example, if fairly distributed between the sexes, cooking from scratch can be dignified and use fewer resources than the frozen instant meal. Just so, communities that turn main streets into walking zones where local artisans and farmers display their products while artists, musicians, and theater troupes perform can provide a richness of human interaction that shopping malls will never match.

60   There could be many more people ready to begin saying "enough" than prevailing opinion suggests. After all, much of what

we consume is wasted or unwanted in the first place. How much of the packaging that wraps products we consume each year—462 pounds per capita in the United States—would we rather never see? How many of the distant farms turned to suburban housing developments could have been left in crops if we insisted on well-planned land use inside city limits?

How many of the unsolicited sales pitches each American receives each day in the mail—37 percent of all mail—are nothing but bothersome junk? How much of the advertising in our morning newspaper—covering 65 percent of the newsprint in American papers—would we not gladly see left out? 61

How many of the miles we drive—almost 6,000 a year apiece in the United States—would we not happily give up if livable neighborhoods were closer to work, a variety of local merchants closer to home, streets safe to walk and bicycle, and public transit easier and faster? How much of the fossil energy we use is wasted because utility companies fail to put money into efficient renewable energy systems before building new coal plants? 62

In the final analysis, accepting and living by sufficiency rather than excess offers a return to what is, culturally speaking, the human home: the ancient order of family, community, good work and good life; to a reverence for excellence of craftsmanship; to a true materialism that does not just care *about* things but cares *for* them; to communities worth spending a lifetime in. 63

Maybe Henry David Thoreau had it right when he scribbled in his notebook beside Walden Pond, "A man is rich in proportion to the things he can afford to let alone." 64

QUESTIONS ON SUBJECT AND PURPOSE

1. How would Durning answer the question "How much is 'enough'?"

2. At three points in his essay, Durning includes tables of information. That information could easily be presented in prose. Why put it into tabular form?

3. What would Durning like to see happen? What possible solutions might there be to the problems that he describes?

QUESTIONS ON STRATEGY AND AUDIENCE

1. In an essay as long as this, what problems does Durning face?

2. Durning both begins and ends his essay with a quotation. How effective is each?

3. What could Durning assume about his audience?

QUESTIONS ON VOCABULARY AND STYLE

1. Why might Durning title his essay "How Much is 'Enough'?"

2. Toward the end of the essay (paragraphs 60–62), Durning poses a series of questions. Why?

3. Be prepared to define the following words: *affluence* (paragraph 1), *profligate* (4), *echelon* (4), *avarice* (8), *insatiable* (8), *insidiously* (9), *supplanted* (10), *egregious* (12), *augmented* (15), *atrophies* (23), *biomass* (41), *gigajoule* (43), *credo* (55).

WRITING SUGGESTIONS

1. For your Journal. In paragraph 57, Durning writes of the need to widen the circle of those "practicing voluntary simplicity." Assuming that you feel some sympathy with the position that Durning is advocating, make a list of ways in which you might practice "voluntary simplicity" or "personal restraint." Try to make your list meaningful, but also realistic.

2. For a Paragraph. Select one of the alternatives that you found in your journal writing and expand that idea into a paragraph in which you attempt to persuade others to join you in this particular act of "simplicity" or "restraint."

3. For an Essay. In citing examples of excessive consumption, Durning covers complex institutionalized practices which individuals might feel helpless to control, as well as fairly simple practices that individuals could in fact change. Select one or more of these simple suggestions—or another you think of—and write an essay in which you try to persuade your audience to adopt a particular course of action. You might, for example, consider one or more of the following:

a. Drinking tap water instead of soda (pop, soft drinks) or bottled water

b. Riding a bicycle or using public transit instead of driving

c. Cooking from "scratch" instead of using prepared foods

d. Modifying diet

e. Not using disposable single-roll cameras and other such single-use products

Argument and Persuasion

Prewriting:

a. Make a list of possible courses of action. Jot down ideas over a two-day period.

b. Select the four best actions and freewrite on each topic for fifteen minutes. Do not stop; do not edit. Just allow your mind and hand to explore the topic.

c. Make a list of all the possible objections that your audience might have to your proposals. Jot down a sentence or two in response to each objection.

Rewriting:

a. Look carefully at your language. Have you invited your reader's support and concern, or have you attacked your reader?

b. Try to anticipate your audience's response by asking several classmates or friends to read your essay. Do they find your argument convincing? Are they likely to change their behavior in these areas? Why or why not? Use that information to rethink your strategy in the essay.

c. Conclusions are particularly important in argumentative and persuasive essays. Look at what you have written. Did you, for example, spend as much time on the conclusion as you did on the introduction? Do you end forcefully? Do you clearly state what you would like your reader to do?

4. For Research. The goal toward which Durning wants his readers to strive is that of a "sustainable society," one that "meets its needs without jeopardizing the prospects of future generations." Given the current consumption of the United States, what will happen to future generations? Select a single topic of concern—for example, air pollution, water pollution, energy consumption, raw material consumption—and research the predictions that scientists make for our future generations. When will we "run out"? When will future generations suffer? Once you have that background information, write a research paper in which you argue for specific changes in our society. Be sure to document your sources wherever appropriate.

NONE OF THIS IS FAIR

Richard Rodriguez

Born in 1944 in San Francisco to Spanish-speaking Mexican-American parents, Richard Rodriguez first learned English in grade school. Educated in English literature at Stanford, Columbia University, and the University of California at Berkeley, Rodriguez is best known for his conservative opinions on bilingual education and affirmative action and in "None of This Is Fair" he uses his personal experience to argue that affirmative action programs are ineffective in reaching those who are seriously disadvantaged. Yet, he also suggests in his two autobiographical works, Hunger of Memory: The Education of Richard Rodriguez *(1982) and* Days of Obligation: An Argument with My Mexican Father *(1992), that he harbors deep regret at losing his own Hispanic heritage when he became assimilated into the English-speaking world.*

Basically, the phrase "affirmative action" refers to policies and programs that try to redress past discrimination by increasing opportunities for underrepresented (or minority) groups. In the United States, the major classifications affected by affirmative action are defined by age, race, religion, national origin, and sex. The phrase was coined in 1965 in an executive order issued by President Lyndon Johnson that required any contractor dealing with the federal government to "take affirmative action to ensure that applicants are employed . . . without regard to their race, creed, color, or national origin." A wide range of court cases have affected, defined, and broadened affirmative action guidelines since then. Affirmative action requirements were extended to educational institutions with the passage of the Equal Employment Act of 1972, as a result of which U.S. colleges and universities increased enrollments of previously underrepresented students.

BEFORE READING

Connecting: To what extent has your education—in elementary and secondary schools—provided you with opportunities that others have not had?

Anticipating: Why did it trouble Rodriguez to be labeled as a "minority student"?

1 My plan to become a professor of English—my ambition during long years in college at Stanford, then in graduate school at Columbia and

Berkeley—was complicated by feelings of embarrassment and guilt. So many times I would see other Mexican-Americans and know we were alike only in race. And yet, simply because our race was the same, I was, during the last years of my schooling, the beneficiary of their situation. Affirmative Action programs had made it all possible. The disadvantages of others permitted my promotion; the absence of many Mexican-Americans from academic life allowed my designation as a "minority student."

For me opportunities had been extravagant. There were fel- 2 lowships, summer research grants, and teaching assistantships. After only two years in graduate school, I was offered teaching jobs by several colleges. Invitations to Washington conferences arrived and I had the chance to travel abroad as a "Mexican-American representative." The benefits were often, however, too gaudy to please. In three published essays, in conversations with teachers, in letters to politicians and at conferences, I worried the issue of Affirmative Action. Often I proposed contradictory opinions. Though consistent was the admission that—because of an early, excellent education—I was no longer a principal victim of racism or any other social oppression. I said that but still I continued to indicate on applications for financial aid that I was a Hispanic-American. It didn't really occur to me to say anything else, or to leave the question unanswered.

Thus I complied with and encouraged the odd bureaucratic 3 logic of Affirmative Action. I let government officials treat the disadvantaged condition of many Mexican-Americans with my advancement. Each fall my presence was noted by Health, Education, and Welfare department statisticians. As I pursued advanced literary studies and learned the skill of reading Spenser and Wordsworth and Empson, I would hear myself numbered among the culturally disadvantaged. Still, silent, I didn't object.

But the irony cut deep. And guilt would not be evaded by avert- 4 ing my glance when I confronted a face like my own in a crowd. By late 1975, nearing the completion of my graduate studies at Berkeley, I was so wary of the benefits of Affirmative Action that I feared my inevitable success as an applicant for a teaching position. The months of fall—traditionally that time of academic job-searching—passed without my applying to a single school. When one of my professors chanced to learn this in late November, he was astonished, then furious. He yelled at me: Did I think that because I was a minority student jobs would just come looking for me? What was I thinking? Did I realize that he and several other faculty members had already written letters on my behalf? Was I going to start acting like some other minority students he had known? They struggled for success and then when it was almost within reach, grew strangely afraid and let it pass. Was that it? Was I determined to fail?

5   I did not respond to his questions. I didn't want to admit to him, and thus to myself, the reason I delayed.

6   I merely agreed to write to several schools. (In my letter I wrote: "I cannot claim to represent disadvantaged Mexican-Americans. The very fact that I am in a position to apply for this job should make that clear.") After two or three days, there were telegrams and phone calls, invitations to interviews, then airplane trips. A blur of faces and the murmur of their soft questions. And, over someone's shoulder, the sight of campus buildings shadowing pictures I had seen years before when I leafed through Ivy League catalogues with great expectations. At the end of each visit, interviewers would smile and wonder if I had any questions. A few times I quietly wondered what advantage my race had given me over other applicants. But that was an impossible question for them to answer without embarrassing me. Quickly, several persons insisted that my ethnic identity had given me no more than a "foot inside the door"; at most, I had a "slight edge" over other applicants. "We just looked at your dossier with extra care and we liked what we saw. There was never any question of having to alter our standards. You can be certain of that."

7   In the early part of January, offers arrived on stiffly elegant stationery. Most schools promised terms appropriate for any new assistant professor. A few made matters worse—and almost more tempting—by offering more: the use of university housing; an unusually large starting salary; a reduced teaching schedule. As the stack of letters mounted, my hesitation increased. I started calling department chairmen to ask for another week, then 10 more days—"more time to reach a decision"—to avoid the decision I would need to make.

8   At school, meantime, some students hadn't received a single job offer. One man, probably the best student in the department, did not even get a request for his dossier. He and I met outside a classroom one day and he asked about my opportunities. He seemed happy for me. Faculty members beamed. They said they had expected it. "After all, not many schools are going to pass up getting a Chicano with a Ph.D. in Renaissance literature," somebody said, laughing. Friends wanted to know which of the offers I was going to accept. But I couldn't make up my mind. February came and I was running out of time and excuses. (One chairman guessed my delay was a bargaining ploy and increased his offer with each of my calls.) I had to promise a decision by the 10th; the 12th at the very latest.

9   On the 18th of February, late in the afternoon, I was in the office I shared with several other teaching assistants. Another graduate student was sitting across the room at his desk. When I got up to leave,

he looked over to say in an uneventful voice that he had some big news. He had finally decided to accept a position at a faraway university. It was not a job he especially wanted, he admitted. But he had to take it because there hadn't been any other offers. He felt trapped, and depressed, since his job would separate him from his young daughter.

I tried to encourage him by remarking that he was lucky at least   10
to have found a job. So many others hadn't been able to get anything. But before I finished speaking I realized that I had said the wrong thing. And I anticipated his next question.

"What are your plans?" he wanted to know. "Is it true you've   11
gotten an offer from Yale?"

I said that it was. "Only, I still haven't made up my mind."   12

He stared at me as I put on my jacket. And smiling, then un-   13
smiling, he asked if I knew that he too had written to Yale. In his case, however, no one had bothered to acknowledge his letter with even a postcard. What did I think of that?

He gave me no time to answer.   14

"Damn!" he said sharply and his chair rasped the floor as he   15
pushed himself back. Suddenly, it was to *me* that he was complaining. "It's just not right, Richard. None of this is fair. You've done some good work, but so have I. I'll bet our records are just about equal. But when we look for jobs this year, it's a different story. You get all of the breaks."

To evade his criticism, I wanted to side with him. I was about to   16
admit the injustice of Affirmative Action. But he went on, his voice hard with accusation. "It's all very simple this year. You're a Chicano. And I am a Jew. That's the only real difference between us."

His words stung me: there was nothing he was telling me that I   17
didn't know. I had admitted everything already. But to hear someone else say these things, and in such an accusing tone, was suddenly hard to take. In a deceptively calm voice, I responded that he had simplified the whole issue. The phrases came like bubbles to the tip of my tongue: "new blood"; "the importance of cultural diversity"; "the goal of racial integration." These were all the arguments I had proposed several years ago—and had long since abandoned. Of course the offers were unjustifiable. I knew that. All I was saying amounted to a frantic self-defense. I tried to find an end to a sentence. My voice faltered to a stop.

"Yeah, sure," he said. "I've heard all that before. Nothing you   18
say really changes the fact that Affirmative Action is unfair. You see that, don't you? There isn't any way for me to compete with you. Once there were quotas to keep my parents out of certain schools; now there are quotas to get you in and the effect on me is the same as it was for them."

19   I listened to every word he spoke. But my mind was really on something else. I knew at that moment that I would reject all of the offers. I stood there silently surprised by what an easy conclusion it was. Having prepared for so many years to teach, having trained myself to do nothing else, I had hesitated out of practical fear. But now that it was made, the decision came with relief. I immediately knew I had made the right choice.

20   My colleague continued talking and I realized that he was simply right. Affirmative Action programs *are* unfair to white students. But as I listened to him assert his rights, I thought of the seriously disadvantaged. How different they were from white, middle-class students who come armed with the testimony of their grades and aptitude scores and self-confidence to complain about the unequal treatment they now receive. I listen to them. I do not want to be careless about what they say. Their rights are important to protect. But inevitably when I hear them or their lawyers, I think about the most seriously disadvantaged, not simply Mexican-Americans, but of all those who do not ever imagine themselves going to college or becoming doctors: white, black, brown. Always poor. Silent. They are not plaintiffs before the court or against the misdirection of Affirmative Action. They lack the confidence (my confidence!) to assume their right to a good education. They lack the confidence and skills a good primary and secondary education provides and which are prerequisites for informed public life. They remain silent.

21   The debate drones on and surrounds them in stillness. They are distant, faraway figures like the boys I have seen peering down from freeway overpasses in some other part of town.

QUESTIONS ON SUBJECT AND PURPOSE

1. In paragraph 4, Rodriguez makes reference to the "irony" of the situation. In what ways was it ironic?
2. Why does Rodriguez decide to reject all of the offers?
3. Is Rodriguez criticizing affirmative action policies? How could such policies reach or change the lives of those who are really seriously disadvantaged?

QUESTIONS ON STRATEGY AND AUDIENCE

1. To what extent does Rodriguez present a formal argument based on an appeal to reason? To what extent does he attempt to persuade through an appeal to emotion? Which element is stronger in the piece?

2. What is the difference between objectively stating an opinion and narrating a personal experience? Do we as readers react any differently to Rodriguez's story as a result?

3. What expectations does Rodriguez have of his audience? How do you know that?

QUESTIONS ON VOCABULARY AND STYLE

1. In paragraphs 11 through 18, Rodriguez dramatizes a scene with a fellow student. He could have just summarized what was said without using dialogue. What advantage is gained by developing the scene?

2. Be prepared to discuss the significance of the following sentences:

   a. "For me opportunities had been extravagant" (paragraph 2).

   b. "The benefits were often, however, too gaudy to please" (paragraph 2).

   c. "The phrases came like bubbles to the tip of my tongue" (paragraph 17).

   d. "Always poor. Silent" (paragraph 20).

3. What is the effect of the simile ("like the boys I have seen . . .") Rodriguez uses in the final line?

WRITING SUGGESTIONS

1. **For your Journal**. What made you stay in (or return to) school? What are the important motivating factors in your choosing to continue or resume your education? Explore the questions in your journal.

2. **For a Paragraph**. Describe a time when you encountered an obstacle because of your age, gender, race, religion, physical ability, physical appearance, or socioeconomic status. Describe the experience briefly and then argue against the unfairness of such discrimination.

3. **For an Essay**. Are minorities and women fairly represented on the faculty of your college or university? Check the proportion of white males to minority and women faculty member, looking not only at raw numbers but also at rank, tenure, and so forth. Then, in an essay, argue for or against the need to achieve a better balance.

Prewriting:

a. Before you begin writing, you will need accurate information. The Affirmative Action Office at your school can provide those statistics. Check a campus telephone directory to locate that office.

b. Statistics about the undergraduate population of your college will also help. The admissions office or the dean of students should be able to provide a breakdown of the student body.

c. On the basis of your evidence and your own feelings, decide upon a position. Make a list of the evidence and the reasons you will use. Then try to anticipate the objections that your audience will have to your position.

Rewriting:

a. Find a classmate or roommate to read your essay. Ask that reader to evaluate your position. Does your reader agree with you? Why or why not? Listen carefully to your reader's reaction and try to use that response in revising your paper.

b. Is your essay structured inductively or deductively? Briefly outline a new strategy. Which of the two arrangements seems more effective?

c. Look at your conclusion. Arguments—either emotional or logical—need to end forcefully. Freewrite a totally different ending to your essay. Ask your reader to evaluate both.

4. For Research. Rodriguez feels that as a result of "an early, excellent education" (paragraph 2), he was no longer "a principal victim of racism or any other social oppression." If the key to helping the "seriously disadvantaged" lies in improving the quality of elementary and secondary education, how successful have American schools been? Has the quality of education for the disadvantaged improved in the last 20 years? Research the problem, and then write an essay in which you evaluate some existing programs and make recommendations about continuing, expanding, modifying, or dropping them. Be sure to document your sources wherever appropriate.

GREETINGS FROM THE
ELECTRONIC PLANTATION
Roger Swardson

As he explains in the following article, Richard Swardson has worked as a telephone representative for Wireless, a mail-order company affiliated with Minnesota Public Radio. The original version was published in the Minneapolis–St. Paul-based City Pages, *an alternative newspaper, to which Swardson is a regular contributor; this edited version appeared in the* Utne Reader.

In "Greetings from the Electronic Plantation," Swardson details a typical day's experiences as a telephone service representative, calling attention to the repetition and monotony, impermanence, lack of benefits, and low pay that characterize many of the "temporary" jobs that have become so common in American business and industry. His persuasive strategy here is an interesting one in that he advocates no specific course of action; his goal seems to be to sow the seeds of change by bringing the plight of workers in this and related industries to the attention of those who might be able to affect public policy.

BEFORE READING

Connecting: What expectations do you have of the career opportunities that await you when you graduate from college?

Anticipating: What aspects of Swardson's job would you find the most troubling personally?

Out in the economic sector where you work all week but can't make a living, lots of us are fastened like barnacles to the bottom of the computer revolution. Soldering tiny leads on circuit boards. Plugging data into terminals. All sorts of things that tend to share one characteristic: repetition. Some of the jobs, like mine, consist of sitting in a chair while, all day long, people call you from all over the country to buy things like T-shirts that read "Compost Happens." 1

Just after 9 a.m., a tireless recorded voice in my headset tips me off. A catalog shopper is coming my way from across the continent. I press the appropriate key and say, "Good morning, welcome to Wireless. My name is Roger. How can I help you?" 2

3   Wireless is one of five direct-mail catalogs operated by River-town Trading Company, a shirttail relation of Minnesota Public Radio, the spawning ground of Garrison Keillor.

4   This morning I walk through a new industrial park to the clusters of smokers hanging around the lone door in the block-long wall of a warehouse. Once inside I show my picture ID to the guard behind the glass window and stick another plastic card in the time clock.

5   I initial the sheet that tells me when to take my morning and afternoon 15-minute breaks and half-hour lunch period. I nod good morning to two women at the group leader station that overlooks the room. They smile and nod back. Both are concentrating on computer terminals that identify scores of telephone service representatives (TSRs) like me who have logged onto the system this morning. The screens tell the group leaders exactly what all the TSRs are doing in the system and for how many seconds they have been doing it. In a seven-day period prior to Christmas 1991, despite the lousy economy, about 300 of us in two shifts wrote 87,642 mail or credit card orders, up 47 percent from the year before.

6   One supervisor in a headset has a distant look on her face. She's monitoring a TSR, tapping into a customer call to check on two dozen points that must be covered. The TSR will be told the results later in the day.

7   I fill up my coffee mug and check the printout taped to the wall next to the time card rack. The printout summarizes the results of our weekly monitorings. Ideally we should get 24 pieces of information from the customer (like home phone, work address, whether or not they want to be on our mailing list) during the course of the conversation. During the monitorings, we are graded according to how much of the data we have gotten, which is a difficult task when you've got a customer on the other end of the line who just wants to make a purchase and hang up without being asked a bunch of questions. We are expected to maintain an average above 90 percent. The names of all TSRs in the 90s have been highlighted with a blue marker. I'm at 89.6 percent. It has been suggested that I could use additional training.

8   I head down a double row of 20 stalls where the backsides of seated people stick out like the rumps of Guernsey cows. The room is done in tones of gray, and merchandise is pinned to white walls. The 80 stalls I can see are mostly occupied. There is a continuous yammer like audience noise before a concert. On two walls electronic scoreboards flash the number of calls completed for each of five catalogs. The total is around 2,200. A busy morning. Must have been a big catalog mailing.

9   I find an open stall, adjust the chair height, get my headset on, and log onto the phone and computer systems, using my password.

An orange light on my console indicates that there are callers on hold.

I bring up the initial screen of the order process and tap the button on my phone to signal that I'm ready to take a customer call. A recorded voice instantly says "Wireless." 10

I swing right into it. "Good morning. Welcome to Wireless. My name is Roger. How can I help you?" 11

A woman from New Jersey is distressed. 12

"You have to help me." 13

"Sure, what's the problem?" 14

"I ordered a ring for my husband for our anniversary. Last night we went out and I gave it to him before dinner. Well, he's put on a little weight and it didn't fit. The poor man was so upset he couldn't eat his dinner. Today he's out there running around the neighborhood and getting red in the face." 15

"That's terrible. What can I do?" 16

"Well, I looked at the ring this morning and I ordered a size too small." 17

"Send it back. We'll send you another one right away." 18

"How long will it take?" 19

"If you want to pay extra I can send it overnight air. Regular delivery is 10 working days." 20

"Make it the 10-day. It won't kill him." 21

"Interface" is a word that tells millions of American workers where we fit. We are devices between you and a computer system. Various terms further identify the device: data entry, customer service, word processing, telemarketing, and others. We take reservations. We do market research. We sell people aluminum siding the minute they sit down to dinner. Every night we update computer records so that multinational corporations can begin the day on top of things. We type most of today's business communications. We do all those mundane tasks that provide computer systems with the raw data that makes them useful. 22

Even so, most of us are among the more than 14 million Americans who work every week but are still classified by the government as poor. The people Ross Perot talks about when he says, "I suppose when they are up to six bucks an hour in Mexico and down to six bucks here, American corporations will again begin creating jobs in this country." 23

Here's another way we are classified. The first sentence of my employee handbook tells me that the company "believes in the practice of employment at will, which means that employment is ter- 24 minable by either the employee or the company at any time, for any reason." We are devices that accommodate the economic needs of our era. Flexible. Disposable.

25   Even recyclable.

26   Say a company is "downsizing" or "delayering" or whatever other term describes job cuts. Through a combination of early retirement, attrition, and layoffs they manage to take 200 current semi-skilled employees off the payroll over the course of a year. Say those employees were paid an average of $12 an hour with full benefits. The company then hires a temporary agency to fill openings as they occur. The agency may even have an office in the company's building. Job qualifications are determined, and the agency finds the people and trains them if necessary. The jobs will pay from $5 to $7 an hour. Even with the agency's commission, the company has just saved around $2 million annually in wages and benefits.

27   Improbable? A want ad placed by a temporary employment agency in my St. Paul newspaper lists four major corporations that need temporary workers. The agency is offering a $25 bonus to people with prior experience with any of the listed companies. Today, through the wonders of current economic policy, it is possible to replace yourself at a bargain rate.

28   Here's another way the system works. You have a data entry barn where the job routine is easy and repetitious. The problem is that your volume is changeable, with big bulges around some of the holidays. A permanent work force would be awkward, so you have a standing order with three temporary agencies.

29   When your temporaries show up, they are told their hours will vary as necessary with one week's advance notice. The temps will rarely get a full week's work. They can be sent home any time during the day or let go permanently for any reason. They will receive no benefits. They are subject to a probationary period and can be dropped with a call to the agency. In a relatively short time you have a high-performance, completely flexible work force. You can even offer the best of them permanent part-time jobs, again with no benefits but with a raise in pay. (This actually amounts to a savings, since you no longer have to pay the agency commission.)

30   Look at the costs and problems you have eliminated. Look how easy the system is to manage. All you have to do is keep weeding.

31   This is the employment system of the 1990s, made possible by a bankrupt economy and an increasingly desperate work force.

32   We are the vocational descendants of the dapper clerks in the better stores who knew your sizes and decided when your son ought to be ready for his first suit. Our voices, regardless of how we happen to look or feel that day, are fresh and animated and friendly. We just

happen to be sitting here in jeans and a sweatshirt talking into a little foam ball.

After a while you get into a rhythm. You learn to judge how the calls will go. Women in California invariably say they have shopped with us before when they have not, men everywhere say they have no idea whether they've shopped with us before though many of them are repeaters. 33

Southern women sign off with "Ba-Ba" except for Texans, who just say "Ba," and people from Alaska sound like friends you can rely on, which seems fortunate in that kind of country. I never heard a shrill voice from Alaska. 34

You can easily tell people who are ordering with a purpose and people who love to shop or do it to feel better. One day a woman browsed through the catalog for 18 minutes and ordered more than 3,000 bucks' worth of stuff. I had a pretty good idea the order wouldn't go through, but she had a wonderful time. 35

This two-week pay period I'm able to get in 74 hours at $6 an hour. My take-home, after federal and state taxes and Social Security, is $355.48. With another good pay period plus the 5 percent commission I make by selling merchandise on the specials list, I could net $800 this month. 36

On this particular day I take 57 calls from 23 states. I write $4,096.59 in orders. The biggest is from a guy in California for a selection of videotapes that includes complete sets of the British television shows *Reilly, Ace of Spies* and *Rumpole of the Bailey*. 37

In just over eight months, working at a pace where I am either available for or taking orders more than 90 percent of the time I am logged on, I have taken 4,462 orders and booked nearly $300,000. 38

Even so, many jobs like mine, especially in urban America, are at risk. Workers in American cities cost more than elsewhere simply because it costs more to live here. As a result, there is a kind of ongoing economic cleansing. Software "upgrades" constantly eliminate some jobs, data barns move to cheaper rural locations, and the Caribbean and Mexico are claiming jobs. 39

In the meantime, take that $6-an-hour job that provides about $800 a month if you can get 40 hours a week in, and then add up rent, utilities, phone, food, and transportation. Then try adding a family. 40

It doesn't add up. 41

"Recovery" is a wishful term. It is also a word that means something understandable. Most of us can tell whether we are recovering. Thirty-eight million people below the poverty line is not a persuasive definition of an economic "recovery." 42

43   Leading economic indicators are used by economists to describe conditions as they may be six to nine months in the future. How, if the present constantly worsens, can the future remain perpetually bright? Even schoolchildren can see that that's denial.

44   How else could "downsizing" be heralded for improving corporate profits and aiding the "recovery"? Fewer livelihoods mean "recovery"? For whom?

45   The same with "diminished expectations" or lesser livelihoods. That must mean those economic refugees from companies that let $12-an-hour people go and replaced them with $6 temporaries. These resettled workers are a non-statistical phenomenon. They are employed. But because millions of dollars have been hacked out of their paychecks, they no longer qualify for mortgages, car loans, or credit cards no matter what the interest rate. Who will spend us into the "recovery"?

46   Workers are getting pushed farther down the economic ladder as laid-off skilled workers and recent college graduates secure even the menial jobs. And, on the bottom, public assistance is breaking its seams.

47   Surely, the term "recovery" has become a mockery of the way millions of Americans now live.

48   The rest of us come and go. The young. Men without jobs. People picking up some extra money. But women between 40 and 60 are always there, plugging away at countless uninspiring jobs that need doing day in and day out, year in and year out.

49   On break they sit together eating homemade food out of Tupperware while the rest of us use the vending machines. They show each other craft handiwork. They bring packets of photos. They take work seriously and talk about the merchandise and what kind of a day they're having. They do well at jobs many make fun of or would not do. And they succeed at life as it is.

50   I left a temp job at an insurance company at dusk. A woman was sitting at a terminal in word processing wearing a smock. I said something sprightly like "Working late, huh?" And that started a conversation. It happens easily with night-shift people.

51   Her husband put in 27 years on the production line of a company that went broke and then cheated him out of his pension. She worked for a small office-equipment firm and the same thing happened. He is now a part-time security guard. She holds down two temporary jobs. Their jobs don't provide health insurance, and they can't afford it. They put in a lifetime working, raising their kids, and they must continue working indefinitely. I was enraged but she passed it off. Gave me a brownie. Then in the lighted corner of the darkened office floor she went to work, producing letters from dictation. As I

left I could hear the tape of some dayside junior exec talking through his nose about yet another intolerable situation that had come to his attention.

The caller's voice does not hold together well. I can tell he is quite old and not well. He is calling from Maryland. 52

"I want four boxes of the Nut Goodies," he rasps at me after giving me his credit card information in a faltering hurry. 53

"There are 24 bars in each box" I say in case he doesn't know the magnitude of his order. Nut Goodies are made here in St. Paul and consist of a patty of maple cream covered with milk chocolate and peanuts. Sort of a Norwegian praline. 54

"OK, then make it five boxes but hurry this up before my nurse gets back." 55

He wants the order billed to a home address but sent to a nursing home. 56

"I've got Parkinson's," he says. "I'm 84." 57

"OK, sir. I think I've got it all. They're on the way." I put a rush on it. 58

"Right. Bye," he says, and in the pause when he is concentrating God knows how much energy on getting the receiver back in its cradle, I hear a long, dry chuckle. 59

One hundred and twenty Nut Goodies. 60

Way to go, buddy. 61

During our time together I am not sucking cough drops and scratching for rent money and she, with her mellow alto, is not calling from a condo at Sea Island. We are two grandparents talking over the selection of videos for her grandson's seventh birthday. We settle on classics, among them *The Red Balloon*, *Old Yeller*, and *Fantasia*. 62

I say "we" because when I'm on the phone I identify with the people I speak with; I'm no longer an electronic menial. And it's not just me. We all do it. I can hear my neighbors. You'd think we were at a Newport garden party. 63

We identify with wealth because none of us, moneyless, think of ourselves as poor. We'll be on this plantation another month. Maybe two. That $10 job will come through. That ominous feeling around the tooth will go away. The car won't break again. We'll be on our way presently. 64

Except there's a feeling these days that's hard to pin down. A detachment that comes out now and then as rage or despair. Many of the people I work with are bone-tired from just trying to make it week by week. A lot of people have just plain stopped believing any politician. 65

66   For years the working poor in this country have felt they had a pact with the powerful. Work hard and you'll be OK. Do your job well and you'll have the basics and a chance to move up. The rich and powerful, because they run the system, have been stewards of that promise. It means when the chips are down, the preservation of opportunity is supposed to come before the cultivation of privilege.

67   On the bus and in the break room today there is a great deal of frustration. The promise has been broken and people don't really know what they can do about it. Another system has taken the place of the old pact. Those who have found a secure place in the suburbs, in government, in the corporations, in wealth, have redefined the country under a different set of rules. It is a smug new club. And those riding the bus and sitting in the break room need not apply.

68   At the end of my shift I log off the computer and phone system, nod good-bye to the two women at the supervisory station, punch out, open my backpack for the guard so he knows I'm not stealing anything, and head for the bus.

69   Not a bad day. Remarkably like yesterday.

QUESTIONS ON SUBJECT AND PURPOSE

1. What associations do you make with the word "plantation"? Why might Swardson choose to use that word?

2. Why does Swardson describe in some detail the environment in which he works?

3. Swardson never argues for a specific reform of the system in which he is caught. Why then might he have written the essay?

QUESTIONS ON STRATEGY AND AUDIENCE

1. Swardson includes two conversations that he has with customers (paragraphs 11–21, and 52–61). Why?

2. At a number of points (for example, paragraphs 5, 7, 8, 36–38), Swardson includes very precise details. What is the effect of such a strategy?

3. What expectations might Swardson have about his audience?

QUESTIONS ON VOCABULARY AND STYLE

1. In what other context might you find the phrase "greetings from . . ."?

2. When Swardson goes to his computer terminal, he writes: "I head down a double row of 20 stalls where the backsides of seated people stick out like the rumps of Guernsey cows" (paragraph 8). What is this figure of speech?

3. Be prepared to define the following words: *mundane* (paragraph 22), *attrition* (26), *dapper* (32), *menial* (46), *stewards* (66).

WRITING SUGGESTIONS

1. For your Journal. Think about a job that you either have had or now have. What were the conditions under which you worked? What were the economic realities? Jot down a series of observations that could be used in an essay similar to Swardson's.

2. For a Paragraph. Using your notes from your journal entry, write a paragraph in which you describe the job's working conditions. Your paragraph, like Swardson's essay, ought to have a persuasive edge, although like Swardson you should try to allow the conditions to reveal your argument rather than explicitly stating it.

3. For an Essay. Do American workers have the "right" to a permanent job with benefits that pays more than the minimum wage? Is it fair that there are 14 million Americans "who work every week but are still classified by the government as poor"? Can American businesses only compete if labor costs are controlled? Should executive salaries be so much greater than those of workers? In an essay, argue the "cause" of either the worker or of American business.

Prewriting:

a. Brainstorm on both sides of the argument regardless of the position that you intend to take. Remember that the quality of your argument is always improved when you understand the issues from both points of view.

b. Write a specific statement of the action or reaction that you want to elicit from your audience. As you are writing, use that statement as a way of checking your developing argument.

c. Pay particular attention to how your essay concludes. What would you like your readers to do? How do you want them to feel? Remember that persuasive essays ought to end forcefully.

Rewriting:

a. Make a copy of your essay and highlight in another color all emotionally charged words and phrases. Look carefully at those highlighted sections. How will your audience react to them? Have you avoided distorted or inflammatory statements?

b. An effective title is important to an essay. It should not only represent the essay but also attract a reader's attention. Write several possible titles for your essay. Ask a friend or classmate to comment on each.

c. Look carefully at how you structured your essay. Did you begin with a position and then provide evidence? Did you begin with specific examples and then draw your conclusion? Is the structure you chose the right one for your essay? If you are working on a word processor, block and move your paragraphs to try the opposite structural pattern.

4. For Research. The problems about which Swardson writes are well known to most Americans—either from firsthand experience or from media coverage. How, though, might these problems be solved or at least improved? Research one of the problems of the "working poor" and suggest some possible solutions. Remember to narrow your subject. You might want to focus on the problems of finding affordable day care, diminished health or retirement benefits, the loss of American jobs to foreign countries. Be sure to present a possible strategy for dealing with the problem, and remember to persuade your audience of the wisdom embodied in this strategy. Acknowledge your sources wherever appropriate.

REVISING

Not even the best professional writers produce only perfect sentences and paragraphs. Good writing almost always results from rewriting or revising. Although the words "rewriting" and "revising" are interchangeable, "revising" suggests some important aspects of this vital stage of your writing process: a "re-vision" is a re-seeing of what you have written. In its broadest sense, this "re-seeing" can be a complete rethinking of a paper from idea through execution. As such, revising a paper is quite different from proofreading it for mechanical and grammatical errors. When you proofread, you are mostly looking for small things—misspellings or typographical errors, incorrect punctuation, awkwardly constructed sentences. When you revise, however, you look for larger concerns as well—such things as a clear thesis, an effective structure, or adequate and relevant details.

Revising does not occur only after you have written a complete draft of a paper. In fact, many writers revise as they draft. They may write a sentence, then stop to change its structure, even erase it and start over; they may shift the positions of sentences and paragraphs or delete them altogether. In this search for the right words, the graceful sentence, the clear structure, writers constantly revise.

As essential as this ongoing process is, rewriting should not just be limited to making corrections while writing a first draft. For one thing, this type of revision usually focuses only on the sentence or paragraph being composed. When you are struggling to find the right word or the right sentence structure, you're probably not thinking much about the larger whole.

Consequently, allowing some time to elapse between drafts of your paper is important. You need to put the draft aside for a while if you are to get a perspective on what you have written and read your paper objectively. For this reason, it is important to finish a complete draft at least one day before you have to hand in the paper. If circumstances prevent you from finishing a paper until an hour or two before class, you will not have a chance to revise. The most that you can do is proofread.

ANALYZING YOUR OWN WRITING

The key to improving your writing is self-awareness. You have to look carefully and critically at what you have written, locate those areas that caused you the most problems, and then work to correct them. Most writers are, in fact, able to identify the key problems that they faced in a particular paper or in writing in general, even though they might not know how to solve those problems. Knowing what causes you problems is the essential first step toward solving them.

When you analyze the first draft of a paper, begin by asking a series of specific questions, starting with the larger issues and working toward the smaller. Ideally, you should write out your answers—doing so will force you to have a specific response. Here are some questions you might consider:

1. What were you asked to do in this paper? Look again at the assignment. Circle the key action words, verbs such as "analyze," "argue," "classify," "compare," "criticize," "define," "describe," "evaluate," "narrate," "recommend," "summarize." Have you done what you were asked to do?

2. What is the thesis of your paper? Can you find a single sentence in your essay that sums up that thesis? If so, underline it. If not, write a one-sentence thesis statement.

3. How have you organized your paper? That organization ought to be conveyed in the way the paper has been paragraphed. Make an outline that contains only as many subdivisions as you have paragraphs.

4. Is each paragraph focussed around a single idea? Is there an explicit statement of that idea? If so, underline it. If not, jot down in the margin the key word or words. Should that idea be specifically stated in the paragraph? Is that idea developed

adequately? Are there enough supporting details and examples?

5. What strategies did you use to begin and end your essay? Does your introduction seem likely to catch the reader's attention? Do you have a concluding paragraph or do you just stop?

Only after you have asked and answered these kinds of questions about the larger elements of your paper should you move to questions directed toward style, grammar, and mechanics:

6. Is everything you punctuated as a sentence in fact a complete sentence? Check each sentence to make sure.

7. Look carefully at every mark of punctuation. Is it the right choice for this place in the sentence?

8. Check your choice of words. Are you certain of what each word means? Are there any words that might be too informal or too colloquial (words that are appropriate in a conversation with friends but not in academic writing)? Is every word spelled correctly? (If you have *any* doubt about *any* word, look it up in a dictionary.)

KEEPING A REVISION LOG

Keeping a log of writing problems you most often encounter is an excellent way of promoting self-awareness. Your log should include subdivisions for a wide range of writing problems, not just grammatical and mechanical errors. The log will help you keep track of the areas that you know you have trouble with and those your instructor, peer readers, or writing tutors point out as needing improvement. Do you have a tendency to overparagraph? To stop rather than conclude? To have trouble with parallelism? Each time you discover a problem or one is pointed out to you, list it in your log. Then, as you revise your papers, look back through your revision log to remind yourself of these frequent problems and look closely for them in your current draft.

If a revision log seems a lot of trouble, remember that only you can improve your own writing. Improvement, in turn, only comes with recognizing your weaknesses and working to correct them.

Most of the writing you'll do in school is aimed toward only one reader—a teacher. Writing just for a teacher has both advantages and disadvantages. On one hand, a teacher is a critical reader who evaluates your paper by a set of standards. A teacher, though, can also be a sympathetic reader, one who understands the difficulties of writing and is patient with the problems that writers have. Classmates, colleagues, or supervisors can be just as critical as teachers but less sympathetic.

Only in school, however, do you have someone who will read everything that you write and offer constructive comments. After you graduate, your letters and reports will be read by many different readers, but you will no longer have a teacher to offer advice or a tutor to conference with you. Instead, you will have to rely on your own analysis of your writing and on the advice of your fellow workers. For this reason, learning to use a peer reader as a resource in your revising process is extremely important. At first, you might feel a little uncomfortable asking someone other than your instructor to read your papers, but after some experience you will feel better about sharing. Remember that every reader is potentially a valuable resource for suggestions.

PEER EDITING

Many college writing courses use peer editing as a regular classroom activity. On a peer editing day, students swap papers with their classmates and then critique one another's work, typically using a list of peer editing guidelines. But you don't have to do peer editing in class to reap the benefits of such an arrangement. If your instructor approves, you can arrange to swap papers with a classmate outside of class or you can ask a roommate or a friend to do a peer reading for you.

From the start, though, several ground rules are important. First, when you ask a peer to edit your paper, you are asking for criticism. You want advice; you want reaction. You cannot expect that your reader will love everything that you have written.

Second, peer editing is not proofreading. You should not just ask your reader to look for misspelled words and missing commas. Rather, you want your reader to react to the whole paper. Is the thesis clear? Does the structure seem appropriate? Are there enough examples or details? Does the introduction catch the reader's attention and make him or her want to keep reading? You need to keep your reader's attention focussed on these larger, significant issues. One good way to do so is to give your reader a checksheet or a set of questions that reflect the criteria appropriate for evaluating this kind of paper.

Third, you want a peer reader to offer specific and constructive criticism. To get that type of response, you must ask questions that invite—or even require—a reader to comment in more than "yes" and "no" answers. For example, do not ask your reader, "Is the thesis clear?"; instead ask, "What is the thesis of this paper?" If your reader has trouble answering that question or if his or her answer differs from your answer, you know that this aspect of your paper needs more work.

GROUP EDITING

Sharing your writing in a small group is another good way to get reader reaction to your papers. Such an editing activity can take place either inside or outside of the classroom. In either case, you can prepare for a group editing session in the same way. Plan to form a group of four or five students and make enough copies of your paper for each group member. If possible, distribute those copies prior to the group editing session so that each member will have a chance to read and prepare some comments for the discussion. Then follow these guidelines:

Before the group editing session

1. Read each paper carefully, marking or underlining the writer's main idea and key supporting points. Make any other notes about the paper that seem appropriate.
2. On a separate sheet, comment specifically on one or two aspects of the paper that most need improvement.

At the group editing session

1. When it is your turn, read your own paper aloud to the group. Since you might hear problems as you read, keep a pen or pencil handy to jot down notes.
2. When you are finished, tell the group what you would like them to comment on.
3. Listen to their remarks and make notes. Feel free to ask group members to explain or expand on their observations. Remember, you want as much advice as you can get.
4. Collect the copies of your paper and the sheets on which the group members have commented on specific areas that need improvement.

After the group editing session

1. Carefully consider both the oral and written comments of your group. You may not agree with everything that was said, but you need to weigh each comment.

2. Revise your paper. Remember that you are responsible for your own work. No one else—not your instructor, your peer editors, your group readers—can or should tell you *everything* that you need to change.

Using Your School's Writing Center or a Writing Tutor

Most colleges operate writing centers, writing labs, or writing tutor programs. Their purpose is to provide individual assistance to any student who has a question about writing. They are staffed by trained tutors who want to help you. In part, such services are intended to supplement the instruction that you receive in a writing class, since most writing teachers have too many students to be able to offer extensive help outside of class to everyone. These services also exist to provide advice to students writing papers for courses in other disciplines where writing might be required, but not discussed.

If you are having trouble with grammar or mechanics, if you consistently have problems with beginnings, or middles, or ends of papers, if you are baffled by a particular assignment, do not be afraid to ask for help. After all, every writer can benefit from constructive advice or additional explanations, and writing centers and tutors exist to provide that help. Remember, though, that a writing tutor is a teacher whose job is to explain and to instruct. You do not drop off your paper at the writing center like you drop off your automobile at the service station. Your tutor will suggest ways that *you* can improve your paper or follow a particular convention. A tutor will not do the work for you.

Come to your appointment with a specific set of questions or problems. Why are you there? What do you want to discuss? What don't you understand? After all, when you have a medical problem, you make an appointment with a doctor to discuss a specific set of symptoms. A conference with a writing tutor should work in a similar way.

Finally, make sure that you keep some form of written record of your conference. Jot down the tutor's advice and explanations.

Those notes will serve as a valuable reminder of what to do when you are revising your paper.

CONFERENCING WITH YOUR INSTRUCTOR

Your instructor in a writing class is always willing to talk with you about your writing. You can, of course, visit your instructor during scheduled office hours. In addition, many instructors, provided that their teaching schedule permits it, will schedule a set of regular conference times spaced throughout the semester. Whatever the arrangement, such a conference is an opportunity for you to ask questions about your writing in general or about a particular paper.

Whether you have asked for the conference or the instructor has scheduled it as a part of the class requirements, several ground rules apply. As with a tutoring session, you should always come to an instructor conference with a definite agenda in mind and a specific set of questions to ask. Writing these questions out is an excellent way to prepare for a conference. Generally, a conference is intended to be a dialogue, and so your active participation is expected. Do not be surprised, for example, if your instructor begins by asking you what you want to talk about. Since time is always limited (remember that your instructor might have to see dozens of students), you will not be able to ask about everything. Try to concentrate on those issues that trouble you the most.

Instructors like to use conferences as opportunities to discuss the larger issues of a paper: Is the thesis well defined? Is the structure as clear as it might be? Are there adequate transitions? Although your instructor will be happy to explain a troublesome grammatical or mechanical problem, do not expect your instructor to find and fix every mistake in your paper. A conference is not a proofreading session.

A conference is also not a oral grading of your paper. Grading a paper is a complicated task and one that frequently involves seeing your essay in the context of the other papers from the class. As a result, your instructor can not make a quick judgment. Do not ask what grade the paper will receive.

As the conference proceeds, make notes for yourself about what is said. Do not rely on your memory. Those notes will constitute a plan for revising your paper.

At one point or another, virtually everyone has had the injunction "proofread!" written on a paper. (The word "proofreading" is derived from printing terminology: a printer reads and corrects "proofs"— trial impressions made of the pages of set type—before printing a job.) You probably stared in dismay at those obvious slips that somehow managed to escape your eye. Why, you may have asked yourself, was I penalized for what were obviously just careless mistakes? In response, you could ask another question: Why do businesses and industries spend so much money making sure that their final written products are as free from errors as possible?

Basically, the answer is related to an audience's perception of the writer (or the business). If a paper, letter, report, or advertisement contains even minor mistakes, they act as a form of "static" that interferes with the communication process. The reader's attention is shifted away from the message to some fundamental questions about the writer. A reader might wonder why you did not have enough pride in your work to check it before handing it in. Even worse, a reader might question your basic competency as a writer and researcher. As the number of errors in proportion to the total number of words rises, the reader's distraction grows. In college such "static" can have serious consequences. Studies conducted in New York City colleges, for example, revealed that readers would tolerate on the average only five to six basic errors in a 300-word passage before assigning a student to a semester-long remedial English course. The point is that careless mistakes are rhetorically damaging to you as a writer: they undermine your "voice" and authority.

Once you have revised your paper thoroughly, considering the effectiveness of the thesis, the clarity of the organization, the strength of the opening and the conclusion, and any other problems in previous papers that you have listed in your revision log, you are ready to proofread. The secret of proofreading is to make sure that you read each word as you have written it. If you read too quickly, your mind often "corrects" or skips over problems. Force yourself to read each word exactly by moving a ruler or a piece of paper slowly down the page, reading aloud as you go. When you combine looking at the page with listening to the words, you increase your chances of catching mistakes that are visual (such as misspellings) and those that are aural (such as awkward phrasings).

Misspellings are so common that they need special attention. Everyone misspells some words; even the most experienced writer, teacher, or editor, has to check a dictionary for correct spellings of certain words. English is a particularly tricky language, for words are not always spelled the way in which they are pronounced. English has silent "e's" as in "live"; "ph's" and "gh's" that sound like "f's" as in "phone" and "tough"; silent "ough's" and "gh's" as in "through" and "bright." It is easy to get confused about when to double consonants before adding "–ed" to the end of a word or when to drop the final "e" before adding "–able." All of these difficulties are perfectly natural and common. No one expects you to remember how to spell every word in your speaking vocabulary, but people do expect that you will check your writing for misspelled words.

Most misspellings can be eliminated if you do two things. First, recognize the words or kinds of words you are likely to misspell; learn when not to trust your instinct, particularly with words that sound alike, such as *there* and *their* and *its* and *it's*. Second, once you have finished your paper, go back and check your spelling. If you have written your paper on a word processor that has a spell check function, be sure to run it. However, do not rely on that type of checking alone; for example, spell checkers won't show you that you've used *there* when you mean *their*. Always have a dictionary at hand. Go through your essay and look up every word that might be a problem. Doing these two things will go a long way toward eliminating misspellings in your papers.

REVISERS AT WORK

To help you think about what is involved in revising and to help you see how it actually takes place, earlier chapters of this text include draft and final revised versions of student papers. In this chapter you can see professional revisers at work.

The selections in this chapter are arranged in two groups. The first three readings—Peter Elbow's "Quick Revising," William Zinsser's "Simplicity," and Donald M. Murray's "Repeat to Revise"—present advice from distinguished writers and teachers. Elbow explains how to achieve a "quick" revision when we "can't afford to re-see, re-think, and re-write completely." Zinsser insists that the "secret" of good writing is simplicity, something which we can achieve by stripping "every sentence to its cleanest components"; Zinsser not only shares this secret, but he also shows us two sample pages of his own revised prose. Murray argues for revision not as a final, separate stage in the writing process—one practiced only when we have a "finished" draft—but as the repetition of each stage of the process: drafts, he argues, are "experiments in meaning" that are perfected by a series of increasingly specific revisions.

The second section of this chapter offers the final published versions of four popular and widely read essays along with earlier drafts of either the whole essay or of sections of the essay. Just as writers use a variety of composing strategies, they also approach the problem of revising in vastly different ways. For some, the process of composition is so painstaking and logical that a single draft is sometimes sufficient. The revision has taken place in small steps as the writing occurred. For other writers, draft follows draft. One writer, when asked to contribute to this chapter, remarked, "Usually I take many, many drafts, even with simple-minded prose. But as I am sure you know, one cannot really just turn over *actual* drafts, not most of the time. . . . One would have to edit them and so forth."

In the four essays included here you'll see writers revising by adding paragraphs (N. Scott Momaday in "The Way to Rainy Mountain"), reworking an introduction (Nora Ephron in "Revision and Life"), deleting paragraphs (Brent Staples in "Black Men and Public Space"), and rewriting a conclusion (Patricia McLaughlin in "Sis Boom Bah Humbug").

QUICK REVISING

Peter Elbow

Born in New York in 1935, Peter Elbow received a B.A. from Williams College, a B.A. and an M.A. from Exeter College, Oxford, and a Ph.D. in 1969 from Brandeis University. Elbow has held various teaching positions at the Massachusetts Institute of Technology, Franconia College, and Evergreen State College. Currently, he is professor of English at the University of Massachusetts. An insightful analyst of the writing process, Elbow is author, coauthor, or editor of nine books, including Writing Without Teachers *(1973) and* Writing with Power *(1981).*

Elbow once commented, "I got interested in writing because of my own difficulties with it." His interest in problem solving in writing is evident in "Quick Revising": "It is 10:30 P.M. now and you have only ten pages of helter-skelter thinking on paper [and] you need an excellent, polished, full report by tomorrow morning." What do you do? You use Elbow's method of "quick revising."

BEFORE READING

Connecting: Do you always allow time to revise your essays? How much time do you regard as enough in which to do an adequate job of revising?

Anticipating: If you had to distill Elbow's advice about "quick revising" into a sentence or two, what would you say? For Elbow, what are the most important things to worry about when doing a "quick" revision?

The point of quick revising is to turn out a clean, clear, professional final draft without taking as much time as you would need for major rethinking and reorganizing. It is a clean-and-polish operation, not a growing-and-transforming one. You specifically refrain from meddling with any deeper problems of organization or reconceptualization. 1

The best time to use quick revising is when the results don't matter too much. Perhaps you are not preparing a final, finished product but rather a draft for friends. It has to be clear, easy to read— if possible even a pleasure to read. But it needn't be your best work or 2 your final thinking. Perhaps it's a draft for discussion or perhaps just a chance for people to learn your thinking about some matter as though you were writing a letter to them. Or perhaps you are just writing for yourself but you want to clean up your draft so that it will be easier and more productive to read when you come back to it.

3 But there is another situation when you can use quick revising and unfortunately it is the one when you are most likely to use it: an occasion that is *very* important when the writing *has* to work for an important audience, but you lack time. You can't afford to re-see, re-think, and re-write completely your raw writing in the amount of time you have left. Maybe it was your fault and now you are kicking yourself; maybe it was unavoidable. But either way you are stuck. It is 10:30 P.M. now and you have only ten pages of helter-skelter thinking on paper, you need an excellent, polished, full report by tomorrow morning, and you care very much how the reader reacts to it. In such situations you have to contend with anxiety as well as lack of time. You need the discipline of the quick revising process. I will describe it here as though you are preparing a substantial piece of writing for tomorrow morning for an important audience because I want to stress the experience of battle conditions with live ammunition. (If it is a small job such as writing that memo in thirty minutes, you probably won't go through all the separate steps I describe below. You'll probably just stand up and stretch now after your fifteen minutes of raw writing, and use your remaining time to look with fresh eyes through what you've written, figure out what you really want to say, and just write out your final draft—perhaps using substantial portions of your raw writing unchanged.)

4 Quick revising is simple and minimal. A lot depends on having the right spirit: businesslike and detached. A certain ruthlessness is best of all. Not desperate-ruthless, "Oh God, this is *awful*, I've *got* to change *everything*," but breezy-ruthless, "Yes, this certainly does have some problems. I wish I could start over and get the whole thing right, but not this time. I guess I'll just have to put the best face on things." If you are too worried about what you wrote or too involved with it, you'll have to work overtime to get the right spirit. You need to stand outside yourself and be someone else.

5 First, if this piece is for an audience, think about who that audience is and what your purpose is in writing to it. You had the luxury of putting aside all thoughts of audience and purpose during the producing stage (if that helped you think and write better), but now you must keep them in mind as you make critical decisions in revising. Try to see your audience before you as you revise. It's no good ending up with a piece of writing that's good-in-general—whatever that means. You need something that is good for your purpose with your audience. . . .

Next, read through all your raw writing and find the good   6
pieces. When I do it, I just mark them with a line in the margin.
Don't worry about the criteria for choosing them. It's fine to be intuitive. If the sentence or passage feels good for this purpose or seems
important for this audience, mark it.

Next, figure out your single main point and arrange your best   7
bits in the best order. It's easiest if you can figure out your main point
first. That gives you leverage for figuring out what order to put things
in. But sometimes your main point refuses to reveal itself—the one
thing you are really trying to *say* here, the point that sums up everything else. All your writing may be circling around or leading up to a
main idea that you can't quite figure out yet. In such a dilemma, move
on to the job of working out the best order for your good passages.
That ordering process—that search for sequence and priorities—will
often flush your main point out of hiding.

You can just put numbers in the margin next to the good bits to   8
indicate the right order if your piece is short and comfortable for you.
But if it is long or difficult you need to make an outline before you
can really work out the best order. It helps most to make an outline
consist of complete assertions with verbs—*thoughts*, not just *areas*.

And of course as you work out this order or outline you will   9
think of things you left out—ideas or issues that belong in your final
draft that weren't in your raw writing. You can now indicate each of
them with a sentence.

If after all this—after getting, as it were, *all* your points and get-   10
ting them in the right order—you still lack the most important idea
or assertion that ties them all together into a unity; if you have connected all this stuff but you cannot find the single thought that pulls
it all together, and of course this sometimes happens, you simply have
to move on. You have a deadline. There is a good chance that your
main idea or center of gravity will emerge later, and even if it doesn't
you have other options.

The next step is to write out a clean-but-not-quite-final draft of   11
the whole piece—excluding the very beginning. That is, don't write
your first paragraph or section now unless it comes to you easily. Wait
till you have a draft of the main body before deciding how to lead up
to it—or whether it *needs* leading up to. How can you clearly or comfortably introduce something before you know precisely what it is
you are introducing? So just begin this draft with your first definite
point. Out of the blue. Start even with your second or third point if
the first one raises confusing clouds of "how-do-I-get-started."

Perhaps you can use the good passages almost as they are—   12
copy them or use scissors—and only write transitional elements to
get you from one to another. Or perhaps you need to write out most

of it fresh. But you can go fast because you have all your points in mind and in order, and probably you have a clearly stated, single main idea holding it all together.

13   If you don't yet know your single main point, there is a very good chance that it will come to you as you are writing this draft. The process of writing the real thing to the real audience will often drive you to say, "What I'm really trying to make clear to you is . . ." and *there* is your main point. This is especially likely to happen toward the end of your piece as you are trying to sum things up or say why all this is important or makes sense. When your main point emerges late in this way, you may have to go back and fiddle a bit with your structure. It is very common that the last paragraph you write, when you finally say exactly what you mean in the fewest words, is just what you need (with perhaps a minor adjustment) for your first paragraph.

14   On rare occasions you still won't be able to find your main point. You know this is a coherent train of thought, and you know you are saying something, but you cannot sum it up in one sentence. You are stuck and you now have to make some choices. You can open or close your piece with a clear admission that you haven't focused it yet. This is usually the most helpful strategy when you are writing for yourself. (Sometimes, in fact, stating your dilemma—as dilemma—as accurately as you can, serves to produce the solution.) Or you can just present your train of thought without any statement at all of a single main idea. Or you can try to trick the reader into a feeling of unity with a vague, waffling pseudo-summary. But this is dangerous. If a reader sees you waffling he is liable to be mad or contemptuous, and even if he is not conscious of what you are doing he is liable to be irritated. If it is important—for this audience and situation—to end up with a piece of writing that is genuinely unified and focused, there is nothing for it but radical surgery. Settle for the best idea you *can* find in your writing and make that your main point. Organize what goes with it and throw away everything else. This usually hurts because it means throwing away some of your best bits.

15   So now you have a draft and a clear statement of your main idea. Finally you can write what you need for an introductory paragraph or section. Almost certainly you need something that gives the reader a clear sense of your main point—where you are going. If you have been writing under the pressure of a tight deadline your final draft will probably have some problems, and so this is no time for tricky strategies or leaving the reader in the dark. Subtlety is for when you can get everything just right.

16   This is also the time to make sure you have a satisfactory conclusion: a final passage that sums up everything you have said with the precision and complexity that is only possible now that the reader has

read and understood all the details. For example you have to begin an essay for most readers with a general statement that is easy to understand, such as "I want to explain how atomic bombs work," but at the end you can sum up your point more quickly and precisely: "In short, $E = mc^2$."

Now you have a draft of the whole thing that probably comes close to what you'll end up with. The next step is to change from writer-consciousness to reader-consciousness. For in writing that draft you were, obviously enough, functioning as a writer: a person trying to put down on paper what you had finally gotten clear in your own mind. Now you should read through this draft *as a reader*. The best way to do this is to read your draft *out loud*: you won't have to search for places that are unclear or awkward or lacking in life, you will *hear* them. If you are in an office or a library or some other place unsuitable for declaiming, you can get almost as much benefit by silently mouthing or whispering your draft as though you were speaking. If you put your fingers in your ears at the same time, you will actually hear your words good and loud. It is the *hearing* of your own words that serves to get you out of the writer-consciousness and into the audience-consciousness.   17

Finally, get rid of mistakes in grammar and usage. . . .   18

Certain people on certain occasions can afford to collapse some of these steps together and type out their final, clean copy after they have settled on their main idea and numbered or outlined their best bits. But this means paying attention to spelling, grammar, and usage while you are engaged in trying to write clear language: focusing simultaneously on the pane of glass and on the scene beyond it. It's not a wise or efficient thing to do unless you are an exceptionally fluent and polished writer. Most people—and that includes myself—save time by waiting to the very end before worrying about mistakes in grammar and usage.   19

Even if you are writing informally for friends you must take care to get rid of these mistakes. Your friends may say, "Oh, who cares about trivial details of correctness," but in fact most people are prejudiced, even if unconsciously, against writing flawed in this way. They are more apt to patronize your writing or take it less seriously or hold back from experiencing what you are saying if there are mistakes in mechanics.   20

In thinking about the whole process of quick revising, you should realize that the essential act is *cutting*. Learn to leave out everything that isn't already good or easily made good. Learn the pleasures of the knife. Learn to retreat, to cut your losses, to be   21 chicken. Learn to say, "Yes, I *care* more about this passage than about any other, I'm involved in it, but for that very reason, I can't make it work right. Out it goes!" Of course you don't need to be so ruthless about cutting if you are writing something to share informally among friends or to save for yourself. You can retain sections that feel important but don't quite work or don't quite fit. You can let your piece be an interesting muddle organizationally or conceptually—*so long as it's not muddled in wording or sentences*. Friends are willing to ponder your not-quite-digested thinking so long as your sentences and paragraphs are clear and easy to understand.

22   When you have *lots* of time for revising you tend to finish with something longer than you have expected. The thing cooks and grows on its own and you have time to integrate that growth. But quick revising usually produces something shorter than you had expected. The reader should probably finish a bit startled: "Done already? This seems a bit skimpy. Still, everything here is well done. Actually, it's not too bad." Better to give your reader mild disappointment at a certain tight skimpiness than to bog him down in a mess so that he stops paying attention or even stops reading.

23   In the last analysis, the main thing for quick revising is to get into the right spirit. Be your brisk, kindly, British aunt who is also a nurse: "Yes. Not to worry. I know it's a mess. But we'll clean it up and make it presentable in no time. It won't be a work of art, ducks, but it'll do just fine."

QUESTIONS ON SUBJECT AND PURPOSE

1. How does a "quick revision" differ from a "major rethinking and reorganizing" (paragraph 1)?

2. Why does Elbow caution against trying to write an opening paragraph too soon?

3. What is involved in changing from "writer-consciousness" to "reader-consciousness" (paragraph 17)?

QUESTIONS ON STRATEGY AND AUDIENCE

1. This is an example of a process essay (see Chapter 6). How does Elbow organize his process? Does he use any step or sequence markers?

2. What is the effect of using metaphors and images when describing the process of writing and revising? Consider each of the following:

a. "Clean-and-polish operation, not a growing-and-transforming one" (paragraph 1)
b. "Raw writing" (3)
c. "Experience of battle conditions with live ammunition" (3)
d. "Flush your main point out of hiding" (7)
e. "Radical surgery" (14)
f. "Focusing simultaneously on the pane of glass and on the scene beyond it" (19)
g. "The thing cooks and grows on its own" (22)

3. Elbow says: "Try to see your audience before you as you revise." Does Elbow seem to see his audience? Who comprises that audience? How do you know?

QUESTIONS ON VOCABULARY AND STYLE

1. Characterize Elbow's tone in the essay. How does he sound? What techniques does Elbow use to develop that tone?
2. Does Elbow ever use sentence fragments? How many?
3. How appropriate is Elbow's conclusion? Does it coincide with the advice that he gives?
4. Be able to define the following words: *refrain* (paragraph 1), *helter-skelter* (3), *intuitive* (6), *leverage* (7), *waffling* (14), *declaiming* (17), *patronize* (20).

WRITING SUGGESTIONS

1. **For your Journal**. Think about the last paragraph or paper you wrote for this course. How much revising did you do? When did you do it? That is, did you revise as you wrote each paragraph or did you revise once you had a complete draft? In your journal, comment on your revising strategies. After you have finished each paragraph or paper in this course, make a similar entry in your journal so that you have a record of how and what you revise.

2. **For a Paragraph**. Go through Elbow's essay and make a list of the steps involved in "quick revising." Then summarize his procedure in a process paragraph. Assume that your summary will be handed out to your classmates as a revision guide.

3. **For an Essay**. Using the material provided in Elbow's essay and your own writing experience, write an essay about how to revise a paper.

Prewriting:

a. Begin by taking notes on Elbow's essay. Add to this material anything else that works for you.

b. Organize the notes into an outline. Remember, you need to order the notes in an appropriate sequence. For example, are the steps chronological (do this, then that)?

c. Make sure that you have provided adequate transitional step or sequence markers. Underline those that you already have, and, if necessary, add others.

Rewriting:

a. Look back over Elbow's essay, and follow his advice in revising your essay.

b. Elbow's essay is very "reader friendly." He tries to make the process sound easy; he is very reassuring. Is that an effective strategy to use in a process essay? What about your essay? What is its tone? Does it sound helpful? Interesting? Or does it sound boring? Ask a peer reader to characterize the tone of your paper.

4. **For Research.** Interview twenty students, asking them what revision means and how they revise their papers. Try to get a mix of students, not just the students in your English class. Use your interviews to write an essay titled "Revising and the College Writer."

SIMPLICITY

William Zinsser

William Zinsser's "The Transaction: Two Writing Processes" is one of the readings in Chapter 5, and biographical information about Zinsser can be found in that headnote.

    Zinsser's "Simplicity," which is excerpted from his book On Writing Well, *advocates writing that is simple, clear, and direct. Noting that the language of commerce and enterprise is marred by excessive verbiage, Zinsser argues that "fuzzy" writing—found in anything from business memos to descriptions of insurance plans to instructions for assembling children's toys—results in "meaningless jargon," loses readers, and spawns frustration. Zinsser once observed: "What writers owe their readers is the distilled version of what is finally important." "In fact," he continued, "writing is strong in proportion to the amount from which the writer chooses and distills the best."*

BEFORE READING

Connecting: If someone urged you to "simplify" your writing, how would you interpret that advice? What would you do to "simplify" it?

Anticipating: What does Zinsser mean when he urges you to "simplify"? Is his sense of that concept different from your original expectations?

Clutter is the disease of American writing. We are a society strangling in unnecessary words, circular constructions, pompous frills and meaningless jargon.

    Who can understand the viscous language of everyday American commerce and enterprise: the business letter, the interoffice memo, the corporation report, the notice from the bank explaining its latest "simplified" statement? What member of an insurance or medical plan can decipher the brochure that describes what the costs and benefits are? What father or mother can put together a child's toy—on Christmas Eve or any other eve—from the instructions on the box? Our national tendency is to inflate and thereby sound important. The airline pilot who announces that he is presently anticipating experiencing considerable precipitation wouldn't dream of saying that it may rain. The sentence is too simple—there must be something wrong with it.

3   But the secret of good writing is to strip every sentence to its cleanest components. Every word that serves no function, every long word that could be a short word, every adverb that carries the same meaning that's already in the verb, every passive construction that leaves the reader unsure of who is doing what—these are the thousand and one adulterants that weaken the strength of a sentence. And they usually occur, ironically, in proportion to education and rank.

4   During the late 1960s the president of a major university wrote a letter to mollify the alumni after a spell of campus unrest. "You are probably aware," he began, "that we have been experiencing very considerable potentially explosive expressions of dissatisfaction on issues only partially related." He meant that the students had been hassling them about different things. I was far more upset by the president's English than by the students' potentially explosive expressions of dissatisfaction. I would have preferred the presidential approach taken by Franklin D. Roosevelt when he tried to convert into English his own government's memos, such as this blackout order of 1942:

> Such preparations shall be made as will completely obscure all Federal buildings and non-Federal buildings occupied by the Federal government during an air raid for any period of time from visibility by reason of internal or external illumination.

5   "Tell them," Roosevelt said, "that in buildings where they have to keep the work going to put something across the windows."

6   Simplify, simplify. Thoreau said it, as we are so often reminded, and no American writer more consistently practiced what he preached. Open *Walden* to any page and you will find a man saying in a plain and orderly way what is on his mind:

> I went to the woods because I wished to live deliberately, to front only the essential facts of life, and see if I could not learn what it had to teach, and not, when I came to die, discover that I had not lived. I did not wish to live what was not life, living is so dear; nor did I wish to practice resignation, unless it was quite necessary. I wanted to live deep and suck out all the marrow of life, to live so sturdily and Spartan-like as to put to rout all that was not life, to cut a broad swath and shave close, to drive life into a corner, and reduce it to its lowest terms, and, if it proved to be mean, why then to get the whole and genuine meanness of it, and publish its meanness to the world; or if it were sublime, to know it by experience, and be able to give a true account of it.

7   How can the rest of us achieve such enviable freedom from clutter? The answer is to clear our heads of clutter. Clear thinking be-

comes clear writing; one can't exist without the other. It's impossible for a muddy thinker to write good English. You may get away with it for a paragraph or two, but soon the reader will be lost, and there's no sin so grave, for the reader will not easily be lured back.

Who is this elusive creature, the reader? The reader is someone 8 with an attention span of about sixty seconds—a person assailed by forces competing for the minutes that might otherwise be spent on a magazine or a book. At one time these forces weren't so numerous or so possessive: newspapers, radio, spouse, home, children. Today they also include a "home entertainment center" (TV, VCR, video camera, tapes and CDs), pets, a fitness program, a lawn and a garden and all the gadgets that have been bought to keep them spruce, and that most potent of competitors, sleep. The person snoozing in a chair, holding a magazine or a book, is a person who was being given too much unnecessary trouble by the writer.

It won't do to say that the reader is too dumb or too lazy to keep 9 pace with the train of thought. If the reader is lost, it's usually because the writer hasn't been careful enough. The carelessness can take any number of forms. Perhaps a sentence is so excessively cluttered that the reader, hacking through the verbiage, simply doesn't know what it means. Perhaps a sentence has been so shoddily constructed that the reader could read it in any of several ways. Perhaps the writer has switched pronouns in midsentence, or has switched tenses, so the reader loses track of who is talking or when the action took place. Perhaps Sentence B is not a logical sequel to Sentence A—the writer, in whose head the connection is clear, hasn't bothered to provide the missing link. Perhaps the writer has used an important word incorrectly by not taking the trouble to look it up. The writer may think that "sanguine" and "sanguinary" mean the same thing, but the difference is a bloody big one. The reader can only infer (speaking of big differences) what the writer is trying to imply.

Faced with such obstacles, readers are at first remarkably tena- 10 cious. They blame themselves—they obviously missed something, and they go back over the mystifying sentence, or over the whole paragraph, piecing it out like an ancient rune, making guesses and moving on. But they won't do this for long. The writer is making them work too hard, and they will look for one who is better at the craft.

Writers must therefore constantly ask: What am I trying to say? 11 Surprisingly often they don't know. Then they must look at what they have written and ask: Have I said it? Is it clear to someone encountering the subject for the first time? If it's not, that's because some fuzz has worked its way into the machinery. The clear writer is someone clearheaded enough to see this stuff for what it is: fuzz.

12   I don't mean that some people are born clearheaded and are therefore natural writers, whereas others are naturally fuzzy and will never write well. Thinking clearly is a conscious act that writers must force upon themselves, just as if they were embarking on any other project that requires logic: adding up a laundry list or doing an algebra problem. Good writing doesn't come naturally, though most people obviously think it does. The professional writer is constantly being bearded by strangers who say they'd like to "try a little writing sometime"—meaning when they retire from their real profession, like insurance or real estate. Or they say, "I could write a book about that." I doubt it.

13   Writing is hard work. A clear sentence is no accident. Very few sentences come out right the first time, or even the third time. Remember this as a consolation in moments of despair. If you find that writing is hard, it's because it *is* hard. It's one of the hardest things that people do.

Following are two pages of the final manuscript of this chapter from the First Edition of *On Writing Well*. Although they look like a first draft, they had already been rewritten and retyped—like almost every other page—four or five times. With each rewrite I try to make what I have written tighter, stronger and more precise, eliminating every element that is not doing useful work. Then I go over it once more, reading it aloud, and am always amazed at how much clutter can still be cut. In this Fourth Edition I've eliminated the sexist pronoun "he" to denote "the writer" and "the reader."

```
is too dumb or too lazy to keep pace with the
writer's train of thought. My sympathies are
entirely with him. He's not so dumb. If the reader
is lost, it is generally because the writer of the
article has not been careful enough to keep him on
the proper path.
     This carelessness can take any number of
different forms. Perhaps a sentence is so
excessively long and cluttered that the reader,
```

hacking his way through the verbiage, simply doesn't know what it means. Perhaps a sentence has been so shoddily constructed that the reader could read it in any of several ways. Perhaps the writer has switched pronouns in mid-sentence, or has switched tenses, so the reader loses track of who is talking or when the action took place. Perhaps Sentence B is not a logical sequel to Sentence A--the writer, in whose head the connection is clear, has not bothered to provide the missing link. Perhaps the writer has used an important word incorrectly by not taking the trouble to look it up. He may think that "sanguine" and "sanguinary" mean the same thing, but the difference is a bloody big one. The reader can only infer (speaking of big differences) what the writer is trying to imply.

Faced with these obstacles, the reader is at first a remarkably tenacious bird. He blame himself. He obviously missed something, and he goes back over the mystifying sentence, or over the whole paragraph, piecing it out like an ancient rune, making guesses and moving on. But he won't do this for long. The writer is making him work too hard--harder than he should have to.

and the reader will look for one who is better at his craft.

The writer must therefore constantly ask himself: What am I trying to say? Surprisingly often, he doesn't know. Then he must look at what he has written and ask: Have I said it? Is it clear to someone encountering the subject for the first time? If it's not, it is because some fuzz has worked its way into the machinery. The clear writer is a person clear-headed enough to see this stuff for what it is: fuzz.

I don't mean that some people are born clear-headed and are therefore natural writers, whereas others are naturally fuzzy and will never write well. Thinking clearly is a conscious act that the writer must force upon himself, just as if he were embarking on any other project that requires logic: adding up a laundry list or doing an algebra problem. Good writing doesn't come naturally, though most people obviously think it does. The professional

QUESTIONS ON SUBJECT AND PURPOSE

1. Zinsser observes that clutter usually increases in proportion to the writer's "education and rank" (paragraph 3). Why would that be so?
2. Why else might writers fail to simplify?
3. Zinsser's observations in his final paragraph are hardly consoling. How does it make you feel to be told that writing is "one

of the hardest things that people do"? Why would Zinsser write that in a book that offers advice to writers?

QUESTIONS ON STRATEGY AND AUDIENCE

1. How does the title of this selection agree with the point that Zinsser is trying to make? What if Zinsser had titled it, "Some Observations on the Art of Achieving Simplicity in Your Own Writing."

2. Why might Zinsser choose to include two sample pages of his own revised prose?

3. What expectations does Zinsser have about his readers or about readers in general?

QUESTIONS ON VOCABULARY AND STYLE

1. Zinsser observes that a writer, in revising, ought to strip every sentence of "every long word that could be a short word." Does he always seem to follow his own advice?

2. In paragraph 11, Zinsser provides the following example: "The writer may think that 'sanguine' and 'sanguinary' mean the same thing, but the difference is a bloody big one." What does he mean?

3. Be prepared to define the following words: *viscous* (paragraph 2), *mollify* (4), *spruce* (8), *verbiage* (9), *tenacious* (10), *rune* (10), *bearded* (12).

WRITING SUGGESTIONS

1. **For your Journal.** Copy into your journal several sentences or a paragraph from a recent paper you wrote in this course. Now try to apply Zinsser's advice. How can you simplify your writing?

2. **For a Paragraph.** Study the changes that Zinsser made in the sample pages of typescript that he reproduces. Formulate a thesis about the reason(s) for one or more of those changes. Then in a paragraph assert your thesis and support it with evidence from the text.

3. **For an Essay.** Zinsser offers general principles about revising, but not much specific advice. On the basis of your experience with your journal, your own writing, and the paragraph as-

signment above on the changes Zinsser made, write a process essay in which you offer specific, step-by-step advice for writers on how to achieve simplicity in their writing. Think of your audience as other students enrolled in freshman writing classes.

Prewriting:

a. Before you begin to plan your essay, review the advice in Chapter 6 (Process) of this text.

b. Brainstorm a list of possible, specific steps. For each one, make sure that you have a specific example. For instance, if you say "remove passive constructions," you will have to define passive constructions for your reader and give an example of how they can be changed.

c. Study the two pages that Zinsser reproduces of his own writing. Try to categorize each change that he makes. What are the principles behind his revision? Doing this analysis will help you to find additional, specific advice.

Rewriting:

a. Have you provided definitions and examples for each piece of advice? Go through the draft of your essay and underline each definition and example.

b. Make a list of the characteristics of your audience. Now look again at the draft of your paper. Have your written with that specific audience in mind?

c. Ask a friend or classmate to read your essay. Is each piece of advice clear? Does your reader understand what you are saying and how to make the changes that you suggest?

4. **For Research.** In your college library catalog, look under Library of Congress Subject Headings such as "English language—rhetoric—study and teaching" and "English language—style" for books that deal with the art of revision. Research the topic and see what others have said about revising. Use the best of this information in a research paper that discusses the art of revising prose. Be sure to document your sources wherever appropriate.

REPEAT TO REVISE

Donald M. Murray

Donald Murray is Professor of English at the University of New Hampshire, as well as a monthly columnist for The Boston Globe. *His editorial writing for the* Globe *earned him a Pulitzer Prize. A widely admired and deeply respected teacher, Murray is the author of short stories, novels, poetry, and a number of books on writing.*

In "Repeat to Revise," which appeared in one of his textbooks, A Writer Teaches Writing, *Murray shares his thoughts and experiences on the art of revision. Positioning revision not as a separate part of the writing process but a repetition of that process, Murray identifies strategies geared toward helping writers interested in learning how to revise effectively.*

BEFORE READING

Connecting: Have you ever thought of the act of writing as egocentric or arrogant?

Anticipating: What does Murray mean by his title "Repeat to Revise?"

Until I started to write the new version of this book I considered revision an integral part of the writing process. . . . Suddenly I realized what was instantly obvious to me, and hadn't been obvious before (and may not be obvious by the time I write about the writing process again). I saw revision as simply that. It is not another step in the process, it is the process repeated as many times as is necessary. . . . I no longer see revision as a separate part of the process but merely as a repetition of the process until a draft is ready for editing. 1

THE CRAFT OF REVISION

The writer creates a draft: 2

COLLECT   PLAN   DEVELOP   =   Draft

Then the writer passes through the same sequence, again and again, emphasizing one stage of the process, or two, or all three—or even part of a stage—doing what is necessary to produce increasingly effective drafts:

<u>COLLECT</u>	PLAN	DEVELOP	=	Second draft
COLLECT	<u>PLAN</u>	DEVELOP	=	Third draft
COLLECT	PLAN	<u>DEVELOP</u>	=	Fourth draft

That might be one sequence, an unusually logical one, in which the emphasis moves from collect to plan to develop as indicated by the underlining. The important thing the writer must know is that there is an inventory of writing tools available to perform the task necessary to make each draft work better than the last one.

3   As the writer moves from early draft to late draft, there is an increasing emphasis on the specific. At first the writer pays attention to the global concerns of subject and truth and point of view and organization, but as the larger problems are solved, the writer moves in close, paying attention to detail, picking every nit so that nothing will get between the reader and the subject. This parallels an increasing attention to audience. In the early drafts, the writer is his or her own reader, but as the draft evolves, the writer stands back to see how it will communicate to a reader.

4   Students may find it helpful during the revision process to use the following checklist:

- *"Do I have enough information?* If not, then I will have to COLLECT more information.
- *"Do I say one thing? Can I answer the question, "What does this mean?"* If not, then I will have to PLAN a new *focus.*
- *"Do I speak in an appropriate voice? Does the writing sound right?* If not, then I will have to PLAN how to *rehearse* so that I will hear an appropriate voice.
- *"Do I answer the reader's questions as they occur to the reader?* If not, then I will have to PLAN so that I can create a design that answers the reader's questions.
- *"Do I deliver enough information to satisfy the reader?* If not, then I will have to DEVELOP the piece more fully.

READING AS A WRITER

5   The writer's first reader is the writer. Too often people forget how much reading is involved in the writing course. It is possible to teach a reading or literature course without writing, but it is impossible to teach writing without reading. The writer must be able to

read a draft in such a way that the writer is able to make another draft more effective. This reading while writing is a sophisticated form of reading that is essential to the writing process.

The first problem the student writer faces is achieving enough distance to read what the reader will see on the page, not what the writer hopes is on the page. When young children write they think whatever they put down is wonderful. As they begin to grow, they become less egocentric and more aware of readers. This causes anxiety and, often, paralysis. They go from being proud of everything to being proud of nothing. Writers veer between excessive pride and excessive despair all their lives. It is understandable; writing is a private act with a public result. 6

The writer must be egocentric to write. It is a profession of arrogance. But then the writer must stand back and become the reader, and that requires an objectivity and distance essential to the craft of writing. Ray Bradbury allegedly puts each manuscript away in a file drawer and takes it out a year after it has been drafted. I don't know any other writer who is organized enough to even consider that technique. Most professionals write the way students write: to deadline. The writer has to develop some methods of distancing that will work in a short period of time. Some ways to achieve distancing include: 7

- "Role-play a specific reader. Become someone you know who is not knowledgeable about the subject you are writing about and read as that person.
- "Read fast, as a reader will read.
- "Read out loud. Tape-record the piece and play it back, or have a friend read it so that you hear it.
- "Have a friend read the piece, asking the friend to tell you what works and what needs work, what is on the page and what needs to be on the page. Be sure to use a friend who makes you want to write when you return to your writing desk.

It's important for the writer to concentrate first on what works. Too often we concentrate only on what is wrong, ignoring what is right. Yet the most successful revision comes when we identify something that works—a strong voice, a pace that moves the reader right along, a structure that clarifies a complicated subject—and build on that strength. 8

It is too easy to identify all the things that are wrong and to be discouraged and unable to produce a more effective draft. Of course there will come a time to deal with what is wrong or what doesn't work, but the solutions to the problems in the piece come from the 9 points of strength. What can we do to make the piece consistent with the good parts? What can we do to bring all parts of the piece up to the level of the best parts?

10   Many pieces of writing fail because the writer does not take advantage of what is already working well in a draft. For example, I may read a draft and feel despair. I'm good at despair. Nothing seems to work. But if I remember my craft I scan the disaster draft and see that, indeed, it is badly organized; that it does include too many undeveloped topics and lacks focus; that its proportions are all wrong—too much description and too little documentation; that the language is uneven, clumsy, stumbling at times and then, yes, there are moments when the language works, when I can hear a clear and strong voice. I read the strong parts aloud and work—cutting, adding, reordering, shaping, fitting, polishing—to make the voice consistent and strong. As I work on the draft line by line, I find I am following the clear sound of the voice I heard in fragments of the draft; I make one sentence clear and direct, and then another, and another. The draft begins to become better organized. I cut what doesn't belong and achieve focus; I pare back the description; I build up documentation. I work on what is most effective in the draft, and as I make that even more effective the writing that surrounds it gets attention and begins to improve.

11   Notice that the writer really looks for what *may* work. As I attacked my disaster draft, the voice was pretty uneven and downright poor most of the time, but I grabbed hold of those few moments of potential success and took advantage of them. They gave me a clue as to how I might improve the draft, and that was enough to get going. It's hard to look through the underbrush of messed up typography, misspellings, tangled syntax, wordiness, and writing that runs off in five directions at once, to see what might work. But that is what the writer has to do. And the writer can best do it by scanning, reading loosely, looking for what meaning lies behind the tangled text.

12   Writers have to keep reminding themselves that a draft is an experiment in meaning. In the early stages it's important to get beyond the etiquette of writing to see where the draft is pointing the writer. I'm intrigued by the fact that my students often make the most significant breakthroughs towards meaning where syntax breaks down—and I do too. We are obviously reaching for a meaning that is just beyond our ability to express. What I have to do and what my students have to do is to identify that potential meaning. Once we know where we are going we may be able to figure out how to get there.

13   The reading writer also has to see what doesn't work: to recognize that the beginning simply delays and the piece starts on page four, that the first-person piece would be more effective in the third

person, that the essay can't say three things of equal importance but has to have one dominant meaning, that the point of view is built on unfounded assumptions, that the draft is voiceless.

The writer reads, above all, to discover the text beyond the draft, to glimpse the potential text which may appear upon passing through the writing process again, and, perhaps, again and again. 14

QUESTIONS ON SUBJECT AND PURPOSE

1. Murray writes, "I no longer see revision as a separate part of the [writing] process but as a repetition of the process" (paragraph 1). What does he mean by that statement?
2. In what sense must a writer be egocentric (7)?
3. How would you characterize Murray's tone in this selection? Check the Glossary for a definition of tone.

QUESTIONS ON STRATEGY AND AUDIENCE

1. Murray uses a range of typographical devices to break his text apart—spacing, capital letters, lists, italics. Why?
2. What is the relationship between the section "The Craft of Revision" and the section "Reading as a Writer"?
3. In what sort of publication would you expect to find Murray's advice?

QUESTIONS ON VOCABULARY AND STYLE

1. What devices does Murray use to make his prose "reader friendly"?
2. When Murray notes that the writer must move in close, "picking every nit" (paragraph 3), what does he mean?
3. Be prepared to define the following words: *egocentric* (6), *veer* (6), *pare* (10).

WRITING SUGGESTIONS

1. **For your Journal.** Murray implies that as children grow up they become more anxious about their writing, going from being proud of everything to being proud of nothing. Did that happen to you? Try to remember what it was like to write when you were in elementary or middle school, in high

school, now in college. Jot down your memories or impressions. Have things gotten harder?

2. **For a Paragraph**. Go through this selection and make a list of the specific advice about revising that Murray offers to his readers. Select one of the topics that Murray covers and then summarize his advice on that one topic in a process paragraph (see Chapter 6). Assume that the paragraph will be handed out to your classmates as a guide to the process of revising.

3. **For an Essay**. Expand the paragraph you wrote for suggestion 2 into an essay by treating not just one aspect of Murray's advice, but rather all aspects. Write to your classmates in your writing course.

Prewriting:

a. Make notes on the specific advice that Murray offers. Do not try to record everything he says but rather focus on his advice about revising.

b. Think of your audience. Do you need to elaborate or interpret what Murray says? Does everything seem clear enough?

c. Remember that you do not need to follow the order that Murray uses in his essay. Make a couple of sketchy outlines of the points that you want to include. Try switching around the order of those points.

Rewriting:

a. Have you phrased every piece of advice in clear, "here's how to do it" prose? Are the pieces of advice phrased in parallel form. (Check the Glossary if you are uncertain about parallelism.)

b. Look again at your title. (You should not use Murray's title.) Is it interesting, provocative? Ask a couple of friends to evaluate your title and listen to their reactions.

c. Are you completely convinced that you give the advice in the most effective order? What if you arranged that advice in another way? Try a different order now that you have a complete draft of the essay.

4. **For Research**. Murray writes, "When young children write they think whatever they put down is wonderful. As they begin to grow, they become less egocentric and more aware of readers." Research that observation. Do young children see writing in a different way from older children or young adults? If so, why? If there are changes, why do those changes

occur? When do they occur? In addition to using books, ask your reference librarian if your library has access to ERIC (Educational Resources Information Center) documents. Be sure to document your sources wherever appropriate.

THE WAY TO RAINY MOUNTAIN

N. Scott Momaday

N(avarre) Scott Momaday was born in Lawton, Oklahoma, in 1934. He earned a B.A. from the University of New Mexico and a Ph.D. in English from Stanford University. A professor of English, artist, editor, poet, and novelist, N. Scott Momaday is above all a storyteller committed to preserving and interpreting the rich oral history of the Kiowa Indians. His work includes a book of Kiowa folktales, The Journey of Tai-Me *(1967), which he revised as* The Way to Rainy Mountain *(1969), and the Pulitzer Prize-winning novel,* House Made of Dawn *(1968).*

This essay originally appeared in the magazine The Reporter *in 1967, but Momaday revised it and used it as the introduction to his book* The Way to Rainy Mountain. *Momaday uses the occasion of a visit to the grave of his grandmother in Oklahoma to reflect upon the migration of his people, the Kiowas, from the high country of western Montana to the plains of Oklahoma. "To look upon that landscape in the early morning," writes Momaday, "with the sun at your back, is to lose the sense of proportion. Your imagination comes to life, and this, you think, is where Creation was begun."*

BEFORE READING

Connecting: In what way does one of your relatives, perhaps a grandparent or a great-grandparent, connect you to a part of your family's past?

Anticipating: How and why does Momaday interlink descriptions of the landscape with descriptions of his grandmother?

REVISED DRAFT

1   A single knoll rises out of the plain in Oklahoma, north and west of the Wichita Range. For my people, the Kiowas, it is an old landmark, and they gave it the name Rainy Mountain. The hardest weather in the world is there. Winter brings blizzards, hot tornadic winds arise in the spring, and in summer the prairie is an anvil's edge.

The grass turns brittle and brown, and it cracks beneath your feet. There are green belts along the rivers and creeks, linear groves of hickory and pecan, willow and witch hazel. At a distance in July or August the steaming foliage seems almost to writhe in fire. Great green and yellow grasshoppers are everywhere in the tall grass, popping up like corn to sting the flesh, and tortoises crawl about on the red earth, going nowhere in the plenty of time. Loneliness is an aspect of the land. All things in the plain are isolate; there is no confusion of objects in the eye, but one hill or one tree or one man. To look upon that landscape in the early morning, with the sun at your back, is to lose the sense of proportion. Your imagination comes to life, and this, you think, is where Creation was begun.

I returned to Rainy Mountain in July. My grandmother had died 2 in the spring, and I wanted to be at her grave. She had lived to be very old and at last infirm. Her only living daughter was with her when she died, and I was told that in death her face was that of a child.

I like to think of her as a child. When she was born, the Kiowas 3 were living the last great moment of their history. For more than a hundred years they had controlled the open range from the Smoky Hill River to the Red, from the headwaters of the Canadian to the fork of the Arkansas and Cimarron. In alliance with the Comanches, they had ruled the whole of the southern Plains. War was their sacred business, and they were among the finest horsemen the world has ever known. But warfare for the Kiowas was preeminently a matter of disposition rather than of survival, and they never understood the grim, unrelenting advance of the U.S. Cavalry. When at last, divided and ill-provisioned, they were driven onto the Staked Plains in the cold rains of autumn, they fell into panic. In Palo Duro Canyon they abandoned their crucial stores to pillage and had nothing then but their lives. In order to save themselves, they surrendered to the soldiers at Fort Sill and were imprisoned in the old stone corral that now stands as a military museum. My grandmother was spared the humiliation of those high gray walls by eight or ten years, but she must have known from birth the affliction of defeat, the dark brooding of old warriors.

Her name was Aho, and she belonged to the last culture to 4 evolve in North America. Her forebears came down from the high country in western Montana nearly three centuries ago. They were a mountain people, a mysterious tribe of hunters whose language has never been positively classified in any major group. In the late seventeenth century they began a long migration to the south and east. It was a journey toward the dawn, and it led to a golden age. Along the way the Kiowas were befriended by the Crows, who gave them the culture and religion of the Plains. They acquired horses, and their ancient nomadic spirit was suddenly free of the ground. They acquired

Tai-me, the sacred Sun Dance doll, from that moment the object and symbol of their worship, and so shared in the divinity of the sun. Not least, they acquired the sense of destiny, therefore courage and pride. When they entered upon the southern Plains they had been transformed. No longer were they slaves to the simple necessity of survival; they were a lordly and dangerous society of fighters and thieves, hunters and priests of the sun. According to their origin myth, they entered the world through a hollow log. From one point of view, their migration was the fruit of an old prophecy, for indeed they emerged from a sunless world.

5　　Although my grandmother lived out her long life in the shadow of Rainy Mountain, the immense landscape of the continental interior lay like memory in her blood. She could tell of the Crows, whom she had never seen, and of the Black Hills, where she had never been. I wanted to see in reality what she had seen more perfectly in the mind's eye, and traveled fifteen hundred miles to begin my pilgrimage.

6　　Yellowstone, it seemed to me, was the top of the world, a region of deep lakes and dark timber, canyons and waterfalls. But, beautiful as it is, one might have the sense of confinement there. The skyline in all directions is close at hand, the high wall of the woods and deep cleavages of shade. There is a perfect freedom in the mountains, but it belongs to the eagle and the elk, the badger and the bear. The Kiowas reckoned their stature by the distance they could see, and they were bent and blind in the wilderness.

7　　Descending eastward, the highland meadows are a stairway to the plain. In July the inland slope of the Rockies is luxuriant with flax and buckwheat, stonecrop and larkspur. The earth unfolds and the limit of the land recedes. Clusters of trees, and animals grazing far in the distance, cause the vision to reach away and wonder to build upon the mind. The sun follows a longer course in the day, and the sky is immense beyond all comparison. The great billowing clouds that sail upon it are shadows that move upon the grain like water, dividing light. Farther down, in the land of the Crows and Blackfeet, the plain is yellow. Sweet clover takes hold of the hills and bends upon itself to cover and seal the soil. There the Kiowas paused on their way; they had come to the place where they must change their lives. The sun is at home on the plains. Precisely there does it have the certain character of a god. When the Kiowas came to the land of the Crows, they could see the dark lees of the hills at dawn across the Bighorn River, the profusion of light on the grain shelves, the oldest deity ranging after the solstices. Not yet would they veer southward to the caldron of the land that lay below; they must wean their blood from the northern winter and hold the mountains a while longer in their view. They bore Tai-me in procession to the east.

A dark mist lay over the Black Hills, and the land was like iron. 8
At the top of a ridge I caught sight of Devil's Tower up-thrust against the gray sky as if in the birth of time the core of the earth had broken through its crust and the motion of the world was begun. There are things in nature that engender an awful quiet in the heart of man; Devil's Tower is one of them. Two centuries ago, because they could not do otherwise, the Kiowas made a legend at the base of the rock. My grandmother said:

Eight children were there at play, seven sisters and their brother. Suddenly the boy was struck dumb; he trembled and began to run upon his hands and feet. His fingers became claws, and his body was covered with fur. Directly there was a bear where the boy had been. The sisters were terrified; they ran, and the bear after them. They came to the stump of a great tree, and the tree spoke to them. It bade them climb upon it, and as they did so it began to rise into the air. The bear came to kill them, but they were just beyond its reach. It reared against the tree and scored the bark all around with its claws. The seven sisters were borne into the sky, and they became the stars of the Big Dipper.

From that moment, and so long as the legend lives, the Kiowas have kinsmen in the night sky. Whatever they were in the mountains, they could be no more. However tenuous their well-being, however much they had suffered and would suffer again, they had found a way out of the wilderness.

My grandmother had a reverence for the sun, a holy regard that 9
now is all but gone out of mankind. There was a wariness in her, and an ancient awe. She was a Christian in her later years, but she had come a long way about, and she never forgot her birthright. As a child she had been to the Sun Dances; she had taken part in those annual rites, and by them she had learned the restoration of her people in the presence of Tai-me. She was about seven when the last Kiowa Sun Dance was held in 1887 on the Washita River above Rainy Mountain Creek. The buffalo were gone. In order to consummate the ancient sacrifice—to impale the head of a buffalo bull upon the medicine tree—a delegation of old men journeyed into Texas, there to beg and barter for an animal from the Goodnight herd. She was ten when the Kiowas came together for the last time as a living Sun Dance culture. They could find no buffalo; they had to hang an old hide from the sacred tree. Before the dance could begin, a company of soldiers rode out from Fort Sill under orders to disperse the tribe. Forbidden without cause the essential act of their faith, having seen the wild herds slaughtered and left to rot upon the ground, the Kiowas backed away forever from the medicine tree. That was July 20, 1890, at the great bend of the Washita. My grandmother was there. Without bitterness, and for as long as she lived, she bore a vision of deicide.

10   Now that I can have her only in memory, I see my grandmother in the several postures that were peculiar to her: standing at the wood stove on a winter morning and turning meat in a great iron skillet; sitting at the south window, bent above her beadwork, and afterwards, when her vision failed, looking down for a long time into the fold of her hands; going out upon a cane, very slowly as she did when the weight of age came upon her; praying. I remember her most often at prayer. She made long, rambling prayers out of suffering and hope, having seen many things. I was never sure that I had the right to hear, so exclusive were they of all mere custom and company. The last time I saw her she prayed standing by the side of her bed at night, naked to the waist, the light of a kerosene lamp moving upon her dark skin. Her long, black hair, always drawn and braided in the day, lay upon her shoulders and against her breasts like a shawl. I do not speak Kiowa, and I never understood her prayers, but there was something inherently sad in the sound, some merest hesitation upon the syllables of sorrow. She began in a high and descending pitch, exhausting her breath to silence; then again and again—and always the same intensity of effort, of something that is, and is not, like urgency in the human voice. Transported so in the dancing light among the shadows of her room, she seemed beyond the reach of time. But that was illusion; I think I knew then that I should not see her again.

11   Houses are like sentinels in the plain, old keepers of the weather watch. There, in a very little while, wood takes on the appearance of great age. All colors wear soon away in the wind and rain, and then the wood is burned gray and the grain appears and the nails turn red with rust. The windowpanes are black and opaque; you imagine there is nothing within, and indeed there are many ghosts, bones given up to the land. They stand here and there against the sky, and you approach them for a longer time than you expect. They belong in the distance; it is their domain.

12   Once there was a lot of sound in my grandmother's house, a lot of coming and going, feasting and talk. The summers there were full of excitement and reunion. The Kiowas are a summer people; they abide the cold and keep to themselves, but when the season turns and the land becomes warm and vital they cannot hold still; an old love of going returns upon them. The aged visitors who came to my grandmother's house when I was a child were made of lean and leather, and they bore themselves upright. They wore great black hats and bright ample shirts that shook in the wind. They rubbed fat upon their hair and wound their braids with strips of colored cloth. Some of them painted their faces and carried the scars of old and cherished enmities. They were an old council of warlords, come to remind and be

reminded of who they were. Their wives and daughters served them well. The women might indulge themselves; gossip was at once the mark and compensation of their servitude. They made loud and elaborate talk among themselves, full of jest and gesture, fright and false alarm. They went abroad in fringed and flowered shawls, bright beadwork and German silver. They were at home in the kitchen, and they prepared meals that were banquets.

There were frequent prayer meetings, and great nocturnal 13 feasts. When I was a child I played with my cousins outside, where the lamplight fell upon the ground and the singing of the old people rose up around us and carried away into the darkness. There were a lot of good things to eat, a lot of laughter and surprise. And afterwards, when the quiet returned, I lay down with my grandmother and could hear the frogs away by the river and feel the motion of the air.

Now there is a funeral silence in the rooms, the endless wake of 14 some final word. The walls have closed in upon my grandmother's house. When I returned to it in mourning, I saw for the first time in my life how small it was. It was late at night, and there was a white moon, nearly full. I sat for a long time on the stone steps by the kitchen door. From there I could see out across the land; I could see the long row of trees by the creek, the low light upon the rolling plains, and the stars of the Big Dipper. Once I looked at the moon and caught sight of a strange thing. A cricket had perched upon the handrail, only a few inches away from me. My line of vision was such that the creature filled the moon like a fossil. It had gone there, I thought, to live and die, for there, of all places, was its small definition made whole and eternal. A warm wind rose up and purled like the longing within me.

The next morning I awoke at dawn and went out on the dirt 15 road to Rainy Mountain. It was already hot, and the grasshoppers began to fill the air. Still, it was early in the morning, and the birds sang out of the shadows. The long yellow grass on the mountain shone in the bright light, and a scissortail hied above the land. There, where it ought to be, at the end of a long and legendary way, was my grandmother's grave. Here and there on the dark stones were ancestral names. Looking back once, I saw the mountain and came away.

QUESTIONS FOR DISCUSSION

1. What event triggers Momaday's essay?
2. How many "journeys" are involved in Momaday's story?

3. Why might Momaday have titled the essay "The Way to Rainy Mountain"? Why not, for example, refer more specifically to the event that has brought him back?

4. Why might Momaday retell the legend of the "seven sisters" (paragraph 8)? How does that fit into his essay?

5. How much descriptive detail does Momaday give of his grandmother? Go through the essay and isolate each physical detail the reader is given.

6. What expectations might Momaday have of his audience? How might those expectations affect the essay?

7. Be prepared to define the following words: *knoll* (paragraph 1), *writhe* (1), *pillage* (3), *nomadic* (4), *luxuriant* (7), *lees* (7), *solstices* (7), *veer* (7), *tenuous* (8), *deicide* (9), *enmities* (12), *purled* (14), *hied* (15).

NOTE ON EARLIER DRAFT

Between the first appearance of "The Way to Rainy Mountain" in the magazine *The Reporter* in January 1967 and its publication as part of *The Way to Rainy Mountain* (Albuquerque: Univ. of New Mexico Press, 1969), Momaday made one major change. He added what are now paragraphs 6 and 7.

QUESTIONS ON THE REVISION

1. Why might Momaday have decided to add paragraphs 6 and 7? What do they contribute to the essay?

2. What is the effect of these other minor changes that Momaday made?

   a. Final: "They were driven onto the Staked Plains in the cold rains of autumn" (paragraph 3).

   Earlier: "They were driven onto the Staked Plains in the cold of autumn."

   b. Final: "As a child she had been to the Sun Dances; she had taken part in those annual rites" (paragraph 9).

   Earlier: "As a child she had been to the Sun Dances; she had taken part in that annual rite."

   c. Final: "In order to consummate the ancient sacrifice—to impale the head of a buffalo bull upon the medicine tree" (paragraph 9).

Earlier: "In order to consummate the ancient sacrifice—to impale the head of a buffalo bull upon the Tai-me tree."

WRITING SUGGESTIONS

1. **For your Journal.** What memories do you have of a grandparent or a great-grandparent? When you think of that person, what comes to mind? In your journal make a list of those memories—sights, sounds, smells, associations of any sort.

2. **For a Paragraph.** In a substantial paragraph analyze the effects that Momaday achieved by adding paragraphs 6 and 7 to the essay.

3. **For an Essay.** Momaday once told an interviewer, "I believe that the Indian has an understanding of the physical world and of the earth as a spiritual entity that is his, very much his own. The non-Indian can benefit a good deal by having that perception revealed to him." What do such perceptions reveal to the non-Indian?

Prewriting:

a. Reread Momaday's essay carefully, looking for evidence of how he perceives the physical world. How does he describe the physical world? What does he seem to "see" in nature? How does his "seeing" differ from that of a scientist?

b. On the basis of what he says, try to finish the following sentence, "Momaday sees nature as . . ."

c. Brainstorm about the possible benefits to you from seeing things as Momaday sees them. Try to list a number of possibilities. What might you do differently?

Rewriting:

a. Look carefully at how you have structured the body of your essay. Probably you either began with the most significant point or ended with it. Would the essay work better if the order were changed?

b. Look again at your introduction. Have you begun with something that might catch your reader's attention? Try to avoid beginning with just a thesis statement.

c. Carefully examine every sentence in your essay. Is each a complete sentence? Do the sentences have some variety in both structure and length?

4. **For Research.** Observation of the natural world is central to both Gretel Ehrlich in "A River's Route" (Chapter 3) and

Momaday. Compare and contrast how these two writers see the natural world. You can extend your research beyond these two selections by reading other books by the two writers. See the biographical headnotes to each selection and check your library's catalog for references to their other books.

REVISION AND LIFE: TAKE IT FROM THE TOP—AGAIN

Nora Ephron

Nora Ephron was born in 1941 in New York City. After she received her B.A. from Wellesley College in 1962, Ephron worked as a journalist and columnist for the New York Post, New York *magazine, and* Esquire, *where she developed her reporting and interviewing skills. She quickly established a reputation as a writer who brought snappy wit, cutting insight, and bare-all candor to any subject she wrote about. In recent years Ephron has become a successful screenplay writer, penning such films as* Silkwood *(1983),* When Harry Met Sally *(1989), and* Sleepless in Seattle *(1993), which she also directed. Her books include* Wallflower at the Orgy *(1970) and a novel,* Heartburn *(1983).*

"Revision and Life," written in response to an invitation to participate in this textbook, was originally published in The New York Times Book Review. *As the title suggests, for Ephron, revision and life are closely linked. When she was a college student, with the limitless potential of youth, her goal was "to get to the end"—to finish the piece, to get on with life. As she has grown older, however, revision has come to mean that more lies ahead. "By the time you reach middle age," she observes, "you want more than anything for things not to come to an end; and as long as you're still revising, they don't."*

BEFORE READING

Connecting: When it comes to writing, what does the word "revision" suggest to you?

Anticipating: When Ephron observes, "A gift for revision may be a developmental stage," what does she mean?

REVISED DRAFT

I have been asked to write something for a textbook that is meant to teach college students something about writing and revision. I am happy to do this because I believe in revision. I have also been asked to save the early drafts of whatever I write, presumably to show these students the actual process of revision. This too I am happy to do. On the other hand, I suspect that there is just so much you can teach college students about revision; a gift for revision may be a developmental stage—like a 2-year-old's sudden ability to place one block on top of another—that comes along somewhat later, in one's mid-20s, say; most people may not be particularly good at it, or even interested in it, until then.

2   When I was in college, I revised nothing. I wrote out my papers in longhand, typed them up and turned them in. It would never have crossed my mind that what I had produced was only a first draft and that I had more work to do; the idea was to get to the end, and once you had got to the end you were finished. The same thinking, I might add, applied in life: I went pell-mell through my four years in college without a thought about whether I ought to do anything differently; the idea was to get to the end—to get out of school and become a journalist.

3   Which I became, in fairly short order. I learned as a journalist to revise on deadline. I learned to write an article a paragraph at a time—and I arrived at the kind of writing and revising I do, which is basically a kind of typing and retyping. I am a great believer in this technique for the simple reason that I type faster than the wind. What I generally do is to start an article and get as far as I can—sometimes no farther in than a sentence or two—before running out of steam, ripping the piece of paper from the typewriter and starting all over again. I type over and over until I have got the beginning of the piece to the point where I am happy with it. I then am ready to plunge into the body of the article itself. This plunge usually requires something known as a transition. I approach a transition by completely retyping the opening of the article leading up to it in the hope that the ferocious speed of my typing will somehow catapult me into the next section of the piece. This does not work—what in fact catapults me into the next section is a concrete thought about what the next section ought to be about—but until I have the thought the typing keeps me busy, and keeps me from feeling something known as blocked.

4   Typing and retyping as if you know where you're going is a version of what therapists tell you to do when they suggest that you try changing from the outside in—that if you can't master the total commitment to whatever change you want to make, you can at least do all the extraneous things connected with it, which make it that much easier to get there. I was 25 years old the first time a therapist suggested that I try changing from the outside in. In those days, I

used to spend quite a lot of time lying awake at night wondering what I should have said earlier in the evening and revising my lines. I mention this not just because it's a way of illustrating that a gift for revision is practically instinctive, but also (once again) because it's possible that a genuine ability at it doesn't really come into play until one is older—or at least older than 25, when it seemed to me that all that was required in my life and my work was the chance to change a few lines.

In my 30's, I began to write essays, one a month for *Esquire* 5 magazine, and I am not exaggerating when I say that in the course of writing a short essay—1,500 words, that's only six double-spaced typewritten pages—I often used 300 or 400 pieces of typing paper, so often did I type and retype and catapult and recatapult myself, sometimes on each retyping moving not even a sentence farther from the spot I had reached the last time through. At the same time, though, I was polishing what I had already written: as I struggled with the middle of the article, I kept putting the beginning through the typewriter; as I approached the ending, the middle got its turn. (This is a kind of polishing that the word processor all but eliminates, which is why I don't use one. Word processors make it possible for a writer to change the sentences that clearly need changing without having to retype the rest, but I believe that you can't always tell whether a sentence needs work until it rises up in revolt against your fingers as you retype it.) By the time I had produced what you might call a first draft—an entire article with a beginning, middle and end—the beginning was in more like 45th draft, the middle in 20th, and the end was almost newborn. For this reason, the beginnings of my essays are considerably better written than the ends, although I like to think no one ever notices this but me.

As I learned the essay form, writing became harder for me. I 6 was finding a personal style, a voice if you will, a way of writing that looked chatty and informal. That wasn't the hard part—the hard part was that having found a voice, I had to work hard month to month not to seem as if I were repeating myself. At this point in this essay it will not surprise you to learn that the same sort of thing was operating in my life. I don't mean that my life had become harder—but that it was becoming clear that I had many more choices than had occurred to me when I was marching through my 20's. I no longer lost sleep over what I should have said. Not that I didn't care—it was just that I had moved to a new plane of late-night anxiety: I now wondered what I should have done. Whole areas of possible revision opened before me. What should I have done instead? What could I have done? What if I hadn't done it the way I did? What if I had a chance to do it over? What if I had a chance to do it over as a different person? These were the sorts of questions that kept me awake and led me into fiction, which at the very least (the level at which I practice it) is a chance to rework the events of your life so that you give the illusion of being the intelligence at the center of it, simultaneously managing to slip in all the lines that occurred to you later. Fiction, I suppose, is the ultimate shot at revision.

7   Now I am in my 40's and I write screenplays. Screenplays—if they are made into movies—are essentially collaborations, and movies are not a writer's medium, we all know this, and I don't want to dwell on the craft of screenwriting except insofar as it relates to revision. Because the moment you stop work on a script seems to be determined not by whether you think the draft is good but simply by whether shooting is about to begin: if it is, you get to call your script a final draft; and if it's not, you can always write another revision. This might seem to be a hateful way to live, but the odd thing is that it's somehow comforting; as long as you're revising, the project isn't dead. And by the same token, neither are you.

8   It was, as it happens, while thinking about all this one recent sleepless night that I figured out how to write this particular essay. I say "recent" in order to give a sense of immediacy and energy to the preceding sentence, but the truth is that I am finishing this article four months after the sleepless night in question, and the letter asking me to write it, from George Miller of the University of Delaware, arrived almost two years ago, so for all I know Mr. Miller has managed to assemble his textbook on revision without me.

9   Oh, well. That's how it goes when you start thinking about revision. That's the danger of it, in fact. You can spend so much time thinking about how to switch things around that the main event has passed you by. But it doesn't matter. Because by the time you reach middle age, you want more than anything for things not to come to an end; and as long as you're still revising, they don't.

10   I'm sorry to end so morbidly—dancing as I am around the subject of death—but there are advantages to it. For one thing, I have managed to move fairly effortlessly and logically from the beginning of this piece through the middle and to the end. And for another, I am able to close with an exhortation, something I rarely manage, which is this: Revise now, before it's too late.

QUESTIONS FOR DISCUSSION

1. What links does Ephron see between revision and life?
2. How does Ephron structure her essay? What principle of order does she follow?

3. It would have been a simple matter for Ephron to omit the references to this textbook (paragraphs 1 and 8). The *New York Times* audience, for example, would not be interested in knowing these details. Why might she have chosen to include these references in her essay?

4. Why is fiction the "ultimate shot at revision" (6)?

5. What might Ephron mean by her final sentence ("Revise now, before it's too late")?

6. Be able to define the following words: *pell-mell* (paragraph 2), *extraneous* (4), *exhortation* (10).

EARLIER DRAFT

Corresponds to paragraphs 1 and 2

I have been asked to write something that will show college students   1
something about writing and revision. I am happy to do this because I believe in revision. I have been asked to write something and save all the early drafts, which I am also happy to do. On the other hand, I believe there is just so much you can teach college students about revision, that an ability for revision is something (a Piaget stage, like a 2 1/2 year old's sudden ability to put one block on top of another) that is acquired slightly later, and that most people aren't particularly good at it or even interested in it until then.

When I was in college, I revised almost nothing. It seems to   2
me (I know my memory isn't what it used to be but I'm fairly sure about this) I typed papers and pretty much turned them in. The same thing I might add applied in life: I pretty much went pell mell through my four years of higher education without a thought about whether I ought to have done anything differently. The things I wrote were a means to an end—to turn in the assignment, I suppose—and so was the way I lived my life—to get out of school and become a journalist.

QUESTIONS ON THE REVISION

1. In the revised draft, Ephron omits the reference to Piaget (paragraph 1). Who was Piaget? Why eliminate the reference?

2. In the revised draft, Ephron suggests when it might be that people acquire an interest in revising ("in one's mid-20's, say"). Why add that detail?

3. What changes occur in the following passage from one draft to another? What is the effect of those changes?

EARLIER DRAFT

When I was in college, I revised almost nothing. It seems to me (I know my memory isn't what it used to be but I'm fairly sure about this) I typed papers and pretty much turned them in.

REVISED DRAFT

When I was in college, I revised nothing. I wrote out my papers in longhand, typed them up and turned them in. It would never have crossed my mind that what I had produced was only a first draft and that I had more work to do; the idea was to get to the end, and once you had got to the end you were finished.

4. What is the effect of changing "four years of higher education" to "four years in college"?

WRITING SUGGESTIONS

1. **For your Journal**. What obstacles do you face when you try to revise something that you have written? Make a list of the ones that immediately come to mind. Add to your list as you finish each paragraph and essay during this course.

2. **For a Paragraph**. Study the two versions of the opening of Ephron's essay. Formulate a thesis about her revision strategy. In a paragraph assert your thesis and support it with appropriate evidence.

3. **For an Essay**. On the basis of your own experience as a writer and as a student in this course, argue for or against *requiring* revision in a college writing course. Should a student be forced to do it? Does revision always produce a better paper?

Prewriting:
a. Remember that regardless of your stand, your argument should be based on solid, meaningful reasons. For example, you should not argue that revision is too much trouble or that it will please your instructor and get you a higher grade. Make a list of reasons.

b. Interview classmates and friends for their experiences and opinions. Remember to take notes.

c. Plan a possible organization for your essay. Does an inductive or a deductive approach seem better? In what order will you arrange your reasons? Will you start or end with the strongest reason?

Rewriting:

a. Check your tone in the essay. Do you sound convincing? Reasonable? Ask a friend or classmate to read your essay and to characterize its tone.

b. Have you avoided emotionally charged language? Examine your word choice carefully. Underline any words that might seem distorted, inaccurate, or too emotional.

c. Titles are an important part of any essay. An effective title should clearly signal the essay's subject and should also arouse the reader's interest. Look carefully at your original title. Does it meet those tests? Try writing some alternative titles.

4. For Research. What role does revision play in the writing process of faculty and staff at your college or university? Interview a range of people—faculty (especially professors in disciplines other than English) and other professional staff members who write as a regular part of their job (for example, librarians, information officers, and admissions officers). Using notes from your interviews, write an essay about the revision practices of these writers. Your essay could be a feature article in the campus newspaper.

BLACK MEN AND PUBLIC SPACE
Brent Staples

Born in Chester, Pennsylvania, Brent Staples graduated from Widener University in 1973 and earned a Ph.D. in psychology from the University of Chicago in 1982. He worked for the Chicago Sun-Times *as a reporter before moving to* The New York Times *in 1985. At the* Times *he was initially an editor on the* Book Review, *then first assistant metropolitan editor. He is now a member of the editorial board, writing on politics and culture. In 1994 he published a memoir,* Parallel Time: Growing Up in Black and White, *which tells the story of his childhood in Chester, a mixed-race, economically declining town. The book focuses on his younger brother, a drug dealer who died of gunshot wounds at 22.*

"Black Men and Public Space" was originally published in the "Can Men Have It All?" section of Ms. *magazine as, "Just Walk on By: A Black Man Ponders His Power to Alter Public Space." In revised and edited form, it was reprinted in* Harper's *under the new title "Black Men and Public Space."*

BEFORE READING

Connecting: What precautions do you take if you have to walk at night in public spaces?

Anticipating: Why does Staples whistle melodies from classical music when he walks at night? What effect does that particular "cowbell" have on people?

REVISED DRAFT

1   My first victim was a woman—white, well dressed, probably in her early twenties. I came upon her late one evening on a deserted street in Hyde Park, a relatively affluent neighborhood in an otherwise mean, impoverished section of Chicago. As I swung onto the avenue behind her, there seemed to be a discreet, uninflammatory distance between us. Not so. She cast back a worried glance. To her, the

youngish black man—a broad six feet two inches with a beard and billowing hair, both hands shoved into the pockets of a bulky military jacket—seemed menacingly close. After a few more quick glimpses, she picked up her pace and was soon running in earnest. Within seconds she disappeared into a cross street.

That was more than a decade ago. I was twenty-two years old, 2 a graduate student newly arrived at the University of Chicago. It was in the echo of that terrified woman's footfalls that I first began to know the unwieldy inheritance I'd come into—the ability to alter public space in ugly ways. It was clear that she thought herself the quarry of a mugger, a rapist, or worse. Suffering a bout of insomnia, however, I was stalking sleep, not defenseless wayfarers. As a softy who is scarcely able to take a knife to a raw chicken—let alone hold one to a person's throat—I was surprised, embarrassed, and dismayed all at once. Her flight made me feel like an accomplice in tyranny. It also made it clear that I was indistinguishable from the muggers who occasionally seeped into the area from the surrounding ghetto. That first encounter, and those that followed, signified that a vast, unnerving gulf lay between nighttime pedestrians—particularly women— and me. And I soon gathered that being perceived as dangerous is a hazard in itself. I only needed to turn a corner into a dicey situation, or crowd some frightened, armed person in a foyer somewhere, or make an errant move after being pulled over by a policeman. Where fear and weapons meet—and they often do in urban America—there is always the possibility of death.

In that first year, my first away from my hometown, I was to be- 3 come thoroughly familiar with the language of fear. At dark, shadowy intersections, I could cross in front of a car stopped at a traffic light and elicit the *thunk, thunk, thunk, thunk* of the driver—black, white, male, or female—hammering down the door locks. On less traveled streets after dark, I grew accustomed to but never comfortable with people crossing to the other side of the street rather than pass me. Then there were the standard unpleasantries with policemen, doormen, bouncers, cabdrivers, and others whose business it is to screen out troublesome individuals *before* there is any nastiness.

I moved to New York nearly two years ago and I have remained 4 an avid night walker. In central Manhattan, the near-constant crowd cover minimizes tense one-on-one street encounters. Elsewhere—in SoHo, for example, where sidewalks are narrow and tightly spaced buildings shut out the sky—things can get very taut indeed.

After dark, on the warrenlike streets of Brooklyn where I live, I 5 often see women who fear the worst from me. They seem to have set their faces on neutral, and with their purse straps strung across their chests bandolier-style, they forge ahead as though bracing themselves against being tackled. I understand, of course, that the danger they perceive is not a hallucination. Women are particularly vulnerable to street violence, and young black males are drastically overrepresented among the perpetrators of that violence. Yet these truths are no solace against the kind of alienation that comes of being ever the suspect, a fearsome entity with whom pedestrians avoid making eye contact.

6   It is not altogether clear to me how I reached the ripe old age of twenty-two without being conscious of the lethality nighttime pedestrians attributed to me. Perhaps it was because in Chester, Pennsylvania, the small, angry industrial town where I came of age in the 1960s, I was scarcely noticeable against a backdrop of gang warfare, street knifings, and murders. I grew up one of the good boys, had perhaps a half-dozen fistfights. In retrospect, my shyness of combat has clear sources.

7   As a boy, I saw countless tough guys locked away; I have since buried several, too. They were babies, really—a teenage cousin, a brother of twenty-two, a childhood friend in his mid-twenties—all gone down in episodes of bravado played out in the streets. I came to doubt the virtues of intimidation early on. I chose, perhaps unconsciously, to remain a shadow—timid, but a survivor.

8   The fearsomeness mistakenly attributed to me in public places often has a perilous flavor. The most frightening of these confusions occurred in the late 1970s and early 1980s, when I worked as a journalist in Chicago. One day, rushing into the office of a magazine I was writing for with a deadline story in hand, I was mistaken for a burglar. The office manager called security and, with an ad hoc posse, pursued me through the labyrinthine halls, nearly to my editor's door. I had no way of proving who I was. I could only move briskly toward the company of someone who knew me.

9   Another time I was on assignment for a local paper and killing time before an interview. I entered a jewelry store on the city's affluent Near North Side. The proprietor excused herself and returned with an enormous red Doberman pinscher straining at the end of a leash. She stood, the dog extended toward me, silent to my questions, her eyes bulging nearly out of her head. I took a cursory look around, nodded, and bade her good night.

10   Relatively speaking, however, I never fared as badly as another black male journalist. He went to nearby Waukegan, Illinois, a couple of summers ago to work on a story about a murderer who was born there. Mistaking the reporter for the killer, police officers hauled him from his car at gunpoint and but for his press credentials would probably have tried to book him. Such episodes are not uncommon. Black men trade tales like this all the time.

Over the years, I learned to smother the rage I felt at so often being taken for a criminal. Not to do so would surely have led to madness. I now take precautions to make myself less threatening. I move about with care, particularly late in the evening. I give a wide berth to nervous people on subway platforms during the wee hours, particularly when I have exchanged business clothes for jeans. If I happen to be entering a building behind some people who appear skittish, I may walk by, letting them clear the lobby before I return, so as not to seem to be following them. I have been calm and extremely congenial on those rare occasions when I've been pulled over by the police.

And on late-evening constitutionals I employ what has proved to be an excellent tension-reducing measure: I whistle melodies from Beethoven and Vivaldi and the more popular classical composers. Even steely New Yorkers hunching toward nighttime destinations seem to relax, and occasionally they even join in the tune. Virtually everybody seems to sense that a mugger wouldn't be warbling bright, sunny selections from Vivaldi's *Four Seasons*. It is my equivalent of the cowbell that hikers wear when they know they are in bear country.

QUESTIONS FOR DISCUSSION

1. What does Staples mean by the phrase "public space?" In what way is he capable of altering it?
2. What is the effect of Staples's opening sentences in the essay?
3. What type of evidence does Staples provide to illustrate his point—that black men alter public space?
4. What purpose might Staples have had in writing the essay?
5. Staples's essay originally appeared in *Ms.* magazine. What assumptions could Staples have made about his audience?
6. Be prepared to define the following words: *discreet* (paragraph 1), *dicey* (2), *errant* (2), *taut* (4), *warrenlike* (5), *bandolier* (5), *solace* (5), *entity* (5), *bravado* (7), *ad hoc* (8), *cursory* (9), *skittish* (11), *congenial* (11), *constitutionals* (12).

EARLIER DRAFT

Paragraph A (in the *Ms.* version this appeared between paragraphs 4 and 5 of the *Harper's* version)

Black men have a firm place in New York mugging literature. Norman Podhoretz in his famed (or infamous) 1963 essay, "My

Negro Problem—And Ours," recalls growing up in the terror of black males; they "were tougher than we were, more ruthless," he writes—and as an adult on the Upper West Side of Manhattan, he continues, he cannot constrain his nervousness when he meets black men on certain streets. Similarly, a decade later, the essayist and novelist Edward Hoagland extols a New York where once "Negro bitterness bore down mainly on other Negroes." Where some see mere panhandlers, Hoagland sees "a mugger who is clearly screwing up his nerve to do more than just *ask* for money." But Hoagland has "the New Yorker's quick-hunch posture for broken-field maneuvering" and the bad guy swerves away.

Paragraph B (in the *Ms.* version this appeared between paragraphs 6 and 7 of the *Harper's* version)

Many things go into the making of a young thug. One of those things is the consummation of the male romance with the power to intimidate. An infant discovers that random flailings send the baby bottle flying out of the crib and crashing to the floor. Delighted, the joyful babe repeats those motions again and again, seeking to duplicate the feat. Just so, I recall the point at which some of my boyhood friends were finally seduced by the perception of themselves as tough guys. When a mark cowered and surrendered his money without resistance, myth and reality merged—and paid off. It is, after all, only manly to embrace the power to frighten and intimidate. We, as men, are not supposed to give an inch of our lane on the highway; we are to seize the fighter's edge in work and in play and even in love; we are to be valiant in the face of hostile forces.

Unfortunately, poor and powerless young men seem to take all of this nonsense literally. . . .

QUESTIONS ON THE REVISED DRAFT

1. When the earlier draft was first published in *Ms.*, it was titled "Just Walk on By." When it appeared in *Harper's* (revised draft), it was retitled "Black Men and Public Space." Why might the title have been changed?

2. The whole of paragraph A (reproduced above) in the earlier draft was deleted when the essay appeared in *Harper's*. Why? What does Staples do in that paragraph that he does not do elsewhere?

3. The whole of paragraph B (reproduced above) in the earlier draft was also deleted when the essay appeared in *Harper's*. Why?

WRITING SUGGESTIONS

1. **For your Journal.** Have you ever been frightened in a public space? Explore your memories—or your recent experiences—and jot down a few such times. Try to capture a few details about each of those experiences.

2. **For a Paragraph.** Select one of the experiences you entered in your journal for suggestion 1, and narrate that experience in a paragraph. Why did you react as you did? Was your fear justified? You can also turn the topic around and describe a time when your presence frightened someone else while in a public space.

3. **For an Essay.** Regardless of our age or sex or color, we all provoke reactions from people who do not know us. Sometimes, in fact, we go out of our way to elicit a reaction—dressing in a certain way, driving a particular type of car, engaging in an unusual activity, wearing our hair in a peculiar style. Describe your image and behavior, and analyze how people react to you and why they react as they do.

Prewriting:

a. Think about the image that you either consciously or unconsciously project. Try to define that image in a couple of sentences. How do you create that image?

b. Make a list of people's reactions to you. What have you noticed about their responses? What is typical? Make a list of those reactions and then jot down next to each item a possible explanation for that reaction.

c. Ask some friends, or even some casual acquaintances, how they respond to you and why. Be sure to explain to them why you want to know—that might encourage them to respond in a helpful manner. Be prepared to be surprised.

Rewriting:

a. Try to find an effective incident with which to begin. Do not try to imitate Staples's introduction, especially his suspenseful example.

b. Be sure that you have offered explanations for why people react to you as they do.

c. Remember that your analysis of reactions needs to be organized in a logical manner. Why have you chosen the order you have? Is there any other way in which those reactions could be organized?

4. **For Research**. Who mugs whom? Research the problem of assault or mugging either in the country as a whole or in your own community. What are your chances of being mugged? Who is likely to do it to you? Where is it most likely to happen? If you decide to focus on your own community or college campus, remember to interview the local police.

SIS BOOM BAH HUMBUG

Patricia McLaughlin

Patricia McLaughlin was born in Boston in 1945. She was educated at Rosemont College, Boston University, and the Annenberg School of Communications at the University of Pennsylvania. Her writing career began when she won a writing contest for Vogue *magazine while still in college. Since 1983 McLaughlin has written a column called "Lifestyle," which has been syndicated since 1988, for the Philadelphia* Inquirer.

"Sis Boom Bah Humbug" originally appeared in the Sunday magazine section of the Philadelphia Inquirer. *In discussing how the essay evolved through several drafts, McLaughlin revealed that advice from a reader and an editor helped shape the final version: "I wasn't happy with the first draft, and asked a friend to read it. She found it infuriating that the task force would tell the bump-and-grinders they couldn't bump and grind, both because of the implication that campus rape was their fault, and because it abridged their freedom. It was just the idea I needed—I agreed with her, and besides, I love being able to disagree with both sides at once. But my editor thought the last two grafs [paragraphs] . . . not only made the column too long, but weakened what sounded to him like the real ending, the indictment of the values the Illinettes [the University of Illinois' "squad of pompom girls"] embody and the advice to transfer to charm school, so he cut it. I wanted the idea back in, so we came up with a way to put it in the middle in the* Inquirer *version, and let the indictment of Illinette values stand as the ending. But I still wasn't completely happy with it, so I rewrote it a little more before I sent it to the syndicate, giving more weight to the abridgment-of-women's freedom issue, and changing the ending a little."*

BEFORE READING

Connecting: Do female cheerleaders, members of a dance club, or majorettes project an image of women as sexual objects?

Anticipating: Why does McLaughlin object to the claim that the Illinettes are "role models" for women on campus?

1 Things don't get ritualized at random. It's no accident that, when you go to a football game, you see testosterone-crazed, bulked-up young males trying to pound each other into jelly out on the field while, on the sidelines, lissome young females prance around with hardly any clothes on, swiveling their pelvises and hollering in unison about how wonderful and important and thrilling the efforts of the young males are.

2 Imagine the reverse: fierce, muscular young women slamming into each other out on the playing field while pretty, scantily clad young men gyrate on the sidelines, urging the young women on to victory. Now imagine it happening every fall Saturday afternoon on campuses all over America and, on TV, with a somewhat older cast, on Sunday afternoons and Monday nights.

3 No way. One of the reasons football is so satisfying—to those it satisfies, at least—is that it rhymes with the way we think things should be: men doing things, women looking pretty, men at the center of attention, women on the sidelines, men in charge of the violence, women there to provide a sexual charge.

4 Of course, by some people's lights, the sex roles football reflects are obsolete, which makes some of those people despise football, and makes others want to change it.

5 For instance, last winter the University of Illinois Campus Task Force on Sexual Assault, Abuse and Violence recommended that the University ban dancing by the Illinettes, its squad of pompom girls, as one of the campus "activities that project women as sexual objects." The Task Force had been convened after a survey of women students found that nearly one in six had been the victim of a criminal sexual assault.

6 The Illinettes, naturally, failed to see that the appallingly high campus rape rate was their fault. And they were right. Telling them their line-dancers can't bump and grind at football games is a totally screwy way to prevent rape. It drags up the old idea that rape is women's fault—that short skirts or sexy dancing or practically anything that reminds a man that a woman is female can drive him so totally gaga that he simply can't help himself. No reasonable person believes this. Besides, it's just not fair to restrict women's freedom in order to keep men from committing crimes. Carry the Illinois ban on sexy dancing to its extreme, and you have women in purdah, so constrained by fear of men's supposedly ungovernable sexual impulses that they have no lives left.

7 On the other hand, it's not easy to swallow the Illinettes' contention that what they do is "a serious sport."

I'm not saying it doesn't take muscles and talent and practice. 8
Indeed, bump-and-grind line dancing is gaining adherents—and
causing controversy—at schools across the country; there are even
national competitions. But how many serious sports require sparkly
Spandex chorus-girl costumes and high-heeled white boots and Dynasty hair? Even more to the point, how many serious sports exist
mainly to glorify the accomplishments of people participating in a
whole different sport?

Withal, the Illinettes contend that they're "role models" for 9
women on campus. God forbid.

The trouble with pompom girls—whether they bump and 10
grind or not—is that they reflect a destructively narrow view of what
women are good for and what they better be good at. The values they
embody are: being thin, being beautiful, being coordinated, having
white teeth and lots of hair and lots of energy, smiling, staying in
shape, and wearing sexy little costumes. The role they play at football
games suggests that a woman's principal role in life should be encouraging men, and supporting them, and making them feel good
about themselves, and telling them how great they are, and getting
everybody else to say so too.

If Illinois' women students can't come up with better role mod- 11
els, they may as well pack up and transfer to charm school.

QUESTIONS FOR DISCUSSION

1. What does McLaughlin mean when she writes, "Things don't
   get ritualized at random"?
2. Why does McLaughlin object to "pompom" girls?
3. Although she finds such activities offensive, McLaughlin does
   not support a campus ban on such organizations. Why?
4. What does McLaughlin's title suggest? Is it an effective title
   for the essay?
5. Be prepared to define the following words: *lissome* (paragraph
   1), *gyrate* (2), *gaga* (6), *purdah* (6).

EARLIER DRAFT

*The only substantive changes that McLaughlin made in the essay from the
first draft to the last occurred in the second half of the essay, from paragraph
6 on. That section of the first draft is reproduced below.*

The Illinettes (correctly) failed to see that this was any of their fault
and, though they agreed to quit doing the bump-and-grind line danc-

ing that worried the task force, they still don't see why they should have to. "We consider this a serious sport," Illinettes captain Pam Withers told *Time* magazine last winter. Indeed, bump-and-grind line dancing is gaining adherents at schools across the country; there are even national competitions.

I'm not saying it doesn't take muscles and talent and practice. But how many serious sports require sparkly Spandex chorus-girl costumes and high-heeled white boots and Dynasty hair? Even more to the point, how many serious sports exist mainly to glorify the accomplishments of people participating in a whole different sport?

The task force wanted to ban the Illinettes for fear they'd give male college students the idea that women are sex objects. I worry more about the ideas they might give little girls.

Withers, defending the Illinettes, said they're campus role models, and no doubt they are. But what kind of role models are they? What kind of message are they sending about what girls should value about themselves, and what their possibilities are? The values the Illinettes embody are: being thin, being beautiful, being coordinated, having white teeth and lots of hair and lots of energy, smiling, staying in shape, and wearing sexy little costumes. The role they play at football games suggests that a woman's principal role in life should be encouraging men, and supporting them, and making them feel good about themselves, and telling them how great they are, and getting everybody else to say so too.

These values make a lot of sense for a society looking to produce more Vanna Whites and Marla Mapleses. But if we're looking for Marie Curies and Georgia O'Keeffes and Edith Whartons, maybe it's time to change channels.

QUESTIONS ON THE REVISION

1. Why might McLaughlin have eliminated the references to Pam Withers, the captain of the Illinettes?

2. Focus just on paragraph 6 in the first draft and in the final version. Specifically, what was the nature of the changes that McLaughlin introduced?

3. McLaughlin completely rewrote the ending of the essay. Why might she have dropped the first draft ending—with its references to specific women?

4. In a second draft of the essay, McLaughlin substituted still another ending, which was then later worked into an earlier section of the essay. How effective is this second draft version as a conclusion to the essay?

As my friend Paula asked, Why do they figure the only way to keep men from committing crimes is to restrict women's freedom? It's insidious, because it begins to suggest that rape is women's own fault, and that the only way to protect them from men's presumably ungovernable sexual appetites is to restrict their freedom. Carried to its extreme, it leaves women in purdah, so constrained by the presumably ungovernable sexual appetites of men that they have no lives.

WRITING SUGGESTIONS

1. **For your Journal**. Male cheerleaders wear long pants; drum majors wear long pants. Female cheerleaders wear short skirts; majorettes or baton twirlers wear body suits. Doesn't this sound sexist? Speculate on this idea in your journal.

2. **For a Paragraph**. Study the changes that McLaughlin made in the second half of the essay. Formulate a thesis about the reason(s) for one or more of those changes. Then, in a paragraph, assert your thesis and support it with evidence from the text.

3. **For an Essay**. In a serious essay, respond to McLaughlin's argument. Your essay might take several possible forms:

   a. Disagree with her position and argue in support of such "pompom" squads.

   b. Agree with her position, but suggest a compromise alternative to such practices.

   c. Agree with her position and write an essay in which you try to dissuade young women from joining such activities.

   Prewriting:

   a. Regardless of the position you plan to take, make a list of all the reasons you can think of for both sides of the argument. Which reasons seem the most effective?

   b. Brainstorm about your audience—how are they likely to feel about the position you are taking? Jot down what you anticipate and then try out your argument on friends. How do they react?

   c. Remember that the first section of your essay should have two parts—one that introduces the subject to your reader in an interesting, readable way and one that summarizes McLaughlin's position. Do you have both sections?

Rewriting:

a. Look again at how you structured your essay. Have you started or ended with your strongest point? If you reversed the order, would your paper be more effective? Try it.

b. Check through your essay line by line. Mark any words or phrases that might be ineffective or might detract from your argument. Ask a classmate, friend, your instructor, or a tutor from your writing center to evaluate each marked example.

c. Check your language. Have you used words that are too emotionally charged? Remember that calling people names or distorting the opposition's position might make you feel better, but it will never help you persuade an audience.

4. For Research. You have been asked by the dean of students at your college or university to prepare a report making recommendations about campus activities that appear to portray women in sexist roles (for example, cheerleaders, majorettes, homecoming or campus queens). The dean wants you to include research about what other colleges or universities have done with this issue. Research the problem through the various periodicals that deal with feminist issues and higher education (such as *The Chronicle of Higher Education*). You might interview your own dean of students as well. Has this ever been an issue on your campus?

FINDING, USING, AND DOCUMENTING SOURCES

FINDING SOURCES

All effective writing involves some form of research. To write a laboratory report in chemistry, you use the information gathered from performing the experiment. To write an article for the student newspaper on your college's latest tuition increase, you include information gathered in interviews with those involved in making that decision. To answer a mid-term examination, you marshal evidence from lecture notes and from required reading.

As these examples demonstrate, you may use a wide variety of sources when you research any particular topic.

> **Firsthand knowledge.** Your own observations and experience play a major role in much of your writing. Such knowledge can be simple and acquired easily (before writing a review of a restaurant, you would sample the cuisine and service) or complex and gathered laboriously (scientists will study the AIDS virus for years, gathering information and testing out hypotheses by performing experiments).
>
> **Printed knowledge.** The bulk of your knowledge for the papers you will typically write in college comes from printed sources, including
>
> **a.** reference works such as dictionaries and encyclopedias
> **b.** books
> **c.** articles in magazines and journals
> **d.** articles in newspapers
> **e.** government documents

Interviewing. On many topics you can gather information through talking with those involved. A newspaper reporter writing about the latest tuition increase, for example, would have to rely on information provided by administrators and budget analysts.

Although all writing uses sources, not all writing meets the special considerations that we associate with a research paper. Not only does a research paper document its sources, it also exhibits a particular approach to its subject. A research paper is not just a collection of information about a subject. Instead, a research paper poses a particular question or thesis about its subject and then sets out to answer that question or test the validity of that thesis.

In some important ways you should approach the research that you do for a college paper in the same way that a scientist sets about exploring a problem. The idea behind research—all research—is to isolate a particular aspect of a subject, to become an expert in that defined area, and to present an original or new conclusion about that material. Because research papers have a thesis, they differ significantly from the informational overviews that we find in encyclopedia articles. Many writers confuse the two forms of writing. The confusion probably dates back to grade school when a teacher assigned a report on, say, Jupiter. What most of us did was go to the *World Book* or another encyclopedia, look up "Jupiter," and then copy down the entry. That might have been an appropriate response for a grade school assignment, but such a strategy will never work for a college research paper.

USING REFERENCE BOOKS AS A STARTING POINT: ENCYCLOPEDIAS AND DICTIONARIES

If you do not already have a fairly detailed knowledge about your subject, encyclopedias and dictionaries can be good places to begin your research. Before using such reference works, however, you should remember two important points. First, encyclopedias and dictionaries are only good as starting points, providing just a basic overview of a subject. You will never be able to rely solely on such sources for college-level research. Second, encyclopedias and dictionaries range from general works that cover a wide range of subjects (such as the *Encyclopedia Britannica*, *Encyclopedia Americana*, and *Collier's Encyclopedia*) to highly specialized works focused around a single area or subject.

Because general encyclopedias provide information about a variety of subjects, they can never contain as much information about a single subject as you can find in a encyclopedia that specializes in that subject. For this reason, you might begin any search with a specialized encyclopedia. The word "specialized" in this sense refers primarily to the more focused subject coverage that these works offer; most of the articles are still written in nontechnical language. The word "dictionary," as it is used in the titles of these works, means essentially the same thing as encyclopedia—a collection of articles of varying lengths arranged alphabetically.

Your school is likely to have a wide range of specialized encyclopedias and dictionaries. In order to locate these reference tools, try the following steps:

1. Consult a guide to reference works. The following guides to reference books are widely available in college and university libraries. Use one or more of them to establish a list of possible works to consult.

   Annie M. Brewer, *Dictionaries, Encyclopedias, and other Word-Related Books* (3 vols), 3rd ed. (1982). Volume 1 is devoted to English-language sources.

   Kenneth F. Kister, *Best Encyclopedias: A Guide to General and Specialized Encyclopedias*, (1986). Detailed descriptions of over 500 works.

   Eugene Sheehy, *Guide to Reference Books*, 10th ed. (1986). *Supplement, 1985–1990* (1992).

   Walford's Concise Guide to Reference Material, 2nd ed. (1992).

2. Check in the library's catalogue under the headings "[Your subject]—Dictionaries" and "[Your subject]—Dictionaries and Encyclopedias."

3. Ask a reference librarian for advice on the specialized sources likely to be relevant to your topic.

FINDING BOOKS:
YOUR LIBRARY'S CATALOG

Every library has an index or catalog that lists the material contained in its collections. Each item is entered by author's name, by title, and generally by a few of the most important subject headings. Library catalogs come in a variety of forms. Traditional catalogs consist of 3" by 5" card files arranged alphabetically in drawers; the author, title, and subject cards may all be filed together, or the catalog may be divided into two sections—one that lists authors and titles and another that lists subjects. In most college and university libraries, however, computers are changing the form of library catalogs. With all information about each item contained in one large data-base, users can access holdings through a computer terminal, searching by author, title, or subject. Some of these *on-line catalogs* not only display call numbers, but also tell you whether the item you want has been checked out or is on the shelves.

When you start a search for books in your library's catalog, remember these key points:

- All catalogs—whether filed in drawers or stored on-line—list only material owned by that particular library or other libraries in the area or state. No library owns a copy of every book.

- Library catalogs list books (by author, title, and a few subject headings) and journals (*only* by title). Library catalogs never include the authors or titles of individual articles contained within journals or magazines.

- Much information on any subject—and generally the most current information—is found in journal articles, not in books. Remember as well that certain subjects may not be treated in books. For example, if a subject is very current or too specialized, no book may have been written about it. Therefore, a search for sources should *never* be limited to those references found in a library catalog.

- In initial searches for information, you are typically looking for subjects—that is, you do not yet have a specific title or author to look up. Searching for subjects in a library catalog can be considerably more complicated than it might initially seem since the subject headings used in library catalogs are often not what you might expect. Unless you use the subject heading or key word that the catalog uses, you will not find what you are looking for. The next section offers some advice about subject headings.

CHOOSING THE RIGHT SUBJECT HEADING

The success of any research paper depends in part upon finding reliable and appropriate sources of information. For most college papers, your information will come from *secondary* sources, typically books and articles that report the research done by others. Depending upon your subject, you might also be able to use *primary* sources—original documents (historical records, letters, works of literature) or the results of original research (laboratory experiments, interviews, questionnaires).

Finding sources is not hard—no matter what your subject—but it does require knowing *how* and *where* to look. A quick tour of your college or university library, with its rows of shelves, is a vivid proof that you need a *search strategy*. The first step in that strategy is to locate subject headings and key words that can be used to retrieve information.

The subject headings used in library catalogs and periodical indexes are part of a fixed, interlocking system that is both logically organized and highly structured. The idea is not to list every possible subject heading under which a particular subject might be found, but to establish general headings under which related subjects can be grouped. Most libraries use the subject headings suggested by the Library of Congress and published in the *Library of Congress Subject Headings* (LCSH), a four-volume set of books typically found near your library's catalog or in the reference area. In addition, most periodical indexes also use either the same system or one so similar that the LCSH headings will still serve your purpose. As a result, the most efficient way to begin a subject search is to check the LCSH for appropriate subject headings under which books and articles on your subject will be listed.

For example, suppose that as you read Gloria Steinem's "Why Young Women Are More Conservative" (Chapter 7), you were surprised to discover that when Steinem wrote her article, women earned only about 75 percent of what men earned. So you decided to do some research to discover the extent to which that disparity still exists. Exactly what key words or subject headings would you look under in a catalog or periodical index to find appropriate sources: Women? Work? Job discrimination? Salaries? Unless you know where to begin, you might waste a considerable amount of time guessing randomly or conclude (quite wrongly) that your library had no information on the topic.

If you consulted the *Library of Congress Subject Headings* you would find cross references that would lead you to the following:

> Equal pay for work of comparable value
>> USE Pay equity
> **Equal pay for equal work** *(May Subd Geog)*
>> Here are entered works on equal pay for jobs that require identical skills, responsibilities, and effort. Works on comparable pay for jobs that require comparable skills, responsibilities, effort, and working conditions are entered under Pay equity.
>> BT   Discrimination in employment
>>   Wages
>> RT   Women—Employment
>> **—Law and registration** *(May Subd Geog)*
>> BT   Labor laws and legislation
> Equal pay for work of comparable value
>> USE Pay equity

The Library of Congress Subject Headings use three sets of abbreviations to indicate the relationships among subjects. By following the cross references, you can conduct a more thorough search. The relationships that are signaled include

Equivalence: USE
Hierarchy: BT(broader term)
            NT (narrower term)
Association: RT (related term)

Having checked the key to using the headings, you know from these entries not to search under "Equal pay for comparable work" since the heading is not in bold type; instead, you are told to use "Pay Equity." The best heading under which to search for books and articles related to your topic is **"Equal pay for equal work."** The abbreviation, "May Subd Geog," indicates that the heading might be subdivided geographically, for example, "Equal pay for equal work—Delaware." The LC Subject Headings also suggest other possibilities: for a broader term (BT) use "Discrimination in employment" or "Wages"; for a related term, use "Woman—Employment." You will find relevant information under all of these possible headings. In general, no one subject heading will retrieve all of the books that your library has on a particular topic.

Here are a few cautions to keep in mind when using subject headings:

1. Always check the *Library of Congress Subject Headings* first to find the best headings to use for your subject. The quickest way to short-circuit your search strategy is to begin with a heading that you think will work, find nothing, and then assume that no information exists in your library on that topic.

2. Remember that the headings used might not be as specific as you want. You might need to browse through a group of related materials to find the more precise information you are seeking.

Subject headings use a *controlled vocabulary*; that is, all information about a particular subject is grouped under a single heading with appropriate cross references from other related headings. For example, if your subject was "capital punishment," you would not also need to look under the headings "the death penalty," "execution," or "death row." Controlled vocabularies do, however, place some restrictions on your search strategy. As we've mentioned, subject headings aren't always as precise as you would like them to be. Furthermore, "new" subjects might not appear within the scheme for several years. For example, although "glasnost" is a common term today, it is not a heading used by the Library of Congress.

An alternative to subject heading searching is *key word* searching. A key word is a significant word, almost always a noun, that is used in the titles of books, reports, or articles. By combining key words you can conduct very precise searches. Key words are often used in computerized searches, including searches of computerized library catalogs.

Using Your Search for Subject Headings and Key Words to Revise Your Topic

Your search for subject headings and key words is also a valuable tool in helping you sharpen and define your topic. Typically, despite the most diligent efforts to find a truly specific topic within a larger subject, you will begin your research strategy with a topic that is really still a subject, too large to research effectively or write about within the limits of a freshman English research paper. If the subject headings you use yield a mountain of published research, obviously you need to focus your topic more precisely.

Finding Magazines, Journals, and Newspapers

The greater amount of information on almost any topic will be found not in books but in magazines and journals. (College and university libraries generally do not use the term "magazine"; instead, they refer to "periodicals" or "serials"; these two terms indicate that the publication appears periodically or that it is an installment of a larger whole.) You'll find that most of the thousands of magazines sold at your local newsstand—whether issued weekly, biweekly, or monthly —cannot be found in your college or university library. Correspondingly, most of the journals found in your college's periodical room cannot be purchased on a newsstand. They are too specialized; they appeal to too limited an audience. Most, if not all, of your research for college papers should be done in the journals that your library holds.

Unfortunately, there is no single index to all periodical literature. (Similarly, most newspapers, with the exception of some large ones such as *The New York Times*, are not indexed at all.) You will, therefore, have to consult a variety of indexes depending upon the particular subject you are researching. Until recently, most periodical's indexes were printed volumes updated on a regular basis. Increasingly, however, periodicals' indexes are computerized, particularly on CD-ROM disks. Both types of indexes are described below. Check with your reference librarian to see what indexes to periodical literature your library owns.

GENERAL PERIODICALS INDEXES

- *The Readers' Guide to Periodical Literature* (1900-). Indexes about 180 popular periodicals, most of which can be purchased at newsstands.
- *InfoTrac.* A computerized data base on CD-ROM that comprises a number of different data bases, the most widely held of which are **Academic Index** (1987), an index to about 400 scholarly and general interest journals on the humanities, the social sciences, the general sciences, and current events (also available as an Expanded Academic Index with over 960 journals); the **Business Index** (1982-), which includes about 800 journals on business, management, and trade; and the **National Newspaper Index** (1991), which includes major newspapers such as *The New York Times, The Christian Science Monitor,* the *Wall Street Journal,* and the *Washington Post.*
- *Business Index* (1979-). A microfiche index to more than 810 business periodicals available on microfilm.
- *Magazine Index* (1977-). A microfiche index to over 400 popular periodicals (including all of those in the *Readers' Guide*) that are available on microfilm.
- *The New York Times Index* (1851-). A bound index of news and articles appearing in *The New York Times.* Since many libraries subscribe to the *Times* on microfilm, this can be a useful source of information.

SPECIALIZED PERIODICALS INDEXES

- *America: History and Life* (1964-). Indexes about 140 journals and magazines publishing articles on North American history and life.
- *Art Index* (1929-). Indexes about 200 journals and bulletins in fields such as archeology, architecture, art history, city planning, fine and graphic arts, industrial design, interior and landscape design, photography, and film.

- *Applied Science and Technology Index* (1958–). Indexes about 300 periodicals in fields such as aeronautics, chemistry, computer science, energy resources, engineering, nutrition, oceanography, plastics, telecommunications, textiles, and transportation.
- *Biography Index* (1946–). Indexes biographical information appearing in more than 3,000 periodicals, standard biographical reference books (such as *Who's Who*), and *The New York Times* obituaries. The place to begin any search for biographical information.
- *Biological and Agricultural Index* (1964–). Indexes about 180 periodicals in biology and agriculture.
- *Business Periodicals Index* (1958–). Indexes about 300 periodicals in business fields such as accounting, advertising, banking, communications, economics, finance, insurance, labor, marketing, and public relations.
- *Education Index* (1929-). Indexes approximately 330 periodicals in all areas of education.
- *Current Index to Journals in Education* (1969-). Indexes about 750 education journals.
- *General Sciences Index* (1978-). Indexes about 90 periodicals in fields such as astronomy, biology, chemistry, earth and environmental sciences, genetics, mathematics, medicine, psychology, and zoology.
- *Humanities Index* (1974-). Indexes about 300 periodicals in fields such as criticism, folklore, history, language and literature, performing arts, philosophy, and religion.
- *Index Medicus* (1960-). Indexes approximately 2,750 biomedical journals.
- *Index to Legal Periodicals* (1908-). Indexes over 460 law periodicals and certain other law publications.
- *MLA International Bibliography of Books and Articles in the Modern Languages and Literatures* (1922-). Indexes books and articles (over 3,100 periodicals) on the modern languages, literature, folklore, and linguistics. The bibliography from 1981 is also available on CD-ROM.
- *Music Index* (1949-). Indexes about 370 periodicals on different aspects of music including bluegrass, classical, folk, jazz, opera, and rock.
- *Social Sciences Index* (1974-). Indexes about 300 periodicals in fields such as anthropology, criminology, economics, geography, international relations, nursing, political science, psychiatry, psychology, social work, sociology, and urban studies.

The United States government is the world's largest publisher of statistical information. On many research topics, government documents represent an excellent source of information. Most college libraries house collections of such documents, often located in a special area. Government documents are arranged by a Superintendent of Documents call number system which indicates the agency that released the document. Check with your reference or government documents librarian for help in locating relevant documents for your research. Depending on what indexes your library owns, the following are good starting points for research.

- *Government Documents Catalog Service* (GDCS). The Government Printing Office Index on CD-ROM. Indexes government publications catalogued by the Government Printing Office from June 1976 to the present.
- *Public Affairs Information Service International* (PAIS). Available on CD-ROM, indexing English-language source material since 1976; also available as a printed text, *PAIS International* (1915-). Indexes and abstracts books, government publications, and scholarly journals in the fields of public policy and international affairs.
- *Monthly Catalog of United States Government Publications.* Printed catalog held in most libraries, running from 1895-.
- *Congressional Information Service Index* and *Abstracts* (CIS). Indexes and abstracts documents from Congressional Committees (1970-).

INTERVIEWING

Depending upon your topic, you may find that people—and not just books and articles—will be an important source of information. To gain insight into the phenomenon of using barely dressed male models in advertisements, for example, Judith Gaines interviewed sociologists, advertising executives, and consumers for her article "The 'Beefcake Years'" (Chapter 7). In researching the production of new series for her article "Birth of a TV Show" (Chapter 6), Elizabeth Kolbert relied exclusively on interviews with writers and network executives.

If you decide to interview someone in the course of your research, you must first choose a person who has special credentials or knowledge about the subject. For example, while working on an essay about campus drinking, you might realize that it would be valuable and interesting to include specific information about the incidence of drinking at your school. To get such data, you could talk to the Dean of Students or the Director of Health Services. Additionally, you might also talk to students who acknowledge that they have had problems with alcohol.

Once you have drawn up a list of possible people to interview, you need to plan your interviewing strategy. When you first contact someone to request an interview, always explain who you are, what you want to know, and how you will use the information. Establish any crucial guidelines for the interview—students who have problems with binge drinking, for instance, would probably not want to have their real names used in an essay. Remember to arrive at the interview on time and to be prepared, having already done some fairly thorough research about the topic. Do not impose on your interviewee by stating, "I've just started to research this problem, and I would like you to tell me everything you know about it." Prepare a list of questions in advance, the more specific the better. (This does not mean limiting yourself to simple "yes-no" or single answer questions; in fact, questions that ask the interviewee to elaborate on a response or to speculate on an issue can be especially effective.) Take notes, but expand those notes as soon as you leave the interview, while the conversation is still fresh in your mind. You might also be able to use a tape recorder, but only if you ask permission first. Keep attention focused on the information that you need, and do not be afraid to ask follow-up questions that will keep your interviewee focused on your subject. If you plan to use direct quotations, make sure that the wording is accurate. If possible, check the quotations with your source one final time.

Quotations from interviews should be integrated into your text in the same way as quotations from printed texts—make sure they are essential to your paper, keep them short, use ellipses if necessary, and try to position them at the ends of your sentences. When you are quoting someone who is an expert or an authority, it is best to include a reference to his or her position within your text, setting off that description or job title with commas:

> Explaining the network's concession to Ms. Kauffman and Mr. Crane, Warren Littlefield, the president of NBC Entertainment, said, "You have to make a substantial commitment to be in business with them."
>
> Elizabeth Kolbert, "Birth of a TV Show" (Chapter 6)

Most researched writing—and virtually every college research paper—needs to be based on a variety of sources, not simply one or two. A single source always represents only one point of view and necessarily contains a limited amount of information. In fact, a wide range of sources are available for any subject—encyclopedias and other reference tools; books; articles in specialized journals, popular magazines, and newspapers; pamphlets; government documents; interviews; research experiments or studies. Your instructor might specify both the number and the nature of the sources that you are to use, but even if the choice is up to you, make sure that you have a varied set of sources.

Evaluating Sources

Primarily, you want your sources to be accurate, specific, up-to-date, and unbiased. Not every source will meet those criteria. Just because something is in print doesn't mean that it is true or accurate—just think of the tabloids displayed at any supermarket checkout. In your search for information, you need to evaluate the reliability and accuracy of each source, because you don't want to base your paper on inaccurate, distorted, or biased information.

Obviously, evaluating sources is less difficult if you are already an expert on the subject you are researching. But how can you evaluate sources when you first start to gather information? The problem is not as formidable as it at first seems for you regularly evaluate written sources when you try to answer day-to-day questions.

For example, if you are interested in information about the best way to lose weight, which of the following sources would you be most likely to trust?

- an article in the *National Enquirer* ("Lose 10 Pounds this Weekend on the Amazing Prune Diet!")
- an article in a popular magazine ("How to Lose a Pound a Week")
- a brochure urging the value of a particular weight-reduction program (for example, electrotherapy treatments, a liquid diet plan, or wraps)
- a newspaper article offering advice on weight loss
- a magazine article published in 1930 dealing with diets
- a book written by medical doctors, dietitians, and fitness experts published in 1994

You would probably reject the *National Enquirer* article (not necessarily objective, accurate, or reliable), the brochure (potentially biased and likely to exaggerate the value of that particular treatment), and the article published in 1930 (out-of-date). The articles in the popular magazine and the newspaper might have some value but, given the limitations of space and the interests of their audiences, would probably be too general and too sketchy to be of much use. Presumably, the best source of information would be the new book written by obvious experts.

Evaluating printed sources for a research paper is pretty much a comparable activity. A good source must meet the following tests:

1. **Is the source objective?** You can assess objectivity in several ways. For example, does the language used in the work, and even in its title, seem sensational or biased? Is the work published by an organization that might have a special, biased interest in the subject? Does it contain documented facts? Are there bibliographical references, footnotes, and lists of works consulted? How reliable are the "authorities" quoted? Are their titles or credentials cited? The more scholarly and impartial the source seems, the greater the likelihood that the information it contains can be trusted.

2. **Is the source accurate?** Reputable newspapers and magazines make serious efforts to ensure that what they publish is accurate. Similarly, books published by university presses or by large, well-known publishing houses are probably reliable, and journals published by scholarly or professional organizations very likely contain accurate information. As a rule, the more specialized the readership of the work, the more you can trust it. For books, you could locate reviews to see critical readers' evaluations. The *Book Review Index* and the *Book Review Digest* can be found in your library's reference room.

3. **Is the source current?** In general, the more current the source, the greater the likelihood that new discoveries will be considered. Current information might not be crucial in discussing literary works, but it makes a great deal of difference in many other fields.

4. **Is the author an authority?** What can you find out about the author's credentials? Are they cited anywhere? What does the nature of the source tell you about the author's expertise?

Even though much of the information in a research paper—facts, opinions, statistics, and so forth—will be taken from outside sources, a research paper should never be just a cut-and-paste collection of quotations with a few bridge sentences written by you. The major part of your research paper should be in *your* own words. You can achieve this balance by remembering several points:

- Ask yourself if the quotation is really necessary. If something is "common" knowledge, you do not need to quote an authority for that information; any information that is widely known or that can be found in general reference works may be included in your own words.

- Keep your quotations as short as possible. Use large chunks of indented direct quotations sparingly, if at all.

- Avoid strings of quotations. You should never pile up quotations in a row. Rather, you should interpret and control the material that you are using and provide transitions for the reader that tie the quotations into your text.

- Learn to paraphrase and summarize instead of giving direct quotations. What is generally important is the idea or the facts that you find in your sources, not the exact words. Paraphrasing means putting the source material into your own words; summarizing goes even further in that you try to condense the quotation into the fewest possible words.

- Learn to use an ellipsis to shorten a quotation. An ellipsis consists of three spaced periods. It is used to indicate that a word, part of a sentence, a whole sentence, or a group of sentences has been omitted from the quotation.

WORKING QUOTATIONS INTO YOUR TEXT

Unless the quotation is only a few words long, try to place it at the end of your sentence. Avoid "sandwich" sentences in which a quotation comes between two parts of your own sentence. If you introduce a several-line quotation into the middle of a sentence, by the end of the sentence the reader will probably have forgotten how your sentence began.

When you place a quotation at the end of a sentence, use a colon or a comma to introduce it. The colon signals that the quotation supports, clarifies, or illustrates the point being made.

John Barker, vice president of the National Consumers League, said: "There's no reason someone shouldn't send stuff into Publisher's Clearing House. It's harmless."

Tim Johnson, "You Have Definitely Won!" (Chapter 1)

One advice book, *Common Sense for Maid, Wife, and Mother* stated: "Heated discussion and quarrels, fretfulness and sullen taciturnity while eating, are as unwholesome as they are unchristian."

Joan Jacobs Brumberg, "The Origins of Anorexia Nervosa: (Chapter 7)

If the introductory statement is not a dependent clause, always use a comma before the quotation. For example, in the following sentence, the introductory clause ("As . . . Barthes writes") is not a complete sentence.

As French philosopher Roland Barthes writes, "cars today are almost the exact equivalent of the great Gothic catherdrals . . . the supreme creation of an era, conceived with passion by unknown artists, and consumed in image if not in usage by a whole population which appropriates them as purely magical objects."

Alan Durning, "How Much is 'Enough'?" (Chapter 9)

If a complete sentence follows the colon, the first word after the colon may or may not be capitalized. The choice is yours, but be consistent. However, if the colon introduces a quotation, then the first word following that colon is capitalized.

DOCUMENTING YOUR SOURCES

Research papers require documentation—that is, you need to document or acknowledge those pieces of information that you have taken from your sources. The documentation serves two purposes. First, it acknowledges your use of someone else's work. Whenever you take something from a published source—statistics, ideas, or opinions, whether quoted or in your own words—you must acknowledge where it comes from (in other words, that it is not your original work). Otherwise, you will be guilty of academic dishonesty. Students who borrow material from sources without acknowledgement—that is, plagiarize—are subject to some form of academic penalty. Writers and people in the business world who do so can be sued. Documentation is necessary if a researcher is to maintain his or her honesty and integrity. Documentation also serves a second purpose, however: It gives you greater credibility because your reader knows he or she can locate and evaluate the sources that you used.

Although different disciplines use different citation systems, in most introductory writing classes you will be asked to use either the MLA or the APA form of documentation. MLA stands for the Modern Language Association, an organization of teachers of modern foreign languages and of English. A full guide to that system can be found in the *MLA Handbook for Writers of Research Papers* (3rd edition, 1988). APA is the American Psychological Association and its style guide, *Publication Manual of the American Psychological Association* (3rd edition, 1983) is widely used by teachers of the social sciences.

Documentation systems are standardized; that is, the systems have a fixed order and form in which the bibliographical information about the source is given. Even the marks of punctuation are specified. No one, however, expects you to memorize, for example, the MLA citation system. Rather, the style guides are models. You should look at each of your sources, noting its particular features (for example, what type of source was it? how many authors did it have? in what type of book or journal did it appear?). You should then locate a similar example from the citation system that you are using, and use that sample as a model for your own citation. Citation formats for the sources most commonly used in a freshman English research paper are given below. But because the range of possible sources on any topic is very large, you might have a source that does not match any of these common examples. For a complete guide consult either the *MLA Handbook* or the APA *Publication Manual*. Both can be found in the reference area of your school's library.

ACKNOWLEDGING SOURCES IN YOUR TEXT

Both the MLA and APA systems acknowledge sources with brief parenthetical citations in the text. The reader can then check the "List of Words Cited" (the MLA title) or "References" (the APA title) at the end of the paper for the full bibliographical reference. In the MLA system the author's last name is included along with the number of the page on which the information appears. In the APA system the author's last name is included, along with the year the source was published and, for direct quotations, the page number. Notice in the following examples that the punctuation within the parentheses varies from MLA to APA.

Here is how a quotation from an article, "Immuno-Logistics," written by Gary Stix, that appeared in the June 1994 issue of *Scientific American* would be cited in the two systems:

MLA: The major vaccines—those for diphtheria, pertussis, tetanus, polio, measles, and tuberculosis—cost less to make than they do to distribute: "The United Nations Children's Fund, for example, spends a total of $1.50 on the vaccines. . . . A tenth of what a government then has to disburse for labor, transportation, training and refrigeration to get these vaccines to infants and young children" (Stix 102).

APA: The major vaccines—those for diptheria, pertussis, tetanus, polio, measles, and tuberculosis—cost less to make than they do to distribute: "The United Nations Children's Fund, for example, spends a total of $1.50 on the vaccines. . . . A tenth of what a government then has to disburse for labor, transportation, training and refrigeration to get these vaccines to infants and young children" (Stix, 1994, p.102).

Note that in both cases the parenthetical citation comes before any final punctuation.

If you include the author's name in your sentence, then you omit that part of the reference within the parentheses.

MLA: According to Gary Stix, the major vaccines—those for diptheria, pertussis, tetanus, polio, measles, and tuberculosis—cost less to make than they do to distribute: "The United Nations Children's Fund, for example, spends a total of $1.50 on the vaccines. . . . A tenth of what a government then has to disburse for labor, transportation, training and refrigeration to get these vaccines to infants and young children" (102).

APA: According to Gary Stix (1994), the major vaccines—those for diphtheria, pertussis, tetanus, polio, measles, and tuberculosis—cost less to make than they do to distribute: "The United Nations Children's Fund, for example, spends a total of $1.50 on the vaccines. . . . A tenth of what a government then has to disburse for labor, transportation, training and refrigeration to get these vaccines to infants and young children" (p.102).

Note that in the APA system the date in such cases goes in parentheses after the author's name in the text.

A quotation of four lines or more should be indented or set off from your text. In such cases, the parenthetical citation comes after the indented quotation. Here is how a quotation from "A Weight That Women Carry" by Sallie Tisdale, which appeared in the March 1993 issue of *Harper's* magazine, would be cited in the two systems:

MLA: Sallie Tisdale points out the links between weight "reduction" and the "smallness" that society presses upon women:

> Small is what feminism strives against, the smallness that women confront everywhere. All of women's spaces are smaller than those of men, often inadequate, without privacy. Furniture designers distinguish between a man's and a woman's chair, because women don't spread out like men. (A sprawling woman means only one thing.) Even our voices are kept down. (53)

APA: Sallie Tisdale (1993) points out the links between weight "reduction" and the "smallness" that society presses upon women:

> Small is what feminism strives against, the smallness that women confront everywhere. All of women's spaces are smaller than those of men, often inadequate, without privacy. Furniture designers distinguish between a man's and a woman's chair, because women don't spread out like men. (A sprawling woman means only one thing.) Even our voices are kept down. (p. 53)

Note in both cases that the parenthetical citation comes after the final period.

If you are quoting material that has been quoted by someone else, cite the secondary source from which you took the material. Do not cite the original if you did not directly consult it. Here is how a quotation from an original source—a nuclear strategist writing in 1967—quoted on page 357 in a 1985 book written by Paul Boyer and titled By the Bomb's Early Light: American Thought and Culture at the Dawn of the Atomic Age would be cited.

MLA: Explaining how Americans' views of the atom bomb shifted during the 1950's, Albert Wohlstetter, a nuclear strategist, commented in 1967: "Bright hopes for civilian nuclear energy" proved to be "an emotional counterweight to . . . nuclear destruction" (qtd. in Boyer 357).

APA: Explaining how Americans' views of the atom bomb

shifted during the 1950's, Albert Wohlstetter, a nuclear strategist, commented in 1967: "Bright hopes for civilian nuclear energy" proved to be "an emotional counterweight to . . . nuclear destruction" (cited in Boyer, 1985, p. 357).

In certain situations you may need to include additional or slightly different information in your parenthetical citation. For example, when two or more sources on your list of references are by the same author, your citation will need to make clear to which of these you are referring; in the MLA system you do this by including a brief version of the title along with the author and page number: (Tisdale, "Weight," 53). (Note that this is generally not a problem in the APA system because works by the same author will already be distinguished by date.) For works that do not indicate an author, mention the title fully in your text or include a brief version in the parenthetical citation: (*MLA Handbook* 166).

THE "LIST OF WORKS CITED" OR "REFERENCES" PAGE

At the end of your essay, on a separate sheet of paper, you should list all of those works that you cited in your paper. In the MLA system this page is titled "List of Works Cited" (with no quotation marks); in the APA system, it is titled "References" (also no quotation marks). The list should be alphabetized by the authors' last names so that readers can easily find full information about particular sources. Both systems provide essentially the same information:

Books

- *For books*: the author's or authors' names, the title, the place of publication, the publisher's name, and the year of publication.
- *For articles*: the author's or authors' names, the title, the name of the journal, the volume number and/or the date of that issue, and the pages on which the article appeared.

Note in the following sample entries that in MLA style, the first line of each entry is flush with the left margin and subsequent lines are indented five spaces; in APA style, the first line also is flush left and subsequent lines are indented three spaces.

A book by a single author

MLA: Boyer, Paul. *By the Bomb's Early Light: American Thought and Culture at the Dawn of the Atomic Age.* New York: Random House, 1985.

APA: Boyer, P. (1985). *By the bomb's early light: American thought and culture at the dawn of the atomic age.* New York: Random House.

An anthology

MLA: Ibieta, Gabriella, ed. *Latin American Writers: Thirty Stories.* New York: St. Martin's, 1993.

APA: Ibieta, G. (Ed.). (1993). *Latin American writers: Thirty stories.* New York: St. Martin's.

A book by multiple authors

MLA: Burns, Ailsa, and Cath Scott. *Mother-Headed Families and Why They Have Increased.* Hillsdale, NJ: Lawrence Erlbaum, 1994.

APA: Burns, A., & Scott, C. (1994). *Mother-headed families and why they have increased.* Hillsdale, NJ: Lawrence Erlbaum.

A book with no author's name

MLA: *Native American Directory.* San Carlos, AZ: National Native American Co-operative, 1982.

APA: *Native American Directory.* (1982). San Carlos, AZ: National Native American Co-operative.

An article or story in an edited anthology

MLA: Quartermaine, Peter. "Margaret Atwood's *Surfacing*: Strange Familiarity." *Margaret Atwood: Writing and Subjectivity.* Ed. Colin Nicholson. New York: St. Martin's, 1994. 119–32.

APA: Quartermaine, P. (1994). Margaret Atwood's *Surfacing:* Strange familiarity. In C. Nicholson (Ed.), *Margaret Atwood: Writing and subjectivity* (pp. 119–32). New York: St. Martin's.

An article in a reference work

MLA: "Film Noir.": *Oxford Companion to Film.* Ed. Liz-Anne Bawden. New York: Oxford, 1976. 249.

APA: Film Noir. (1976). In L. Bawden (Ed.), *Oxford companion to film* (p. 249). New York: Oxford.

Articles

An article in a journal that is continuously paginated (that is, issues after the first in a year do not start at page 1)

MLA: Meyer, David S. "Political Opportunity after the Cold War." *Peace & Change* 19 (1994): 114–40.

APA: Meyer, D. (1994). Political opportunity after the cold war. *Peace & Change, 19,* 114–40.

Note: When each issue of a journal does begin with page 1, also indicate the issue number after the volume number. For MLA style, separate the two with a period: 9.2. For APA style, use parentheses: *9*(2).

An article in a monthly magazine

MLA: Hubbell, Sue. "You Can Still Get It at the 'Dime Store,' but not for a Dime." *Smithsonian* June 1994: 104–12.

APA: Hubbell, S. (1994, June). You can still get it at the 'dime store,' but not for a dime. *Smithsonian,* pp. 104–12.

An article in a weekly or biweekly magazine

MLA: Bruck, Connie. "Hillary the Pol." *The New Yorker* 30 May 1994: 58–96.

APA: Bruck, C. (1994, May 30). Hillary the pol. *The New Yorker,* pp. 58–96.

An article in a daily newspaper

MLA: Feldmann, Linda. "Efforts to Revamp Superfund May Be Running Out of Time." *The Christian Science Monitor* 9 June 1994: 3.

APA: Feldmann, L. (1994, June 9). Efforts to revamp superfund may be running out of time. *The Christian Science Monitor,* p. 3.

An editorial in a newspaper

MLA: "Reaching Drunk Drivers Early." Editorial. *Chicago Tribune* 8 June 1994, sec. 1: 12.

APA: Reaching drunk drivers early. (1994, June 8). [Editorial]. *Chicago Tribune,* Section I, p. 12.

A review

MLA: Tinder, Glenn. "Liberalism and Its Enemies." Rev. of *The Anatomy of Antiliberalism,* by Stephen Holmes. *Atlantic* Oct. 1993: 116–22.

APA: Tinder, G. (1993, October). Liberalism and its enemies. [Review of *The anatomy of antiliberalism,* by Stephen Holmes]. *Atlantic,* pp. 116–22.

Other sources

An interview

MLA: Quintana, Alvina. Personal interview. 13 June 1994. Worthington, Joanne. Telephone interview. 12 Dec. 1993.

Note: APA style does not include personal interviews on the Reference list, but rather cites pertinent information parenthetically in the text.

A film

MLA: *Silkwood*. Writ. Nora Ephron and Alice Arden. Dir. Mike Nichols. With Meryl Streep. ABC, 1983.

APA: Ephron, N. (Writer), & Nichols, M. (Director). (1983). *Silkwood* [Film]. Hollywood: ABC.

More than one work by the same author(s)

MLA: Didion, Joan. *Miami*. New York: Simon and Schuster, 1987.
————. "Why I Write."" *New York Times Book Review* 9 Dec. 1976: 22.

APA: Didion, J. (1976, December 9). Why I write. *The New York Times Book Review*, p. 22.
Didion, J. (1987). *Miami*. New York, Simon and Schuster.

Note: MLA style lists multiple works by the same author alphabetically by title. APA style lists such works chronologically beginning with the earliest.

SAMPLE STUDENT RESEARCH PAPER: MLA DOCUMENTATION STYLE

The following paper was written to fulfill the research component of a freshman composition course and is documented according to the guidelines of the Modern Language Association, as required by the instructor. Be sure to consult with your instructor to determine which documentation style he or she prefers.

This paper has been annotated to point out important conventions of research writing and documentation. Note that it does not begin with a title page. If, however, your instructor requires an introductory outline, then your first page should be a title page (ask him or her for a preferred format) and the first page of the paper should be headed with only the title of the essay.

Walker 1

1. Page numbers in upper right corner, with author's last name.

Kristen E. Walker

English 101, sec. 33

Professor Bator

8 December 19XX

2. Double-spacing throughout.

I'd Toddle . . . er . . . Walk a Mile for a Camel!

3. Title centered.

Responding to recent trends in cigarette advertising that appear to target minors, Representative Henry Waxman recalls the headline of an early R.J. Reynolds Tobacco Company advertisement: "More Doctors Smoke Camels Than Any Other Cigarette". In an editorial in *The Journal of the American Medical Association*, Waxman observes that the implication was that cigarette smoking was safe—after all, if medical doctors smoked, cigarettes must not be harmful. As Waxman notes, in today's advertising "physicians in white coats have been replaced by cartoon animals in bright, pre-school colors" designed to appeal to young children and adolescents (3195). One of the most popular and successful of these cartoon figures is R.J. Reynolds' Old Joe Camel.

4. Introduction: background with specific example to get reader's attention. Parenthetical cite includes only the page number because the author's name mentioned in text.

Old Joe Camel, a "smooth character" modeled after James Bond and Don Johnson of the *Miami Vice* television series, was part of an advertising campaign

5. Histori-
cal back-
ground.
Selective
use of
direct
quotation.
Et al. in cite
and Works
Cited
indicates
more than
three
authors.
for Camel cigarettes created in 1988 to boost sagging
cigarette sales (DiFranza et al. 3149). In a study published in *The Journal of the American Medical Association*,
Joseph DiFranza and his colleagues report, "Many industry analysts believe the major goal of [the Old Joe]
campaign is to reposition Camel to compete with
Philip Morris' Marlboro brand for the illegal children's market segment" (3149). Ever since the dangers
of smoking became public and caused a sharp decline
in the number of adult smokers, the recruiting of new
and younger smokers by cigarette companies has been
on the rise. Joe Camel is by far the most influential of
cigarette advertising campaigns in encouraging children and teenagers to smoke. Regardless of the tobacco industry's claims that it does not seek to interest

6. Thesis
statement.
children in smoking, exposure to cigarette advertising
—with its captivating images and slick slogans—places
children at risk by enticing them to start smoking.

In 1971, cigarette advertisements were banned
from television. However, this did not stop Camel
from advertising its product. In fact, since that time
Camel has employed virtually every advertising technique known, including the recent strategies such as
Old Joe Camel which target a much younger generation. Since 90 percent of all new smokers are children
and teenagers (DiFranza et al. 3149), the reasons for
targeting the younger generation are clear. The most
frequently seen advertisements—with slogans such as
"Light up the Night" or "There's something for every-

one at Joe's place"—are found at sports stadiums and malls, on billboards, t-shirts, and caps, and in magazines, all easily accessible to children and adolescents. But these techniques are only part of the arsenal tobacco companies use to sell cigarettes to minors. They have other tactics designed to entice even more.

In the *Joe's Place Catalog*, for example, Camel offers free Camel merchandise in exchange for Camel Cash enclosed with each pack of cigarettes. This "cash," or C-Notes, as they are called, can be exchanged for smoking accessories, clothing, jewelry, dart sets, beach towels, and other miscellanea, all reflecting the Camel logo. A special V.I.P. card can even be ordered at no extra cost by calling Camel's toll free information hotline (1-800-CAMEL-CASH). The card entitles its holder to free C-Notes, significant discounts, private sales, and the use of the V.I.P. hotline which gives details on events and Smokin' Joe's racing schedule (*Joe's Place Catalog*).

7. Use of primary sources as evidence.

Camel even has its own magazine—*Smooth*. The premier issue featured Old Joe with the caption "Character of the Year." *Smooth* includes letters to the editor, brightly colored pull-outs of Joe and his friends, and Joe's personal Smooth Philosophy. Joe's advice for dating includes the following: "When all else fails, pick up a pack of Camels." Although each page of the magazine has a printed warning by the Surgeon General on the dangers of smoking, the warnings are insignificant juxtaposed to the flashy print, colors, and slogans promoting the Camel brand. Merchandise attracts children to products, and cigarette manufacturers capitalize on that—and profit from it.

Nevertheless, R.J. Reynolds' Camel cigarette advertising is increasingly being exposed as a "thinly veiled attempt to lure children to start smoking" (Green 22). In an open letter to R.J. Reynolds, Mark Green, the New York City Commissioner of Consumer Affairs, told the cigarette manufacturer that their Old Joe advertisements were "unconscionable because they appear to be targeted to unsophisticated minors who feel immortal" (22). As Joseph DiFranza notes in his study, young children are often "too immature to understand the purpose of advertising" (3149). Stating that the Old Joe advertisements are misleading because their images imply that "smoking a Camel leads to social success and happiness, not to disease and death," Green points out that young children are attracted to the brightly colored cartoon camel, while teenagers are drawn to Old Joe's "cool" image (22).

Over the past several years members of the public health community have become concerned with the images used by Camel to attract minors to cigarettes. As a result, studies have been undertaken to determine whether Old Joe encourages children to smoke. According to Steven Colford and Ira Teinowitz, recent studies on the ages of Camel smokers confirm that

Camel smokers are younger today (37). In 1991, for example, a study by the Simmons Market Research Bureau found that 78.3 percent of Camel smokers were under the age of 50, an increase of 15.5 percent from 1988 (qtd. in Colford and Teinowitz 37). As Colford and Teinowitz point out, this increase occurred within one year of the debut of the Old Joe Camel advertising campaign (37).

8. Reference to indirect source. Walker found the Simmons study in another source, indicated by *qtd. in* ("quoted in").

Joseph DiFranza and his colleagues observe in their study that while only 2.7 percent of smokers aged 17 to 24 years of age chose Camels prior to the Old Joe campaign, 32.8 percent of smokers younger than 18 years old preferred the brand in a 1991 study (3149–51). Furthermore, DiFranza and his researchers found that children (97.7 percent) are much more likely than adults (72.2 percent) to recognize the Old Joe character (3150), demonstrating the influence the campaign has had on children's smoking behavior.

9. Summary and paraphrase clearly documented.

A study published in *The Journal of the American Medical Association* indicated that Camel's market share among children rose significantly—from .5 percent to 32 percent—within only three years after the Old Joe campaign began (Clowe). According to John Clowe in a letter to the editor of the *Philadelphia Inquirer*, R.J. Reynolds has only augmented the campaign since the release of the results of this study, so that each day 3,000 more children will smoke their first cigarette. Another study published in *The Journal of the American*

Medical Association found that children between the ages of three and six were as captivated by Old Joe Camel promoting cigarettes as they were by Mickey Mouse in advertisements for the Disney Channel (Fischer et al. 3146).

Spokespersons for Camel cigarettes claim that the four billion dollars they spend each year on advertising and promotion is not intended to encourage young people to smoke. Cigarette manufacturers have maintained that peer pressure and parent and sibling example are the major influences on children, not advertising. Nevertheless, cigarette companies earn hundreds of millions of dollars in revenues each year from the sale of cigarettes to minors (Dribben). And, even if some children are unable to buy cigarettes directly, they are resourceful enough to get them other ways (Schroeder 74).

10. Walker offers "common knowledge" and her own opinions regarding possible regulation of tobacco advertising. No documentation needed.

While the First Amendment to the Constitution of the United States generally permits advertising of products, the government also has an interest in protecting minors. Requiring tobacco companies to place a label on their cigarette packages clearly outlining the hazards of smoking may not be enough. Other measures that might be effective in curbing smoking include banning distribution of free samples to avoid inadvertently disbursing cigarettes to minors. Also, advertising at places where young people typically congregate, such as sports stadiums, movie theaters, and shopping areas should be restricted. Cigarette vending machines, which make cigarettes accessible to anyone, should be outlawed altogether. And advertising sponsored by tobacco companies at events which children or adolescents are likely to attend—such as sporting events—should be prohibited. Tobacco companies that sell merchandise, such as the Camel company with its line of accessories, should be required to put warning labels on any merchandise that carries their logo.

Ultimately, the Federal Trade Commission needs to address cigarette marketing either by banning cigarette advertising or setting strict, clear guidelines that would restrict minors' exposure. As Joseph DiFranza observes,

> In countries where advertising has been totally banned or severely restricted, the percentage of young people who smoke has decreased more rapidly than in countries where tobacco promotion has been less restricted. (3152)

11. Indented block format for quotation of four lines or more. Parenthetical cite follows period.

Although no efforts toward restricting or banning cigarette advertising have occurred, the Old Joe Camel advertising has "ignited outrage" in the medical community. George Lundberg, a physician, believes that Old Joe "will turn out to be the metaphorical straw that broke the advertising camel's back," which will, Lundberg hopes, "start the dominoes falling on *all* cigarette advertising" (qtd. in Whelan 22). In the past, Surgeon General Antonia Novella observes, "R.J. Reynolds would have us walk a mile for a Camel. Today, it's time we invite 'Old Joe' Camel himself to take a hike."

12. Conclusion offers strong, pointed quotations from acknowledged experts to support Walker's thesis.

13. Untitled letter to the editor. Clowe, John L. Letter. *Philadelphia Inquirer* 21 Sept. 1993: A14.

Colford, Steven W. and Ira Teinowitz. "Old Joe a Winner Even With Ad Ban." *Advertising Age* 16 August 1993: 1, 37.

14. Article by three or more authors; *et al.* substitutes for authors' names after the first. DiFranza, Joseph, et al. "RJR Nabisco's Cartoon Camel Promotes Camel Cigarettes to Children." *The Journal of the American Medical Association* 22 (1991): 3149–52.

Dribben, Melissa. "Adults Heed the Warnings." *Philadelphia Inquirer* 1 March 1993: B1.

Fischer, Paul M., et al. "Brand Logo Recognition by Children Aged 3 to 6 Years." *The Journal of the American Medical Association* 22 (1991): 3145–48.

Green, Mark. Letter. *Business and Society Review* 73 (1990): 22–26.

15. Work without named author listed by title. *Joe's Place Catalog.* R.J. Reynolds Tobacco Company, 1994.

Lewis, Claude. "Cigarette Companies are Looking for New Customers to Kill Off." *Philadelphia Inquirer* 7 April 1993: A13.

Novella, Antonia C. "Abolition of 'Joe Camel' Ads Asked." *Facts on File* 52 (1992): 452.

Schroeder, Ken. "Getting 'Em Young."
Education Digest 57 (1992): 74–75.

Smooth. R.J. Reynolds Tobacco Company,
1990.

Waxman, Henry A. "Tobacco Marketing:
Profiteering from Children." Editorial.
*The Journal of the American Medical
Association* 22 (1991): 3185–86.

Whelan, Elizabeth M. "Against Old Joe: It's
the Final Straw." *Advertising Age* 27
(1992): 22.

16. *Editorial* designation, if appropriate, comes after title.

GLOSSARY

Abstract words refer to ideas or generalities—words such as "truth," "beauty," and "justice." The opposite of an abstract word is a *concrete* one. Margaret Atwood in "The Female Body" (p. 414) explores the abstract phrase "female body," offering a series of more concrete examples or perspectives on the topic.

Allusion is a reference to an actual or fictional person, object, or event. The assumption is that the reference will be understood or recognized by the reader. For that reason, allusions work best when they draw upon a shared experience or heritage. Allusions to famous literary works or to historically prominent people or events are likely to have meaning for many readers for an extended period of time. Martin Luther King, Jr., in "I Have a Dream" (p. 443) alludes to biblical verses, spirituals, and patriotic songs. If an allusion is no longer recognized by an audience, it loses its effectiveness in conjuring up a series of significant associations.

Analogy is an extended comparison in which an unfamiliar or complex object or event is likened to a familiar or simple one in order to make the former more vivid and more easily understood. Inappropriate or superficially similar analogies should not be used, especially as evidence in an argument. See *Faulty analogy* in the list of logical fallacies on pp. 425-26.

Argumentation or **persuasion** seeks to move a reader, to gain support, to advocate a particular type of action. Traditionally, argumentation appeals to logic and reason, while persuasion appeals to emotion and sometimes prejudice. See the introduction to Chapter 9.

Cause and effect analyses explain why something happened or what the consequences are or will be from a particular occurrence. See the introduction to Chapter 7.

Classification is a form of division, but instead of starting with a single subject as a *division* does, classification starts with many items, and groups or classifies them in categories. See the introduction to Chapter 4.

Cliché is an overused common expression. The term is derived from a French word for a stereotype printing block. Just as many identical copies can be made from such a block, so clichés are typically words and phrases used so frequently that they become stale and ineffective. Everyone uses clichés in speech: "in less than no time" they "spring to mind" but "in the last analysis" a writer ought to "avoid them like the plague," even though they always seem "to hit the nail on the head." Theodore Bernstein offers a good definition and many examples in "Clichés" (p. 386).

Coherence is achieved when all parts of a piece of writing work together as a harmonious whole. If a paper has a well-defined thesis that controls its structure, coherence will follow. In addition, relationships between sentences, paragraphs, and ideas can be made clearer for the reader by using pronoun references, parallel structures (see *Parallelism*), and transitional words and phrases (see *Transitions*).

Colloquial expressions are informal words and phrases used in conversation, but inappropriate for more formal writing situations. Occasionally, professional writers use colloquial expressions in order to create an intentional informality. Paul Bodanis in "What's in Your Toothpaste" (p. 183) mixes colloquial words ("gob," "stuff," "goodies," "glop") with formal words ("abrading," "gustatory," "intrudant").

Comparison involves finding similarities between two or more things, people, or ideas. See the introduction to Chapter 5.

Conclusions should always leave the reader feeling that a paper has come to a logical and inevitable end, that the communication is now complete. As a result, an essay that simply stops, or weakly trails off, or moves into a previously unexplored area, or raises new or distracting problems lacks that necessary sense of closure. Endings often cause problems because they are written last and, therefore, are often rushed. With proper planning, you can always write an effective and appropriate ending. Keep the following points and strategies in mind:

1. An effective conclusion grows out of a paper—it needs to be logically related to what has been said. It might restate the thesis, summarize the exposition or argument, apply or reflect upon the subject under discussion, tell a related story, call for a course of action, or state the significance of the subject.

2. The extent to which a conclusion can repeat or summarize is determined in large part by the length of the paper. A short paper should not have a conclusion that repeats, in slightly varied words, the introduction. A long essay, however, often needs a conclusion that conveniently summarizes the significant facts or points discussed in the paper.

3. The appropriateness of a particular type of ending is related to a paper's purpose. An argumentative or persuasive essay—one that asks the reader to do or believe something—can always conclude with a statement of the desired action—vote for, do this, do not support. A narrative essay can end at the climactic moment in the action, such as E.B. White's recognition of mortality in "Once More to the Lake" (p. 120). An expository essay in which points are arranged according to significance can end with the major point.

4. The introduction and conclusion can be used as a related pair to frame the body of an essay. Frequently in a conclusion you can return to or allude to an idea, an expression, or an illustration used at the beginning of the paper and so enclose the body.

Concrete words describe things that exist and can be experienced through the senses. Abstractions are rendered understandable and specific through concrete examples. See *Abstract*.

Connotation and **denotation** refer to two different types of definition of words. A dictionary definition is denotative—it offers a literal and explicit definition of a word. But words often have more than just literal meanings, for they can carry positive or negative associations or connotations. The denotative definition of "wife" is "a woman married to a man," but as Judy Brady shows in "I Want a Wife" (p. 395), the word *wife* carries a series of connotative associations as well.

Contrast involves finding differences between two or more things, people, or ideas. See the introduction to Chapter 5.

Deduction is the form of argument that starts with a general truth and then moves to a specific application of that truth. See the introduction to Chapter 9.

Definition involves placing a word first in a general class and then adding distinguishing features that set it apart from other members of that class: "A dalmation is a breed of dog (general class) with a white, short-haired coat and dark spots (distinguishing feature)." Most college writing assignments in definition require extended definitions in which a subject is analyzed with appropriate examples and details. See the introduction to Chapter 8.

Denotation. See *Connotation and denotation*.

Description is the re-creation of sense impressions in words. See the introduction to Chapter 3.

Dialect. See *Diction*.

Diction is the choice of words used in speaking or writing. It is frequently divided into four levels: formal, informal, colloquial, and slang. Formal diction is found in traditional academic writing, such as books and scholarly articles; informal diction, generally characterized by words common in conversation contexts, by contractions, and by the use of the first person ("I"), is found in articles in popular magazines. Bernard R. Berelson's "The Value of Children" (p. 219) exhibits formal diction; Judith Viorst's "How Books Helped Shape My Life" (p. 310), informal. See *Colloquial expressions* and *Slang*.

Two other commonly used labels are also applied to diction:

> **Nonstandard.** Words or expressions not normally used by educated speakers. An example would be *ain't*.
>
> **Dialect.** Regional or social differences in a language exhibited in word choice, grammatical usage, and pronunciation. Dialects are primarily spoken rather than written, but are often reproduced or imitated in narratives. William Least Heat-Moon in "Nameless, Tennessee" (p. 150) captures the dialect of his speakers.

Division breaks a subject into parts. It starts with a single subject and then subdivides that whole into smaller units. See the introduction to Chapter 4.

Essay literally means an attempt, and in writing courses the word is used to refer to brief papers, generally between 500 to 1000 words, on restricted subjects. Essays can be formal and academic, like Bernard Berelson's "The Value of Children" (p. 219), or informal and humorous, like Suzanne Britt Jordan's "That Lean and Hungry Look" (p. 248).

Example is a specific instance used to illustrate a general idea or statement. Effective writing requires examples to make generalizations clear and vivid to a reader. Deborah Tannen's "Wears Jump Suit" (p. 60) is comprised of a series of examples of the ways women in our culture are "marked" by the way they dress and wear their hair. See the introduction to Chapter 1.

Exposition comes from a Latin word meaning "to expound or explain." It is one of the four modes into which writing is subdivided —the other three being *narration, description,* and *argumentation.* Expository writing is information-conveying; its purpose is to inform its reader. This purpose is achieved through a variety of organizational patterns including *division and classification, comparison and contrast, process analysis, cause and effect,* and *definition.*

Figures of speech are deliberate departures from the ordinary and literal meanings of words in order to provide fresh, insightful perspectives or emphasis. Figures of speech are most commonly used in descriptive passages and include the following:

> **Simile.** A comparison of two dissimilar things generally introduced by the words "as" or "like." Annie Dillard in "On Being Chased" (p. 103) describes the result of automobile tires passing through snow on a Pittsburgh street by using a simile: "The cars' tires laid behind them on the snowy street a complex trail of beige chunks like crenellated castle walls."

> **Metaphor.** An analogy that directly identifies one thing with another. After Scott Russell Sanders in "The Inheritance of Tools" (p. 164) accidentally strikes his thumb with a hammer, he describes the resulting scar using a metaphor: "A white scar in the shape of a crescent moon began to show above the cuticle, and month by month it rose across the pink sky of my thumbnail."

> **Personification** An attribution of human qualities to an animal, idea, abstraction, or inanimate object. Gretel Ehrlich in "A River's Route" (p. 158) describes the layers of rock over which the river runs as "brown bellies."

> **Hyperbole.** A deliberate exaggeration, often done to provide emphasis or humor. Margaret Atwood in comparing the female brain with the male brain (pp. 416-17) resorts to hyperbole: "[Female brains are] joined together by a thick cord; neural pathways flow from one to the other, sparkles of electronic information washing to and fro . . . The male brain, now, that's a different matter. Only a thin connection. Space over here, time over here, music and arithmetic in their sealed

compartments. The right brain doesn't know what the left brain is doing."

Understatement. The opposite of hyperbole, or a deliberate minimizing done to provide emphasis or humor. In William Least Heat-Moon's "Nameless, Tennessee" (p. 150), Miss Ginny Watts explains how she asked her husband to call the doctor unless he wanted to be "shut of" (rid of) her. Her husband, Thurmond, humorously uses understatement in his reply: "I studied on it."

Rhetorical questions. Questions not meant to be answered, but instead to provoke thought. At several points in his essay "How Much Is 'Enough'?" (p. 456), Alan Durning poses strings of rhetorical questions.

Paradox. A seeming contradiction used to catch a reader's attention. An element of truth or rightness often lurks beneath the contradiction. Tracy Kidder in "Linda Manor" (p. 142) explores the paradox of a new building housing the elderly: "It seemed so new a place for people so old."

Generalizations are assertions or conclusions based upon some specific instances. The value of a generalization is determined by the quality and quantity of examples upon which it is based. Bob Greene in "Cut" (p. 52) formulates a generalization—being cut from an athletic team makes men superachievers later in life—on the basis of five examples. For such a generalization to have validity, however, a proper statistical sample would be essential.

Hyperbole. See *Figures of speech.*

Illustration is providing specific examples for general words or ideas. A writer illustrates by using *examples.*

Induction is the form of argument that begins with specific evidence and then moves to a generalized conclusion that accounts for the evidence. See the introduction to Chapter 9.

Introductions need to do two essential things: first, catch or arouse a reader's interest, and second, state the thesis of the paper. In achieving both objectives, an introduction can occupy a single paragraph or several. The length of an introduction should always be proportional to the length of the essay—short papers should not have long introductions. Because an introduction introduces what follows, it is always easier to write after a draft of the body of the paper has been completed. When writing an introduction, keep the following strategies in mind:

1. Look for an interesting aspect of the subject that might arouse the reader's curiosity. It could be a quotation, an unusual statistic, a narrative, a provocative question or statement. It should be something that will make the reader want to continue reading, and it should be appropriate to the subject at hand.

2. Provide a clear statement of purpose and thesis, explaining what you are writing about and why.

3. Remember that an introduction establishes a tone or point of view for what follows, so be consistent—an informal personal essay can have a casual, anecdotal beginning, but a serious academic essay needs a serious, formal introduction.

4. Suggest to the reader the structure of the essay that follows. Knowing what to expect makes it easier for the audience to read actively.

Irony occurs when a writer says one thing but means another. E.M. Forster ends "My Wood" (p. 338) ironically by imagining a time when he will "wall in and fence out until I really taste the sweets of property"—which is actually the opposite of the point he is making.

Metaphor. See *Figures of speech*.

Narration involves telling a story, and all stories—whether they are personal experience essays, imaginative fiction, or historical narratives—have the same essential ingredients: a series of events arranged in an order and told by a narrator for some particular purpose. See the introduction to Chapter 2.

Nonstandard diction. See *Diction*.

Objective writing is an impersonal, factual approach to a particular subject. Bernard Berelson's "The Value of Children" (p. 219) is primarily objective in its approach. Writing frequently blends the objective and subjective together. See *Subjective*.

Paradox. See *Figures of speech*.

Parallelism places words, phrases, clauses, sentences, or even paragraphs equal in importance in equivalent grammatical form. The similar forms make it easier for the reader to see the relationships that exist among the parts; they add force to the expression. Martin Luther King, Jr.'s "I Have a Dream" speech (p. 443) exhibits each level of parallelism: words ("When all God's children, black and white men, Jews and Gentiles, Protestants and Catholics"), phrases ("With this faith, we will be able to work together, to pray together, to struggle together, to go to jail together, to stand up for freedom together"), clauses ("Go back to Mississippi, go back to Alabama, go back to South Carolina, go back to Georgia, go back to Louisiana, go back to the slums and ghettos of our northern cities"), sentences (the "one hundred years later" pattern in paragraph 2), and paragraphs (the "I have a dream" pattern in paragraphs 11 to 18).

Person is a grammatical term used to refer to a speaker, the individual being addressed, or the individual being referred to. English has three persons: first (I or we), second (you), and third (he, she, it, or they).

Personification. See *Figures of speech.*

Persuasion. See *Argumentation and persuasion.*

Point of view is the perspective or angle the writer adopts toward a subject. In narratives, point of view is either first person (I) or third person (he, she it). First-person narration implies a *subjective* approach to a subject; third-person narration promotes an *objective* approach. Point of view can be limited (revealing only what the narrator knows) or omniscient (revealing what anyone else in the narrative thinks or feels). Sometimes the phrase "point of view" is used simply to describe the writer's attitude toward the subject.

Premise in logic is a proposition—a statement of a truth—that is used to support or help support a conclusion. For an illustration, see p. 427.

Process analysis takes two forms: a set of directions intended to allow a reader to duplicate a particular action, or a description intended to tell a reader how something happens. See the introduction to Chapter 6.

Proofreading is a systematic check of a piece of writing to make sure that it contains no grammatical or mechanical errors. A proofreading is something quite different from a revision. See *Revision.*

Purpose is intention or the reason why a writer writes. Three purposes are fundamental: to entertain, to inform, or to persuade. Purposes are not necessarily separate or discrete; all can be combined together. An effective piece of writing has a well-defined purpose.

Revision means "to see again." A revision involves a careful, active scrutiny of every aspect of a paper—subject, audience, thesis, paragraph structures, sentence constructions, and word choice. Revising a piece of writing involves something more complicated and more wide-ranging than proofreading. See *Proofreading.*

Rhetorical questions. See *Figures of speech.*

Satire pokes fun a human behavior or institutions in order to correct them. Judy Brady in "I Want a Wife" (p. 395) satirizes the stereotypical male demands of a wife, implying that marriage should be a more understanding partnership. In "Hair" (p. 267), Marcia Aldrich satires her mother's obsession with having her hair done.

Simile. See *Figures of speech.*

Slang is common, casual, conversational language that is inappropriate in formal speaking or writing. Slang is frequently used to make or define social groups—a private, shared language not understood by outsiders. Slang changes constantly and is, therefore, always dated. For that reason alone, it is always best to avoid using slang in writing.

Style is the arrangement of words that a writer uses to express meaning. The study of an author's style would include an examination of diction or word choice, figures of speech, sentence constructions, and paragraph divisions.

Subject is what a piece of writing is about. See also *Thesis.* Bruce Catton's subject in "Grant and Lee" (p. 253) is the two generals; his thesis is that the two represented or symbolized "two diametrically opposed elements in American life."

Subjective writing expresses an author's feelings or opinions about a particular subject. Editorials or columns in newspapers and personal essays tend to rely on subjective judgments. Senator Don Nickles and Aimee Berenson's debate, "Should HIV-Infected Immigrants Be Barred from the United States?" (p. 432), and Patricia McLaughlin's "Sis Boom Bah Humbug" (p. 543) are examples of subjective journalism. Writing frequently blends the subjective and objective together. See *Objective.*

Syllogism is a three-step deductive argument including a major premise, a minor premise, and a conclusion. For an illustration, see p. 427.

Thesis is a particular idea or assertion about a subject. Effective writing will always have an explicit or implicit statement of thesis; it is the central and controlling idea, the thread that holds the essay together. Frequently a thesis is stated in a thesis or *topic sentence.* See *Subject.*

Tone refers to a writer's or speaker's attitude toward a subject and audience. Tone reflects human emotions and so can be characterized or described in a wide variety of ways, including serious, sincere, concerned, humorous, sympathetic, ironic, indignant, sarcastic.

Topic sentence is a single sentence in a paragraph that contains a statement of *subject* or *thesis*. The topic sentence is to the paragraph what the theses statement is to an essay—the thread that holds the whole together, a device to provide clarity and unity. Because paragraphs have various purposes, not every paragraph will have a topic sentence. When they do, topic sentences are frequently found at the beginnings or ends of paragraphs.

Transitions are links or connections made between sentences, paragraphs, or groups of paragraphs. By using transitions, a writer achieves *coherence* and *unity*. Transitional devices include the following:

1. Repeated words, phrases, or clauses.
2. Transitional sentences or paragraphs that act as bridges from one section or idea to the next.
3. Transition-making words and phrases such as those of
   ADDITION—again, next, furthermore, last
   TIME—soon, after, then, later, meanwhile
   COMPARISON—but, still, nonetheless, on the other hand
   EXAMPLE—for instance, for example
   CONCLUSION—in conclusion, finally, as a result
   CONCESSION—granted, of course

Understatement. See *Figures of speech.*

Unity is a oneness in which all of the individual parts of a piece of writing work together to form a cohesive and complete whole. It is best achieved by having a clearly stated *purpose* and *thesis* against which every sentence and paragraph can be tested for relevance.

CREDITS

Ackerman, Diane, "Why Leaves Turn Color in the Fall." From *A Natural History of the Senses* by Diane Ackerman. Copyright © 1990 by Diane Ackerman. Reprinted by permission of Random House, Inc.

Aldrich, Marcia, "Hair." From *Northwest Review*, 1993. Reprinted by permission of the author.

Angelou, Maya, "Sister Monroe." From *I Know Why the Caged Bird Sings* by Maya Angelou. Copyright © 1969 by Maya Angelou. Reprinted by permission of Random House, Inc.

Asturias, Elena, "Growing Up in the U.S.A.: A First Generation Look." Reprinted by permission of the author.

Atwood, Margaret, "The Female Body." From *Good Bones by* Margaret Atwood (Coach House Press, 1993). Copyright © 1992 by O.W. Toad, Ltd. Reprinted by permission of Phoebe Larmore Agency and Coach House Press.

Berelson, Bernard R., "The Value of Children: A Taxonomical Essay." From *The Population Council Annual Report, 1972.* Reprinted by permission of the Population Council.

Bernstein, Theodore M., "Clichés." From *The Careful Writer: A Modern Guide to English Usage* by Theodore M. Bernstein. Copyright © 1965 by Theodore M. Bernstein. Reprinted by permission of Atheneum Publishers, an imprint of Macmillan Publishing Company.

Berry, Wendell, "They Knew but Had Little." From "A Native Hill" in *Recollected Essays, 1965-1980* by Wendell Berry. Copyright © 1981 by Wendell Berry. Reprinted by permission of North Point Press, a division of Farrar, Straus and Giroux, Inc.

Bodanis, David, "What's in your Toothpaste." From *The Secret House* by David Bodanis. Copyright © 1986 by David Bodanis. Reprinted by permission of Simon & Schuster, Inc.

Brady, Judy, "I Want a Wife." From "Why I Want a Wife," *Ms.*, December 31, 1971. Reprinted by permission of the author.

Britt Jordan, Suzanne, "That Lean and Hungry Look." From *Newsweek*, "My Turn," October 9, 1978. Copyright © 1978 by *Newsweek*. Reprinted by permission of the author, Suzanne Britt.

Brumberg, Joan Jacobs, "The Origins of Anorexia Nervosa." From *Fasting Girls: The Emergence of Anorexia Nervosa as a Modern Disease* by Joan Jacobs Brumberg. Copyright © 1988 by the President and Fellows of Harvard College. Reprinted by permission of the publisher, Harvard University Press.

Butterfield, Fox, "Why They Excel." From *Parade*, January 21, 1991. Copyright © 1991 by *Parade*. Reprinted by permission of *Parade* and the author.

Cannon, Carl M., "Honey, I Warped the Kids." From *Mother Jones*, July/August 1993. Reprinted by permission of the author.

Catton, Bruce, "Grant and Lee: A Study in Contrasts." From *The American Story*, edited by Earl Schenck Miers. Reprinted by permission of the U.S. Capitol Historical Society.

Cofer, Judith Ortiz, "Silent Dancing." From *Silent Dancing: A Partial Remembrance of a Puerto Rican Childhood* by Judith Ortiz Cofer. Reprinted by permission of the publisher, Arte Publico Press-University of Houston, 1990.

Cole, Diane, "Don't Just Stand There." From "A World of Difference," a special supplement to *The New York Times*, April 16, 1989. Copyright © 1989 by The New York Times Company. Reprinted by permission of the author.

Didion, Joan, "On Keeping a Notebook." From *Slouching Towards Bethlehem* by Joan Didion. Copyright © 1966, 1968 by Joan Didion. Reprinted by permission of Farrar, Straus and Giroux, Inc.

Dillard, Annie, "On Being Chased (Throwing Snowballs)." From *An American Childhood* by Annie Dillard. Copyright © 1987 by Annie Dillard. Reprinted by permission of HarperCollins Publishers, Inc.

Durning, Alan, "How Much is 'Enough'." From *Worldwatch*, November/December 1990. Reprinted by permission of the Worldwatch Institute.

Ehrlich, Gretel, "A River's Route." From *Introduction to the 1989 Sierra Club Wilderness Wall Calendar* by Gretel Ehrlich. Copyright © 1989 by Gretel Ehrlich. Reprinted by permission of the author.

Eighner, Lars, "On Dumpster Diving." From *Travels with Lizbeth* by Lars Eighner. Copyright © 1993 by Lars Eighner. Reprinted by permission of St. Martin's Press, New York, NY. This article first appeared in *The Threepenny Review*, Fall 1991.

Elbow, Peter, "Quick Revising." From *Writing with Power: Techniques for Mastering the Writing Process* by Peter Elbow. Copyright © 1981 by Oxford University Press Inc. Reprinted by permission of the publisher.

Ephron, Nora, "Revision and Life: Take It from the Top—Again." From *The New York Times Book Review*, November 9, 1986. Copyright © 1986 by The New York Times Company. Reprinted by permission of International Creative Management, Inc. and the author.

Forster, E.M., "My Wood." From *Abinger Harvest* by E.M. Forster, Copyright © 1936 and renewed 1964 by Edward Morgan Forster. Reprinted by permission of Harcourt Brace Jovanovich, Inc., King's College, Cambridge, and the Society of Authors, literary representative of the Estate of E.M. Forster.

Gaines, Judith, "The Beefcake Years." From *The Boston Globe*, September 5, 1993. Reprinted by permission of *The Boston Globe*.

Greene, Bob, "Cut." From *Esquire*, July 1984. Copyright © 1984 by Bob Greene. Reprinted by permission of John Deadline Enterprises, Inc.

Guilbault, Rose Del Castillo, "Americanization is Tough on 'Macho'." From "This World," *San Francisco Chronicle*, August 20, 1989. Reprinted by permission of the author.

Heat-Moon, William Least, "Nameless, Tennessee." From *Blue Highways: A Journey into America* by William Least Heat-Moon. Copyright © 1982 by William Least Heat-Moon. Reprinted by permission of Little, Brown and Company.

Hughes, Langston, "Salvation." From *The Big Sea* by Langston Hughes. Copyright © 1940 by Langston Hughes; renewal copyright © 1968 by Arna Boutmeps and George Houston Bass. Reprinted by permission of Hill and Wang, a division of Farrar, Straus and Giroux, Inc.

Johnson, Tim, "You Have Definitely Won." From *The Philadelphia Inquirer Sunday Magazine*, January 16, 1994. Reprinted by permission of the author.

Keen, Sam, "Faces of the Enemy." From *Esquire*, February 1984. Copyright © 1984 by Esquire. Reprinted by permission of the author.